# Router Magic

## Jigs, Fixtures, and Tricks to Unleash Your Router's FULL Potential

**Bill Hylton**

Photographs by **Mitch Mandel**

Illustrations by **Bill Hylton and Frank Rohrbach**

Reader's Digest

THE READER'S DIGEST ASSOCIATION, INC.
Pleasantville, New York/Montreal

Until now, it's gone without saying.

To Judi. Always to Judi.

The author and editors who compiled this book have tried to make
all of the contents as accurate and as correct as possible. Plans,
illustrations, photographs, and text have all been carefully checked
and cross-checked. However, due to the variability of local conditions,
construction materials, personal skills, and so on, neither the author
nor Reader's Digest assumes any responsibility for any injuries
suffered or for damages or other losses incurred that result from the
material presented herein. All instructions and plans should be
carefully studied and clearly understood before beginning construction.

Library of Congress Cataloging in Publication Data

Hylton, Bill.
    Router magic : jigs, fixtures, and tricks to unleash your router's
    full potential  / Bill Hylton ; photographs by Mitch Mandel ;
    illustrations by Bill Hylton and Frank Rohrbach.
        p.        cm.
    ISBN 0-7621-0185-7 (paperback)
    1. Routers (Tools)    2. Woodwork.      3. Jigs and fixtures.
I. Title.
TT203.3.H94      1999
684 '.083–dc21                                          99-24915

READER'S DIGEST ILLUSTRATED REFERENCE BOOKS
    **Editor-in-Chief** Christopher Cavanaugh
    **Art Director** Joan Mazzeo
    **Operations Manager** William J. Cassidy

Address any comments about *Router Magic* to:
Reader's Digest
Editor-in-Chief, Illustrated Reference Books
Reader's Digest Road
Pleasantville, NY 10570

Visit our website at: www.readersdigest.com

Printed in the United States of America
Second Printing, February 2001

# Contents

# Introduction

Abracadabra! It's magic!

Kind of a hackneyed device, isn't it? It seemed good as I started this book project. But as I collected and refined the ideas and plans for the jigs and fixtures and gizmos in this book, I heard every putdown and jibe and smug joke the theme could evoke.

"Wooo! It's maagic."

But as the book nears completion, the theme still works for me. When I get into the shop and try out a new router gizmo I've made—and it WORKS!—well, there is a magical feeling to it.

But the "magic" theme goes beyond a self-satisfied feeling when I accomplish something in the shop. It acknowledges that a lot of the successes we all experience in woodworking stem just from *knowing the trick.*

There are three kinds of magic, in my mind.

1. illusion
2. sleight-of-hand
3. trickery

**Illusion** is simply that. *Illusion.* It's hocus-pocus. What you are seeing is not what's really happening. At the family picnic, Uncle Bud absolutely *wows* the little kids by pulling off his thumb tip momentarily, then putting it back. It's just in the way he holds his hands, we older kids realize.

There's none of this hocus-pocus here, because I've kept the illusions out of *Router Magic.* It's just good, hard-core, down-to-earth, practical-as-dirt woodworking using a router.

**Sleight-of-hand** is common in woodworking. To me, sleight-of-hand is handling a taxing, intricate operation so quickly and fluidly that it seems easy. It's handling the task in a way that provokes the "How'd he *do* that!?" response. The way some woodworkers chop out dovetails qualifies as sleight-of-hand.

The catch with sleight-of-hand, and the reason I've left it out of *Router Magic,* is that it grows out of dedicated, almost obsessive practice. If you'd hand cut dovetails for a half-dozen drawers every working day for 25 or 30 years, you'd become adroit at it, too.

**Trickery** is what this book is all about. Trickery is simply executing a well-devised strategem, putting a gimmick to work, making use of a special device or apparatus. This is the foundation of both great magic and great woodworking.

Here's a trick, the sort you've seen performed on television by one flamboyant showman or another. He trusses up his young assistant, puts her in a wooden crate, then pushes it off the bridge into the river below. As the water closes over the crate, a limo pulls up. The showman turns, opens the back door, and helps his young assistant alight. And you say, "How'd he *do* that!?" Let me assure you, it is a trick. If you know the trick, you don't need any special skills to replicate the performance. In this particular case, you need special equipment: twins.

What I've put in *Router Magic* is strictly trickery. And of course, the point is to tell you exactly what the gimmick is. While I do want you to be dazzled, I also want to you say, "Hey! I can do that!!"

*Router Magic* is a whole bag of neat tricks for doing woodworking using a router. It's for the busy person who wants to know the tricks so he can cut to the chase, so she can get more done in less time. It's for the woodworker who already has a router and bits and uses them regularly in his or her woodworking. But *Router Magic* is also for the woodworker who has the router sitting on a shelf while he waits for it to show off its much-touted versatility. If you fit this latter description, this is the book that'll turn you into a router wizard.

If you are just starting out, for example, you may want to stop at the jigs and fixtures marked with the "Trick-Bag Basic" symbol. The symbol identifies the router accessories that my woodworking colleagues and I selected as the most useful for the average woodworker to have in his bag o' router tricks.

## Trick-Bag Basic

Leaf through the book and take a look at these projects. You'll find them relatively quick and easy to build, often of scraps you already have in your shop. Let me emphasize here that this is not *The Magic Router.* It is NOT "neat stuff you can do with this incredible router from another galaxy!" Your standard router will do just fine for most of these jigs.

If you work through the book and stock your bag o' router tricks with just these basics, you'll begin to appreciate the versatility of your router. Using the "Trick-Bag Basic" accessories, you'll be able to perform a significant range of operations.

With jigs like the T-Squares and the Fractionating Baseplate, you'll rout precisely positioned and sized dadoes, grooves, and rabbets. The multipurpose Surfacing Baseplate equips your router for planing lumber, forming tapers, even cutting circles and shaping edges without the snipes caused by bobbles and tips of the router. The Flush-Trimming Baseplate will help you to pare plugs and through tenons and to trim edge-banding.

I especially like the Trammel Baseplate because it is just such a great trammel. With it, you can cut disks (or holes) ranging in diameter from 1 inch up to about 24 inches. Believe me, this is a very handy range, especially on the low end. Cutting circles is one of the things that routers do best. This is a relatively small project—modest amount of material, only a few steps—but it will have a big impact on your woodworking.

Another of my trick-bag favorites is the Mortising Jig. Mortising is something that plunge routers do especially well. This jig is great because it is quite simple to make, it is solid and durable as the Rock of Gibraltar, and it is easy to use. Take five or ten minutes to set it up, then you can knock out a mortise-a-minute. And every mortise will be the same.

Beyond the "Trick-Bag Basics," you'll find a dozen or more solid accessories that enable you to use that router in different and certainly unexpected ways. The tricks you perform—boring holes, for example, or making dowels and dowel joints—will make it clear to you just how versatile the router can be. And as you tackle these operations, your router know-how will become more advanced.

But maybe you feel you've already mastered the router. Perhaps you already use your router for the kinds of operations I've cited. Don't put the book down yet, for I'd like to think that even a seasoned woodworker will discover new tricks and techniques in *Router Magic*.

You see, I picture this book as a magic workshop, a show for insiders, an opportunity for the performers to exchange information and ideas with an audience of their peers. You know, there's no better audience for a magic show than other magicians. Sure, the audience will know a lot of the tricks and will be able to pick apart a performance to figure out the other tricks. But magicians—like woodworkers—are always on the lookout for new twists, subtle improvements, and especially innovations.

In this light, a woodworker will look at a jig or fixture he or she sees and evaluate it. Has it been seen before? Does it WORK? Is it really *better*? Or just different? Does it have some flexibility, or are its applications very specific? Is it something to keep in mind? Or something to be built straightaway?

You experienced woodworkers should study each jig and fixture in this book with a critical eye. I certainly have, and so have my woodworking colleagues.

The ideas for these jigs, fixtures, and tricks come from a variety of sources. My job for the past year has been to find, develop, test, and fine-tune these devices. I not only looked in books and magazines for ideas, I contacted woodworkers far and wide, looking for creative glimmers and bursts. The best of these projects, I think, were generated by a small circle of woodworking colleagues here at Rodale Press. I'd say to a friend, "What if you wanted to use the router to…?" And we'd turn the idea around and roll it over, and tickle its chin and kick its butt, stroke it a little and chase it around the block. I'd sketch a plan and build and try it. Often, I'd ask a respected colleague to come up with a prototype. There were collaborations, where one person would build a basic jig and others would offer suggestions for improvements and enhancements. I borrowed unabashedly. There are, after all, few ideas that the sun hasn't already shone upon.

In the end, I got a swell collection of magic apparatus and router tricks. Like a good magic show, *Router Magic* is a mixture of basic tricks and some unusual stunts. I openly admit, some of the jigs herein reprise old standards. You'll see jigs and tricks here that you've seen elsewhere. But I think you'll embrace the approaches taken here; they are solid and no-nonsense. I've avoided screwing up a good jig just for the sake of making it a little different.

This is part of the book's emphasis on fundamentals. To pull off the advanced tricks, you have to have a mastery of the basics. So here and there in the book are chapters that examine fundamental router jig making. "The Generic Baseplate" is a good example. About a dozen of the router fixtures in this book involve making a replacement baseplate for your router. The job is easy, but seldom as easy as most woodworking books make it seem. "The Generic Baseplate" details how to go about this essential work. And when I say it *details* how to do it, I mean it gives you *all* the particulars.

*Router Magic* also focuses on contemporary materials and technologies. Knowing about modern materials and hardware (and where to get them) is important to a magician. Phenolic plastic. MDF. Toggle clamps. Easy-on-the-hands plastic knobs. And knowing about unusual technologies that are within the reach of the small-shop professional and the hobby woodworker is important, too. Using vacuum for clamping. Using forced-air flow to lift stuff and help you move it.

With all the stress on fundamentals and materials and technology, don't think this is stodgy stuff. In every good show, there's at least one extravaganza that positively rolls your socks down. And I've got three or four of 'em in here.

Look at the fifth chapter, "Router Duplicator." Maybe you've seen similar devices in woodworking catalogs. The idea is to create an object in wood—a carving, a sign, a hollowed seat, a shallow plate or bowl—through the parallel movements of the duplicator's two beams. As you "trace" a three-dimensional pattern with a stylus mounted on one beam, the second beam duplicates the movements of the first, causing the router mounted on it to reproduce the object being traced. It's a whiz-bang trick.

And to make it better, the Router Magic duplicator isn't trapped on rails or mounted on a stand. It literally floats on air. That IS magic!

Now you can buy a duplicator if you have enough money, or you can make the Router Magic duplicator for a remarkably modest amount of money and shop time. As with all the projects in *Router Magic*, the plans for building and using the duplicator are detailed and tested.

(Let me note parenthetically that all of the project chapters include a list of the parts and the hardware you need for building the item in question. The construction directions are methodical and thorough. Lots of drawings and photos of pertinent procedures are included. The directions for using each jig or fixture are likewise thorough and sequential. I don't *think* you can go wrong.

Practical detail is a special characteristic of *Router Magic*. I get needled by my colleagues for being long-winded, and I am. But I'm trying to make sure I've explained the full intricacies of each project. Often, when I read through woodworking books, I get frustrated by the missing pieces of information—those vital details and subtle nuances of technique that make the difference between success and frustration. I've tried to focus *Router Magic* on the gritty details that make the real difference.)

A major portion of *Router Magic* is given over to router tables and router table accessories. This is an extravaganza of shop-made tables and accessories, ranging from two different ways—one horizontal and one vertical—to mount the router to the table saw, through a variety of sleds and featherboards, to a nifty bench-top router table.

Let me talk some about the Bench-Top Router Table. While it may not *stop* the show for you, it may turn out later to have *stolen* it for you. In a small shop, this router table is great because it is compact and doesn't occupy its own piece of the floor. Set on a workbench, it is elevated above the standard working height, putting the action closer to you. It's very portable, so you can carry it to a remodeling site or a backyard job. I even incorporated three hand-grip openings in the base to make it easy to carry (or to hang on a stout nail for storage).

But three design features make this router table genuinely special.

First, it's designed around a small, fixed-base router, which a lot of hobby woodworkers have.

Second, you can install and retrieve the router from the table in ten seconds. In other words, the router isn't "tied up" when it's in this router table, which is invariably the case with other router table designs. (As you know, you usually have to unscrew three or four screws, remove the router from the mounting plate, then reinstall the stock baseplate by redriving those three or four screws. Takes three to five minutes and a screwdriver.) A couple of toggle clamps hold the router underneath this router table's top. You don't even remove the stock baseplate to mount the router under the tabletop.

Third, a lift-top feature makes it super-easy to make bit changes and bit-height adjustments. This is a feature UNIQUE to shop-built router tables.

The real show-stopper *Router Magic* table is the fabulous Floor-Standing Router Table. It has the lift-top feature, a shop-made router adjustment crank, router bit storage, dust and chip collection, and more.

All in all, these are unique router tables. You can't buy anything like them ANYWHERE!

*Router Magic*'s bravura act has to be the Router Lathe. With this shop-built mechanism, you can "router-turn" posts and legs and spindles and finials with rings and coves and tapers. But its real specialty is spirals, which are beyond the capabilities of even the most expensive lathes and the most skilled turners. You either cut these kinds of turnings on a device like this, or you carve them by hand.

If you want to buy one of these devices, you have two choices—an incredibly expensive industrial machine or a cheap-o-shoddy one. Our router lathe is quite easy to build using some bicycle sprockets and chain, some off-the-shelf bearings and gears, and some plywood. It's durable, flexible, and unique. No one has published plans for such a device. You may never build one, but it will be sure to grab your attention.

If ever there was a magical, gee-whiz router gizmo, this is it.

Before turning you loose in the shop, let me say that the first step to becoming a certified router wizard is to get that router off the shelf. Then you've got to fill that bag o' router tricks. You can buy a lot of gizmos out of catalogs, but the sweetest, most fulfilling tricks are those you create yourself.

So take this book into the shop and get busy.

*Bill Hylton*

# Crosshair Baseplate

**Catch layout marks in your router's crosshairs to plunge-bore on-target holes.**

Though it will never replace the drill and drill press, the plunge router is an excellent boring tool. Sure, its range and flexibility are somewhat limited, but there are some applications in which it outperforms drills. And if you don't have a drill press, it can sometimes be a workable substitute.

The advantage of the plunge router over the portable electric drill, of course, is that it bores a hole that's perfectly square to the work surface. And although it can't bore a deep hole, it can bore to a preestablished depth.

This special baseplate can make it easier to accurately place the holes you bore with a plunge router. When using a plunge router, it's difficult to eyeball the exact location of the hole. The bit doesn't have a centerpoint to line up on a mark, and the bulk of the motor makes it impossible to sight down on the bit. The crosshair baseplate helps overcome this problem. I call it the crosshair baseplate because it is simply a piece of clear plastic with crosshairs delineating the centerpoint of the bit.

To use the baseplate, you must lay out hole locations on the workpiece using two lines crossing at right angles. Set the router on the work, and line up the baseplate's crosshairs over the layout. Flick on the router and plunge. The hole will be just where you want it.

This baseplate works especially well with trigger-switch routers, like the Bosch plungers, which allow you to switch the router on and off the way you would a drill.

## Making the Baseplate

It should be obvious that you must use a clear plastic for the baseplate. You can use either acrylic or polycarbonate. I used acrylic.

Tips on working thermosetting plastics can be found in the appendix.

**1. Cut the blank.** Cut a square slightly larger than your plunger router's baseplate. Make sure the blank is really square. Leave the paper facing on the blank.

**2. Mount it on the router.** Remove the router's baseplate and, using doubled-sided tape, bond it to the blank. Guided by the mounting-screw holes in the stock baseplate, select the appropriate-size drill and bore holes in

## CROSSHAIR BASEPLATE LAYOUT

Baseplate blank is sized to fit router's base.

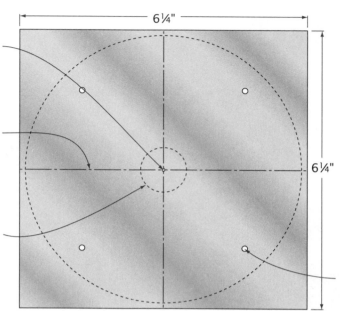

Dimple center of baseplate with V-grooving bit when baseplate is attached to the router.

Scribe crosshairs through the centermark using a scratch awl.

Plunge-bore the bit opening after scribing crosshairs.

6¼"

6¼"

Drill holes for mounting screws.

**Drilling thermosetting plastic** requires a high chuck speed and a rapid in-and-out feed action. Feed the bit sharply for only a moment, then retract it clear of the plastic. Feed sharply again, but only briefly. Retract the bit. This in-and-out action keeps the bit cool enough that it won't melt the plastic.

| Cutting List | | | |
|---|---|---|---|
| **Part** | **Qty.** | **Dimensions** | **Material** |
| Baseplate | 1 | ¼" × 6¼" × 6¼" | Clear plastic* |

*You can use acrylic or polycarbonate for this baseplate.

the blank. Switch to a countersink, and countersink the holes so the flathead screws you use will set below the baseplate surface.

Separate the blank from the stock baseplate. The protective paper will probably peel off the blank with the carpet tape; that's okay. Mount the blank on the router.

**3. Mark the bit opening centerpoint.** Fit a V-grooving bit in the router. Plunge the bit against the blank. Don't even plug the router in; just turn the bit a few times by hand, scoring a centermark into the blank.

Remove the blank from the router. On the drill press, drill the smallest-diameter hole you can through the blank at the centermark.

**4. Scribe the crosshairs.** Peel the protective paper from the blank (if it isn't already removed). Using a square and a scratch awl, score the crosshairs on the bottom of the blank. Apply dark-colored paint to the scored lines with a fine brush, then wipe the baseplate clean. The paint will cling to the scratches, highlighting the lines. (As an alternative, you can try using a fine-tipped marker to color and highlight the scratched crosshair lines.)

**5. Bore the bit opening.** You can bore this hole on the drill press with a large-diameter bit. Or remount the new baseplate on the router, and plunge-bore the bit opening with a large-diameter straight bit.

## Using the Baseplate

Is this an easy operation? You bet it is. Set up the router with the crosshair baseplate and the correct bit; then set the correct plunge depth.

The site of every hole must be laid out with crossed layout lines. Set the router over the marks, and get the baseplate's crossed hairs directly over the layout marks. Switch the router on and plunge the bit.

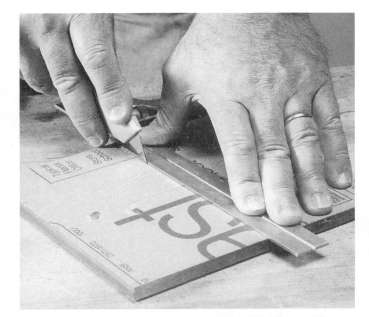

**To create the crosshairs,** work in good light with a square and scratch awl (*top*). Line up the square so it bisects the tiny centermark hole. Then draw the awl firmly along the square's blade, scoring the plastic as deeply as possible. After both lines are scratched into the baseplate, highlight them with dark-colored paint (*bottom*). Use a tiny artist's brush to apply a bead of paint along the scratched lines. Wipe the excess from the plastic, leaving just a thread of it in the scratches.

**It's going to be a bull's-eye!** You can't look directly down on the crosshairs and see without distortion how they line up with the layout lines. But the crosshairs of this baseplate make it dramatically easier to line up the router for plunge-boring.

# Slotted Pilot Template

**Now pilot *slots* are as easy to make as pilot holes.**

In building furniture, there are times when you need to confine a panel that changes width seasonally or fasten a panel that changes width to a structure that doesn't. If you don't make any allowance for this movement, surfaces buckle and joints break, doors won't open and drawers jam. If the member that moves is fastened to the fixed member with screws, the screw shank and head should slide in an elongated channel or slot.

The trick is: how to make the very narrow slots that are required. Try drilling several holes in a line, especially using a ⅛-inch-diameter bit. It doesn't work, because the bit wants to skitter off the mark into the previously drilled hole.

Here's the magical solution: the plunge router. It is the ideal tool to cut these slots. All you need is a simple template to guide the machine.

## Making the Template

The template is easy to make. Before beginning the work, study the template layout shown in the drawing.

**1. Cut the template blank.** Make the template out of ⅜- or ½-inch-thick plywood, hardboard, or acrylic. Plywood is probably the most practical. I like to jot notes and layout marks on templates, and I find it difficult to see any marks made on hardboard. Positioning an acrylic template is easy because it is clear, but be careful with clamps: Acrylic can be broken.

The template should be at least twice as long as the diameter of your router base and 1½ times wider. The template shown in the drawings is larger than that. But it provides plenty of clamping surface, so you can clamp it to the work without interfering with router movement.

**2. Scribe the crosshairs.** You can incorporate these helpful alignment lines only if you are making your template out of clear plastic. Incise the lines with a utility knife or a scratch awl and a square. Cut right through the masking paper that protects the plastic's surface.

**3. Rout the slots.** Guiding your router against a straightedge, rout a slot in the center of the template with a ⅝-inch-diameter straight bit to match a ⅝-inch-diameter guide bushing.

## SLOTTED PILOT TEMPLATE LAYOUT

Scribe crosshairs before routing template slots.

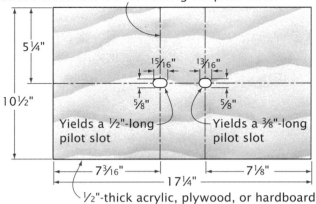

5 1/4"

10 1/2"

15/16"    13/16"

5/8"    5/8"

Yields a 1/2"-long pilot slot

Yields a 3/8"-long pilot slot

7 3/16"    7 1/8"

17 1/4"

1/2"-thick acrylic, plywood, or hardboard

### Cutting List

| Part | Qty. | Dimensions | Material |
|------|------|-----------|----------|
| Baseplate | 1 | 1/2" × 10 1/2" × 17 1/4" | Plywood |

## Using the Template

The typical 5/8-inch guide bushing has a collar that's 9/16 inch long. Before you can use a template thinner than that—and that's what I've directed you to make—you need to grind down the collar.

**1. Set up the router.** To rout a slot, you'll need a plunge router, one template guide (the 5/8-inch-O.D. size), and two straight bits—one for the counterbore for the screw head and a different one for the screw shank slot. For a #10 roundhead screw, use a 3/8-inch-diameter bit to cut the counterbore and a 3/16-inch-diameter bit for the shank slot. For a #8 or #6 screw, use the 3/16-inch bit for the counterbore and a 1/8-inch bit for the shank slot.

**2. Clamp the template to the workpiece.** Line up the template over the layout mark for the slot. Position the clamps where they won't interfere with the router.

**3. Rout the counterbore.** Chuck the larger bit in the router. Set the cutting depth stop to 1/4 inch beyond the thickness of the template. Set the router on the template, with the guide in the template's slot. Switch on the router, plunge the cutter, and rout.

**4. Rout the slot.** Switch to the smaller bit. Reset the cutting depth stop to the thickness of the workpiece plus that of the template. Rout the slot.

As you cut, remember that you are using a really frail bit. It is very easy to shear off the cutting tip of a 1/8-inch or 3/16-inch bit. So make a series of very shallow cuts to rout the slot.

**Rout slotted pilots in the cleats** that you use in attaching a tabletop to the leg-and-apron assembly. The screws driven through the cleat into the tabletop thus will be able to move a little as the top expands and contracts.

## TEMPLATE CUTAWAY

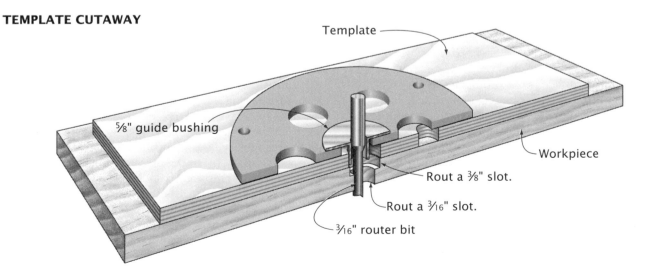

Template

5/8" guide bushing

Workpiece

Rout a 3/8" slot.

Rout a 3/16" slot.

3/16" router bit

# Boring Templates

**Routing holes may be boring, but with each of these templates, you can get some pretty exciting results: different sizes, through or blind holes, flat or stepped bottoms, even circular grooves.**

Large-diameter holes are bored with Forstner bits, hole saws, and flycutters. You can use a router and trammel (and frankly, we have a couple of good trammels in this book).

Of course, any boring operation has a limitation or two. For example:

- If you use a drill press, you have to be able to perch the work on the machine's little table. If the workpiece is too big or unwieldy, if the hole isn't relatively close to the workpiece edge, the drill press can't do the job.
- If you use a hand-held drill, making sure the hole is square to the surface is the problem.
- You can't use a flycutter in a hand-held drill.
- Large-diameter Forstner bits are costly, nonadjustable, and single-purpose. So it costs a lot to bore a hole of a one specific diameter.
- Neither a hole saw nor a flycutter can create a stopped hole.

The list could go on (if I'd really think about it). But rather than belabor it, let me say that a router and template can produce a large-diameter hole for you when other approaches are stymied by their limitations.

Shown here are a batch of templates with holes cut in them. To rout a matching hole, you simply clamp the template to the work, fit a pattern bit in your router, and let the template guide the router through the cut. If you need a through hole, just keep cutting deeper until the disk of waste is cut free of the workpiece. If a stopped hole is what you need, rout around the perimeter of the template hole until you've cut to the final depth, then work back and forth to excavate all the waste.

Now don't think you are limited to reproducing the hole in the template. If you use a guide bushing, which offsets the bit from the template edge, the hole size is reduced. You can use almost any groove-forming bit with a guide bushing. By using different guide bushing/straight bit combinations, you can use each template hole to rout at least seven different sizes of hole. If you use a ¼-inch bit with a guide bushing with an outside diameter of ¾ inch, it reduces the diameter of the template hole by ½ inch.

The table "Template Size Ranges" on page 11 lays out the specifics for you. It lists the sizes of holes that can be routed using the templates, and it is long. But to cut all 77 of these hole sizes, you need only three guide bushings and four bits, all common sizes.

One last thing. Several of the templates have rounded

corners. Those corners aren't rounded just for looks; they have a purpose. Clamp a template at a corner of something like a tabletop, and you can round the corner using your router and pattern bit. No saw marks to sand away, no ripples or flat spots. Use the same template at each corner on the tabletop, for example, and you can round the corners smoothly and consistently.

The templates give you corner-round guides starting at a ¾-inch radius and jumping in ¼-inch increments to 3 inches.

To make it a little easier to position the corner-rounding templates, I made little plastic stops that you attach to the edges of the templates. The idea is that you make two, then attach them on each side of whichever corner pattern you are using. When you use a different-radius corner, just move the stops. The mounting "screws" have plastic knobs that make it easy.

| Cutting List | | | |
|---|---|---|---|
| **Part** | **Qty.** | **Dimensions** | **Material** |
| Template 1 | 1 | ½" × 6" × 18" | MDF |
| Template 2–5 | 4 | ½" × 12" × 14" | MDF |
| Stops | 2 | ⅜" × 2" × 3" | Plastic |
| **Hardware** | | | |

2 hanger bolts, ¼" × 2"

2 hex nuts, ¼"

2 knurled plastic knobs,
1" dia. with ¼" threaded insert;
#DK-32 from Reid Tool Supply Co. (800-253-0421)

4 flathead wood screws, #6 × ¾"

## Making the Templates

This is a simple matter. Template layouts are shown in the drawing. You *can* make individual templates—one for each size of hole—but ganging the smaller holes gives you space-efficient clamping area without wasting template stock and without making the templates unwieldy.

**1. Cut the blanks.** Templates are usually made of plywood, medium-density fiberboard (MDF), or particleboard. The stock should be at least ½ inch thick. If you are reproducing the template set shown in the drawing *Circle Template Layouts,* cut the blanks to the sizes specified by the Cutting List.

**2. Drill or rout the holes.** You can make the holes in several ways. I used a couple. I used Forstner bits in a drill press to bore the four smallest holes. For the larger ones, I used a router equipped with the Trammel Baseplate on page 39. You can also use a flycutter in a drill press, or even hole saws.

Lay out the centerpoints on the various templates. Bore those that you are making with Forstner bits, a flycutter, or hole saws. Remember that the holes must be precisely *sized* but not precisely located.

For those that will be routed, locate and drill ⅛-inch-diameter pivot holes. Set up the router and trammel, and rout the holes. I found it beneficial to set up the router and make a test pass on scrap to ensure that the trammel setting was exactly what I needed.

**3. Round the corners.** Two approaches come to mind here. I used the trammel, but you can also simply sand the corners to a layout line. The truth is, it's tough to completely avoid dinging the edges when routing the corners,

**CIRCLE TEMPLATE LAYOUTS**

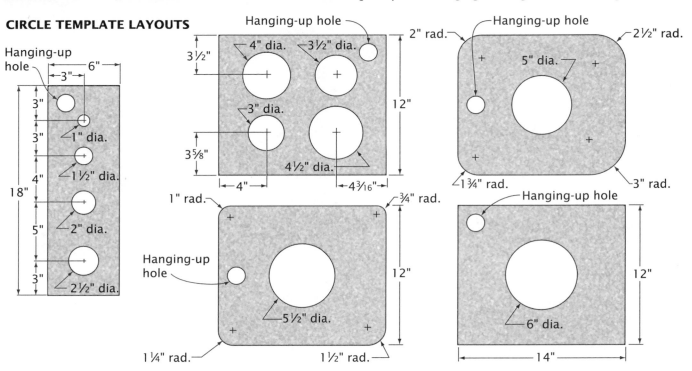

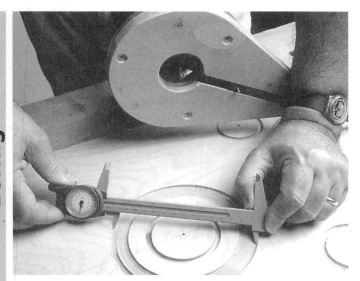

**Accurately sized template holes** are essential. When using a trammel, it's worth the trouble to make a test cut in scrap and measure it before cutting the template.

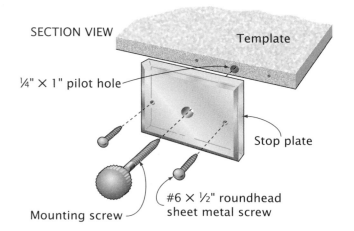

Plastic knob (Reid #DK-32)

Hex nut

¼" × 2" hanger bolt

Clearance hole for mounting screw

Pilot for screw

PLATE LAYOUT

MOUNTING SCREW

SECTION VIEW

Template

¼" × 1" pilot hole

Stop plate

Mounting screw

#6 × ½" roundhead sheet metal screw

so some sanding is inevitable. You do need smooth, nick-free edges for the templates to be worth using.

**4. Drill hanging holes.** If you plan to store the templates by hanging them up, by all means make a hole in each specifically for that. The hanging hole invariably gets nicks and dents from the shank of the nail from which it hangs. You don't want those injuries inflicted on the template hole, because they'll transfer to the holes you rout.

**5. Make the stop plates.** What you need are two 2 × 3-inch pieces of scrap. I used plastic left over from making baseplates because I had it and it looks cool. But plywood would work swell, as would thin hardwood scraps.

The stop plate has two points on each side of a mounting-screw hole. The points dig into the template as the mounting screw is tightened, thus preventing the stop from twisting.

Cut the scraps to size, chamfer the edges on the router table, then lay out the holes, as shown in the drawing *Stop Detail*. The center hole must provide clearance for the mounting knob, so it should be bigger than the threaded section of the shank. Drill pilots for the two sheet-metal screws.

Drive the screws into the latter two holes.

**6. Install the stops.** To mount the stops, I wanted to have a screw with a plastic knob on it. No one (that I know of ) makes a studded plastic knob with a tapered thread. So I used a hanger bolt, which has a machine thread on one end, a tapered thread on the other. Turn a nut on the shank, then the knob. Jam the nut against the knob.

Bore the pilot holes into the template edges for the stops. To mount a stop, hold it in position, insert the screw shank into the hole, and tighten the screw.

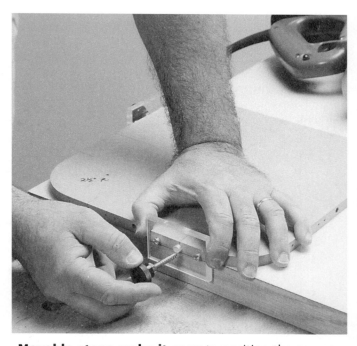

**Movable stops make it easy** to position the corner-rounding templates. A "screw," made up of a hanger bolt and a plastic knob, is turned by hand into a pilot hole in the edge of the template, attaching the plastic stop. The stops catch on the edges of the workpiece, ensuring that the template is aligned flush.

# Using the Templates

The basic technique is straightforward: Clamp the template to the workpiece, set up the router, and rout.

When you do this, you get a circle. Cut completely through the workpiece, and it is a big hole. Cut partway through the workpiece, and it's a groove or a recess. Use a groove-forming bit with a profile—a core-box bit, for example, or a plunging round-over bit—and you can form decorative bull's-eyes or rosettes.

**1. Clamp the template to the workpiece.** Depending upon where the circular cut must be made, any of a variety of clamping techniques may be in order. If the location is close to an edge, you can simply clamp the template to the workpiece. If it is beyond a clamp's reach, use carpet tape or hot-melt glue.

Lining up the template for a cut that must be placed precisely is a little tricky. You can scribe crosshairs on the template, then try to align them with similar marks on the workpiece. You can also scribe a circle on the workpiece that is the same size as the template opening. Line up the template on the circle.

**2. Set up the router.** Do your math, or consult the size table on page 11. Select the bit and the guide bushing combination needed for the size hole you are going to rout. Chuck the bit in the collet, and fit the bushing to the baseplate. Set the plunge depth.

**3. Rout the hole.** Set the router on the template with the collar tight against the edge. Switch on the router, plunge the bit, and feed the router clockwise around the template. Keep the collar tight against the template edge as you work. Plunge a little deeper for the second revolution, and go to the full depth for the third round.

If you are merely routing a recess, setting the depth of cut is pretty important. Plunge to that depth and rout around the template. Then move the router back and forth, clearing the waste from the middle of the recess. The template and guide bushing will ensure that you don't wander out of the defined area (something that's easy to do when freehanding a recess).

## Rounding Corners

The same templates can be used to round off the corners of tabletops, counters, and other panels. Instead of using a guide bushing, you use a pattern bit, which has a shank-mounted bearing that rides on the template to guide the cut.

**1. Attach the stops to the template.** Pick the template corner that has the radius you want to use. Attach a stop on each side of the corner. Insert the mounting screw through the hole in the stop, and feed it into the pilot hole in the template edge. As you tighten the screw, the screw points on each side of the mounting screw will dig into the template edge to keep the stop from rotating.

**2. Clamp the template to the workpiece.** The stops make positioning the template easy. Set the template on the workpiece and slide it diagonally onto the surface until both stops contact the edges on each side of the corner. Then apply a couple of clamps where they won't interfere with the router.

**3. Set up the router.** As noted, you use a pattern bit for this operation. The cutting edge doesn't need to be longer than the stock thickness, but the bearing must be in contact with the template on every pass. So in adjusting the cutting depth, you really have to simply extend the bit fully, so the shank-mounted bearing is exposed and can contact the template.

**4. Rout the corner away.** What I usually do is take shallow cuts back and forth, nibbling away at the corner of the workpiece. I have the baseplate flat on the template, but the bearing isn't against the template; the bit is out at the edge of the workpiece. As the corner is routed away, the bearing catches on the template, and a final pass along the template completes the cut.

Now, about bit length. If you have a pattern bit with a 1-inch cutting length, you have to make a full-depth cut; you can't creep down to full depth in increments, which is the usual routing approach. With a short bit, cut as deep as you must on the first pass, then remove the template and guide the second cut by riding the bearing on the edge routed on the first pass.

You can confine your work to the very corner, or you can rout from stop to stop, which will help blend the radius into the flats.

**The results are anything but boring,** but you've got to be imaginative in your choices of bits and guide bushings. The boring templates can help you produce through holes, stepped holes, recesses, grooves, and arcs, in all sorts of profiles.

## How It Works

To give you the idea of how using these templates works, here's a listing of the guide/bit combinations used, with the differential between the outside diameter of the guide and the diameter of the bit. What I am calling the "differential" is twice the *offset*. When using a particular guide/bit combination with a circle template, you can calculate the size of the hole you'll cut by subtracting the differential from the diameter of the hole in the template.

You will note that NO combination gives you a $\frac{1}{16}$-inch differential. Can't be done with guide bushings; the collar has to have *some* wall thickness. The consequence, which you will note in the extrapolated table, "Template Size Ranges," is that you cannot rout the $\frac{7}{16}$-inch and $\frac{15}{16}$-inch increments. But you can try this: Buy a $\frac{1}{4}$-inch-I.D. × $\frac{3}{8}$-inch-O.D. bearing and put it on the shank of a $\frac{5}{16}$-inch straight bit. Use the bearing to guide the cut, rather than a guide bushing. (Eagle America stocks a bearing of this size: catalog number 196-0620. Call 800-872-2511.)

| Guide Bushing | Bit Diameter | Differential |
|---------------|--------------|--------------|
| $\frac{3}{4}$" O.D. | $\frac{1}{4}$" | $\frac{1}{2}$" |
| $\frac{3}{4}$" O.D. | $\frac{5}{16}$" | $\frac{7}{16}$" |
| $\frac{5}{8}$" O.D. | $\frac{1}{4}$" | $\frac{3}{8}$" |
| $\frac{5}{8}$" O.D. | $\frac{5}{16}$" | $\frac{5}{16}$" |
| $\frac{5}{8}$" O.D. | $\frac{3}{8}$" | $\frac{1}{4}$" |
| $\frac{1}{2}$" O.D. | $\frac{5}{16}$" | $\frac{3}{16}$" |
| $\frac{5}{8}$" O.D. | $\frac{1}{2}$" | $\frac{1}{8}$" |

**HOW IT WORKS**

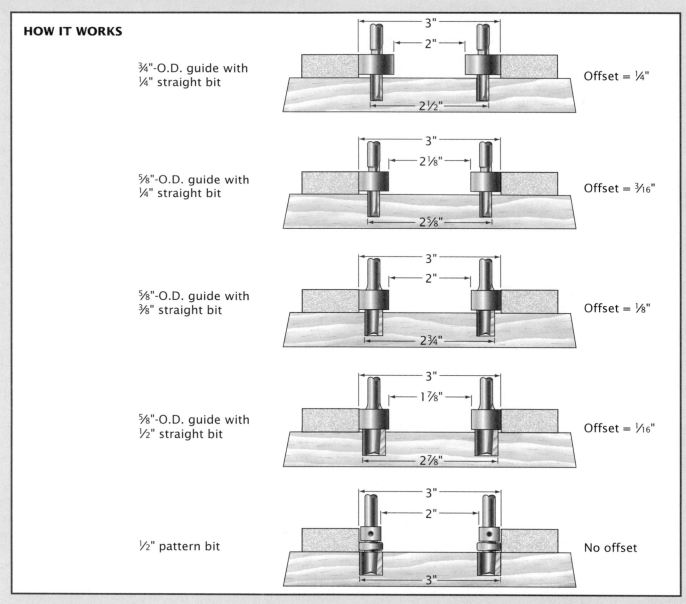

$\frac{3}{4}$"-O.D. guide with $\frac{1}{4}$" straight bit — Offset = $\frac{1}{4}$"

$\frac{5}{8}$"-O.D. guide with $\frac{1}{4}$" straight bit — Offset = $\frac{3}{16}$"

$\frac{5}{8}$"-O.D. guide with $\frac{3}{8}$" straight bit — Offset = $\frac{1}{8}$"

$\frac{5}{8}$"-O.D. guide with $\frac{1}{2}$" straight bit — Offset = $\frac{1}{16}$"

$\frac{1}{2}$" pattern bit — No offset

## Template Size Ranges

| Template Diameter | Guide Bushing O.D. | Bit Diameter | Hole Diameter | Template Diameter | Guide Bushing O.D. | Bit Diameter | Hole Diameter |
|---|---|---|---|---|---|---|---|
| 1" hole | ¾" | ¼" | ½" | 4" hole | ¾" | ¼" | 3½" |
|  | ¾" | 5⁄16" | 9⁄16" |  | ¾" | 5⁄16" | 3 9⁄16" |
|  | 5⁄8" | ¼" | 5⁄8" |  | 5⁄8" | ¼" | 3 5⁄8" |
|  | 5⁄8" | 5⁄16" | 11⁄16" |  | 5⁄8" | 5⁄16" | 3 11⁄16" |
|  | 5⁄8" | 3⁄8" | ¾" |  | 5⁄8" | 3⁄8" | 3¾" |
|  | ½" | 5⁄16" | 13⁄16" |  | ½" | 5⁄16" | 3 13⁄16" |
|  | 5⁄8" | ½" | 7⁄8" |  | 5⁄8" | ½" | 3 7⁄8" |
| 1½" hole | ¾" | ¼" | 1" | 4½" hole | ¾" | ¼" | 4" |
|  | ¾" | 5⁄16" | 1 1⁄16" |  | ¾" | 5⁄16" | 4 1⁄16" |
|  | 5⁄8" | ¼" | 1 1⁄8" |  | 5⁄8" | ¼" | 4 1⁄8" |
|  | 5⁄8" | 5⁄16" | 1 3⁄16" |  | 5⁄8" | 5⁄16" | 4 3⁄16" |
|  | 5⁄8" | 3⁄8" | 1 1⁄4" |  | 5⁄8" | 3⁄8" | 4 1⁄4" |
|  | ½" | 5⁄16" | 1 5⁄16" |  | ½" | 5⁄16" | 4 5⁄16" |
|  | 5⁄8" | ½" | 1 3⁄8" |  | 5⁄8" | ½" | 4 3⁄8" |
| 2" hole | ¾" | ¼" | 1 1⁄2" | 5" hole | ¾" | ¼" | 4½" |
|  | ¾" | 5⁄16" | 1 9⁄16" |  | ¾" | 5⁄16" | 4 9⁄16" |
|  | 5⁄8" | ¼" | 1 5⁄8" |  | 5⁄8" | ¼" | 4 5⁄8" |
|  | 5⁄8" | 5⁄16" | 1 11⁄16" |  | 5⁄8" | 5⁄16" | 4 11⁄16" |
|  | 5⁄8" | 3⁄8" | 1 3⁄4" |  | 5⁄8" | 3⁄8" | 4¾" |
|  | ½" | 5⁄16" | 1 13⁄16" |  | ½" | 5⁄16" | 4 13⁄16" |
|  | 5⁄8" | ½" | 1 7⁄8" |  | 5⁄8" | ½" | 4 7⁄8" |
| 2½" hole | ¾" | ¼" | 2" | 5½" hole | ¾" | ¼" | 5" |
|  | ¾" | 5⁄16" | 2 1⁄16" |  | ¾" | 5⁄16" | 5 1⁄16" |
|  | 5⁄8" | ¼" | 2 1⁄8" |  | 5⁄8" | ¼" | 5 1⁄8" |
|  | 5⁄8" | 5⁄16" | 2 3⁄16" |  | 5⁄8" | 5⁄16" | 5 3⁄16" |
|  | 5⁄8" | 3⁄8" | 2 1⁄4" |  | 5⁄8" | 3⁄8" | 5 1⁄4" |
|  | ½" | 5⁄16" | 2 5⁄16" |  | ½" | 5⁄16" | 5 5⁄16" |
|  | 5⁄8" | ½" | 2 3⁄8" |  | 5⁄8" | ½" | 5 3⁄8" |
| 3" hole | ¾" | ¼" | 2 1⁄2" | 6" hole | ¾" | ¼" | 5½" |
|  | ¾" | 5⁄16" | 2 9⁄16" |  | ¾" | 5⁄16" | 5 9⁄16" |
|  | 5⁄8" | ¼" | 2 5⁄8" |  | 5⁄8" | ¼" | 5 5⁄8" |
|  | 5⁄8" | 5⁄16" | 2 11⁄16" |  | 5⁄8" | 5⁄16" | 5 11⁄16" |
|  | 5⁄8" | 3⁄8" | 2 3⁄4" |  | 5⁄8" | 3⁄8" | 5 3⁄4" |
|  | ½" | 5⁄16" | 2 13⁄16" |  | ½" | 5⁄16" | 5 13⁄16" |
|  | 5⁄8" | ½" | 2 7⁄8" |  | 5⁄8" | ½" | 5 7⁄8" |
| 3½" hole | ¾" | ¼" | 3" |  |  |  |  |
|  | ¾" | 5⁄16" | 3 1⁄16" |  |  |  |  |
|  | 5⁄8" | ¼" | 3 1⁄8" |  |  |  |  |
|  | 5⁄8" | 5⁄16" | 3 3⁄16" |  |  |  |  |
|  | 5⁄8" | 3⁄8" | 3 1⁄4" |  |  |  |  |
|  | ½" | 5⁄16" | 3 5⁄16" |  |  |  |  |
|  | 5⁄8" | ½" | 3 3⁄8" |  |  |  |  |

# Shelf Support Template

**A shop-made template, a guide bushing, and a plunge router are all you need to bore clean, accurate, precisely placed support-pin holes for adjustable shelving.**

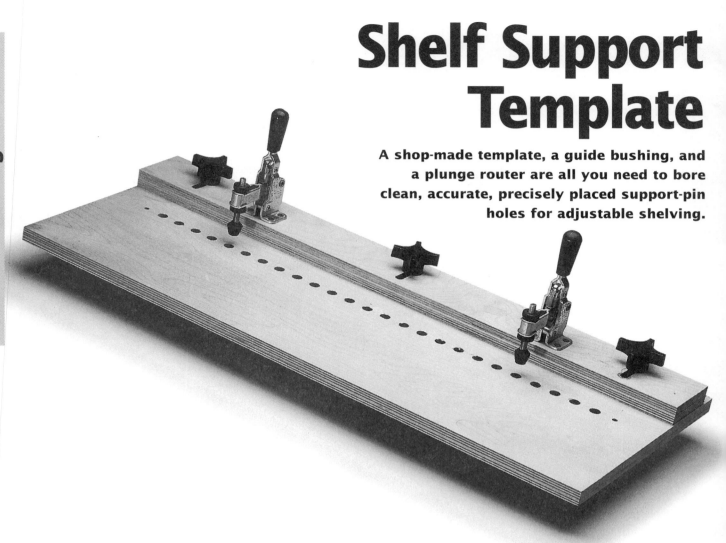

Here's a jig to make boring ranks of holes for adjustable shelving a whole lot easier and more accurate. It's a template that clamps to the work-piece. You use a plunge router with a ½-inch template guide and a ¼-inch straight bit to actually bore the holes.

With this shelf adjustment approach, of course, you have sets of four holes, two in each of two sides, and all are in the same level plane. A pin in each hole will support a shelf. Wanna move that shelf up or down a little? Need to make headroom for a new book that's an inch taller than the others? Move the four pins to a different set of holes and move the shelf.

The hitch is that stipulation that each set of four holes must all be in the same level plane. If the ranks of holes in one side are a fraction out of line with those in the other side, the shelves won't be level. Worse, if one side's two ranks of holes are slightly out of alignment with each other, each shelf will be supported by only three pins. It'll be unsteady and rattly.

Nevertheless, this approach for providing adjustability in shelving and cabinetry is flexible and popular. If you use wooden pegs rather than manufactured pins, the materials bill is low. On the other hand, it's fairly labor-intensive. (So a pro may choose plastic or metal shelf standards, which require less labor.)

If you are like me, you've seen different gizmos and tricks for boring these holes. Most depend upon a portable drill to bore the holes. Such approaches have never proved satisfactory to me. The tool wavers as I drill hole after hole, so the holes aren't consistently square to the surface. The bottoms aren't flat. Whatever jig I use gets worn and distorted by the drill bit, and eventually, the holes that are drilled get out of alignment. It's a messy business.

This jig solves these problems.

A router bit bores a clean, flat-bottomed hole. No tear-out around the surface edge. The plunge router's structure guarantees that the holes will be perpendicular to the surface. Its depth stop ensures that all the holes will be the same depth. Because the bit never touches the template (the template guide does), the template doesn't get worn. Because the template doesn't get worn, the holes are in consistent alignment.

## Making the Jig

You can make this jig either of two ways, and error can creep in no matter how you do it.

The easy way is to lay out the template holes, then drill

## SHELF SUPPORT TEMPLATE EXPLODED VIEW

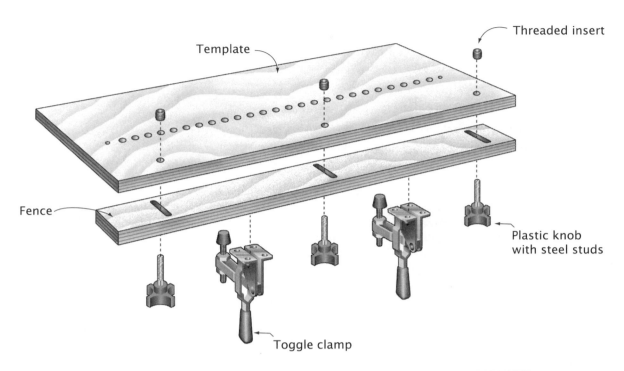

Threaded insert

Template

Fence

Plastic knob
with steel studs

Toggle clamp

## Cutting List

| Part | Qty. | Dimensions | Material |
|------|------|-----------|----------|
| Baseplate | 1 | ½" × 10" × 10" | Plywood |
| Indexing pin | 1 | ½" dia. × 1" | Hardwood dowel |
| Template | 1 | ¾" × 14" × 32" | Plywood |
| Fence | 1 | 1" × 3" × 30" | Plywood |

## Hardware

3 brass threaded inserts, ⅜"-16

3 plastic knobs with steel studs, ⅜"-16 × 1½";
#DK-97 from Reid Tool Supply Co. (800-253-0421)

2 toggle clamps (De-Sta-Co #TC-207-U)

2 spindles, ⁵⁄₁₆"-18 × 2³⁄₁₆";
#TC-225208 from Reid Tool Supply Co.

8 panhead screws, #8 × ¾" (for mounting the clamps)

2 hex-head bolts, ¼" × 1½" (to serve as
indexing pins)

## INCREMENTAL BORING BASEPLATE

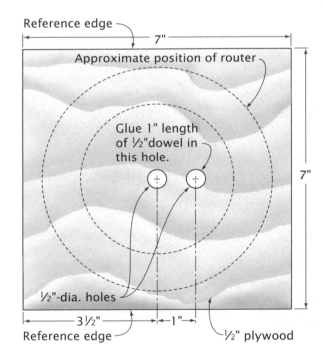

Reference edge

7"

Approximate position of router

Glue 1" length
of ½"dowel in
this hole.

7"

½"-dia. holes

3½"  1"

Reference edge

½" plywood

them on the drill press. This is fast. You can get the holes in a straight line, and you can get the first and last holes exactly 24 inches apart. But the spacing of holes between the first and last can vary. That spacing inconsistency can lead to tippy, rattling shelves, I think.

So I'm recommending that you make and use a special baseplate, which I call the incremental boring baseplate.

You use it to guide the router when boring the template holes. If error creeps into the making of the baseplate, it doesn't matter (in my opinion), because the hole spacing on the template will be consistent. The hitch is that the first and last template holes may be more or less than 24 inches apart: You have cumulative error.

Here's an example. If, to be extreme, your baseplate

ends up spacing the template holes consistently ⅞ inch apart instead of 1 inch apart, your template will measure 21 inches from first hole to last, not 24 inches. I don't view this as a problem, because the holes are spaced consistently, and the template can be repositioned to extend the ranks of holes. The incremental spacing will be consistent, though the cumulative spacing may not be dead-on. So don't be surprised.

## Making the Baseplate

The parts for this baseplate are included on the Cutting List, even though, once the template is built, you don't need the baseplate anymore.

**1. Cut the baseplate parts.** The baseplate is a plywood square, larger than your plunge router's base. On the Cutting List, I spec'd it as a 10-inch square, while the drawing shows it as a 7-inch square. Start with the 10-inch square; after the necessary holes are bored and the indexing pin is installed, cut it down to the 7-inch-square size. (Of course, if your plunge router has a larger footprint, by all means increase the finished size of this baseplate.) The indexing pin is a 1-inch-long piece of ½-inch-diameter hardwood dowel.

**2. Mount the baseplate blank on the router.** Remove the factory baseplate from your plunge router, and roughly center it in the baseplate blank. Transfer the mounting-screw locations. (Position the mounting holes so the router will be comfortably oriented when you are plunge-routing the holes in the template.) Drill the holes, countersink them, and attach the blank to the router in place of the stock baseplate.

**Boring the indexing pin hole** is easy if you plan ahead. Before removing the baseplate from the router, set the edge guide against the baseplate edge. That will ensure that both holes will be the same distance from the edge. Next, pencil an alignment mark for the router so the second hole will be 1 inch from the first, as shown. *Then* unscrew the baseplate and proceed to bore the hole.

**3. Plunge-bore the bit opening and pin hole.** The baseplate has two ½-inch-diameter holes in it, 1 inch apart: one for the bit, the other for the indexing pin. The holes must be the same distance from one edge of the baseplate.

To bore the bit opening, simply fit a ½-inch straight bit into the router collet and plunge-bore the hole. Boring the indexing pin hole is a bit more involved.

Do this first: Fit the edge guide to the router, and snug it up against the plywood baseplate. Using the edge guide will ensure that the pin hole will be the same distance from that edge as the bit opening.

Now put a reference mark on the baseplate, so you know how far to move the router so the pin hole will be 1 inch from the bit opening. Butt a rule against the router base, and mark 1 inch from the base on the baseplate.

Next, remove the baseplate from the router and bond it to a large scrap clamped to the workbench. Use carpet tape to secure the baseplate.

Finally, bore the pin hole. Set the router on the baseplate. Snug its edge guide tight against the baseplate's edge. Slide the router to the mark penciled on the baseplate. Now switch on the router and plunge-bore the hole.

**4. Complete the baseplate.** Glue the pin in the pin hole.

If you want, cut down the baseplate to a manageable size. As you do this, make very sure that the reference edges (see the baseplate drawing) remain parallel to the line between the bit opening and the pin. You can save yourself a little finagling later, when you bore the last hole in the template, if you make these edges equidistant from the bit opening now.

Hold off on remounting the baseplate on the router until after the first template hole is bored.

## Making the Template

With the special baseplate completed, you can now turn to the template itself.

**1. Cut the template blank.** As with the special baseplate, the template blank should be a bit oversized. In this case, the reason has to do with getting the edges square to the centerline of the template holes. So, despite what the *Template Plan Views* drawing suggests, cut the template to the size specified by the Cutting List.

**2. Bore the first hole.** Check the drawing, then lay out the location of the first ½-inch-diameter hole in the column. Scribe the centerline of the column of holes as you do this. Remember that you'll cut down the template after all the holes are bored, so lay out the first hole and the centerline accordingly. Set the router over the hole location and plunge-bore it. (The Crosshair Baseplate can help you locate this hole precisely; see page 1.)

**3. Clamp the fence in place.** *Now* mount that incremental boring baseplate on the router. Set the router on the blank, and catch the pin in the first hole. Swing the

**TEMPLATE PLAN VIEWS**

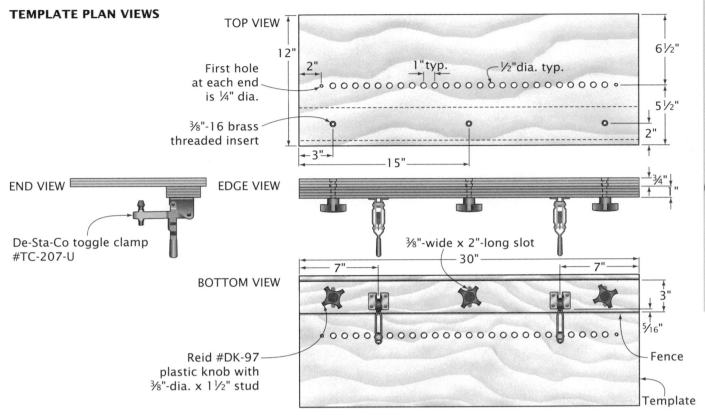

TOP VIEW

12"

First hole at each end is ¼" dia.

⅜"-16 brass threaded insert

6½"

5½"

2"

2"

1"typ.

½"dia. typ.

3"

15"

END VIEW

EDGE VIEW

¾"

1"

De-Sta-Co toggle clamp #TC-207-U

⅜"-wide x 2"-long slot

BOTTOM VIEW

30"

7"

7"

3"

5/16"

Reid #DK-97 plastic knob with ⅜"-dia. x 1½" stud

Fence

Template

router to align the bit over the centerline.

Slide the fence up to the baseplate's edge, and clamp it to the workpiece. The fence should be parallel to the centerline.

**4. Plunge-bore the holes.** Switch on the router and plunge-bore the second hole. The baseplate should be against the fence, and the indexing pin should be captured in the first hole you bored. Retract the bit and shift the router again.

Repeat the process until all the ½-inch holes are bored.

**5. Plunge-bore the end holes.** Switch to a ¼-inch-diameter bit. Bore the first of the two ¼-inch holes, with the base tight against the fence and the indexing bit caught in the last ½-inch hole.

To bore the second ¼-inch hole, you may need to shift the fence slightly, depending upon the precision of your incremental boring baseplate. Both ¼-inch holes *must be*

**Using the incremental boring baseplate:** This custom baseplate has a pin projecting from it a short distance from the bit opening (*right*). With that indexing pin captured in a hole, the router is essentially on a trammel and can only swing in an arc around that hole. Bring a fence against the router base, and you establish exactly where the next hole will be bored.

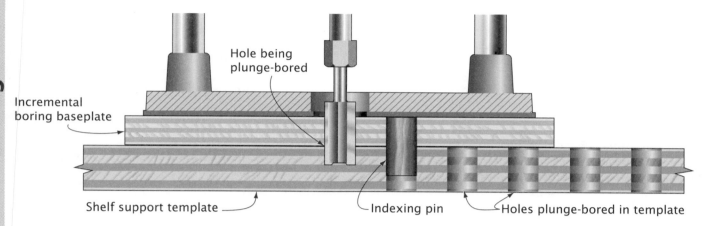

Incremental boring baseplate

Hole being plunge-bored

Shelf support template

Indexing pin

Holes plunge-bored in template

perfectly aligned on the centerline shared by all the other holes. And to bore that last hole, you have to turn the router 180 degrees, so the indexing pin is on the opposite side of the bit.

If need be, ensure that the fence is properly aligned for the last hole by fitting the ½-inch bit in the router. Orient the router as it will be when boring that last hole. With the router turned *off*, plunge the bit and fit it into a hole, with the indexing pin fitting into the adjacent hole. If you can do that, and the fence is tight against the baseplate, you are set. But if the fence is out of position in any way, unclamp it, shift it so it is tightly against the baseplate, and reclamp it. Now switch back to the ¼-inch bit and bore the last hole.

Yes, this is a lot of busywork. But you only have to do it once to get the template right. And having the template right will ensure that you save time every time you use the template.

**6. Trim the template.** Before unclamping the fence, strike a pencil line along its edge. Remove the fence, and use the pencil line—which parallels the centerline of the template holes—to trim the template to its final size.

## Making the Fence

The last part to make is the fence. It positions the template on the workpiece and is the base for the toggle clamps, which secure the template on the work.

**1. Make the fence blank.** Cut two strips of ½-inch plywood to the dimensions specified by the Cutting List. Glue them face to face to form the 1-inch-thick blank for the fence.

**2. Cut the adjustment slots.** The fence has three 2-inch slots routed in it, so it can be moved up to 2 inches. Thus, the holes in a shelf side can be positioned anywhere between 1 and 3 inches from the side's edge.

Probably the best way to rout the holes is with a hand-held plunge router, guided along a fence clamped across the workpiece. It's a good idea to clamp scraps along each side of the workpiece to provide more bearing for the router. And remember to slide scrap underneath the work-piece so you won't rout into the bench top.

Take the slot locations from the *Template Fence Detail* drawing, and transfer them to the workpiece. Then set up and rout the slots.

**3. Attach the toggle clamps.** I used De-Sta-Co clamps, though other brands, including Taiwanese knock-offs, are sold by a number of mail-order vendors. The model I chose has a T-handle and a long U-bar for the spindle. The U-bar configuration allows you to vary the spindle position. The reach of the TC-207 series provides good flexibility in clamping. In a fairly typical setup, the spindle pressure is applied on the far side of the template holes, although that

## TEMPLATE FENCE DETAIL

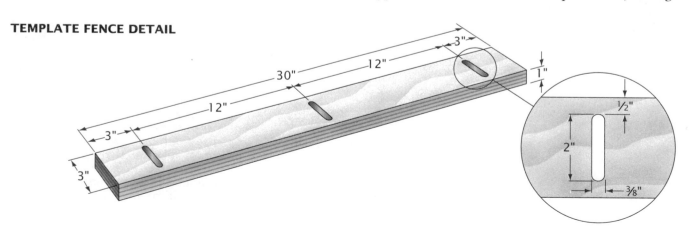

30"

12"

12"

3"

3"

3"

1"

½"

2"

⅜"

wouldn't necessarily be the case in every situation. For example, with the fence set as far from the template holes as it'll go, the spindles will be almost directly on a template hole. Watch out for that! You'll damage both the spindle and the bit if they collide.

This particular De-Sta-Co comes without a spindle. The spindle I selected is specified by the Cutting List.

The positions for the clamps are delineated on the *Bottom View* drawing. Mount each with four panhead screws.

**4. Assemble the template.** Clamp the fence to the template, and transfer the slot locations to the template. Mark where you'll bore pilot holes for the threaded inserts, then bore these holes. Install the inserts.

Fasten the fence to the template with the studded knobs. The template is completed.

## Using the Jig

As I mentioned, the template is easier to use than it is to make. Set the fence square; set the router. Then pop the template on the workpiece, and bore away. Here, step by step, is how to do it.

**1. Lay out one side.** Layout is primarily a matter of deciding

- How far from the workpiece edges you want the holes to be.
- How far from the top edge the holes should begin.
- How close to the bottom edge they should end.

You might scribe a couple of lines on one of the shelf or cabinet sides to help you set up the template. Beyond that, it's all in the template for all subsequent pieces you work.

**2. Set the template fence position.** It's easiest if you use the same offset from both front and back edges. That way you don't have to work your way through the stack of workpieces twice. If, for example, you were building standard 12-inch-deep wall cabinets for a kitchen or bath, you might set the offset at $1\frac{1}{2}$ inches. You'd have a line of holes $1\frac{1}{2}$ inches from the front edge and another $1\frac{1}{2}$ inches from the back edge.

The fence determines where the line of holes will fall on the workpiece. Measure from the holes to position the fence, and tighten the knobs firmly, so the fence won't shift as you move the template from workpiece to workpiece and slam it into place. And make darn certain the fence is parallel to that centerline. Otherwise, you'll have the holes on a skewed line. And no, that's not pretty.

**3. Clamp the template to the workpiece.** The toggle clamps on the fence are what hold the template on the workpiece. As you set the template on the first workpiece, take the time to adjust the spindles so that the clamps snap closed, and so that when they do, the template and the

work are really clamped tightly together.

Usually, I like to use check nuts on toggle-clamp spindles because it makes it easy to reposition the spindle. But it's hard to jam them tightly enough to hold a setting over a period of prolonged use. In this application, I use hex nuts and tighten them with wrenches.

Once the clamp spindles are adjusted and set, give a moment's attention to the position of the template on the work. With the clamps open, insert one of the bolts that serve as indexing pins into the ¼-inch hole. Slide the

**Set the fence parallel to the line of holes.** To do this, use two ¼-inch bolts and a couple of scraps ripped to the width of the offset. Insert a bolt through each indexing hole, as shown. Set a spacer block against each bolt, then slide the fence against the blocks. Tighten the clamping knobs, and the fence is set parallel to the line of holes.

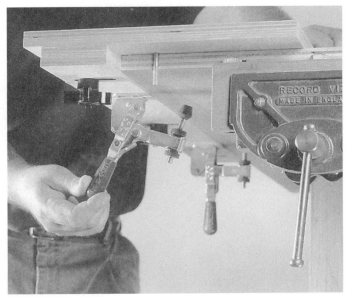

**With the workpiece overhanging the workbench edge,** position the template on it. The template's fence and an indexing bolt dropped through the end hole position the template on the work. Snap the clamps closed to secure the template.

template down the workpiece until the bolt/pin contacts the work's top edge. Check that the fence is flat against the workpiece. Both the fence and the bolt must be against the work to position it.

Snap the toggle clamps closed.

**4. Set up the router.** Because the template has ½-inch holes in it, the router has to be set up with a ½-inch-diameter (O.D.) template guide. You can use any size bit that will fit into this guide, but the size that's usually used is ¼ inch. Clamp the chosen bit in the collet, and install the ½-inch template guide.

Now set the depth stop on the plunge router. Set the router on the template, with the guide in a hole. Bottom the bit and lock the plunge mechanism. Drop the stop rod onto the turret, then raise it ¼ inch (or whatever depth you want the holes to be). Lock the rod and unlock the plunge mechanism. The router is set.

I think it's worth mentioning that a good router to use with this jig is a plunge router with a trigger switch. Rather than keeping the router running as you move it from position to position, you can turn it on and off, as you would a drill if you were drilling a series of holes. Bosch is the only maker I can think of who makes trigger-switch plunge routers.

**5. Plunge-bore the holes.** Plug in the router and get to work! Set the router on the template with its guide extending into the template hole. Switch on the router and plunge. Retract the bit and move the router to the next hole.

Tedious? Perhaps. But difficult? Nah.

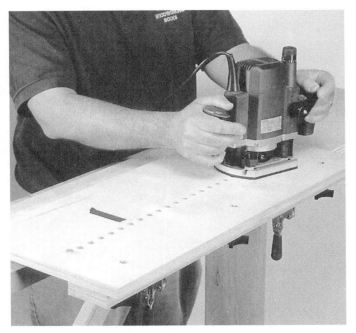

**Any plunge router can produce the holes.** Fit the proper bit and guide in the router, and set the depth stop. Boring each pin hole is a matter of dropping the guide into a template hole, turning on the router, then plunging the bit into the work.

**6. (optional) Shift the template position to extend the run of holes.** If the line of holes must be longer than 24 inches, just move the template. The indexing pin will ensure that the spacing of holes will remain consistent.

Open the toggle clamps. Pull up the bolt from the indexing hole so you can slide the template down the workpiece. Line up the index hole over the last hole you bored, and push the bolt down into the index hole and one into the hole in the workpiece. Nudge the fence tight against the workpiece edge, and close the toggle clamps.

Now keep boring.

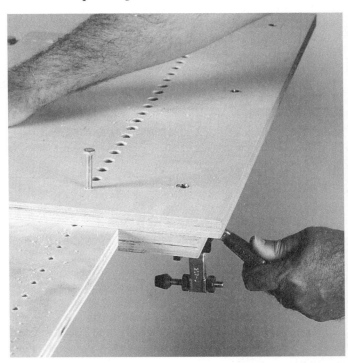

**Extending the run of support-pin holes** is easy. All you do is reposition the template. To align it in relation to the already-routed holes, insert a bolt through the template's indexing hole and into the last pin routed in the workpiece, as shown.

**7. Switch the template to the back edge of the workpiece.** You shift to the back edge by unclamping the template and walking it around to the other side. Move the index pin from one ¼-inch hole to the other. The fence setting remains the same, and the positioning routine remains the same.

# Router Duplicator

**As a kind of woodworking Xerox machine, this device helps you duplicate shallow carvings and curved moldings, hollowed chair seats, and even signs. And it does all this while floating on a thin cushion of air.**

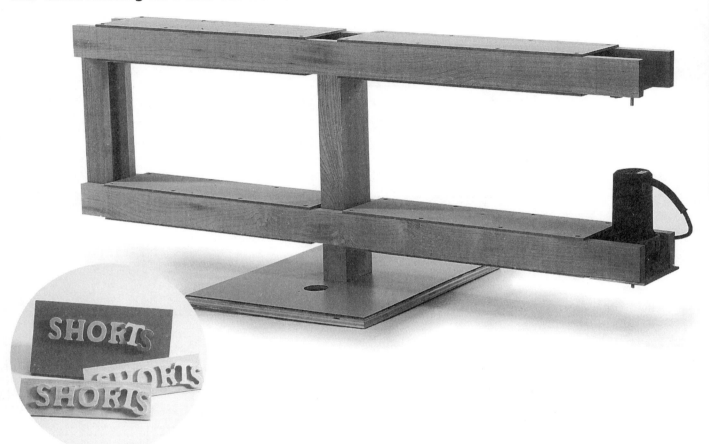

The most arresting thing about this device is not how gawky it is. It isn't the mystery of WHAT, exactly, it IS. What stops you in your tracks is this: It's a hovercraft! It's a fantastical woodshop hovercraft! It isn't on wheels or casters. It isn't sliding on a smooth, slick surface. It is literally FLOATING ON AIR!

Of course, once you get your brain restarted, you DO want to know just what this ungainly device is. The answer is: It is a shop-built router duplicator. If you have a three-dimensional object, for example, a shallow carving or a sign, you can make a copy with this device.

The duplicator consists of two horizontal beams and two vertical columns, all joined to an air-flotation platen. The upper beam has a stylus mounted at its front end. A lightweight laminate trimmer is mounted in the corresponding position on the lower beam. A central column, rising from the platen and joined to the beams through ball-bearing pivots, supports both beams. A second column, attached with pivots to the ends of the two beams, keeps them parallel as they tilt up and down. The platen allows the device to be moved to and fro over a smooth, flat surface.

Once the duplicator, the original (or pattern), and the working stock are set up, duplicating is a matter of tracing over every inch of the original's surface with the stylus. As you do this, the router's bit is carving out a duplicate.

This is possible because the device holds the stylus at a fixed distance directly over the bit. (The distance *is* slightly adjustable during setup; but once setup is completed, the distance is *fixed.*) The stylus and bit can rise and fall, but they do so together and they always share the same axis. That's the magic of the pivoting beam-and-column design. The platen allows the duplicator to swing side to side and to advance and retreat on its cushion of air, but the beam-and-column structure maintains the stylus-bit axis.

While the dynamic of the superstructure is quickly evi-
*continued*

**ROUTER DUPLICATOR PLAN VIEWS**

TOP VIEW

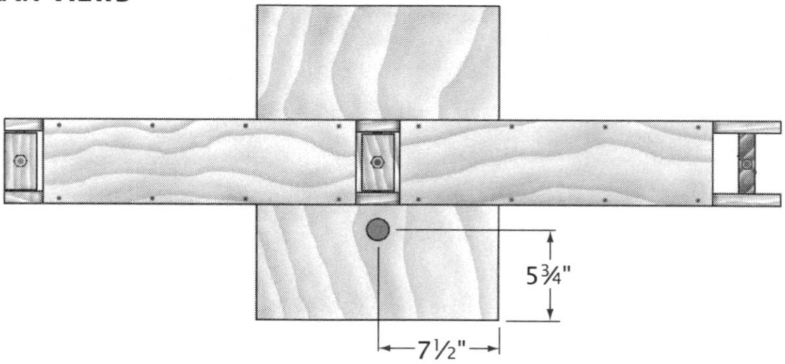
5¾"
7½"

SIDE VIEW

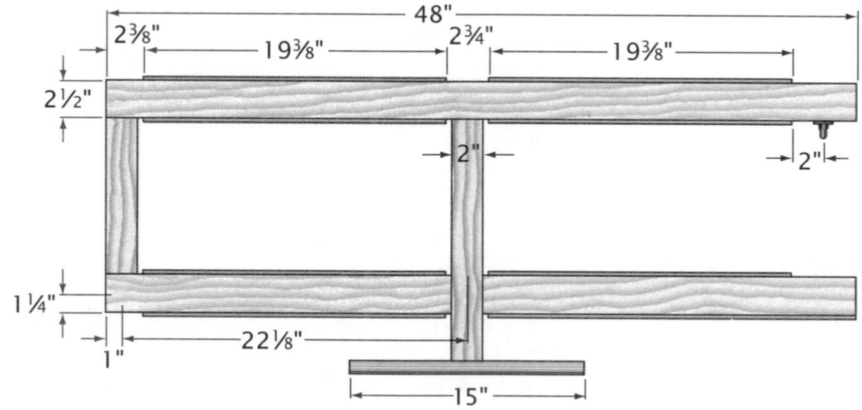
48"
2⅜"
19⅜"
2¾"
19⅜"
2½"
2"
2"
1¼"
1"
22⅛"
15"

BOTTOM VIEW

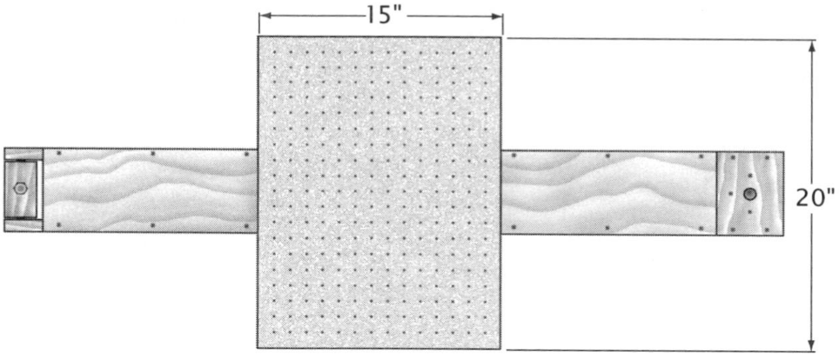
15"
20"

| Cutting List | | | |
|---|---|---|---|
| **Part** | **Qty.** | **Dimensions** | **Material** |
| Pivot blocks | 4 | ¾" × 2" × 4½" | Hardwood |
| Beam sides | 4 | ¾" × 2½" × 48" | Hardwood |
| Beam webs | 8 | ¼" × 5⅜" × 19⅜" | Plywood |
| Column sides | 6* | ¾" × 2" × 12" | Hardwood |
| Platen-mount column sides | 3* | ¾" × 2" × 4" | Hardwood |
| Platen | 1 | ¾" × 15" × 20" | Plywood |
| Platen surface | 1 | 1⁄16" × 16" × 21" | Plastic laminate |
| Attachment block | 1 | ¾" × 1¼" × 2" | Hardwood |
| Mounting bar | 1 | ¼" × 1¼" × 5⅜" | Plywood |

FRONT VIEW

BACK VIEW

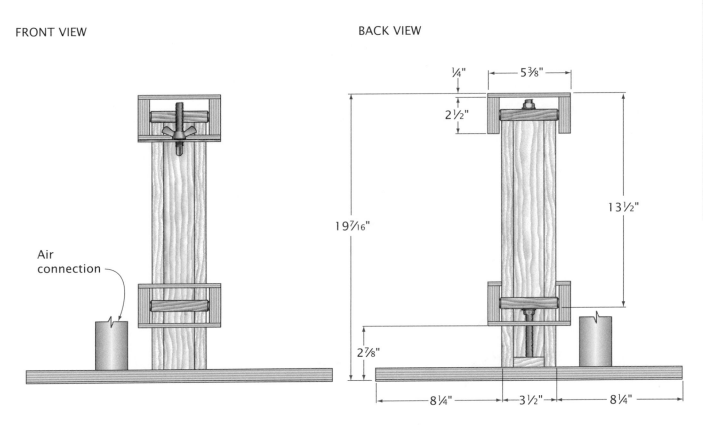

Air connection

¼"      5⅜"

2½"

19⁷⁄₁₆"

13½"

2⅞"

8¼"     3½"     8¼"

## Hardware

8 ball bearings, ½" bore × 1⅛" O.D. × ⅜" long

8 O-rings, ½" dia.

drywall screws, #6 × 1"

1 T-nut, ⁵⁄₁₆"-18

1 threaded rod, ⁵⁄₁₆"-18 × 14½"

1 threaded rod, ⁵⁄₁₆"-18 × 18"

4 hex nuts, ⁵⁄₁₆"-18

1 steel bar, ⅛" × 1" × 5 ⅜"

1 bolt, dia. to match router bit, 3" long

1 wing nut, size to match bolt OR 2 hex nuts, size to match bolt

*Prepare the column sides and platen-mount column sides as three pieces ¾" × 2" × 30" as described in the text.*

**Carving**

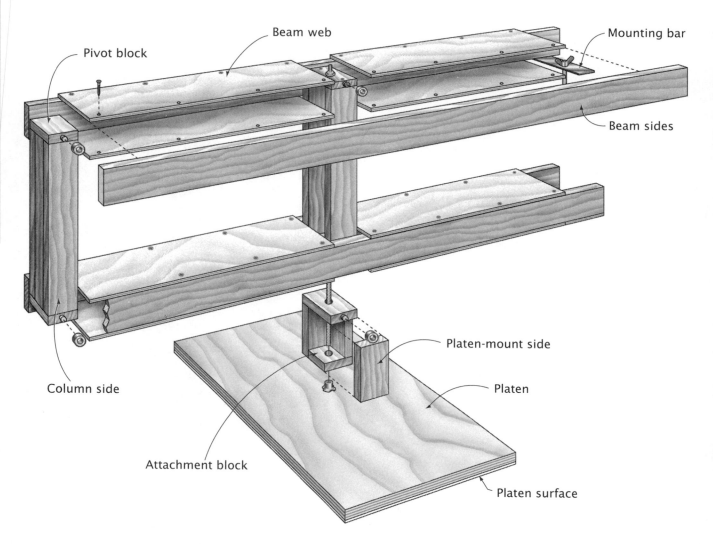

Pivot block

Beam web

Mounting bar

Beam sides

Column side

Platen-mount side

Platen

Attachment block

Platen surface

dent, the inconspicuous rectangular base may actually be the most fascinating part of the duplicator. It distributes a cushion of air between the jig and the surface that it's parked on, virtually eliminating all friction. This allows the router and its overhead stylus to move with the greatest of ease in a horizontal plane. The best part is that the air cushion has its origins in the "lungs" of a shop vacuum.

You probably don't think of your shop vac as a source of positive air flow. But all the air it draws in has to go somewhere, and that somewhere is out the exhaust port. Connect the hose to the exhaust port, and you have air streaming out of it. Connect the free end of the hose to the platen, which distributes the air across a surface with one tiny hole per square inch. The air gushing through these holes has enough force to raise the platen and whatever is resting on it. It doesn't raise it far—maybe $\frac{1}{16}$

inch—but that's enough to move it freely across a flat, smooth surface.

The duplicator is the result of a collaboration between Fred Matlack, creative maven of the Rodale Press Design Shop, and Bob Moran, a woodworking writer and editor. I urged Fred to come up with a router duplicator to produce signs, copy simple carvings, and hollow out seats for stools or chairs. I had copies of photos of commercial duplicators and articles about what they'd do, and even some information about a shop-built duplicator from a British book.

Next thing I knew, Fred had a prototype suspended from the shop ceiling. The key, he explained, is keeping the stylus, with which you trace the original or pattern, and the router bit, which cuts along whatever line the stylus follows, in perfect alignment, both always in the same axis.

Hanging the superstructure from the ceiling worked, but limited the horizontal range of the device.

A few days later, a working prototype of the duplicator you see here was rolling back and forth on a workbench on huge, cartoonish wheels that seemed to be going in at least three different directions at once. Eventually, Bob entered this particular picture and contributed the idea for the air-cushion platen as a replacement for the cartoon wheels. He also contributed the idea of assembling the beams and the columns with threaded rods and nuts. Thus assembled, the superstructure is a knockdown unit. Broken down into beams and columns and platen, the duplicator is far easier to store. The columns and hardware can nest inside the beams.

Okay, you say, it's really cool. But what practical good is it?

Reproducing carvings, I've mentioned. If you have letter-and-numeral stencils, you can make signs. You can reproduce carved and/or curved moldings. You can hollow out chair and bench seats, shallow bowls, and the like. Anything that can be viewed as a bas-relief carving is fodder for the duplicator.

The dictionary defines bas-relief as "sculptural relief in which the projection from the surrounding surface is slight and no part of the modeled form is undercut." In this case the "slight projection" is limited to a couple of inches and the proscription against undercuts can only be violated to the slightest degree by using a ball mill in the router and a corresponding stylus.

If this were a factory or professional-shop duplicator with a four- or five-figure price tag, it would be interesting to read about how it works. The pleasant surprise is that this home-built duplicator does what the commercial equipment does, includes the sophisticated air-cushion device (you won't find *that* on those commercial models), but doesn't cost nearly what a purchased duplicator will.

This duplicator is built of commonplace hardwood lumber and plywood, uses off-the-shelf bearings and hardware, and requires a shop vac and a laminate trimmer. The shop vac must have a provision for connecting the hose to the exhaust port, and most vacs do. You *don't* need the biggest, most powerful vac. The laminate trimmer is not a whoppin' great pair-of-Clydesdales router, but you will discover it to be a very practical router, useful for all sorts of general-purpose routing.

You don't need oddball, hard-to-find router bits. An assortment of core-box (or roundnose) bits, V-groovers, and veining bits—commonplace all—will suffice. You do need to make a stylus for each bit you use; and as you gain experience, you'll find that you use several bits on each project. You'll start with a fairly large-diameter bit to clear broader areas, a small core-box to rough out lines, and a veiner to refine those lines and etch in fine detail.

You just might find the duplicator useful in conjunction with hand tools. To reproduce chair seats, for example, you can use the duplicator first to cut a series of gauging grooves. Then you can gouge out the waste with the duplicator, and finally smooth things out with a spokeshave, a travisher, and abrasives.

# Building the Duplicator

The joinery in this rig is not sophisticated. Butt joints, glue, and screws account for most of it, and a couple of threaded rods tie the rest together. Marrying ball bearings, which we normally associate with metal constructions, to a wooden structure is easy and straightforward but requires some bits and cutters that you may not have. Specifically, you'll need a drill bit that cuts a clean hole 1⅛ inches in diameter to seat the outer race of the ball bearings, and a plug or tenon cutter that cuts tenons with parallel sides (not tapered) ½ inch in diameter to fit the inner races.

Begin building the duplicator by making the box beams that form the top and bottom of the parallelogram, including the pivot joints. Then make the U-shaped columns that form the remaining sides of the parallelogram. The air-cushion platen comes next. Making this platen is a simple matter of routing a grid of grooves in a piece of plywood, applying plastic laminate over the grooves, and drilling tiny holes through the laminate into the grooves. Attach the platen to the beam-and-column parallelogram, mount the router and stylus, and the duplicator itself is completed.

## Making the Beam-and-Column Assembly

The beam-and-column assembly is the structure that holds the router and the stylus, keeping one perfectly aligned in relation to the other. Despite its looks, it is very simple to build if you take your time and set up each operation carefully.

**1. Cut the pivot blocks.** I'd recommend preparing a single piece of straight-grained stock to the thickness and width specified by the Cutting List for the pivot blocks. It should be a couple of feet long. Crosscut the board into five pieces 4½ inches long. The extra piece will allow you the luxury of ruining one when setting up for cutting the tenons on the ends.

**The pivot block tenons** are cut with a plug cutter chucked in your drill press. Setting fences to secure the workpieces is the painstaking part. The cutter itself makes the tenon-forming work foolproof.

**2. Form the tenons on the pivot blocks.** Because this is a drill press operation, the initial task is to set up that machine. The pivot block has to be aligned with the axis of the chuck. Chuck a small-diameter bit or a centering pin in the drill press. Draw diagonals across the end of a pivot block to find the center. Align this pivot block under the drill bit, taking the time to center the piece perfectly. Then clamp fences to the drill press table so each block can be placed in the same position.

Now chuck a plug cutter or tenon cutter in the drill press. Since you're going to cut a round tenon to fit the inner race of a ball bearing (and not a plug to bung a hole), you don't want to use a plug cutter that cuts a tapered plug. Use the more conventional type of plug cutter that produces plugs with parallel sides, or one of the longer plug, tenon, and dowel cutters. Set the drill press's depth stop so the cutter will cut ⅜ inch into the ends of the blocks. Cut a test tenon on the extra pivot-block blank to check this setting.

With the correctness of the setup confirmed, cut tenons on both ends of all the blocks (including the test block). If there is any tendency for the blocks to move or vibrate while you are cutting the tenons, clamp them to the fences. This will give you smoother and more precise tenons that will fit into the bearings better.

**3. Trim the pivot blocks to their final shape.** This is best done with a smooth-cutting crosscut blade on the table saw. Guide the workpiece with the miter gauge; it should have an auxiliary facing for this operation.

Adjust the blade height to ¾ inch, or maybe a skosh less. (The blade should reach the tenon when the block is on edge, but not cut into it.) To position the blocks for these trim cuts, clamp a stop block to the miter gauge facing exactly 4⅛ inches from the blade. Make sure the stop

block is positioned so the *tenon* contacts it. If only the waste touches the stop block, it will be useless when you go to trim the second end of a block.

If the plug cutter cuts a narrow groove around the tenon, the trim cuts may leave little nubbins of waste standing guard around each tenon. These can be pared off with a chisel.

**4. Install tenon O-rings.** The O-ring ensures that only the inner race of the bearing contacts the pivot block. This is important.

### PIVOT BLOCK DETAIL

TOP VIEW

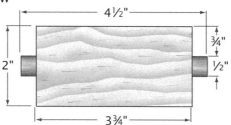

FRONT VIEW

END VIEW

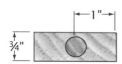

SECTION VIEW

1⅛"-dia. bore, ⅜" deep, houses outer race of bearing.

Off-the-shelf ball bearings, ½" bore, 1⅛" O.D., ⅜" long

Rubber O-ring shims bearing away from shoulder of pivot block.

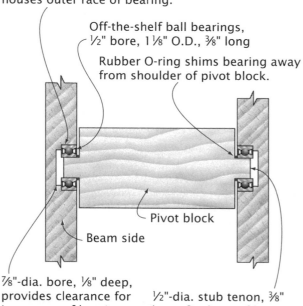

Pivot block

Beam side

⅞"-dia. bore, ⅛" deep, provides clearance for inner race of bearing.

½"-dia. stub tenon, ⅜" long, fits bore of bearing.

**Trim the shoulders of the pivot-block tenons** on the table saw. With a stop block clamped to the miter gauge or cutoff box facing, the blocks are automatically positioned for the cuts. Note that the cuts are made with the blocks standing on edge.

Consult the drawing *Pivot Block Detail.* You'll see that if you would push the bearings all the way onto the tenons, the outer races would rub on the blocks instead of turning freely. The solution to this problem is to slip a ½-inch-diameter O-ring onto each tenon before installing the bearings. The O-ring provides the needed clearance, as shown in the drawing.

An effective alternative to the O-rings is a piece of stout cotton cord (about 1⁄16-inch diameter) wetted with glue. Wrap it around the base of the tenon, and hold it in place with the bearing while the glue dries.

**5. Drill the mounting-rod holes through the pivot blocks.** These 5⁄16-inch holes are for the threaded rods that help hold the rig together. The hole must be in the center of the block's face. To find the centerpoint, draw diagonal lines across the pivot block face.

As you did in setting up to cut the tenons, align the pivot block under a drill bit, then clamp fences to the drill press table to hold the block secure while you drill. These fences will also serve to position the other blocks for drilling, so you only have to lay out the center of the first block.

Drill the holes.

**6. Cut the beam parts.** The beams are the top and bottom (roughly horizontal) members of the parallelogram that keeps the router in line with the stylus. The beam sides house the outer races of the bearings. The webs tie the pairs of sides together, forming the beams.

Check the dimensions specified by the Cutting List for the beam sides and webs, bearing in mind that the list presents the final dimensions of these parts. While the webs ultimately will be 5⅜ inches wide, you'll get a neater job if you trim the webs flush with the sides *after* assembly. Therefore, it's better to cut them 5½ inches wide at this point. The sides, on the other hand, must be cut to their final size now.

**7. Bore the bearing recesses in the sides.** These recesses are stepped—counterbored, in effect—so they'll hold the bearing tightly but provide clearance for the inner race. The hole that houses the bearing is 1⅛ inches in diameter and ⅜ inch deep. The clearance recess is concentric; it is ⅞ inch in diameter and 1⁄16 inch deep.

Begin the work by laying out the centers of the two bearing recesses that must be bored in each side. The locations are shown in the *Side View* of the drawing *Router Duplicator Plan Views.* The holes are centered between the edges of the sides. This is convenient because it means that the four pieces are identical rather than symmetrical. You don't have to keep track of almost-the-same parts.

Drill the recesses on the drill press using a 1⅛-inch-diameter Forstner bit. Clamp a fence to the drill press table to position the workpieces, and adjust the depth stop so the holes will be exactly ⅜ inch deep. Check and confirm the depth stop setting by pressing a bearing into a test hole.

**Use a fence to locate the workpieces,** and boring the stepped holes for the bearings becomes easy. Both holes are on the same axis. Take the time to set the fence carefully, so the holes are centered across the beam sides. Then drill all the bearing holes. After switching bits, drill all the clearance holes, as shown here.

The bearing should be flush with the beam side when it's fully seated in the hole.

After drilling all the bearing holes, switch bits and drill the inner-race clearance recesses. Don't move the fence; it's in the right position to give you clearance recesses that are concentric with the bearing holes. Use a ⅞-inch Forstner bit. You don't need to remove a lot of material, remember. Just 1⁄16 inch is deep enough.

**8. Assemble the beams.** Assembly captures the bearings and pivot blocks, so you want to get the unit working smoothly before making this incarceration permanent. For this reason I suggest you assemble the beams with screws only. After the duplicator is completely assembled and tested, but before you put it to heavy use, glue the webs and trim them. To do this, remove one web at a time, apply glue, and redrive the screws in the same holes. This ensures that the web is being returned to its exact, tested-and-proven position. After all the webs are thus permanently fixed, use a router with a flush-trimming bit to shear the webs even with the sides (you cut the webs a little wide, remember).

But I'm getting ahead of us.

Begin the assembly work by pressing a bearing fully into each recess in the beam sides. Make sure they are flush with the surface of the beam sides and that the inner races turn freely.

Now install the pivot blocks. Check that your O-rings (or glued-cord shims) are in place on the tenons. With one of the sides laid flat on the bench top, insert a pivot block into each of its bearings. Set another side in place, seating

**Assembling a beam** doesn't really require three or four hands. Lay a side on the workbench, and insert bearings in the recesses. Press a pivot block into each bearing. Fit a second side, with its bearings in place, onto the pivot blocks. Right the assembly, and apply a clamp over each pivot block, as shown here, to hold the assembly while you screw the webs in place.

this side's bearings over the projecting tenons on the pivot blocks. Make sure the tenons go all the way into the inner races of the bearings so the O-rings contact both the tenon shoulders and the bearing inner races.

Right the assembly, and lightly clamp the sides together, placing the clamps directly over the bearings. This will ensure that there is absolutely no side-to-side play. Place two of the webs on the assembly, as shown in the *Side View*, and screw them in place. Use 1-inch drywall screws. Turn the assembly over, and screw the other two webs in place. The pivot blocks should turn freely in the bearings when you are done and have removed the clamps. (If they don't, disassemble the beam and try again. This is why you don't glue the webs in place.)

Assemble the second beam in the same way.

**9. Make a column blank.** Although there are three different columns in the assembly, it is easiest to glue up one long column, then crosscut it into the three pieces needed.

Begin by milling and ripping three pieces of straight-grained hardwood stock to the thickness and width specified by the Cutting List. Each of these pieces should be crosscut to a 30-inch length.

**Lay the beams and columns on the workbench** to assemble them. Line up these subassemblies, insert the threaded rods, and tighten the nuts finger-tight. After thus tying the parts together, refine the alignment of the parts as necessary, then drive screws through the pivot blocks into the columns.

Glue the pieces together, forming a single U-section column. The drawing *Column Assembly Detail* shows the arrangement of the parts.

If you find it more convenient to screw the parts together than to clamp them while the glue dries, make sure the screws don't lie in the path of the cuts you'll make in the next step.

**10. Cut the columns to length.** When the glue is dry, trim one end of the long column square, then saw it into two 12-inch-long pieces and one 4-inch-long piece.

When making these cuts, make sure your blade is perpendicular to the saw table and that your miter gauge fence is perpendicular to the miter gauge bar, because you want the cuts to be as square to the axis of the column as you can get them.

**11. Assemble the beams and columns.** Assuming that you bought a 36-inch length of threaded rod, saw it into one piece 14½ inches long and one 18 inches long. Assemble the box beams, columns, and threaded rods as shown in the *Router Duplicator Exploded View*.

You'll have to make one departure from what you

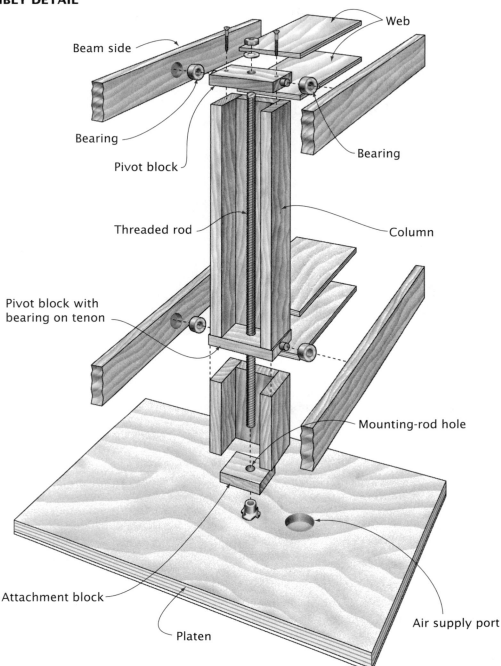

Beam side

Web

Bearing

Bearing

Pivot block

Threaded rod

Column

Pivot block with bearing on tenon

Mounting-rod hole

Attachment block

Air supply port

Platen

see in the *Exploded View:* The longer rod can't screw into the T-nut on the platen because you haven't made those parts yet. Just thread an extra nut onto the rod for the time being.

With the nuts on the threaded rod snug against the pivot blocks but not overly tight, lay the assembly on its side on a flat surface, like your saw table. Now nudge and tap the columns into exact position, centered on the pivot blocks and not touching the box beams. When you have them just right, tighten the nuts to hold them securely in place, then drill pilot holes and screw the pivot blocks to the columns. The screws will keep the columns from twisting on the pivot blocks, thus main-

taining the accuracy of the jig, while the threaded rod will keep the screws from being pulled out of the end grain of the columns.

You can use glue and less hardware if you like, but then you won't be able to disassemble the duplicator for storage.

## Making the Platen

You are about to construct that magic carpet upon whch the duplicator floats. This is really the most magical part of this jig. Like most apparatus used by magicians, it is elegantly simple.

In the course of just a few steps, you transform a piece of ordinary plywood into a levitation device by routing

Carving

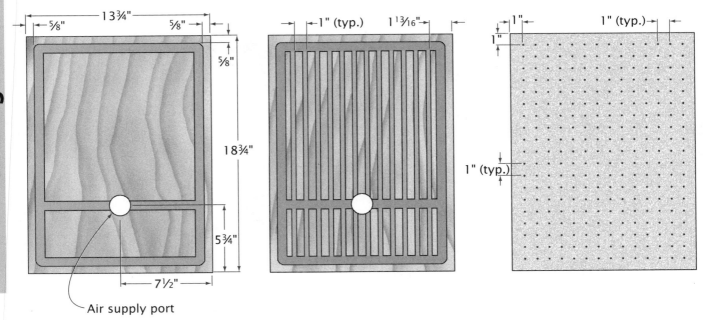

Air supply port

1. After boring the air supply port, rout ¾-inch-wide, ½"-deep grooves bisecting the port and paralleling the platen's edges.

2. Rout ⅜"-wide, ⅜"-deep grooves.

3. Lay out the air holes on the plastic laminate, arranging them on a 1" grid. Drill the holes with a ³⁄₃₂" bit. Apply the plastic laminate to the platen so the holes line up over the grooves.

grooves in it, covering the grooves with plastic laminate, then riddling the laminate with holes. You have to be asking yourself, does something this simple really work?

Yes, it does. Just you wait…

**1. Cut the platen blank.** As I said, the platen is a piece of ¾-inch plywood. To work properly, the platen must be dead flat, so select your plywood carefully. Cut it to the dimensions specified by the Cutting List.

**2. Bore the air supply port.** The air is supplied by your shop vacuum. For the air to get into the passages that you will be routing into the platen in the next step, you have to bore a hole in the platen that's big enough for the shop vac's hose. Because the connector can extend only ⅜ inch into the platen, it's important that the port closely match the connector's diameter.

Begin by determining how big the hole must be. Measure the outside diameter of the connector on the hose with a pair of calipers. Bore a test hole with a Forstner or multi-spur bit as close as possible to the measured size of the connector. A large hose might require that you use a hole saw.

If the hole is slightly too small, you can file it larger with a half-round rasp. If it's too large, you can wrap tape

around the end of the connector. The hose must fit reasonably air-tight.

After you've decided on the bit you'll use, lay out the center of the air supply port, following the drawing *Platen Detail*. Then bore the port. You can bore completely through the platen.

**3. Lay out and rout the air passages.** The air is dispersed across the platen through a grid of grooves routed into the platen's bottom. The drawing *Platen Detail* shows these air passages. Note that there is a ¾-inch-wide × ½-inch-deep perimeter groove and a similarly sized one extending from side to side through the air supply port. Completing the grid are a dozen ⅜-inch-wide × ⅜-inch-deep grooves routed from end to end. None of these grooves, of course, breaks through the edge of the platen.

How you produce the grooves may have a bearing on how you lay them out. It is useful, later on, to know where the grooves are, so you do want mark the groove centerlines on the platen edges. Rout the grooves with a plunge router equipped with an edge guide, or on the router table.

Rout the large air columns first. Use a ¾-inch straight bit. Adjust the depth stop for a ½-inch-deep cut. Set the edge guide so the centerline of the cut is 1 inch from the stock's edge. Rout the perimeter air passage. Don't forget that these

**Use a hand-held router with an edge guide** to cut the air-passage grooves. Set the edge guide to rout the perimeter grooves first. Don't fuss with stop blocks; just lay out the inside corners of these grooves, then rout from mark to mark. To start the cut, tip the router so the bit is clear of the work, as shown here. Then begin advancing the router as you lower it into the work (here I am pulling the router toward me).

grooves stop short of the edges of the stock. You'll find it easiest to rout these grooves in three or more passes of increasing depth.

Reset the edge guide, and rout the air passage that bisects the air supply port. Rout across the width of the platen, from the perimeter groove along one side to the one along the other side.

Now rout the small air columns. Switch to a ⅜-inch straight bit, and reset the depth stop to produce a ⅜-inch-deep cut. Set the edge guide position to rout the two grooves closest to the platen edges. What you do is rout two grooves, one referencing each edge of the platen. Then reset the edge guide and rout two more grooves. Keep resetting and routing until all the grooves have been cut.

Just remember: DON'T break through the edges. You want air escaping only through the tiny holes you will be drilling through the plastic laminate you will be applying.

**4. Apply the plastic laminate to the platen's top.** As I mentioned, the platen must be flat to work, and if you cover only the bottom surface with laminate, the platen is almost certain to cup. So cut two pieces of laminate to the dimensions specified by the Cutting List, holding one for the next step.

Apply contact cement to the laminate and to the top of the platen. When the cement is dry, apply the laminate to the platen. With a router and flush-trimming bit, trim the laminate overhang. Drill a hole through the laminate covering the air supply port, and insert the bit through the hole

so you can open up the port. Switch to a chamfering bit and make another pass around the perimeter of the platen, eliminating the sharp laminate edge.

**5. Drill the air holes in the plastic laminate.** The many holes in the platen's plastic laminate bottom must be drilled *before* it is applied. If you drill them after it is applied, all the dust and chips created will collect in the air passages, and they may restrict air flow.

Now I know the usual approach to laminate work is to cut the laminate oversized and apply it to the substrate with some overhang around all four edges. In this case, simply plan to align one edge of the laminate flush to the substrate edge, and have the overhang only on the other three edges. Cut the plastic laminate to the dimensions specified by the Cutting List. These dimensions provide leeway for you to trim it flush after it is cemented in place.

Given the application approach, you simply have to lay out the holes, working from the "flush" edge. As the drawing *Platen Detail* shows, the air holes are drilled on a grid of 1-inch squares. Find the center midpoint along the flush edge, and lay out the grid from that point. Use a pencil and a framing square to extend lines across the laminate. Then turn the laminate 90 degrees and pencil lines from side to side, forming a grid with 1-inch squares. At each grid intersection, you must drill a hole through the laminate.

Back up the laminate with a clean, solid piece of scrap—plywood or medium-density fiberboard. Drill the holes using a ³⁄₃₂-inch twist-drill bit in a portable drill. The holes don't need to be located with absolute precision. It isn't hard, just tedious.

**6. Apply the plastic laminate to the bottom.** Despite the grooved substrate and the perforated laminate, this is really a straightforward job. Set up first. Clamp a straightedge that's thicker than the platen to the workbench between you and the platen. Pull the platen tight against it, and mark the center of one or two air passages on the top of the fence. You are going to use these marks to align the laminate, and you are going to align the laminate's "flush" edge with this fence, so make sure you have the platen oriented appropriately.

Now apply the contact cement. As you spread it on the grooved platen, try to avoid getting too much down in the grooves where it might obstruct the flow of air. This isn't difficult. What is tricky is applying the cement to the laminate. You have to kind of paint stripes of the cement between the holes. You don't want a film of cement gumming up the air holes. I found that a disposable bristle brush worked just fine for applying the cement in this particular situation. Allow the cement to dry sufficiently.

Now apply the laminate to the platen. Stand its flush edge on the platen, tight against the fence, and make sure the appropriate strings of air holes are aligned with your alignment marks on the fence. Flex the laminate so it bows, and gradually lay it onto the platen. Burnish it down with a J-roller or the heel of your hand.

Set up your laminate trimmer or router with a flush-

**Advance planning is the key** to successfully laminating the platen. The grid of air holes must be laid out from a "flush" edge, then drilled through the laminate. The edge of the platen corresponding to the "flush" edge of the laminate must be butted against a fence. Alignment marks must be scribed on the fence and the laminate (on the masking tape). The laminate can then be "rolled" down onto the platen, as shown, with the laminate's air holes aligned over the platen's air passages.

trimming bit, and trim the laminate edges flush with the platen edges. Switch bits and rout a narrow bevel around the edges to finish off the job.

**7. Take a test drive with your platen.** This is a deviation from proper step-by-step decorum, I admit. But this is so cool you need to try it out right away. And now that you have the air holes drilled, you can get it afloat on a cushion of air.

So stick one end of the hose in the shop vac's exhaust port, the other in the air supply port on the platen. Turn on the vac and see how nicely the platen floats. Pile some tools on it, and see how it reacts. Call the family together and show it off. It's a great trick.

Okay, break's over. Back to work.

**8. Make and install the attachment block.** Cut the block to the dimensions specified by the Cutting List.

Lay out the hole for the mounting rod. Note, in the drawing *Column Assembly Detail,* the general location of this hole. It is equidistant from the ends and 1 inch back from one edge. At that spot, drill a counterbore just deep enough to recess the flange on a T-nut. Then bore through the block for the body of the T-nut. Tap the T-nut into the hole, and check to make sure that no part of it projects above the face of the block.

Turn the platen over (so the side with the laminate is down), and work out the best location for the attachment block. The location is important, but positioning the

block with great precision is not necessary.

Mark the center of the platen surface. Plug the air hose into the air supply port. Now place the remaining 4-inch section of column around the attachment block, and position the two at or near the centermark. The face of the block with the T-nut should be down.

Adjust the column and block away from the center of the platen, if necessary, to ensure that the air hose won't interfere with the movement of the beams. As you can see from the *Front View* of the *Router Duplicator Plan Views,* the column should be at least 1¼ inches away from the hose connector. When you're happy with the location, mark it. Then glue and screw the attachment block to the platen. A couple of 1-inch drywall screws are sufficient. Avoid longer screws unless you're quite certain they won't be penetrating an air passage in the platen. The column section, by the way, remains unattached.

## Assembling the Duplicator

This is when the machine really comes together. Because the major unit, the beam-and-column assembly, has already been constructed, you have a sense of what the duplicator is going to look like. But now you are going to mount it on the platen, install the router and the stylus, and ready it for its maiden voyage across your workbench.

**1. Join the beam-and-column assembly to the platen.** These two major elements are cinched together with the threaded rod that extends through the main column.

**To mount the beam-and-column unit** on the platen, you must remove the bottom nut on the center column's threaded rod. (The screws will hold the unit together when you do this.) Turn the rod into the attachment block on the platen as far as it will go. Holding the rod with locking-grip pliers, as shown, tighten the top nut to secure the assembly.

Carving

The first thing to do is to place that short column section back around the attachment block on the platen. Don't glue it there—don't fasten it in any way.

Next, remove the bottom-end nut from the 18-inch threaded rod. Turn the top-end nut out near the end of the rod. Right the beam-and-column assembly, and stand it on the short column that's on the platen. Thread the rod well into the T-nut in the attachment block.

To tighten up the assembly, you have to tighten the nut on the rod's top end down against the upper pivot block. Before doing this, check that the short column at the platen is centered on the lower pivot block and that the beam-and-column assembly works freely. When all is aligned, tighten the nut on the top of the threaded rod, clamping the beam assembly to the platen. You may need to hold the rod with pliers as you tighten the nut.

**2. Make the router mounting plate.** As noted at the beginning of this chapter, the best router for this jig is a laminate trimmer. In fact, because the router is mounted between the beam sides, you can't use anything but a laminate trimmer because it won't fit.

To mount the trimmer, you make what amounts to an oversized baseplate and screw that to the bottom edges of the beam sides. Make the mounting plate from a scrap of ¼-inch plywood. Cut it to the dimensions specified by the Cutting List.

Remove the factory baseplate from the laminate trimmer, and bond it to the mounting plate blank using carpet tape. Make every effort to align the baseplate's bit opening over the centerpoint of the mounting plate. If you don't, you'll have a hard time aligning the bit in the router directly under the stylus. You can find tips for doing this in the chapter "The Generic Baseplate" on page 63. Use the baseplate as a guide in drilling mounting-screw holes and a bit opening.

**3. Install the mounting plate.** Screw the plate to the bottom edges of the beam sides, as shown in the *Router Duplicator Exploded View*. Screwing, but not gluing, the plate in place allows you the option of removing or replacing it at a future time. Gluing might make the mounting a wee bit more rigid, but it isn't essential.

**4. Choose a stylus configuration.** One of the keys to accurate duplication is to use a stylus of the same size and shape as the router bit. The best router bit to use depends on whether you're removing large amounts of stock or reproducing fine detail. A ⅜-inch core-box bit does a good job of removing waste, while a veining, V-grooving, or sign-making bit will duplicate finer detail. If your work requires both extensive stock removal and fine detail, you'll want to use both kinds of bit and will need a separate stylus and mounting bar for each bit.

Each stylus is made from a bolt. Choose one with an unthreaded shank diameter at least as great as the maximum cutting diameter of the bit. The length of the bolt, not including the head, should be at least as great as the overall length of the router bit. Extra length is not a problem—the excess will simply project up from the mounting bar.

**5. Make the stylus.** Start by sawing the head off the bolt with a hacksaw.

Next, chuck the threaded end of the bolt in your drill press. Since you'll need to run nuts down these threads when you install the stylus, you want to avoid distorting the threads with excessive tightening of the chuck. A couple of layers of masking tape on the threads provide some insurance against distortion.

Now file the end of the bolt to the shape of your router bit. This is a simple, if somewhat tedious, task. Set the drill press speed quite slow, swing the table out of the way, and file against the rotation of the bolt with a flat mill file. While you're not hand-tooling a part to space-age tolerances, bear in mind that the more accurately you reproduce the router bit's profile, the more accurately your duplicator will duplicate.

**6. Make the stylus mounting bar.** This bar is a 5⅜-inch-long strip of steel with a hole drilled through it for the stylus. The width of the bar is not critical; anything ¾ inch or more in width will do fine. But try to find a piece at least ⅛ inch thick. A mounting bar that flexes will give you distorted duplicates, which is especially vexing if you're trying to reproduce fine detail.

Cut the strip to the appropriate length, then lay out and drill the hole for the stylus. Begin with a ⅛-inch-diameter pilot hole, then enlarge the hole with the appropriate-sized twist-drill bit. Be sure to clamp the bar to the drill press table while drilling so the drill bit won't yank it out of your hand.

While you are at the drill press, lay out and drill the two *continued*

**Shape the stylus** by filing the end of a bolt while the bolt turns in the drill press. Hold the file against the bolt end, and move it around as necessary to shape the bolt end to match the "companion" router bit's contour.

# A Stock-and-Pattern Table

This two-tiered little table is a very important adjunct to the router duplicator. It holds both the pattern (the object being copied) and the workpiece (the wood into which the laminate trimmer is cutting). Use of the table makes it quick and easy to position and align these two pieces, a not inconsiderable achievement.

The thing is that for the duplicator to do its work, both the pattern to be duplicated and the stock to be routed must be held rigidly. Neither must be able to wiggle or shift. The upper surfaces of the two must be 12¾ inches apart, and the pattern must be directly above the stock. Moreover, the sizes and shapes of the workpieces will undoubtedly vary greatly from project to project.

This stock-and-pattern table designed by Fred Matlack and Bob Moran is a simple response to the need. Because the design is so simple, it is adaptable to a variety of specific needs. The drawing *Stock-and-Pattern Table Plans* shows the details of the table. Notice that two different leg arrangements are shown.

*(continued)*

## STOCK-AND PATTERN TABLE Cutting List

| Part | Qty. | Dimensions | Material |
|---|---|---|---|
| Tabletops | 2 | ¾" × 16" × 20" | Plywood |
| Leg sides* | 8 | ¾" × 2¾" × 13½" | Hardwood |
| Straight dogs | 2 | ½" × 1½" × 14" | Plywood |
| Taper dogs/Wedges | 2 | ½" × 3" × 14" | Plywood |
| Dowels | 8 | ⅜" dia. × 1½" | Hardwood |

## Hardware

drywall screws, #6 × 1⅝"

*The length specified is for the short-legged version of the table. For the long-legged version, make the leg sides 15 inches long.*

**The stock-and-pattern table** is a good way to hold both the pattern and the working stock. It's easy to make and easy to use.

Carving

## STOCK-AND-PATTERN TABLE PLANS

FRONT VIEW

END VIEW

2¾"

¾"

13½"

15"

2¾"

¾"

12¾"

TOP VIEW

2"

1" typ.

4"

8"

16"

20"

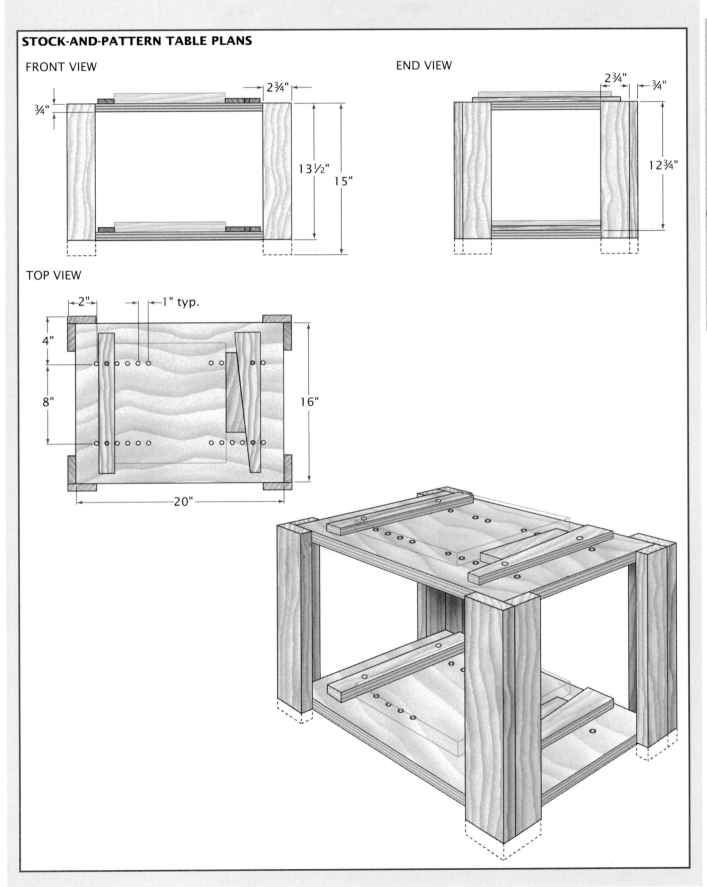

# A Stock-and-Pattern Table—Continued

## DOG-AND-WEDGE DETAIL

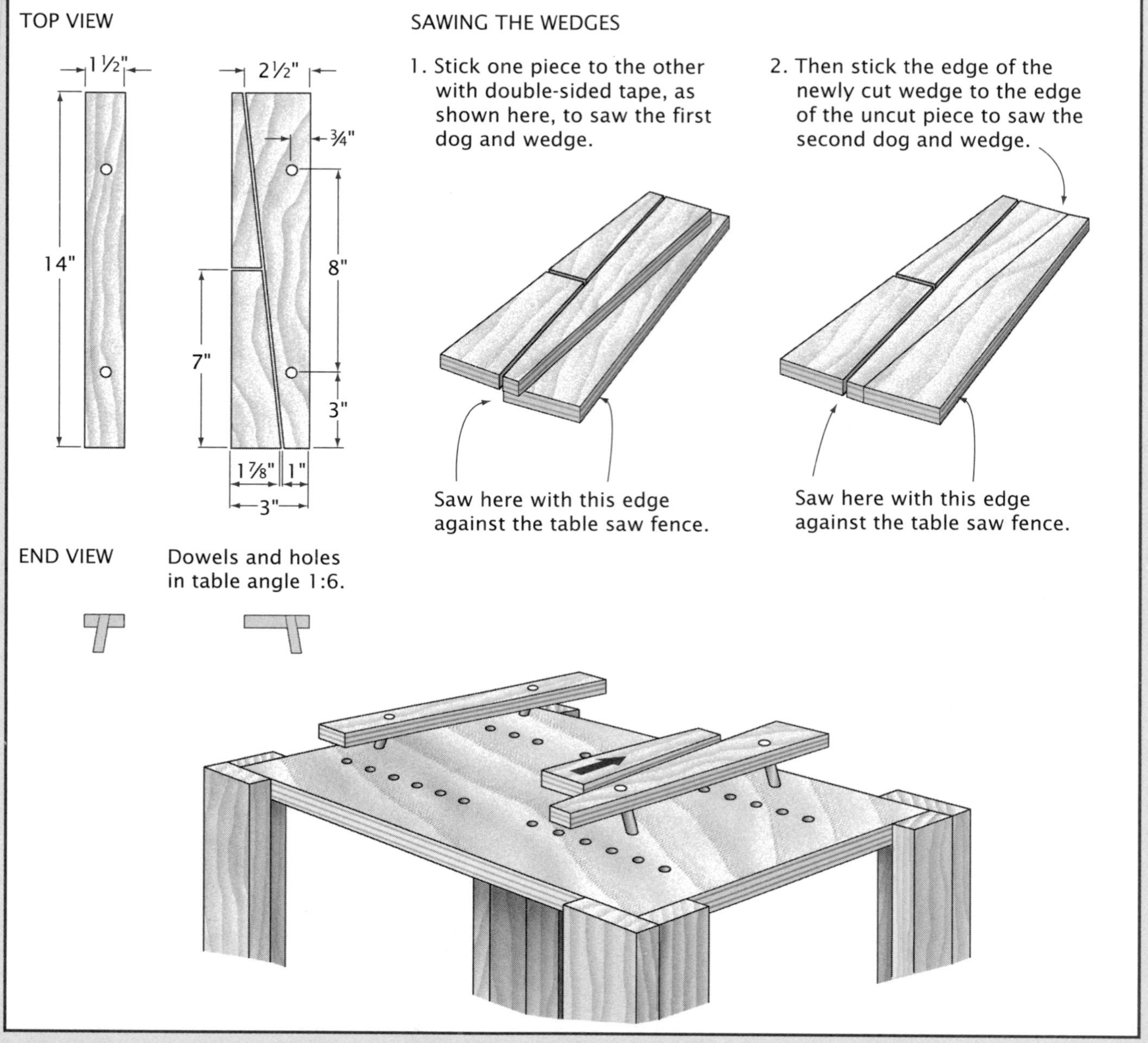

TOP VIEW

SAWING THE WEDGES

1½"   2½"   ¾"

14"   8"   7"   3"

1⅞"   1"   3"

END VIEW   Dowels and holes
in table angle 1:6.

1. Stick one piece to the other
with double-sided tape, as
shown here, to saw the first
dog and wedge.

2. Then stick the edge of the
newly cut wedge to the edge
of the uncut piece to saw the
second dog and wedge.

Saw here with this edge
against the table saw fence.

Saw here with this edge
against the table saw fence.

---

The short-legged version accommodates thicker stock and patterns and is easier to clamp to a table or workbench. The long-legged version allows you to reproduce shallow carvings with more precision because the beams of the duplicator will remain more nearly parallel to the surfaces of the pattern and the stock. If you anticipate a need for both versions, make the short one and, when you need the taller version, block it up off the workbench.

The drawing *Dog-and-Wedge Detail* shows one means of clamping the pattern and the stock to the tables. Because it doesn't project above the surface of

the stock, this clamping system doesn't interfere with the duplicator. If your stock and pattern are significantly larger than the actual carved area, you can use just about any clamps you want. And if you're just anxious to run the duplicator through its paces without taking the time to make your own clamping device, stick the pattern and stock to their respective tables with double-sided tape.

**1. Cut the table parts.** The tabletops, dogs, and wedges are plywood; the legs, hardwood. Cut these parts to the dimensions specified by the Cutting List.

**2. Assemble the legs.** Glue and nail or screw the eight leg pieces into four legs, as shown in the drawing *Stock-and-Pattern Table Plans*.

**3. Lay out and drill the dog holes.** The locations are shown in the drawing *Stock-and-Pattern Table*. Before you drill the holes, however, notice in the drawing *Dog-and-Wedge Detail* that the holes enter the stock at an angle and that the set of holes on one side must angle in one direction while the holes on the other side angle in the opposite direction. These angles ensure that the dogs remain down tight against the table when the wedge is tapped into place and that they won't creep up while you're routing a copy into some very expensive stock.

The actual angle of the holes is not critical. The 1:6 specification is there only to give you an idea of roughly how much angle is appropriate in case you aren't familiar with workbench dogs. It *is* important that all the holes have the same angle and that the dowel holes in the dogs themselves have this same angle. It is also important that the holes in each pair be equidistant.

The way to drill these holes is not with a drill press but with a hand-held drill. You use a simple jig to guide the bit and position the holes.

Make yourself this jig guide by drilling two holes through a 2-inch-square piece of hardwood. The holes must be 8 inches apart. Then bevel an edge of the hardwood strip with the table saw blade tilted to 83 degrees. With the beveled face resting on the workpiece, the jig will tilt the drill bit to the proper angle for the holes you want to bore. And the jig will ensure that all the holes in each pair will be equidistant.

**4. Glue and screw the tables to the legs.** If you haven't kept track of which surfaces of the tables are the tops, mark them now. The tops are the surfaces where the two innermost pairs of holes are closest together; that is, the holes flare out at the bottom like the legs of some tables.

Place one of the tables top-down on your workbench, and stand the legs on end at the four corners, positioned as shown in the drawings. Note that the wide sides of the legs go on the ends of the table, while the narrow sides of the legs go on the front and back. This gives the lower beam of the duplicator the maximum-sized "window" to work through. Glue and screw the legs in place.

Now place the remaining table top-up on your workbench. If you've made the legs to the long dimension shown, prop the table up 1½ inches on a couple thicknesses of ¾-inch-thick stock. Place the assembled table and legs upright on the bench with the legs straddling the second table. Check that the distance from one tabletop to the other is 12¾ inches, then glue and screw the second table in place.

**5. Make the dogs and wedges.** The angle of the wedges needs to match the angle of the tapered dogs quite accurately. To achieve this without undue fuss, start with two pieces of stock 3 inches wide for both the wedges and the tapered dogs and two pieces half that width for the untapered dogs. Lay out and bore the holes for the dowels the same way you bored the dog holes in the tables.

Now rip the 3-inch-wide pieces into wedges and dogs with a tapering jig on the table saw. If you don't have a tapering jig, stick one piece to the other piece with carpet tape, as shown in the drawing *Dog-and-Wedge Detail*. Then make the cuts.

Glue the dowels into the holes in the dogs, and you're done.

Well, almost done. You'll probably find that the dowels need a bit of shaving in order to fit easily into the dog holes in the tables.

**Here's the setup for drilling angled dog holes.** The workpiece is resting on a scrap piece of plywood. The hardwood drill guide is clamped at one end, held firmly at the other. The masking-tape flag on the drill bit is a depth gauge aimed at preventing damage to the bench top. When the flag sweeps the surface of the guide, the bit has penetrated the workpiece (but not the scrap beneath it).

# Using the Duplicator

**Carving**

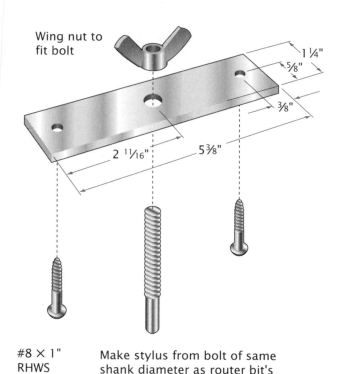

Wing nut to fit bolt

1 ¼"

⅝"

⅜"

2 ¹¹⁄₁₆"          5 ⅜"

#8 × 1" RHWS

Make stylus from bolt of same shank diameter as router bit's cutting diameter.

Your duplicator is built. The laminate trimmer is mounted at the end of the lower beam. You've got a bas-relief carving you want to copy. And now you pause.

Look at it. It certainly *looks* as gawky as Ichabod Crane, all elbows and knees. Is this sucker really gonna work? you ask yourself. You've got time and money tied up in it, so it better.

I think it will. It did for Fred and Bob. And it did for me.

What you have to do is the same thing you do with all these magical, mystical routing machines: Experiment. You have to learn through experience what it is like to maneuver this ungainly device. You have to steer this vessel with just the stylus, and feel the tug and resistance created by the router's energy and the force of the spinning, cutting bit. Sure it's ungraceful, but it is literally FLOATING ON AIR! The 15- or 20-pound device you lift onto the workbench sheds all that weight as soon as you flick on the shop vac.

It's a whopping good trick!

So now you want to go to work. Here's how to set up and rout a copy of a bas-relief carving.

**1. Choose your work surface.** The duplicator requires a smooth, flat, level surface; smooth and flat so the platen moves about freely without hanging up on irregularities in the surface, level so it doesn't tend to slide off downhill. (Remember, there is virtually no friction between the platen and the surface it's riding on once you turn on the air.) A well-maintained workbench makes a good work surface. A flat sheet of plywood over a lousy workbench or table also works fine.

**2. Decide how to stage the workpieces.** When you use the duplicator, you have two "workpieces" you are addressing simultaneously. One is the pattern, the other is the stock being routed.

As in a template-routing operation, a very particular relationship must be maintained between the pattern and the working stock. But unlike the template operation, where the template and the stock are sandwiched together, the two workpieces must be separated for the duplicator. Working out a tidy way of positioning and securing the pattern and the working stock can be a major challenge. And this is true when using any router duplicator, not just this one.

With this duplicator, the challenge is compounded by the fact that the pattern must be suspended directly *above* the stock to be routed. The distance between the two working surfaces must be 12¾ inches.

Once in a while, the workpieces lend themselves to some job-specific staging that can be cobbled up to support the pattern above the working stock. But more often than not, a tidy and flexible two-level table is what you need. I recommend that you spend the time right now, before you really do any purposeful duplicating work, to build the auxiliary project, "A Stock-and-Pattern Table," presented on page 32. Bob and Fred collaborated on its design, and it has worked well for the jobs that I've tackled with the duplicator.

mounting-screw holes, as shown in the drawing *Stylus and Mounting Bar Detail*.

If you want, if you think it will make it easier to use, you can tap the stylus hole. That way you can simply turn the stylus itself to adjust its length to match the router bit setting. To lock it in position, you jam a wing nut that's been turned onto the stylus against the mounting bar. You do not, however, have to tap the hole. Instead, you can drill the mounting bar to the outside diameter of the stylus and mount the stylus with two nuts, one above the bar and one below.

In either case, remember that you must always match the stylus extension to the router bit extension. Remember also that you need a different mounting bar for every different diameter of stylus you use.

**7. Install the mounting bar and stylus.** As long as your router is accurately mounted in the center of the mounting plate, as shown in the drawings, the stylus mounting bar's correct mounting position is 2 inches from the web, as shown in the *Side View* drawing. If for some reason you've done things differently, make sure that the stylus mounts directly above the router bit. Screw the mounting bar to the underside of the box beam sides. If you anticipate frequently changing the mounting bar to accomodate a stylus of a different diameter, consider using small hanger bolts and wing nuts instead of screws.

Your duplicator is now complete. Why don't you hook it up to the shop vac and take it for a spin up and down the workbench?

**The dog-and-wedge setup** makes it easy to clamp both the pattern and the work to the table. Lay the pattern on the upper tabletop, tight against the straight dog. Set the tapered dog into a set of holes close to the workpiece's edge, then tap the wedge into the gap between the dog and the work.

**Adjust the bit and stylus settings** using the stock and the pattern after they've been dogged to the table. Adjust the bit, and position the duplicator so the bit rests on the stock, as shown. The device's balance is such that it will settle onto the bit; you don't have to hold it. Then adjust the stylus so it is in contact with the upper tabletop.

Park the table on the workbench, but don't clamp anything just yet. The setup requires a little trial and error, and it can get a little fussy. To position the work, you need to have the duplicator set up with the bit and stylus. Having done that, you'll be able position and wedge the pattern and the work to the table. Then you can run through the limits of movement that will be necessary, and see if you can complete the router-carving operation with the table in one position. So…

**3. Pick your bit (and complementary stylus).** Take a good, long, judgmental look at the pattern. Take the bits and styluses to the pattern, and see which bit is best to use to copy the pattern. If you have a lot of material to hog away, obviously you want to start with a big bit. To trace the details, you need a small-diameter bit, maybe a veiner or a V-groover.

Having selected the bit, chuck it in the laminate trimmer. Remove the motor from the base, tighten the bit in the collet, and return the motor to the base.

Mount the stylus that goes with the chosen bit on the duplicator. This likely means you must screw a mounting bar with the appropriate stylus to the upper beam.

**4. Connect the air supply.** The air that floats the duplicator comes from your shop vac, as I've said repeatedly. You have to have a vac that has an exhaust port into which the hose can be inserted. Most do, though not all.

Plug in the vac and position it beside the workbench, though out of the way of your movements as much as possible. Plug one end of the hose into the exhaust port, the other into the duplicator's air supply port. It should seal

tightly without entering the port more than ⅜ inch. A turn or two of masking tape around the connector should tighten it up if it goes in too far.

Hold on to the duplicator with one hand, while you turn on the vac. If everything is working as it should, the only noticeable resistance to the jig sliding around will be the dragging and flexing of the vacuum hose. If you discover, when you switch on the vac, that the duplicator is suddenly stuck solidly to the work surface, you've connected it to the vac's suction port.

**5. Dog the pattern and stock in place.** Whenever possible, make setup easy by making the stock the same size as the pattern. That way, you can wedge the pattern on its table, then use the duplicator itself to position the stock on the stock table.

Using this technique to position the workpieces doesn't commit you to having the table in a particular location. You are aligning the pattern and stock with one another, which is essential. Once they are aligned and wedged to the table, they are set. You can clear the table from the workbench and do something completely different. Move them back to the bench two weeks later, and they'll still be properly aligned with one another.

So here's how to do it. With the router turned off, position the stock so the router bit slides along two of its edges while the stylus is sliding along the corresponding two edges of the pattern. Then clamp the stock in place. You don't need to be overly precise in this positioning—nobody is likely to notice if the position of a carving in the stock is off by a small fraction of an inch.

Now the workpieces are ready.

**Here's the overall setup.** The stock-and-pattern table is clamped at the edge of the workbench. On the far side of the table, occupying the center of the workbench, is the duplicator. The shop vacuum is to the side. The operator, suited out with ear muffs, safety glasses, and nuisance dust mask, is seated by the work.

**6. Adjust extension of the bit and the stylus.** If both the pattern and the workpiece are the same thickness, you can make this adjustment using the tabletops as reference points. But the best way to do it is after you've dogged the pattern and workpiece to their respective tabletops.

Extend the bit as far as it can be extended, then rest it on the workpiece. Now move the duplicator around so the stylus just touches the highest spot on the pattern. Adjust the stylus extension so that, when the stylus is touching that high point, the bit is resting on the workpiece. To accomplish this, it may be necessary to readjust the bit extension.

**7. Clamp the stock-and-pattern table.** With the shop vac running and the duplicator thus mobile, but with the router NOT running, trace around the pattern to see how best to orient the stock-and-pattern table. You don't need to be too obsessive, since you can move the table without needing to readjust the bit and stylus settings and without needing to realign the pattern and the stock. But a little experimenting now may save you two or three table shifts after you get started.

**8. Rout.** Actual experience is by far the best teacher for using this jig. Since the jig maintains the spatial relationship between the stylus and the router bit, you can guide the cuts by holding the stylus and moving it or by holding the router and moving it while watching where the stylus is going.

The latter approach provides much better control. Use both hands. Grip the duplicator on either side of the laminate trimmer, but watch the stylus. Guide it by moving the router. Don't rush; take your time. You want to trim away the wood a little at a time, rather than burrowing into it. Glancing at the stock occasionally will reassure you that the duplication is progressing as intended. It probably will reveal from time to time that you've missed an area. Just keep at it until the stylus has traced all the ins and outs of the pattern.

The quickest carvings to duplicate are those that retain the carver's original gouge marks. By using a bit and stylus that closely match the curve of the carver's gouge, you can follow right down the carver's strokes with the stylus, reproducing each of the original gouge marks in your duplicate.

If a carving has been smoothed out, you can usually rough out the duplicate with core-box bits, then smooth out these "gouge" marks with rasps and abrasives, presumably the way the carver did the original.

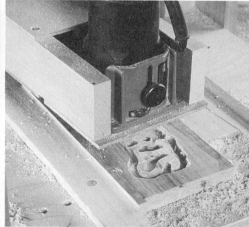

**Keep your eyes on the pattern** as you work. With practice you'll gain confidence and feel comfortable using the duplicator even though you can't see both the stock and the pattern at the same time. Every movement of the stylus will be replicated by the router (*right*).

# Trammel Baseplate

**Every router magician's basic bag o' tricks has a trammel in it. Here's a great one for *your* bag o' tricks.**

For routing smallish disks and holes, ranging from a 1-inch diameter up to about 16 inches in diameter, this is the ideal trammel. What I like most is its ability to do those small-diameter cuts—the 1- and 2-inch ones. The fact that it's got good range beyond is merely a plus.

The prototype is in the *working* half of the Rodale woodworking shop, the half where Phil Gehret spends each day building furniture and tchotchkes, cabinets and garden contraptions, industrial displays and a whole lot more. Phil designed and made the original trammel for his Porter-Cable 100. I've borrowed it innumerable times; it just works for me.

Eventually I made my own, fitting it to a small Bosch plunge router.

The trammel is a roughly teardrop-shaped baseplate made of ¾-inch plywood. A 5½-inch-long T-slot, extending from the bit opening out to the most distant edge, houses a slide with a pivot-nail driven through one end. Move the slide in or out to adjust the radius of the cut, then fix its position by tightening the locking knob.

A small router works best on the trammel, and a plunge router has the ability to initiate and deepen a cut easily. That's why I fitted my trammel baseplate to a small plunge router. To me, routing 1½-inch disks with a 3½-

horsepower router is like commuting across town in a Peterbilt truck.

## Making the Baseplate

The baseplate shown is Apple Ply, which I'd characterize as an American-made version of Baltic Birch plywood. It has 11 plies rather than the 7 plies typical of regular ¾-inch birch plywood. The slide is walnut. Hardware needed includes a T-nut, a thumbscrew or studded plastic knob, an 8d common nail, and extra-long mounting screws, all commonplace stuff.

**1. Lay out the baseplate.** The goal is to have a 6½-inch span from the bit axis to the tail end of the baseplate. The length of baseplate needed to achieve this goal changes in proportion to the diameter of the router base.

Begin by removing the factory baseplate from the router you'll use on the trammel. Measure its radius, and add 6½ inches to that. Cut a blank: The width equals the diameter of the base, and the length equals the base radius plus 6½ inches.

Use carpet tape to attach the factory baseplate to the blank, as shown in the drawing *Baseplate Layout*. With a

## Cutting List

| Part | Qty. | Dimensions | Material |
|------|------|-----------|----------|
| Base | 1 | ¾" × 6½" × 9¾" | Plywood |
| Slide | 1 | ⅜" × ¾" × 8" | Hardwood |

## Hardware

1 T-nut, ¼"-20

1 thumbscrew, ¼"-20 × 1"

1 common nail, 8d

3 extra-long mounting screws (size needed will vary by brand and model of router)

## BASEPLATE LAYOUT

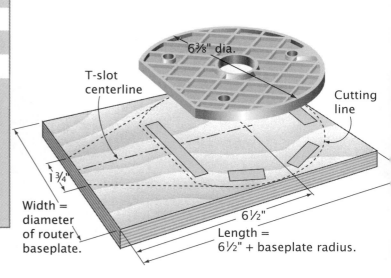

To guide the drilling of mounting-screw holes and a bit opening, stick the factory baseplate to the blank with carpet tape.

## TRAMMEL BASEPLATE PLAN VIEWS

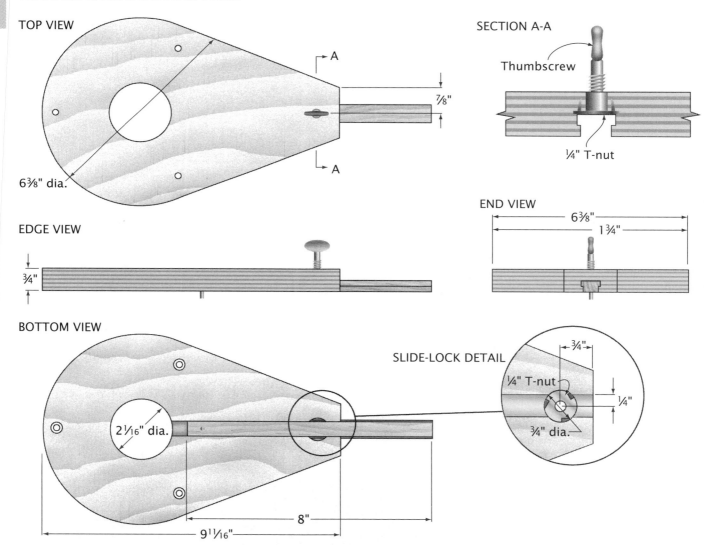

# ROUTING THE T-SLOT

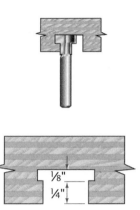

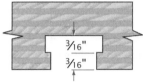

A. With a ½" straight bit in a table-mounted router, plow a groove ⅜" deep.

B. Switch to a ⅜" keyhole bit. Raise the bit flush with the bottom of the groove. Adjust the fence so the bit cuts a notch in the sidewall farthest from the fence. Make the cut into both sidewalls.

C. Lower the bit ¹⁄₁₆" and make a second pass on each side, increasing the height of the notch.

pencil and straightedge, lay out the tangents and the slot.

**2. Drill the holes for the router.** Using the holes in the factory baseplate as drill guides, drill holes for the mounting screws. Mark the location of the bit opening. Remove the factory baseplate from the blank. Then countersink the mounting-screw holes, and bore a large-diameter hole (about 2 inches) for the bit opening.

**The T-nut for the slide-lock** sits in a counterbored hole drilled in the baseplate near the tail end of the slot. To seat the T-nut's prongs, thread a bolt into the T-nut, as shown, and tap on the bolt head with a hammer. (Note that the necessary hole is larger than the slot.)

**3. Rout the T-slot.** This is a good router table operation. Begin by routing a ½-inch-wide × ⅜-inch-deep groove at the position shown in the layout drawings. Switch to either a T-slot bit or a ½-inch keyhole bit. Adjust the fence so this bit will be cutting into the outside sidewall of the groove (the sidewall farthest from the fence). The neck of this bit should be flush with the groove's sidewall, so its wing can cap the T. Make a cut into each sidewall of the groove. The proper feed direction, by the way, is right to left. For one side, plow from end to bit opening; for the other, from bit opening to edge.

**4. Drill for and install the T-nut.** As noted, the slide is fixed in position by a thumbscrew that's run through a T-nut. The tip of the screw presses against the slide, jamming it. You have to drill a pilot for the T-nut, plus a counterbore for the T-nut flange. Work very carefully, since you don't have much thickness with which to work.

Set the baseplate on the drill press table, with the slot up. Align it for drilling the T-nut pilot, and clamp it to the table. Drill the appropriately sized pilot hole. Switch to a ⅞-inch Forstner bit, and drill a counterbore deep enough for the T-nut flange. Test the depth by setting the T-nut into it, upside down, and seeing if the flange is flush with the bottom of the slot.

Tap the T-nut carefully into place. Turn the thumbscrew into the T-nut.

## T-Slide Tester Tip

To help fit the slide, cut a T-slot in an extra piece of the baseplate stock. Make this tester as you rout the T-slot in the base, using the same setups. As you refine the slide, check how it fits in this tester. When you can pass the slide through the tester's slot, it's ready to use in the baseplate.

**5. Cut the baseplate to shape.** With the T-slot cut and the slide lock installed, you can trim the baseplate's rectilinear form to the more teardrop shape. This is done quickly and easily on the band saw. If you don't have a band saw, use a saber saw. Then sand the edges square with a belt sander.

**6. Make and fit the slide.** The slide is formed by routing two rabbets into an edge of a hardwood strip, forming a tongue between them. For safety's sake, this operation should be performed on a workpiece that's 2 inches or more wide. After cutting the rabbets, check the fit of the tongue in the already-cut T-slot. If it won't fit the slot, make the rabbets a bit wider. If it is too loose, start over, making the rabbets narrower.

When the tongue fits the slot, rip the slide from the workpiece. Set up the ripping cut so the slide will fall to the outside of the blade. Fit the slide to the T-slot. With a block plane, remove shavings from the slide's back and the

### MAKING THE SLIDE

A. Rabbet the edges of a 2"-wide workpiece, forming a tongue.

B. Check the fit of the tongue in the T-slot. Re-rout the rabbets to reduce tongue width. Start over if the tongue is too narrow.

Tongue too wide    Tongue too narrow    Just right

C. Rip the slide from the workpiece.

D. Fit the slide to the T-slot by planing top and edges of the flanges with a block plane.

Plane the edges of the flange to reduce overall width of the slide.

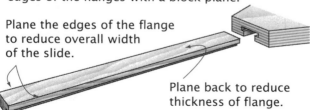

Plane back to reduce thickness of flange.

tips of the its wings as necessary to get it to fit.

When it fits perfectly, drill and counterbore the hole for the pivot.

To make the pivot, cut the shank from an 8d common nail, leaving it about ⅝ inch long. Press the pivot into the hole, and slip the slide into the baseplate.

## Using the Baseplate

Using a trammel seems pretty intuitive. It's like using a compass, isn't it? Set the compass for the desired radius, stick its pivot into the work, and spin it. But we don't usually have to account for the thickness of the pencil line a compass makes, or protect the surface beneath the work. Make a mistake with a compass, and you can erase the arc and redraw it. Make a mistake with a router and trammel, and you pretty much have to toss the work and start over.

**1. Chuck a bit in the collet.** My instinct is to talk in straight-bit terms. But you may be routing a decorative profile with an unpiloted profile cutter. So choose your bit and fit it in the router.

If you are routing a hole or making a disk, I'd recommend a spiral upcut bit. It will run cooler because it tends to auger the chips up and out of the cut.

While you are setting up the router, adjust the plunge depth if you are using a plunge router. If you are routing completely through the stock, set the plunge depth to the stock thickness plus no more than 1/16 inch.

**2. Set the slide position for the desired cutting radius.** Loosen the thumbscrew, move the slide, and tighten the thumbscrew.

Here's where you account for the diameter of the bit. If cutting a disk, *exclude* the bit from the radius; measure from the center of the pivot to the closest point on the bit. If cut-

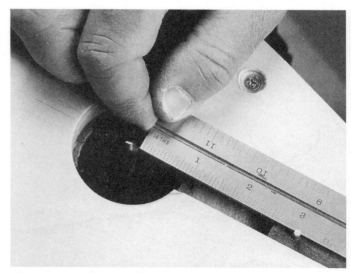

**Set the cutting radius** by measuring from bit to pivot. Use a metal ruler for this. Turn the bit by hand to ensure that you are measuring from the cutting edge, and not the body of the bit. Measure from the center of the pivot.

ting a hole, *include* the bit in the radius; measure from the pivot center to the farthest point of the bit. See the drawing *Setting the Cutting Radius*.

For best accuracy, use a metal rule, rather than a tape measure, to set the slide.

## SETTING THE CUTTING RADIUS

WANT THE DISK?

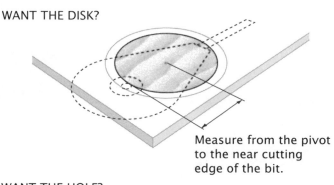

Measure from the pivot to the near cutting edge of the bit.

WANT THE HOLE?

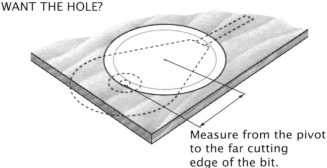

Measure from the pivot to the far cutting edge of the bit.

**3. Drill the pivot hole in the workpiece.** You can't get around needing a pivot hole in the work. It doesn't need to be too deep, since the pivot is little more than a nubbin. Use a ⅛-inch drill bit, and bore only ¼ inch deep. Keep the drill perpendicular to the work.

**4. Clamp the workpiece.** If you are routing a through hole, you need to secure the work and, at the same time, protect the surface beneath it. Moreover, you definitely don't want the pivot point to move as you complete the cut.

What to do? Slide a piece of expendable material—¼-inch plywood, for example—under the workpiece. That'll protect the workbench beneath the workpiece. To immobilize the piece that will be cut free, bond it to the backup with carpet tape. With this done, clamp the workpiece and its backup to the workbench, positioning the clamps where they won't interfere with the trammel's travel.

**5. Set the router in place, and rout.** With everything set up, set the router on the work, and work the pivot into the pivot hole.

With a plunge router, the operation involves no more than switching on the router, plunging the bit into the work, and swinging the machine around the pivot.

Fixed-base routers are a bit more problematic, and you may need to experiment a bit with the router you have to

determine the best avenue of attack. You may be able to switch on the motor with the bit retracted within the base, then loosen the lock mechanism, plunge the bit into the work, and tighten the lock. Doesn't work for you? Try setting the cutting depth to about ¼ inch, then catching the pivot in its hole while keeping the router base tipped up from the workpiece so the bit is clear of the work. Switch on the router and lower it onto the work, plunging the bit. Still uncomfortable? Here's a third option: Drill a starting hole the same diameter as the bit. Set the depth of cut; position the router with the pivot in its pilot and the bit in its starting hole. Now switch on the router.

With the cut started, it is a simple matter to swing the router—*counterclockwise* is the correct feed direction—through a complete circle. Increase the cutting depth, and take another lap. Keep it up, and you'll get there.

**A perfect circle is the end result.** Whether you want a disk or a hole, the trammel baseplate will serve you. The effective range of the jig is evident: The groove is the largest arc you can produce, while the disk and hole represent the smallest.

# Vacuum Trammel

**Rout a circle without leaving a mark at the pivot point. Vacuum pressure holds this trammel's pivot to the work.**

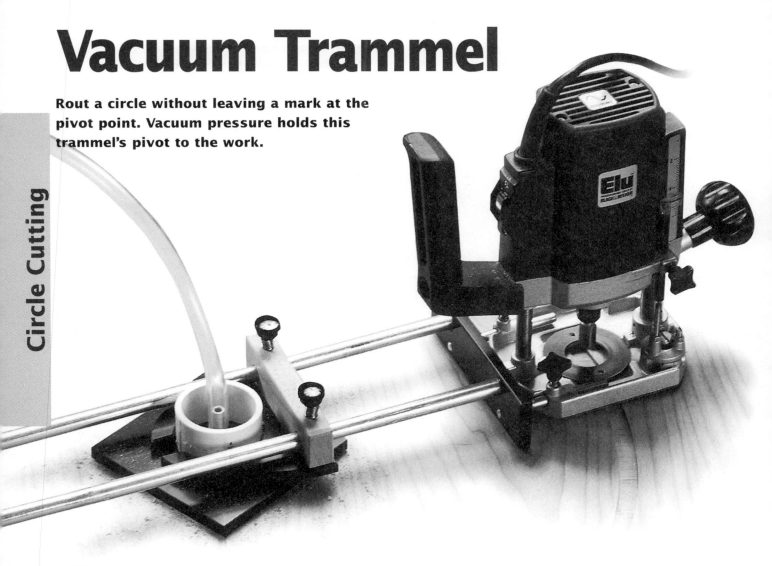

A trammel puts a router on a compass. Instead of simply drawing arcs and circles, it enables you to *cut* them.

If you've been working wood and reading about woodworking for a couple of years, you've surely seen a score of trammel setups. On the low end of the trammel scale is the strip of ¼-inch plywood with a pivot screw at one end and a router carpet-taped to the other. The trammel baseplate shown in the previous chapter is somewhere in the middle of the scale. A beautifully machined and finished commercial trammel like Micro-Fence's circle jig has to represent the high end.

The trammel presented here is a "niche fixture." It's a good general-purpose trammel, but it's special because it allows you to rout a circle without making a pivot hole anywhere in the workpiece. (It's also special because it needs a vacuum system to work as just advertised.)

The critical element here is the pivot. It is a vacuum jig; vacuum sucks it to the work. You position the pivot base, pull a vacuum, and it instantly grabs the work and won't let it go. You hang the trammel on the pivot, set the radius, and make the cut. Then you cut the vacuum, and the pivot base instantly releases from the work. No fuss, no marks, no nasty residue.

I was spurred to make this fixture by Ed Ferri of Quality VAKuum Products, who introduced me to the realm of vacuum clamping. (See the next chapter, "Vacuum Clamping," on page 50.) The examples of vacuum trammels that I've seen have a smallish pivot plate with a right-angle vacuum port. The vacuum hose thus attaches to a fitting in the edge of the pivot base, making the vacuum hose an obstacle. If you do snag that hose while making a cut, you'll lose your pivot instantly, and very probably botch the cut and the workpiece. This is trouble a woodworker doesn't need. I figure there are enough obstacles in trammel-routing, so why introduce another on the pretext of making the process easier?

So I came up with a design that has the fitting in the center of the pivot itself. The hose can be dropped down from overhead (suspend it from a shop skyhook) so that you rout around it. It's never in the way.

Because routing and vacuum clamping are contemporary woodworking methods, it seems right to me that the vacuum trammel be made with contemporary materials and approaches. As a consequence, the only bit of wood in this fixture is roughly an inch square and 5 inches long. The rest of the trammel is metal and plastic. The only glue used is a high-tech glue formulated specifically to bond disparate kinds of plastic.

Nevertheless, with the exception of cutting threads, the techniques applied and the tools used are conventional woodworking techniques and tools.

Before detailing how to make and use the vacuum trammel, I should emphasize that you need some special equipment to create the vacuum that holds the pivot base to the work. Details on this are in the next chapter, "Vacuum Clamping," on page 50. If you don't have a vacuum system, there's no point in making this trammel.

## Making the Trammel

It's ironic, I think, that we have this shop-made wood-working fixture here, and it has almost no wood in it. It's a good example of how high-tech materials and techniques are becoming more accessible, even to the hobby wood-worker. You can easily substitute wood for almost all the plastic parts in this fixture—and in fact, you might make

something quite handsome, even something in the tradition of eighteenth-century joiners and cabinetmakers.

But wouldn't *that* be ironic! A state-of-the-art router mounted to a high-tech vacuum-clamped trammel lovingly handcrafted of exotic woods.

**1. Cut the pivot collar.** The key component is the short piece of PVC pipe that serves as the pivot collar. The drawings and Cutting List are for a trammel built around $1\frac{1}{2}$-inch-I.D. pipe. To be honest, the trammel shown in the photos has a 2-inch-I.D. pipe as its collar. Obviously, either size pipe works; but if you do use the larger-diameter pipe, you must adjust the dimensions of all the parts.

Cut the pipe to length, and clean the burrs from the edges. Measure it carefully with calipers, determining both the inside and outside diameters.

**2. Cut the pivot base.** I made the base from phe-

### VACUUM TRAMMEL EXPLODED VIEW

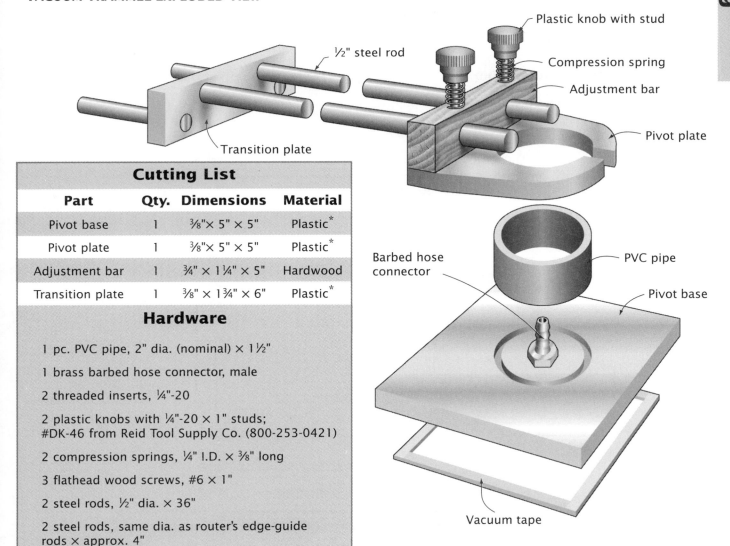

### Cutting List

| Part | Qty. | Dimensions | Material |
|---|---|---|---|
| Pivot base | 1 | $\frac{3}{8}$"× 5" × 5" | Plastic* |
| Pivot plate | 1 | $\frac{3}{8}$"× 5" × 5" | Plastic* |
| Adjustment bar | 1 | $\frac{3}{4}$" × $1\frac{1}{4}$" × 5" | Hardwood |
| Transition plate | 1 | $\frac{3}{8}$" × $1\frac{3}{4}$" × 6" | Plastic* |

### Hardware

1 pc. PVC pipe, 2" dia. (nominal) × $1\frac{1}{2}$"

1 brass barbed hose connector, male

2 threaded inserts, $\frac{1}{4}$"-20

2 plastic knobs with $\frac{1}{4}$"-20 × 1" studs;
#DK-46 from Reid Tool Supply Co. (800-253-0421)

2 compression springs, $\frac{1}{4}$" I.D. × $\frac{3}{8}$" long

3 flathead wood screws, #6 × 1"

2 steel rods, $\frac{1}{2}$" dia. × 36"

2 steel rods, same dia. as router's edge-guide rods × approx. 4"

*Phenolic and polycarbonate are recommended. Acrylic is acceptable.*

nolic, though a base made from clear polycarbonate or acrylic might be easier to position. Cut the pivot base to the dimensions specified by the Cutting List. You want to be able to use the corners of the base to align it on a pivot point marked (with crosshairs) on a workpiece. Thus, you must be certain that the base is square, but also that the center of the square is marked. (If you are using polycarbonate or acrylic, leave the protective masking paper on it and make all the layout marks on it. Apply a strip of masking tape to the phenolic, and make the mark on it.) Carefully drill a ⅛-inch-diameter hole through the plate at that point.

**3. Rout the circular groove for the pivot collar.** Use the Trammel Baseplate on page 39 on a plunge router for this operation. Use a bit that matches the wall thickness of the PVC pipe as closely as possible. I used a ⅛-inch bit. Set up the trammel baseplate by cutting test rings in scrap material, then fitting the PVC pipe into them. When you've achieved a good fit, rout the groove in the pivot base, using the hole drilled in the center as your pivot. Make the groove only ⅛ inch deep, just enough to catch the pipe and serve as a reservoir for the special glue that will bond the pipe to the plate.

**4. Drill and thread the vacuum port.** Make the port by redrilling the center hole (the one you just used as a pivot). Determine the size of hole needed for the vacuum connector you will use (I used a brass barbed hose connector with a ¼-inch-18 NPT male thread on it), and drill out the hole to that size. Then tap the hole for the connector. Note that National Pipe Thread (NPT) is significantly different from the National Coarse threads on fasteners, so use the correct tap. See the section "Cutting Threads" in the appendix.

**5. Glue the post to the pivot base.** I experimented with several glues before settling on Devcon's Plastic Welder which I bought at the local hardware store. Mix the glue's two constituents and spread it in the circular groove in the pivot base. Set the collar into place. Use a small-diameter dowel to build up a fillet of glue around the inside and outside of the collar, to reinforce the joint.

Set the assembly aside while the glue cures. No clamping is necessary.

**6. Cut the pivot plate.** This is the plate that fits over the pivot post, tying the router to the pivot. It, too, is plastic in my prototype, though you could make it of plywood.

**7. Shape the pivot plate.** Lay out the shape of the

## VACUUM TRAMMEL PLAN VIEWS

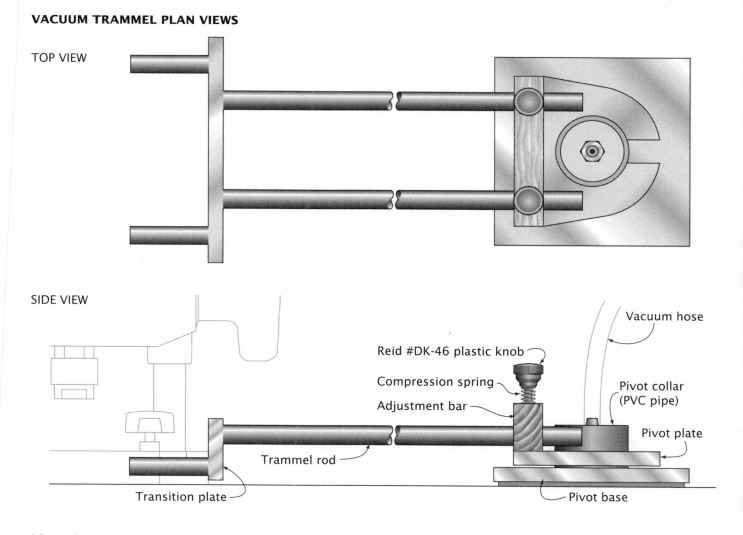

TOP VIEW

SIDE VIEW

Vacuum hose

Reid #DK-46 plastic knob

Compression spring

Adjustment bar

Pivot collar (PVC pipe)

Pivot plate

Trammel rod

Transition plate

Pivot base

## PIVOT BASE PLAN

### TOP VIEW

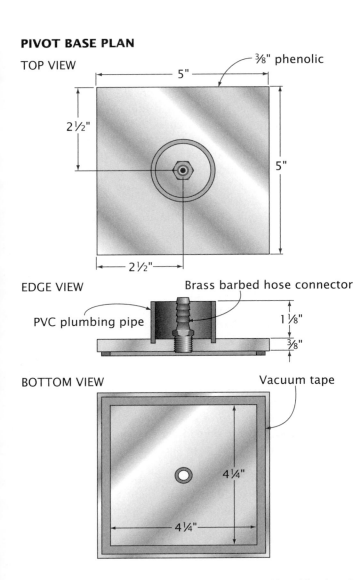

⅜" phenolic

5"

2½"

5"

2½"

### EDGE VIEW

Brass barbed hose connector

PVC plumbing pipe

1⅛"

⅜"

### BOTTOM VIEW

Vacuum tape

4¼"

4¼"

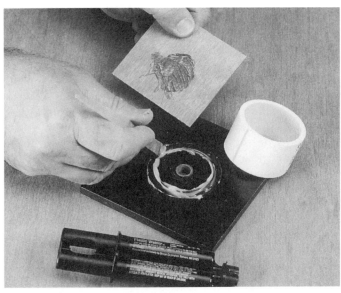

**Glue the collar to the base** using a special two-part glue called Devcon's Plastic Welder. Pushing a plunger on the package dispenses equal amounts of the two constituents, which must be mixed. Spread the thoroughly mixed glue on the bottom edge of the collar and in the groove in the base. Then press the two parts together.

## PIVOT PLATE PLAN

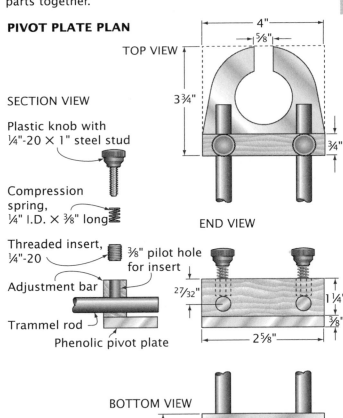

### TOP VIEW

4"

⅝"

3¾"

### SECTION VIEW

Plastic knob with
¼"-20 × 1" steel stud

Compression spring,
¼" I.D. × ⅜" long

Threaded insert,
¼"-20

⅜" pilot hole for insert

Adjustment bar

Trammel rod

Phenolic pivot plate

### END VIEW

¾"

27/32"

1¼"

⅜"

2⅝"

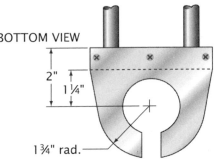

### BOTTOM VIEW

2"

1¼"

1¾" rad.

plate as shown in the drawing *Pivot Plate Plan.* The break in the ring allows you to fit the trammel on the pivot base *after* it's been vacuum-set on the workpiece. The slot is wide enough for the vacuum hose to pass through.

On black phenolic, you aren't going to be able to see any layout lines. So apply strips of masking tape to the plastic before doing the layout work. An alternative is to apply a sheet of paper to the plastic with artist's spray adhesive.

Drill a ⅛-inch-diameter hole at the pivot point indicated in the *Bottom View* of the *Pivot Plate Plan* drawing.

Lay out the arc and the tangents that extend from the arc to the corners of the adjustment bar. Cut the tangents; the band saw is ideal for this, though other tools with do the job.

Next use carpet tape to bond the plate to a backup scrap that's big enough to be clamped or dogged to the workbench. (This may seem an ironic approach, since we're talking about a vacuum-clamped jig. But the truth is, vacuum clamping doesn't work in every situation, and this is one in which it won't work.)

Using the trammel baseplate, rout the arc. Later, after you've separated the plate from the scrap, you can file or sand the edge to fair and smooth the transition from arc to tangent, and to buff up the appearance of the plate's edges. For now, leave the plate stuck to the scrap.

**8. Rout the pivot hole.** Use the plunge router fitted with the trammel baseplate for this operation. As you did when routing the groove in the pivot base, make test cuts in scrap to adjust the router and trammel. You want a fairly tight fit of the post in the hole. A bit of resistance as the plate turns on the post isn't a problem, but slop is. If the plate can rattle a bit on the post, you will not get satisfactory cuts using the trammel. So make sure the trammel adjustment is just right before making the cut in the plate.

After routing the hole, separate the plate from the backup scrap. Cut the hose-clearance slot on the band saw or with a saber saw. File the corners of this slot to soften them, and smooth the transitions from arcs to straights. Clean the edges of the plate using fine sandpaper or a scraper.

**9. Make the adjustment bar.** Cut the hardwood to size. I used cherry, but many other hardwoods will do just fine.

Lay out and drill the holes for the trammel rods, as well as for the locking knobs. Opting for sturdiness, I used ½-inch rods. I bored ³³⁄₆₄-inch-diameter holes for them in the adjustment bar. To lock the pivot plate in position on the rods, I used small plastic knobs with ¼-inch-diameter, 1-inch-long studs turned into threaded inserts.

Drill the pilot holes, using the drill size specified for the inserts you use. Drive the inserts.

**10. Mount the bar on the pivot plate.** Clamp the parts together. Lay out, drill, and countersink pilots for the mounting screws. Drive the screws.

**11. Make the rods.** The trammel assembly has two sets of rods. One is set is the pair of trammel rods that extend from the transition plate to the pivot plate. I used ½-inch steel rods for this purpose; you can certainly substitute smaller-diameter rods. The Hardware List specifies 36-inch-long rods. You can make them longer or shorter, as you

desire. (Because these rods can be unscrewed from the transition plate as easily as they are screwed into it, you can make a pair of short rods to supplement the rods specified.)

The second set of rods connects the trammel to the router. The specifications of these router rods depend upon the router. Some machines, such as the Freud, Hitachi, and Ryobi routers, use quite large-diameter rods. The D-handled Makita uses only one rod, and it's pretty hefty. Porter-Cable, DeWalt, and other brands and models use twin rods, but the spacing and rod diameter vary. So use your router as a guide here.

The router rods shouldn't be too long. You'll get the minimum flex in the structure if the transition plate can be snugged against the router base. Ergo, the rods need only be long enough to reach from the transition plate to an inch or so beyond the router's locking screws or knobs.

After selecting and cutting the two sets of rods to length, use a die to cut threads on one end of each rod. Since the transition plate is only ⅜ inch thick, you need only thread a ⅜-inch-long section of each rod.

**12. Make the transition plate.** The transition plate has to be customized to accommodate your router. The holes for the trammel rods can be laid out and drilled based on the drawing *Transition Plate Layout*. But the holes for the router rods have to be laid out from your router.

After the holes have been laid out, drill and tap them.

**13. Assemble the trammel.** Turn the trammel rods and router rods into the transition plate. Slide the trammel rods into the adjustment bar. Drop a small compression spring over the stud of each lock knob, and thread the studs into the inserts in the adjustment bar. (The purpose of the springs is to prevent the locking knobs from vibrating loose during use.) Tighten them down on the trammel rods, locking their positions.

Turn the vacuum fitting into the the vacuum port in the pivot base. Apply the vacuum tape to the bottom surface of the pivot base.

You are ready to rout circles!

## TRANSITION PLATE LAYOUT

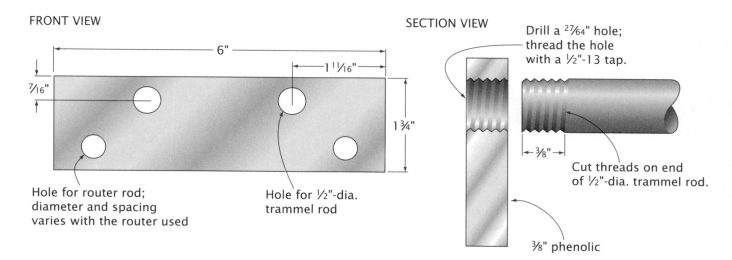

FRONT VIEW

6"

1¹¹⁄₁₆"

⁷⁄₁₆"

1¾"

Hole for router rod; diameter and spacing varies with the router used

Hole for ½"-dia. trammel rod

SECTION VIEW

Drill a ²⁷⁄₆₄" hole; thread the hole with a ½"-13 tap.

⅜"

Cut threads on end of ½"-dia. trammel rod.

⅜" phenolic

# Using the Vacuum Trammel

You *can* use the trammel with a fixed-base router, but circle cutting is generally easier with a plunge router. You don't have to flex and twist the trammel to keep the bit free of the work as you start the router. You don't have difficulty plunging the bit to start the cut. And changing the depth of cut between passes is easier to accomplish, too. So I'd recommend a plunge router.

**1. Lay out the cut.** Because the trammel has a nearly 2-inch-diameter pivot hole, it's darn hard to set the cutting radius using a tape measure. You need to lay out an arc of the intended cut, set the pivot base, and adjust the trammel to position the router on the layout line. You don't have to do the entire cut, just enough of an arc to set up the trammel.

So mark the center of the arc, which will be the pivot point, and scribe a bit of the cut arc.

**2. Set up the router.** To do this, select the bit for the job and tighten it in the router's collet. Next, set the plunge depth. Finally, connect the router to the trammel. You can roughly adjust the cutting radius.

**3. Set the pivot base.** Because the pivot base is a square, it can be positioned accurately on a pivot point. All you have to do is delineate the point with crosshairs penciled on the workpiece (and of course they must be at right angles to each other). Align the base so each corner is on a crosshair line. The pivot axis will be exactly on the desired pivot point.

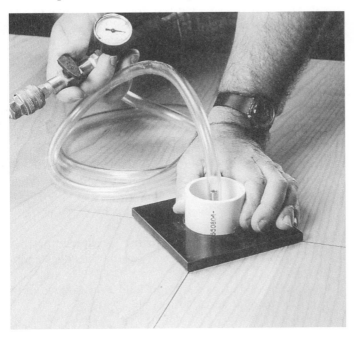

**To set the pivot base,** scribe crosshairs on the workpiece, marking the desired pivot point. Line up the corners of the base on the lines, as shown, which will place the axis of the pivot collar directly over the desired pivot point. Turning the valve on the vacuum pump will pull the vacuum, sucking the base to the work.

With the vacuum hose on the base's vacuum fitting, and the base properly aligned, pull the vacuum. The base will be firmly fixed in place.

**4. Adjust the cutting radius.** Adjustment of the cutting radius is accomplished by loosening the locking knobs on the adjustment bar. Then the router can be moved in and out in relation to the pivot.

Hook the pivot plate over the base's pivot collar. Plunge the bit to the surface of the workpiece (with the router switched off, of course). Loosen the locking knobs and move the router in or out as necessary to align it on the laid-out arc. That done, tighten the locking knobs, plug in the router, and you are ready to cut.

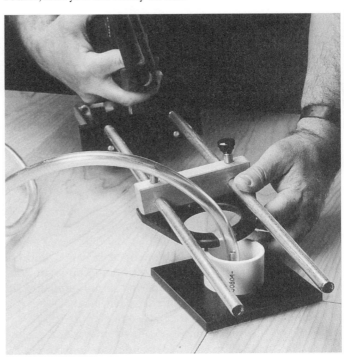

**To mount the trammel on the pivot base,** hook the pivot plate around the vacuum hose, as shown, and settle it onto the pivot collar.

**5. Rout the arc.** Switch on the router, plunge the bit about ¼ inch into the work, and feed the router counterclockwise. If you are cutting completely through the work, plunge the bit deeper at the end of the first lap, and make a second lap. Always feed the router counterclockwise.

# Vacuum Clamping

**Clamps in the way of your routing? Here's how you can use atmospheric pressure to displace those clamps and clear a path for your router.**

You were a geek in junior high school, weren't you? Come on, admit it. In the cafeteria, you'd impress your friends by sucking a drinking cup onto your face. You'd hold it over your chin and mouth and suck all the air out, and it'd just hang there. Oh, man! Don't you remember how impressed they all were?

Well, now you can impress your woodworking friends with a similar bit of magic. Use vacuum pressure to hold a workpiece while you rout it.

"Gee, Mr. Wizard," you're saying just now, "what's the trick?"

No trickery, just simple science. The woodshop principle involved is the same one that prevailed in the junior high cafeteria. Remove the air between the workpiece (that cup) and the workbench (your face), and they will stick to each other. Let the air seep back between the two, and they separate. In the workshop context, it's usually called vacuum clamping.

Look at the most straightforward vacuum-clamping device, the vacuum plate. The plate is a thick board with a hole drilled through it. A vacuum hose is inserted into the hole. Then special tape is applied around the perimeter of the board, forming a very shallow recess. You lay the workpiece on top of the plate, completely covering the recess and turning it into a "chamber." Suck the air out of the chamber, and it becomes a vacuum chamber. Allahkazam! The workpiece and the plate will be stuck together.

Because you don't need C-clamps or hand screws or any other mechanical clamps to keep the two pieces bonded together, the router's got a clear pathway to do its work. In this regard, vacuum clamping is in the style of using carpet tape, but it doesn't require you to pry the pieces apart with a chisel when you are done, and it leaves no sticky residue.

Consider these possibilities: You can make

- a plate to hold a workpiece in place on a bench (on the horizontal or vertical) so you can rout dadoes or grooves into the surface, or rout a profile on the edge;
- a T-square that attaches itself to the work without router-obstructing mechanical clamps;
- featherboards and other hold-downs that attach themselves almost instantly to a router table (or other power-tool worktable);
- a trammel whose pivot attaches to the work without nails, screws, or sticky tape;
- templates that stick firmly to the workpiece or that hold the work tight to a bench, leaving the edges unobstructed;
- push blocks that pick up and hold a workpiece until *you* are ready to let go of it.

This is a pretty intoxicating variety of vacuum-clamping jigs. And I repeat that you make them yourself, customizing them to your job, your tools, your work habits. You do have to be selective about the materials you use for the jigs, and you do have to buy some special equipment. You can't make the device that produces the vacuum, for example; you have to buy it. You need to buy "plumbing" to link the vacuum

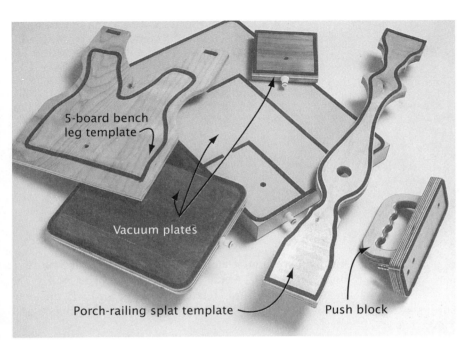

**Powerful vacuum clamps** can secure your work to a bench or a template to the work. Each is custom-made using common woodworking materials, vacuum tape, and a vacuum fitting.

5-board bench leg template

Vacuum plates

Porch-railing splat template

Push block

valve to the jig. And to "power" the vacuum-producing device, you have to have an air compressor. Quite frankly, I don't think you can justify the outlay necessary for both the vacuum system and an air compressor strictly on the basis of its clamping capabilities unless you are a pro. But if you already have an air compressor, you should look closely at the clamping devices shown in the following pages and seriously consider investing in the necessary vacuum-producing equipment.

## Vacuum Hardware

The essential device here is one that will create a vacuum you can turn on and off at will. You may already have read or heard about electric vacuum pumps, which aren't dependent on an air compressor. These devices are designed for veneer clamping rather than the type of clamping needed in router woodworking. What you need for clamping operations is a gizmo that converts a stream of compressed air into a vacuum. And no, it isn't magic (though it sure seems that it is).

The critical component is called a vacuum venturi valve. Some manufacturers call it a vacuum pump. Whatever it's called, it's really a chunk of aluminum (or plastic) with a little gauge stuck on it. It has three ports, two threaded for ¼-inch or ⅛-inch NPT (National Pipe Thread) fittings. Inside is a venturi, which is essentially a funnel. A venturi speeds up air flow; and in this device, the air flow is abetted by the fact that the air is already under pressure, since it's coming from a compressor. It rushes through the venturi so rapidly that as it roars past the adjacent vacuum port, it sucks the air right out of the port, thus creating a vacuum. After it passes the vacuum port, the air hisses out the exhaust port. The hiss can be really annoying, by the way, and most vacuum valves—but not all—incorporate a muffler.

To take advantage of the vacuum created by the valve,

you run a plastic hose from your clamping fixture and connect it to the vacuum port. To prevent sawdust that gets sucked into the system from clogging the valve, some systems include a filter. Others are easily disassembled and cleaned.

Although manufacturers offer a range of systems for vacuum clamping, the vacuum venturi valve is the key component in all of them. At least one manufacturer, Quality VAKuum Products, of Concord, Massachusetts (800-547-5484), allows you to trade up from the lowest-

### VACUUM SYSTEM SCHEMATIC

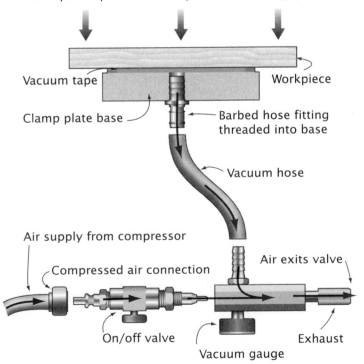

Atmospheric pressure "clamps" work to clamp plate.

Vacuum tape

Workpiece

Clamp plate base

Barbed hose fitting threaded into base

Vacuum hose

Air supply from compressor

Air exits valve

Compressed air connection

On/off valve

Vacuum gauge

Exhaust

**A vacuum venturi valve** is the heart of all vacuum clamping systems. The compressed air enters this valve on the left; speeds up as it passes through the venturi inside the device, pulling the air in through the connection opposite the gauge and thus creating a vacuum at that port; then whistles on out the port at right.

priced system, crediting you for the initial cost of the valve. But bear in mind that as you move up, you may need more air compressor to drive the vacuum system.

The valve must be matched to the air compressor. At a price hovering around $100, you can get a valve that will convert the 1 or 2 cubic feet per minute (cfm) of air flow produced by a ½-horsepower compressor into a very usable vacuum. As you get into multiple-clamp applications and a need to clamp more-porous materials, you need a system running on 4 cfm or more. It takes a 1½- to 2-horsepower compressor to generate and sustain that volume of air flow.

What happens if the vacuum system needs more air flow than the compressor produces? You don't get a very good vacuum, meaning the holding force is reduced. It takes longer (by a matter of 2 or 3 seconds) to evacuate the air from a jig, and the system has less ability to overcome air leaks. If the mismatch between vacuum valve and air compressor is pronounced, you simply may not get enough vacuum to activate the clamp.

### Jigmaking Basics

Making vacuum-clamping jigs involves woodworking familiars like solid wood, plywood, and plastic laminate, and some acquaintances like acrylic, polycarbonate, and phenolic plastics. But strangers must be involved, too: vinyl hose, barbed hose connectors and related fittings, and special vacuum tape.

Don't worry too much about the unfamiliar supplies you need. When you buy a vacuum system, you'll undoubtedly get a roll of vacuum tape, a small assortment of fittings, and a length of suitable hose. After you've made a few jigs, you can buy more tape from the original vendor. Fittings and hose you can probably buy for less money at a local hardware or auto parts store. Just match the stuff you got in the original purchase.

The familiars and acquaintances are used for the jig bases. This is where the issue of porosity comes up. To create a vacuum, you suck all the air out of the vacuum chamber. To maintain the vacuum, you do two things: one, prevent air from seeping back in, and two, continue to draw air out. To prevent air from seeping back into the vacuum chamber, the chamber's parts must be nonporous. Thus, the best materials to use for those parts of a clamping jig that

form the vacuum chamber are plastics—acrylic, polycarbonate, phenolic, even plastic laminate. The worst are man-made wood products like particleboard and medium-density fiberboard (MDF). In between are solid wood and plywood.

Unprompted, you may not think of wood as being particularly porous; I certainly don't. You know, *solid* wood! But consider wood's structure, and then, well, it does make sense that it would be porous. So when you think of a wood structure as a vacuum vessel, as a barrier keeping air out of the vessel, you can see that air leakage has to be expected.

This doesn't mean you can't use wood; it just means that it isn't ideal. You should seal it with several coats of a film finish, like shellac, polyurethane, or paint, or cover it with plastic laminate. Plywood should be void-free. Apple Ply and Baltic Birch plywood are very good, though lesser plywoods must be sealed carefully. Be especially vigilant about filling voids in the edges. If you use particleboard, use a melamine-covered variety.

A final note on the base material: For a vacuum jig, you

**Seal wooden vacuum jigs** with shellac, polyurethane, or some other film finish. Thus sealed, jigs made of solid wood and man-made wood products, which all tend to be porous to some degree, will be less likely to leak air. Apply two or three coats to be sure the jig is sealed.

need a *flat* base. Solid wood does come and go with changes in temperature and humidity. A loose board may cup or warp. For this reason, you should favor plywood or laminate-covered MDF or particleboard for a wooden base.

The capacity of the vacuum valve also plays a role here. Phase 2 of maintaining a vacuum, after all, is continuing to draw out air. If your valve moves a lot of air—and thus pulls a lot of vacuum—you can succeed with somewhat porous materials. To make best use of a small valve, though, you need to be rigorous about using nonporous materials in making your jigs.

In addition, the workpiece is a cast member. It forms half of the vacuum chamber, remember. You don't want to seal it, of course; so the high-volume valve is a plus when you are working MDF and other man-made materials.

To form the recess that, when the workpiece is laid over it, becomes the vacuum chamber, you outline an area of the base using vacuum tape. This is a high-density relative of closed-cell foam weather stripping, with which you may be familiar. Typically, vacuum tape is $\frac{1}{8}$ inch thick and $\frac{1}{4}$ inch wide. It has pressure-sensitive adhesive (PSA) on one side. The $\frac{1}{8}$-inch-thick tape is the best all-around and is the standard tape supplied with most vacuum-system packages. You may find tape that's $\frac{1}{4}$ inch thick; some woodworkers prefer this tape for large work, since it bridges minor warps and irregularities better. But steer clear of any thicker tape, since it can allow lateral movement between the clamping jig and the workpiece.

I mentioned that vacuum tape is similar to closed-cell foam weather stripping. You *can* use the weather stripping, but it isn't as resilient as vacuum tape, and it won't be as long-lasting. After it has been vacuum-crushed several times, it stays crushed and doesn't rebound when the pressure is removed. So employ it for limited-use templates but not for clamping plates and other jigs that will see a lot of use.

To apply the tape, you simply peel the waxy paper off the PSA backing and apply the tape to the (sealed) base. Obviously, the tape must completely encircle the vacuum area, and any joints between pieces of tape must be butted just as tightly as possible. You'll see, in looking at the jigs shown in the next few pages, that I try to encircle the vacuum area with a single, continuous strip, so I have only one such joint. It isn't always possible, of course. Moreover, you'll see a couple of instances where the total area is partitioned into zones, with breaks in the partition strips. A strip of the tape is positioned to serve as a vac-gate; you close the gate to limit the area of the vacuum, open the gate to extend it.

## VACUUM PORT ALTERNATIVES

THROUGH PORT

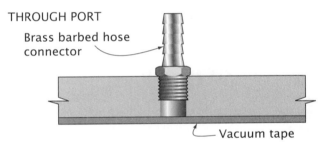

Bore a hole through the face of the base.

RIGHT-ANGLE PORT

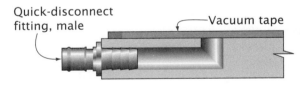

Bore a stopped hole into the base's edge. Bore a hole into the base's face, just deep enough to intersect the first hole.

T-PORT

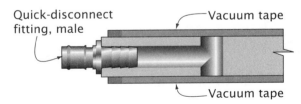

Bore a hole through the face of the base. Bore a hole into the edge, drilling just deep enough to intersect the through hole.

## Making a Self-Tapping Fitting

File a notch across the threads of a brass hose fitting, as shown in the photo, and it will cut its own threads in the vacuum port. It will even cut threads into a wooden base.

Brass is soft, and the notch is easy to make. But once the fitting is installed, leave it in place. The notch will cut each time you turn it into the hole. Removing and reinstalling the fitting too many times will result in a loose fit (and a vacuum leak).

The final step is to plumb the jig, so the vacuum valve can evacuate the air from the vacuum chamber. First, you have to drill a vacuum port, a hole that extends from the exterior of the jig into that vacuum chamber. The placement of the hole isn't critical; it just has to reach inside the chamber. Three alternatives spring to mind, and they are shown in the drawing *Vacuum Port Alternatives*.

After boring the port that's appropriate for the jig, you install a fitting, usually a barbed hose connector. The plastic "quick-disconnect" fittings that typically come with the vacuum kits must be sealed into the port with a silicone

caulk. I've also used threaded brass and nylon fittings. Use a tap of the appropriate thread to cut threads in the port, then install the fitting.

To carry the air from the jig to the vacuum valve (you remove the air from the chamber to create the vacuum, remember), use any rubber, vinyl, or plastic hose that's stout enough to withstand a vacuum without collapsing. The hose supplied with the system I use is 5/16-inch-inside-diameter, 7/16-inch-outside-diameter clear vinyl hose. It works perfectly with the quick-disconnect fittings, as well as with the brass and nylon fittings. And the local hardware store has yards of the same hose for half what the vac-pump maker charges.

If you choose to use the quick-disconnect fittings, you plug a male fitting into the jig and a female into the hose. Then you just disconnect the hose from one jig and reconnect it to another. What I've found is that the hose slides onto barbed fittings easily, and it can be removed from them just as easily. So you can use the same length of hose with different jigs whether you use the quick-disconnect or the regular fittings.

## TYPICAL VACUUM-SYSTEM FITTINGS

**Quick-disconnect fittings**

male      female

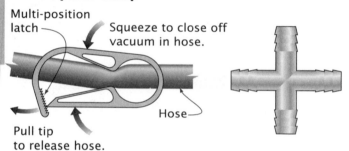

Press latch to release female connector from male.

**Plastic T-connector**

**Plastic pinch clamp**

Multi-position latch

Squeeze to close off vacuum in hose.

Hose

Pull tip to release hose.

**Plastic 4-way connector**

**Brass barbed hose connector**

**Brass coupling, male/male**

**Brass nipple, male/male**

**Brass tee, female**

**Brass 90° elbow, female**

**Brass 90° elbow, male/female**

**Brass stop cock (closed)**

**Brass stop cock (open)**

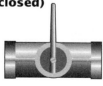

## Vacuum Testing Routines

In theory, a perfect vacuum at sea level will result in an atmospheric pressure on the workpiece of about 15 pounds per square inch (psi). In reality, however, you have to factor in material porosity, the tightness of fittings and

---

## Math in a Vacuum

It's useful to calculate the force holding your workpiece, especially when you first start working with vacuum clamping. It will help you develop some vacuum savvy—how large a workpiece can be secured with a given plate; how small a plate you can make that will still work; what you have to do to secure particleboard and MDF workpieces; and so forth.

Use the following formula: Divide the vacuum level (the inches of mercury indicated in the gauge) by 2, and multiply the quotient by the number of square inches enclosed by the vacuum tape.

***An example:*** If the gauge reads 22 inches of mercury and the tape encloses an 8 × 10-inch area, the holding force is 880 pounds on the entire workpiece. That's figured: 22 ÷ 2 = 11. Then 8 × 10 = 80. Then 80 × 11 = 880.

The vacuum level will tell you something about the porosity of the workpiece. You can test the clamping plate and get a baseline vacuum-level reading. Then recheck the vacuum level when using the plate with different workpieces. You'll see the vacuum level vary from one material to another. Don't assume that the holding force will be the same with a given plate, regardless of the material being worked. That isn't true, and this little computation will prove it.

seals, and even the vac-valve's efficiency. Thus, you'll doubtless end up with about half the theoretical pressure. But that's still about a half-ton of pressure per square foot.

It's a good idea to run a quick test on every new jig you make. Here's how:

1. Check the vacuum valve by connecting it to the compressed air line. Turn on the air, and cover the device's vacuum port with your finger. The gauge should read 26 to 28 inches of mercury. (For every 1000 feet above sea level, subtract 1 inch of mercury.) If the reading isn't in this range, or if the pump makes a fluttering noise, you need to adjust the line pressure up or down.

2. Connect the jig to the valve with the vacuum hose next. Turn on the valve, "pulling" the vacuum. Cover the jig's vacuum port with your finger. If the material is nonporous and the pump has tested properly, you should achieve 25 inches of mercury or better. If you don't get it, there is leakage in the system: Either the plumbing leaks or the base material is porous. To achieve the highest vacuum level possible, try to isolate and correct the problem. Check the fittings, and make sure they are seated firmly and seal properly. Apply silicone caulk to the barbs or threads to improve the seal. If the base is a wood product, apply additional coats of sealer to it.

## The Clamp Plate

The primary shop-made vacuum-clamping device is what I call a clamp plate. As I noted earlier, it is simply a board or plastic panel with vacuum tape outlining a vacuum chamber (or series of connected chambers) on one side. A

vacuum port allows you to pull the air out of the chamber, sucking the work to the plate.

This is a whole lot better way to secure workpieces for routing operations than using those router pads. One big advantage is that the work is elevated above the workbench by the plate thickness, so you have a little clearance for a pilot bearing when doing edge-forming cuts. (But hey, don't rout through the vacuum hose!)

The clamp plate does need to be anchored to a workbench in some way to prevent it from pushing away from you. You can dog it, for example. You can attach it to a workbench with screws. It doesn't have to be mounted on the horizontal, either. Mounted on the end of a workbench, a

### ROUTER-TABLE CLAMP PLATE PLAN
TOP VIEW

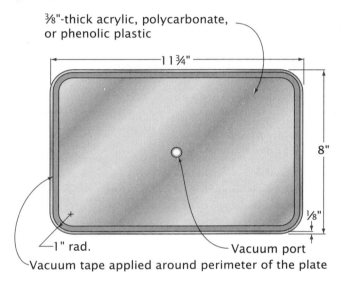

⅜"-thick acrylic, polycarbonate, or phenolic plastic

11¾"

8"

⅛"

Vacuum port

1" rad.

Vacuum tape applied around perimeter of the plate

EDGE VIEW

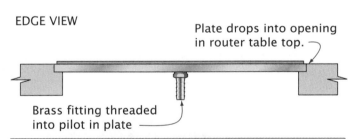

Plate drops into opening in router table top.

Brass fitting threaded into pilot in plate

### ROUTER-TABLE CLAMP PLATE
### Cutting List

| Part | Qty. | Dimensions | Material |
|------|------|------------|----------|
| Plate | 1 | ⅜" × 8" × 11¾" | Plastic* |

### Hardware

Vacuum tape, ⅛" × ¼", approx. 42"

Brass vacuum fitting, male

*Acrylic, polycarbonate, and phenolic are all suitable for this application.

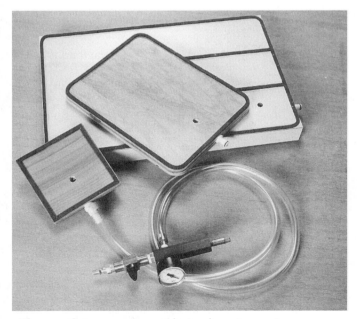

**Clamp plates** can be made in almost any size, as these examples demonstrate. Both the smallest plate and the medium-sized one are heavily polyurethaned Baltic Birch plywood. The largest is two pieces of MDF, glued face-to-face and covered with plastic laminate.

## MINI-PLATE Cutting List

| Part | Qty. | Dimensions | Material |
|------|------|------------|----------|
| Plate | 1 | ¾" × 5" × 5" | Void-free plywood |

### Hardware

Vacuum tape, ⅛" × ¼", approx. 42"

Quick-disconnect fitting, male

**MINI-PLATE PLAN**

TOP VIEW

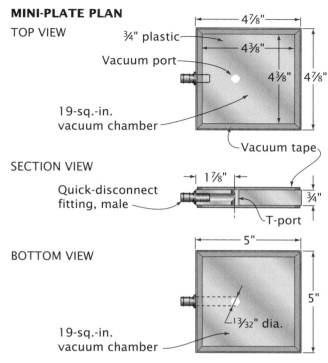

¾" plastic

Vacuum port

4⅞"

4⅜"

4⅜"

4⅞"

19-sq.-in. vacuum chamber

Vacuum tape

SECTION VIEW

Quick-disconnect fitting, male

1⅞"

¾"

T-port

BOTTOM VIEW

5"

5"

¹³/₃₂" dia.

19-sq.-in. vacuum chamber

**MIDI-PLATE PLAN**

TOP VIEW

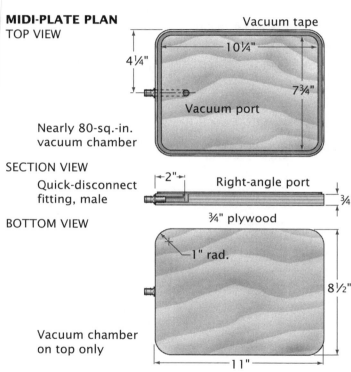

Vacuum tape

10¼"

4¼"

7¾"

Vacuum port

Nearly 80-sq.-in. vacuum chamber

SECTION VIEW

Quick-disconnect fitting, male

2"

Right-angle port

¾"

BOTTOM VIEW

¾" plywood

1" rad.

8½"

11"

Vacuum chamber on top only

## MIDI-PLATE Cutting List

| Part | Qty. | Dimensions | Material |
|------|------|------------|----------|
| Plate | 1 | ¾" × 8½" × 11" | Void-free plywood |

### Hardware

Vacuum tape, ⅛" × ¼", approx. 42"

Quick-disconnect fitting, male

**MAXI-PLATE PLAN**

TOP VIEW

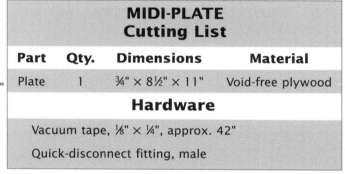

Vacuum tape

17¼"

11¼"

Vacuum port

2½"

SECTION VIEW

Plastic laminate seals edges, top, and bottom.

Quick-disconnect fitting, male

2½"

T-port

2-layered substrate

BOTTOM VIEW

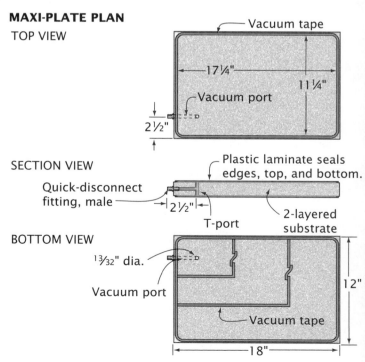

¹³/₃₂" dia.

Vacuum port

Vacuum tape

12"

18"

## MAXI-PLATE Cutting List

| Part | Qty. | Dimensions | Material |
|------|------|------------|----------|
| Plate plies | 2 | ¾" × 12" × 18" | MDF |

### Hardware

2 pcs. plastic laminate, 1¾" × 12½"

2 pcs. plastic laminate, 12½" × 18½"

Vacuum tape, ⅛" × ¼", approx. 14'

Quick-disconnect fitting, male

clamping plate can serve as a vacuum vise. Just seal fasteners with silicone caulk so air doesn't leak around them into the vacuum chamber.

The magic of the vacuum-clamp plate, of course, is that you can outline vacuum chambers on both faces of the plate. Then, by using a T-port, you can simultaneously suck the work to the plate and the plate to the bench.

Here are plans and cutting lists for four slightly different turns on the clamping-plate form.

The first is a plate that replaces the mounting table in a router table. Pop the router out of the router table and drop this plate into its place. It will hold a workpiece so you can rout around the edges, rout grooves and dadoes, sand it, and perform other operations that apply only downward or lateral forces. If you lift the workpiece, the plate will, of course, pull up out of the router table. The router table clamp plate is not a hold-down.

The next three plates are the same but for their sizes and materials. I just want to demonstrate the range of materials that can be used, as well as the configurations that are possible. The mini-plate and the maxi-plate have vacuum chambers on both faces, while the midi-plate has a vacuum chamber on one side only. To use it, you must dog it to a workbench.

## Making a Clamp Plate

Here are the basic steps to making a clamp plate of any size and any material.

**1. Cut the base.** Select your material. Remember that plastics are best because they are flat and non-porous. Man-made sheet goods are flat but vary in their porosity and will undoubtedly need to be sealed. For some applications, solid wood is okay, though it does tend to warp and it will need to be sealed.

Depending upon the material and the style of vacuum port, the plate can be as thin as ⅜ inch but may need to be as thick as ¾ inch. And to boost the height of the work above the work surface, you may want to make the base more than ¾ inch thick. To achieve these greater heights, you probably will need to glue-laminate two or more layers.

Given these parameters, determine how big your base will be, and cut the base (or base plies). Glue-laminate the layers if necessary, then trim the edges square and flat.

**2. Seal the base.** If you are using plywood, go over the edges carefully, filling in any gaps between plies with wood putty or sealer.

Wood and plywood can be sealed satisfactorily with a film finish. But don't be hasty or haphazard; get the base throughly sealed. Shellac dries quickly, so you can apply two or three coats in fairly short order. Most polyurethanes take 12 to 24 hours to dry between coats. Latex paint dries fairly quickly but may leave colored scuffs on workpieces.

MDF and particleboard need to be covered with plastic laminate—top, bottom, and edges. This can be done faster, I think, than shellacking or painting, and it ensures that the plate will remain flat. And it *really seals* the plate.

Detailed information on applying plastic laminate can be found in the chapter "Custom Router Table Top" on page 156. Follow the drawing *Laminating Sequence* as you apply and trim the plastic laminate.

Of course, if you are using plastic for the base, you can skip straight to Step 3.

**LAMINATING SEQUENCE**

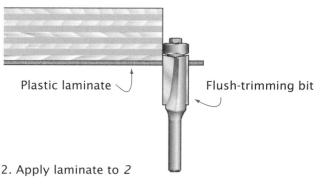

1. Apply laminate to the bottom, and trim the laminate flush.

Plastic laminate

Flush-trimming bit

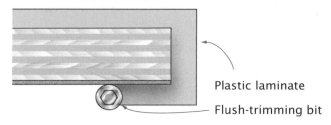

2. Apply laminate to *2 opposite* edges, and trim the laminate flush.

Plastic laminate

Flush-trimming bit

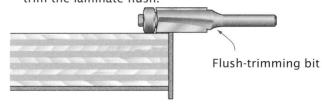

3. Apply laminate to the 2 remaining edges, and trim the laminate flush.

Flush-trimming bit

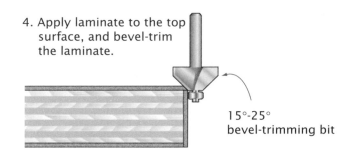

4. Apply laminate to the top surface, and bevel-trim the laminate.

15°-25° bevel-trimming bit

**3. Drill the vacuum port.** A through port is easy to drill, of course. A right-angle port or a T-port demands that you drill into the edges of the base to insect a hole drilled through the surface. Just match the diameter of the hole to the size and style of the fitting you will be using.

**4. Install the vacuum connector.** A plastic quick-disconnect fitting is a press fit in the proper-sized hole. To seal the connection between the fitting and the plate—and to bond the fitting to the plate—apply a discrete amount of silicone caulk to the fitting's barbs before thrusting it into the vacuum port.

A threaded fitting is a good connector to use in a plastic base since you can cut threads in the plastic with a tap. Though you can't cut threads in wood with a tap, you can modify the fitting's threaded section so it will cut its own threads. (See "Making a Self-Tapping Fitting" on page 53.) In any case, a thin coating of silicone sealant on the threads will solidify the seal.

**5. Outline the vacuum chamber with vacuum tape.** On a small plate, you'll have only a single line of vacuum tape. On a large plate, you may choose to outline several perimeters, so the plate can be used with small, medium, or large workpieces. (See the *Bottom View* of the drawing *Maxi-Plate Plan.*)

Use true vacuum tape on a clamp plate, since it is destined to be used frequently. Make sure the surface is clean before applying the tape. Make sure the ends butt tightly together: no gaps that will leak air.

## Using a Clamp Plate

The basic procedure has been outlined several times already.

Connect the plate to the vacuum system. With the vacuum off, set the plate on a nonporous surface—a workbench, a router table top, a countertop, even the floor. Lay the workpiece on top of the plate.

Turn on the vacuum system and pull the vacuum. The work will be sucked to the work surface by the clamp plate.

Here are some commonsense guidelines.

- The underside vacuum chamber must be covered completely by the work surface (meaning that you can't have the plate extending beyond the benchtop edge), and the topside vacuum chamber likewise must be completely covered by the workpiece.
- You have to maintain the vacuum throughout your routing operation. In other words, as soon as you pinch off the vacuum line or turn off the vacuum pump, the holding force disappears.
- You have to maintain the integrity of the vacuum chambers. If you plunge through the workpiece, for example, you cannot plunge through it into the area covering the clamp plate, or the vacuum will be breached, and the holding force will disappear.

With some experience, you'll develop a sense of what you can and can't do. You can't expect to hold a large workpiece with a small plate, for example, or to work too aggressively on a piece held by a small plate.

# The Vacuum Push Block

Though I'm calling this a push block, it's really a double-purpose jig. And that's what I like about it.

You can use it as a pusher, provided the workpiece is wide enough to provide a tight seal to the vacuum chamber. It's useful in doing edge-forming work on smallish workpieces, meaning pieces that are bigger than the shoe but smaller than you want to maneuver around a piloted bit with your fingers. Suck that workpiece to the pusher, and you can work all around the edge with your hand on the jig's handle, up away from the cutter.

But where it's really useful is clamped in a vise. There it serves as a small clamping plate.

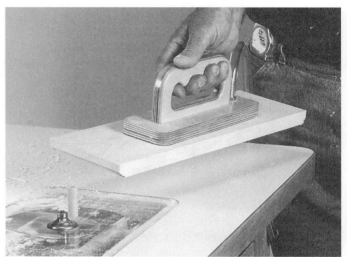

**Put a handle on your workpiece** by using the vacuum push block. Here I'm profiling all four edges of a small board on the router table. With the vacuum push block, I have complete control of the work, even to the extent of lifting it clear of the tabletop. And my hand is always well clear of the bit.

**Clamp the vacuum push block in a vise,** with its bottom up, to create a quick-release work-holder. As you can see, the work will be held above the bench and vise, clear of the vacuum line, so you have unobstructed access to the upper surface as well as all four edges.

## Making the Push Block

I made this push block fairly large. That's good for its secondary application—as a vise-held clamp plate—but I admit it limits the jig's utility as a pusher. A narrow base—or a narrow vacuum chamber on the same base—might increase its usefulness. As you gain experience with vacuum work, you'll develop a sense of how small you can make a pusher and still have enough holding force to do useful work.

**1. Cut the parts.** For this jig, I used Apple Ply because of its plywood strength and its low porosity. It has a great many thin plies and no voids. You can make the base of plastic, and use a wood handle. Or you can make the entire jig of wood.

Choose your material, and cut the parts to the dimensions specified by the Cutting List. Radius the corners of the base, either by routing them using the templates described in the chapter "Boring Templates" on page 6 or by sanding them on a belt sander.

### VACUUM PUSH BLOCK PLAN

TOP VIEW

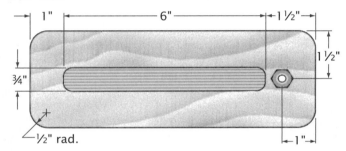

SIDE VIEW

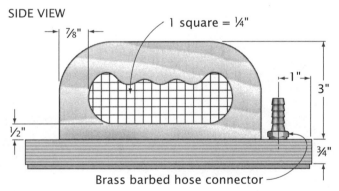

Brass barbed hose connector

BOTTOM VIEW

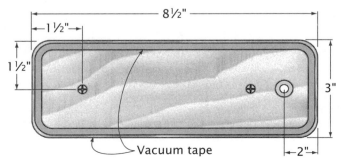

**2. Shape the hand grip.** To be truthful, I shaped a prototype handle by bonding a paper layout to a block of wood with spray adhesive and then cutting it on the band saw. Then I sanded to the pattern's lines on an oscillating spindle sander. And having done that, I could confirm that the handle was properly sized for my hand and was comfortable to grip. But I also determined that the handle should be taller, with the hand grip a hole, rather than a cutout.

To make the handle on the push block shown in the photos, I made a template in hardboard and used a plunge router with a template guide to rough out the shape.

To make the template, enlarge and apply the pattern to the template stock. As you do this, pull the cut edge back 1/16 inch to allow for the offset between the guide bushing and the bit. Bit/guide bushing combinations that will yield 1/16 inch of offset include (but are not limited to):

- 1/4-inch bit with a 3/8-inch-O.D. bushing
- 1/2-inch bit with a 1/2-inch-O.D. bushing
- 5/8-inch bit with a 3/4-inch-O.D. bushing

Form the hand-grip opening in the template by drilling some starting holes, then cut out the waste with a saber saw. Cut the radii on the top corners with the saber saw, too. Then refine the shape and smooth the edges with files and sandpaper.

To cut the handle itself, bond the blank to a large piece of scrap that's dogged or clamped to the workbench. Use carpet tape for this, and to bond the template to the scrap. Set up the router with the bit and bushing, and rout out the handles. Pry the template off the handle. Switch to the roundover bit, and radius the exposed edges of the handle. Pry it from the scrap, turn it over, and radius the edges on the other side. Sand the finished handle.

**3. Assemble the push block.** Glue the handle to the base. Drill pilot holes and drive drywall screws through the base into the handle. To prevent air leaks, apply a little silicone sealer to the screws before driving them.

**4. Drill the vacuum port.** The vacuum port is located at the end of the handle so it won't be in the way

### VACUUM PUSH BLOCK Cutting List

| Part | Qty. | Dimensions | Material |
|------|------|-----------|----------|
| Sole | 1 | 3/4" × 3" × 8 1/2" | Apple Ply |
| Handle | 1 | 3/4" × 3" × 6" | Apple Ply |

### Hardware

2 drywall screws, #6 × 5/8"

Brass barbed hose connector, male

Vacuum tape, 1/8" × 1/4", approx. 24"

when the push block is clamped by its handle in a vise. Determine the diameter of the pilot hole needed for the fitting you'll use, and drill through the base.

**5. Seal the jig.** Use shellac or a varnish to seal the entire jig. Apply two or three coats. While it's good to try to seal the inner surface of the vacuum port, you don't want to clog the port.

**6. Install the vacuum connector.** If you use a plastic quick-disconnect fitting, use the male. Apply a bit of silicone sealer to the barbs, and press the fitting into the hole.

I used a brass connector, which has a threaded body to turn into the port. File a notch across the threads so the fitting can cut its own threads, and turn the fitting into the port. A bit of silicone sealer on the threads will ensure a good seal.

**7. Apply the vacuum tape.** Lay out the vacuum area on the bottom of the jig, and apply vacuum tape around the perimeter.

### Using the Vacuum Push Block

To use the vacuum push block, you have to adjust your work habits somewhat. You can't start a cut, bring in the pusher, and complete the cut exactly the way you can with an ordinary push stick. If you touch the pusher to the work and pull the vacuum in mid-cut, you may jerk the work enough to botch the cut (depending on just what manner of cut you are making). Moreover, the act of pulling the vacuum will distract you from the business of making the cut if you are using a stop cock or pinch clamp to open the vacuum line.

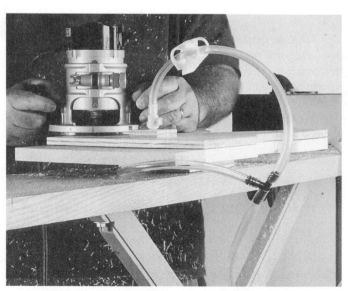

**This leg template for a five-board bench** is used with a router set up with a pattern bit. I clamp the work to a workbench with a clamp plate, then suck the template to the work. With the hoses extending away from the top edge of the work, as shown here, I can rout both side contours and the foot cutout in one pass.

When using the vacuum pusher, make it a habit to suck the jig to the work before beginning the cut, even before turning on the router. And if you can afford the equipment, use a pedal-actuated vacuum pump.

## The Vacuum Template

A vacuum template is simply a template that uses vacuum to suck itself to the workpiece. It can take one of three forms.

A. *A template that mounts atop the workpiece to guide the router.* The workpiece must still be clamped to a workbench in some way. All the template does is guide the cut.
B. *A template that doubles as a clamp plate.* This form of template is placed over a vacuum port. The workpiece is laid on top. The vacuum is pulled, sucking the template and the work to the bench. Then you make the cut using a piloted bit (with the pilot riding on the template, of course).
C. *A template that doubles as a sled or pusher.* Used on a router table, this template is a lot like the first template form, except that it has some sort of handle or grip to aid in maneuvering it around the bit.

In each form, the purpose of the template is what you expect—to enable you to generate duplicate parts with relative ease. To use it, you equip your router with a guide bushing, which rides along the edge of the template, so that the bit duplicates every curve and corner as it cuts the workpiece. Or you chuck a piloted bit of some sort—a flush-trimming bit, or a piloted profile bit, or a pattern bit

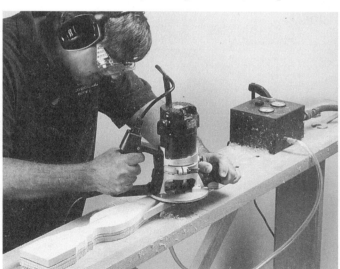

**A template that doubles as a clamp plate** minimizes the vacuum piping and thus much of the hassle. In the setup being used here, the vacuum fitting has been inserted in one of the bench's dog holes, while the other dog holes have been covered with common packing tape. Pulling the vacuum clamps the work to the template and the template to the bench. The edges are clear, and I can run a flush-trimming bit completely around the perimeter without stopping.

## VACUUM TEMPLATE FORMS

A. TEMPLATE MOUNTS ATOP THE WORKPIECE TO GUIDE THE ROUTER.

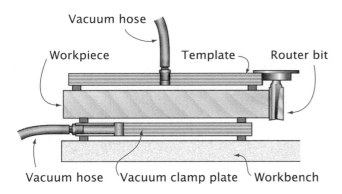

Vacuum hose

Workpiece — Template — Router bit

Vacuum hose — Vacuum clamp plate — Workbench

B. TEMPLATE DOUBLES AS A VACUUM CLAMP PLATE.

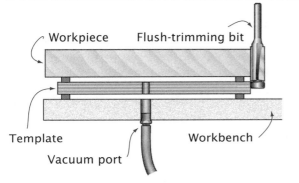

Workpiece — Flush-trimming bit

Template — Workbench

Vacuum port

C. TEMPLATE DOUBLES AS A SLED OR PUSHER.

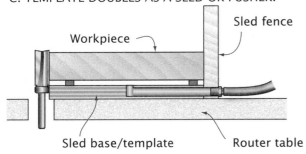

Sled fence

Workpiece

Sled base/template — Router table

with a shank-mounted bearing—in your router's collet. The bearing rides along the template's edge, guiding the cut in the workpiece.

If you've done template work, you know the template sometimes must be between the router and the work. Other times, it must be on the opposite side of the work from the router. The former prevails when you use a guide bushing or a pattern bit, the latter when you use a standard piloted bit (including flush-trimming bits and piloted profile cutters). With vacuum clamping the template to the work, you can have it both ways.

I can't give you plans for a particular vacuum template that will have any relevance to you, obviously. There are a couple examples shown in use, which convey

**Template routing on the router table** is enhanced if you have vacuum-clamping equipment. Here the edge and end of a board are being shaped with a pattern bit. The template is the base of the sled that holds the workpiece. The work is set on the template, tight against the back and end stops, and the vacuum pulled. The sled can be moved free around the bit.

the general idea, though. The essence of the job is this: Making a vacuum template is almost exactly like making a clamp plate. (See "The Clamp Plate" on page 55.) The only difference is the contour or shape of the plate. The rules that apply to making clamp plates apply to making vacuum templates.

For the template, use nonporous material. Plastic is ideal. High-quality plywood is good. MDF and particleboard are only fair and must be well sealed with a nonporous film finish.

The minimum thickness of the template depends upon the surface area of the template, upon the template material's stiffness, and upon the kind of vacuum port you are using. With a stiff plastic, a medium-sized template, and a through port, you can get by with ⅜-inch-thick stuff. In plywood, ½ inch is the minimum, and ⅝ or ¾ inch is better. Most fittings have a large diameter of ½ inch, so trying to fit them into the edge of a ½-inch-thick template is perilous.

Make the vacuum template the same way you'd make any template. If you are making it to use with a guide bushing, be mindful of offset. In all cases, make the edges as smooth as possible. Pay attention to minimum radii of inside corners. All that template stuff.

Apply the vacuum tape. This is what turns an ordinary template into a vacuum template. If you have any through holes—mortise windows, hand-grip cutouts, and the like, be sure to surround them with the tape. If the template is to fit between the work and the bench top, apply the tape to both faces.

Here's a quick but useful tip: If the vacuum chamber is vast, it's a good idea to spot little patches of tape here and there in the interior to act as pillars, preventing the template (or a thin workpiece) from bowing under vacuum. In extreme situations, a thin template (or workpiece) can collapse onto the vacuum port, breaking the vacuum. It's an unhappy surprise for the woodworker.

Plan ahead in positioning the vacuum port. If it is a through port, you have to ask, Will the fitting and vacuum hose be in the way of the router? If it is a right angle or T-port, you have to ask, Will the bit hit the fitting?

## Using a Vacuum Template

What can I tell you about using vacuum templates that I haven't told you already? No struggling with a cartload of bar clamps and C-clamps. Connect the template to your vacuum system. Position it on the work, and pull the vacuum. Then get busy with your router. It's just that simple.

Clamping Systems

# A Vacuum Manifold

Do you like a switch on the lamp fixture? Or on the lamp cord, somewhere between the lamp itself and the plug? Do you like fumbling in the dark, finding the cord, then running your fingers along the cord until they come upon the switch?

Yeah, I like the switch on the lamp better, too. It's always there on the lamp, and knowing where the lamp is, I know where the switch is. No fumbling. I don't even have to look directly at that lamp to find the switch and flick on the light.

The vacuum manifold is the same way. My vacuum manifold, shown in the drawing, gives me several vacuum circuits, each with an on/off valve (or stop cock). I can set a series of jigs, one by one, because the manifold provides a separate on/off valve for each jig.

Sure, pinch clamps on vacuum lines do the same thing. Sure they're cheap. But finding them to open a vacuum line when you are concentrating on keeping two parts in alignment is a needless frustration, like finding the Switch-on-a-Cord. The vacuum manifold, mounted next to the vacuum pump on your workbench or router table, is always there. Use it a half-dozen times, and you'll find yourself reaching out—without even looking—and turning a valve to pull a vacuum.

The nice thing about the manifold is that it's assembled from stock fittings I bought at the local hardware store (which is no House o' Bargains). I spent roughly $20 for a two-line manifold, and I can expand it for about $10 per line. All the fittings are for ¼-inch pipe; all are made of brass. You just screw them together and tighten 'em with a wrench. Mount the manifold beside the vacuum pump. Run a vinyl hose from the pump to the appropriate barbed connector. Run hoses from the other connectors to the particular jigs being used.

The vac-pump and manifold are constants in your system, while the jigs can be changed as necessary.

**MANIFOLD ASSEMBLY**

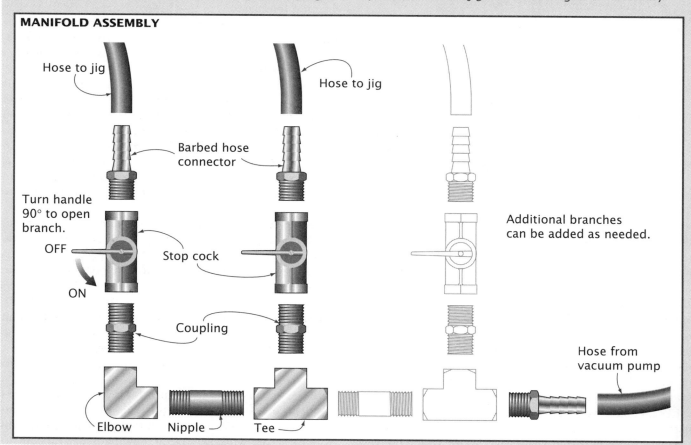

Hose to jig

Hose to jig

Barbed hose connector

Turn handle 90° to open branch.

OFF

ON

Stop cock

Additional branches can be added as needed.

Coupling

Hose from vacuum pump

Elbow   Nipple   Tee

# The Generic Baseplate

**Router jig making often involves fabricating a substitute for the factory baseplate. So making a precision plate should be routine. Here's the essential savvy.**

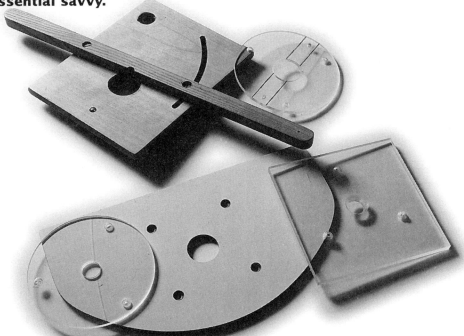

**W**ant to replace your router's baseplate? Maybe you want something that's clear so that you can see the work better. Maybe it's a larger baseplate you are after. Or one with a long, straight edge to ride along a fence. In any case, it's a baseplate that provides a function that the factory baseplate does not.

Baseplates are easy to make, and for some applications, precision doesn't matter. You bore mounting-screw holes, you bore an opening for the bit. Attach it with the factory-supplied screws, and you are ready to rout.

But for some applications, precision *does* count. Examples: a baseplate for use with template guides, or the Crosshair Baseplate on page 1. What are the characteristics of a precision baseplate?

- The bit opening must be precisely sized.
- The bit opening must be concentric with the bit axis.
- The baseplate must settle into the same position on the router each time it is installed.

Achieving this precision is not difficult. But you do have to incorporate certain principles in your design. And of course you must work carefully.

Let's make a generic baseplate with a bit opening that will center itself on the bit axis every time. Once you've mastered the craft of fitting such a baseplate to your router, you'll be able to apply the skill when making other custom baseplates in this book. Bear in mind that there's no one best way to do it. It varies according to the tools you have

to work with, your intentions, and the skills you've already mastered. I'll explain the choices that will present themselves as you work; make the choices that will work for you.

## Design Keys

1. *Always use flathead screws to attach the baseplate.* Very likely, your router has panhead screws securing the baseplate. This works with the factory baseplate because that baseplate has integral locating pins that fit into hollows cast into the base itself. That baseplate generally will fit onto the base only one way. The screws don't position the baseplate; they merely keep it from falling off.

    But with a shop-made baseplate, the screws must position the baseplate as well as secure it. A roundhead or panhead screw, which has no taper incorporated into its head design, won't position a baseplate consistently and accurately unless the hole in the baseplate exactly matches the screw shank's diameter—and won't wear. A flathead screw, on the other hand, has a head that tapers into the shank. If the hole for it is tapered, the screw will center itself.

2. *Always use the router itself to locate the bit opening's centerpoint.* To do this, attach the baseplate to the router with the mounting screws, then prick it with a V-grooving bit. If the baseplate has found its center on the router via the flathead-screw mounting, then the point of the bit will mark the center of the bit axis.

# Making a Baseplate

A good long look at your router, its baseplate, and the mounting screws is the starting point. That informs you about the extent of the job: Are you only making a baseplate, or are you also doing some work on the router base? Then you select the material and really get down to making dirt.

**1. Evaluate the baseplate-mounting screws.** You may well need to replace them. Check the screws on the router, and determine whether or not they will suffice for the new baseplate:

- Are they flathead?
- Are they long enough to use with a thicker baseplate?
- Are they sturdy enough?

If your router already has long, sturdy, flathead screws, you are set. If not, consider your options:

- Order a set of longer screws for your router from a mail-order vendor, like Woodhaven (800-344-6657) or Eagle America (800-872-2511).
- Take your router to the local hardware store and find flathead screws that fit.
- Upgrade your router by drilling out and tapping the base to accept larger-diameter screws.

The first two options are easy. If you exercise the third option, here are a couple of tips. First, when you redrill the screw holes, bore all the way through the base flange. That way you won't discover that the screws bottom out before their heads seat. Second, you may want to get a set of pan-head screws of the larger size so you can continue to use the factory baseplate.

The section "Cutting Threads" in the appendix will give you information on drilling and tapping holes.

**2. Select the baseplate material.** Router bases can be made from a variety of materials, all of which have advantages and disadvantages. Among the most popular are acrylic and polycarbonate, two common plastics, both of which are available in clear, foot-square pieces from mail-

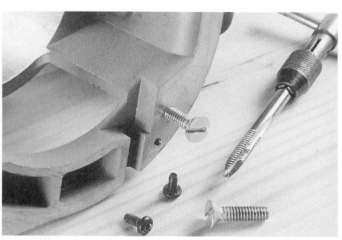

**Upgrade your router's baseplate-mounting screws.** I replaced this router's tiny screws (the black ones) with ¼-inchers. To do it, I drilled new holes through the router base, close beside the original mounting-screw holes. Then I cut threads in the new holes using the proper tap.

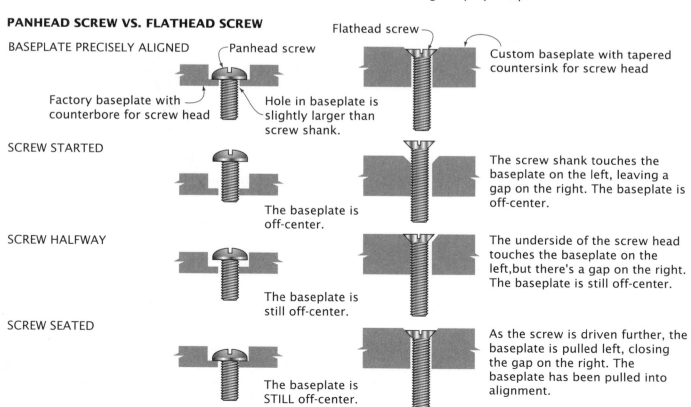

**PANHEAD SCREW VS. FLATHEAD SCREW**

BASEPLATE PRECISELY ALIGNED — Panhead screw

Factory baseplate with counterbore for screw head

Hole in baseplate is slightly larger than screw shank.

Flathead screw

Custom baseplate with tapered countersink for screw head

SCREW STARTED

The baseplate is off-center.

The screw shank touches the baseplate on the left, leaving a gap on the right. The baseplate is off-center.

SCREW HALFWAY

The baseplate is still off-center.

The underside of the screw head touches the baseplate on the left, but there's a gap on the right. The baseplate is still off-center.

SCREW SEATED

The baseplate is STILL off-center.

As the screw is driven further, the baseplate is pulled left, closing the gap on the right. The baseplate has been pulled into alignment.

order woodworking tool outlets. More information about these and other appropriate materials can be found in the appendix.

Since we are making a generic baseplate here, let's at least make it clear, so it's an improvement over the factory baseplate.

**3. Cut the blank.** Almost any rigid plastic, from a laminate to an acrylic to a phenolic, can be cut on your table saw with a carbide-tipped combination or crosscut blade (one with a lot of teeth). The band saw cuts plastics well, especially if fitted with a metal-cutting blade. And don't forget the router. Even to cut the basic blank, you can use a router and straight bit, guided by a T-square or other straightedge.

Acrylics and polycarbonates are thermoplastics, which means they are sensitive to heat. Generate too much heat in working them, and they'll gum up that work. I have never had a problem in this regard on the table saw. On the band saw, the length of the blade keeps it cool. (In addition, the band saw blade clears chips well, producing a very smooth cut.)

**4. Drill the mounting holes.** The trickiest part of this task is getting the holes in the correct spots. The most reliable approach is to bond the factory baseplate to the blank temporarily with carpet tape (which is sticky on both sides). Then you can use the mounting holes in it as guides.

Before you do anything else, select the bit. I've found that common brad-point bits work just fine for drilling in plastic. Use the factory baseplate to choose the correct bit size.

Now there are two ways you can go about positioning the factory baseplate on the blank. With the generic clear baseplate we're making, you can simply plunk the the factory part anywhere on the blank. Eventually, you'll trim the custom baseplate to duplicate the factory one, and the bit opening will end up centered in the plate.

*Aligning the baseplate on a spot:* Suppose there's a sound reason why you have to center the factory baseplate over a particular point on the blank. The factory plate has a bit opening that suddenly seems huge, and it has no lines to help you align it on a point. Now what?

Try this.

With the factory plate on the router, and a very small diameter bit in the collet, stretch masking tape over the bit opening. Turn on the router and bore a hole in the tape. (This is easy with a plunge router, more problematic with a fixed-base router. In the latter situation, clamp the router motor in a vise, and loosen the depth-of-cut adjuster. Now turn on the router and move the depth adjuster to make the hole.) The trick, of course, is to bore a clean hole without tearing the tape. You may need to apply several layers of tape. Or use duct tape.

Remove the plate from the router. Sight through the hole in the tape, and center the hole on the blank's centerpoint. You may say this is imprecise, and to some degree it is. But I think if you try it, you'll find it works well.

*Here's a positioning tip:* With some custom baseplates, you want to orient the router handles a particular way. The orientation of the handles is not always evident when you look at just the factory baseplate. In those situations, check back and forth between the router, factory baseplate, and blank so that when you are all done, the router handles will be oriented the way you want them.

## THE PLUNK METHOD

A. Use baseplate to select the proper drill bit for the mounting-screw holes.

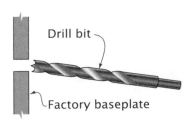

Drill bit

Factory baseplate

B. Stick carpet tape to the baseplate and plunk it face down on the plastic blank.

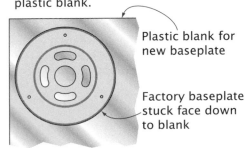

Plastic blank for new baseplate

Factory baseplate stuck face down to blank

C. Using the baseplate as a guide, drill the mounting-screw holes in the blank.

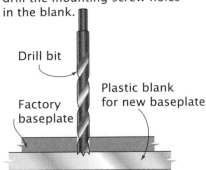

Drill bit

Factory baseplate

Plastic blank for new baseplate

D. With a saber saw, trim the blank to within 1/8" of the factory baseplate.

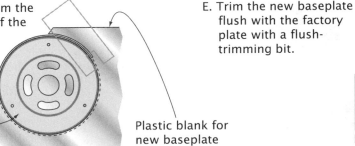

Factory baseplate stuck face down to blank

Plastic blank for new baseplate

E. Trim the new baseplate flush with the factory plate with a flush-trimming bit.

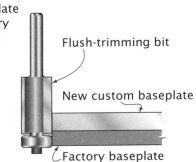

Flush-trimming bit

New custom baseplate

Factory baseplate

## THE HOLE-IN-TAPE METHOD

A. Apply 2 or 3 layers of masking tape across the bit opening on the factory baseplate. Plunge-bore a hole in the tape with a small-diameter bit.

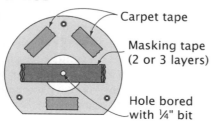

Carpet tape

Masking tape (2 or 3 layers)

Hole bored with ¼" bit

B. Cut the custom baseplate blank to rough size. With a pencil and straightedge, draw diagonals to mark the center of the desired bit opening.

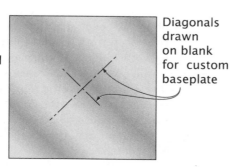

Diagonals drawn on blank for custom baseplate

C. Apply patches of carpet tape to the baseplate, and remove it from the router. Align the hole in the tape over the centermark by eye. Then press the baseplate firmly to the blank.

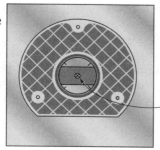

Align hole in tape over centermark by eye.

*What if I have no baseplate?* If you have no pattern that you are comfortable using, go to Plan B. It's extra work, maybe, but it is precise and it does have appeal. You need an expendable set of mounting screws, as well as a centering pin to chuck in the router collet. (You can buy a centering pin from CMT Tools (800-531-5559), Eagle America (800-872-2511), and other bit and router accessory vendors. The pin does have other uses; you won't be wasting $5 or $10 on a tool good for only one procedure.)

Cut the heads off the screws, and file or grind a point where the head was. Thread the screws into the appropriate holes in the router's base, with all the points protruding an equal amount. Chuck the centering pin in the collet.

**File points on headless screws on the drill press.** After cutting the heads from long-shanked screws of the same size as the baseplate-mounting screws, chuck one in the drill press, as shown. With the drill press running at a low speed, hold a flat file against the tip. A centered point will quickly develop. Do the rest of the screws, in turn, in the same way.

## THE POKE METHOD

A. Cut the heads from extra baseplate-mounting screws. File or grind points on the shanks. Use 1" or longer screw.

File the cut end to a point. Center the point on the shank.

B. Turn the pointed screw shanks into the router base. Chuck a centering pin in the router's collet.

Centering pin

Pointed screw shank

C. Set the router on the custom baseplate blank. Press down on the router to mark the blank.

Custom baseplate blank

D. The points on the screw shanks and the centering pin will dimple the blank. The marks are the centerpoints of the mounting screw holes and the bit opening.

Bit opening centerpoint

Mounting screw locations

Line up the centering pin on the designated spot on the blank, and set the router gently on the blank. Then push down hard on the router to dimple the blank with all the points—the centering pin's point as well as every one of the screws. (A side benefit of this approach is that you can orient the router just the way you want it on the new baseplate.)

*Bore the mounting-screw holes.* Back up the workpiece with a clean board, and if you clamp it, protect it from the clamp jaws with another wood scrap. Set the drill's speed to between 500 and 1,000 rpm. Feed the bit into the work slowly and steadily. When working with a thermoplastic, back the bit out often to clear the chips. Don't stop the bit in the hole; it may get stuck there. As the tip nears the breakthrough point, slow the bit even more.

After boring the holes, countersink them just enough that the mounting screw will be below the surface. A standard countersink works just fine in plastic.

**5. Trim the blank to size.** How you do this depends to some extent upon the final shape. If the baseplate you're making is indeed generic, it probably will duplicate the shape of the factory plate. If that's the case, leave the factory plate stuck to the new plate. Put a pattern bit or a flush-trimming bit in your router. Orient the two-plate sandwich so the pilot bearing rides on the factory plate, and trim the new plate.

If the new plate will be some shape other than that of the factory baseplate, or if you aren't using the factory plate as a pattern, then trim the new baseplate on the table saw or band saw or with a saber saw or router. See the appendix for more specific tips on cutting the material you are using.

**6. Locate the bit opening.** Fit a V-grooving bit in the router's collet. Mount the new baseplate—still without a bit opening—on the router. Don't even plug the router in. This is a hand-powered operation. Bring the tip of the

bit in contact with the baseplate, and turn the bit a couple of revolutions with your hand.

**7. Bore the bit opening.** Three options for doing this come to mind.

1. Use the V-grooving bit that's already in the router. Just plunge-bore with it.
2. Chuck a different bit in the router, and plunge-bore a zero-clearance hole for that particular bit.
3. Remove the plate from the router and drill a bit opening.

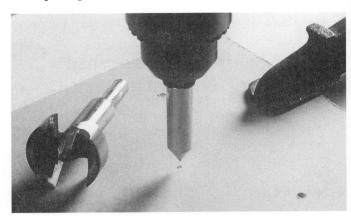

**Aligning the blank under the drill perfectly** is essential. With a centering pin in the chuck, lower and lock the quill just a hair shy of the workpiece. Shift the workpiece until your centermark is directly under the pin's point, as here. Clamp the workpiece to the drill press table. Then unlock the quill, change to the appropriate bit, and drill the hole.

## A Zero-Clearance Opening for a Piloted Bit

Bore the hole in two steps. First bore a clearance hole for the pilot bearing with a ⅝-inch bit. Then switch to the piloted bit. The bearing passes through the first hole, as shown, and the bit's cutting edges expand the opening just enough to pass through. It's a zero-clearance opening.

**Plunge-boring the bit opening with a fixed-base router** is not too difficult. But use care. Here the router has been set on scrap stock, and the base clamped to the worktable. The motor clamp is loose, so the motor can be raised and lowered. Take it slow; don't just auger straight in.

By exercising either of the first two options, you will ensure that the bit opening is centered perfectly. If you use the V-grooving bit, it will give you a fairly large-diameter opening.

When the router is a plunge model, boring the opening is straightforward. Just set the router on an expendable scrap of wood, and rout. Of course, you don't want the bit to "weld" itself into the baseplate, so bore the opening in increments. Plunge and feed sharply for a double-instant, then retract the bit and allow the work to cool momentarily. Then plunge again. Eventually you'll break through.

When the router is a fixed-base model, the work is a little more complicated, if only because the machine isn't designed for *any* plunge cuts. You have to clamp the router by its motor, and work the base up and down on the motor housing using the depth-of-cut mechanism. Since the mechanism, regardless of the style, wasn't designed for this operation, it won't necessarily go smoothly. The bit tends to grab, and that jerks the base. Moveover, there's usually play in the mechanism, and this makes it darn hard to rout a true zero-clearance opening. But clamp the machine securely, and the operation will work fine.

Drilling the opening on the drill press is a fine approach. If precise centering is a goal, use a centering pin or a small-diameter bit to help you position the baseplate accurately under the bit. Be sure you clamp the workpiece once it is positioned. Then change to the bit needed to create the proper-sized hole, and drill.

## Making a Baseplate for Template Work

You can make a custom baseplate that'll accommodate standard template guide bushings. To bore the rabbeted bit opening, use two Forstner bits.

To ensure that the opening is concentric with the bit axis, mount the blank on the router and use a V-grooving bit to just mark the center of the opening. Remove the baseplate from the router.

Chuck a centering pin in the drill press. Set the baseplate on the table, and position its centermark precisely beneath the centering pin's point. Clamp the baseplate in place.

Chuck a 1⅜-inch Forstner bit in the drill press, replacing the centering pit. With an in-and-out feed action, drill the counterbore. Be sure you don't bore all the way through the plate, but do bore deep enough that the bushing's flange will be flush with or below the surface.

Complete the hole with a 1¼-inch Forstner bit. Don't move the workpiece, of course. Just remove the 1⅜-inch bit from the chuck, and replace it with the 1¼-inch bit. When drilling, feed the bit hard for a second, then back it completely out of the work. Feed again briefly, then back out. Repeat this in-and-out action until the bit completely penetrates the plastic.

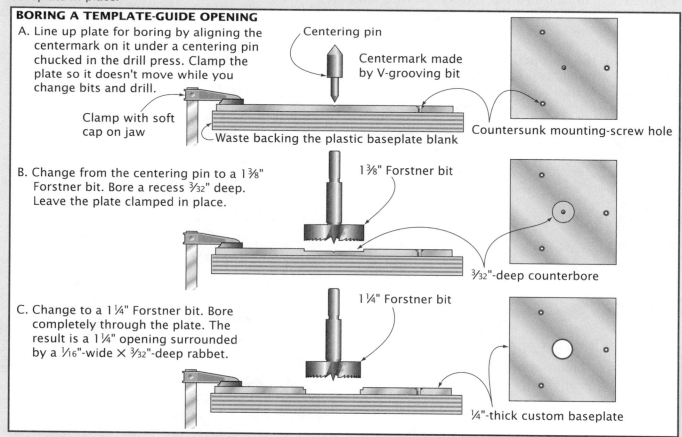

**BORING A TEMPLATE-GUIDE OPENING**

A. Line up plate for boring by aligning the centermark on it under a centering pin chucked in the drill press. Clamp the plate so it doesn't move while you change bits and drill.

Centering pin

Centermark made by V-grooving bit

Clamp with soft cap on jaw

Waste backing the plastic baseplate blank

Countersunk mounting-screw hole

B. Change from the centering pin to a 1⅜" Forstner bit. Bore a recess 3/32" deep. Leave the plate clamped in place.

1⅜" Forstner bit

3/32"-deep counterbore

C. Change to a 1¼" Forstner bit. Bore completely through the plate. The result is a 1¼" opening surrounded by a 1/16"-wide × 3/32"-deep rabbet.

1¼" Forstner bit

¼"-thick custom baseplate

# T-Square

**Step past the scrap-board fence. Make yourself a T-square to guide those casework dadoes.**

**A** T-square is made of two pieces fastened together to form a T. It's a basic, basic router woodworking tool. Make yourself one. Believe me, you'll get use out of it.

And it is kind of magical how easy it becomes to set up a dado cut. The T-square saves setup time. That's its big advantage. You don't have to mark the full length of the dado, then painstakingly align and clamp a straightedge to guide the router. With a T-square, a single tick mark usually is sufficient. So long as the T-square's fence is perpendicular to its crossbar, you can be assured that the dado will be square to the edge.

In addition, the crossbar acts as a brace, allowing you to secure the typical T-square with a single clamp. If you were to guide a router along an unadorned board fence secured with a single clamp, that clamp would become a pivot. With the crossbar butted firmly against the workpiece edge, that pivoting can't happen.

Making a T-square, of course, is really tough. (Wink, wink.) You have to glue and screw two straight-and-true scraps together in a T-shape. One piece, called the crossbar or the head, butts against the edge of the workpiece; and the other, called the fence or the guide or the blade, extends at a right angle across the workpiece surface.

The typical T-square—check out the drawing—has a fence between 30 and 36 inches long and a crossbar between 8 and 12 inches long. For narrow work, a smaller guide is more manageable. If you do a lot of cabinet work, make a really big T-square, and cut both case sides at one time.

A lot of woodworkers make their T-squares like capital Ts, which is to say without extensions. My T-squares have fences that extend 3 to 6 inches beyond the crossbar to steady the router as it exits a cut. This is particularly useful with big routers and with those with straight-edged or over-sized baseplates.

Once you get into the habit of using a T-square for routing dadoes and grooves, you may begin to dream about tweaking the T-square to make it even easier to use. That's what I did, and the results are included here. First I added clamp blocks—like those used on a router-table fence. No more fumbling with loose clamps. Then, after I got hooked on vacuum clamping, I made a vacuum T-square.

But let's start with a plain vanilla T-square.

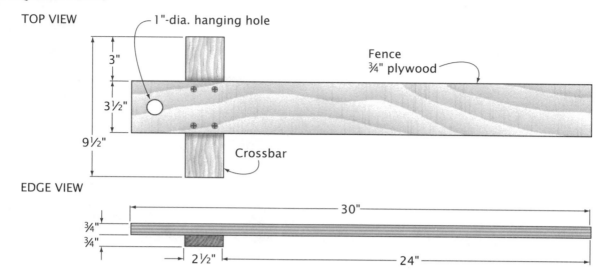

TOP VIEW

1"-dia. hanging hole

3"

3½"

9½"

Fence
¾" plywood

Crossbar

EDGE VIEW

¾"
¾"

30"

2½"

24"

## Making the T-Square

This is one of those projects that can cause no end of grief because it seems too easy. You just slap a couple boards together, not noticing that the edges of the fence weren't parallel, or that you didn't get the crossbar absolutely square to the fence.

Don't lose your focus. This *is* easy, but you gotta do it right.

**1. Cut the parts.** You can make a T-square from straight, defect-free hardwood scrap; but I use plywood for the fence, if not for the crossbar. Plywood is strong and stable. Half-inch material is satisfactory for the typical fence, in my experience; but by all means use ¾-inch material if you are concerned about deflection. The crossbar should be ¾-inch stock. When you cut the fence and the crossbar, be sure the edges are perfectly parallel.

**2. Assemble the fence and crossbar.** Glue and clamp the pieces together, and check to be sure they are exactly square. An out-of-square T isn't a jig, it's scrap. When the glue dries, drill pilot holes and drive three or four screws of the appropriate length to reinforce the glue joint.

## Adding Clamps

The T-square is a classic jig. It has only two parts, neither of them moving. It has a singular purpose that it fulfills faultlessly. The one way you can improve it is to add clamps. So I did.

The clamp block configuration is borrowed from the split fence. Two are used, as you can see. One, a fixed clamp, is located directly under the intersection of the fence and the crossbar. The second clamp moves in a slot routed in the fence. To use this T-square, you set the crossbar firmly against the edge of the work, and tighten the fixed clamp. Then you slide the second clamp into position and tighten it.

| Part | Qty. | Dimensions | Material |
|---|---|---|---|
| **BASIC T-SQUARE Cutting List** | | | |
| Fence | 1 | ¾" × 3½" × 30" | Plywood |
| Crossbar | 1 | ¾" × 2½" × 9½" | Hardwood |
| **Hardware** | | | |
| 4 drywall screws, #6 × 1" | | | |

While it is easier to rout the slot in the fence *before* assembling the T-square, there's no reason why you can't retrofit clamps to an old T-square.

### Making the Clamps

While you don't need much stock to make the clamp blocks, it should be thick. If you don't see an 8/4 (eight-quarter) hardwood in your scrap bin, then glue-laminate thinner stock. You can even use plywood.

**1. Cut and shape the clamp blocks.** The contour and dimensions of the clamp blocks are shown in the drawing *Clamp Detail*. Note that the two clamp blocks are slightly different.

The clamps are easiest to form with a band saw and stationary sander. You can enlarge the pattern, transfer it to a single board of the correct thickness, then saw out the blocks. The sander will make quick work of smoothing and blending the edges.

Alternatives? You can saw out the clamp blocks with a table-mounted saber saw. You can rough them out on the table saw; the details of doing this are related in the directions for making the Split Fence on page 237.

Finish shaping the clamp blocks by sanding or filing a narrow flat at the jaw's tip. Then round-over the

Dadoing & Grooving

# T-SQUARE WITH CLAMPS

## TOP VIEW

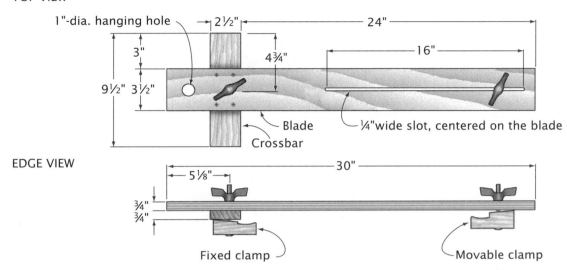

1"-dia. hanging hole
2½"
24"
3"
4¾"
16"
9½"  3½"
Blade
Crossbar
¼"wide slot, centered on the blade

## EDGE VIEW

30"
5⅛"
¾"
¾"
Fixed clamp
Movable clamp

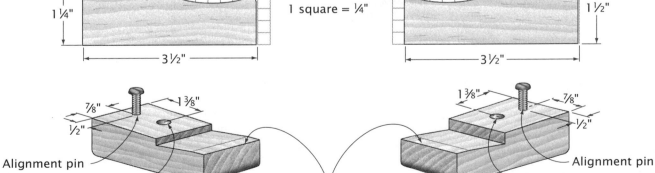

exposed edges with sandpaper or a file.

**2. Drill the holes in the blocks.** The clamp blocks are mounted to the T-square with ¼-inch carriage bolts. Left at that, the blocks would easily twist out of position, which would be pretty annoying when you are trying to set the clamps. Each clamp block therefore has an alignment pin protruding from the top. On the fixed clamp, the pin is actually a panhead screw. This screw projects into a hole in the crossbar, keeping the block from twisting. On the movable clamp, the pin is a short piece of ¼-inch dowel that projects into the slot.

To provide a little play for the mounting bolts, bore a ⁵⁄₁₆-inch hole (for one bolt) through each block, as shown in the drawing *Clamp Detail*.

Drill a pilot hole for the alignment screw in the fixed clamp block, then drive a panhead screw into it, as shown in the drawing. Leave the head protruding about ³⁄₁₆ inch.

Drill a pilot hole for the alignment pin in the movable

### T-SQUARE WITH CLAMPS
### Cutting List

| Part | Qty. | Dimensions | Material |
|------|------|------------|----------|
| Clamp blocks | 2 | 1½" × 1½" × 3½" | Hardwood |
| Alignment pin | 1 | ¼" dia. × 1¼" | Dowel |

### Hardware

1 panhead screw, #8 × 1"

1 carriage bolt, ¼"-20 × 3½"

1 carriage bolt, ¼"-20 × 4½"

2 compression springs, ¼" I.D. × 1" long

2 flat washers, ¼" I.D.

2 plastic wing nuts with ¼"-20 threaded inserts

## CLAMP DETAIL

PATTERNS

1 square = ¼"

1¼"
3½"

1½"
3½"

Alignment pin
⁵⁄₁₆" hole for bolt
⅞"
1⅜"
½"
FIXED CLAMP

Sand a flat on tip of the jaw.

1⅜"
⅞"
½"
Alignment pin
⁵⁄₁₆" hole for bolt
MOVABLE CLAMP

clamp block, then glue a short piece of dowel into it. Leave the dowel protruding about ⅝ inch.

**3. Prepare the T-square.** The slot can be routed on the router table or with a edge guide–equipped portable router. And you can do it after the T-square is assembled. The specifics of the slot are shown in the drawing *T-Square with Clamps.*

Lay out and drill the mounting-bolt hole in the crossbar *after* the T-square is assembled. Temporarily install the fixed clamp to mark the location of the alignment-screw hole in the crossbar. Just press the clamp hard against the crossbar, and the screw head will dent the wood where you need to drill the hole.

**4. Mount the clamps.** Insert the bolts in the holes in the clamp blocks and seat the heads with a hammer blow. Slip the bolts through the T-square, drop a flat washer over the shank of each, and turn the wing nuts onto the bolts. Align the screw and pin to align the blocks.

To pop the clamps free of the workpiece, slip a compression spring over the bolt before feeding it into the T-square. The spring will push the block away from the T-square.

## Using the T-Square

Here's how it works. Hook the T-square over the workpiece so that the jaw of the fixed clamp is against the bottom surface. Use your offset gauge to position the T-square. Keep the crossbar against the workpiece edge. Tighten the fixed clamp.

Slide the movable clamp tight against the back edge, then tighten the wing nut. The T-square is locked in place, ready to guide the router.

You can see that the workpiece must be supported in a way that provides access for the clamps. Here the work is dogged to the workbench.

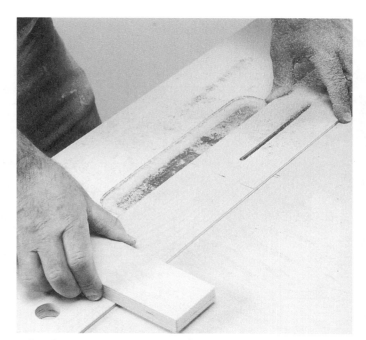

**Slotting an already-assembled T-square** can be done on the router table. Guide the work along a fence that's thinner than the T-square's blade. Mark the center of the bit on the fence, and the ends of the slot on the T-square blade. Lower the work onto the bit, and rout until the bit mark and the end mark align, then tip the work up off the bit. Take two or three passes to rout the slot.

# Vacuum T-Square

Vacuum pressure is a great way to hold a T-square on a workpiece so you can rout a groove or dado.

The most common T-square hassle, in my experience, is getting both it and the workpiece clamped. Typically, the square needs to be clamped at both ends to really hold its position, and that can be problematic when you have a 12-inch-wide workpiece resting on a 24-inch-wide workbench. Even with the T-square with integral clamps (see above), you have to have access at and underneath the workpiece edges.

Not so with a vacuum T-square. Just set the square in place and apply the vacuum. Rout your dado. Release the vacuum, move the square to the next spot, and reapply the vacuum. Obviously, you need a vacuum system. Get the vacuum details in the chapter "Vacuum Clamping" on page 50.

### Making the Vacuum T-Square

The square shown in the plans drawing is the same one presented at the beginning of this chapter. Follow those directions for cutting the parts and assembling the basic square. For the best vacuum, you need to use a high-quality, void-free plywood for the fence. Though you probably wouldn't apply a finish to the T-square under normal circumstances, you ought to in this situation, just to seal the surfaces and prevent air leaks.

When that is done, install the vacuum accessories.

## VACUUM T-SQUARE PLANS

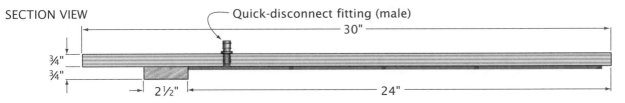

SECTION VIEW — Quick-disconnect fitting (male)

30"

¾"
¾"

2½"    24"

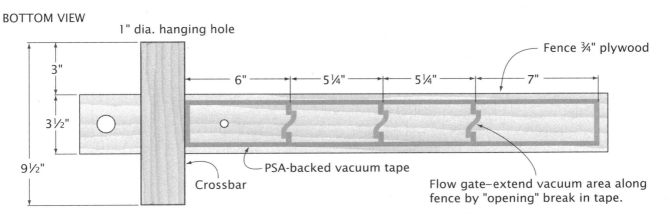

BOTTOM VIEW

1" dia. hanging hole

3"

3½"

9½"

Crossbar

6"    5¼"    5¼"    7"

Fence ¾" plywood

PSA-backed vacuum tape

Flow gate—extend vacuum area along fence by "opening" break in tape.

**1. Install the vacuum port.** Drill a hole for the fitting roughly where shown in the drawing. Apply an economical bead of silicone sealant to the barbed end of the male fitting, and insert it in the hole.

**2. Apply the vacuum tape.** As you can see from the drawing, the vacuum zone is divided into four chambers. Apply the vacuum tape to the bottom of the fence. You can joint the corners carefully, as shown in the drawing, or you can use a continuous run of the tape, bending around the corners. Once you have the entire perimeter taped, add the dividers and the closure strips (which I call "flow gates" on the drawing).

For a 6- to 11-inch-wide workpiece, use only the first chamber. As the workpiece width increases, you open more of the chambers to the vacuum.

### Using the Vacuum T-Square

Presumably, if you are using vacuum for clamping, you've got the vacuum pump conveniently located on your workbench and hooked up to your air compressor. Setting up the T-square, then, is nothing more than switching the hose from one jig to another—like switching bits in your router.

Clamp the workpiece to the bench (you can use vacuum to do this, of course) so it won't slide away from you. Position the T-square in relation to the layout lines for the cut (using an offset gauge), pull a vacuum, and you are ready to rout.

**Apply that sucker just about anywhere!** You don't have to fuss and finagle to get the workpiece positioned where there's room for a couple of clamps. Vacuum sucks this T-square tight to the workpiece. Once it's placed, the T-square's only obstruction is its vacuum hose, and that is flexible enough to be directed out of your way and the router's path.

### VACUUM T-SQUARE Cutting List

| Part | Qty. | Dimensions | Material |
|---|---|---|---|
| Fence | 1 | ¾" × 3½" × 30" | Plywood |
| Crossbar | 1 | ¾" × 2½" × 9½" | Hardwood |

### Hardware

4 drywall screws, #6 × 1¼"

Vacuum tape, ⅛" × ¼", approx. 36"

Quick-disconnect fitting, male

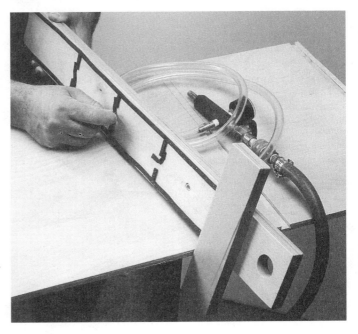

# Offset Gauge

A 6- to 12-inch-long strip of material is all it is. But an offset gauge allows you to position a T-square speedily and accurately, using a mark for the dado's edge as a starting point. The gauge's trick is this: It is exactly the same width as the distance from the bit's cutting edge to the baseplate's edge.

**To make the jig,** clamp a fence near the edge of a workbench. Butt the gauge stock to the fence, and tack it down with a couple of brads or stick it down with carpet tape. Guide the router along the fence, cutting through the stock. Pry up the gauge. You now have a way to position your T-square when using the router-and-bit combination used to make the gauge.

Mark the gauge indelibly with the bit and router used. I like to drill a "hanging hole" in the jig, too.

**To use the jig,** measure and mark one edge of the dado. You don't have to square a line across the workpiece. You don't have to mark both edges. Just a single tick mark per dado is all you need.

Align one edge of the offset gauge with the mark, and butt the T-square against the other edge. The T-square's crossbar ensures that the fence is square to the edge. The offset gauge ensures that the fence is the proper distance from the dado location.

Quick, simple, and direct.

If you feel like being picky, make sure you have a different jig for each dado-cutting bit in your collection. This doesn't mean simply one for each *size* bit you have, but one for every *individual* straight. Your ½-inch-shank ¾-inch straight may actually be slightly different in cutting diameter than your ¼-inch-shank bit of the same size. And it should go without saying—but I'll say it anyway—that you can't use a gauge cut with one router to set the T-square for use with a different router.

**Want to know how far to offset the T-square?** Make a trial cut through a scrap of hardboard or thin plywood. Set a fence a couple of inches from the workbench edge. Stick a scrap to the bench top with carpet tape, putting it tight against the fence. Run the router along the fence, cutting through the scrap. The remaining stock is the offset gauge.

**Using the offset gauge** is as simple as aligning one of its edges with the layout mark, then butting the T-square against the other edge. The T-square's crossbar will ensure that the fence is square to the edge.

# Routing Straightedge

**Deceptively easy to use, this self-clamping straightedge saves time in setting up and making straight-line router cuts.**

To guide the router when making straight cuts, there's a straightedge with built-in clamps. The clamps pinch in on the edges of the workpiece, securing the straightedge so you can slide the router along the edge.

For years, I worked with a T-square or whatever straight scrap I had at hand as a clamp-on fence. It seemed the quick-and-easy thing to do, but it wasn't always so. If the workpiece was narrow, for example, getting a clamp on each end of my straightedge could be a challenge. I'd clamp one end, then realize I couldn't reach the other end with a clamp. So I'd undo the first clamp and start pushing the work and the straightedge around on the bench top. Angle it across a corner? No. Push it further to the end? Hmmm, maybe. Eventually I'd get it done.

So this accessory is a wonderful time-saver. Dog or clamp the workpiece to the bench top, then clamp the straightedge to the workpiece. The clamp blocks or jaws are thin enough that I can attach it to a ¾-inch-thick workpiece that's lying flat on the bench top. It is easy to move from place to place on a workpiece without having to reclamp the workpiece itself.

Quite frankly, this is a routing accessory that you can buy. And the one you buy is darn grand. But every time I look in my wallet, I say to myself, "Man, it sure is empty in there." So naturally, I'm continually struggling to make my woodworking dollars go further. (Sound familiar?)

One way to do that is to *make* some accessories. I can't make a router bit or a saw blade, but I can make a clamp-on guide for straight router cuts. Instead of investing $40 in a commercial unit, I put about $12 into common hardware and a couple of comfortable plastic knobs. The wood came from my odds-and-ends collection. I spent about two hours making the jig. The money I *didn't* spend on this guide I did spend on tools that I can't make.

Dadoing & Grooving

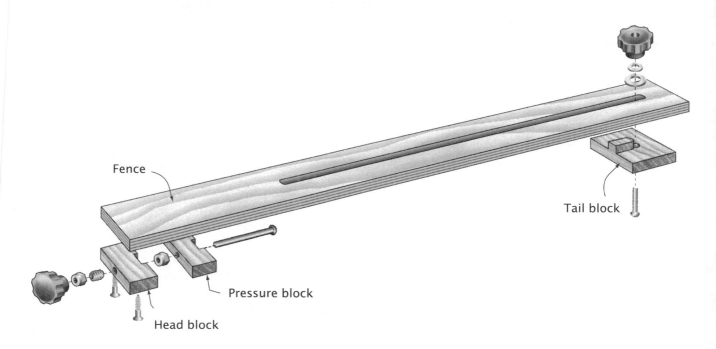

Fence

Tail block

Pressure block

Head block

## Cutting List

| Part | Qty. | Dimensions | Material |
|---|---|---|---|
| Fence | 1 | ¾" × 4" × 44" | Plywood |
| Head block | 1 | ¾" × 2" × 4" | Hardwood |
| Pressure block | 1 | ¾" × 1½" × 4" | Hardwood |
| Tail block | 1 | 1¼" × 4" × 4" | Hardwood |

## Hardware

1 brass threaded insert, ⅜"-16

1 carriage bolt, ⅜"-16 × 5½"

2 nylon-insert stop nuts, ⅜"-16

1 fluted plastic knob, 2⁵⁄₁₆" dia. with ⅜"-16 blind brass threaded insert; #DK-3 from Reid Tool Supply Co. (800-253-0421)

4 drywall screws, #6 × 1¼"

1 carriage bolt, ⅜"-16 × 2"

1 fender washer, ⅜" I.D.

1 flat washer, ⅜" I.D.

1 fluted plastic knob, 2⁵⁄₁₆" dia. with ⅜"-16 through brass threaded insert; #DK-121 from Reid Tool Supply Co.

PSA sandpaper

# Making the Straightedge

This jig is simply a plywood straightedge or fence with some home-brewed clamping blocks attached to the bottom.

In concept, it's like a pipe clamp. Here the work of the pipe is done by the plywood fence. At one end is a fixed head block. A threaded rod extends through this head block. The rod has a pressure block on one end, a knob on the other. Turn the knob clockwise, and the pressure block moves away from the head block. Turn it the other way, and the pressure block pulls back toward the head block.

At the opposite end of the fence is a tail block. This block is attached to the jig by a single bolt that extends through a long adjustment slot in the fence. Loosen the knob on that bolt, and you can slide the tail block back and forth on the fence.

To use the jig, set it on the workpiece, just as you would a pipe clamp. Move the tail block against the edge of the work and set it. Then turn the knob to apply pressure at the head end, and pinch the workpiece tightly.

What's appealing about this jig is that the pressure-application mechanism uses standard hardware—a carriage bolt, stop nuts, and a threaded insert. It's stuff that's available and cheap. And the mechanism works!

**1. Collect the hardware.** It's always a good idea to do your shopping before you begin. You may already have most of the hardware in your shop. Go out now and buy what you don't have. The local hardware will have everything but the knobs. And you just may find suitable substitutes there.

TOP VIEW

EDGE VIEW

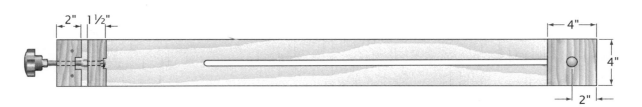

BOTTOM VIEW

If you've a mind to, go ahead and make your own wooden knobs. I happen to like the big plastic knobs that are becoming more and more common in woodworking catalogs. They are durable, provide great leverage, are easy-on-the-hands, and are not all that expensive.

**2. Make the fence.** I used shop-grade birch plywood. Substitutions are okay, but I'd recommend some type of plywood because it is stable and strong.

Cut your material to the dimensions specified by the Cutting List. You can, of course, make the fence longer or shorter. If you make it about 56 inches long, you'll be able to use the finished guide across standard-sized sheet goods. But for smaller workpieces, you may find the extra length a nuisance. The range of the guide shown is $6\frac{1}{2}$ inches up to 36 inches.

Rout the slot next. I did this on the router table with a $\frac{1}{2}$-inch straight bit. Scribe lines across the straightedge, marking the ends of the slot. On masking tape applied to the router table fence, mark the width of the router bit. Line up the appropriate marks, plunge the work onto the bit, rout until the end marks line up, then tip the work up off the bit. Repeat the process, making incrementally deeper cuts until the slot is completed.

**3. (optional) Apply laminate to the edges.** I actu-

ally used my straightedge for quite some time before deciding to laminate the edges—to grease the skid, so to speak. The laminate dresses up the plywood edges, too.

Simply coat the edges with contact cement, and apply it to the backs of the plastic laminate strips, too. When the cement is dry, stick the laminate to the plywood, burnish it with a J-roller, then trim the edges flush with a flush-trimming bit. Do the ends first. After they've been trimmed, apply the laminate to the long edges. That way, the long laminate strips will overlap the ends of the short laminate strips.

**4. Cut the clamping blocks.** Use hardwood, though it doesn't matter particularly what hardwood. I made the head and pressure blocks from oak. For the tail block, I rescued a poplar offcut from the scrap bin because it was just the right thickness and length. Cut these parts to the dimensions specified by the Cutting List. Note the grain direction.

**5. Form the spine on the tail block.** This block has a ridge or spine that fits into the straightedge's slot to keep the jaw from twisting.

To form the spine, I cut two rabbets on the table saw. With a backsaw, I trimmed the spine back on one end, leaving it just under 2 inches long. So that the spine would nestle into the rounded end of the slot, I rounded the front end of the spine with a file.

Dadoing & Grooving

**The ridge left between two rabbets** locks into the straightedge's slot, keeping the tail block aligned. Cut the rabbets on the table saw. After making the shallow shoulder cuts, raise the blade and adjust the rip fence for the base cuts. Cut so the waste falls to the outside of the blade, rather than being trapped between the blade and the fence (which would lead to kickback).

**Improve the clamp's grip with sandpaper.** The short-coming of the jig's compression clamping system is the lack of traction on smooth wood surfaces. To keep the jaws from slipping out of position on the straightedge, and to improve the jaws' grip on the workpiece, glue sandpaper to the the jaws, as shown.

**6. Install the tail block.** The block is, of course, fitted into the straightedge slot, then held in place with a carriage bolt and plastic knob.

Counterbore and drill the bolt hole. On the back of the block, locate the exact center of the piece. With a ⅞-inch Forstner bit, drill a ³⁄₁₆-inch-deep counterbore so that the carriage bolt head will be recessed. Switch to a ⅜-inch bit, and drill the shank hole. This hole should emerge at the back end of the spine. To steady the workpiece while you drill, set it into the straightedge slot and put both parts on the drill press table.

Drive the carriage bolt into the hole, then insert it through the straightedge. Drop on the large fender washer, then thread the knob onto the end.

**7. Drill the adjustment-bolt holes in the head and pressure blocks.** As shown in the drawing *Assembly Detail,* the bolt that provides the pressure extends through holes drilled through the middle of the blocks. The head block has a two-part hole. The first inch is bored as a pilot hole for the threaded insert, while the remaining length is bored as a clearance hole for the bolt. The hole in the pressure block is a clearance hole for the bolt.

To ensure the holes will be properly aligned, set up a fence and stop block on the drill press table to position and hold the block being drilled.

Do the head block first. Chuck the bit for the insert pilot hole in the drill press. (The size of bit to use should be specified on the insert. The ⅜-inch inserts I use require a

¹⁵⁄₃₂-inch-diameter pilot hole.) Position the block under the bit, then bring the fence and stop block into place and clamp them. Clamp the workpiece to the fence. Bore the pilot just deep enough for the insert.

Switch to the bit for the clearance hole. If you need to, move the workpiece; but don't touch the fence or stop block. Drill the hole through. Set the head block aside. Pop the pressure block into place, and drill the clearance hole through it.

**8. Notch the blocks.** Both blocks must be notched to provide clearance for parts of the pressure mechanism, as you can see from *Assembly Detail.* Notch the head block for the stop nut, and the pressure block for the bolt head. The notches are the same width but different depths.

I cut the notches on the table saw. Set the blade height to match the depth of the notch. Stand the block on edge, and guide it across the blade with the miter gauge. Make repeated cuts to clear the waste.

**9. Drive the threaded insert.** This is a somewhat dicey operation, because there is but a thin wall between the pilot hole and the surface of the block. It's easy to blow out that wall while driving the insert.

For a driver, use a short bolt with two nuts on the shank. Thread the bolt, with the two nuts already on it, into the insert. Jam one nut against the insert, then the second nut against the first. Clamp the block in a vise. Use a wrench to turn the insert and bolt, and drive it into the hole. When it is fully driven, unjam the nuts so the bolt can be

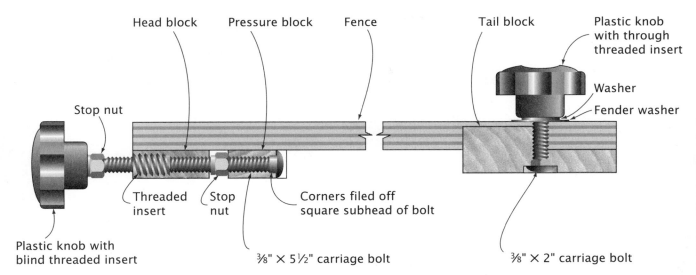

Head block | Pressure block | Fence | Tail block | Plastic knob with through threaded insert

Stop nut

Washer
Fender washer

Stop nut

Threaded insert | Stop nut | Corners filed off square subhead of bolt

Plastic knob with blind threaded insert

⅜" × 5½" carriage bolt

⅜" × 2" carriage bolt

**Dadoing & Grooving**

unthreaded *without* backing the insert out of the block.

**10. Assemble the pressure mechanism.** The idea is to insert the bolt through the pressure block and trap the block between the bolt head and a stop nut. The bolt must be free to spin in the block, so you can't jam the nut against the block.

I used a carriage bolt here. To allow the bolt to spin freely, I filed off the corners of the bolt's square "subhead." Compare a long hex-head bolt with a carriage bolt of the same length. You'll see that the hex bolt has only a short section of threads, while the carriage bolt is threaded right up to the head. The application requires more threads than the hex bolt offers. Hence, the choice of carriage bolt.

Insert the bolt, and thread the stop nut onto it. A stop nut has a nylon insert that prevents it from loosening. Consequently, a stop nut is hard to thread. Once the insert engages the bolt's threads, you have to turn it with a wrench; you can't do it with your fingers.

Fit the head block onto the bolt next. Add a second stop nut, then the plastic knob. Turn the knob onto the bolt until it seats. Then back the stop nut up to the knob, and jam it against the knob.

**11. Mount the head block on the straightedge.** You can glue and screw the head block to the straightedge. I used screws only, and that's been satisfactory.

Position the head block, as shown in the drawings. Secure it with a clamp while you drill pilot holes and drive drywall screws. I drove two screws through the block into the straightedge, then flipped the unit over and drove two

more screws through the straightedge into the block.

To finish, I glued sandpaper to the working edge of the pressure block, just as I did to the tail block.

## Using the Straightedge

The routing straightedge is easy to use, almost deceptively so. You adjust the tail block roughly for the width of the workpiece, set the jig in place, then tighten the pressure block.

But you do have to measure and lay out its position vis-à-vis the location of the intended cut. The straightedge is *not* a T-square. It won't set itself square to the edge of the workpiece.

Moreover, the width of the cut and the size of the router base enter into the setup, just as they do with a T-square or other router guide. Here are my two suggestions:

A. *Set up from the center line of the cut.* This is easy to do if the base diameter of your router is a nice round number—like 6 inches or 7 inches. You mark the cut's center line, then offset 3 inches or 3½ inches or whatever to mark the straightedge location. Regardless of the width of the cut, the offset from the center line is always the same.

B. *Make offset gauges.* An offset gauge is a piece of hardboard or the like. Its width is the amount the straightedge must be offset from the edge of the cut. You lay one edge of the gauge right on the layout line for the cut, then bring the straightedge up to the other edge of the gauge. Gauges are easy to make; see "Offset Gauge" on page 74.

**Laying out the fence position** requires you to measure and lay out the cut first. Because the straight-edge won't square itself, you need to extend the lines across the workpiece. Then you need to offset from the cut and mark the fence position. When clamping the straightedge be sure to align both its ends with the layout marks.

**Setting the straightedge with an offset gauge** eliminates the need to calculate and measure the offset from the cut. But you still must lay out the cut across the workpiece. Use the gauge at both ends of the straightedge before tightening the clamp.

# Fractionating Baseplate

**This scrap of plastic will add new dimensions to your straight bits.**

It sure *looks* square, but this baseplate is a trickster. The measurement from the axis of the bit to each of the four baseplate edges is different. With this baseplate, you expand the cutting width of any straight bit in your collection, and you give yourself the ability to produce a greater incremental range of cuts.

This clever baseplate was developed by Nick Engler, a prolific writer of woodworking books.

Here's how it works: Use a straight bit and make a pass with the baseplate's "zero" side against the fence. Then turn the router so the "+⅛" side is against the fence, and make a second pass. The additional ⅛ inch between the bit and the fence adds ⅛ inch to the width of the cut. Other sides of the baseplate add ¹⁄₁₆ inch and ³⁄₁₆ inch to the zero cut.

Thus, a ½-inch bit could produce ½-inch-wide dadoes, ⁹⁄₁₆-inch-wide dadoes, ⅝-inch-wide dadoes, and ¹¹⁄₁₆-inch-wide dadoes. It's as simple as turning the router to reference a different edge against the guide fence.

Using a ¾-inch bit with this base gives you dado widths of ¾ inch, ¹³⁄₁₆ inch, ⅞ inch, and ¹⁵⁄₁₆ inch. A ¼-inch bit yields widths of ¼ inch, ⁵⁄₁₆ inch, ⅜ inch, and ⁷⁄₁₆ inch.

If you are *really* clever, you'll see that Nick's idea is an inexpensive solution to undersized plywood. One of the shortcomings of plywood, especially hardwood stuff, is that it's typically a 64th or a 32nd undersized. For instance, ¾-inch plywood is more likely ²³⁄₃₂ inch or ⁴⁷⁄₆₄ inch. It rattles in the dado you cut for it with your ¾-inch straight. Maddening.

One solution is to buy special dadoing bits that *are* ²³⁄₃₂ inch. But a less costly solution is to make a version of this fractionating baseplate that'll allow you to make those off-sized dadoes in two passes with a ⅜-inch or ⅝-inch bit.

## Making the Baseplate

In this situation very accurate work is essential. Because it is tough to get the baseplate trimmed dead-on with your first attempt, I've included tips on fine-tuning the baseplate.

**1. Cut and mount the blank.** Cut a square of acrylic or polycarbonate, making it about an inch or so larger than the factory baseplate. Leave the protective paper bonded to the plastic for now. Drill mounting holes, using the factory baseplate as a template. For the baseplate to be self-centering on the router base, you have to mount it using flathead screws. (See the chapter "Center-Finding Baseplate" on page 85.) This baseplate especially needs to be self-centering, so countersink the mounting holes.

Mount the baseplate blank on the router.

**FRACTIONATING BASEPLATE LAYOUT**

For a Milwaukee router
(with a 6¹⁄₁₆"-dia. baseplate)

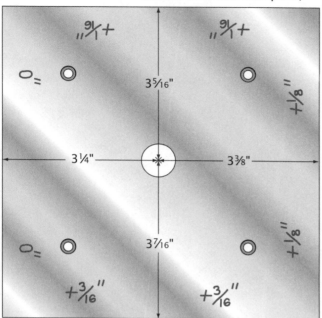

| Cutting List | | | |
|---|---|---|---|
| **Part** | **Qty.** | **Dimensions** | **Material** |
| Baseplate | 1 | ¼" × 7" × 7" | Plastic* |

*Acrylic, polycarbonate, and phenolic are all suitable.*

**2. Mark the centerpoint.** Mount the baseplate blank on the router. Chuck a V-grooving bit in the router. Lower the bit 'til it touches the blank. Turn the bit a few times by hand, marking the centerpoint. For the sake of accuracy, keep the mark as small as possible.

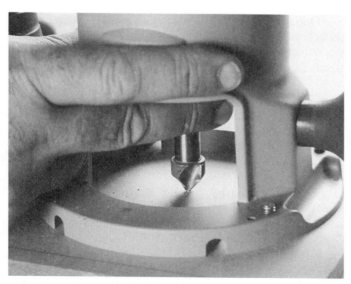

**Mark the baseplate blank's centerpoint** by lowering a V-grooving bit to the blank, then turning it by hand. You neither need nor want a large mark, so don't overdo it.

**3. Trim the baseplate.** Remove the blank from the router. Measure from the centerpoint to the first side and mark it for trimming. (Have this be the zero side.) I found it helpful, in laying out the cuts, to pencil perpendiculars (not diagonals) through the centerpoint. In addition, I found that measuring one side and immediately cutting that side minimized confusion. As you trim a side, mark which side it is (zero, +¹⁄₁₆, and so forth). I made these cuts on the table saw.

When the trim cuts are done, peel the protective paper from the baseplate. As you do so, transfer the labels from the paper to the plastic itself. A permanent marker, such as Sanford's Sharpie, will do the job.

**4. Bore the bit opening.** With the baseplate trimmed, bore the bit opening. You can do this with a large-diameter bit on the drill press or by remounting the baseplate and plunge-boring with a large-diameter straight bit.

**5. Test the baseplate.** The proof of your work is in the dadoing. Do the following. Clamp a T-square to a 6- to 8-inch-wide scrap. (See "T-Square" on page 69 for plans.) With the zero side riding this fence, rout a dado across the board. Turn the router to reference the fence with the "+¹⁄₁₆" side, and rout about three-quarters of the way across the board, widening the dado. Repeat with the "+¹⁄₈" side, going about halfway. Finally, rout about a quarter of the way with the "+³⁄₁₆" side.

Set the router aside, and very carefully measure the widths of the four different sections. Dial calipers will give you a very accurate measurement. If you hit the increments on the nose, pat yourself on the back. But if you missed them, do a little fine-tuning.

**The proof of your baseplate's accuracy** lies in actual cuts. Here, I'm measuring a test cut made using each edge of the baseplate, and I'm jotting down the measurements so I can assess the needed fine-tuning. The zero edge cut will equal the bit diameter, no matter what. It is ½ inch here. Both the +¹⁄₁₆ and +¹⁄₈ edges are ¹⁄₆₄ inch under. If the +³⁄₁₆ edge is also ¹⁄₆₄ inch under, only the zero edge will have to be jointed.

## BASEPLATE FABRICATION SEQUENCE

For Milwaukee router

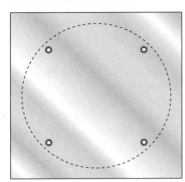

1. Mount an oversized square of ¼" or ⅜" acrylic plastic to the router base. (In this case, a 7" square is used in place of a 6"-dia. stock baseplate.) Use flathead screws for this regardless of the style used to attach the stock baseplate.

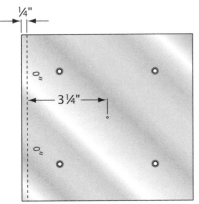

2. With the blank attached to the router base, install a V-grooving bit in the router. Turn on the router and adjust the cutting depth so the bit just touches the baseplate, marking the centerpoint.

3. Remove the blank from the router, and trim it. Lay out and cut the "0" edge first. Measure from the centerpoint, trimming ¼" from the edge. Label that edge "0".

¼"

0"

3¼"

0"

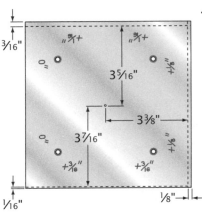

4. Trim the other three edges in the same fashion. Take ³⁄₁₆" from the second edge, ⅛" from the third edge, and only ¹⁄₁₆" from the fourth. Label the edges, as shown.

³⁄₁₆"

"³⁄₁₆+

"³⁄₁₆+

0"

3⁵⁄₁₆"

+⅛"

3⅜"

0"

3⁷⁄₁₆"

+⅛"

+³⁄₁₆"

+³⁄₁₆"

¹⁄₁₆"

⅛"

# Fine-Tuning the Baseplate

This is the ticklish phase of the work. Take your time and work methodically.

**1. Assess the situation.** Begin by jotting down the widths of the dado segments and assessing the nature of the tuning that's needed. If all the pluses are over, you simply need to skim material from each of those edges. But if one or more is *under,* you have to trim the zero edge first.

When I say trim and skim, I'm presuming you aren't out a 16th. Rather, I'm talking 32nds and 64ths. Such cuts are too fine to be made on the table saw. Acrylic, polycarb, and phenolic are all murder on jointer knives. So what to do? Joint the edges on your router table.

**2. Set up the router table for jointing.** Use the Split Fence presented on page 237 to guide the cuts. To joint with this fence, you need to shim out the outfeed section of its facing (the left half) while keeping the infeed section (the right half) zeroed. I measured several thicknesses of notebook paper with my dial calipers, using enough sheets to shim out the outfeed section ¹⁄₆₄ inch. (Later, when I needed to take around ¹⁄₁₂₈ inch from an edge to bring it to perfection, I applied two layers of masking tape to the infeed half of the fence. It worked.)

With the fence facings set, adjust the fence position in relation to the bit, setting it so the outfeed section of the fence is tangent to the circumference of the bit.

**3. Trim the edge.** The most accurate and reliable way to assess your progress is to rout dadoes with the baseplate and then measure them. Work one edge into perfect trim at a time. Make a test cut, measure the cut width, and trim the edge as needed. Then make a test cut, measure the cut width, and trim the edge as needed. It's repetitive, yes, and a little tedious.

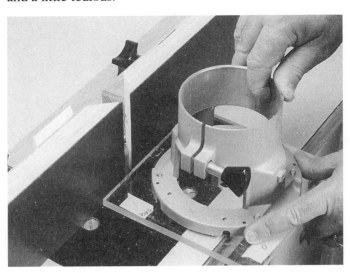

**Jointing on the router table** is the best way to make the fine cuts needed to fine-tune your baseplate. Note that with its knobs removed, the base can be left on the baseplate while the jointing is done.

If you are working with a fixed-base router, and if the knobs can be removed, you shouldn't have to remove the baseplate from the base to trim it. Just pull the base from the router motor.

After the first edge is just right, turn to the second edge and tune it in the same way. Finally, do the third "plus" edge.

## Using the Baseplate

Once you've tested and fine-tuned the baseplate, you know how to use it. But, to repeat, you make a cut, guiding the router along a fence. Then you turn the router so a different baseplate edge bears against the fence, and make a second cut.

What may not be evident is that matter of feed direction. If you make the first pass with the zero edge against the fence, the second pass should be fed in the opposite direction. That's because, as the drawing *Feed Direction Savvy* makes clear, the second pass would be cutting on the side of the dado opposite the fence.

If you want to make both passes in the same direction, be sure you make the cut with the "+" edge first. Make the cut with the zero edge second. That way, you'll be widening the cut toward the fence, rather than away from the fence.

### FEED DIRECTION SAAVY

FIRST PASS

"Zero" edge is against the fence.
Feed direction is left to right.

SECOND PASS

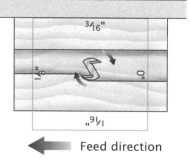

"+" edge is against the fence.
Feed direction is right to left.

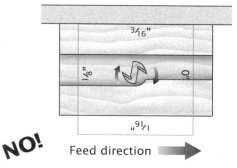

**NO!** Feed direction

This is a climb cut. The bit wants to pull the router through the cut.

FIRST PASS

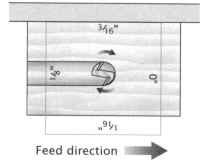

Feed direction

"+" edge is against the fence.
Feed direction is left to right.

SECOND PASS

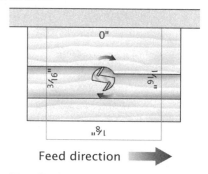

Feed direction

"Zero" edge is against the fence.
Feed direction is left to right.

# Center-Finding Baseplate

**Magical though it seems, a simple geometric principle is the secret behind this fixture. With it, the bit can easily be centered across the workpiece.**

Centering a hole or a mortise or a groove on the edge of a workpiece is always tough. Measuring and scribing layout lines isn't error-free. Setting up a guide can't be error-free. You can get the cut *close* to center, but it is seldom really on center.

Here's a simple baseplate that can be made in a short time. And it will almost magically center a cut on a workpiece. The baseplate has two pins projecting from it. You set the router atop the workpiece, with a pin on each side. Twist the router to bring both pins in contact with the work; the bit will automatically be centered on the work.

The trick is simple geometry. The pins must be equidistant from the bit axis and must be on a straight line that passes through the bit axis. The bit will always be equidistant from them, regardless of the angle from which you measure.

As in all magic, precision apparatus used with well-practiced skill is the key to success. In making the baseplate, you must be precise. Lay out and drill all the necessary holes carefully. Before using the baseplate on good work, practice. Use of the baseplate requires steadiness. The fixture is firmly attached to the router, but it doesn't fix the router to the workpiece. Keeping the router square on the work and the pins in contact with the work is the operator's job.

I've seen this sort of baseplate fitted to a fixed-base router, but there's more sense, I think, in using it on a plunge router. You can't make a through cut with it, simply because both pins must be in contact with the work. Depending upon the pin placement, you must begin and end any cut 2 to 3 inches from the end of the work. Stopped cuts like these are the stuff of the plunge router, not the fixed-base router.

## Making the Baseplate

Each "pin" is really a sleeve or bushing over a bolt. The bolt threads into a hole in the plate. I located the pins outside the perimeter of the router base, which provides a wide stance that's stable but doesn't let you rout too close to the ends of the workpiece. If you want to, you can reposition the holes closer to the bit (or drill and tap several pairs of holes).

Accuracy is critical. The pin holes must be exactly equidistant from the bit axis, and they must be perpendicular to the plate surface.

**1. Collect the hardware for the pins.** You *can* get by with dowels as pins. But I used a router bit's pilot as a paradigm; a bearing—not a solid pin—is pretty much the

## CENTER-FINDING BASEPLATE LAYOUT

for Bosch plunge router

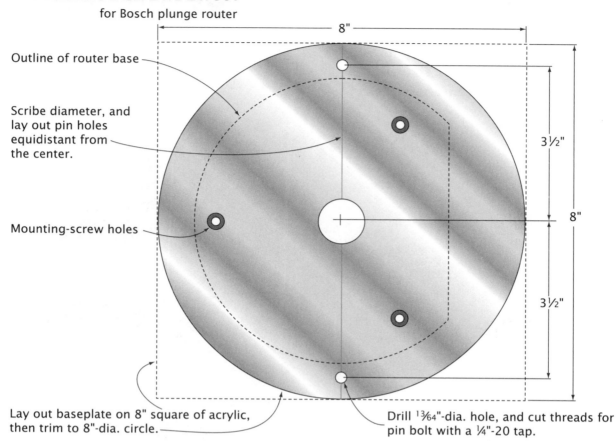

8"

Outline of router base

Scribe diameter, and lay out pin holes equidistant from the center.

3½"

Mounting-screw holes

8"

3½"

Lay out baseplate on 8" square of acrylic, then trim to 8"-dia. circle.

Drill ¹³⁄₆₄"-dia. hole, and cut threads for pin bolt with a ¼"-20 tap.

| Cutting List | | | |
|---|---|---|---|
| Part | Qty. | Dimensions | Material |
| Baseplate | 1 | ⅜" × 8" × 8" | Acrylic |
| **Hardware** | | | |
| 2 roundhead stove bolts, ¼"-20 × 2" | | | |
| 2 hex nuts, ¼"-20 | | | |
| 2 plastic sleeves, ¼" I.D. × ½" O.D. × 1" long | | | |

## PIN ASSEMBLY DETAIL

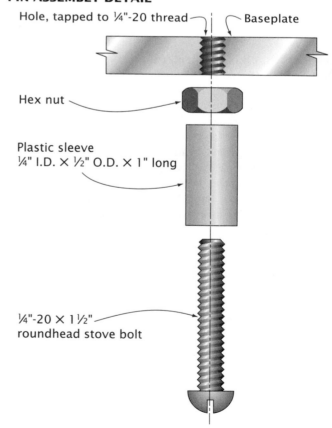

Hole, tapped to ¼"-20 thread

Baseplate

Hex nut

Plastic sleeve ¼" I.D. × ½" O.D. × 1" long

¼"-20 × 1½" roundhead stove bolt

standard these days. So I made pins with "sleeve bearings," using oddments from the local hardware store.

Buy a couple of roundhead stove bolts with a nut for each. The sleeves can be bronze bushings or simple plastic spacers. Here are three options:

1. Use a ¼-inch-I.D. × ½-inch-O.D. × 1-inch-long plastic sleeve as the bearing. Cost: about 20 cents each.
2. Use a ¼-inch-I.D. × ½-inch-O.D. × 1-inch-long bronze bushing. Cost: about $1.20 each.
3. Use a ¼-inch-I.D. × ⅜-inch-O.D. × 1-inch-long bronze bushing inside a ⅜-inch-I.D. × ½-inch-O.D. × 1-inch-long bronze bushing. Cost: about $3.50 for each pair.

**2. Make the baseplate.** Refer to the chapter "The Generic Baseplate" on page 63 for the details of how to

## DRILLING SEQUENCE

1. Set stop blocks against both edges of blank, with bit hole directly under the drill bit.

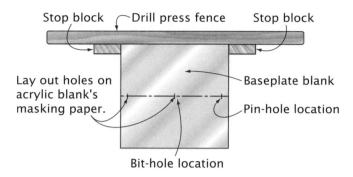

Stop block — Drill press fence — Stop block

Lay out holes on acrylic blank's masking paper.

Baseplate blank

Pin-hole location

Bit-hole location

2. After drilling trammel-pivot hole at bit-hole location, move the right-hand stop block. Insert a 3½"-wide spacer against the blank, and reset the stop block against it.

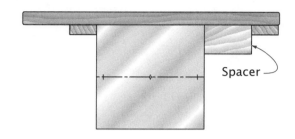

Spacer

3. Shift blank against the right stop block, and drill the first pin hole.

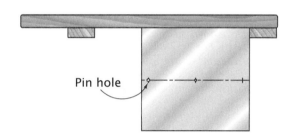

Pin hole

4. Return the blank to its starting position, and reset the right stop. Move the left stop and use the spacer to reset it. Shift the blank to the left, against the stop, and drill the second pin hole.

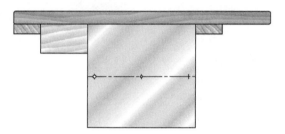

mount the baseplate on your router and mark the bit opening. This is one of those baseplates that has to center itself on the bit axis every time it's installed, so use care in laying it out and drilling the mounting-screw holes. At the same time, try to orient the router so the plane of the handles will be parallel to an edge of the square baseplate blank.

After you've marked the center of the bit opening, but *before* you've bored it, scribe a diameter, as shown in the layout drawing. This diameter must be parallel to an edge. Measure and mark the pin locations. Make sure the pins are equidistant from the bit.

Drill and tap the holes for the pins. The drawing *Drilling Sequence* shows a good way to drill the holes and ensure that they are properly positioned. To cut threads in the pin holes, I used a ¼-inch-20 tap. The pilot hole for this tap can be $^{13}\!/_{64}$ inch in diameter. Be extremely careful to keep the tap perpendicular as you begin to cut the threads. This is where you get the hole out of alignment. The result is a cocked pin, which botches the accuracy of the fixture.

At the center of the baseplate, drill a ⅛-inch-diameter hole for a trammel pivot. Using a router and trammel, trim the baseplate to an 8-inch-diameter circle. Then redrill the bit hole for the largest bit you are likely to use with the baseplate.

**3. Install the pins.** Slip the sleeve over the bolt.

Thread a nut onto the bolt; but don't jam it against the sleeve, which would prevent the sleeve from rotating. Thread the bolt into the hole. Turn the bolt until it almost seats, then tighten the nut against the baseplate. The bolt should be tight, but the sleeve must rotate freely.

# Using the Baseplate

The baseplate can be used to plunge-bore holes, to cut mortises, and to plow grooves. The operating principles are the same for all three chores. The difference is in whether or not to actually feed the router laterally, and if you do, how far. Here's how to do it, step by step.

**1. Set up the router.** Naturally, you need to install the baseplate. Select the bit you need to use, and chuck it in the router. Set the plunge stop.

**2. Lay out the cut.** Remember that the closest you can rout to the workpiece's end is about 3½ inches. Mark the beginning and end of the desired cut. If the cut is a simple hole, mark it with an "X."

Clamp the workpiece in some way that provides unobstructed access to both surfaces that the pins must reference.

**3. Make the cut.** Set the router in place. Twist it so the pins come into firm contact with the workpiece. Align

the bit over the start of the cut. Switch on the router, plunge the bit, and make the cut.

*Troubleshooting:* If you discover that your plate making wasn't as accurate as you would have liked, and your cut isn't perfectly centered, you can salvage the workpiece. The cut will be wider than the bit, but it will be centered.

Lift the router and reposition it so pins are on the opposite sides of the workpiece than they were before, and take a second pass. Now don't simply reverse the direction in which you twisted the router. If you do this, the pins will remain on the same sides of the workpiece, and the bit will still be off-center toward the same edge. So that won't work.

To repeat myself, you have to move the pins so they reference different sides of the workpiece in the second pass than they did in the first. That is all it takes. But to rectify the problem for the long term, make yourself a new baseplate. Just work a little more carefully the second time. Hey, I had to make mine twice, so don't feel too bad if you do too.

**Center cuts on an edge** don't need a lot of setup fiddling. Whether the cut is a hole, a mortise, or a slot, the center-finding baseplate will position it equidistant from the arrises of the workpiece. The trick behind this magic is that the positioning pins attached to the baseplate are themselves equidistant from the bit axis.

## CUT SCHEMATIC

Twist router 'til BOTH pins contact workpiece. Hold pins firmly against the workpiece as you feed the router and make the cut.

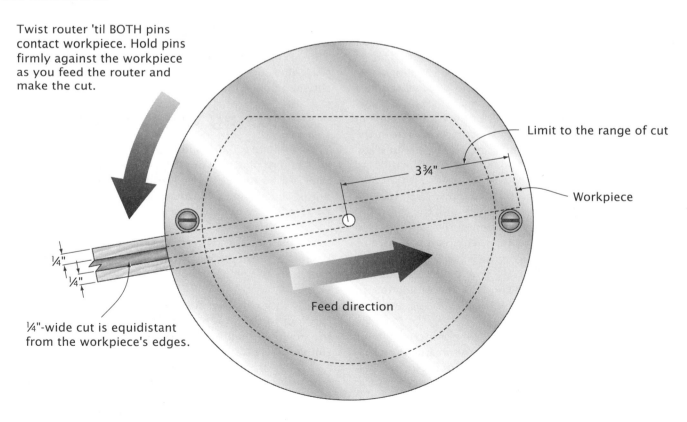

Limit to the range of cut

3¾"

Workpiece

¼"

¼"

¼"-wide cut is equidistant from the workpiece's edges.

Feed direction

# Doweling Jig

**Boring dowel joinery *can* be a fulfilling experience. Use your plunge router with this precision jig. The jig makes it hard to go wrong.**

Dowel joinery was one of the things I tried early in my woodworking experience. What I had were carpentry tools; but I was making a vanity, and I wanted to join the rails and stiles of a face frame. Dowel joints *seemed* like the way to go for me—just buy a doweling jig and use the portable drill and twist bits I already had.

What a disappointment! Maybe it was me, and maybe it was the jig, but I never did master dowel joinery with a drill and a doweling jig. It just never worked for me the way I thought it should. The holes in the rails just would never match up with the holes in the stiles. They'd be a bit too far apart or too close together. And jig or not, at least one of the holes would be cocked.

Twenty years later, I'm using a plunge router with my shop-made doweling jig with far better results. After a bit of setup, I can knock out whole sets of dowel-jointed face frames, with all the holes aligned, square, and perfectly and consistently positioned.

The trick is a template that has several holes bored in it. The workpieces are clamped beneath the template. You use a plunge router fitted with a guide bushing to bore the dowel holes. An adjustable workpiece stop ensures that each workpiece will be clamped in the same position, and template adjusters help you fine-tune the template so the holes are dead-center on the workpiece.

If you are making a traditional frame with rails and stiles, the stiles are clamped horizontally beneath the template; the rails, vertically. A toggle clamp makes workpiece changeover fast and easy, yet it holds the work very securely. The clamp is screwed to a pad that makes it easy to shift the clamp's position to accommodate different sizes of workpieces.

An innovative feature of this jig, contributed by Fred Matlack of Rodale's Design Shop, is that adjustable workpiece stop I mentioned. You move it from one end of the jig to the other, depending upon which end of a frame member is being worked. Once adjusted for a job, you make use of the same setting at both positions.

The jig is not infinitely variable. The template has four evenly spaced holes. If you are working 1½-inch-wide stock, for example, you would use two of the holes, and your dowel holes would be ¾ inch apart (center-to-center). If the working stock is wider and can accommodate three holes on the ¾-inch center-to-center spacing, then you'd use three of the template holes, and so on.

But the jig can and must be tuned precisely.

A hitch with any router doweling jig is that you can't orient the workpieces so the same face of each is against the jig. If you place the reference face of the stiles in (against the jig), then the reference face of the rails must be out. That's just the way it is. So the jig must be adjustable in such a way that the dowel holes can be placed precisely. And this jig is that adjustable.

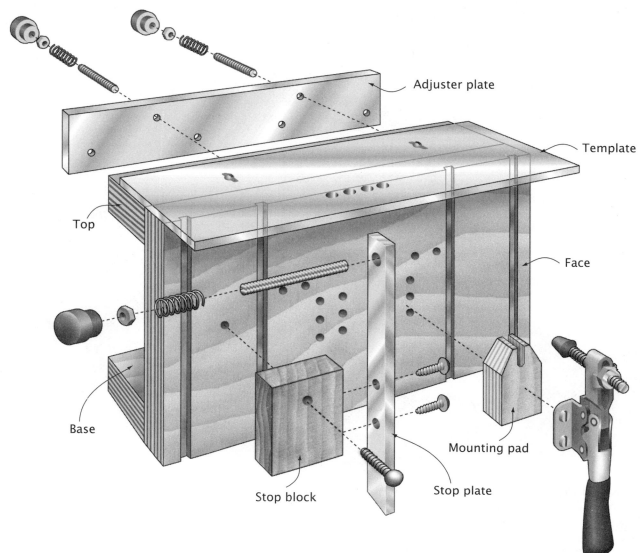

Adjuster plate

Template

Top

Face

Base

Stop block

Mounting pad

Stop plate

The template can be shifted in and out on the body, and screw adjusters allow for controlled, almost infinitesimal movements of the template. The same is true of the workpiece stop, which is used to position the workpieces. It is a screw adjuster.

## Making the Jig

The doweling jig is a mixed-media creation. I used plastic for several of the parts. The clear plastic used for the template lets you see the work, which makes setup much easier. The plastic adjuster plates can be threaded, so you don't have to fiddle with T-nuts or inserts.

Overall, I think the plastic works. It is the right stuff for this application, and it looks slick. You can work the stuff with your woodworking tools. The appendix has general information on buying and working the plastics that are suitable for this jig.

**1. Make the body.** I made the jig body by laminating two layers of ¾-inch Baltic Birch plywood, which

add up to a thickness just under 1½ inches. This makes the unit more stable than if I had used a solid wood construction. Cut and glue-laminate plywood for the face, base, and top, then trim them to the dimensions specified by the Cutting List.

Glue up the parts, as indicated by the *End View* of the *Plan Views* drawings. Check the assembly carefully as you clamp it to ensure that it is square. After the glue sets, remove the clamps and scrape off any squeeze-out. Square the ends, and sand the top smooth and square to the face.

Lay out and rout the dadoes for the workpiece stop next. Ideally, you should do this on a router table, but you can use a router equipped with an edge guide. You need the stop to be equidistant from the center of the jig, regardless of which end it is on, so you must position the dadoes to ensure that it will be.

Finally, lay out and drill the holes for mounting the workpiece stop and the toggle clamp. Do a few preliminary holes now, then add others as dictated by the work situations that come up.

## DOWELING JIG PLAN VIEWS

TOP VIEW

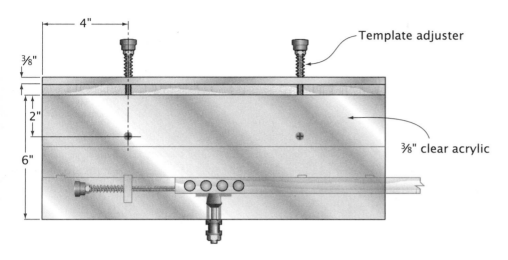

4"

3/8"

2"

6"

Template adjuster

3/8" clear acrylic

FRONT VIEW

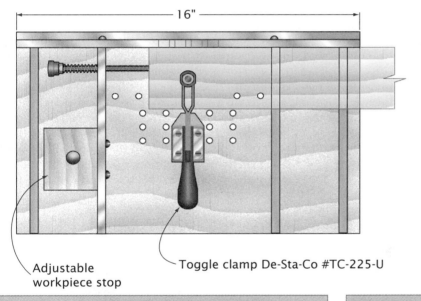

16"

Adjustable
workpiece stop

Toggle clamp De-Sta-Co #TC-225-U

END VIEW

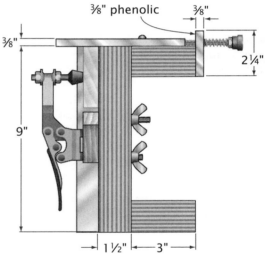

3/8" phenolic

3/8"

3/8"

2¼"

9"

1½"

3"

| Cutting List | | | |
|---|---|---|---|
| Part | Qty. | Dimensions | Material |
| Face | 1 | 1½" × 9" × 16" | Baltic Birch plywood |
| Base/Top | 2 | 1½" × 3" × 16" | Baltic Birch plywood |
| Stop block | 1 | 1" × 2⅜" × 3" | Hardwood |
| Mounting pad | 1 | ¾" × 1½" × 2⅜" | Baltic Birch plywood |
| Template | 1 | ⅜" × 6" × 16" | Clear acrylic |
| Adjuster plate | 1 | ⅜" × 2¼" × 16" | Plastic* |
| Stop plate | 1 | ⅜" × 1¼" × 8¾" | Plastic* |

*Acrylic, polycarbonate, and phenolic are all suitable for
this application.

## Hardware

Threaded rod, ¼"-20 × 12"

3 hex nuts, ¼"-20

3 plastic knobs, ¾" dia. with ¼"-20 insert; item
#DK-42 from Reid Tool Supply Co. (800-253-0421)

3 compression springs, ¼" I.D. × 1" long

8 panhead screws, #8 × 1"

2 carriage bolts, ¼"-20 × 3"

2 flat washers, ¼" I.D.

2 wing nuts, ¼"-20

Toggle clamp, De-Sta-Co #TC-225-U

4 panhead screws, #8 × ¾"

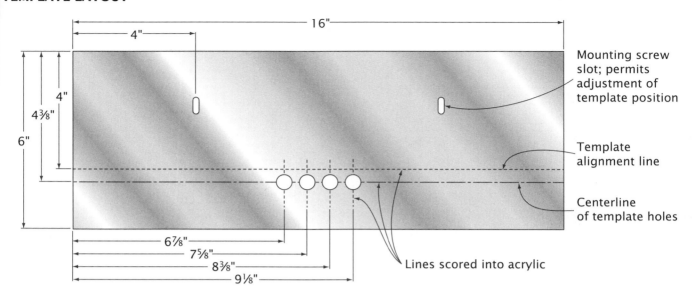

- 16"
- 4"
- 4"
- 4⅜"
- 6"
- 6⅞"
- 7⅝"
- 8⅜"
- 9⅛"

Mounting screw slot; permits adjustment of template position

Template alignment line

Centerline of template holes

Lines scored into acrylic

**Dowel Joinery**

**2. Cut and lay out the template.** Clear acrylic is the best material for the template. You can see through it to help yourself align workpieces. You can etch alignment lines in it with a scratch awl or a utility knife. And it looks sharp, kinda high-tech. Cut the template blank to size on the table saw.

Lay out the lines shown in the *Template Layout* drawing right on the masking paper that protects the acrylic. Precision here is vital. The alignment line and the centerline must be parallel, the crosshairs for the holes evenly spaced. With a scratch awl or utility knife, score the lines, cutting right through the masking paper and etching the plastic. Also mark the locations of the mounting-screw slots.

**3. Bore the holes.** Set up your drill press with a fence to do this, and take the time to get that first hole perfectly aligned under the bit before boring it.

To ensure that the holes are evenly spaced, make three spacers. Mill a strip of ¾-inch stock, then crosscut it into three pieces. Line up the template blank under the drill bit, tight against the fence. Butt the three spacers against the blank, and clamp a stop block against the outside one. Drill the first hole in the blank. Remove one spacer, and slide the blank over against the remaining two. Drill the second hole. Remove another spacer, and again slide the blank over. Drill the third hole. Remove the last spacer, and slide the blank over against the stop block. Drill the fourth hole.

**Lines etched into the template** help you set up and use the jig. Because they are scored into the surface, they can't be worn or scuffed off. Use a square and a utility knife to scribe the lines, as shown, cutting right through the protective masking paper.

**Boring the template holes** should be done on the drill press, using a fence and spacer blocks to eliminate variables in placement of the holes. The fence ensures that all the holes will be an equal distance from the template edge. The blocks, seen in front, position the template in relation to the stop block.

## ADJUSTER DETAILS

### TEMPLATE ADJUSTER PLATE

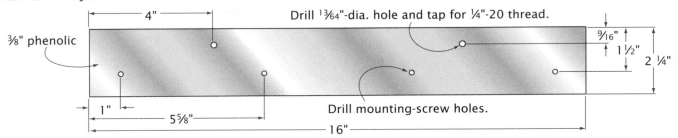

3/8" phenolic

Drill $^{13}/_{64}$"-dia. hole and tap for 1/4"-20 thread.

Drill mounting-screw holes.

4"

9/16"
1 1/2"
2 1/4"

1"
5 5/8"
16"

### ADJUSTABLE WORKPIECE STOP

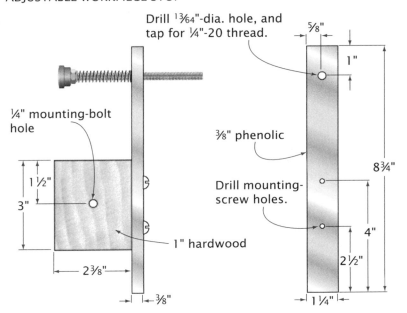

Drill $^{13}/_{64}$"-dia. hole, and tap for 1/4"-20 thread.

1/4" mounting-bolt hole

3/8" phenolic

Drill mounting-screw holes.

1" hardwood

1 1/2"
3"
2 3/8"
3/8"

5/8"
1"
8 3/4"
4"
2 1/2"
1 1/4"

### ADJUSTER ASSEMBLY (typ.)

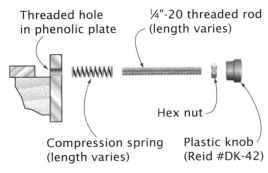

Threaded hole in phenolic plate

1/4"-20 threaded rod (length varies)

Hex nut

Compression spring (length varies)

Plastic knob (Reid #DK-42)

**Dowel Joinery**

---

Use the Slotted Pilot Template on page 4 to rout the mounting slots.

To dress up the appearance of the template, chamfer the sharp edges on the router table. Then use a cabinet scraper to remove saw marks. Finally, flame-polish those edges 'til they shine.

**4. Make the adjuster plate.** Any number of different materials can be used for the adjuster plate. A material that you can cut threads into is best, which means you can use a variety of plastics or metals. If you are most comfortable using wood, use threaded inserts. I used 3/8-inch phenolic.

Cut the plate to size, and lay out the mounting holes and the holes for the adjusters, as shown in the drawing *Template Layout*. Bore the holes.

Tap the adjuster holes next. The process is detailed in the section "Cutting Threads" in the appendix.

To enhance the appearance of the jig, if you want it to look spiffy, chamfer the edges just enough to soften their sharpness. Use a cabinet scraper to remove saw marks.

**5. Make the workpiece stop.** This is a wood and plastic assembly that is bolted to the jig body. Begin making it by checking out the layout drawing. Cut the plastic plate

and the hardwood block to the dimensions specified by the Cutting List.

Lay out and drill the holes in these parts. The adjuster hole in the plate must be tapped with a 1/4-inch-20 thread. "Buff" the edges of the stop plate, as you did the edges of the template and the adjuster plate, by chamfering the edges and scraping off saw marks.

Screw the stop plate to the stop block.

**6. Assemble the jig.** This is largely a matter of screwing the various parts and subassemblies to the jig body.

Mount the template and adjuster plate on the jig body with panhead screws. Install the workpiece stop to the face by fitting the stop plate into the dado, then bolting the stop body to the jig body. (The stop must be moved and removed often; you ought to use a wing nut or a studded plastic knob instead of a nut so it doesn't take a wrench to mount and dismount it.)

Now make up the adjuster screws. Cut three pieces of 1/4-inch threaded rod, two that are 2 1/2 inches long for the template adjusters, one that is 4 1/2 inches long for the work-piece stop adjuster. Use a very small file, like an auger-bit file, to remove burrs from the cut ends of the threads. Turn a hex nut and a plastic knob onto one end of each rod. Seat

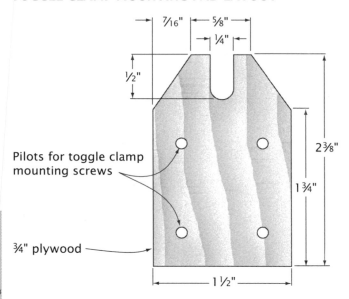

Pilots for toggle clamp mounting screws

¾" plywood

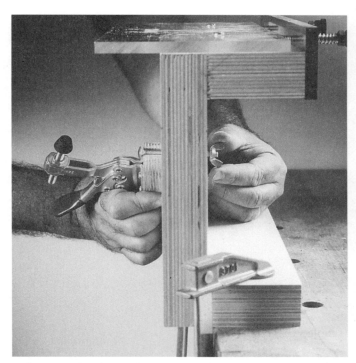

**The toggle clamp is easy to position** and repo-sition because it is screwed to a small pad that's separate from the jig. Catch the pad's mounting slot on a carriage bolt inserted through the appropriate hole in the jig body, then tighten the wing nut to secure the clamp. Orient the clamp so its spindle applies pressure directly on the workpiece, just below the template holes.

the knob, then jam the nut against it very tightly to keep it from unthreading.

Install these screws and tension springs. The role of the springs is to keep the screws from rattling out of the position you set. Visit the hardware store and sort through the assortment of compression springs until you find a style that's the correct inside diameter, the correct length, and an appropriate stiffness.

**7. Mount the toggle clamp.** As noted, the toggle clamp is attached to a pad, which is in turn bolted to the jig. This arrangement allows me to shift the toggle clamp position more easily than if I had to withdraw and drive four mounting screws. I used a De-Sta-Co clamp—the model number is in the Hardware List—with a "reach" of about 2 to 2½ inches. To me, reach is the distance from the clamp's mounting flange to the end of the bar to which the spindle is attached. You don't want to use too small a clamp. If you dowel wide frames, use a larger clamp, and shift the locations of the inserts so the clamp doesn't conflict with the template.

Cut the pad to the shape shown in the layout drawing. Clean up the edges. Screw the clamp to the pad, then mount the toggle on the jig.

The jig is ready for some doweling.

## Using the Jig

The jig isn't difficult to use, but it may take a bit of time to tune the setup, especially the first time you use it. But if you are doweling a batch of face frames, the speed and accuracy with which you can plunge-bore the dowel holes makes this extra setup time a worthwhile invest-ment. If you use the jig primarily for ¾-inch stock, and if you work with consistently thicknessed material, then once the jig is set up, any adjustment from job to job will be minimal.

**1. Set up the jig.** Clamp it to the workbench to begin.

Next set the template. Loosen the set screws. Align the etched line on template with the face edge of jig, then retighten the screws. Set the adjusters against the edge of the template.

Mount the toggle clamp next. There's one position that's suitable for both rails and stiles, provided they aren't too wide. If you are working a job with frame members that are 3 inches wide, you will probably have to switch the toggle clamp back and forth between a position that works for the stiles and one that works for the rails. (The switching is nettlesome during test cuts, but less so when you are doing the actual job.)

Finally, mount the workpiece stop.

**2. Set up the router.** The jig is designed to be used with a ½-inch template guide, so install that guide bushing on the router. Select the correct bit size for the dowels you are using, and chuck it in the collet.

Finally, set the plunge depth. To do this, clamp a scrap in the jig, set the router on the jig, and bottom the bit against the scrap. Drop the stop rod onto the turret, then raise it a distance equal to the depth of the dowel hole you want to bore. A typical depth is 1 inch.

**3. Make test bores.** You need to work with scraps of the actual working stock, of course, and you must make a

Dowel Joinery

complete joint so you can assemble it and evaluate the alignment of the parts.

Lay out the two pieces and mark where the "rail" intersects the "stile." Bearing in mind the template's hole spacing, lay out the dowel positions on both pieces. Finally, mark the reference face of both pieces (the reference face being the one that's up as you lay out the joint).

Clamp the test "stile" in the jig, orienting the reference face out. Align the layout marks with the lines etched into the template. Then spin the workpiece adjuster until it gently seats against the end of the test piece.

Set the router on the template with its guide bushing in one of the holes. Plunge-bore the hole. Move the router to the next hole, and plunge-bore a hole. Keep going until all the holes you will be boring are done.

Now switch test pieces. This time, orient the reference face in. Butt the end of the test "rail" squarely against the template, and slide it left until it contacts the stop. Clamp it. Bore the holes.

**4. Assemble and evaluate the test joint.** Insert dowels—no glue, of course—into the test bores, and assemble the joint. The reference face of both pieces should be up.

Evaluate the joint. Are the faces flush? Do the assembled pieces form a flat surface? If it were a complete face frame, in other words, would that face frame be flat? Are the surface planes misaligned? Are the edges properly aligned?

**5. Fine-tune the jig setup.** Of course, if the joint is perfect on this first try, pat yourself on the back and get busy on the real workpieces. But more than likely, especially

**Adjusting the template position** is easy with these screw adjusters. The plastic knobs are easy on the fingers, and the compression springs keep the screw's setting, even when the router vibrates the jig.

on first use, some minor fine-tuning will be needed. You may have to move the template in or out, or adjust the workpiece stop. You make these adjustments based on your analysis of the joint alignment in relation to the way in which the parts were clamped in the jig.

*The faces are skewed:* The template is cocked. Study the holes in the test pieces, determine which one is off the centerline, and adjust the appropriate end of the template.

*The faces aren't flush:* You need to move the entire template in or out. Look at the test pieces as they were clamped in the jig.

- If the holes are closer to the reference face, the template needs to be pushed back.
- If they are closer to the back face, the template must be pushed forward.

*The edges don't line up:* The workpiece stop must be adjusted in or out.

- If the edge of the rail overhangs the end of the stile, the adjuster screw must be retracted.
- If the stile overhangs the rail, the adjuster screw must be advanced.

*All of the above:* Deal with the problems one at a time. Square the template first, then get it adjusted in or out. Finally, adjust the workpiece stop.

To adjust the template, you must first loosen the mounting screws, of course. To move it back, you back both adjusters away from the edge of the template an equal amount, then push the template back against them. To move it forward, you turn both adjusters so they push against the template.

Because we are dealing with two workpieces, the impact of each template movement will be doubled. Thus in most situations, you will want to move the template a mere fraction of an inch, which translates into a mere fraction of a turn. With the 20-threads-per-inch (tpi) adjusters, a quarter-turn will move the tip of the screw 1/80 inch.

The same is true of the workpiece stop. Very small adjustments of the screw will yield significant shifts of the workpieces.

**6. Rout the dowel holes in the workpieces.** You can follow whatever routine is most productive or comfortable for you. See the drawing *Doweling Sequence.* As the jig now is set up, you can bore the dowel holes in one end of each stile and rail. To do the other ends, switch the workpiece stop to the other position. Regardless of where the workpiece stop is positioned, the stiles are oriented horizontally with their reference faces out, the rails vertically with their reference faces in.

After all the joints at the ends of the workpieces are done, you can remove the workpiece stop so you can do the rest of the joints. These have to be aligned under the template holes by eye. But if the layout marks on the workpieces are accurate, you shouldn't have any difficulty.

## DOWELING SEQUENCE

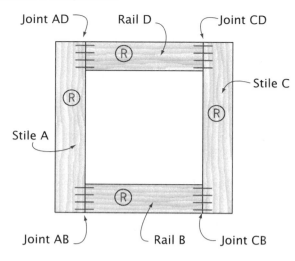

Joint AD — Rail D — Joint CD

Stile C

Stile A

Joint AB — Rail B — Joint CB

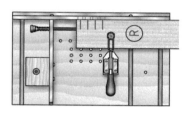

**Stiles**
for Joints AD and CB
- Stop on the left
- Reference face OUT

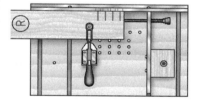

**Stiles**
for Joints AB and CD
- Stop on right
- Reference face OUT

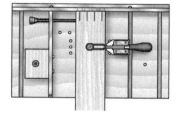

**Rails**
for Joints AD and CB
- Stop on the left
- Reference face IN

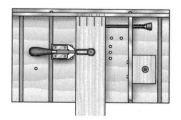

**Rails**
for Joints AB and CD
- Stop on the right
- Reference face IN

**Fast workpiece handling** is a major benefit of the router doweling jig. A rail is positioned vertically, so the holes can be bored into the end. It is aligned by squaring the butt end against the underside of the template, then sliding it against the workpiece stop. The toggle clamp snaps home to hold it in place.

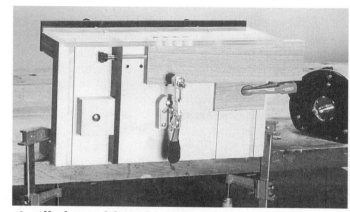

**A stile is positioned horizontally** beneath the template. While the clamp will secure most such workpieces, very long stiles may need a template ledger to support them, as shown here. All you need is a thin block clamped to the jig body, where it will support the workpiece without interfering with workpiece exchange.

**Not every dowel joint** is at the end of the frame member. To bore those dowel holes, you have to remove the workpiece stop and align the workpiece under the template holes using layout marks and the lines etched in the template. The toggle clamp can be repositioned if that helps hold the workpiece.

# Dowel-Making Fixture

**This simple, shop-made apparatus, deftly manipulated by a router magician (that's *you!*), turns square blanks into rounds. Yes, it's a trick, but it's a trick *you* can perform.**

**G**enuine magic. What else can you call this gizmo? It's just a block of wood. You poke a square stick into a round hole in it. When the stick comes out the other side, *it's round!* And hey! It's not a fancy-schmancy block of space-age plastic or exotic Baltic Birch plywood. It's just an ordinary hardwood block.

So what else can it be but some of that router magic?

Oh, I love this fixture just because it *is* so simple, so practical, so effective. It is what magic is: A simple piece of apparatus, deftly manipulated by a practiced magician to produce an engaging illusion. And yeah, it is a trick. I'm going to tell you what it is.

The trick is that the holes in the apparatus are precisely sized and precisely placed in relation to one another. One is the infeed hole. It gives way to the outfeed hole. And intersecting these two is the bit hole. (Of course there's a router involved!)

Chuck the appropriate bit—when the time comes, I'll explain what bit is appropriate, and I'm going to get to what bit is appropriate in a minute—in a table-mounted router. Next, you set the fixture over the bit and clamp it. Set the bit height just so, of course. Switch on the router, and poke that stick in the infeed hole.

Let me explain how to make the fixture, then I'll detail how to use it and how to achieve the best results.

But before I do, let me answer your question: You rout your own dowels when you need walnut dowels, or oak dowels, or cherry dowels. You rout your own when commonplace birch dowels, available for cheap at any lumberyard and many hardware stores, won't do. And once you discover how easy it is to rout your own, you may choose to perform this little magic act whenever you need a dowel.

## Making the Jig

The jig consists of a base and a block. You need to make a different block for each different diameter of dowel you want to rout. You use the same base for all the blocks. To change from one size to another, just undo the fasteners that secure the block on the base, and switch blocks.

**1. Pick the hole sizes.** As I said, there are three holes in the block. Two are stone simple to size. The *outfeed hole* must be the same diameter as the dowel you want to produce. The *bit hole* is no more than a 1/16 bigger in diameter than the bit you will use.

The third hole is the *infeed hole*. Its diameter must match the diagonal measurement of the square dowel blank. For example, if you want to rout a 1/2-inch-diameter dowel, you'd cut a blank that's 1/2 inch square (and maybe a

97

## DOWEL-MAKING FIXTURE EXPLODED VIEW

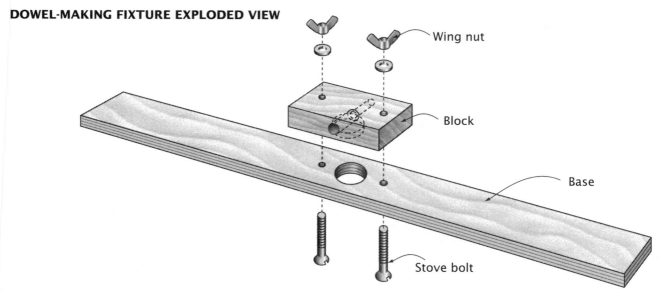

Wing nut

Block

Base

Stove bolt

| Cutting List | | | |
|---|---|---|---|
| **Part** | **Qty.** | **Dimensions** | **Material** |
| Block* | 1 | 1¼" × 3" × 6" | Hardwood |
| Base | 1 | ½" × 3" × 36"† | Plywood |

### Hardware

2 flathead stove bolts, ¼" × 2"

2 washers, ¼" I.D.

2 wing nuts, ¼"

*Cut one such block for each different diameter of dowel
you wish to rout.

†Alter the base length as necessary to fit your router table.

skosh over that). But you wouldn't be able to force that square stick into a ½-inch-diameter hole. And that's because, measured on the diagonal from corner to corner, it's ¾ inch across. So the infeed hole must match the diagonal measurement of the blank.

Refer to the "Dowel Blank/Feed Hole Sizing" chart on page 100 to determine how big the infeed and outfeed holes should be.

**2. Cut the parts.** The fixture consists of a hardwood block, which has the three holes, and a plywood base, which positions and secures the block on the router table. While you can use most any wood, hard or soft, for the block, hardwood will be more durable in the long run.

I'd suggest making several blocks right from the get-go, so you can make more than one size of dowel. Start with a 6/4 (six-quarter) hardwood board about 18 inches long. Flatten one face on the jointer, square an edge to that face, and plane the board to the thickness specified by the Cutting List. Then crosscut the board into three blocks, each about 6 inches long.

For the plywood base, measure the width of your

router table top (from side to side). Cut the plywood the same width as the blocks, and crosscut it to match the router table width.

**3. Drill the feed holes.** The two holes must be bored on the same axis, as shown in the drawing *Dowel-Making Fixture Layouts.* It's important to drill these holes before the bit hole so that the bit isn't deflected by the bit hole.

By all means, drill the hole on the drill press. Set up the

**Drilling two holes on the same axis** is easy with the correct setup. Use a fence on the drill press to center the workpiece under the bit. Crank up the table as close to the bit as you can before starting to drill; you need to use as much stroke as your drill press has to bore a 3-inch-deep hole. Butt a stop block against the end of the workpiece, and clamp it to the fence. Drill the infeed segment of the hole first, boring about 1½ inches deep. To change bits, remove the work from the drill press. The stop block and fence will enable you return it to exactly the same position for continuing the hole with the smaller-diameter bit.

## DOWEL-MAKING FIXTURE LAYOUTS

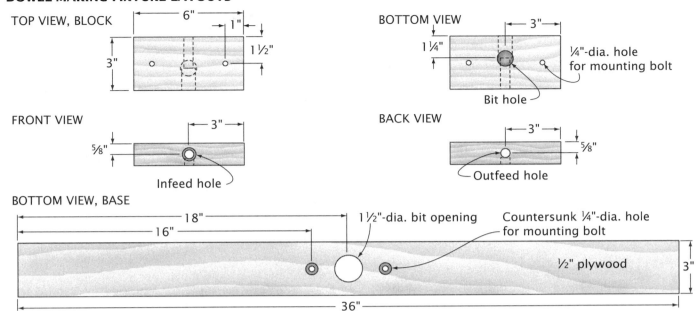

TOP VIEW, BLOCK

6"
1"
3"
1½"

BOTTOM VIEW
3"
1¼"
¼"-dia. hole for mounting bolt
Bit hole

FRONT VIEW
3"
⅝"
Infeed hole

BACK VIEW
3"
⅝"
Outfeed hole

BOTTOM VIEW, BASE
18"
16"
1½"-dia. bit opening
Countersunk ¼"-dia. hole for mounting bolt
½" plywood
3"
36"

table with a fence and stop block to position the workpiece. Drill the larger-diameter hole first, boring about 1½ inches deep. Then switch bits and finish the hole with the smaller-diameter bit, boring the rest of the way through the block. The fence and stop block allow you to move the workpiece out of the way when you change bits, yet ensure that you can return it to exactly the same position. That is essential if the two holes are to share the same axis.

**4. Select a bit and bore the bit hole.** You need to select the bit now, since it must fit the bit hole in the block almost without clearance.

You can use a large-diameter core-box (or roundnose) bit, a bottom-cleaning bit, a mortising bit, or a dish cutter.

**The intersection of the fixture's three holes** can be seen here. The bit hole should just break into the outfeed hole. You don't need to drill any deeper than this.

I've used them all, and I haven't discerned much difference in the finished product, regardless of the bit used. I'd suggest you go with whichever of these bits you have.

The bit hole is a stopped hole, as you can see from the drawing. It is the same diameter as the bit you will use. Position the hole as shown in the drawing, and bore just deep enough to break through the wall of the outfeed hole.

**5. Mount the block on the base.** Lay out the block position on the base, and transfer the location of the block's bit hole to the base. At that spot, bore an oversized hole so the bit can extend through the base into the block.

Drill mounting-bolt holes, as shown in the layout drawing, in both the block and the base. Countersink the holes in the base. Insert flathead stove bolts through the base, fit the block over them, add washers, and then thread a wing nut onto each bolt.

## Routing Dowels

I tried making dowels out of oak, ash, cherry, soft maple, poplar, walnut, and mahogany. All these woods run through the dowel-making fixture without a hitch, so long as the blank is straight-grained. Any twists, dips, or waves lead to chip-out and splintering. Examine your stock carefully, and be selective for best results.

**1. Cut the dowel blanks.** Check the dowel chart for the specs of the dowel you want. Rip a test blank to the dimensions specified for the desired dowel diameter. Now check its fit in the *infeed* hole. It must be snug, but not so snug that you can't turn it by hand.

*If it is too tight,* re-rip the blank, making it slightly smaller.

*If it is too loose,* rip another blank, making it slightly larger.

## DOWEL BLANK/FEED HOLE SIZING DIAGRAM

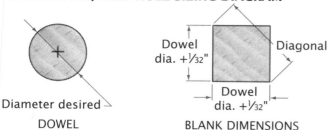

Diameter desired — **DOWEL**

Dowel dia. +1/32" / Diagonal / Dowel dia. +1/32" — **BLANK DIMENSIONS**

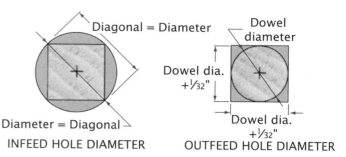

Diagonal = Diameter / Diameter = Diagonal — **INFEED HOLE DIAMETER**

Dowel diameter / Dowel dia. +1/32" / Dowel dia. +1/32" — **OUTFEED HOLE DIAMETER**

### Dowel Blank/Feed Hole Sizing

| Dowel Size | Blank Size | Infeed Hole | Outfeed Hole |
|---|---|---|---|
| 1/4" dia. | 9/32" sq. | 13/32" dia. | 1/4" dia. |
| 3/8" dia. | 13/32" sq. | 5/8" dia. | 3/8" dia. |
| 1/2" dia. | 17/32" sq. | 3/4" dia. | 1/2" dia. |
| 5/8" dia. | 21/32" sq. | 15/16" dia. | 5/8" dia. |
| 3/4" dia. | 25/32" sq. | 1 1/8" dia. | 3/4" dia. |
| 7/8" dia. | 29/32" sq. | 1 5/16" dia. | 7/8" dia. |
| 1" dia. | 1 1/32" sq. | 1 1/2" dia. | 1" dia. |

When you've established the correct blank size, rip all the blanks you need, plus a few spares, to that size. Hang on to the correctly sized test blank, too, so you can use it to tune and fine-tune the fixture setup.

Be sensible about the length of the blanks. I cut them 4 to 6 inches longer than what I absolutely need. There's usually an unusable section at the end that gets chucked in the "power feeder." But I also endeavor to keep them as short as possible. Trying to rout a several-foot-long 1/4-inch-diameter dowel is overreaching.

**2. Set up the fixture.** Chuck the bit in the table-mounted router, and raise it just enough to capture the

fixture on it. Next, set the fixture over the bit, center it, and clamp it to the router table.

Adjust the bit height by sighting through the *outfeed* hole. Raise the bit until its tip is flush with the bottom surface of the outfeed hole.

**3. Fine-tune the setup.** Rout a section of the test blank to check the bit height setting. Switch on the router, and feed the blank into the fixture. As you do this, turn the blank by hand. You'll find that it "threads" itself through the fixture. In other words, you don't have to push it, because as you turn the blank, it will feed itself.

When the leading end of the blank emerges from the outfeed hole, switch off the router. Pull the blank out of the fixture. Don't be overly concerned with the test dowel's finish at this point, since a hand-fed dowel tends to be rough. Rather, focus on how it fits the outfeed hole. The tighter the dowel's fit in the outfeed hole, the better the finish you'll get.

*If the blank can't be fed through the fixture at all,* the bit is too low. It isn't reducing the blank's diameter to equal that of the outfeed hole.

*If the blank binds in the outfeed hole,* the bit is too low. Raise the bit very slightly. (Remember, there's a doubling effect at work here. If you raise the bit 1/64 inch, you reduce the dowel's diameter by 1/32 inch.)

*If the dowel is less than snug in the outfeed hole,* the bit is too high. It is removing too much material. As the disparity between the dowel's and the hole's diameters

## TUNING THE SETUP

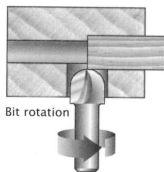

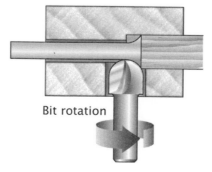

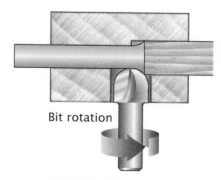

**BIT TOO LOW**
The bit is not removing material from the blank; the blank can't fit into the outfeed hole.

**BIT TOO HIGH**
The bit is removing too much material; the dowel is smaller than the outfeed hole.

**PERFECT SETUP**
The bit is removing just the right amount of material, so the dowel is the same diameter as the outfeed hole.

**Dowel Making**

increases, the dowel starts to chatter and whip. The spiral texture of the dowel's surface gets more coarse. If these effects are evident, lower the bit.

Retest the setup. And keep testing and adjusting until you're satisfied that it is as good as you can make it. And you'll feel it when the setup is right. The blank will seemingly disappear into the fixture, no chatter, no binding.

**4. Set up the "power feeder."** The best finish is achieved by increasing the speed that the stock turns as it moves past the bit. The way to do this is to chuck the blank in a power drill, and spin it at 600 to 800 rpm.

I use a ½-inch portable drill for this. It provides maximum chuck capacity, and its speed is limited—according to the spec plate on it—to 800 rpm. Small dowel blanks fit right into the chuck. Large ones must be whittled down to fit. You only need to whittle a short section on one end of the blank. After the dowel is formed, you trim that part off.

**5. Rout the dowel.** It goes quickly, once you have the fixture set up and fine-tuned. Here's the drill:

A. Chuck a blank in the drill.
B. Switch on the router.
C. Insert the end of the blank into the infeed hole.
D. Squeeze the drill's trigger and simultaneously feed the blank into the hole.
E. When you've fed as much of the blank through the fixture as you can, cut the power to the router, then to the drill.
F. Extract the dowel from the fixture.
G. Take it out of the drill chuck and fit a new blank into the chuck. Return to A.

The nature of this routine is such that a foot-switch on the router is a big plus. You get the drill with the blank all ready, then step on the pedal. And when you are ready to cut the power, you don't have to let go of the drill to do it.

**Rout just the end** before chucking the blank in your "power feeder." You'll then be able to get the dowel started more easily if you shape just about the length shown here. Turn the blank by hand to do this.

**Yes, it's magic!** Switch on the router, and insert the blank's tip in the infeed hole. Quickly trigger the drill to spin the blank, and simultaneously push the blank into the hole. With a little experience, you'll develop a feel for the best feed rate.

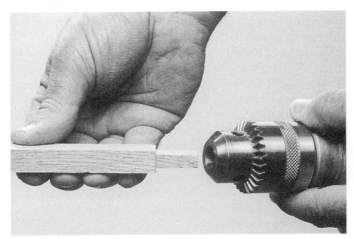

**The fixture's power feeder** is your electric drill. Spinning the dowel blank with the drill as the bit cuts it produces the best finish on the dowel. To fit a large dowel blank in the drill chuck, you have to whittle the end.

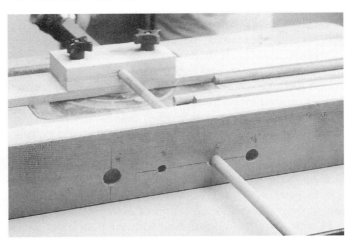

**To keep a long, slender dowel from whipping,** feed its finished end into a steady rest block clamped to the back of the router table top. The steady rest is no more than a block with a hole the diameter of the dowel drilled through it.

# Dowel-Turning Jig

**Here's a turnabout on the woodworking convention. Turn the workpiece by hand in this jig while using your router to shape it round and smooth.**

**F**at dowels, simple round tapers, and even modestly ornamented spindles can be produced with a router and this primitive lathe. It is simple to make (as all good jigs are), yet it has a lot of potential.

I've called it a *dowel*-turning jig because that's what the woodworker who told me about it used it for: making dowels. And it *is* a turning operation. You turn the spindle blank as the cutter moves along its axis. This makes it round. After I made the jig to try out, I realized that it could be customized for some other operations as well.

This jig got its start when San Francisco woodworker Yeung Chan needed a 4-inch-diameter dowel for a table base. When he couldn't find what he needed ready-made, and because he didn't have a lathe, Chan turned to his router. The version of the jig shown is my interpretation of Chan's jig.

In brief, what he did was to screw together a four-sided plywood box. In the center of each end, Chan drilled a ⅜-inch hole. He mounted a blank for his dowel inside the box by driving lengths of threaded rod through the holes and into the ends of the blank. He also mounted an improvised handle on one rod so he could turn the blank.

Then Chan made a new plywood baseplate for his router, one wide enough to span the width of the box.

To fix the router over the axis of the blank, he attached guide strips to the plywood baseplate.

To turn the dowel, all he had to do was set up the router with a straight bit, switch it on, and very slowly feed it along the top of the box while he simultaneously cranked the blank around and around.

Chan's jig, it seems, is a job-specific solution to an immediate problem. But it holds potential for a somewhat more flexible jig, one that's a little less improvised, one that's a keeper. After noodling with the basic design and trying a few ideas that didn't pan out, I came to the conclusion that you can't really design a dowel-turning jig that will accommodate every job. You are going to have to move the end pieces to accommodate different spindle lengths. You will want to drill the end pieces specifically for tapering jobs.

In other words, keep the jig, but figure on doing a little cutting or drilling to adapt it to the job at hand.

## Building the Jig

The jig presented here will take a blank up to 32 inches long. If you want a jig that will do a longer blank, or if you know that 32 inches is much too long for the needs you

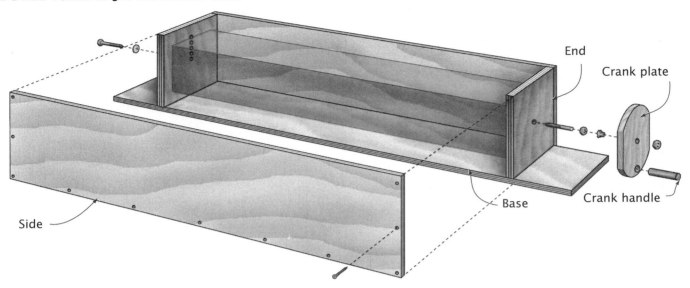

Side

End

Crank plate

Crank handle

Base

anticipate, then modify the dimensions, making the jig longer or shorter.

**1. Cut the parts.** I made my jig mostly from plywood leftovers. The dimensions of the parts are specified by the Cutting List. Cut the base, sides, and ends for the box, as well as the baseplate for the router. I used a piece of acrylic for the baseplate.

**2. Bore the spindle holes in the ends.** Study the drawing *Crank Layout*. I made each end piece with a series of spindle holes so that several different diameters of dowel can be produced without necessarily remaking the end pieces. For the jig to work properly, the axis of each hole in one end piece must match the axis of the corresponding hole in the other end piece.

Lay out the holes, and drill them on the drill press.

**3. Assemble the box.** This is as simple as lining up the parts, drilling pilot holes, and driving screws. I attached the sides to the base, then fitted the ends between the sides. Make sure the sides and ends are flush around their top edges.

**4. Make the crank.** Study the drawing *Crank Layout*. The crank plate is ¾-inch hardwood. It is basically a disk, though the width of the scrap I used was less than the diameter of the circle I routed. The crank is mounted on a ¼-inch × 3-inch hanger bolt using a T-nut and two stop nuts. To accommodate both the crank plate and two nuts on the machine-threaded section of the hanger bolt, you have to drill a ⅜-inch-deep counterbore, as shown in the drawing.

Find a suitable scrap, about 4¼ inches wide, and locate the centerpoint. With a ¾-inch Forstner bit, drill the counterbore on the centerpoint. Switch to a ⅛-inch bit and drill through the workpiece, making a pivot hole. Lay out and

| Cutting List | | | |
|---|---|---|---|
| **Part** | **Qty.** | **Dimensions** | **Material** |
| Base | 1 | ¾" × 6" × 44" | Plywood |
| Sides | 2 | ½" × 6¾" × 34" | Plywood |
| Ends | 2 | ¾" × 6" × 6" | Plywood |
| Baseplate | 1 | ¼" × 6" × 8½" | Acrylic |
| Crank plate | 1 | ¾" × 4¼" × 5" | Hardwood |
| Crank handle | 1 | ½" dia. × 4" | Dowel |
| Guide strips | 2 | ¾" × ¾" × 6" | Hardwood |
| Locking-pin grip | 1 | ½" dia. × 2" | Dowel |
| Locking-pin shank | 1 | ¼" dia. × 2" | Dowel |

## Hardware

21+ drywall screws, #6 × 2"

1 hanger bolt, ¼"-20 × 3"

2 stop nuts, ¼"-20

1 T-nut, ¼"-20

1 lag screw, ¼" × 2"

4–8 flat washers, ¼"

bore the ½-inch-diameter hole for the crank handle.

Set up the Trammel Baseplate (page 39) to cut a 2½-inch-radius arc. Set the trammel's pivot in the center hole, and rout the shape of the crank plate. Having done that, redrill the pivot hole to a ⁷⁄₁₆-inch diameter to accommodate the T-nut. Drive the T-nut in place. Glue the handle in place.

## DOWEL-TURNING JIG PLAN VIEWS

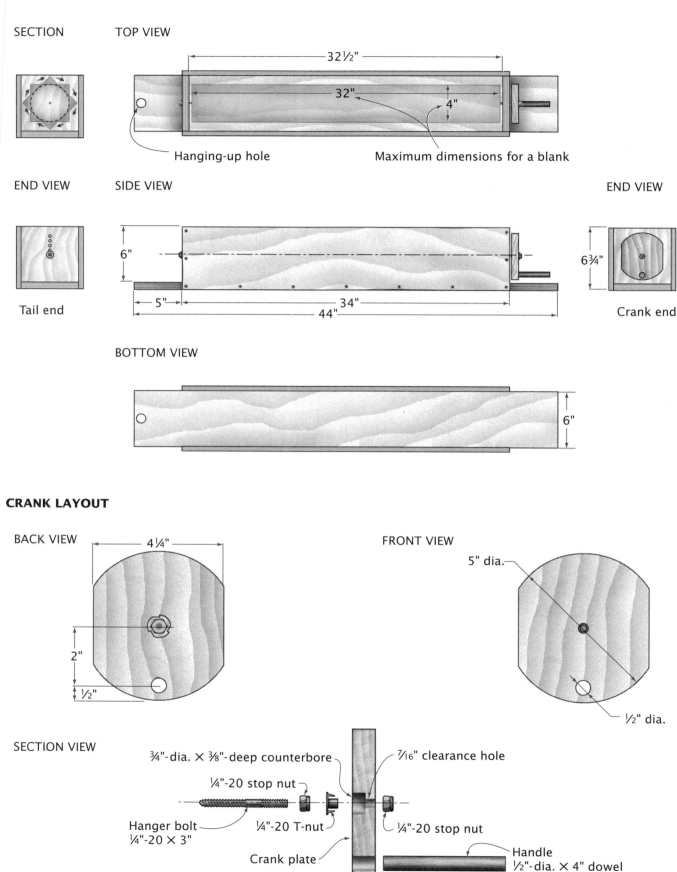

SECTION   TOP VIEW

32½"

32"

4"

Hanging-up hole          Maximum dimensions for a blank

END VIEW   SIDE VIEW                                      END VIEW

6"                                                          6¾"

Tail end                                                  Crank end

5"

34"

44"

BOTTOM VIEW

6"

## CRANK LAYOUT

BACK VIEW   4¼"                    FRONT VIEW

5" dia.

2"

½"                                                ½" dia.

SECTION VIEW

¾"-dia. × ⅜"-deep counterbore          7/16" clearance hole

¼"-20 stop nut

¼"-20 stop nut

Hanger bolt
¼"-20 × 3"          ¼"-20 T-nut

Crank plate

Handle
½"-dia. × 4" dowel

**Dowel Making**

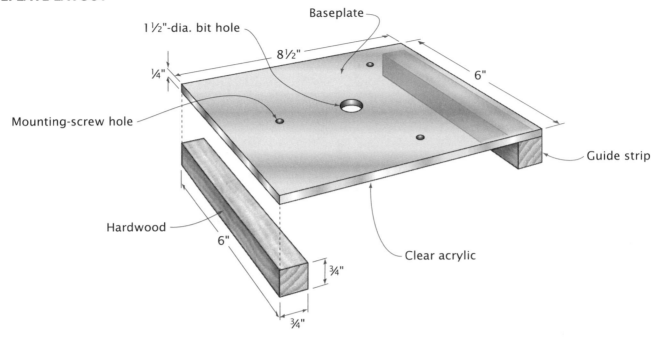

1 1/2"-dia. bit hole
8 1/2"
1/4"
Baseplate
6"
Mounting-screw hole
Guide strip
Hardwood
6"
3/4"
3/4"
Clear acrylic

Now bolt everything together. Thread a stop nut onto the hanger bolt; you'll need to grip the bolt in a pair of Vise-Grips and turn the nut with a wrench. Turn the nut as far as it will go. Now turn the crank onto the bolt, tightening it against the stop nut. Add the second stop nut.

**5. Make the baseplate.** The baseplate is necessary for any router with a baseplate diameter under 7 inches, which is to say, darn near *every* router. It suspends the router on the top edges of the box, with the bit directly over the blank's axis. The guides glued to the baseplate trap the baseplate, allowing it to be slid from end to end but not side to side.

Cut the baseplate from 1/4-inch material. I used a piece of acrylic so I could see the bit relatively easily, but plywood would also be suitable. (I don't think it's necessary to buy a piece of acrylic just for this application if you have usable scraps of plywood.) Use the router's factory baseplate as a pattern for drilling the mounting-screw holes and the bit opening. Attach the baseplate to the router.

To position the guide strips, which can be fashioned from scrap rippings, chuck a small-diameter straight bit or a V-grooving bit in the collet. Set the router on the jig, and align it directly above the holes in one end. Apply a little glue to the guides, and apply them to the underside of the baseplate, tight against the sides of the box. Clamp them with spring clamps. (To attach the strips to my acrylic base-plate, I drove small screws through the baseplate into the guide strips.)

## Using the Jig

Before getting to the specifics of router-turning a dowel, let me mention the jig's capacities.

The jig shown in the plans will accommodate a blank that is 4 inches square. Under the best conditions, this will yield a 4-inch-diameter dowel. If you trim a blank to an octagon before mounting it in the jig, you can produce a dowel around 5 1/2 inches in diameter, max. (Of course, you can enlarge the jig if you need an even larger round.)

To turn a smaller-diameter dowel, you should raise the turning axis. The bit can't be extended very far below the baseplate; so the closer to the jig's top edges the blank is, the better. A reasonable rule of thumb is half the diagonal of the square blank, and drop the head and tail spindle holes that distance from the top edge of the ends.

The longest blank the jig will accommodate is 32 inches. By extending the sides (and, if necessary, the bottom), you can mount a longer blank, of course. To handle a shorter blank (why turn more than you need?), move the tail end closer to the crank end. All you have to do is pull six screws to free the end piece, remember.

Bear in mind that you can't rout the entire length. If you get too close to the blank's ends, you risk gouging the jig's end pieces. So you will have a bit of waste to trim from the completed dowel.

**1. Set up the jig.** The diameter and length of the dowel you want must be considered at the outset. Calculate the girth and length of the blank needed. Determine the best position for the spindle holes in the jig's end pieces.

Clamp the jig to the workbench. The jig was designed with an extra-long base specifically for clamping. Make sure the clamp at the crank end doesn't interfere with the crank.

If necessary, remove the end pieces and drill 1/4-inch-diameter spindle holes. Sandwich the ends and drill the holes in both at one time.

Reinstall the ends. If the blank will be shorter than 32 inches, shift the tail end closer to the crank end as appropriate.

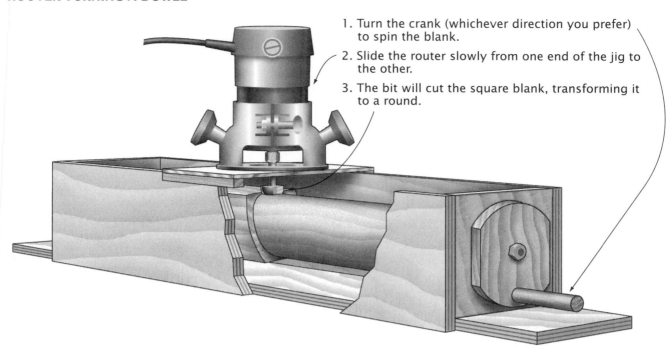

1. Turn the crank (whichever direction you prefer) to spin the blank.

2. Slide the router slowly from one end of the jig to the other.

3. The bit will cut the square blank, transforming it to a round.

**Dowel Making**

**2. Cut and mount the blank.** Cut the blank(s) to size. You *can* save some turning time by ripping the blank to an octagon. But frankly, you'll just be trading time on one machine for time on another; suit yourself. The *best* reason for doing this is to fit a 5½-inch square to the jig.

Scribe diagonals on the blank's ends, and drill ³⁄₁₆-inch-diameter pilots into the ends for the mounting spindles. The more accurately you can align these holes, the better.

I use washers to offset the blank from the jig's ends. Slide the crank spindle through the hole in the jig's end,

hang a washer on the spindle tip, then fit the blank in position. Turn the crank and drive the spindle into the pilot in the blank. Drive the lag screw through the jig's tail end and into the tail end of the blank.

**3. Set up the router.** Remove the factory baseplate, and attach the jig's baseplate.

Choose your bit, and chuck it in the router's collet.

What bit should you use? My choice is the dish cutter (also called a bowl bit). It is designed for cutting a surface

**Adjust the jig to accommodate the blank.** To rout a small-diameter dowel or spindle, as at left, the blank must be positioned high in the jig. A fairly large-diameter blank will be suspended from the middle of the end pieces. For a short blank, the tail end can simply be moved closer to the crank end, as at right.

perpendicular to the bit axis (as opposed to one parallel to the bit axis). But the cutting edges are radiused at their extremities so the horizontal surface of the cut blends into the vertical, rather than making a sharp, right-angle change. In use, this bit seems to leave a smoother, more even surface.

Core-box or roundnose bits, straight bits, bottom-cleaning bits, and mortising bits can all be used. I recommend that you try whichever of these bits you have. If you have them all, try them all. Then use the one that produces the best surface.

With the bit in the router, set the router on the jig and adjust the bit extension. To start, turn the blank so a flat surface is up. Set the router in position and extend the bit 'til it bottoms on the blank. At this setting, your first pass will hog away the corners of the blank.

**4. Rout the blank.** The first time you use the jig, experiment to develop a sense of the operation. Crank the blank clockwise and feed the router to the left. Then feed it to the right. Then crank the blank counterclockwise and feed the router from right to left and left to right. You'll pick up on when the router is self-feeding, which isn't desirable.

Vary the rate of your cranking. How does the speed of rotation impact on the smoothness and evenness of the cut surface? My experience is that the faster you crank, the smoother the surface.

I work from the right toward the left, cranking the blank clockwise. To begin, tip the router a little so the bit is clear of the work. Switch it on, then set it back on the jig. Start cranking the blank, and steadily move the router. You don't need to move the router slowly.

After you've cleaned the corners from the blank, roughing it to a round, adjust the bit extension to achieve

the diameter of dowel you want. Remember that you are changing the *radius* of the dowel when you alter the bit extension. The diameter is *twice the radius*. The diameter of the dowel will be reduced by *twice* the distance you move the bit.

To measure the diameter of the dowel while it is still in the jig, use calipers.

When you are done, remove the dowel from the jig,

**The finished dowel's surface** may not be perfect. For the best surface finish possible, make a very light cut on the final pass, moving the router quite slowly but cranking the blank furiously. A light sanding should clean off the minute ridges and imperfections. (Of course, the character of the wood you use will have a lot to do with the quality of the final surface.)

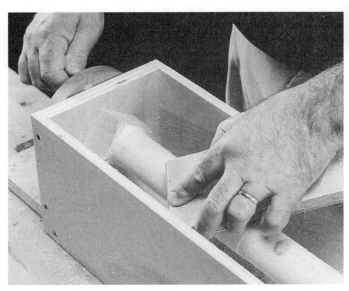

**Sand the dowel.** A turner sands his turned spindle while it's still mounted in the lathe, and I found that that's the easiest way to sand a dowel, too. Hold a sanding block against the dowel, and turn the crank. It works with a pad sander, though a belt sander is too crude and a random-orbit sander is too erratic.

**A good first pass** will clean off the corners of the blank, as you can see. It won't necessarily produce a nice, even round.

TAPER LAYOUT

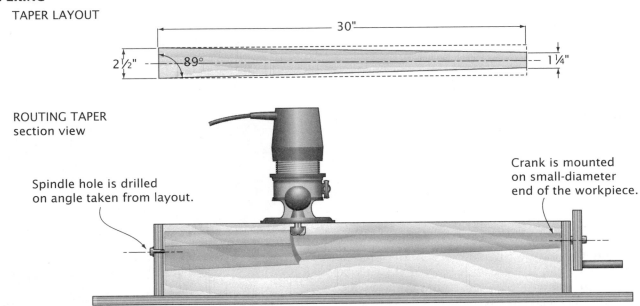

ROUTING TAPER
section view

Spindle hole is drilled
on angle taken from layout.

Crank is mounted
on small-diameter
end of the workpiece.

## Tapering

trim the ends, and put it to use in your project.

Routing a tapered spindle is accomplished simply by tilting the axis of the blank in the jig. One end is high, the other low. The router moves back and forth in the same level plane; but because the blank is angled, the result is a tapered spindle.

This is a case where you need to customize the end pieces for the project. For the blank to be rotated without binding or jiggling, the pivot holes in the jig ends should be angled. So that the crank doesn't bind on the end piece, it is best to have it on the high end of the blank, as shown in the drawing *Tapering*.

On paper or a scrap board, draw the taper full-sized.

Sketch in the jig and the spindle bolts. Determine the drop from the top edge of the jig ends to the pivot holes, and the angle of the spindles. As you work out these details, keep the size of the necessary blank in mind. If you can taper the blank on the table saw or jointer before you mount it in the jig, you'll save some router work. If you can't, you may need to make two pairs of pivot holes. Otherwise you risk having one end of the blank sticking up out of the jig, while the other end is at the limits of the bit's reach. One set of pivot holes allows you to rough the blank to a taper, while the second set of holes repositions the workpiece so it can be reduced to finished size.

In any case, lay out the holes on the ends, and drill them at the proper angle. Then install the ends in the jig.

**Mounting a blank for tapering** requires the tail spindle to be higher in its jig end than the crank spindle. The spindle holes in the blank are still located dead-center, however.

**The process is the same,** but the result is a little different. Turn the crank and move the router. You get a taper. Note that the narrow end of the blank is round here, while the fat end still has broad flats.

Mount the blank in the jig, set up the router, and rout the spindle as you would in making a straight dowel.

## Simple Turning

Once you've mastered the process of turning blanks into rounds and tapered rounds, you'll see that, with the right bits, you can produce some rudimentary embellishments, particularly rings and coves.

Rather than repeat a lot of information, let me refer you to the chapter on making and using the Router Lathe (page 269). That device is more involved to build and will do much more sophisticated turnings, but the bits and many of the techniques used can be carried over to this more simple jig.

# Fluting

To flute a round, you need an indexing wheel. This is a disk marked off in regular increments, which you attach to the blank in place of the crank. The index wheel allows you to rotate the blank a specific number of degrees, then lock it. You can then make a straight cut the length of the blank.

If you use a straight, mortising, or bottom-cleaning bit, you can create pentagonal, hexagonal, or octagonal billets. With a core-box, you can rout traditional, deep flutes into a spindle. With a coving bit, you can create broad, shallow flutes. With a plunge-point roundover bit, you can rout beads. What's more, if the jig is set up for tapering, you can easily perform these cuts on tapered spindles.

## Making the Indexing Wheel

Layout is the biggest part of the job. The drawing *Index Wheel Layout Tricks* depicts how to use a compass to segment the wheel as you lay it out. I suppose you could use a protractor and lay out a wheel with a couple of dozen

| Number of Segments | Degrees |
|---|---|
| 5 segments | 72° each |
| 6 segments | 60° each |
| 8 segments | 45° each |
| 12 segments | 30° each |
| 24 segments | 15° each |

**INDEX WHEEL LAYOUT**

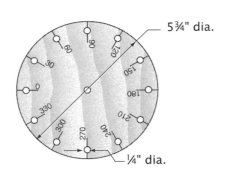

5¾" dia.

¼" dia.

indexing marks, but simpler is better, to my mind. I'd recommend making a wheel with only those marks you'll need for the job at hand. When a new project demands different segmentation, heck—make a new wheel. It doesn't take long.

**1. Lay out the wheel.** Use ¾-inch plywood or medium-density fiberboard (MDF); for layout purposes, start with a 12-inch square. Locate the center of the square; using a compass, scribe a 6-inch-diameter circle.

You can divide up the circle in a variety of ways. Don't get carried away and mark too many segments, though. Pick your arrangement and follow the appropriate sequence shown in the drawings. Once you've stepped off the segments, label them with degrees. The table on this page converts the number of segments into degrees for you.

**2. Rout out the disk.** With the layout work done, drill a ⅛-inch pivot hole on the centermark. Set up your router and trammel, and cut the disk.

**3. Drill the locking-pin holes.** You have to be able to lock the wheel in specific positions. The locking system I used is really simple and works just fine. At each of 12

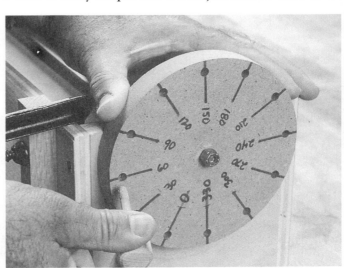

**The indexing wheel** replaces the crank for fluting and beading. This one is laid out with 12 positions, each with a locking-pin hole. By inserting the locking pin through a hole in the wheel into a hole in the jig end, as shown, you lock the blank.

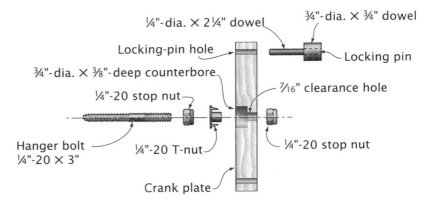

¼"-dia. × 2¼" dowel

¾"-dia. × ¾" dowel

Locking-pin hole

Locking pin

¾"-dia. × ⅜"-deep counterbore

7/16" clearance hole

¼"-20 stop nut

¼"-20 T-nut

¼"-20 stop nut

Hanger bolt ¼"-20 × 3"

Crank plate

**Dowel Making**

5/10 segments

6/12 segments

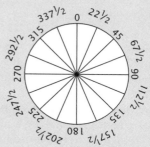

8/16 segments

A. Draw a circle and two diameters at right angles to each other. Find the midpoint of a radius, as shown at M.

A. Scribe a circle. Keep the compass set to the circle's radius throughout the layout process.

A. Start with a square. Quarter it, then scribe diagonals. A circle scribed in the square will have its circumference divided into eight equal segments.

B. Set a compass to radius AM. With the compass point on M, strike an arc, locating P.

B. Mark a point–any point–on the circumference. Label it #1. Step off five more points around the circumference.

B. To get 16 segments, set a compass to half the length of a diagonal. Set the compass on each corner and mark each adjoining side.

C. Reset the compass to radius AP. Start at A, and step off four additional points around the circle's circumference.

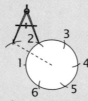

C. Split the arc between two points. With the compass on point #1, strike an arc outside the circle. Move the compass to point #2, and strike an arc across the first. Use a straightedge to connect the arcs' intersection to the circle's centerpoint.

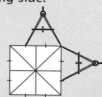

C. By this process, each side will get two new marks, bringing the total to 16.

D. To double the number of points, set the compass on Z, which evenly divides one of the five segments. Step off four additional points around the circle's circumference. Extend a radius from the center to each mark on the perimeter.

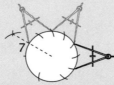

D. Put the compass on point #7, and step off five more points around the circumference. You can now scribe radii from the center to the 12 circumferential marks.

D. Scribe a circle. Extend a radius from the center to each mark.

spots, I drilled a ¼-inch hole through the disk. I also drilled a hole in the jig's end piece. A dowel thrust through the hole in the wheel into the end pins the wheel and prevents it from rotating as I rout.

Drill the holes on the drill press. Clamp a scrap to the drill press table. Chuck the appropriate bit in the machine, and line up the disk for the drilling of the first hole. Then run a screw through the disk's pivot hole into the scrap worktable. Drill the first hole. Turn the wheel to line up the next hole, and drill it. Keep going until all the holes are drilled.

**4. Make the locking pin.** The pin I use is made from two pieces of dowel. I drilled a stopped hole into the end of a length of ½-inch dowel, then glued a piece of ¼-inch dowel into the hole. I trimmed the grip to a 1-inch length, and the shank to a 1½-inch length.

**5. Mount the wheel.** The indexing wheel is mounted the same way as the crank. Drill the necessary counterbore, and open up the small pivot hole for the ¼-inch-diameter hanger bolt.

Assemble the hardware as you did the crank hardware, and install it in the wheel.

### Using the Indexing Wheel

Before you actually use the jig for fluting, you need to sketch out what the finished part should look like. How

**To rout flutes or beads into a spindle,** use the indexing wheel to distribute the cuts evenly, as well as to lock the workpiece. Feed the router from one end of the jig to the other, making the cut. Note the stop clamped to the side of the jig.

many segments? What bit will you use? How deep should the cut be? With these guidelines in hand, you can set up and use the jig.

**1. Mount the blank in the jig.** The technique is the same as for mounting a blank for rounding. Instead of the crank, use the indexing wheel.

You do have to drill the locking-pin hole in the jig's end. The position of this hole depends on the height of the blank in the jig. Best approach: Mount the blank, then use one of the locking-pin holes in the wheel as a guide in drilling the end. Obviously, the hole should coincide with an appropriate alignment point on the end.

**2. Set up the router.** Mount the baseplate on the router. Select the appropriate bit for the cut you want to make (a core-box for fluting, for example), and chuck it in the router. Adjust the bit extension. Caution growing out of inexperience suggests keeping the first pass cuts shallow. After you have a feel for the operation, you probably can get the depth of cut set correctly at the outset and make each cut in one pass.

**3. Make the first pass.** Tip the router up so the bit is clear of the workpiece. Try tipping it along the axis of the blank, so when you lower it, the bit will sweep into the cut on the correct line, rather than across it.

Switch on the router and lower the bit. Slide the router along the jig, making the cut. As you reach the end of the cut, switch off the router and lift the bit clear of the workpiece. Set the router clear of the work.

Pull the locking pin, and rotate the wheel to the next position. Reinsert the pin, locking the blank. Put the router back on the jig, its bit clear of the workpiece. Switch it on and rout. Keep repeating this sequence until you've make a first pass on each segment of the blank.

**4. Make additional passes.** Assess the condition of the workpiece. If your first cuts were shallow, adjust the router's depth of cut. Rotate the blank to the starting point and lock it in position with the pin. Make a second, and if necessary a third, series of passes in the same manner as the first passes.

### Squaring an Irregular Workpiece

As strange as it may seem, you can also use this turning jig to plane a round or irregular workpiece flat and square. Here's an example: You get your hands on some small-diameter logs that you want to turn into lumber.

Here's how you do it. Drill spindle holes in the log. Mount it in the dowel-turning jig, but lock it so it won't turn. Remove the guide strips from the router baseplate so that you can move the router side to side on the jig as well as end to end. Rout a flat surface on the log.

Unlock the workpiece and rotate it 90 degrees. Relock it. Now rout a second flat on the workpiece, this one at a right angle to the first. Finish up the job by routing the remaining two sides in the same manner.

# Slot-Cutter Drawer Joinery

**Cut drawer joints with one setup of one cutter. Two simple jigs help you do it.**

Drawer Making

The drawer lock joint is a machine-cut joint used in making drawers. You've probably seen it in showings of different woodworking joints, but it may be that you've never tried or used it.

It's a strong joint because the two parts interlock. The drawer front is given a rabbet with a little tongue that fits into a slot in the drawer side. Unlike a plain rabbet joint, the parts are hooked together mechanically, even before you drive nails or brads into the joint. It doesn't look any better or worse at the front of a drawer than a rabbet joint. The drawback for me has always been mental: It seemed to involve a lot of setups.

Then someone showed me an approach that suddenly made the drawer lock joint a whole lot more attractive. That's because with this setup, it is a whole lot easier and faster to make.

The joinery is cut with a ⅛-inch slot cutter chucked in a table-mounted router. You set the bit, position the fence, and forget them. Each joint is cut in four passes, all with the bit and fence in the same position. To make the system work, you need two extremely simple jigs: an auxiliary facing for the router table fence and a booster sled.

Although the drawer lock joint can be customized to work with all sorts of stock thicknesses and drawer configurations, this particular setup does have limitations. It works with ½-inch stock. You can use thicker stock for the fronts, but the sides must be ½-inch thick, no more and no less. It produces a flush drawer. If you want an overlapping front, you have to add a false front after the drawer trays are assembled. On the plus side, you can use this joint between the back and sides, as well as between the front and sides.

## Making the Jigs

Only a few scraps of wood and some commonplace hardware is needed to build the two necessary jigs. And if you study the drawings, you may find ways to simplify the jigs even more than I have.

**1. Make the sled.** Cut the hardboard sole and the hardwood heel to the dimensions specified by the Cutting List. Glue and nail the heel to the sole, using 1-inch brads. (See the drawing *Booster Sled Plan.*) Make sure the brads are sunk flush, so they won't drag on the router table top when the sled is being used.

**2. Cut the parts for the auxiliary facing.** The critical piece is the facing itself. It must be ⅜ inch thick. Select a straight-grained piece of hardwood for this part. Joint and plane the facing to the specified thickness. If you don't have

## BOOSTER SLED PLAN

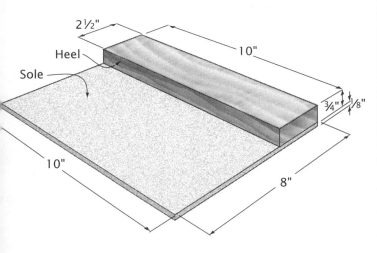

**BOOSTER SLED Cutting List**

| Part | Qty. | Dimensions | Material |
|------|------|------------|----------|
| Sole | 1 | ⅛" × 8" × 10" | Hardboard |
| Heel | 1 | ¾" × 2½" × 10" | Hardwood |
| **Hardware** | | | |

1" brads

a planer, you can resaw stock on the table saw.

Rip and crosscut the parts to the dimensions specified by the Cutting List.

**3. Install the clamp studs.** The clamping system is shown in the detail of the drawing *Auxiliary Fence Facing Plan.* Drill holes for the T-nuts in the back. The holes should be about 4 inches in from the ends and about ¾ inch up from the bottom edge, though the specific locations are not all that important. Drive the T-nuts. Thread the carriage bolts, used as clamp bolts, into the T-nuts. Thread a hex nut on each bolt, then a plastic knob. Seat the knob, then jam the hex nut against the knob, preventing it from loosening in use.

**4. Assemble the fence facing.** The facing and the back are glued and screwed to the edges of the top, as shown in *Auxiliary Fence Facing Plan.* Be sure to countersink the screws so they won't impede the movement of the drawer parts along the fence when you are cutting the joinery.

## AUXILIARY FENCE FACING PLAN

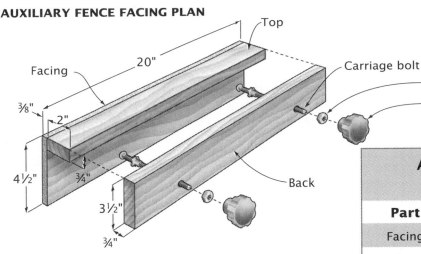

**AUXILIARY FENCE FACING Cutting List**

| Part | Qty. | Dimensions | Material |
|------|------|------------|----------|
| Facing | 1 | ⅜" × 4½" × 20" | Hardboard |
| Top | 1 | ¾" × 2" × 20" | Hardwood |
| Back | 1 | ¾" × 3½" × 20" | Hardwood |
| **Hardware** | | | |

2 T-nuts, ¼"-20

2 carriage bolts, ¼"-20 × 3"

2 hex nuts, ¼"-20

2 knurled plastic knobs, ¾" dia. with ¼"-20 × ⁵⁄₁₆" blind brass insert; #DK-42 from Reid Tool Supply Co. (800-253-0421)

Drywall screws, #6 × 1"

## CLAMP ASSEMBLY DETAIL

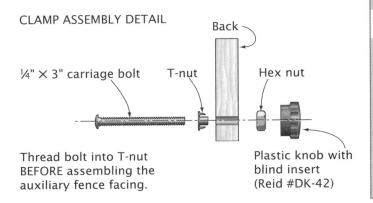

¼" × 3" carriage bolt    T-nut    Hex nut

Plastic knob with blind insert (Reid #DK-42)

Thread bolt into T-nut BEFORE assembling the auxiliary fence facing.

# Cutting a Drawer Lock Joint

Is the principal appeal of this joint the speed with which it is made? Or is it the strength of the assembled joint? While you are working, you'll be pleased at how quickly the work progresses. But after the drawers are assembled, you'll be impressed with how strong they are. So really, it's both.

**1. Set up the router table.** Chuck the ⅛-inch slot cutter in the table-mounted router. Adjust the bit extension so the top edge of the cutting teeth is ⅜ inch above the tabletop.

Bring the fence into position around the cutter. The typical slot cutter makes a ½-inch-deep slot, which is what you want. So position the fence so it will permit this depth of cut.

**2. Install the auxiliary facing on the fence.** Drop the auxiliary facing over the fence's vertical face. The gap between the facing's bottom edge and the tabletop is important. It must be 3/16 to ¼ inch greater than the thickness of the drawer front, since the front must pass beneath it on the first two passes. You can measure the distance with a ruler, or cobble up a couple of spacers. In either case, adjust the facing position and tighten the clamps to secure the auxiliary facing.

**3. Cut the joint.** As shown in the drawing *Routing Sequence,* each joint is cut in four passes. The drawer front is cut first, and three passes are required to complete the joinery on one end. On the fourth pass, the drawer side is slotted. Here are the four passes:

1. With the drawer front flat on the router table top, its exposed face up, slot the end.
2. To raise the workpiece for a second pass, set it on the booster sled. The orientation remains the same. This pass will widen the slot to ¼ inch.
3. Set the sled aside, and stand the workpiece on end with the exposed face out. Slide the workpiece along the auxiliary facing, and trim the slot's wall. This completes the drawer front.
4. Slot the drawer side. Stand the workpiece on end, and feed it along the auxiliary fence to make this cut.

When the two parts are assembled, you have a drawer lock joint.

When making a case full of drawers, it is most expeditious to make the first pass on both ends of each drawer front (and back). Then set the sled on the tabletop and make the second pass on all the pieces. Set the sled aside and complete the fronts (and backs). Set them aside and do the sides.

This approach keeps the work and the routine organized, and minimizes the number of times you fetch and set aside the sled.

**ROUTING SEQUENCE**

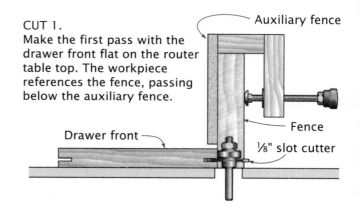

CUT 1.
Make the first pass with the drawer front flat on the router table top. The workpiece references the fence, passing below the auxiliary fence.

Auxiliary fence
Drawer front
Fence
⅛" slot cutter

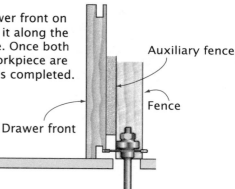

CUT 2.
Place the drawer front on top of the hardboard booster sled and make the second pass. Again, the workpiece is against the fence, below the auxiliary fence.

Auxiliary fence
Fence
Booster sled — Drawer front

CUT 3.
Stand the drawer front on end, and slide it along the auxiliary fence. Once both ends of the workpiece are cut, the front is completed.

Auxiliary fence
Fence
Drawer front

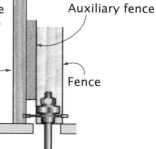

CUT 4.
Slot the drawer side with the workpiece on end and referencing the auxiliary fence.

Auxiliary fence
Fence
Drawer side

# Offset Baseplate

**Are you on the edge? Tense and sweating, teetering, slipping? This outrigger baseplate makes edge-routing more trouble-free by helping you maintain a router's balance.**

So many router operations involve shaping an edge. You perch the machine on the work, but more than half of it is unsupported. Okay, maybe you keep the handles aligned with the edge of the cut. But as often as not, you've got one handle over the work, the other out there in "unsupported" territory. It's a balancing act.

So is it any wonder you occasionally bobble, tipping the router and sniping the edge?

An offset baseplate like this can help you prevent those bobbles. Its oblong shape changes a router's balance. It has a hefty knob at its farthest reach, so you can out-leverage the bobble.

The baseplate is a fairly simple project. If you are not too particular about the detailing, you can cut to the chase, and simply cut a piece of plastic to shape, drill the necessary holes, and mount it on your router. But to produce a precision offset baseplate, one you can use for template work, for example, you should make a template, then make the baseplate from the template.

A benefit of the template approach is that you can easily make more than one baseplate. You can make one baseplate configured to accept template guides, and another to accept fairly large-diameter profile bits.

In the following step-by-step, I'll quickly talk you through the template approach. If you choose to skip the template, go right ahead. Just lay out the baseplate directly on the plastic's masking paper, and work from there. If you aren't completely sure of the procedures, I would encourage you to read through the chapter "The Generic Baseplate" on page 63. It provides a more thorough and detailed sequence for making and fitting a baseplate to a router.

The drawings show two different sizes of offset baseplates. Either one can be made from the nominal foot-square pieces of plastic (acrylic, polycarbonate, and phenolic) that are available from mail-order woodworking sources. The larger baseplate you lay out on a diagonal, as you can see in the drawing, while the smaller one is oriented on the workpiece from side to side.

## Make the Baseplate

Although installing the knob is the last thing you do, *ordering* it is the very first thing you should do. With the hardware in hand, you can make and complete the offset baseplate in just an hour or two.

**1. Cut the template blank.** I used medium-density fiberboard (MDF) for the template because it is smooth and

## OFFSET BASEPLATE LAYOUT VERSION 1.0

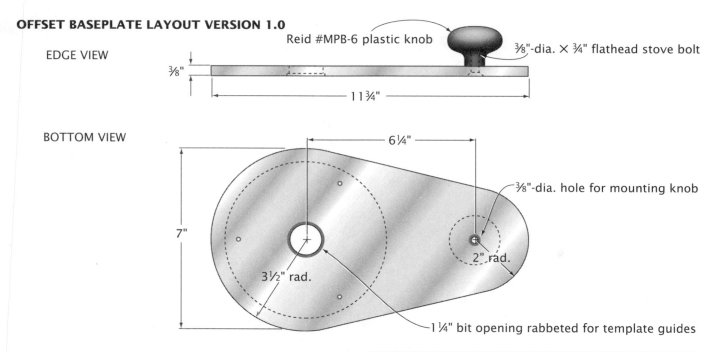

EDGE VIEW

Reid #MPB-6 plastic knob

⅜"-dia. × ¾" flathead stove bolt

⅜"

11¾"

BOTTOM VIEW

6¼"

⅜"-dia. hole for mounting knob

7"

2" rad.

3½" rad.

1¼" bit opening rabbeted for template guides

flat, with a consistent, void-free core and a relatively low price. You can use plywood, so long as it is free of voids, or particleboard. Cut the blank to the dimensions specified by the Cutting List.

**2. Lay out the baseplate on the blank.** Follow the appropriate *Offset Baseplate Layout* drawing. "Appropriate" means: Use version 1.0 for the smaller baseplate, version 2.0 for the larger.

With a compass, scribe a 7-inch-diameter circle at one end of the blank, a 4-inch-diameter circle at the other end. Use a straightedge to guide to scribing of tangents connecting the two circles. Be sure you clearly mark the centerpoints of the circles.

### Cutting List

| Part | Qty. | Dimensions | Material |
|------|------|-----------|----------|
| Template | 1 | ½" × 7" × 14½" | MDF |
| Baseplate | 1 | ⅜" × 11¾" × 11¾" | Plastic* |

### Hardware

1 mushroom-shaped plastic knob, 2½" dia. with ⅜" threaded insert; #MPB-6 from Reid Tool Supply Co. (800-253-0421)

1 flathead stove bolt, ⅜" dia. × ¾"

*Acrylic, polycarbonate, and phenolic are all suitable.*

## LAYOUT OPTIONS

Nominal 12" square of plastic

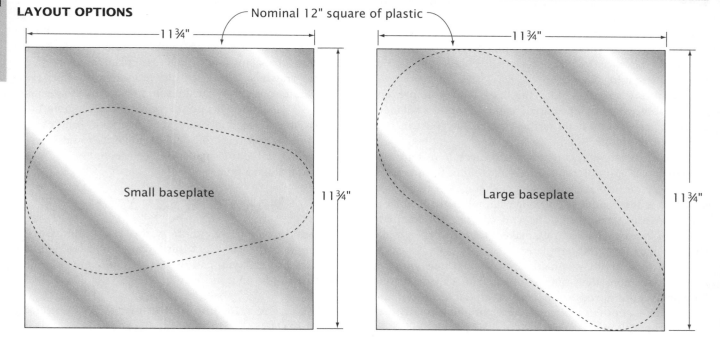

11¾"

11¾"

Small baseplate

11¾"

11¾"

11¾"

Large baseplate

11¾"

## OFFSET BASEPLATE LAYOUT VERSION 2.0

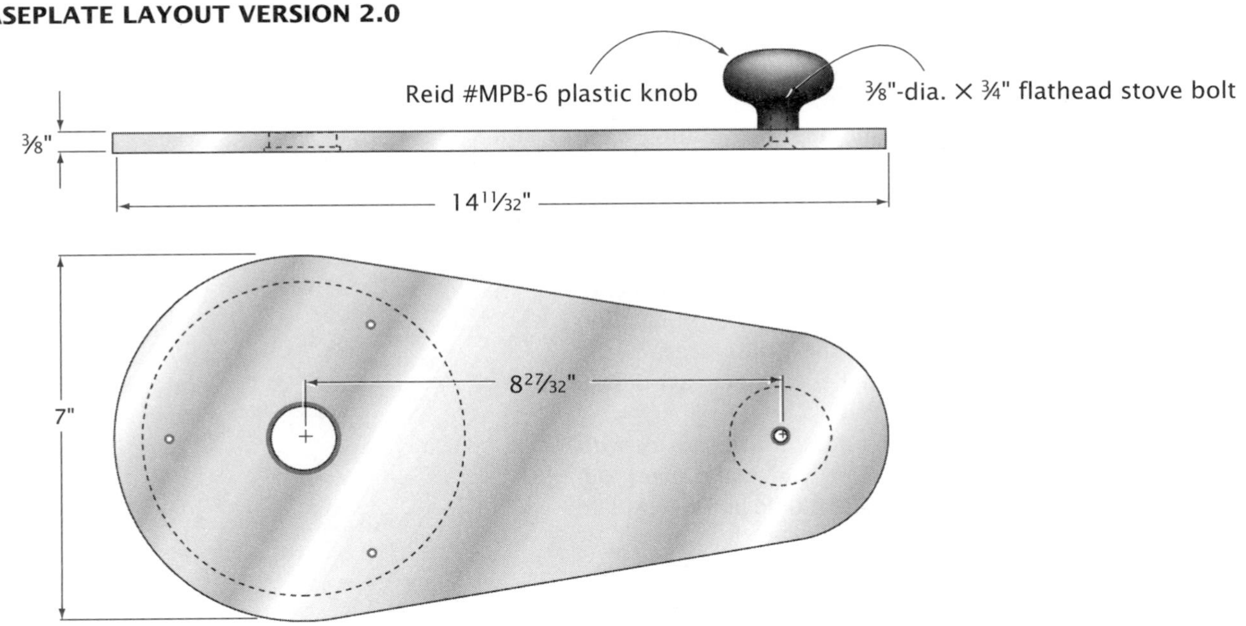

Reid #MPB-6 plastic knob

⅜"-dia. × ¾" flathead stove bolt

⅜"

14¹¹⁄₃₂"

7"

8²⁷⁄₃₂"

**3. Cut out the template.** Use a saber saw or band saw to cut out the baseplate shape.

For the best appearance of the finished baseplate, the template edges must be smooth and fair. I've found that a smooth file is useful in fairing the edges. A portable belt sander is a bit aggressive and difficult to control for something like this, I think, but give it a try if you want. After filing the edges, smooth them with a random-orbit or pad sander.

**4. Bore the holes.** To lay out the mounting-screw holes, use the router's baseplate. Stick two or three small pieces of carpet tape on the router's factory baseplate, line it up on the template, then press it firmly in place. It would be cool, of course, to have the bit axis match the centerpoint of the larger circle, but that alignment may be a bit hard to achieve. In the real world, that match is immaterial.

What is significant is the orientation of the router's handles. The drawing *Handle Orientation* shows the two principal alignments. I like the top one, but you suit yourself. Just align the baseplate on the template so the handles will be where you want them.

Drill holes for the mounting screws, guided by the baseplate. Countersink these holes. Drill a ⅜-inch-diameter hole at the centerpoint of the small arc. This is for the knob's mounting bolt.

**5. Lay out and bore the bit opening.** Fit a V-grooving bit in the router's collet. Mount the template on the router. Don't even plug the router in. Bring the tip of the bit in contact with the baseplate, and turn the bit a couple of revolutions with your hand to make the center of the bit mark the centerpoint.

Remove the template from the router, and bore a 1½-inch-diameter hole though the template. Be sure the hole is centered on the mark made by the bit.

**HANDLE ORIENTATION**

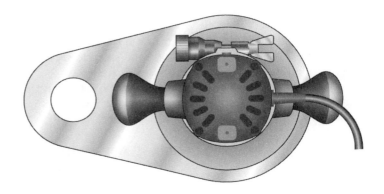

**6. Make the baseplate.** Use carpet tape to bond the template to the square of plastic you've selected for the baseplate. (The appendix has information on the suitable plastics that may help you decide which to use.)

Drill the holes first. Do the mounting-screw holes and the knob-mounting bolt hole. Countersink all the holes.

Rout the bit opening, using a straight bit and a template guide. To make a bit opening for standard Porter-Cable-type template guides, rout a 1¼-inch hole clear through the mounting plate, using a ⅜-inch straight bit in a ⅝-inch-O.D. template guide. Then switch to a ½-inch straight bit in the same template guide, and rabbet the hole. Measure the flange on a guide bushing, and rout the rabbet that depth. It's usually about ³⁄₃₂ inch, but check.

If you want a bit opening of a different size, work with other bit/bushing combinations. You can make many different sizes of holes, using that 1½-inch hole in the template as a guide.

Finally, using a pattern bit or flush-trimming bit in your router, trim the mounting plate to size. Pry the template and the mounting plate apart; this is when the masking paper comes off the mounting plate. Attach the plate to the router.

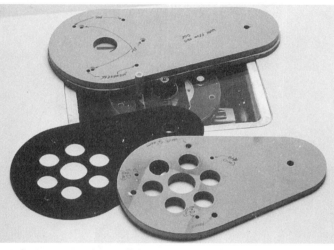

**Using a template** allows you to make multiples quickly and easily. Stick the baseplate material to the template, and feed it around a flush-trimming bit on the router table. You can even adapt a template to more than one model of router, and to both opaque and clear materials.

**7. Install the offset knob.** I selected a mushroom-style plastic knob from the Reid Tool Supply catalog. The design comfortably offsets the grip from the baseplate. Any number of other styles would work, and suitable styles can be found in many woodworking supply catalogs.

The particular knob I chose has ⅜-inch threaded insert, so the knob is attached with a ¾-inch-long flathead stove bolt.

## Using the Offset Baseplate

You probably won't have a great deal of difficulty figuring out how to use your newly made offset baseplate. The most obvious use is in routing edges, as noted at the outset. Just keep the auxiliary knob over the workpiece, and keep a hand on it as you maneuver the router.

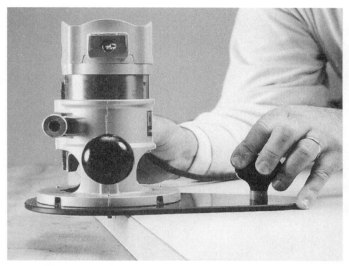

**Troublefree edge-routing** is what the offset baseplate virtually guarantees. Just a light touch on the baseplate's knob counteracts the router's tendency to topple off the work.

## Offset Baseplate on a D-Handled Router

If you are partial to D-handled routers, as I am, you may appreciate this little tip. Make an offset baseplate without an auxiliary knob. Extend the offset under the D-handle. It's a "transparent" modification to the router in most circumstances—you just don't realize it's there.

But when you need that extra baseplate area, you simply shift the position of the router, putting the extra surface where it will do the most good.

# Flush-Trimming Baseplate

**Make an old standard out of contemporary, high-tech materials. It's extra slick, extra tough.**

This is a basic fixture in any router magician's bag o' tricks. What you see is not a revolutionary new design, but a contemporary version of an old standard. What I've done is tweaked the design to extend the reach of the router bit and used high-quality materials that make the fixture smooth-operating and long-lasting.

There are many approaches to flush-trimming jobs, but this baseplate is a great general-purpose fixture because it trims the surface upon which it rests. It's the baseplate I use, for example, to trim wooden edge-banding or plugs concealing screws. The design shines especially brightly when nosing into edge-banded corners, where other flush-trimming approaches generally falter.

The trick is the two-layered design. The router is attached to the upper layer, which I call the sole. Attached to the sole's bottom surface is a shorter layer, which I call the heel. The heel raises the router ⅜ inch above the work surface so it can clear protrusions. The bit extends below the router, set just clear of the work surface, where it engages those protrusions and shears them off. Because the heel is angled back sharply from the bit, the bit can get into corners. As you work, the baseplate can slide onto the newly trimmed surface, and you extend the trimmed area even further.

Two different baseplate sizes are shown. One is for a laminate trimmer, the other for a regular fixed-base router.

## Making the Baseplate

Although the two baseplates are slightly different in configuration, the materials used and the construction sequence and procedures are the same for both.

**1. Cut the heel and sole plates.** I made my two flush-trimming baseplates (one for a laminate trimmer, one for a full-sized router) of plastic. For the laminate trimmer baseplate, I used two layers of ⅜-inch phenolic. Because of the design of the trimmer's base, using clear acrylic wasn't going to provide any more visibility. Clear acrylic does provide more visibility on the full-sized router's baseplate, so I did use it for the sole plate for that router.

Either baseplate, of course, can be made using acrylic or polycarbonate, if that's your preference, or even plywood, medium-density fiberboard (MDF), or hardboard.

If you don't mind wasting a couple of triangles of the plate stock, cut two pieces the same size, that being the dimensions of the sole plate. Any of the materials cited can be cut on the table saw. To trim the prow of the heel plate,

## FLUSH-TRIMMING BASEPLATE FOR LAMINATE TRIMMER

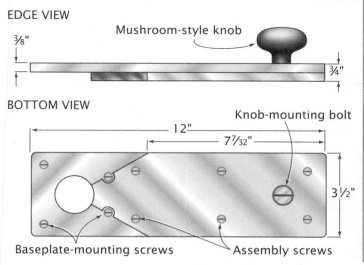

EDGE VIEW

3/8"

Mushroom-style knob

3/4"

BOTTOM VIEW

Knob-mounting bolt

12"

7 7/32"

3 1/2"

Baseplate-mounting screws

Assembly screws

### LAMINATE TRIMMER BASEPLATE
### Cutting List

| Part | Qty. | Dimensions | Material |
|------|------|------------|----------|
| Sole plate | 1 | 3/8" × 3 1/2" × 12" | Phenolic |
| Heel plate | 1 | 1/8" × 3 1/2" × 10 1/4" | Phenolic |

### Hardware

6 flathead machine screws, 10-24 × 3/4"

1 mushroom-style plastic knob, 2 1/32" dia. with 3/8" threaded insert; #MPB-6 from Reid Tool Supply Co. (800-253-0421)

2 plastic spacers, 1/2" O.D. × 3/8" I.D. × 3/16" thick

1 flathead stove bolt, 3/8" dia. × 1 1/2"

## PLATE LAYOUTS FOR LAMINATE TRIMMER

SOLE PLATE

3 1/2"

Mounting-screw holes; use factory baseplate as pattern.

3/8" phenolic

12"

7 3/4"

4 1/4"

3/4"

Assembly-screw holes, tapped for 10-24 machine screw

1 3/4"   3/4"

HEEL PLATE

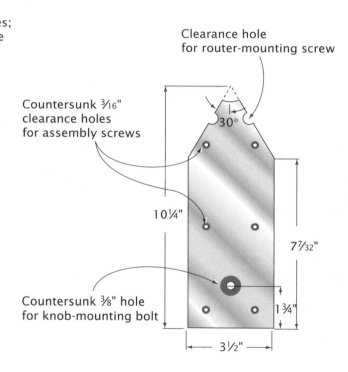

Clearance hole for router-mounting screw

Countersunk 3/16" clearance holes for assembly screws

30°

10 1/4"

7 7/32"

Countersunk 3/8" hole for knob-mounting bolt

1 3/4"

3 1/2"

set the saw's miter gauge to the angle specified in the layout drawings, and cut it to the length shown.

**2. Mount the sole on the router base.** This is a procedure detailed in the chapter "The Generic Baseplate," which begins on page 63. Basically, you use the factory baseplate as a pattern for drilling mounting-screw holes in the blank for the new baseplate. If at all possible, use flathead screws to attach the new baseplate to the router.

You may want to trim the plate to conform to the shape of the router base. The small plate was made for a DeWalt laminate trimmer, which has a square base; the plan reflects that configuration. The larger plate was rounded to match

the shape of a DeWalt DW 610 fixed-base router. To shape your baseplate, you can radius it with a router and trammel, or trim it with a flush-trimming bit, using the factory baseplate as a pattern.

You can mount the sole plate on the router base to check your work, but then remove the plate from the base. You can drill the bit opening now, or wait until the final step, which is what I did. If you do it now, you will later have to trim the tip from the heel plate.

**3. Lay out and drill the assembly-screw holes.** This is a key step, since the two plates are joined with machine screws. To drill the holes so they will line up

Flush-Trimming

## FIXED-BASE ROUTER BASEPLATE
### Cutting List

| Part | Qty. | Dimensions | Material |
|------|------|-----------|----------|
| Sole plate | 1 | $\frac{3}{8}$" × 6" × 11$\frac{3}{4}$" | Clear acrylic |
| Heel plate | 1 | $\frac{3}{8}$" × 6" × 8$\frac{3}{4}$" | Phenolic |

### Hardware

6 flathead machine screws, 10-24 × $\frac{3}{4}$"

1 mushroom-style plastic knob,
2$\frac{1}{32}$" dia. with $\frac{3}{8}$" threaded insert;
#MPB-6 from Reid Tool Supply Co. (800-253-0421)

2 plastic spacers, $\frac{1}{2}$" O.D. × $\frac{3}{8}$" I.D. × $\frac{3}{16}$" thick

1 flathead stove bolt, $\frac{3}{8}$" dia. × 1$\frac{1}{2}$"

## FLUSH-TRIMMING BASEPLATE FOR FULL-SIZED ROUTER

SIDE VIEW

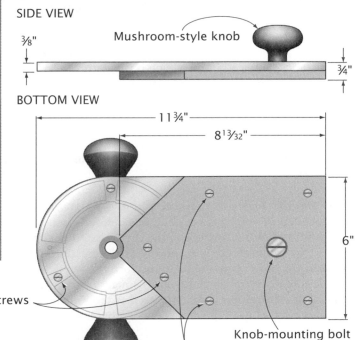

Mushroom-style knob

$\frac{3}{8}$"

$\frac{3}{4}$"

BOTTOM VIEW

11$\frac{3}{4}$"

8$\frac{13}{32}$"

6"

Baseplate-mounting screws

Knob-mounting bolt

Assembly screws

## PLATE LAYOUTS FOR FULL-SIZED ROUTER

SOLE PLATE

Countersunk $\frac{3}{16}$" holes
for mounting screws

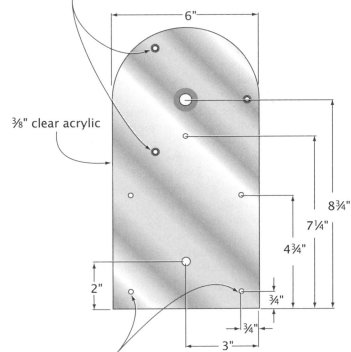

6"

$\frac{3}{8}$" clear acrylic

8$\frac{3}{4}$"

7$\frac{1}{4}$"

4$\frac{3}{4}$"

2"

$\frac{3}{4}$"

$\frac{3}{4}$"

3"

Assembly screw holes,
tapped for 10-24 machine screws

HEEL PLATE

$\frac{3}{8}$" clearance hole
for mounting screw

Countersunk $\frac{3}{16}$" holes
for assembly screws

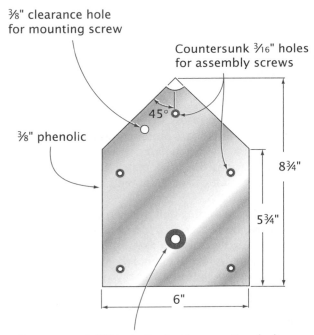

45°

$\frac{3}{8}$" phenolic

8$\frac{3}{4}$"

5$\frac{3}{4}$"

6"

Countersunk $\frac{3}{8}$" hole for knob-mounting bolt

perfectly for assembly, you must drill them in both plates simultaneously. Stick the two plates together with a couple small squares of carpet tape.

Lay out the locations of the screw holes. If you are using black phenolic, mark the spots with a punch or awl. Drill the holes with a #25 drill, which is the correct size for tapping 10-24 threads. Drill the holes on the drill press so they will be square.

If the heel plate covers any mounting-screw holes in the sole plate, you will need to drill clearance holes through the heel plate. Now is the time to locate these holes. Guided by the mounting-screw holes in the sole plate, drill through the heel plate.

**4. Tap the holes in the sole plate.** Use a 10-24 tap. The procedure, if you've never done this before, is detailed in the feature "Cutting Threads" in the appendix. Chuck the tap in a tap wrench. Apply the appropriate lubricant to the tap, insert the tap's tip in the hole, and turn the wrench to start the threads. Make sure the tap is square to the plate. Each couple of turns, back the tap up a quarter- to half-turn to break up the chips. Tap all of the assembly holes in the sole plate.

**5. Redrill and countersink the holes in the heel plate.** The holes in the heel plate are too small for the assembly screws. Drill them with a 3/16 bit, then countersink them. Be sure to bore the countersinks into the surface of the plate that was exposed when you drilled the holes in Step 3. (If you make the countersinks in the wrong side, the holes probably won't line up when you try to assemble the plates.) Bore the countersinks deep enough that the screw heads will seat below the plate surface.

If you have clearance holes to drill for router-mounting screws, do that now. Measure the screw head, and bore a slightly larger hole in the heel plate.

**6. Assemble the baseplate.** This is as simple as driving a few screws. Place the two plates together, insert a 3/4-inch-long 10-24 flathead machine screw into each assembly-screw hole, and tighten it with a screwdriver.

**7. Mount the knob.** I used a mushroom-shaped knob with a 3/8-inch insert. It is mounted on the baseplate with a 3/8-inch-diameter, 1½-inch-long flathead stove bolt. To elevate the knob from the plate, I used a couple of 3/16-inch-thick plastic spacers bought at the local hardware store.

Drill the mounting-bolt hole, then countersink it. A 3/8-inch stove bolt has a darn big head, so a big countersink is required. You may be able to substitute a large V-grooving bit in a plunge router for this job. Again, the countersink must be deep enough that the bolt head seats below the plate surface.

**8. Bore the bit opening.** Depending on the router, you can, with caution, bore the bit opening with it. Chuck the bit in the router, then screw the plate to the router.

Clamp the plate on top of scrap. Switch on the router, and work the cutting depth adjustment mechanism to plunge and retract the bit, thus cutting the opening.

An alternative approach, one that I used, is to bore the opening with a Forstner bit or a hole saw.

**Dress up the rough baseplate edges.** Round the square corners with a roundover bit in a table-mounted router. Stand the baseplate on edge, and back it up with a scrap pusher. To make the cut, feed it along the fence and across the bit.

## Using the Baseplate

Which baseplate to use? The one that fits your router, of course. But if you have a laminate trimmer, I'd recommend that router for this work. It's light and maneuverable. Either way, large or small, the baseplates are used in the same way.

**1. Set up the router.** Remove the factory baseplate, and replace it with the flush-trimming baseplate.

Select an appropriate bit, and chuck it in the router. Depending upon the router, you can use a bottom-cleaning bit, a dado-cleanup bit, a dish cutter, or a mortising bit. All of these are designed for shearing the surface at the bit's tip. You can also use a straight bit.

Adjust the cutting depth by bottoming the bit on a sheet of paper. That means your bit will be a few thousandths shy of the working surface. (My dial calipers tell me that a sheet of typical copier paper is 0.005 inch thick.) This setting will keep the bit from gouging or scuffing a slightly uneven surface, yet allow it to pare the real protrusions. After you trim with this setup, a hit with a sander should bring the surface dead flush.

**2. Trim the nonflush stuff.** Before switching on the router, take note of the machine's balance. Though these plastic baseplates seem to be pretty well balanced, the general tendency with such baseplates is for the machine to tip onto the bit. My point here is that you need to keep the router upright by pressing down on the baseplate's offset knob. Otherwise, the bit will gouge the workpiece.

With one hand pressing down on the knob, switch on the router. Move the router toward the protrusion.

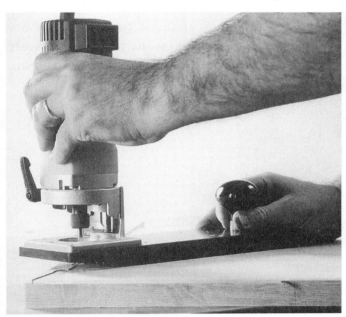

**Equipped with the flush-trimming baseplate,** a laminate trimmer can work places that a piloted flush-trimming bit can't reach. That's because the machine rests on the working surface, and its bit pares away any high spots or ridges. Thus, when trimming edge-banding, as shown, it can cut into both inside and outside corners.

Depending upon what needs to be trimmed, you may slide the router and baseplate sideways, or you may just swing the router in an arc around the knob. Basically, you want to sweep the protrusions off the workpiece. Don't allow the bit to dwell too long in any one spot.

With a little practice, you'll develop a routine and a feel for the movements that contribute to splintering and tear-out.

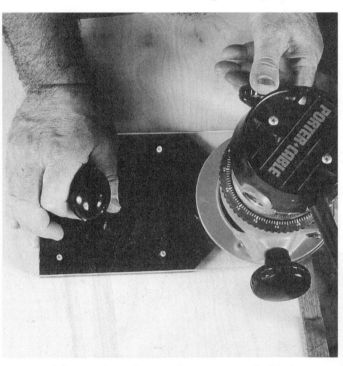

**To avoid gouging the work,** you must hold the router upright by pressing down firmly with one hand at the end of the baseplate extension. Use your other hand to slide the router along the ridge of material to be routed away.

Flush-Trimming

# Mortising Jig

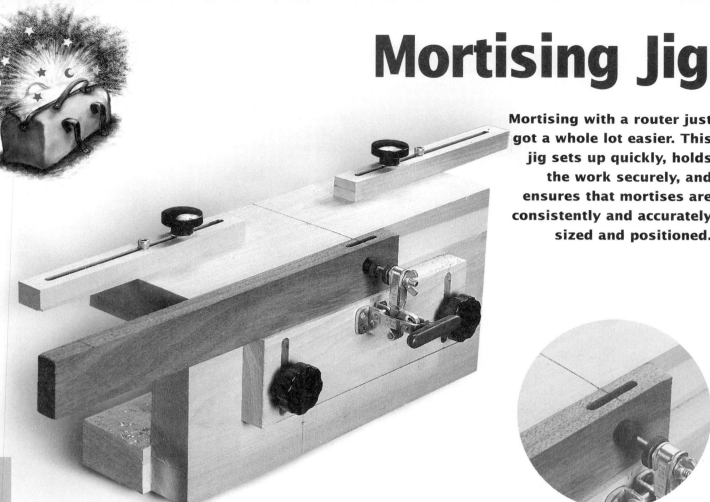

**Mortising with a router just got a whole lot easier. This jig sets up quickly, holds the work securely, and ensures that mortises are consistently and accurately sized and positioned.**

The biggest single challenge in mortising with a plunge router is holding the workpiece while simultaneously supporting and guiding the router. This jig meets the challenge head-on. It is simple to make, easy to set up, and a snap to use.

The mortise-and-tenon is woodworking's essential frame joint, you know. So if you are going to grow as a woodworker and develop your skills, you have to master the making of the mortise-and-tenon joint.

The basic elements are the mortise, which is a hole—round, square, or rectangular—and the tenon, which is a tongue cut on the end of the joining member to fit the mortise. Once assembled with glue or pegs, the mortise-and-tenon joint resists all four types of stress—tension, compression, shear, and racking. And it does it better than any other type of joint.

The main advantages of the router for mortising include the smoothness of its finished cuts and the accuracy of placement and sizing that's possible. The only disadvantage that comes to mind is the limited reach of the router bit. A narrow, deep mortise—¼ inch wide × 1¾ inches or more deep, for example—is problematic for a router. The machine can do it, but its cutters can't. (Given the strength of modern glues, however, even a shallow mortise makes a strong joint.) A plunge router, a spiral or straight bit, and an edge guide will handle most of the mortising you'll *ever* want to do.

To rout a mortise, the first thing you must do is cobble up a mortising jig to hold the workpiece.

The original version of this jig was conceived and built by Ken Burton, Jr., one of Rodale's woodworking book editors. Ken's jig has that real-world look: It's made of scrap wood, not first-class material. It has lots of extra holes, the reminders of, among other things, stops that have been repositioned. There are layout markings left from projects past.

My duplicate, shown in the photos, is a little different, primarily in the hardware and the quality of the material I used. (We want these jigs to *look* good as well as work properly.)

The jig does several things. It

- holds one workpiece at a time so handling is minimized;
- holds the workpiece securely so it doesn't move as you rout;
- allows you to switch workpieces quickly, positioning them consistently;
- provides adequate bearing surface, so no cut is compromised by a router tip or wobble;
- enables you to position the cut consistently from mortise to mortise;
- controls the length of the cut.

Best of all, it's easy to make.

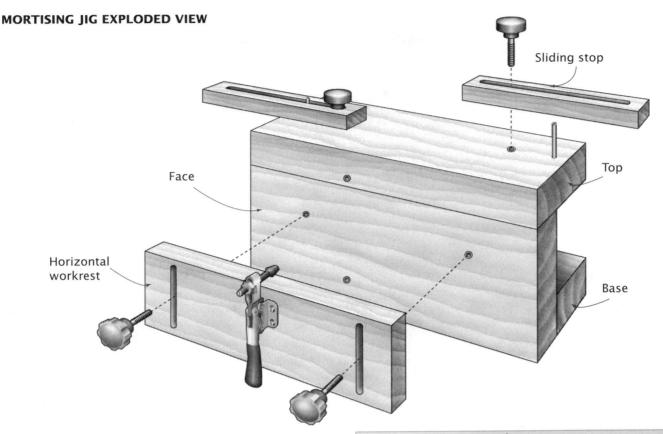

Sliding stop

Face

Top

Horizontal
workrest

Base

## Building the Jig

A reminder to collect all the necessary hardware before you begin is, to me, always appropriate. Some of the hardware can be picked up at the local hardware store. But the jig won't work without the toggle clamps, and it is likely you will have to order them. At the same time, order the plastic knobs. When the stuff arrives, get to work on the jig.

**1. Cut the body parts.** The jig's body, formed of the top, face, and base, is made of thick hardwood. Ken used 1⅜-inch maple; I used 1¾-inch poplar. Use what you have or can get your hands on economically. While the material you use should be somewhere in the 1⅜ to 1¾ realm, the specific thickness of the parts is relatively unimportant. (But remember to adjust dimensions if you do deviate from the 1¾-inch thickness shown in the various drawings.)

Joint and thickness 8/4 (eight-quarter) hardwood to 1¾ inches. Rip and crosscut the body's components to the dimensions specified by the Cutting List.

**2. Glue up the jig body.** Just glue the top to the edge of the face, and glue the bottom to the back of the face, as indicated in the drawing *Plan Views*. There are no special tricks here, but do try to keep the body square as you apply the clamps.

After the glue has cured and the clamps have been removed, scrape off any dried squeeze-out. Then joint the face and top to make these surfaces absolutely square to one another. This is critical.

### Cutting List

| Part | Qty. | Dimensions | Material |
|------|------|-----------|----------|
| Top | 1 | 1¾" × 4¾" × 15½" | Hardwood |
| Face | 1 | 1¾" × 6" × 15½" | Hardwood |
| Base | 1 | 1¾" × 3" × 15½" | Hardwood |
| Horizontal workrest | 1 | 1" × 3¼" × 10½" | Hardwood |
| Vertical workrest | 1 | 1" × 2½" × 7" | Hardwood |
| Sliding stops | 2 | ¾" × 1" × 9" | Hardwood |

### Hardware

2 plastic knobs, 1¾" dia. with ⅜"-16 × 1½" steel stud; #DK-29 from Reid Tool Supply Co. (800-253-0421)

4 brass threaded inserts, ⅜"-16

2 plastic knobs, 1⅜" dia. with ¼"-20 × 1½" steel stud; #DK-20 from Reid Tool Supply Co.

2 brass threaded inserts, ¼"-20

1 toggle clamp (De-Sta-Co #TC-215-U)

4 panhead screws, #8 × ¾"

2 hex-head bolts, ¼" × 1¼"

Make sure the front and back edges of the top are parallel. This too is critical. If necessary, rip the back edge to *make* it parallel.

Mortising

TOP VIEW

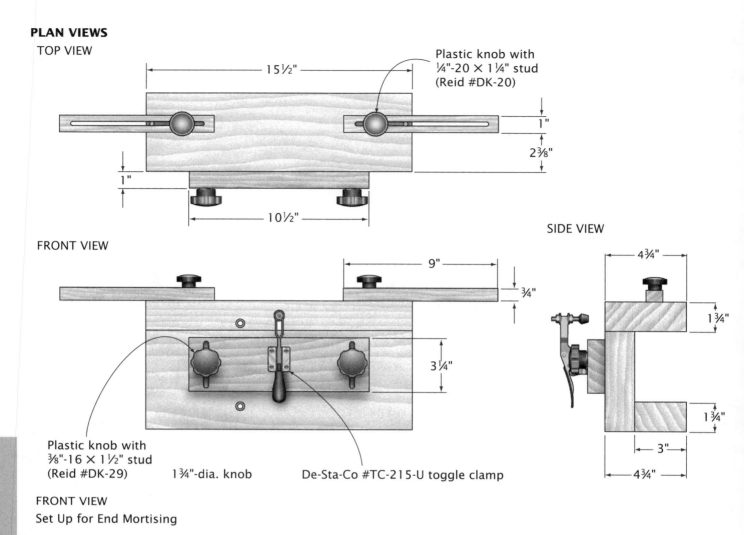

Plastic knob with
¼"-20 × 1¼" stud
(Reid #DK-20)

15½"

1"

2⅜"

1"

10½"

SIDE VIEW

FRONT VIEW

9"

¾"

3¼"

4¾"

1¾"

1¾"

3"

4¾"

Plastic knob with
⅜"-16 × 1½" stud
(Reid #DK-29)

1¾"-dia. knob

De-Sta-Co #TC-215-U toggle clamp

FRONT VIEW
Set Up for End Mortising

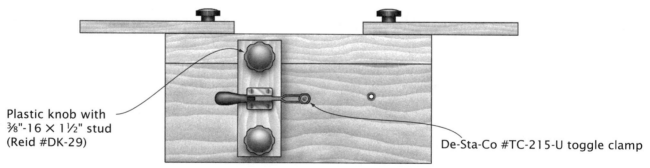

Plastic knob with
⅜"-16 × 1½" stud
(Reid #DK-29)

De-Sta-Co #TC-215-U toggle clamp

While it's not essential, you may want to score a center-line across the top. I find the centerline helps in setting up the jig at the beginning of each mortising project. Just measure 7¾ inches from either end of the jig, and square a line across the top. I used a utility knife to score a shallow V-groove, then inked in the line with an fine-tipped red marker.

**3. Install the threaded inserts.** Lay out locations of the threaded inserts in the face and top, as well as the two holes for the sliding-stop locating pins. The spots are shown in the drawing *Parts Layouts.*

*A couple of caveats:* In use, the sliding stops should contact the edge-guide rods. It is a good idea to set your plunge router—fitted with its edge guide—on the jig, and see if you need to tailor your jig to accommodate your router. If the rods aren't long enough, you will want to rip the jig top to make it narrower. And if the sliding stops, as positioned in the plans, touch the router rather than squarely contacting the rods, you will want to move them.

The locating-pin holes are ¼ inch in diameter. Drill them about 1 inch deep.

Drill pilots for the threaded inserts next. In the top are the two inserts for the sliding stops. In the face, there are two holes for the horizontal workrest and two for the vertical workrest. If you don't know what diameter hole to

## PARTS LAYOUTS

### TOP

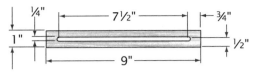

¼"-20 threaded insert

¼"-dia. × ¾" deep hole for locating pin

4¾"

¾"    2½"

15½"

### FACE

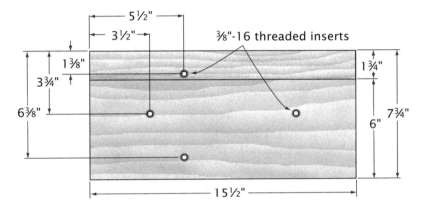

5½"

3½"

⅜"-16 threaded inserts

1⅜"

3¾"

6⅜"

1¾"

6"    7¾"

15½"

### SLIDING STOP

¼"

7½"

¾"

1"

½"

9"

### VERTICAL WORKREST

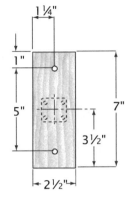

1¼"

1"

5"

7"

3½"

2½"

### HORIZONTAL WORKREST

1"

5¼"

¾"

⅜"

2½"

3¼"

⅜"

10½"

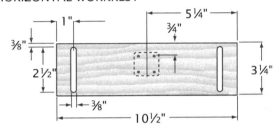

bore for the inserts, measure the root diameter of one with dial calipers. (The root diameter is the diameter of the shank inside the threads.) Note that there are two different sizes of inserts required.

After the holes are bored, drive the inserts. You don't need an expensive insert tool; use a nut and bolt and a wrench. Turn the nut onto the bolt, then add the insert. Jam the nut down against the insert, and start turning the insert into the pilot hole. Once you get the insert started, use the wrench on the nut to turn the assembly.

**4. Make the workrests.** The Cutting List specifies the thickness of the workrests at 1 inch; make them thicker or thinner, as you wish. But in any case, the slots in the horizontal rest are easiest to rout, I think, if you work with a wide board rather than one that's already ripped to finished width.

Rip a board to a width of about 6 inches, and crosscut it to a 10½-inch length. Lay out both the horizontal and vertical rests on it. Rout the slots with a plunge router equipped with an edge guide. Bore the holes in the vertical rest. Rip the two rests from the board, and crosscut the vertical rest to length.

**5. Install the toggle clamps.** Lay out the position of the toggle clamp on each rest. Drill pilot holes and fasten a clamp to each rest with four screws. No, you don't really need two clamps; you can easily work with one clamp,

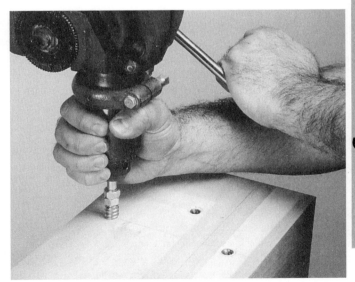

**Use your drill press to drive threaded inserts.**
With the insert threaded onto a bolt, and the bolt chucked in a drill press, it is easy to drive the insert square to the face of the jig. DON'T turn the drill press on; turn the chuck by hand as you advance the quill. Turn two hex nuts onto the bolt and tighten one against the other, jamming them so neither will turn. Turn the insert into the bolt next. The jam nuts prevent the insert from working its way up the bolt as you turn the drill chuck.

**The slots in the horizontal workrest** can be routed with a plunge router with an edge guide, as shown. Work with a wider board than needed, so the router will be adequately supported, then rip it to the final width.

attaching it to whichever rest you are using. Bear in mind, too, that you may need to shift the position of the toggle clamp, depending upon the width of the workpiece being mortised, so its spindle doesn't interfere with the router. Panhead screws lend a stylish appearance to the jig (and I listed them in the Hardware List), but 1-inch drywall screws are more real-world.

**6. Make the sliding stops.** As with the rests, the stops are best made from a workpiece that's bigger than the finished stop. Lay out a stop along each edge of a 4- or 5-inch-wide board, and clamp it to the workbench so the areas to be slotted extend off the bench edge. With a plunge router equipped with a edge guide, cut the slots.

Crosscut the board to length, and rip the stops.

**7. Install the workrest and the stops.** Each workrest is attached to the jig body with studded plastic knobs turned into the appropriate threaded inserts.

The sliding stops are similarly attached. To keep each stop aligned, I used a hex-head bolt as a locating pin, inserting it through the slot into the appropriate hole in the jig top. Ken used dowels for this purpose but then glued them into the holes. Leaving the pins—whether bolts or dowels—loose allows you to sand or joint the jig top to "refresh" that surface. (For the sake of your jointer knives, make sure the inserts are sunk well below the surface before doing this.)

## Using the Jig

The jig is really quite easy to set up and use. Don't be put off by the number of steps. Most take but a moment or two to accomplish.

**1. Lay out a mortise.** Use a scrap of the working stock, and outline the mortise exactly where it is to be cut. Mark the centerline across the mortise.

**2. Clamp the jig to a workbench.** Set the jig at the edge of the workbench, and clamp it with a couple of C-clamps or quick-action bar clamps.

**3. Set the workrest and toggle clamp.** Adjust the workrest so the workpiece will be flush with the top of the jig. If you are using the horizontal rest, make sure it is parallel to the top. If you are using the vertical rest, make sure it's perpendicular to the top.

Adjust the spindle on the toggle clamp as necessary. The clamp should snap smartly and hold the workpiece securely.

**4. Clamp the workpiece to the jig.** Set the test piece on the rest, and line up the centerline of the mortise with the centerline scored across the jig. Snap the toggle clamp closed.

**5. Set the plunge depth stop.** Chuck the appropriate bit in your plunge router. Zero-out the depth scale, then set the depth stop for the depth of mortise you intend to rout.

**6. Adjust the edge guide.** Fit the edge guide to the router. Set the router on the jig, with the guide referencing the back edge of the top. Plunge the bit—with the router *unplugged,* of course—to the workpiece. With the edge guide loose on its rods, adjust the position of the router so the bit is centered within the mortise layout lines. Turn the bit by hand, and observe the cutting flutes to ensure that it really is centered. Slide the guide up against the jig's back edge, and tighten the locking knobs.

Move the router from side to side, with the guide firmly against the jig. The bit should remain centered within the mortise layout lines. If it does not, something is out of whack. Either the edges of the jig top are not parallel, or the faces of the test piece are not parallel, or the mortise layout is skewed.

**7. Adjust the sliding stops.** The lateral movement of the router is arrested when the edge guide rods contact the sliding stops. Move the router left or right to position the bit at the very end of the mortise. Slide the stop against the edge-guide rod on that side, and tighten its knob.

Slide the router so the bit is poised at the other end of the mortise. Bring the stop against that side's rod, and tighten the knob.

**8. Rout the test mortise.** With the workpiece clamped in the fixture, and with the router all set up, rout the mortise.

Plunge-cut the ends of the mortise first. Doing this ensures that the ends of the mortise will be vertical. Then rout out the waste between the ends in a series of passes.

When you cut, be sure you feed the router in the right direction, the one that uses the force of the bit rotation to pull the guide against the work. To do this, you've got to retract the bit between cutting passes. With the edge

## SETTING UP ROUTER AND STOPS

1. Set the workpiece on the workrest, lining up the centerline on it with the centerline on the jig.

2. Move the router to position the bit exactly between the layout lines for the mortise then lock down the edge guide.

3. Move the router to position the bit just inside the layout line at one end of the mortise and adjust the sliding stop against the edge guide's rod.

4. Move the router to position the bit just inside the layout line at the other end of the mortise and adjust the other sliding stop against the edge guide's other rod.

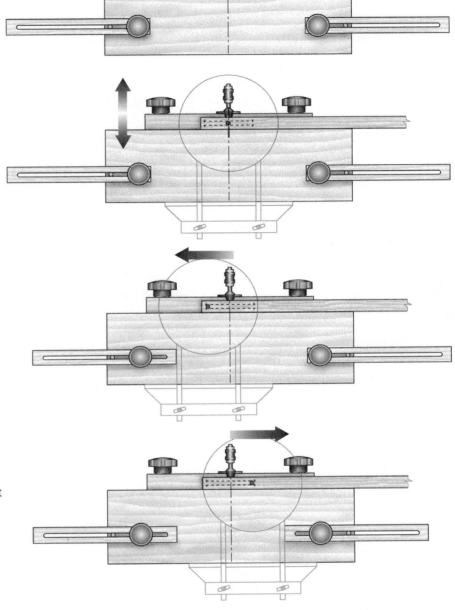

## MORTISE ROUTING SEQUENCE

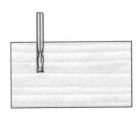

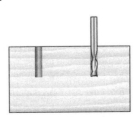

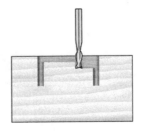

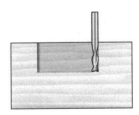

1. Plunge-bore one end of the mortise to the full depth.

2. Plunge-bore the other end to the full depth.

3. Rout the waste from between the two holes, nibbling about ¼" deeper with each pass.

4. Continue this process until the mortise is completed.

guide opposite you, riding along the jig top's back edge, you make the cutting pass by moving the router right to left. Then retract the bit clear of the work and slide the router back to the right. Then replunge the bit for another cutting pass.

**9. Pencil positioning marks on the jig.** Assuming the mortise test turns out just right, you have one more setup task to complete before tackling the actual workpieces. You need to decide what layout marks you will use to position the succession of workpieces being mortised.

**The essential layout mark** is the center (from end to end) of the mortise. There's a centermark on the jig, and you line up the layout mark on the workpiece with it. Because of how you've set up the jig and the router, the mortise will be perfectly positioned.

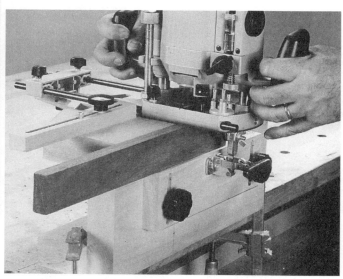

**Routing a mortise** calls for a series of light cuts. Plunge-bore the two ends first to establish the parameters of the finished mortise. Then plunge the bit about ¼ inch and make a pass, cutting from one end to the other. Retract the bit free of the work, and return to the starting point. Plunge a little deeper for the next pass. Repeat this routine until the mortise is cut to its final depth.

You DO NOT need to completely lay out each and every mortise!

You *can* mark the centerline of each mortise, then align the workpiece mark with the scored centerline on the jig. But it may be easier to lay out the ends of each mortise. Usually, you can measure and mark one workpiece, then stack all of them and transfer the marks with a square and a pencil.

Given this approach, you need to lightly pencil on the jig top the ends of the mortise. So before moving the test mortise, use a square and pencil to make these alignment marks on the jig top.

**Loose-tenon joints** are what the vertical workrest is for. To make a loose-tenon joint, you rout mortises in both rail and stile, then insert a separate piece as the tenon when the joint is assembled. Typically, the problem is holding the rail so a mortise can be routed into its end. As shown here, the vertical workrest solves that problem.

**Mortising a table leg** isn't any different, really, than mortising a door stile. The toggle clamp's spindle is easily adjusted to accommodate the greater thickness of the leg.

# Shop-Built Slot Mortiser

**With this fixture, you can use your plunge router to cut mortises—and to rout tenons, slots, and grooves, even to cut moldings and raise panels. It's a Marvelous Machine.**

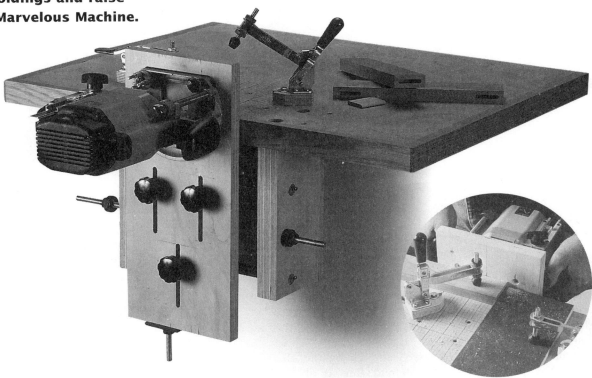

Faced with the need to cut hundreds of mortises, Bob Moran went shopping for a machine to do the job. He discovered, he says, "I had neither the money nor the space for a commercially made slot mortiser." After thinking it all over and listing his requirements and desires, Bob realized that he could better satisfy his needs by simply designing and building his own slot mortiser.

Bob built his fixture around a plunge router. The router is mounted horizontally on a plate that rides back and forth on shafts fixed to a bench. As I'll soon explain in detail, there are several adjustments you can make to control the depth, length, and position of a mortise. To cut a mortise, you clamp the workpiece to the workbench, then plunge the router and slide it along the mortiser's shafts.

Let me tell you, this is one slick-working device. The router and its mount roll effortlessly back and forth on those shafts. The fine adjustments possible are super-precise. Hung at the end of a workbench or the back of a router table, the mortiser doesn't take up valuable shop space. The router can be removed quickly and used for other jobs.

In the many years since Bob designed and built his Marvelous Mortiser, it has proven itself to be extremely reliable, accurate, and convenient. It even beats the commercial ones when mortising large, unwieldy stock because the stock itself is fixed during mortising.

Best of all, it isn't a one-job fixture. It can function in every way that a horizontal router table can. You can cut tenons on it. You can rout grooves and slots, you can raise panels, you can rout moldings.

## How It Works

To be effective, a slot mortiser needs to be able to move or be adjusted in three different directions:

1. in and out for the depth of cut;
2. side to side for the length of cut;
3. up and down for the height of cut.

Bob designed his slot mortiser with these movements in mind.

*In and Out:* The in-and-out movement is performed by the plunging action of the router. Mortise depth is controlled by the bit extension, which is governed by the router's own depth stops.

*Side to Side:* The router moves from side to side by means of three ball-bearing linear-motion pillow blocks that slide along two precision-ground steel shafts. The pillow

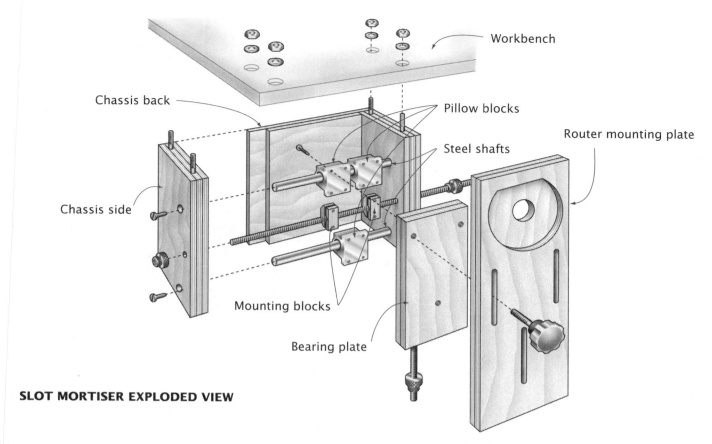

**Workbench**

**Chassis back**

**Pillow blocks**

**Steel shafts**

**Router mounting plate**

**Chassis side**

**Mounting blocks**

**Bearing plate**

**SLOT MORTISER EXPLODED VIEW**

Mortising

blocks are mounted on the back side of the bearing plate, and the router mounting board is attached to the front of that plate. The shafts are mounted within a chassis that is hung beneath a work surface.

Side-to-side travel is coarsely limited by the chassis sides. The maximum mortise length thus is about 4¼ inches (exact length also is affected by the bit diameter). Fine adjustment of lateral travel within that range is provided by stops on a threaded rod that extends from the bearing plate through holes in the chassis sides. Lateral movement halts when the stop contacts the chassis side. By adjusting the stops in and out on the rod, you control how far the router travels from side to side. By seating both stops against the chassis sides, you prevent lateral movement completely.

The stops are special disk-like nuts, often called check nuts by machinists. Because the adjustment rod has 16 threads per inch, the adjustment can be as fine as ¹⁄₆₄ inch. (A full turn moves the nut ¹⁄₁₆ inch, so a quarter-turn moves it only ¹⁄₆₄ inch.) Putting two check nuts together allows you to jam one against the other to hold a setting.

*Up and Down:* Vertical position of the router is established by the position of the router mounting board in relation to the bearing plate. The mounting board is secured to the plate with three plastic knobs with integral studs. The studs extend through slots in the board into inserts in the plate. To make a coarse vertical adjustment of the router, loosen the knobs and raise or lower the mounting board.

Fine vertical adjustment is made the same way lateral-travel adjustment is. A threaded rod projects from the bottom of the bearing plate. A check-nut stop on the rod

**Clear the workbench for other work** by pulling the mounting knobs and lifting the mounting board and router from the chassis. None of the vertical or lateral settings are lost when you do this, because you don't have to tamper with the check nuts to do it. With these parts removed, the mortiser no longer intrudes in the workspace. The chassis is out of the way beneath the bench top.

seats against a slotted plate screwed to the bottom of the router mounting plate. Turning the check nut (after the knobs are loosened) either forces the mounting board up or allows it to descend, thus adjusting the height of the router in increments as fine as 1/64 inch.

## Why It Works

I first read about Moran's Marvelous Mortiser in the pages of *American Woodworker*. When I started screening projects for this collection, it was one of the first that came to mind. After pawing over Bob's original, I set about making my own, except that I felt I could "improve" it.

What had rocked me about the Marvelous Mortiser was the cost of the parts. The particular pillow blocks and shafts Bob selected had cost him about $150 back in the '80s. (Of course, a commercial slot mortiser costs about 6 times that!) My "improvement" would be a "poor man's mortiser," made of standard birch plywood and

bronze bushings in place of the pillow blocks.

But when completed, the poor man's version was no improvement. While it cost significantly less, it took more time and considerably more practiced skills to build, and then it didn't work (which of course was the real killer).

This is a long way around to say two things:

1. The original mortiser is well designed.
2. You get what you pay for.

Bob chose the materials and hardware for specific qualities and characteristics. The high-quality plywood used costs more than standard birch plywood and is less widely available, but it has the stiffness needed to counter the different forces applied to the device during use. Standard birch plywood lacks that stiffness, and when you substitute it for the other, the mortiser you end up with isn't as rigid, and the cuts it makes are not as accurate in all situations.

## Cutting List

| Part | Qty. | Dimensions | Material |
|------|------|------------|----------|
| Router mounting plate plies | 2 | 1/2" × 8" × 18 1/4" | Baltic birch plywood |
| Chassis side plies | 6 | 1/2" × 5" × 10" | Baltic birch plywood |
| Chassis back ply | 1 | 1/2" × 12" × 10" | Baltic birch plywood |
| Chassis back ply | 1 | 1/2" × 9 1/4" × 10" | Baltic birch plywood |
| Bearing plate plies | 2 | 1/2" × 5" × 9" | Baltic birch plywood |
| Mounting blocks | 2 | 7/8" × 3/4" × 2" | Hardwood |
| Vertical-adjustment plate | 1 | 1/8" × 2" × 2 1/2" | Aluminum* |
| Toggle-clamp pads | 4 | 3/4" × 1 1/2" × 2 3/8" | Baltic birch plywood |

## Hardware

4 hex-head bolts, 5/16" × 3 1/2"

4 flat washers, 3/8" I.D.

4 hex nuts, 5/16"

3 knurled nuts, 3/8"-16;
#KN-1 from Reid Tool Supply Co. (800-253-0421)

3 check nuts, 3/8"-16; #V-4 from Reid Tool Supply Co.

3 threaded inserts, 5/16"-18;
#EZ-14 from Reid Tool Supply Co.

10 T-nuts, 1/4"-20

1 threaded rod, 3/8"-16 × 19"

1 threaded rod, 3/8"-16 × 6 1/4"

2 class "L" ground steel shafts, 3/4" × 12";
#QS 3/4" L 12 from Thomson Industries, Inc.
(800-554-8466 for name of a dealer)

3 linear-bearing pillow blocks;
#SPB 12 from Thomson Industries

4 panhead screws, #6 × 3/4"

drywall screws, #6 × 1 5/8"

18 panhead screws, #8 × 1"

16 panhead screws, #8 × 3/4"

3 plastic knobs with studs, 5/16"-18;
#DK-27 from Reid Tool Supply Co.

2 toggle clamps (De-Sta-Co #TL-235-U)

2 toggle clamps (De-Sta-Co #TL-225-U)

*You can also make this plate from 16-gauge steel, 3/8-inch or 1/2-inch plywood, or even phenolic.

Likewise, the pillow blocks Bob selected are specifically designed for *linear* motion. They have recirculating ball bearings, not bushings. They have efficient dust seals, which is important in a woodworking environment. They are perfectly matched to the precision-ground, hardened-steel shafts selected. Yes, they are costly (three blocks and two shafts cost us $170 in late 1995), but they are designed for exactly the kind of work they are doing. And let me tell you, as one who knows from experience: Because they fit the shafts, construction is *greatly* simplified.

## Building the Fixture

A selection of specialized hardware is required to build the mortiser. So the first step in construction should be the purchasing. You can endeavor to substitute for the parts I specify on the Hardware List (which is what my cohorts and I tried the first time around), or you can save yourself some trouble and just buy what I've put on the list.

Telephone-order the plastic knobs with studs and the two kinds of check nuts from Reid Tool Supply. If you can't find brass threaded inserts locally, order them from Reid, too.

Check the Yellow Pages for sources of bearings; then call and see if they stock or can order the required pillow blocks and shafts. Our local source had these parts in hand within a week of ordering them for us. Can't find a source

in the telephone book? Call the manufacturer, Thomson Industries (800-554-8466), for the name of a nearby dealer.

The remainder of the hardware on the list should be stocked by your local hardware store.

Finally, buy a piece of ½-inch Baltic Birch or Apple Ply plywood to use for the wooden structure of the mortiser. In most situations, this material is special-order, but it should be available. If you are stuck for a source, you can order it by mail from Boulter Plywood (617-666-1340) or M. L. Condon (914-946-4111).

## Making the Chassis

With the materials and hardware in hand, get busy in the shop. Build the chassis first, then the router mounting board.

**1. Cut the parts.** I recommended high-quality plywood to you for the wooden components. Here's why:

The plywoods I specified—Baltic Birch and Apple Ply—have a greater number of plies than standard birch plywood (in the ½-inch thickness, nine versus five). And the plies are all void-free. The result is a stiffer material. The key to success in combining precision components such as the linear-motion pillow blocks and steel shafts with a wooden chassis is to use a highly stable and very stiff wood product.

Bob built his mortiser using Baltic Birch plywood, glue-laminating four ¼-inch pieces to form the various

**Mortising**

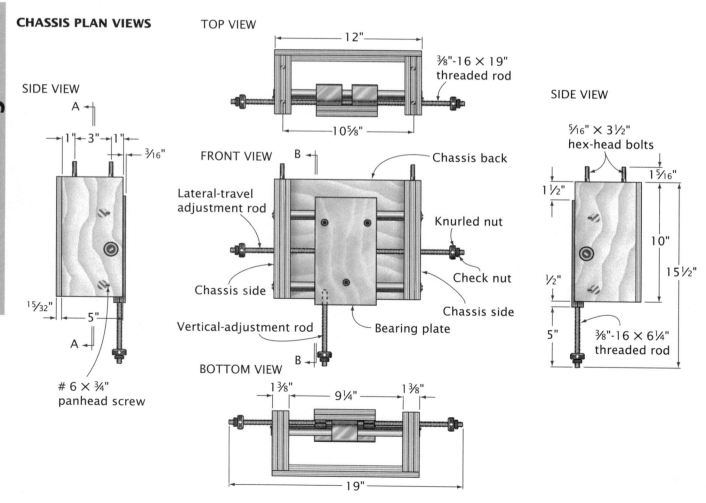

CHASSIS PLAN VIEWS

components. In making the poor man's version, we used ordinary birch plywood. One of the notable failings of the poor man's version was the flexibility of the chassis and the mounting board. For our final version, shown in the various photos, I used Apple Ply and recaptured the rigidity of Bob's original mortiser.

So, from the proper plywood, cut the plies for the chassis parts to the dimensions specified by the Cutting List.

**2. Glue-laminate the chassis sides and bearing plate.** The bearing plate is made up of two plies; each chassis side, of three.

Before glue-laminating the chassis sides, you must slot the middle plies for the mounting bolts, as shown in the drawing *Chassis Side Layout*. This can be done on the router table or on the band saw. The slots are supposed to closely accommodate ⁵⁄₁₆-inch hex-head bolts; don't cut them too loose. The bolt heads should be oriented as shown in the *Assembly Detail* of that drawing, with flats sliding into the notches and with points projecting out of the ply on each side. When the plies are laminated, those points will dig into the outer plies, helping to lock them so the

bolts won't twist. (Such twisting would be a distinct problem when you install the chassis beneath a workbench.) The shank of each bolt should project 1⁵⁄₁₆ inches beyond the open end of its slot. When the completed chassis is mounted under a 1½-inch-thick bench top, the bolts will be recessed about ⅛ to ³⁄₁₆ inch.

With the slots cut, you can glue up the two chassis sides. Spread glue on the appropriate faces of the plies. Slip the mounting bolts in the slots, and sandwich the parts together. Because of the bolts, you won't be able to trim the top edges of the chassis sides, so align the three plies very carefully. You can, of course, true the other three edges after the glue sets.

Glue-laminate the two plies forming the bearing plate.

**3. Drill the chassis sides.** The most critical parts that you'll be making are the chassis sides. They ensure that the shafts are absolutely parallel and that the plane of the bearing plate is perpendicular to the bench top. To achieve the needed accuracy, mark the inner faces, and tape or screw the sides together, inner face to inner face. That way, you can work on them as one unit.

With the sides taped or screwed together, trim them to

## CHASSIS SIDE LAYOUT

### TOP VIEW

Glue up 3 plies to form each chassis side.

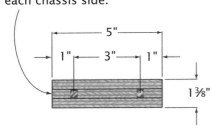

### ASSEMBLY DETAIL

Outer ply

Insert mounting bolt in slot in inner ply, then sandwich it between the outer plies.

⁵⁄₁₆" × 3½" bolt

Inner ply

Outer ply

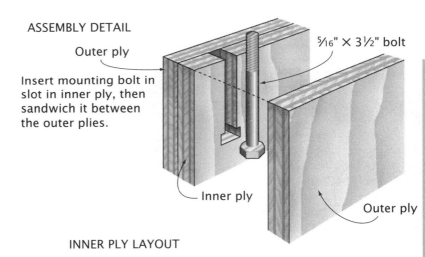

### SIDE VIEW

⁵⁄₁₆" × 3½" hex-head bolt

¾"-dia. hole for shaft

½"-dia. hole for adjustment rod

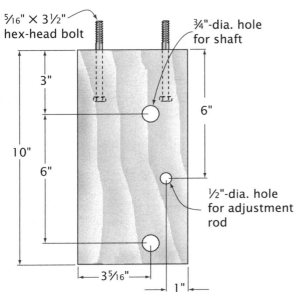

### INNER PLY LAYOUT

Slot for mounting bolt

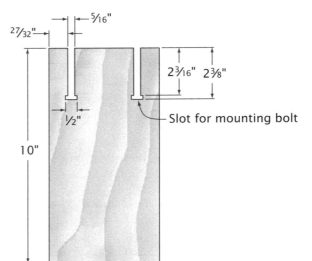

Mortising

**The precision of the chassis sides** is critical to the accuracy of this fixture. To ensure that the holes for the shafts and the lateral-travel adjustment rod align perfectly, tape the sides together and bore these holes in both pieces at the same time. And do the boring on a drill press.

length and width, then lay out the holes shown in *Chassis Side Layout.*

Before boring the holes, check to ensure that your drill press table is perpendicular to the drill, and use a fence when boring the shaft holes to keep them the same distance from the edge. The shafts should fit snugly in their holes.

Then separate the sides.

**4. Install the inserts in the bearing plate.** The router mounting plate is attached to the fixture with three studded knobs that turn into threaded inserts in the bearing plate. Trim the bearing plate to its final size, squaring it in the process. Then drill and install the inserts.

See the drawing *Bearing Plate Layout* for the specific locations of the inserts. Lay out and bore the pilot holes, using the diameter of bit specified for the inserts you are using (a ⁵⁄₁₆-inch insert usually requires a ¹⁄₂-inch-diameter pilot hole). You can bore the holes completely through the plate.

Install the inserts next. A special wrench can be purchased to drive inserts, but a cheap solution is use a hex-head bolt of the appropriate size chucked in a drill press. See the photo on page 127 for details.

Before setting the bearing plate aside, drill the hole for the vertical-travel adjustment rod. Lay out the hole as shown in *Bearing Plate Layout,* then drill it with a ³⁄₈-inch bit.

**5. Assemble the shafts, pillow blocks, and chassis sides.** Unpack the shafts and the pillow blocks. As you do so, bear in mind that the pillow blocks are sensitive to dust and dirt. They have excellent dust seals, which will keep out dirt once they are mounted on the shafts. But you have to keep them clean *before* they are mounted on the shafts. So clean up your work area before you open the packages. And as soon as you unwrap a pillow block, slip it onto a shaft. It's as simple as that.

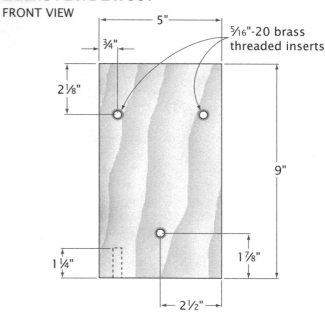

**BEARING PLATE LAYOUT**
FRONT VIEW

⁵⁄₁₆"-20 brass threaded inserts

5"

¾"

2⅛"

9"

1¼"

1⅞"

2½"

BOTTOM VIEW

³⁄₈"-dia. × 1¼"-deep hole for adjustment rod

¾"

½"

1"

Glue up two ½" plies to form the plate.

Stand the chassis sides on their back edges.

Install the lower shaft first. Slide the shaft into the lower hole in one of the sides. Fit a pillow block onto the shaft, then slide the shaft into the lower hole in the other side. Move the two sides as necessary to position the shaft flush with their outer faces.

Poke a ¾-inch-long #6 panhead screw into the seam between the wood and the steel shaft. Drive the screw between the wood and steel; it will bind the two parts together. In the same fashion, drive a screw to lock the other chassis side on this first shaft.

The second shaft is installed in exactly the same way, except that this shaft—the upper one—has two pillow blocks on it.

Once a screw has been driven at each end of both shafts, you'll find that the chassis ends stay in position at the outer ends of the shafts.

**6. Mount the pillow blocks on the bearing plate.** Set the bearing plate face down on the workbench (the face has the inserts in it).

Set the chassis assembly over the plate. Align the pillow blocks on the plate, as shown in the *Section Views.* The upper pillow blocks should be spread apart and positioned all but at the edges of the plate. The lower pillow block should be centered. There should be an equal amount of space above the upper blocks and below the lower block. Most important of all, the plate should be square to the axes of the shafts.

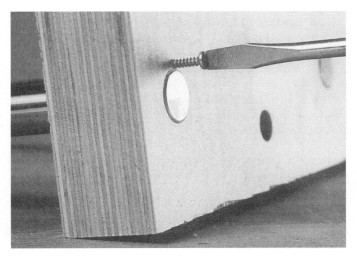

**Locking the shaft in the chassis side** is accomplished with a screw driven into the seam between the parts, as shown. The screw takes up enough space to jam the shaft in the hole, but it can't in any way mar the hardened steel of the shaft.

Because the bearing plate is proud of the chassis sides, the front edges of these parts should be balanced about ³⁄₁₆ inch off the bench top.

Drive a couple of screws into each pillow block to hold their positions. Then slide the chassis back and forth. Make sure the inner faces of the chassis sides are parallel to the edges of the bearing plate. If they aren't, if the

**Mounting the pillow blocks** is a straightforward screw-driving process. With the bearing plate on a flat surface, set the chassis assembly in place, line up the pillow blocks, drill pilot holes, and drive the screws.

chassis is slightly cocked on the plate, withdraw the screws and realign things. Then redrive the screws—run them into different holes on this second try—and check the alignment again.

When the alignment is tested and proven correct, tighten down the screws holding the blocks. Drive and tighten the rest of the screws.

## SECTION VIEWS

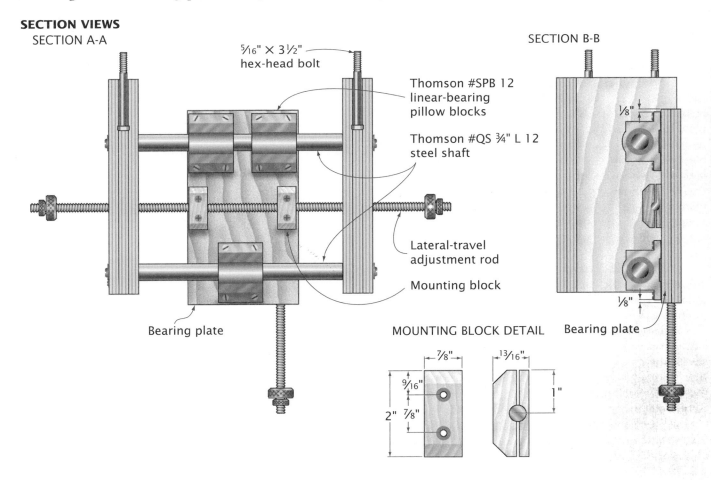

SECTION A-A

SECTION B-B

⁵⁄₁₆" × 3½" hex-head bolt

Thomson #SPB 12 linear-bearing pillow blocks

Thomson #QS ¾" L 12 steel shaft

Lateral-travel adjustment rod

Mounting block

Bearing plate

MOUNTING BLOCK DETAIL

Bearing plate

⅛"

⅛"

⅞"

⁹⁄₁₆"

2"  ⅞"

¹³⁄₁₆"

1"

**Custom-fit the adjustment-rod mounting blocks** to the mortiser as it takes shape. With the rod roughly centered in the chassis-side holes, slide the bottom half of the block under the rod, as shown. If it won't fit, shave the bottom with a block plane. When it fits, set the top half in place and screw the block to the bearing plate.

**7. Install the lateral-travel adjustment rod.** Without moving the chassis assembly, slide the threaded rod that will serve as the lateral-travel adjustment rod through the holes in the chassis sides. The same length of rod should extend beyond the plate on each side, of course. This rod is fastened to the bearing plate with mounting blocks.

Cut the mounting blocks to rough shape, and drill the pilot holes for the mounting screws. But don't drill the holes for the adjustment rod or halve the blocks just yet.

Instead, wedge the adjustment rod so it is roughly centered in the holes in the chassis sides. The idea is that the rod should move back and forth in those holes without restriction when the mortiser is in use. Measure from the plate to the center of the rod (it should be in the neighborhood of $\frac{3}{16}$ inch). Lay out the centerpoint on the mounting blocks, and drill a $\frac{3}{8}$-inch hole through each. Then with a backsaw, saw each block in two, halving this hole.

Slip the bottom parts of the blocks under the rod, locating them at the outer edges of the plate, as shown in the *Section Views*. Set the mounting block tops in place, and drive the screws, securing them and the rod to the bearing plate.

**8. Make and install the back.** Like the rest of the wooden parts, the back is glue-laminated from two pieces of $\frac{1}{2}$-inch plywood. For the best fit, it's best to wait until this point in the project to cut the two plies.

Measure the chassis. One ply fits between the chassis sides, while the second ply overlays them, fitting flush with their outer faces. Cut the parts to the correct sizes, then glue them face to face. A half-dozen small nails driven through the plies will hold them in alignment while the glue sets, and permit you to complete the assembly right away.

Set the back in place and screw it fast. Using just screws—no glue—allows you to remove the back at a later date, should it become necessary.

**9. Epoxy the vertical-adjustment rod into the bearing plate.** This is the last chassis part to be installed. Cut the threaded rod to the specified length, and epoxy it in its stud hole in the bottom edge of the bearing plate.

If your epoxy is the thin, runny kind, paint the inside of the drill holes thoroughly, and leave at least $\frac{1}{2}$ inch of epoxy in the bottom of each hole. Paint the rod end with epoxy, and insert it gently into the hole; don't push it

**ROUTER MOUNTING BOARD LAYOUT**

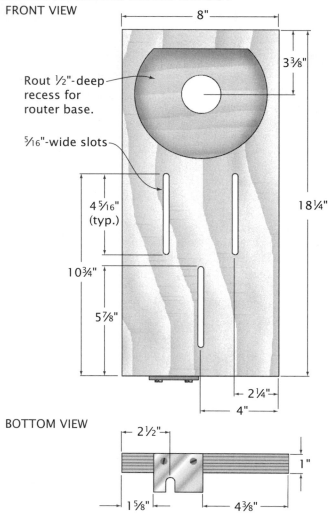

FRONT VIEW

Rout $\frac{1}{2}$"-deep recess for router base.

$\frac{5}{16}$"-wide slots

8"

3$\frac{3}{8}$"

18$\frac{1}{4}$"

4$\frac{5}{16}$" (typ.)

10$\frac{3}{4}$"

5$\frac{7}{8}$"

2$\frac{1}{4}$"

4"

BOTTOM VIEW

2$\frac{1}{2}$"

1"

1$\frac{5}{8}$"

4$\frac{3}{8}$"

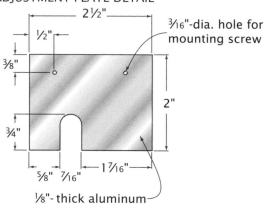

ADJUSTMENT PLATE DETAIL

2$\frac{1}{2}$"

$\frac{1}{2}$"

$\frac{3}{16}$"-dia. hole for mounting screw

$\frac{3}{8}$"

2"

$\frac{3}{4}$"

$\frac{5}{8}$" $\frac{7}{16}$"

1$\frac{7}{16}$"

$\frac{1}{8}$"-thick aluminum

Mortising

down fast, which would force air into the hole and squirt out epoxy.

If your epoxy is the thick, pasty kind, drill a small vent hole into the bottom of the stud hole, and smear both the inside of the stud holes and the rod end with the paste, and then push it in. Wipe up the excess.

Let the epoxy cure at least 24 hours before disturbing the assembly. Epoxy doesn't require any kind of clamping, but it really does take many hours to cure.

After the epoxy cures, turn the pairs of special nuts on the adjustment rods, horizontal as well as vertical. Turn the knurled nut on the rod first, then the check nut. In use, you make the adjustment with the knurled nut, then jam the check nut against it to hold the precise setting.

## Making the Router Mounting Board

The mounting board shown is sized to accommodate the biggest Elu or DeWalt plunge router. It is laid out with the bit axis $3\frac{3}{8}$ inches from the top edge. The adjustment slots provide just over 4 inches of vertical travel. If mounted under a $1\frac{1}{2}$-inch-thick worktable, the bit axis ranges roughly from $\frac{7}{8}$ inches below the table surface to 3-plus inches above the table surface. See the drawing *Vertical Range*.

You may need or want to alter some of the dimensions to accommodate a different router or a thicker worktable. (I wouldn't mount this fixture to anything less than $1\frac{1}{2}$ inches thick.) For a 2-inch-thick worktop, for example, add $\frac{1}{2}$ inch to the mounting board length, and add the space between the slots and the bit opening. That is, lay out the slots by measuring up from the bottom of the board, as shown in the drawing *Router Mounting Board Layout,* and lay out the bit opening by measuring down from the top. The extra length will fall where it should.

**1. Cut the plywood.** Like the chassis sides and bearing plate, the router mounting board is made from two pieces of $\frac{1}{2}$-inch Apple Ply plywood, laminated together. Cut the pieces roughly to the dimensions specified by the Cutting List.

**2. Cut the recess for the router.** Since the recess's depth equals the thickness of one plywood layer, it is easiest to cut the opening before laminating the mounting board.

Lay out the centerpoint of the bit opening. Center the router over the mark, and scribe around the base. Cut the opening. For a shape like that of the Elu and DeWalt routers, rout the straight section, using a clamped-on fence to guide the router. Then set up the router with a trammel, and rout the arc from one end of the straight groove to the other.

**3. Laminate the plies.** With the opening for the router completed, apply glue to the faces of the two panels and clamp them together.

When the glue has cured, trim the mounting board to bring it to its final dimensions and to square it.

**4. Rout the adjustment slots.** This can be done with a plunge router equipped with an edge guide and a $\frac{5}{16}$-inch straight bit. Lay out the slots and rout them.

### VERTICAL RANGE

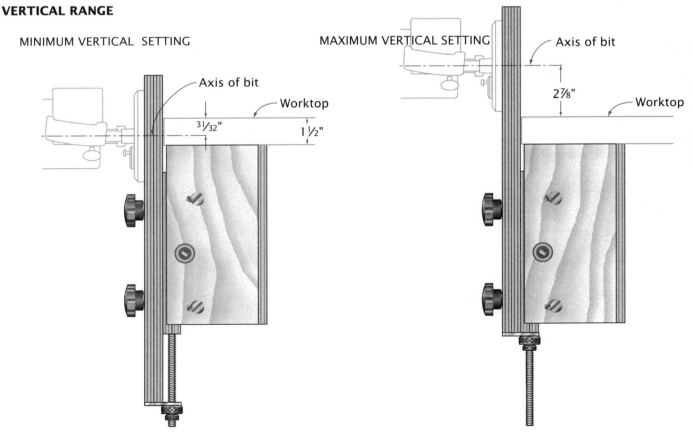

MINIMUM VERTICAL SETTING

Axis of bit

Worktop

$3\frac{1}{32}$"

$1\frac{1}{2}$"

MAXIMUM VERTICAL SETTING

Axis of bit

$2\frac{7}{8}$"

Worktop

Mortising

**5. Make and install the vertical-adjustment plate.** On Bob's original, this plate is ⅛-inch-thick aluminum. The choice of that material seems to have been a function of serendipity. For the job it performs, the plate could just as easily be made of 16-gauge steel, ⅜-inch or ½-inch plywood, or even phenolic, if you have that. I did have some ¼-inch phenolic, so I used that on the slot mortiser shown in the photos.

If you use plywood or phenolic, rout the slot on the router table. If you use metal, drill a ⁷⁄₁₆-inch-diameter hole, then cut into the hole with a hacksaw, forming the slot. Cut the plate to size. Drill the holes for mounting screws. File any rough or sharp edges, as necessary. Attach the plate to the bottom of the mounting plate so the threaded rod fits into the slot.

**6. Install the router.** Remove the router's baseplate. Set it into the recess in the mounting board, and use it as a pattern to drill holes for the baseplate-mounting screws. Countersink the holes. Then mount the router on the board.

Since the router operates in a horizontal position, the return springs can be a nuisance. We followed Bob's lead in removing them.

If the router you use on the mortiser has a spring-loaded plunge lock, you have a decision to make. To Bob, the spring-loaded plunge lock on his Elu was a nuisance, so he disabled it. But he was using his mortiser for mortising only. If you want your slot mortiser to double as a horizontal router table, you will need to use the plunge lock to set the bit extension. Thus, you probably won't want to disable even a spring-loaded plunge lock.

If you decide to remove the plunge springs and the plunge lock, check the parts diagram for your router to figure out how to go about it. Removing these parts doesn't mean that you can no longer use your router separate from this fixture. The parts usually are as simple to replace as they are to remove.

## Outfitting the Worktable

The slot mortiser is useless until it is mounted to the underside of a sturdy worktable. Since you will be pushing and pulling on the router and the fixture it is attached to, the worktable should be rigid and heavy.

You can use a workbench or a substantial router table as the worktable for the slot mortiser. But remember that you have to drill and counterbore mounting holes, as well as holes for threaded inserts. You will surely want to etch a grid into the tabletop to facilitate setups. These add up to alterations you may not want to make to a good workbench or router table. If you have space for it, and if you will use it often enough, you can always build a separate worktable for the slot mortiser. However you choose to deal with this matter, here's how to outfit the worktable, thus completing the fixture.

**1. Mount the mortiser to the worktable.** A couple of points before the actual work begins.

First, the worktop to which you mount the mortiser should be at least 1½ inches thick, and it should be flat with top and bottom surfaces parallel. If it isn't thick enough, the mounting bolts will protrude above the surface. If the surfaces aren't flat and parallel, bolting the mortiser tightly to it will wrack the chassis, throwing your new fixture out of kilter.

The second point has to do with the gap between the chassis's leading edges and the mounting board. The gap will be about ³⁄₁₆ inch, and you probably don't want that much space between the mounting board and the worktop. Therefore, try to set the chassis back from the worktop edge about ⁵⁄₃₂ inch.

I found the easiest way to lay out the holes for the mounting bolts was to make a template from the mortiser. Cut a 5 × 12-inch piece of ¼-inch plywood. Set it on top of the mounting bolts, and align it flush with the front edges of the chassis sides. (Hold a straightedge against the chassis, and slide the plywood template up against it.) Tap on the template at each bolt, denting the template. Flip it over, and drill a ³⁄₃₂-inch hole centered in each dent.

Lay the template on the worktop, and align it. The edge of the template represents the front edge of the chassis, and you want to set that back a bit. By drilling ⅜-inch holes for the ⁵⁄₁₆-inch mounting bolts, you give yourself just a little room for adjustment. So line up the template and clamp it. With a nail or awl, mark through the template on the worktop.

Remove the template to drill a 1-inch-diameter, ½-inch-deep counterbore, centered on each mark. Switch bits, and drill ⅜-inch-diameter through holes for the mounting bolts.

Drop a ⅜-inch-I.D. flat washer into each counterbore. Position the chassis under the worktop, and push the mounting bolts up through the holes. Turn a nut onto each bolt, and lightly seat each. Install the mounting board, and adjust the chassis position under the worktop. You want the face of the mounting board to be parallel to the worktop's edge. When the mortise is so aligned, tighten the nuts on the mounting bolts.

**2. Fine-tune the mounting.** Once you mount the fixture, you need to check it for alignment. There are two ways it can be misaligned:

1. The axis of the router bit can be out of parallel with the bench top.
2. The bearing shafts can be out of parallel with the bench top.

Any misalignment must be corrected by fitting shims between the chassis and the underside of the bench top.

The alignments can be checked by chucking a steel dowel pin, a centering pin, or even a router bit into the router (with the router unplugged) and measuring the height of the dowel pin above the bench top with a depth-measuring vernier or dial calipers. The height, when the router is all the way to the left, must be exactly the same as when it is all the way to the right; the height must be the same whether fully plunged or fully retracted. If it isn't, mark the corners of the chassis where the measurement is high, loosen the nuts holding the chassis, and insert paper shims to shim the

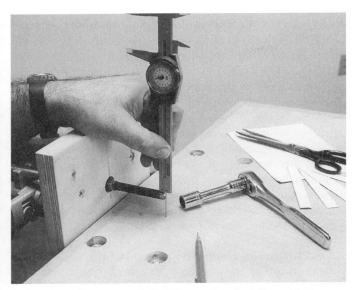

**The mortiser mounting is properly aligned** if measurements taken at the limits of the mortiser's lateral travel and with the router both fully plunged and fully retracted are all exactly the same. Take the measurements from the bit to the tabletop using a pair of depth-measuring dial calipers, as shown.

chassis down at the marked corners. Then tighten it up and check the measurements again. Repeat as necessary until the measurement at all four points is the same.

**3. Grid the worktop.** Using the fixture requires accurately positioning the workpiece on the bench and clamping it there. A grid of reference lines permanently scribed in the bench top is useful. You can adjust the lateral travel according to these lines, as well as position the workpiece to them. I suggest that at first you simply use pencil lines. Once you know what kind of a grid works best for

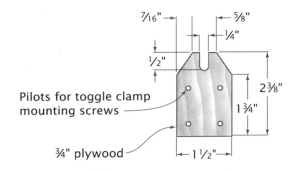

7/16"  5/8"  1/4"  1/2"  2 3/8"  1 3/4"  1 1/2"

Pilots for toggle clamp mounting screws

3/4" plywood

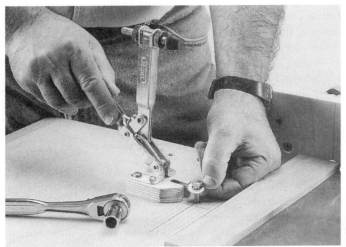

**Mounting a toggle clamp to the worktable** requires only a single bolt turned into a T-nut in the worktop. You can swing the pad-mounted clamp around the bolt, orienting it for the best contact with the work. Big clamps have a longer reach and apply more pressure than small ones. But both can be used productively.

**TABLETOP LAYOUT**

Hole for mounting toggle clamp; T-nut on underside of table.

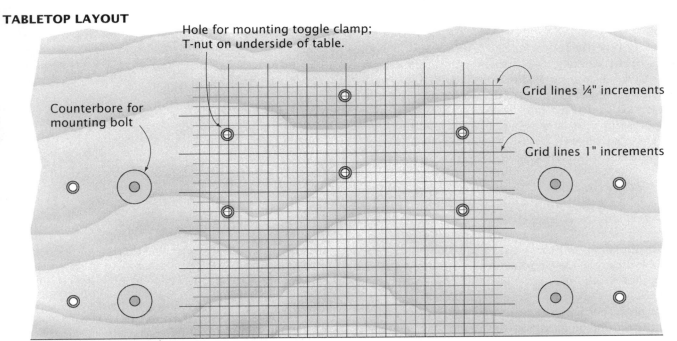

Grid lines 1/4" increments

Grid lines 1" increments

Counterbore for mounting bolt

Edge of tabletop

**Mortising**

your purposes, scratch the lines in with a sharp awl, and fill the scratches with a dark wood filler.

It's important to be able to position clamps on the workpiece as close as possible to the mortise. The most convenient way to clamp is with toggle clamps. But of course, you don't want to clutter the worktop with toggle clamps.

Instead, install T-nuts at key spots on the worktop. (Bore a hole through the tabletop and tap the T-nut into the underside.) Mount a couple of large toggle clamps—I use De-Sta-Co's TC-235-U—on slotted pads made of ¾-inch plywood. Turn a bolt into the T-nut, and catch it in the slot of the toggle clamp's pad. Tighten the bolt, and you've got a toggle clamp just where you need it for the job at hand. You can use the T-nuts directly or via a toggle clamp to secure positioning stops for production runs.

As with the grid, it's probably better to develop a sense for where T-nuts are useful, rather than pock the worktop with them haphazardly. The layout I use is shown in the *Tabletop Layout* drawing.

## Using the Fixture

And now the moment of truth is upon us. You've invested in expensive parts but spent only a couple of evenings putting the mortiser together. How will it work?

Only few minutes are needed to set the mortiser up for a cut, to clamp a test piece in position, and then to actually make that cut. And the truth will be in the cutting.

### Mortising

This is the job for which the fixture was designed. Tackling this operation will expose you to all the workings of the fixture. You have to adjust all three axes of movement (discussed at the beginning of this chapter). You have to work the tabletop grid and set toggle clamps. You have to do the mortising dance.

**1. Lay out the mortise.** This is where it begins. On a piece of the working stock, pencil off the mortise you want, where you want it. Will it follow the Rule of Thirds, having a width equal to one-third the stock's thickness? Will it be centered across the stock thickness? How long will it be? How deep? Your layout should answer the first three questions. The answer to the fourth question will be revealed in setting up the router.

**2. Set up the router.** This is a slot mortiser, cutting mortises in back and forth passes at a given level. Thus, the width of the mortise dictates the diameter of the bit to use.

The conventional wisdom is that spiral upcut bits are best for mortising, and that's true. But you need not feel that's the *only* style of bit you can use. I've used straight bits of every style—straight flue, shear flue, single and double flute.

Equally important as the diameter is the length of the bit. To the desired mortise depth you must add ½ inch for the thickness of the mounting board, maybe ⅛ inch of

space between the mounting board and the collet nut, and at least ½ inch of shank to be gripped by the collet. So the bit needs to be at minimum 1⅛ inches longer than the mortise depth.

Given these guidelines, choose your bit for the mortise and tighten it into the collet.

Now set the plunge router's depth stop for the mortise depth. To do this, you merely have to plunge the router—without the springs, it will stay plunged as far as you push it—and measure the portion of the bit extending from the mounting board. Plunge the router until the correct amount of bit is exposed, then set the depth stop at that point. Then pull the router back, retracting the bit (though not fully), and ready the machine for the next setup step.

**3. Adjust the mounting board height.** Set the stock with the mortise laid out on it beside the bit. Loosen the three knobs securing the mounting board and make a coarse setting, raising or lowering the bit as close as possible between the layout lines. Tighten at least one knob to hold the setting, and spin the check nuts up against the slotted plate.

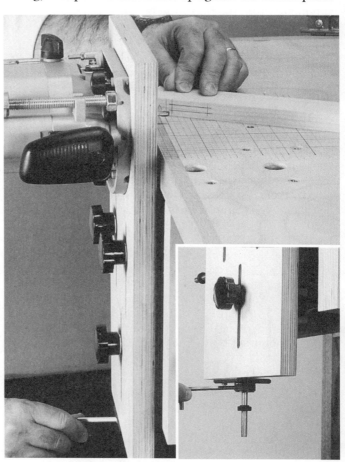

**Setting the mounting board height** can be done with considerable precision, thanks to the number of threads per inch (16) on the adjustment rod and the style of the check nut. With the workpiece beside the bit, turn the nut to raise or lower the bit so it aligns with the layout lines, as shown. The nut (*inset*) has four holes, allowing you to easily "dial" a quarter- or half-turn for very fine adjustment.

Examine the level of the bit against the mortise layout closely. If it seems appropriate, loosen the knob(s) and turn the check nut to raise or lower the bit. When you are comfortable with the setting, tighten all three knobs, and jam the second check nut against the first.

**4. Set the lateral-travel limits.** This can be done using the laid-out mortise or the grid on the worktop, whichever is easier for you.

Setting the stops for the mortise length is easy to do using the grid on the bench top. Pick out the grid lines that represent the extremities of the mortise. With the bit plunged, look down on the grid and align the bit's left edge with the line representing the mortise's left end. Set the stop on the adjustment rod's left to prevent the router from moving any farther in that direction. Slide the router to the right, aligning the bit's right edge with the line representing the mortise's right end. Set the right stop.

**5. Position the work.** The fixture has been set to create a cut of a specific length. The tasks now are to place the workpiece so the mortise will be where you want it, and to position a toggle clamp to lock the workpiece down during the routing operation.

Positioning the workpiece is a matter of aligning the mortise layout lines with the appropriate grid lines. For a production run, it saves time if you clamp a stop block to locate the workpieces automatically. The stop can be clamped with a C-clamp or with a toggle clamp.

The toggle clamp designated to hold the workpiece

**Setting the stops for the mortise length** is done easily using the bench-top grid. Look down on the grid, and align the bit with grid lines that represent the ends of the mortise. With the bit at one mortise-end position, spin the check nut on that side until it seats against the chassis side. Move the bit to the other position, and set the stop on that side.

should be positioned so that its spindle applies pressure to the work as close to the mortise as possible.

**6. Rout a test mortise.** With everything set, lock down the test piece and rout the mortise. Then examine and evaluate the mortise. Measure it. Do any adjustments need to be made? Is it centered in the edge? Is it the correct length? The correct depth?

If necessary, adjust the settings.

**7. Rout the work.** When all is right, get to work on the good stock.

A word or two about technique is in order here. I grasp the router's knobs, one in each hand, but I set my thumbs against the router mounting board. You'll probably find, as I did, that you have smoother control of the plunge action if you apply pressure with your body rather than with your hands. The thumbs set against the mounting board counter this pressure, controlling the rate and depth of plunge. With spiral upcut bits, it seems easier to plunge and cut laterally in one continuous motion, rather than plunging first and then cutting laterally. Just be sure you don't force a bit, especially a solid carbide one.

**End mortises are easy to rout** with the slot mortiser. Turn the workpiece so its end confronts the bit, rather than its side. Though a single toggle clamp will hold the workpiece in place while the mortise is routed, a stop block locates it for the cut automatically.

## Fixed-Position Routing

Under this heading I collect all those horizontal-router-table operations you can do with the slot mortiser. There's a bunch of them: tenoning, slotting and grooving, rabbeting, routing moldings, raising panels.

In each of these operations, the work is fed into or over the bit. So to set up the slot mortiser for them, you set the lateral-travel stops against the chassis sides, locking the router in one position. Then you've got a horizontal router table.

To cut a groove with a straight bit, you adjust the bit extension and the vertical position. Turn on the router, and feed the work across the bit. If you are doing an end-grain cut, as in tenoning, use a push-block sled to feed and back up the workpiece.

Before you embrace these operations, you should weigh the impact of them on the bench under which the mortiser is mounted. In all the mortising operations, the bit is above the tabletop. It never cuts the tabletop. But for nearly all the fixed-position operations, the bit is partially buried in the tabletop.

So the question is: Do I want a bit cutout in the tabletop?

If you do tenoning only, then the injury to the tabletop is fairly modest, a ½-inch-wide, 1- to 1½-inch-long slot. If you raise panels or rout moldings, the tabletop will develop a significant crevice that's an inch or more wide and even longer. I think this is a downside.

These operations are possible. You decide whether they are advisable.

**To rout a groove with the slot mortiser,** lock the router in position, then feed the workpiece past it. Your position behind the router makes the feed action different than with a regular router table.

## Loose-Tenon Joints

The mortise-and-tenon joint is a good joint because it provides relatively large areas of flat-grained gluing surface. It is these large, flat-grained surfaces that make it superior to a dowel joint.

The great feature of a dowel joint, which is really just a specialized mortise-and-tenon joint, is that the rounded hole (the mortise) can be quickly and easily bored and the dowel (the tenon) can be mass-produced.

With an efficient slot mortiser, the advantages of the mortise-and-tenon joint can be combined with the advantages of the dowel joint. The combination is a joinery uniquely suited to the small shop producing one-of-a-kind or limited-production furniture or high-end cabinetry.

Traditionally, mortises were the hard part and tenons were the easy part. Today, it is more efficient (and just as strong) to cut two mortises and use a separate tenon. The mortises are quickly and accurately cut with the slot mortiser, and the tenons are easily mass-produced out of scrap or inexpensive wood in whatever sizes the woodworker needs.

Making up a batch of tenon stock is straightforward:

1. Rip a length of rough stock to the rough width of the tenon.
2. Resaw to just over the desired thickness.
3. Surface to the desired thickness.
4. Joint one edge.
5. Rip to accurate width.
6. Round-over the edges on the router table.

One advantage of loose-tenon joints is that parts no longer need to be sized to include an integral

tenon. That not only saves expensive cabinet wood, but also makes the sizing of pieces more straightforward and makes the woodworker less prone to dumb mistakes. And, once in a while, the savings in wood makes the difference between almost enough and barely enough. These are the occasions when you can gaze at your slot mortiser and smile.

# Template-Mortising

**Guide your router with a template to
cut those hard-to-position mortises.**

Using a template to guide a mortising cut is sometimes the most convenient, accurate, and effective
way to work. You outfit your plunge router with a
guide bushing and a straight bit, then use it with a template
to rout the mortise.

The key is not the router, per se, but the template. A
mortising template, like any other template, can be made of
hardboard, medium-density fiberboard (MDF), plywood, or
plastic. It can be a job-specific jig, made to be used for the
particular application at hand, then tossed. Or it can be a
keeper, one you squirrel away against the day you need to
make that very mortise again.

You can make a template for mortising door frames
or face frames; but frankly, this is mortising work I'd do
using one of the other mortising jigs presented in this
book. To me, there are other woodworking situations to
which the mortising template is better suited, many in
which the template is the only solution. Let me list some
specific applications:

- the through mortise in a panel, such as the mortises in
  a bench seat or a case side;
- a through mortise in a very thick workpiece, which
  requires you to work from both sides of the workpiece.
  An example is a sawbuck leg assembly that has a
  through mortise for a stretcher.
- a mortise in the face of a panel; this is a workpiece that
  can't be clamped in the Mortising Jig on page 124 or

the Shop-Built Slot Mortiser on page 131. I once reproduced a country chest of drawers in which the face
rails were mortised into the sides. To cut the mortises,
I used a template.
- a difficult-to-position mortise, such as one in a round,
  one cut into the arris of a leg, one cut into an already-
  shaped part, or one to be cut at an angle. In these
  situations, the use of a template allows you to make a
  cradle for the workpiece and still provide a flat, sound
  bearing surface for the router. Using a template frees
  you of the need to provide a guide surface for an edge
  guide or the baseplate edge.

What I'm going to do here is explain, step by step, how
to make and use a basic mortising template. This is the sort
of template used in the first example given above, a through
mortise in a bench seat. Then I'll show you the templates
used in the other specific jobs cited above.

## Making a Generic Mortising Template

The exercise here is to make a country-style five-board bench.
The bench's legs each have two tenons as long as the seat is
thick. These tenons extend into mortises cut through the seat
board. The 1⅛-inch-wide × 2¾-inch-long mortises are routed
with a guide bushing–equipped plunge router and a template.

## GENERIC MORTISING TEMPLATE LAYOUT

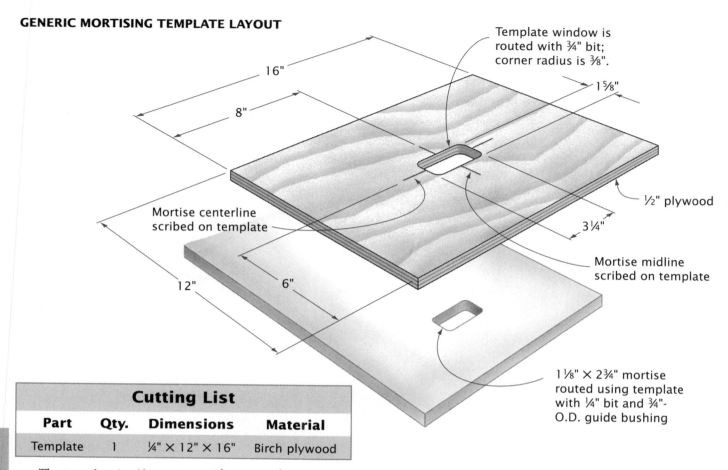

16"

8"

Template window is routed with ¾" bit; corner radius is ⅜".

1⅝"

½" plywood

3¼"

Mortise centerline scribed on template

Mortise midline scribed on template

12"

6"

1⅛" × 2¾" mortise routed using template with ¼" bit and ¾"-O.D. guide bushing

### Cutting List

| Part | Qty. | Dimensions | Material |
|------|------|------------|----------|
| Template | 1 | ¼" × 12" × 16" | Birch plywood |

The template itself is a piece of ¼-inch or ½-inch birch plywood. You set the template on the workpiece (which rests on a piece of scrap) and apply a couple of clamps, securing the template to the work and the work to the workbench. Then rout.

Before making the template, you have to make fundamental decisions about the bushing and the bit you will use. You have to make these decisions up front, because

you must size the window in the template to accommodate the bushing. Too, you have to position the window to account for the offset, which is the difference between the size of the bushing and the size of the bit.

**1. Choose the bit for the mortising operation.** Typically, you use a bit whose diameter matches the desired mortise width. For a ¼-inch-wide mortise, you use a

## CHOOSING A GUIDE BUSHING FOR TEMPLATE-MORTISING

COLLAR LENGTH

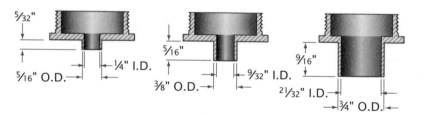

5/32"

5/16" O.D.

¼" I.D.

5/16"

3/8" O.D.

9/32" I.D.

9/16"

21/32" I.D.

¾" O.D.

With standard guide bushings, the collar length increases as the collar diameter increases.

The longer the collar, the thicker the template material must be, and the less deep the bit extending through it can reach.

CHIP CLEARANCE

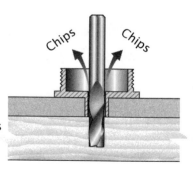

¼"-dia. bit in ⅜"-dia. bushing

Chips    Chips

Tight clearance between the collar and the bit constricts the passage of chips from the cut.

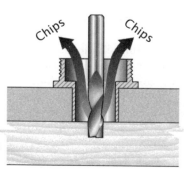

Same ¼"-dia. bit in ⅜"-dia. bushing

Chips    Chips

Ample clearance between the collar and the bit promotes passage of chips out of the cut.

Mortising

¼-inch-diameter bit. If you want a ½-inch-wide mortise, use a ½-inch-diameter bit. In this instance, of course, the mortise is to be 1⅛ inches wide, and it's unlikely you have a straight bit of that diameter. The largest straight in my collection is 1 inch in diameter.

But with a template, you can easily use a ¼-inch or ½-inch bit to produce this mortise. This is because the template, not an edge guide, controls the cut. Instead of making a single straight-line cut, you rout around the inner perimeter of the template, then rout back and forth or end to end to remove the interior waste.

A significant consideration in choosing a bit is the impact the bit diameter has on the mortise's corners. A large-diameter bit hogs out the waste quickly but leaves a substantial web of waste to be removed with a chisel. If you use a small-diameter bit—say, a ¼-inch bit—that web of waste is much smaller, much more easily removed.

The final consideration, and it's a vital one, is the bit's overall length. Tally up the needs: a minimum of ½ inch in the collet + the router base thickness + the thickness of the template + the desired mortise depth. To rout a through mortise in 5/4 (five-quarter) stock using a ¼-inch template means the bit must be a minimum of 2 inches long.

In this instance, I selected a ¼-inch-diameter bit.

**2. Choose the template guide bushing.** In selecting the guide bushing, there are two facets that must be considered: the collar diameter and the collar length.

Perhaps obviously, the inside diameter of the collar must be large enough to accommodate the bit. But you should also consider chip clearance. Using a large-diameter guide bushing with a small-diameter bit provides plenty of clearance for the chips that well out of the cut. If you can manage it, allow at least ³⁄₁₆ inch between the bit and the inside of the collar, which means that the inside diameter of the bushing should be ⅜ inch larger than the bit diameter. An example: For a ¼-inch-diameter bit, use a ¾-inch-O.D. bushing, which typically has a ²¹⁄₃₂-inch inside diameter.

In addition, choose a bushing with a short collar so you can use a thin template. The collar, as you probably know, must be just a skosh less than the template thickness. And the thickness of the template has to be subtracted from the maximum reach of the bit at full plunge, thus limiting the depth of the mortise that can be routed. If your mortise must be more than 1 inch deep and your template is ¾ inch thick, you are going to need an awfully long bit. Every fraction of an inch you shave off the template pushes the mortise deeper.

The hitch, of course, is that large-diameter guide bushings tend to have long collars. A visit to the bench grinder can cut the collar down to a more reasonable length.

For the mortising template shown, use a ¾-inch-O.D. guide bushing, and make sure the collar is no more than ¼ inch long.

**3. Select and cut the template stock.** The template stock, as noted earlier, can be hardboard, MDF, plywood, or

## CHOOSING A BIT FOR TEMPLATE-MORTISING

BIT DIAMETER

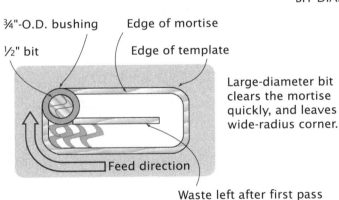

¾"-O.D. bushing
½" bit
Edge of mortise
Edge of template
Feed direction

Large-diameter bit clears the mortise quickly, and leaves wide-radius corner.

Waste left after first pass

¾"-O.D. bushing
¼" bit
Edge of mortise
Edge of template
Feed direction

Small-diameter bit requires more passes to clear the mortise, and leaves tight-radius corners.

Waste still to be routed away

BIT LENGTH

Portion of bit in router collet — ½"  ⅛"
Baseplate/guide-bushing thickness
Template thickness — ⅝"  2½"
Workpiece thickness — 1⅛"
Scrap

## TEMPLATE-MORTISING SCHEMATIC

To the length (or width) of the mortise add twice the offset to determine how long (or wide) the opening in the template must be.

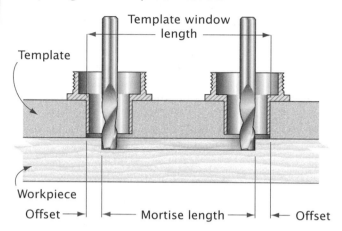

Template window length

Template

Workpiece

Offset — Mortise length — Offset

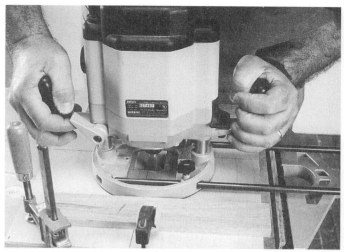

**Routing the template window** is a straightforward operation. The ¼-inch-thick template material is clamped to scrap. The window's length is controlled by the stops clamped to the template material. The router's edge guide positions the window.

plastic. With the length of the guide bushing's collar in mind, check the scrap bin for a usable piece. Failing there, use the least expensive of these materials for your template. This is especially true if the template will be job-specific— that is, made for this particular job and destined for the scrap bin when that job is completed.

For the generic template under consideration here, I used ¼-inch birch plywood. It's a material I had on hand, and it is light-colored, so layout lines show up easily. MDF (medium-density fiberboard) in a ¼-inch or ⅜-inch thickness is an excellent material, as is any good-quality plywood in either of those thicknesses. Hardboard is suitable, but I find it next to impossible to see layout lines drawn on it, so I generally avoid it for applications like this.

Roughly size the template material, making it large enough that clamps can be applied where they won't interfere with the router's movement around the template window. The Cutting List specifies that this template be 12 × 16 inches.

### 4. Lay out the window on the template stock.
The guide window is the opening into which the guide bushing fits. With the bushing trapped in that window, the router's movement is limited. In essence, it can move from one end of the window to the other, from one side to the other. Because the bit is inside the bushing, its range of movement, too, is limited.

The task now is to design and lay out the slot necessary to produce the desired mortise. To start, note the width and length of the desired mortise (in this instance, a 1⅛-inch-wide, 2¾-inch-long one). You've already chosen a ¼-inch-diameter straight bit and a ¾-inch-O.D. guide bushing. Compute the offset, which is determined by subtracting the bit diameter from the bushing diameter and dividing by 2. In this case, the offset is ¼ inch.

Here's how to translate the dimensions of the desired mortise into the dimensions for the necessary template slot. Add twice the offset to the mortise length, as shown in the drawing *Template-Mortising Schematic*. Thus, the

template slot must be 1⅝ inches wide and 3¼ inches long.

Follow the drawing *Generic Mortising Template Layout*. Scribe the centerline of the slot, then add a crosshair at the midpoint. Because these lines will be used again and again to position the completed template on workpieces, the lines should be drawn with a pen or fine-line marker. Then lay out the window from these lines. (If you have trouble seeing your layout lines on hardboard—I always do—try applying strips of masking tape to the hardboard. Then pencil the layout lines on the tape. When you rout, just rout through the tape.)

### 5. Rout the window in the template stock.
A very easy and accurate way to cut the guide window is with a plunge router equipped with an edge guide. You do have to reset the edge guide to get all the waste, but both long edges of the window will be parallel, because both are referenced from the same edge of the template.

To begin, dog or clamp a piece of scrap of the workbench, then clamp the template to it. Arrange the template so the edge you will reference with the router's edge guide projects beyond the scrap's edge. You want to reference the template edge exclusively with the edge guide. (You could also screw the template to the scrap; two or three holes in it won't interfere with the use of the template.)

Tighten a straight bit in the router's collet. Set the plunge depth to just a skosh more than the template thickness. Install the edge guide, and adjust it so the bit will cut one edge of the window, just leaving the layout line. Before routing, set up a pair of stop blocks to prevent you from overshooting either end of the slot.

With the blocks set, rout the first slot. Set the router on the template, switch it on, plunge the bit, and rout from stop to stop. Reset the edge guide, then make a second pass, widening the window. Repeat the process until the window is completed.

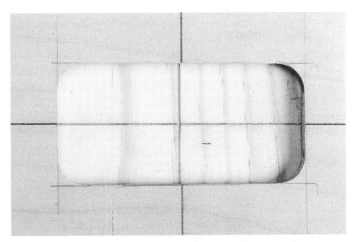

**Crosshairs allow you to position the template** without laying out the mortise completely on the work. Just lay out the centerlines (length and width) of the mortise. Then align the crosshairs on the template with these lines, as shown. The mortise will be perfectly positioned.

# Using the Mortising Template

To use a mortising template successfully, it is important to know which bit and guide bushing to use with it. You won't have difficulty with this when you use the template immediately after having made the template. But how about a year later? Or five years later?

I think it is essential to annotate the templates that are going to be keepers. Just write legibly on the template what bushing/bit combination is supposed to be used with it.

Now, as you prepare to make another five-board bench, you get out the template, then fetch the correct bushing and bit from where they are kept in your shop.

**1. Set up the router.** Start by fitting a ³⁄₄-inch guide bushing into the bit opening in the router baseplate.

Next, tighten a ¹⁄₄-inch straight bit in the collet. A spiral

**The completed mortise** is clean and accurately sized and positioned.

upcut bit is most often recommended for mortising, since its design is calculated to help auger chips up out of the cut. If you've got such a bit and it is long, by all means use it. But overall length is often a more significant consideration in mortising. The longest ¹⁄₄-inch bits I've got—both from Amana—are not spirals. But those are the bits I use most often for mortising.

Finally, set the plunge depth.

## Combining Templates

Saving templates from a project can make it easy to reproduce that project in the future.

But saving templates can also lead to storage woes. If everything you make requires two or three or four templates, it won't be too long before the accumulation pushes out of its little corner and crowds you into the opposite one.

A simple project like my five-board bench involved three templates—one for shaping the legs, another for shaping the apron ends, and a third for routing the mortises. But guess what! All three templates can be one. Check out the photo. The leg shape occupies an end and a side of the template blank. The apron shape occupies the other other side and end. The window for the mortises is in the middle.

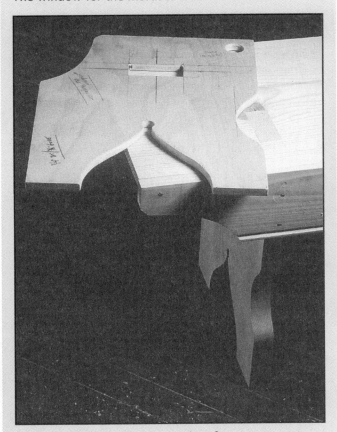

**Three templates in one** makes for easy storage. On the 12 × 15-inch piece of ½-inch plywood (resting on the bench) are the patterns for all the template-guided cuts made in constructing this five-board bench.

**2. Lay out the mortise on the workpiece.** This doesn't mean you must draw rectangles on the workpiece, delineating each mortise to be routed. Rather, it means you should scribe the centerline and midpoint of each mortise on the workpiece, so you can line up the template. If you've made the template with precision, and your layout lines are accurate, the mortises will be properly located.

**3. Position the template.** Lay the workpiece on an expendable piece of scrap that will back it up, eliminating chip-out on the underside of the workpiece and protecting the bench top. Set the template on the work, and align the midpoint mark on the template with the corresponding mark on the work. Apply a couple of clamps, clenching the template, workpiece, and backup scrap to the workbench.

**4. Rout the mortise.** Set the router on the template with the bushing in the slot. Switch on the router, plunge the bit, and rout the mortise. The routine I usually follow is to plunge-bore the corners of the mortise to full depth and then make a series of increasingly deeper passes back and forth,

side to side, nibbling away the waste between the end bores.

The nice thing about using a template for this work is that feed direction confusion is eliminated. Because the bushing is trapped in the template slot, the cut can't wander, even if you feed with the bit rotation rather than against it. (Do that when guiding a mortising cut with an edge guide, and the cut can veer off the centerline.)

## A Base-Guiding Mortising Template

An alternative to the template used with a guide bushing is this template, which incorporates fences that guide the router base. You don't have to use a guide bushing with it. You don't even have to use a plunge router!

What I particularly like about this template is that you don't have to work with a template window that's much larger than the mortise. The window is exactly the same length and width as the mortise. So to position the template, you merely have to set it on the layout lines penciled on the workpieces.

## Choking on Chips

Spiral upcut bits notwithstanding, chips can—and do!—clog the template slot when you are mortising. The result can be a undersized mortise with uneven walls.

What happens is that chips well up in the cut and push up into the template slot. As the guide bushing moves through the slot, it packs chips against the ends. In effect, the slot gets shorter. The result is a stepped mortise—one that's the correct length near the surface, but too short three-quarters of the way down toward the bottom.

The problem is most pronounced, in my estimation, with wide, through mortises, which require side-to-side cutting as well as end-to-end cutting.

What to do?

The best solution is a router-mounted chip-extraction setup. Some manufacturers, notably DeWalt and Bosch, offer such accessories. Typically, a plastic shroud with a vacuum-hose connection is mounted inside the base. The shroud surrounds the bit. The vacuum pulls the chips out of the cut and through the bit opening in the base, then sucks them away to the shop vac.

The alternative is to stop work and vacuum the chips out of the cut. On some occasions, usually when working pine, I've had to use a screwdriver to clean the ledge between the template slot and the mortise to ensure that the guide bushing could get into the corners of the template slot.

**When chips clog the cut,** the resulting mortise is seldom accurate. Usually, this means you have to stop and vacuum the chips out of the cut. But with a vacuum pickup attached to the router, you can suck those chips out of the cut as the router bit produces them.

Mortising

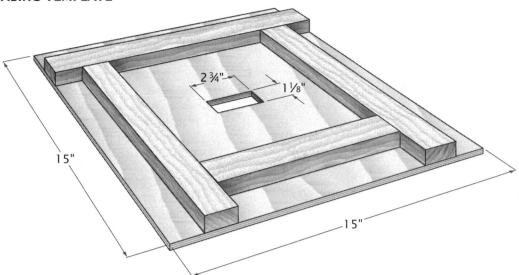

2 ¾"

1 ⅛"

15"

15"

## Cutting List

| Part | Qty. | Dimensions | Material |
|------|------|-----------|----------|
| Template | 1 | ¼" × 15" × 15" | Birch plywood |
| Fence | 1 | ¾" × 1½" × 15" | Hardwood |
| Fences | 2 | ¾" × 1½" × 15"* | Hardwood |
| Fence | 1 | ¾" × 1½" × 15"* | Hardwood |

## Hardware

Drywall screws, #6 × 1"

*Length is approximate. Cut to fit while actually assembling the template.

**A base-guiding mortising template** is simple to make and use. The wooden cleats attached to the template material guide the router as it cuts the window in the template, and also as it cuts the mortise itself.

## Making the Template

Making the template is pretty much a can't-miss proposition. You use an offset gauge, which is most commonly used in positioning straightedges for routing dadoes and grooves. Not only will this technique work for this jig, it's also a good way to guide a router when routing mortising windows in templates intended to be used with guide bushings.

**1. Make an offset gauge.** Cut this using the router and bit you will use with the mortising template that you are about to make. Set up the router. Now cut a 6- to 12-inch-long strip of ¼-inch to ½-inch plywood, MDF or hardboard, ripping it about 4 to 5 inches wide. This is a gauge blank.

Clamp a fence near the edge of a workbench. Butt the gauge blank to the fence; tack it down with a couple of brads, or stick it down with carpet tape. Guide the router along the fence, cutting through the stock. Pry up the gauge. You now have a way to position your template fences.

**2. Cut the parts.** You need a piece of plywood about 15 inches square for the template, and about 4 feet of ¾ × 1½-inch hardwood stock for the fences.

**3. Lay out the window on the template.** Lay a drop-leaf hinge, barrel up, in the center of the plywood and trace around it with a sharp pencil. Mark the centerline of the hinge pin, too, extending this line well beyond the outline of the hinge.

**4. Set the template's fences.** Use the offset gauge for this, as shown in the drawing *Fencing-In Sequence*. Lay the gauge so one edge just covers one of the pencil lines outlining the mortise. Clamp the gauge to the template blank, then butt a strip of the fence stock to its opposite edge. Screw the fence to the template blank (it's best, of course, if you drive the screws through the template stock into the fence stock).

Now use the gauge in the same way to position fences

**Mortising**

## FENCING-IN SEQUENCE

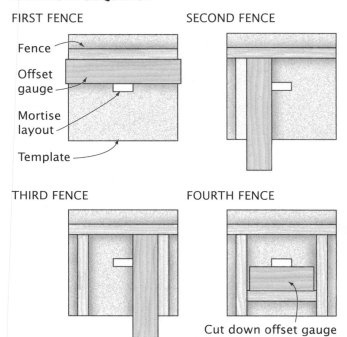

FIRST FENCE

Fence

Offset gauge

Mortise layout

Template

SECOND FENCE

THIRD FENCE

FOURTH FENCE

Cut down offset gauge

at each end of the jig. If necessary, trim the offset gauge to fit between the two end fences, and use it to position the fourth and last fence.

**5. Test the jig.** To do this, cut a piece of ¼-inch plywood or hardboard to just drop inside the fences. Use the chosen router and bit to cut a shallow mortise in this test scrap. (Don't cut into the template stock yet.) Measure the mortise. If it is the correct dimensions, rout through the template, forming the window. On the other hand, if the

**Template-mortising with a fixed-base router** is possible if you use a base-guiding template. With the router tipped so the bit is clear of the work, brace the router's base against the template's fences. Switch on the router, then lower the bit into the work. The fences confine the router, preventing it from cutting outside the mortise.

mortise is too large or too small, adjust the fence positions, and repeat the test procedure.

### Using the Base-Guiding Template

With the template made and successfully tested, routing mortises is a farily simple matter. This template is used in the same way the regular template is, except that you don't need a guide bushing on your router.

Outline the mortise on the workpiece, then align the template over it. Because the template's window has the same dimensions as the mortise, alignment with the layout lines is easy. Clamp the template to the work, and rout.

*If you don't have a plunge router,* this is an excellent way to rout mortises. You should be able to tip the router back enough to have the bit clear of the work, yet still have the router trapped between the fences. The fences then provide enough control that you can turn on the router, lower the bit into the work, and rout the mortise. After this initial pass, switch off the router and lift it clear of the work. Increase the bit extension, and repeat the process to rout a little deeper. Three or four cycles like this should enable you to rout a mortise at least an inch deep.

## A Template-Mortising Sampler

Template-mortising is a very versatile system. The generic mortising templates you've just read about—and actually tried, I hope—are just an introduction. There are other situations in which template-mortising is absolutely the best system. At the beginning of this chapter, I listed several of those applications. In each, the mortise would be difficult, if not impossible, to rout without a template.

The first, of course, has been dealt with by the general mortising templates. But what about those other three applications?

### SAWBUCK LEG ASSEMBLY

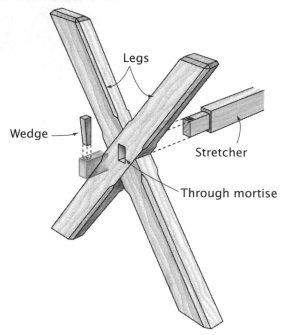

Legs

Wedge

Stretcher

Through mortise

## The Deep Through Mortise

Ordinarily, a through mortise can be routed using the approach described above. But every once in a while, the demands of a mortise go beyond the reach of even the longest of router bits. The right template setup can extend your router's reach.

An example is a knockdown sawbuck table I made a couple of years ago. The underpinnings were two sawbuck leg assemblies joined by a stretcher. Each pair of legs was joined in a crosslap. A tenon on the stretcher passed through a mortise in the legs and was locked in place with a removable wedge or key, as shown in the drawing *Sawbuck Leg Assembly*. Since the legs were 2¾ inches thick, the through mortise was beyond the reach of my longest bit.

By fitting the template with identical positioning blocks on both faces, I was able to do the mortise. The hidden problem here is alignment. If, in shifting the template from one face of the work to the other, you turn over the work or you turn over the template, the template likely will be misaligned. What you have to do is move the template just as though it was a playing card you were moving from the top of the deck to the bottom. *After* you have moved and reclamped the template, turn the whole works over so you can continue routing.

I made the mortising template as shown in the drawing *Sawbuck Leg Mortising Template*. I laid out and cut the window in the center of the template stock—a piece of ½-inch birch plywood. The mortise window was scaled to work with a ½-inch bit/⅝-inch guide bushing combination.

When the template was ready, I laid out the mortise on one leg assembly. Next I cut two triangular positioning blocks to fit into the crotch of the legs, tight against both legs. Now I was ready. I centered the template over the

**Routing a deep through mortise** calls for a mortising template with positioning blocks on both faces. The two blocks allow you to reference the same edges of the workpiece for position when moving the template from one face of the assembly to the other. Here I have routed as deep as I can into a nearly 3-inch-thick leg assembly. The template design allows me to move it underneath the assembly, keeping its orientation essentially unchanged. Then I can turn the whole works over and rout from the second side to complete the mortise.

## SAWBUCK LEG MORTISING TEMPLATE

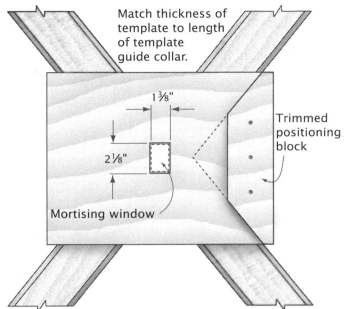

Match thickness of template to length of template guide collar.

1⅜"

2⅛"

Mortising window

Trimmed positioning block

Center template over layout lines for mortise, and clamp it to the legs. Then butt triangular positioning block against the legs and fasten it to the template.

layout and clamped it to the leg assembly. I next fit a positioning block firmly against the legs, then drove screws through the template into this block. I turned the template over and attached the second block, very carefully aligning it with the first positioning block. Then I trimmed the tips off the blocks to provide clearance for the router.

With the plunge router fitted with the appropriate bit and guide, I started routing the mortise. After cutting approximately halfway through the assembly, I unclamped the template, shifted it to the other side of the assembly, turned the leg assembly and template over, and reclamped the template. Finally, I completed the mortise.

This approach won't work for every extremely deep mortise you must rout. The project must present a couple of reference edges that will enable you to switch the template from one face to the other and maintain proper alignment. And if it does, this approach may save your day.

## A Mortise in the Panel's Face

Any time you have a mortise in the face of a panel, you have a situation in which a mortising template can be a benefit. The difficulty, as I noted at the outset of this chapter, is that you can't mount a panel in the typical jig designed to hold stiles and rails for mortising. But with a template, the panel can be dogged to a workbench and the template clamped to it. The template controls the position and length of the mortise.

My example here is a chest of drawers I reproduced for the book *Country Pine* (Rodale Press, 1995). The piece had its face rails mortised into the case sides (and drawer runners mortised into the backs of the rails). There were no stiles extending from top to bottom as in the typical face frame. It would have been possible to use an edge guide and freehand-rout the mortises in the sides, but I was put off from this

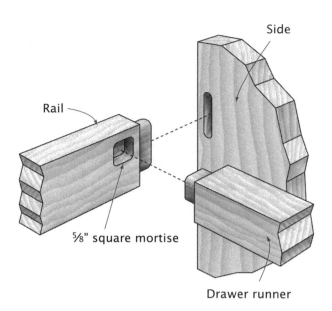

Rail

Side

⅝" square mortise

Drawer runner

approach by the possibility that I'd inadvertently rout too far, making a mortise too long. Instead I used a template, since it would ensure accurate sizing and placement of the mortises.

The template I used had windows in it for the five different mortises required. It is shown in the drawing *Joinery Template*. Because the mortises were only ½ inch deep, the template thickness wasn't a prime consideration; I used ½-inch plywood. All the mortises were routed with a ⅜-inch-diameter guide bushing and a ¼-inch straight bit. To make the template easy to use, I lined up the mortising windows parallel to one edge, my reference edge. Then I attached a fence to the template to locate it in relation to the edge of the workpiece.

To use the template, I laid out each mortise on the workpiece. First, I scribed a centerline from end to end, ⅜ inch from the panel's front edge. Then I marked the midpoint of each mortise. I laid the template on the panel, with the cleat butted against the front edge. Then I lined up the template slot over the layout, centering it by eye. I clamped the template securely, set the router on the template with the guide's collar in the appropriate slot, turned on the router, plunged the bit, and made the cut.

## Template-Mortising Frame Members

Yes, you can use a template to rout mortises in the edges of stiles (and rails) for face frames and door frames. Typically, a cleat is screwed to the template parallel to the mortising slot. The template can then be set on the workpiece with the cleat tight against the workpiece face. Clamps are applied, securing the template to the work. Then you rout the mortise.

Using a thin template with a cleat works well in this situation, but there's a lot of busywork in clamping the work and then positioning the template on it and clamping that. To move the template to a new spot, you usually also have to reposition the work in the vise. But if you can use thicker template stock, say ½-inch or more, you can reduce the busywork and save time.

What you do is make the template large enough to clamp to a workbench, with the mortising slot and the cleat cantilevered off the bench. Then you merely have to push the work against the cleat and the bottom of the template and then clamp it to the cleat. To rout a second or third mortise in the same piece, you simply have to move the work, not the work *and* the template. As I said before, this is the sort of router-mortising work that can be done efficiently using one of the other mortising jigs.

But a variant of this work, a variant in which the template-mortising approach proved its worth, came up in building the reproduction chest of drawers briefly described under "A Mortise in the Panel's Face" on page 153. The drawer runners were mortised into the face rails and the case's back boards. These mortises were ⅝ inch square.

Now if I had tried to rout them using the Mortising Jig on page 124, I either would have had to settle for ⅝-inch-diameter round mortises or I would have had to rout them using two different edge-guide settings. Talk about busywork!

But since I used a square window in the joinery template made for the job and a ¼-inch bit, the mortises turned out square with radiused corners. And by screwing a cleat with a positioning stop under the template, I was able to slap those rails in place, rout the mortise, and efficiently change over to the next rail.

**The template can hold the workpiece** for mortising if it is sturdy enough. Attach a cleat to the bottom of the template to position the workpiece for mortising. Clamp the work to the cleat, as shown, then rout the mortise.

**Mortising**

## JOINERY TEMPLATE

Use ⅜" template guide and ¼" straight bit.

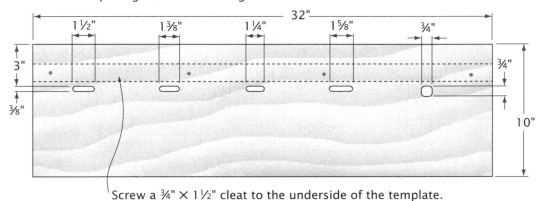

Screw a ¾" × 1½" cleat to the underside of the template.

Adjusting the setup for the next mortise was as simple as freeing the clamps, sliding the template to the next mortise location, then reclamping it. Because the cleat was parallel to the slots, the mortises were all parallel to the side's front edge.

**Rout mortises in the face of a panel** with a template. Here, the template is clamped to the side of the chest of drawers. With a cleat clamped to the bottom of the template, it's easy to slide the template along the workpiece from mortise to mortise. This fence ensures that all will be the same distance from the workpiece's edge. Lining up the slots for the three different rail mortises makes it easier to rout them in the first place and easier also to rout the mortises.

## A Difficult-to-Position Mortise

Routing a mortise in a round post, into the arris of a square billet, into any part of a shaped piece, can be vexing. Use a template both to support the router square to the mortise and to control the width and length of the mortise.

What you must do in these situations is to build a V-block or other cradle to hold the workpiece and then construct a complementary support for the template.

**Mortising a turning is a template job.** Here a turned leg is clamped between two strips of plywood in a vise. The mortising template is aligned over the mortise location, then attached to the plywood strips with drywall screws.

# Custom Router Table Top

**It must be flat, strong, and stable, must both withstand and dampen vibration, and must have a hard, tough, slick surface. Here's how to make the ideal router table top.**

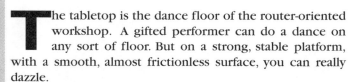

The tabletop is the dance floor of the router-oriented workshop. A gifted performer can do a dance on any sort of floor. But on a strong, stable platform, with a smooth, almost frictionless surface, you can really dazzle.

So what's your pleasure? Do you perform wood-working ballet? Or are you just a down-home clogger? For either extreme, and every style in between, your own personal dance will be most fulfilling on a platform of your own creation. Oh, you can hire a stage, and if it's all you ever use, you'll be happy enough.

But try a surface custom-tailored to your act. If you want it just right, you have to build it yourself. Then you'll have a unique tabletop, one that can't be purchased, not at any store, not from any catalog.

The industry standard for a router table top seems to be a 1⅛-inch-thick × 24-inch-wide × 32-inch-long top. Sized to get six from a 4 × 8 sheet. Medium-density fiberboard (MDF) core with plastic laminate on both sides. Tough polyethylene T-molding edging the top. Available with or without a mounting plate opening and with or without a miter slot. These router table tops are well

made, they are flat, and they are reasonably priced.

But why on earth would you buy one when you can make your own personal, custom-tailored tabletop for less money? It is not difficult. If you can glue two boards together, you can make a laminate-covered router table top. (Come on now, are you a woodworker or a collector of corded tools?)

When you make your own tabletop, you don't have to settle for the one-sixth-of-a-sheet-of-MDF size. You can make it somewhat smaller to fit better in a shop that's cramped for space. You can make it bigger, even big enough to accommodate more than a single router. You can make it thicker or thinner, too.

When you make your own tabletop, you can have a choice of edgings—plastic T-molding, yes, but also plastic laminate or solid-wood edge-banding, in semiconcealed or exposed styles. You can trim it with oak or walnut or, if you want, bubinga.

When you make your own tabletop, you can have any color or pattern of laminate on it you want. Black? You got it. Turquoise? You got it. Granite? Plasti-Wood? Whatever you want! You buy it, you apply it.

# The Custom Tabletop

Consider the criteria for a good, custom router table top. It must be flat, strong, and stable. It must both withstand and dampen vibration. It must have a hard, tough, slick surface.

The ways in which woodworkers fulfill these criteria have evolved over the years. Had you been following woodworking periodicals 10 or 15 years ago, you would have seen plans for smallish benchtop units, much like the Bench-Top Router Table on page 203. Typically, it'd be a three-sided plywood box or a stand with short legs. It would have a ¾-inch plywood tabletop. Often, the router was hung directly from the tabletop—you'd rout a recess in the plywood, leaving ¼ or ⅜ inch of material from which you'd hang your router. Or you'd cut a hole in the plywood, then hang the router from a piece of hardboard with which you covered the entire tabletop. (The tempered hardboard would make the surface slicker than plain plywood.)

At some point, a frugal woodworker modified a sink cutout, purchased cheap at the local lumberyard. He captured the slickness and durability of plastic laminate for his router table top without having to do any laminate work.

More recently, woodworkers have been applying plastic laminate to both sides of a plywood, particleboard, or MDF substrate, then cutting a hole in it and suspending the router from a mounting plate of acrylic, polycarbonate, or even phenolic plastic.

In designing an ideal tabletop, the shop-made custom tabletop, I think one needs to start with the materials. It must be made of fairly commonplace materials, ones that can be purchased in small towns across America and that can be worked in the typical home woodworking shop.

Start with the finished surface. We've moved away from bare wood and wood with a film finish. We've moved away from hardboard, which, though hard and slick, is neither tough nor durable. With a few commercial exceptions, we've moved away from metal as well. Plastic laminate seems to satisfy these criteria. It is hard and durable and slick. It is available everywhere. It's really easy to work.

Then you think about what must underlie plastic laminate. The core can be constructed of three different sheet goods.

*MDF* (medium-density fiberboard) is a good core material. Dense, it is made up of very fine particles. It is very stable and very flat. But, in my experience, it isn't as readily available as birch plywood. If you have access to it, if you like it, then use it. But laminate *both* sides to maintain its flatness. And size the edges before applying edge-banding. To do this, spread a thin coat of white or yellow glue over the edges and let it dry. Then you can glue on the edge-banding.

*Particleboard* is probably okay as a core for your tabletop. While some router woodworkers recommend particleboard for this use, others contend that it disintegrates from the vibrations of a router. My guess is that a behemoth router and a cheap particleboard make a poor partnership. For an occasional-use table equipped with a mid-sized router, particleboard is probably okay. For a heavily used table with a big router, go to plywood. As you may know, particleboard is a sheet product composed primarily of sawdust and glue. It has no grain structure, so it lacks plywood's strength. It's made in a variety of grades for a variety of purposes, but it is a common substrate for laminate-covered kitchen counters.

*Plywood,* in my book, is the ideal substrate. Because its individual veneers have grain direction and strength, and because these veneers crisscross in layers, plywood has great strength that the other sheet goods don't. The big shortcoming of plywood is that it isn't always perfectly flat. You can compensate for this, however, if you glue up a substrate from two pieces of the plywood. You will probably do this, since in most instances you'll want a tabletop at least 1 inch thick.

## Keeping the Top Flat

How many times have you experienced this at the lumberyard? You pull the top sheet from the stack of plywood or particleboard. The exposed face has picked up moisture from the open air, while the other face, having been virtually sealed against the sheet beneath it, has stayed more dry. Is this sheet flat? Though we think of sheet goods as being *flat,* we all know from experience they aren't. One face gets damp, the other stays dry: The sheet cups.

But you want a FLAT tabletop. How to get it? Start with a flat sheet, of course. Don't accept that bowed sheet. Then you get the material into your shop and give it days or weeks to acclimate to the shop's temperature and humidity before working it. When you laminate two layers, always orient any crowning in. The bowing of one layer will counteract that of the other, leaving you with a flat tabletop core.

Then apply plastic laminate to BOTH sides of this core, and seal any exposed edges of the core. If you apply laminate to one side of plywood or particleboard or even MDF, you are setting it up for a warp. The laminated side will stay dry, but the unlaminated side can pick up moisture. The panel is out of balance. The damper side will expand, the

**The tabletop core** can be made of several different materials. You can use MDF (*top*), particleboard (*center top*), plywood (*center bottom*), or Baltic Birch plywood (*bottom*).

## ANATOMY OF A ROUTER TABLE TOP

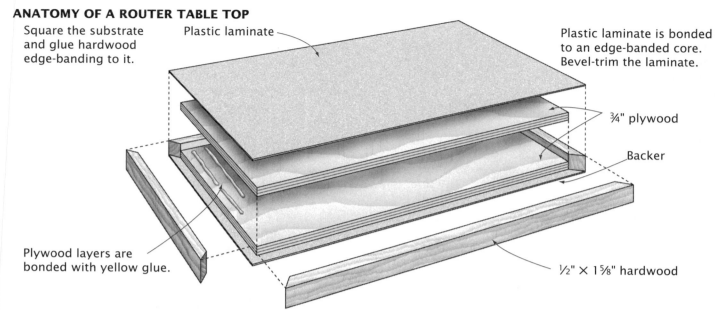

Square the substrate and glue hardwood edge-banding to it.

Plastic laminate

Plastic laminate is bonded to an edge-banded core. Bevel-trim the laminate.

¾" plywood

Backer

Plywood layers are bonded with yellow glue.

½" × 1⅝" hardwood

### Cutting List

| Part | Qty. | Dimensions | Material |
|---|---|---|---|
| Core plies | 2 | ¾" × 23⅝" × 36" | Birch plywood |
| Edge bands | 2 | ¾" × 1⅝" × 37½" | Hardwood |
| Edge bands | 2 | ¾" × 1⅝" × 25⅛" | Hardwood |
| Top surface | 1 | ¹⁄₁₆" × 26" × 38" | Plastic laminate |
| Bottom surface | 1 | ¹⁄₁₆" × 26" × 38" | Backer |

**The tabletop edges** can be finished several ways. You can carefully square the top before applying the laminate, then laminate the edges as well as the faces (*top*). You can apply the laminate, then glue on ½- to 1-inch-thick edge-banding cut from maple, oak, or other durable hardwood (*center*). Or you can edge-band the plywood and run the laminate out to the edge of this assembled core (*bottom*).

panel will cup. In context, your router will be in a subtle saucer. Here's what to do to prevent this:

- Laminate both faces to create a balanced panel that will stay flat.
- Seal the edges as well. If you apply hardwood edge-banding, seal it with a couple of coats of finish.
- Paint or otherwise seal the edges of the mounting-plate opening.
- Skip the miter gauge slot in the tabletop. It's unnecessary, and it breaches the seal.

### My Ideal Tabletop

My ideal tabletop has a 1- to 1½-inch-thick plywood core with plastic laminate on both sides. The dimensions of it, other than the thickness, are pretty much irrelevant. It can be small enough (say, 16 × 20 inches) to be for a benchtop router table, or large enough (say, 30 × 48 inches) to serve also as a table saw outfeed (or as a multirouter workstation). For any configuration, the materials used and the method of construction remain the same.

I like the plywood core because it has structural strength and it has rigidity. A 1½-inch-thick plywood tabletop doesn't need a framework to stiffen it. It won't sag. My router tables tend to be auxiliary workbenches, so these considerations have significance.

The tabletop edges can be finished several ways. You can carefully square the edges before applying the laminate, then apply laminate to the edges as well as the faces. This is known as the "self-edge." In some ways, this is the easiest tabletop to build. At the opposite extreme, you can use exposed edge-banding. Square the core, and apply laminate to the top and bottom. Then glue on ½- to 1-inch-thick edge-banding cut from maple, oak, or other durable hardwood. To complete this tabletop, you must flush-trim the edge-banding and apply a finish to it. The third option is to edge-band the core before applying the laminate, to produce a tabletop with semiconcealed edge-banding. When you apply the laminate, run it out beyond the edge-banding. Flush-trim the laminate, then rout a bevel around the edges. And, of course, apply a finish to the exposed wood.

The last option is my favorite. Here's how to go about building such a tabletop. The Cutting List shows what you'd use to build the tabletop for the Floor-Standing Router Table on page 212. Change the dimensions to suit your custom application, by all means.

## Building the Tabletop

Here are the step-by-step directions for building a tabletop for any of the router tables in this book or for any that you create. Follow these steps to a better tabletop than you can buy.

**1. Cut the layers.** Cut two pieces of plywood, particleboard, or MDF to size. I generally use birch plywood because its faces are smoother than standard fir plywood. Since either face of a piece could end up as the work surface, both faces of each piece should be as smooth and defect-free as possible.

Assess the pieces for crowning and face quality. The crowned face of each piece—regardless of its quality—must be oriented to the inside when you glue them together; this is how you create a flat, balanced top. If both pieces are flat, then orient the best faces out.

**2. Glue up the substrate.** Spread yellow glue on what you've selected as the mating faces. Get on a thin but thorough coating, avoiding dry spots. When both surfaces are ready, lay one carefully atop the other. Slide the top piece around on the bottom piece just a little to

**To spread glue on the tabletop layers,** I dribble glue over the surface, then spread it around with a suitable ripping from the scrap bin. The makeshift trowel does a good job of thinly coating the entire surface. And when the job's done, the scrap goes back in the scrap bin. A roller or brush spreads glue well, but washing it out when the job is done is really onerous.

smear the glue and get the two pieces really stuck together. Since yellow glue sets up pretty fast, don't dilly-dally. Align the edges.

As you apply the clamps along one edge during glue-up, the others will tend to open up. Eventually, the clamps will close the gaps, and the bowing will spread the pressure across the entire surface. The glue bond will be that much better overall.

Let the glue cure overnight with the clamps in place.

**Is your plywood slightly bowed?** Don't worry. Orient the panels with the crowned faces in. As you apply the clamps along one edge during glue-up, the others will tend to open up. Eventually, the clamps will close the gaps, and the bowing will spread the pressure across the entire surface. The glue bond will be that much better overall, and the bowing of one sheet will counteract that of the other, leaving you with a flat tabletop core.

**3. Prepare your edge-banding stock.** It should be a hard, straight-grained hardwood like maple, ash, oak, or birch. It should be wide enough to stand a bit proud of the plywood core on both sides, and about ¾ inch thick. Make it about 1⅝ inches for the 1½-inch core.

**4. Apply the edge-banding.** Remove the clamps from the core. Trim it to make it square and to clean and true the edges.

Cut the edge-banding to fit, mitering it at the corners. Glue it in place. Be sure to align each piece of the banding so it stands proud of the core on both top and bottom.

**5. Flush-trim the edge-banding.** After the glue has dried and you've removed the clamps, you must trim the edge-banding flush with the top and bottom surfaces of the substrate. As with every task in woodworking, there are several ways to do this.

If you have a lightweight router and a means to securely clamp the tabletop on edge, you can use flush-

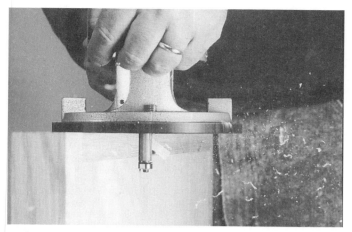

**When using a flush-trimming bit** to trim wooden edge-banding, you need a steady hand. It's best if you can clamp the tabletop on edge so that gravity helps you hold the router on the narrow edge. Take very shallow cuts, feeding in the correct direction. Any jerk or wobble of the router will telegraph into the routed surface in the form of a gouge that you'll be hard-pressed to remove or conceal.

**With a flush-trimming baseplate,** edge-band trimming is less dicey but takes more time. The tabletop not only can, but must, rest flat on the workbench, as shown. With a mortising or bottom-cleaning bit in the router and the baseplate flat on the substrate, work back and forth along the banding, nibbling it flush.

Router Tables

trimming bit to do the job quickly, as shown in the photo at top left. You *can* clamp the tabletop flat, and hold the router horizontally to do this, but I think the likelihood of a wobble that'll gouge the edge increases dramatically.

The other obvious option is to use the flush-trimming baseplate and a mortising or bottom-cleaning bit. With this setup, you can, as shown in the photo at bottom left, do the job with the tabletop setting flat on the workbench. The size of the router you have is less of a factor, too. Plans for the Flush-Trimming Baseplate are shown on page 119.

**6. (optional) Round the tabletop corners.** Rounding the corners of your router table top can save you some painful bruises. You don't need to do this, but if you choose to, this is the time to do it.

I use a corner-rounding template with a pattern bit. Clamp the template to one corner. (See the chapter "Boring Templates" on page 6 for a usable template.) Chuck the pattern bit in the router, and set the depth of cut so the shank-mounted bearing will ride against the template. Don't plow squarely into the waste. There's a lot of material right at the corner to remove, so nibble at it with back-and-forth passes of the router. When the bearing comes into contact with the template, the bit will stop cutting, and you can stop too.

Repeat this process at each corner. Then set aside the template.

You still have waste to remove, of course (unless you have a pattern bit with 1½-inch-long cutting edges). Rout this waste off, using the just-routed edges to guide the pattern bit's bearing.

**7. Apply the laminate and backer.** Now you are ready for the plastic laminate. Cut the two pieces required to make a balanced, stable, warp-resistant top about a half to a full inch larger than the edge-banded core. Because of the irreversible nature of the bonding process, and because you will trim the edges of the laminate after installation anyway, it's best to cut the pieces extra long and wide.

You can saw laminate with carbide-tipped blades, cut it with carbide router bits, or score and break it. For the latter process, use a special scoring tool, which you can buy for three to five dollars. Laminate will chip out quite easily as it's sawed, and the chips are hard and sharp. Wear those safety goggles!

Contact cement is what bonds the laminate to the substrate. It's a sophisticated rubber cement that you spread on the mating pieces and leave to dry. When you touch the dried cement on the laminate to the dried cement on the substrate, they stick—immediately. Therefore, the laminate must be accurately aligned before it can be allowed to touch the substrate.

Spread the cement on the two pieces. A scrap of laminate makes a good trowel-like spreader, but you can use a

## Backer

You can save some money if you cement "backer" to the bottom side of the tabletop. Backer is laminate without the color layer, and it is designed specifically for sealing the bottoms of counters and other laminated surfaces. Though it's kraft-paper brown and only half the thickness of regular laminate, backer nonetheless has the same moisture-resistant qualities, works the same way, and is bonded with the same contact cement.

An advantage backer has over laminate is that it isn't as slippery. Clamps can get a better purchase on it. Thus, a clamped-down fence is somewhat more likely to stay put if the tabletop's underside is backer rather than laminate.

**Spread contact cement** on each of the pieces to be joined. A scrap of laminate makes a good trowel-like spreader for solvent-based cement, but you can use a bristle brush or roller for water-based cement. Thoroughly coat the surfaces and wait for the cement to dry. Do this in a well-ventilated area.

**Bond the laminate** by pulling the spacers one by one and pressing the laminate firmly onto the substrate. It's common to start in the middle, as shown here, and work out toward the ends. Always work from the bonded area out so you don't trap a pocket of air between the laminate and the substrate. When all the spacers are removed, set the bond by pressing the laminate firmly to the substrate with the heel of your hand or a J-roller.

## Making a Tabletop with Exposed Edge-Banding

The procedures for making this style of tabletop are no different than those detailed in this chapter's step-by-step. They simply are performed in a different sequence.

1. Laminate the two layers to form the core, and prepare the edge-banding (Steps 1 through 3 on page 159).
2. After squaring the core, apply the plastic laminate to it.
3. Trim the laminate flush with the edges of the core.
4. Now apply the edge-banding.
5. Trim it flush with the top and bottom surfaces of the tabletop, then apply a finish to it.

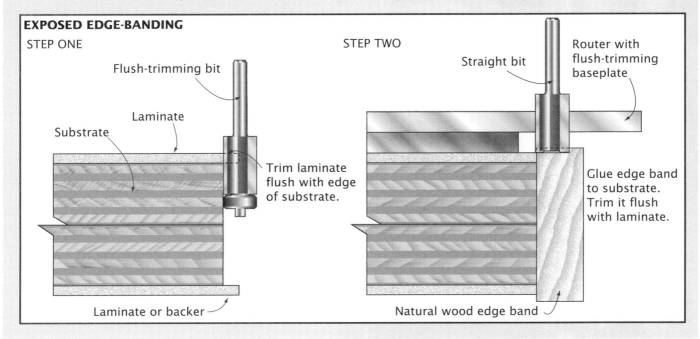

EXPOSED EDGE-BANDING

STEP ONE

Flush-trimming bit

Laminate

Substrate

Trim laminate flush with edge of substrate.

Laminate or backer

STEP TWO

Straight bit

Router with flush-trimming baseplate

Glue edge band to substrate. Trim it flush with laminate.

Natural wood edge band

bristle brush or other applicator. Thoroughly coat the surfaces and wait for the cement to dry. Especially if you use a solvent-based cement, do this in a well-ventilated area.

After the cement has dried, distribute the spacers evenly over the substrate. The spacers can be dowels or narrow rippings from the scrap bin. Position the laminate on the spacers, and center it over the substrate. Pull the spacers one by one, and bond the laminate. I usually start in the middle, pulling one spacer and pressing the laminate down onto the substrate. Then I work out toward the edges. After the laminate is stuck to the substrate, go over the surface with a J-roller, pressing very hard to ensure that the laminate is thoroughly bonded to the substrate. Or just tap a scrap of wood with a hammer as you move it slowly and methodically across the surface.

Flip the tabletop over, and repeat the process to apply laminate or backer to the other side.

**8. Trim and bevel the edges.** Complete the tabletop by trimming the laminate, slightly beveling the edge of the laminate and the hardwood edge-banding. Use a bevel-trimming bit in your router. Set the depth of cut to about ⅛ inch, which is about twice the thickness of the laminate. With the router on the laminate surface and the bit's pilot riding the edge-banding, rout around the tabletop. Turn the top over and trim the other side's laminate.

**9. Apply a finish to the exposed edges.** To completely stabilize the tabletop, the raw wood of the edge-banding must be sealed. A couple coats of polyurethane varnish should preserve the beauty of the wood you've used for the edge-banding, while reducing to the bare minimum its ability to take on and give off moisture.

## Making a Tabletop with a Self-Edge

This style of tabletop doesn't require you to prepare and apply solid-wood edge-banding, but the process of applying and trimming the plastic laminate is more involved. Yet the techniques for doing this are no different than those detailed in this chapter's step-by-step.

1. Laminate the two layers to form the core (Steps 1 and 2 on page 159).
2. After squaring the core, apply the plastic laminate to *two opposite edges*.
3. Trim this laminate flush all around.
4. Apply plastic laminate to the two remaining edges.
5. Trim this laminate flush all around. The ends of these strips will overlap the end edges of the first two strips applied and trimmed.
6. Apply the plastic laminate to the top and bottom surfaces of the tabletop.
7. With a bevel-trimming bit, trim the edges of the laminate. Set the cutter so it bevels the edges of the top and bottom surfaces *without* cutting into the faces of the laminate on the tabletop edges.

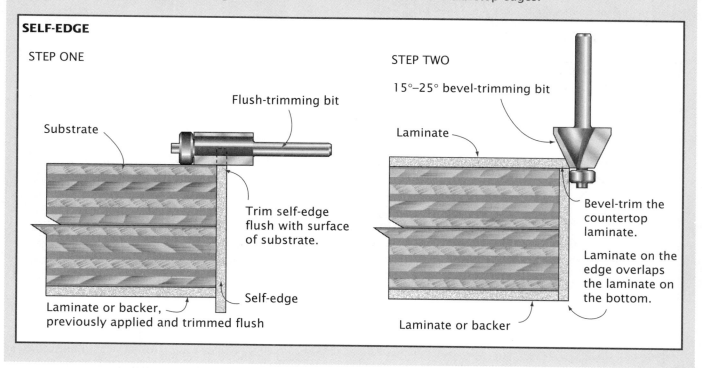

**SELF-EDGE**

STEP ONE

Substrate

Flush-trimming bit

Trim self-edge flush with surface of substrate.

Self-edge

Laminate or backer, previously applied and trimmed flush

STEP TWO

15°–25° bevel-trimming bit

Laminate

Bevel-trim the countertop laminate.

Laminate on the edge overlaps the laminate on the bottom.

Laminate or backer

Router Tables

# Universal Router Mounting Plate

**Work from scratch to make yourself a mounting plate that's fitted precisely to your router and router table.**

**A**ttach the router directly to a piece of plywood. That used to be the typical approach to creating a router table, and it's one that works. Not as well as other, more contemporary approaches. But it works.

Nowadays, of course, the most common way to mount a router in a table is with a mounting plate, which is little more than an oversized baseplate. A rabbeted opening is cut through the tabletop. The opening is big enough to allow the router to drop through, but the plate is caught and supported by the rabbet. The plate ends up flush with the tabletop. The weight of the router keeps the plate in position. A proper fit means there's no sideplay, so the plate doesn't shimmy around in the hole. Because the plate is separate from the table and not fastened down, it—and the router—can be easily removed from the tabletop.

What an improvement over the old approach! You can pop the router out to change bits. And because the plate is probably less than half the thickness of a plywood tabletop, you can wring greater depth of cut from your router.

Obviously, the plate from which the router hangs is a critical component. It has to be flat so that your cuts are consistent. It has to be strong enough to support the router. And because we're all on some kind of budget, it can't come too dear.

You can buy a mounting plate, of course. Commercial mounting plates abound. Most bit sellers have them in their catalogs, as do full-line tool dealers. These plates are not bad, generally.

But my attitude is: Why buy a mounting plate if you can make one? Especially if you are a hobby woodworker, making a mounting plate can introduce you to techniques and procedures that will enhance your "real" woodworking. And it can give you something you probably don't get enough of: practice. Moreover, working from scratch will give you a mounting plate that's fitted precisely to your router; the bit opening will be centered on the bit axis, and that's essential. It will give you a mounting plate that precisely fits the tabletop.

In the following few pages, I'll show you, step by step, how to make a mounting plate. You can make it as big or as small as you like, from whatever (appropriate) material you choose, attach whatever router you have, and make the bit opening as big or small as you desire. I'll also explain how to use the mounting plate to cut the tabletop opening for it.

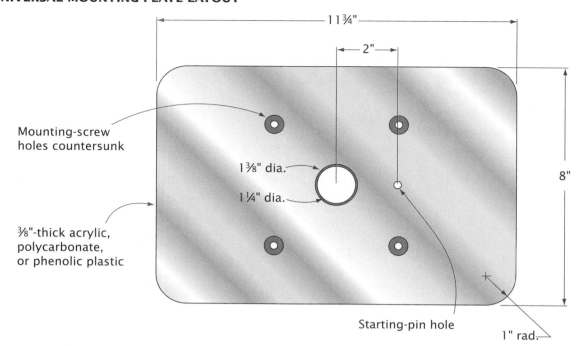

Mounting-screw holes countersunk

1⅜" dia.

1¼" dia.

⅜"-thick acrylic, polycarbonate, or phenolic plastic

11¾"

2"

8"

Starting-pin hole

1" rad.

# Making the Mounting Plate

The approach here will be to make a plywood or medium-density fiberboard (MDF) template or pattern, then use that to make the plastic mounting plate. There are several reasons for this.

- Plywood and MDF are easier to work than plastic. They won't melt, for example, if you sand an edge too aggressively.
- Both wood products cost less than plastic, so if you goof, you aren't writing off a $10 to $15 square of material.
- Both products provide good surfaces for note taking. You can jot directions for using the template right on it. In the future, when you want to make a dupe of your mounting plate, you will be reminded of what bits and guide bushings to use.

But you need not make a template if you don't want to. To make a one-off mounting plate, follow the sequence, but work with the mounting plate blank instead of a template blank.

**1. Select the mounting plate material.** The materials usually used these days are plastic: acrylic, polycarbonate, and phenolic. In three nutshells:

- **Polycarbonate** is easy to work with woodworking tools and is readily available at plastics stores and through mail-order woodworking suppliers. Virtually unbreakable, it is a tad flexible—it gives rather than shatters—and may sag under the weight of a behemoth router. *Third choice.*

## Cutting List

| Part | Qty. | Dimensions | Material |
|---|---|---|---|
| Template | 1 | ½" × 8" × 11¾" | MDF |
| Mounting plate | 1 | ⅜" × 8" × 11¾" | Plastic* |
| Starting pin | 1 | ⅜" dia. × 1¼" | Dowel |

*Acrylic, polycarbonate, and phenolic are all suitable.*

- **Acrylic** also is easy to work with woodworking tools and is readily available at plastics stores and through mail-order woodworking suppliers. It isn't as unbreakable as polycarbonate, but it is more rigid. A ⅜-inch-thick piece will support a screaming 18-pounder without sagging. *Second choice.*
- **Phenolic** is easy to work with woodworking tools, but it is difficult to find; a few mail-order woodworking suppliers carry pieces. It is very strong, very rigid. A ¼-inch-thick piece of the right grade will support that 18-pounder. *First choice.*

More information about the materials and about techniques for working them is in the appendix.

**2. Settle on dimensions for the plate.** How big should the plate be? Just big enough and no bigger. You want to be able to drop the router through the tabletop opening without unnecessary maneuvering. You want to be able to raise the router to its maximum depth of cut without having the handles bottom against the tabletop before you get to the router's limit. But you want the plate as small as possible. The optimum dimensions thus may vary from router to router.

Router Tables

## FITTING PLATE AND TABLE OPENING TO ROUTER

### A. PORTER-CABLE #690 1½-HP FIXED-BASE ROUTER

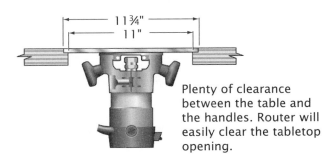

Plenty of clearance between the table and the handles. Router will easily clear the tabletop opening.

### B. PORTER-CABLE #7519 3¼-HP FIXED-BASE ROUTER

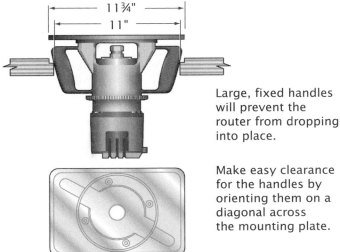

Large, fixed handles will prevent the router from dropping into place.

Make easy clearance for the handles by orienting them on a diagonal across the mounting plate.

### C. RYOBI #RE-600 3-HP PLUNGE ROUTER

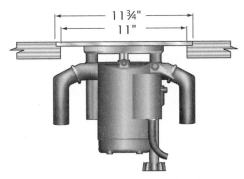

Even at maximum plunge depth, there's plenty of clearance between table and handles. But because of handle design, the router will not easily clear the opening.

### D. HITACHI #M 12V 3¼-HP PLUNGE ROUTER

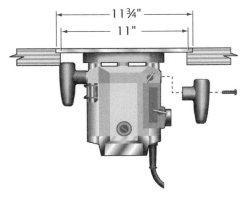

Handles touch tabletop just before router's maximum plunge depth is reached.

An easy solution? Remove the handles. A single screw secures each one. Removal of the router is now easy, too.

As a practical matter, though, it may be best to pick up cues from those mail-order catalogs. I checked several; mounting plates offered ranged from a small of 7¾ × 10¼ inches up to a large of 9 × 12 inches. Bear in mind that most catalogs offer suitable plastics in *nominal* foot-square pieces, meaning that they are 11½ inches square or 11¾ inches square.

So measure the router you've earmarked for the router table. What's the distance from handle to handle? What's the distance from the bottom of the handle to the bottom of the base? (If you are measuring a plunge router, be sure to bottom it out for this measurement.) If you go with 8 × 11¾ inches, can you make it work? The tabletop opening (excluding the rabbet) would be about 7¼ × 11 inches. This is the size I picked as being an appropriate compromise between the size of the routers typically used in router tables and the *nominal* foot-square plastic plates most commonly available.

**3. Cut the plate template.** Make the template out of fine particleboard, MDF, or plywood. Use material that's ½ inch thick.

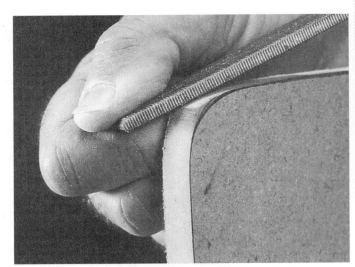

**Smooth mill marks from the template edges.** Any nicks or washboardlike ridges will telegraph into the plastic mounting plate's edges. Since it's easier to file or sand them from MDF than from acrylic or phenolic, do this cosmetic work on the template.

## MANEUVERING ROUTER THROUGH OPENING

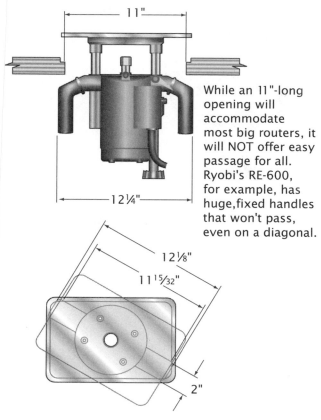

While an 11"-long opening will accommodate most big routers, it will NOT offer easy passage for all. Ryobi's RE-600, for example, has huge, fixed handles that won't pass, even on a diagonal.

What to do?

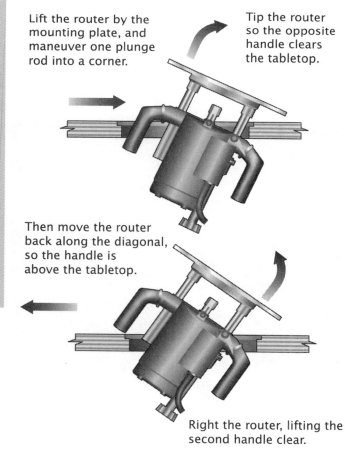

Lift the router by the mounting plate, and maneuver one plunge rod into a corner.

Tip the router so the opposite handle clears the tabletop.

Then move the router back along the diagonal, so the handle is above the tabletop.

Right the router, lifting the second handle clear.

On the table saw, cut the material to the dimensions you've settled on for the mounting plate.

Round the corners. There's a practical reason for this: It's easier to rout the tabletop opening if the opening's corners are radiused. Squaring the corners has to be done with a chisel. The work of rounding the template corners can be done on a stationary sander, but I like to use a template to guide a router and pattern bit. (See "Boring Templates" on page 6 for more information on corner-rounding templates.)

**4. Drill the mounting-screw holes.** You want to be able to use the template to guide the drilling of the mounting-screw holes and the routing of the bit opening. Use the router's factory baseplate as a pattern for the mounting-screw holes.

Remove the baseplate from the router. Use it as a drill gauge to select the proper-sized bit to drill the mounting-screw holes. With the drill selected, stick the baseplate to the template. Although the bit opening must be absolutely concentric with the bit axis if you want to use template guides successfully, it doesn't have to be dead center on the plate. Therefore, you can eyeball the router location on the plate. Apply carpet tape to the factory baseplate, position it on the template, and press it firmly to the template.

Take the template and drill bit to the drill press, and bore the mounting-screw holes. Take your time; get the holes perfectly positioned. Pry the baseplate off the template. Then, strange as it may seem, countersink the holes in the template.

**5. Locate and bore the bit opening.** Now mount the router itself on the template. This is why you countersunk the screw holes; you need to get the screws tight enough to pull the template into position so you can accurately mark the bit opening's center.

Chuck a V-grooving bit in the router's collet. Don't plug in the router, but rather turn the bit by hand, just barely marking the template.

Remove the router from the template, and head back to the drill press. Use a centering pin or a small-diameter bit in the drill press chuck to align the workpiece for boring the bit opening. When the center pin point is right on the centermark, clamp the workpiece. Then switch to a 1½-inch-diameter Forstner bit or hole saw and bore the bit opening in the template.

Depending on the bit and template guide combinations you use, this size template opening can be turned into a mounting-plate bit opening ranging from ¾ inch diameter up to a full 1½ inches.

**6. Locate and drill the starting-pin hole.** The starting pin is called a *starting* pin because it helps at the beginning of a cut. It's a fulcrum for the workpiece when you are routing with a piloted bit but no fence. You brace the work first against the pin, then "lever" it into the bit.

Commonly, a starting pin is a wooden peg or metal or plastic pin projecting from the mounting plate 2 to 4 inches from the bit. The position I recommend is shown in the plate layout drawing. Mark the location on the template, and drill the ¼-inch-diameter hole.

**7. Make the mounting plate.** Use a couple of strips of carpet tape to bond the template to the plastic you've selected for the mounting plate. If the plastic is protected by masking paper, leave the paper in place.

At the drill press, drill the mounting-screw holes. Be careful to center the drill bit in the template's guide holes so you get the holes in the plate perfectly positioned and also so you don't erode the guide holes.

Drill the starting-pin hole.

Set up your router to rout the bit opening. Here are a few bit/guide-bushing combinations to choose from:

- For a ¾-inch opening, use a ¼-inch straight bit in a 1-inch-diameter guide bushing.
- For a 1-inch opening, use a ¼-inch straight bit in a ¾-inch-diameter guide bushing.
- For a 1¼-inch opening, use a ⅜-inch straight bit in a ⅝-inch-diameter guide bushing.
- For a 1½-inch opening, use a pattern bit.

If you want to make a bit opening that will use template guides configured on the Porter-Cable standard, bore a 1¼-inch hole clear through the mounting plate. Then switch to a ½-inch straight bit in the ⅝-inch guide bushing, and rabbet the hole. Measure the flange on a guide bushing, and rout the rabbet that depth. It's usually about 3⁄32 inch, but check.

**Different combinations of template guides and straight bits** enable you to transform the template's 1½-inch-diameter bit opening into one of a smaller size when making a mounting plate. You can even rout a rabbeted bit opening that will accept template guides, as shown here. After routing completely through the mounting plate with one bit/guide bushing combination, you switch bits to rout the rabbet.

# Router-Mounting Screws

Make sure you have reasonably beefy screws holding the router to the mounting plate. Many older routers had only three 8-32 screws holding the baseplate on. That was fine for the use intended, but when you hang the router from the plate, you're better off either drilling out and tapping those holes to a bigger size or drilling and tapping entirely new holes. The Porter-Cable behemoth used in the Rodale Design Shop's router table has four ¼-inch screws holding it to the plate.

By all means, use flathead screws and countersink them so that they are just barely recessed. (Recessing too much not only weakens the plate, it creates a collection point for chips that will invariably catch your work and ruin your cut, if not your fingers.) Flatheads give the best load-spreading grip and are least likely to crack the plate and pull through. Don't use roundhead screws; they require a flat-bottomed counterbore that can seriously compromise the strength of the plate. The counterbores collect a lot of chips, too.

The situation most likely to test the strength of the plate and mountings is when you make a mistake in feed direction. A 3-horsepower router sucking a ¾-inch piece of oak into a ½-inch space between the cutter and the fence can create an amazing amount of pressure. If your router is securely mounted, the fence should give enough to allow the stock to be plucked from your fingers and thrown across the shop. If the router mounts give first, you could end up with an angry router coming out from under the table after you.

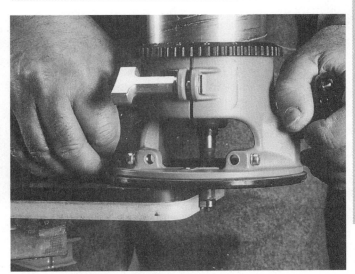

**A duplicate of the mounting-plate template** is produced in a single circuit with a router and flush-trimming bit. Bond mounting-plate material to the template with carpet tape. With the bit's pilot riding on the template, zip around the sandwich, trimming the mounting plate flush with the template, as shown.

Finally, using a pattern bit or flush-trimming bit in your router, trim the mounting plate to size. Pry the template and the mounting plate apart; this is when the masking paper comes off the mounting plate. Attach the plate to the router.

**8. Make the starting pin.** As noted previously, the most common manifestation of the starting pin is a wooden peg or a metal or plastic pin. For this plate, I used a 1¼-inch-length of ⅜-inch hardwood dowel.

Cut the pin to length. With a utility knife, score the pin deeply ⅜ inch from one end. Whittle the pin from the end to the score, reducing the diameter and forming a shank. Periodically test the fit of the shank in the starting-pin hole in the template.

## Installing the Mounting Plate

There's no question that the mounting plate must fit properly in the tabletop. It has to be dead *flush* with the tabletop surface so work doesn't get hung up. If the plate is high or low, there's an edge somewhere to catch and stop work being fed across it. It has to be tight in the opening. If it's loose, the gap between plate and tabletop fills with dust and chips, hindering the smooth movement of the work, perhaps throwing off setups. Moreover, a loose plate can shift position when the router is switched on, again throwing off a precise setup. If the fit is too tight, you may not even get the plate into the opening. If you do, the plate may be distorted.

So the real question is: How do I achieve that just-right fit?

The answer: Use the mounting plate template (or just the mounting plate) to make a new template. Then use the new template to rout the tabletop opening. There are two approaches that will work. In the first approach, you make a template against which the router base rides. In the second, you make a template against which a template guide rides.

I like the second approach, but that doesn't mean you will. To me, its advantage is that you use the mounting plate itself to guide the router as it cuts the template. There are no pencil layouts, no frustrating efforts to saw to a line. You just guide the router around the mounting plate; it cuts the perfect template that'll produce the perfect fit.

The first approach is not without advantages, of course. It allows the router to ride directly on the tabletop surface as it cuts the opening. This affords the best support and accuracy of cutting depth. It can be done with any router and straight bit; you don't need an assortment of template guides and several different straight bits. A less obvious advantage is that the template needn't be finely finished. The large radius of the router base can ride a neatly sawed edge without translating every little saw mark into the cut.

### Using a Base-Guiding Template

This approach can be used with any router, fixed-based or plunger. It can even be used with a laminate trimmer. In fact, the trimmer's smaller baseplate minimizes the size of template needed to guide the cut.

**1. Trace the mounting plate on the template stock.** Make the framelike template from ¼-inch plywood or hardboard. Lay the mounting plate on the template stock, and trace around it with a sharp pencil. If the plate has rounded corners, use a draftsman's circle template to locate the centerpoint of each corner's radius.

**2. Bump up the template outline.** You need to make the template opening larger than the plate to account for the base of the router you'll use to cut the tabletop. Draw lines on the template stock parallel to those traced from the mounting plate. The distance away from the plate tracing that you position these new lines is the difference between the bit's radius and the baseplate's radius, as shown in the drawing *Routing Tabletop Opening with Base-Guiding Template*. If the corners are rounded, use a compass to scribe them, pivoting on the corner centerpoints.

**Laying out a base-guiding template** calls for traditional drafting tools, like a compass, draftsman's circle templates, and a rule. After tracing around the mounting plate on the template stock, you have to draw cut lines, offset from the traced lines. To round the template's corners properly, you must swing the compass on the centerpoint of the mounting plate's corner arcs, as shown.

**3. Cut out the template.** Use a saber saw. While you want to avoid a cut that wanders, little ripples and rough saw marks shouldn't transfer to the router cut (though they would if you were referencing a template guide against the template rather than the router baseplate).

**4. Test the template.** Use a piece of plywood the size of the template. Position the template on the test panel and clamp it. Use the router and a ⅜-inch straight bit to cut a groove. Lay the mounting plate over the test cut; its outside edge should just line up with the outside edge of the groove. If the test cut demonstrates that the template is too big or too small, repeat the whole process to make and test a new template.

## ROUTING TABLETOP OPENING with Base-Guiding Template

### A. DETERMINE THE OFFSET.

Baseplate radius – bit radius = offset
In this example,
$$3" - \tfrac{3}{16}" = 2\tfrac{13}{16}"$$

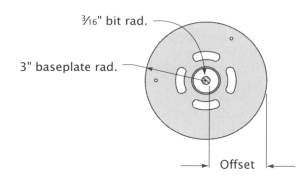

$\tfrac{3}{16}"$ bit rad.

3" baseplate rad.

Offset

### B. BUMP UP THE MOUNTING PLATE TRACING.

Round corners with compass.

Line traced from mounting plate

Scribe lines parallel to traced line.

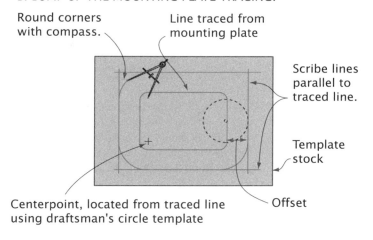

Template stock

Offset

Centerpoint, located from traced line using draftsman's circle template

### C. USE FINISHED TEMPLATE TO ROUT THE GROOVE IN THE TABLETOP.

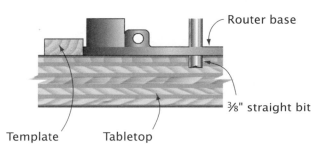

Router base

$\tfrac{3}{8}"$ straight bit

Template    Tabletop

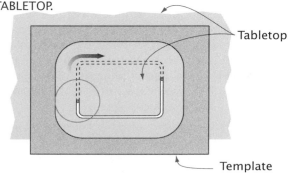

Tabletop

Template

### D. SAW OUT THE WASTE.

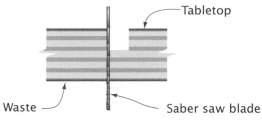

Tabletop

Waste    Saber saw blade

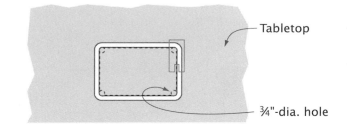

Tabletop

$\tfrac{3}{4}"$-dia. hole

**5. Cut the tabletop opening.** Do this only after the test demonstrates that the template is sized correctly, of course. Position the template on the tabletop, clamp it securely, and use the router to groove the tabletop. This groove eventually becomes the rabbet that supports the mounting plate.

Cut out the waste to complete the opening. Use a saber saw, and guide it along the inner edge of the groove. To start the cut, drill a pilot hole for the saber saw blade. When you are done, the plate should just fit. After all, you've tested it.

**Guide the router against the template's inner edge** to groove the tabletop. The cut isn't too heavy for a laminate trimmer, if you have one. The trimmer's small size is a benefit in this situation because the template doesn't need to be so big. Here, the groove is being routed in a table saw extension tabletop.

## Using a Guide-Bushing Template

I like this approach, as I said, because there's less opportunity for error to creep in. If you work carefully, you are sure to get a perfect fit.

**1. Rout an internal template guided by the mounting plate.** Use a piece of ½-inch plywood, MDF, or particleboard for the template. There's no layout work to perform, but some preparation is necessary.

First bond the mounting plate to the template stock with carpet tape. Use the carpet tape also to bond the template stock—particularly the section beneath the mounting plate—to a piece of expendable material. Do this even though you clamp the template stock to the workbench. The expendable material protects the workbench top. The carpet tape between it and the template keeps the waste, which supports the router, from shifting as it is cut free of the template.

Outfit a plunge router with a ⅜-inch-O.D. template guide and a ¼-inch straight bit. Set the plunge depth stop so the bit will, when bottomed against the stop, just break through the template stock into the waste beneath.

Keeping the template guide tight against the mounting plate, rout around it in the direction indicated in the drawing *Routing Tabletop Opening with Guide-Bushing Template*. Make several passes, plunging a little deeper for each circuit, until the waste is cut free. Unclamp the workpiece. Pry the plate from the waste.

**To make a guide-bushing template,** use the mounting plate itself as a template. Bond it to the template stock, and rout counterclockwise around it, as shown here. Keep the template guide tight against the mounting plate because the template will be ruined if the guide drifts away from the plate.

**2. Rout the plate-support rabbet in the tabletop.** Position the template on the router table top. Clamp it, being sure to position the clamps where they won't interfere with the router as you feed it around the inside edge of the template.

Change the plunge router setup. Chuck a ⅝-inch straight bit in the collet, and install a 1¼-inch-O.D. template guide in the baseplate. Porter-Cable makes this guide; it's

part number 42021. (You can also use a ⅜-inch straight bit in a 1-inch-O.D. template guide. This combination, obviously, will yield a narrower groove.)

Set the plunge depth carefully. The depth of the groove you are about to rout should exactly match the thickness of the mounting plate. You also must account for the thickness of the template. To do this, set the router on the template, and gently bottom the bit against the workpiece. Now rest a corner of the mounting plate on the turret, and drop the depth rod onto it. Lock the rod. You are ready to rout.

Keeping the template guide tight against the template, rout around the inner perimeter in the direction indicated in the drawing. Make several passes, plunging a little deeper for each circuit, until the maximum depth is achieved. Unclamp the template, and clear the chips from the groove.

**Use the mounting plate to set the plunge stop.** After bottoming the bit against the work (stand the router on the template and plunge it 'til the bit touches the tabletop) and locking the plunge, hold the plate between the router's turret and the depth stop rod, as shown. With the plate against the turret, seat the rod on the plate and lock it. Now the router will cut a groove as deep as the plate is thick.

**Grooving the tabletop** is a less ticklish operation than routing the template. Set the router on the template, with the guide collar tight against the template's guiding edge. Plunge the bit, and guide the router clockwise. If you do let the router drift away from the guiding edge, you'll merely be cutting into the waste area.

**ROUTING TABLETOP OPENING with Guide-Bushing Template**

A. MAKE AN INTERNAL TEMPLATE.

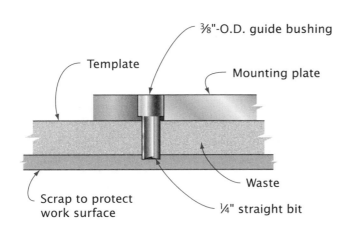

- Template
- ⅜"-O.D. guide bushing
- Mounting plate
- Waste
- ¼" straight bit
- Scrap to protect work surface

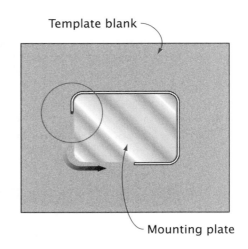

- Template blank
- Mounting plate

B. ROUT THE PLATE-SUPPORT RABBET.

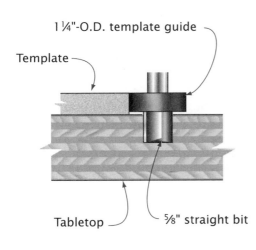

- 1¼"-O.D. template guide
- Template
- Tabletop
- ⅝" straight bit

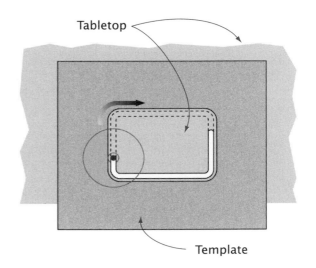

- Tabletop
- Template

C. CUT THE INTERNAL WASTE FREE.

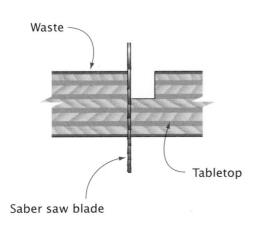

- Waste
- Tabletop
- Saber saw blade

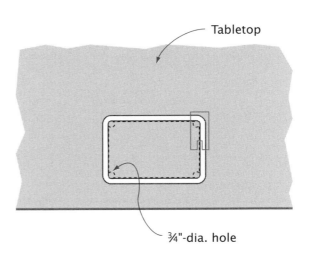

- Tabletop
- ¾"-dia. hole

**Router Tables**

**3. Cut the waste out of the tabletop opening.** Use a saber saw for this operation, cutting roughly along the inner shoulder of the groove. You'll get the cleanest job if you drill ¾-inch-diameter holes at each corner, as shown in the drawing and photo. This way, you can insert the blade into the hole and make a straight cut from one corner to another.

The placement of the saw cut will determine how wide the plate-support rabbet is. If you do cut right at the groove's shoulder, the rabbet will be just under ⅝ inch wide, which is a bit much. A good width for the rabbet is ⅜ inch.

With the waste removed, the mounting plate should fit perfectly, which is to say, just a bit hard. You will be able to set it into the opening, but you'll probably have to smack it with your fist to seat it.

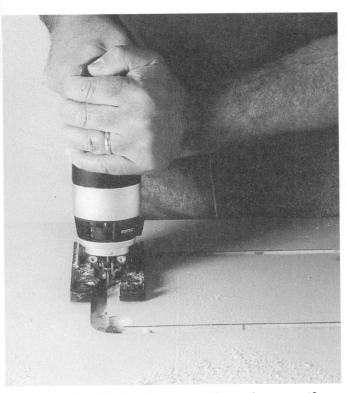

**Cut out the block of waste** with a saber saw. If you drill a large-diameter hole at each corner, as shown, you simply have to make straight cuts from corner to corner. Guide the saw along the inner edge of the groove so a rabbet is left to support the mounting plate.

## Using the Mounting Plate

No particular tricks are involved in using the mounting plate. You simply drive the mounting screws through the appropriate holes into the router base. Maneuver the router through the tabletop opening, and seat the plate in the rabbet. Chuck a bit in the collet, plug in the router, and you are ready for router table work.

The weight of the router will keep the plate in place.

A big advantage this mounting plate design has over the old bolted-to-the-tabletop mounting schemes surfaces when you need to change bits. With the router mounted (more or less permanently) beneath the tabletop, you have to struggle to change bits. Often, you can't see what you are doing, because the tabletop provides no window to the router.

But with the clear plastic mounting plate, you can see through the plate to see where you've got the wrenches. Even better, you can pull the router up out of the tabletop and give yourself easy access for bit changes.

Remember to pull the plug ANY time you change bits.

I can't think of a single instance in which freehand routing on the router table is appropriate. In every operation that comes to mind, you use either a starting pin or a fence, even a sled, a template guide, or an overhead pin, to help you guide and control the workpiece.

Fences that can be used are covered in other chapters: "Table Saw Extension Router Table" on page 183, "Bench-Top Router Table" on page 203, "Floor-Standing Router Table" on page 212, and "Split Fence" on page 237. The point here is the starting pin you made. Whenever you are routing with a piloted bit but no fence, use that starting pin. Brace the work against the pin, then "lever" it into the bit. The pin is fixed, so you can brace the work against it securely. Moreover, the pin gives you leverage, multiplying the strength of your hold on the wood and dampening the cutter's energy. (If you are working without a starting pin, then the spinning bit is your fulcrum.)

Once the cutter is engaged and the work is in firm contact with the pilot, the pin is superfluous. It won't hurt to keep the work against it throughout as much of the cut as possible, but you can't always keep the work against both the pin and the cutter. You'll probably find that if you concentrate on keeping the work against the pin throughout the cut, you'll occasionally let it get away from the pilot, leaving an unfinished feel to the cut.

# Bit Opening Inserts

**Interchangeable inserts scale the mounting plate's bit opening to whatever size bit you are using to keep you routing safely. Here's how to make them for your router table.**

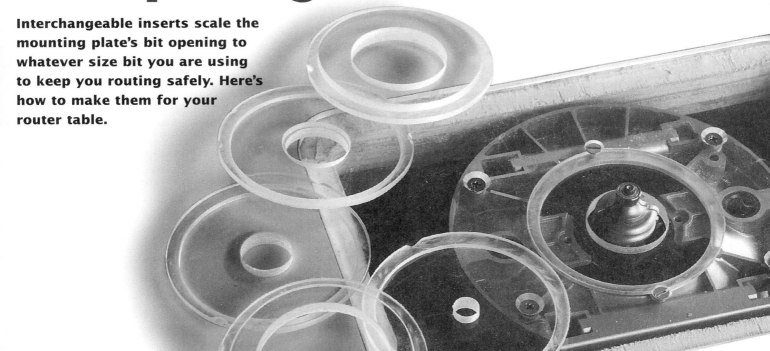

This is safety as much as savvy. You should have the bit opening in the mounting plate closed down around the bit just as closely as possible. This prevents the workpiece from dipping into the bit opening, snagging the edge, maybe stalling the cut.

If you've opened up the bit hole to accommodate a 3-inch (or larger) panel-raising bit, don't then fit a ½-inch dovetail bit or ¼-inch straight bit in the router and expect to rout a groove without hazard or hangup.

A possible solution, especially if you have a mounting-plate template, is to knock out several plates, each with a different size of bit opening.

But an interesting alternative is to make a special mounting plate with a set of bit opening inserts. The dimensions are shown in the drawing *Bit Opening Insert Layouts*. I made the set shown in the photo from ⅜-inch clear acrylic. The basic bit opening in the mounting plate is 3½ inches in diameter, large enough to accommodate the largest panel-raiser in any bit collection. It has a ¼-inch-wide × ³⁄₁₆-inch-deep rabbet around it. The inserts are 4 inches in diameter and are similarly rabbeted so the insert fits into the bit opening and rests flush. The bit openings in the inserts are matched to different, commonly used bit sizes—½-inch, 1-inch, 1⅝-inch, and so on. I've got one that's bored out and rabbeted for template guides.

Both the mounting plate's bit opening and the inserts

**This mismatch of bit to bit opening is trouble.**
With a small bit in a large opening, the work can catch the far side of the bit opening and get hung up. Even worse, it could tip into the void. If you are lucky, it will only ruin the workpiece. But using an insert closes down a hole big enough for a panel-raiser to provide near-zero clearance for a ¼-inch cove bit (*inset*).

are cut using the same template. In fact, you can incorporate the required orifice into the mounting-plate template, thus simplifying the matter of ensuring that the bit opening is concentric with the bit axis.

## BIT OPENING INSERT LAYOUTS

Retaining-screw hole, countersunk and
tapped for 8-32 flathead machine screw

11¾"

4" dia.

8"

⅜"-thick acrylic,
polycarbonate,
or phenolic plastic

3½" dia.

1" rad.

Mounting-screw holes, countersunk

SECTION VIEW

8-32 flathead
machine screw

Insert

Mounting plate

2" dia.          2½" dia.

½" dia.          1" dia.          1¼" dia.          1⅝" dia.

4" dia. (typ.)

1⅜" dia.

## Making Bit Opening Inserts

Having the inserts does you no good unless you also have a mounting plate set up to accommodate them. So make the plate at the same time you make the inserts; you do use the same template. Here's how to make a plate and an insert.

**1. Make the mounting-plate template.** I do hate to do this to you, but. . . . Keep your finger at this page, and turn to the step-by-step text on making the Universal Router Mounting Plate on page 163. Follow the procedure outlined there for making the template.

When you bore the bit opening in the template, make the opening 4½ inches in diameter, not 1½ inches. To cut a hole this large and have it centered perfectly, use a router and trammel (the Trammel Baseplate shown on page 39 is great for this operation) or do it at the drill press with a fly-cutter or hole saw.

**2. Make the mounting plate.** Follow the directions in the "Universal Router Mounting Plate" chapter on page 163 for using the template to make the mounting plate. Drill and countersink the mounting-screw holes for the router, and flush-trim the plate to duplicate the template.

But skip the directions in that chapter on routing the bit opening.

Instead, study the drawing *Making Bit Opening Inserts.* As shown there in part A, use a 1¼-inch-O.D. template guide bushing and a ¼-inch straight bit to rout the opening through

### Cutting List

| Part | Qty. | Dimensions | Material |
|---|---|---|---|
| Mounting plate blank | 1 | ⅜" × 8" × 11¾" | Clear acrylic† |
| Insert blank* | 1 | ⅜" × 12" × 12" | Clear acrylic† |

### Hardware

2 brass flathead machine screws, 8-32 × ½"

*You should get a minimum of four inserts from a blank this size.*

†*Phenolic is also suitable.*

the mounting plate. Note the feed direction specified.

Then switch to a ¾-inch straight bit in the same template guide to rout the ³⁄₁₆-inch-deep rabbet, as shown in part B of the drawing.

At this point, you can pry apart the template and mounting plate.

**3. Cut the insert blank.** The insert must be made from the same material as the mounting plate. Obviously, you can't attach the template to a small square workpiece; so cut as many inserts as you want from one large workpiece. Bond the template to the workpiece with carpet tape, as you did in making the mounting plate. Use the tape to bond the workpiece to some scrap. The scrap will protect the work surface. Taping the workpiece and scrap together keeps the insert blank from shifting as it is cut free; if it would shift, the router bit would gouge it, and thus ruin it.

Set up the router with a ⁵⁄₁₆-inch-O.D. template guide and a ³⁄₁₆-inch straight bit.

Keeping the template guide tight against the inner edge of the template, rout out the insert blank. The plastics typically used for mounting plates are all very hard. A ³⁄₁₆-inch straight bit is thin and consequently frail. So take very shallow cuts, or you risk breaking the bit.

If you are making more than one insert—and surely you are—pry up the template and reposition it to cut the next one. The carpet tape always seems to stick to the wrong part, and when it does, you can't successfully peel it up and reapply it to the right part. So you should figure on using new strips of tape for each new insert.

**4. Rabbet the insert blank.** Each insert must be rabbeted so it will nest into the mounting plate. The depth of the rabbet is critical, since you want the insert neither standing proud of the plate nor setting recessed. It must be perfectly flush.

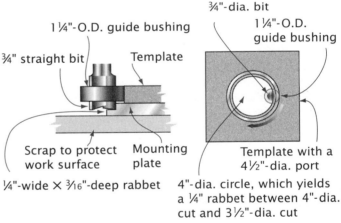

**To hold the insert blank for rabbeting,** attach it to a 2-inch-square post with carpet tape. Clamp the post in a vise, and you have unrestricted access to the blank's edge. Because of its compact size, a laminate trimmer is a dandy router to use for this job. Use a rabbeting bit, of course.

## MAKING BIT OPENING INSERTS

### A. CUT THE BIT OPENING IN THE MOUNTING PLATE.

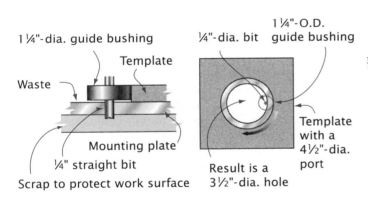

1¼"-dia. guide bushing
Template
Waste
Mounting plate
¼" straight bit
Scrap to protect work surface

¼"-dia. bit
1¼"-O.D. guide bushing
Template with a 4½"-dia. port
Result is a 3½"-dia. hole

### B. ROUT THE RABBET AROUND THE OPENING.

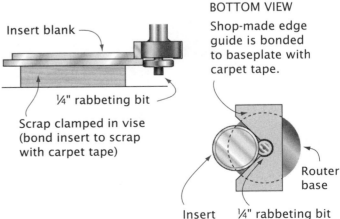

1¼"-O.D. guide bushing
¾" straight bit
Template
Scrap to protect work surface
Mounting plate
¼"-wide × ³⁄₁₆"-deep rabbet

¾"-dia. bit
1¼"-O.D. guide bushing
Template with a 4½"-dia. port
4"-dia. circle, which yields a ¼" rabbet between 4"-dia. cut and 3½"-dia. cut

### C. CUT THE INSERT BLANK.

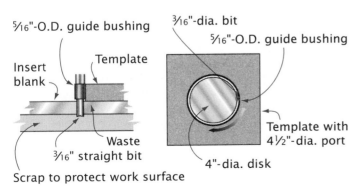

⁵⁄₁₆"-O.D. guide bushing
Template
Insert blank
Waste
³⁄₁₆" straight bit
Scrap to protect work surface

³⁄₁₆"-dia. bit
⁵⁄₁₆"-O.D. guide bushing
Template with 4½"-dia. port
4"-dia. disk

### D. RABBET THE INSERT BLANK.

Insert blank
¼" rabbeting bit
Scrap clamped in vise (bond insert to scrap with carpet tape)

BOTTOM VIEW
Shop-made edge guide is bonded to baseplate with carpet tape.
Router base
Insert
¼" rabbeting bit

**Router Tables**

Chuck a rabbeting bit in the router. Make sure you have the appropriate pilot bearing for making a ¼-inch-wide rabbet. Set the cutting depth, using the mounting plate's rabbet. Set the mounting plate on the baseplate, with the flange formed by the rabbet beside the bit, as shown. Set the height of the bit to exactly equal the thickness of the flange. If you rabbet just this thickness from the insert, it will nest flush into the mounting plate.

The drawing shows a shop-made edge guide stuck to the router's baseplate. This isn't essential, but you may find it helpful in keeping the router steady on the workpiece. The insert blank is small, and you have to work its entire edge. To secure the blank yet minimize the handling, stick it to a block of scrap wood with carpet tape. You can improve the bond if you squeeze the blank to the block momentarily, using a Quick-Grip clamp. (The improved bond, of course, means the insert will be harder to pry off the wood when the routing is done.) Clamp the wood in a vise, and rout the rabbet around the insert.

**5. Drill, countersink, and tap the retaining-screw holes.** Retaining screws are needed to keep the insert in place. Since there's no weight on it, as there is on the mounting plate, the router's vibrations will prompt it to pop out of place—a real disaster.

The screws are located in the seam between the plate and the insert, as shown in the drawing *Bit Opening Insert Layouts.* As you can see, the mounting plate has through holes, while the inserts have only two crescent-shaped notches on the edge. All are slightly countersunk.

Because the holes in the mounting plate are tapped (so the screws thread into them), their diameter has to be coordinated with the tap to be used. Check the tap; the size of the bit to use will be embossed on it. If you are using 8-32 screws, use what's called a #29 bit. (You can buy the tap and the bit at a good hardware store.)

The easiest way to bore the holes is on the drill press. Fit an insert into the mounting plate, and position this workpiece on the drill press table. Drill the two holes, then countersink them. Remove the insert. Tap the holes in the mounting plate. Details on using a tap are found in the

appendix, in the feature "Cutting Threads" on page 304.

Use the insert that's been drilled as a pattern for filing similar notches in any other inserts you are making. Here's the situation: The half-hole or notch in the insert merely provides clearance for the screw shank. The screw head needs a skosh of contact to hold the insert down. But a precise fit isn't that important here. Now it's darn hard to bore half a hole. A Forstner bit will do it, but you won't find a #29 Fortsner. If you fit each insert into the mounting plate and drill all of them, you'll distort the mounting-plate holes, making them impossible to tap. So that's out. A little work with the corner of a file should do the trick.

**6. Bore the bit opening in the insert.** The best way to bore the bit openings is with the router. This will provide true zero-clearance holes in the inserts. Mount the plate on the router. Chuck the bit you want to use in the router's collet. Fit an insert into place and drive in the retaining screws. Turn on the router and plunge-bore through the insert. Because you are boring plastic, you need to bore in increments, plunging and retracting the bit again and again until the insert is penetrated.

Repeat this process with other bits and inserts, as you desire.

For very large openings, bore the holes on the drill press or with a a router and trammel. To mark the insert centerpoint, which you need to do for either of these approaches, install it in the mounting plate. Then use a V-grooving bit, chucked in the router but turned by hand, to dimple the insert.

**If you use the drill press,** use a Forstner bit or fly-cutter to bore the holes. To begin, chuck a centering pin or small-diameter bit in the chuck, and lock the quill just above the insert surface. Line up the insert's centerpoint directly under the bit axis, then clamp the insert. Unlock the quill, and switch to the bit to be used to bore the bit opening.

If you want to make an insert for template guides, this is the approach to use. After the insert is aligned on the drill press table, bore a ³/₃₂-inch-deep counterbore for the template guide flange using a 1³/₈-inch Forstner bit. Then switch to a 1¼-inch Fortsner bit to bore completely through the insert.

**If you use a router and trammel,** you still *should* use a drill press to bore a hole in the insert for the pivot pin. For the trammel to guide a cut that's concentric with the centerpoint, the pivot hole needs to be perpendicular to the insert's face. A drill press will bore such a hole. Lacking a drill press, use a drill equipped with a right-angle guide.

With the pivot hole drilled, bond the insert to a fairly large scrap, which can be clamped to the work surface. Since the pivot is in the waste, you need to ensure that it won't shift when the waste is cut completely free of the insert. And, of course, you don't want the insert to move, either.

Adjust the trammel to the desired radius, and rout the opening.

If you want to try routing a rabbeted opening for template guides, you should rout the larger-diameter circle first, cutting ³/₃₂ inch deep. Then readjust the trammel to rout the smaller-diameter opening.

**Create a countersink arc in the insert** using a round file. Mark the locations of the needed countersinks—two in each insert. A couple of swipes with the file will form the profile needed.

# Router Crank

**Adjust the plunge router in your router table the same way you adjust the blade height in your table saw: by turning a crank. It's fast, smooth, precise. And when you make your own, it's economical.**

It's a good-news, bad-news cliché. The good news is that, mounted in a table, the plunge router provides the means to adjust bit extension very precisely and without the sideplay that plagues many fixed-base routers. The bad news is that, mounted in a table, the plunge router can be a wrist wrencher to adjust.

To extend the bit for a cut, you may need to twist your wrist about 20 to 30 times. Then to lower the router enough to expose the collet so you can change bits, you have to twist that wrist another 30 to 40 times in the other direction. If building forearms like Popeye's is one of your ancillary goals, have at it. If not, try this gizmo.

It's a shop-made variation on the familiar height-adjustment knob that most woodworkers use on table-mounted plunge routers. Instead of giving you a knob to twist, this device gives you a crank to work. Suddenly, raising and lowering your table-mounted router's bit is as simple as raising or lowering your table saw's blade.

This is one of those concepts that's obvious and simple. I had thought about it, yet I didn't actually believe it would work until I had a chance to try out a router table built by master woodworker Nick Engler. Nick's router was fitted with a crank almost exactly like the one shown here, and it moved that router slick as could be. Oh my, 'twas almost magical.

Now you can go two ways on this. You can make a fixture quickly and install it on your router, and it will work okay but never as slick as Nick's. OR you can make a fixture with care, and, before installing it on the router, you can super-tune the router's adjustment mechanisms. Then you'll have something. But the fact of the matter is that the router itself is the linchpin. If the plunge mechanism is sticky and the depth-stop rod is misaligned, no knob or crank will be able to make bit adjustments easy.

So that good-news, bad-news cliché winds all the way through. The good news is, your bit adjustment troubles are over. The bad news is, you gotta tune that router of yours.

## Using the Fixture

While it is simple in concept, this fixture needs to be fitted pretty precisely to the router if it is to work as slick as you want it to. I'm going to flip-flop the usual chapter format in this instance, because I think telling you *how* the fixture works will make it easier for you to understand why you need to make it the way I describe below.

All the crank is is a wooden column bored to fit over the router's height-stop rod. A nut is epoxied into the end of the column. And of course there's that crank atop the column.

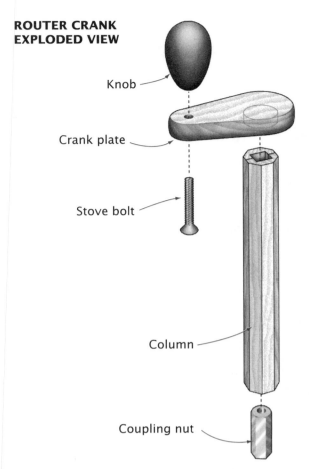

Knob

Crank plate

Stove bolt

Column

Coupling nut

| Cutting List | | | |
|---|---|---|---|
| **Part** | **Qty.** | **Dimensions** | **Material** |
| Column plies | 2 | ¾" × 1½" × 12"* | Hardwood |
| Crank plate | 1 | ¾" × 1¾" × 4¼" | Hardwood |

## Hardware

1 coupling nut (thread to match that of router's height-stop rod)

1 plastic knob, 1⅛" dia. × ⁷⁄₁₆" high with ¼"-20 insert; #ROA-4 from Reid Tool Supply Co. (800-253-0421)

1 flathead stove bolt, ¼"-20 × 1¼"

*Trim to fit the router after assembly.*

To use the fixture, you remove the stop nuts or jam nuts from your router's height-stop rod, just as you do when you need to pull the motor off the plunge rods. Drop a flat washer over the rod, and turn the fixture's nut onto the threaded rod. Start cranking, turning the fixture down onto

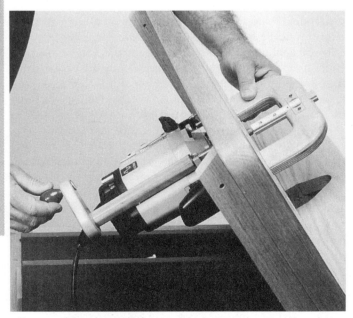

**On a table-mounted router,** the crank expedites bit-extension adjustments. No more wrist wrenching. It's now as easy as adjusting your table saw's blade. Just turn that crank and watch the bit move.

the rod until it seats against the yoke on the motor. Now as you crank, the motor will be driven down the plunge rods. It's just like the commercial adjustment fixtures you can buy, except that you are cranking, not twisting. Cool, huh?

Why don't the commercial accessories have a crank instead of a knob, you ask? Well, take a look at how they are constructed. The typical unit has a barrel-shaped plastic threaded insert stuck into an aluminum tube. When it's turned onto the height-stop rod, the only thing keeping the tube on the same axis as the rod is that plastic insert. Put a crank on top and, when you start grinding, the tube's going to wobble and whip and eventually pop right off the insert.

So here's the secret to cranking success: The crank column has to be closely fitted to that height-stop rod. And the longer that rod is, the better the unit will work. Because of this, you may want to consider replacing the stock rod with a longer one, though you can't do this on all plunge routers. (If you can't find metric threaded rod in your locale, you can order it from Reid Tool Supply Co.: 800-253-0421.)

And if you are going to replace that rod, why not replace it with a ⅜-inch rod, which will have 16 threads per inch. The 16 tpi is really handy since it means, in our router table application, that each full revolution of the crank changes the bit extension $\frac{1}{16}$ inch. A half-turn moves the bit $\frac{1}{32}$ inch. A quarter-turn moves it $\frac{1}{64}$ inch. Such precision!

If you want to tackle this router modification, read the feature "Replacing the Threaded Rod" on page 181.

## Making the Fixture

The critical element is that column. If you've got a lathe and the appropriate know-how, you can make the crank column by boring a 1-inch-diameter dowel on that machine. But I'm not a turner, so I had to find an alternative approach. You might think, as I did 'til I tried it, that the drill press is the right tool for boring the column. But instead, use the approach I settled on after a couple of false starts. It's a bit of that router magic, I think.

Basically, you rout grooves in two pieces of wood, then glue them together. The grooves combine to form a channel for the height-stop rod and a recess for the nut. To make the

Router Tables

## ROUTER CRANK LAYOUTS

FRONT VIEW

SECTION VIEW

END VIEW

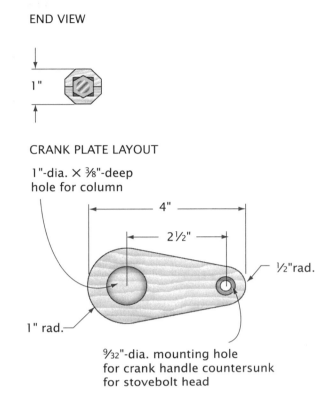

1"

CRANK PLATE LAYOUT

1"-dia. × ⅜"-deep
hole for column

4"

2½"

1" rad.

½"rad.

⁹⁄₃₂"-dia. mounting hole
for crank handle countersunk
for stovebolt head

Channel for
height-stop rod

9"

Epoxy nut in recess.

Coupling nut

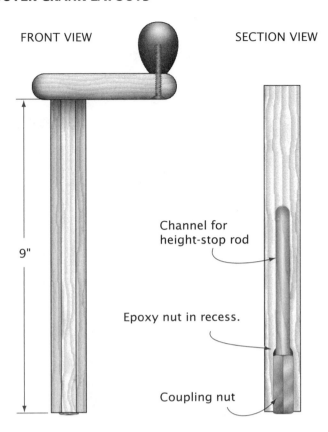

**Measure your router for the crank.** Plunge it as far as it will go, and measure the rod from the yoke to its end, as shown. Also measure from the yoke to the top of the machine.

column fit the router, you rip it down and chamfer or round-over the edges.

**1. Start by measuring your router.** The column must be long enough to clear the top of the motor and the power cord, if it projects out of the top of the motor. (If the crank hits the power cord on every rotation, it will be as nettlesome to use as a wrist-busting knob.) The column must to bored to accommodate the threaded rod, and the diameter of the hole must match the diameter of the rod. (As I explained earlier, if this hole is too much larger than the rod, the whole crank will wobble when you turn it.)

Plunge the router until the motor bottoms on the base, and lock it. Then measure from the yoke through which the threaded rod passes to the highest projection on the router. This is the minimum length of the column. Also measure from the yoke to the top of the rod. This is the minimum depth of the clearance hole that must be bored in the column. Finally, use dial calipers to measure the diameter of the threaded rod.

**2. Buy a coupling nut.** This is an extra-long nut that's usually used to connect two rods that have the same thread. I elected to use this longer nut to help eliminate wobble.

Your local hardware store will undoubtedly have coupling nuts in the the National Coarse thread sizes. But most plunge routers—Porter-Cable is the one exception I can think of—have metric height adjustment rods, so you need

## COLUMN ROUTING SEQUENCE

FIRST CUT

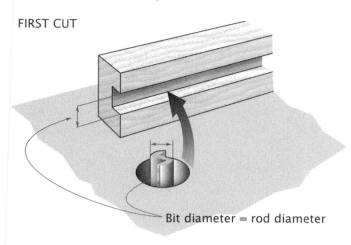

Bit diameter = rod diameter

SECOND CUT

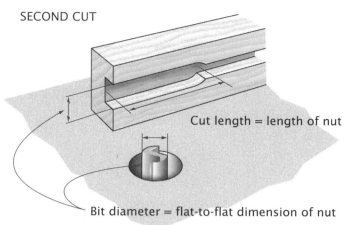

Cut length = length of nut

Bit diameter = flat-to-flat dimension of nut

THIRD CUT

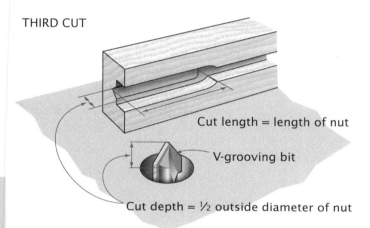

Cut length = length of nut

V-grooving bit

Cut depth = ½ outside diameter of nut

COUPLING NUT          HEIGHT-STOP ROD

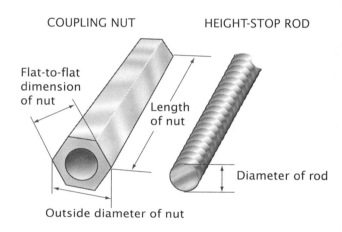

Flat-to-flat dimension of nut

Length of nut

Diameter of rod

Outside diameter of nut

**Here's a good fit** of the rod and nut in the column ply. The rod fits closely in its groove, as does the coupling nut. When both column plies are glued up, the nut will be trapped and unable to rotate in its cavity, even without being epoxied.

a metric coupling nut. Can't find one locally? Try Reid Tool Supply Co. again. While I haven't looked at every plunge router, I can tell you that the Hitachi M 12V takes an M6 thread, the Ryobi RE600 an M10 thread, and the big DeWalt plunger an M12 thread.

The point here is simply that you must have the nut in hand before you make the column.

**3. Cut the column plies.** Start with two pieces ¾ × 1½ × 12 inches. Good, tight-grained hardwood like cherry or maple. After the column is grooved, glued up, and ripped and routed to its final "diameter," you can crosscut it to the proper length for your router.

**4. Rout the grooves for the rod.** Do this on the router table. Use a straight or core-box bit that is the same diameter as the rod, or as close to the diameter as you can come. Set the depth of cut to half the rod's diameter. It's best to creep up on the perfect depth of cut. Groove both pieces, then hold them together and see if the rod fits into the channel. If the channel is too small, make a second pass on each piece, and check the fit again. If the channel is too big, start over.

In making these cuts, set the router table fence so the

grooves are as close to the center of the stock as possible. And once set, leave the fence in the same place for all subsequent cuts.

These initial grooves can be routed through, or they can be stopped.

**5. Rout the grooves for the nut.** This involves rerouting the first 1 to 1½ inches of the groove to widen and deepen it to accommodate the coupling nut. Remember, don't change the fence position from the previous cut: merely change bits. Measure the nut from flat to flat, and use a straight bit whose diameter matches. The depth of cut

should be half the bit diameter. Rout both pieces.

To finish off the grooves for the nut, use a small-diameter V-grooving bit. Rout a V-groove, as shown in the drawing *Column Routing Sequence.*

Check how the nut fits. You may need to cut the V-groove a bit deeper, or even switch back to the straight bit to cut a little deeper. The goal is to get the nut tightly fitted to the column.

**6. Glue up the column.** Line up the grooves as you clamp the two column halves. And don't overspread the glue. You don't want squeeze-out to block the channels.

## Replacing the Threaded Rod

Replacing the Hitachi M12V's height-stop rod with a ⅜-inch-diameter rod with 16 threads per inch (tpi) yields several benefits.

The most obvious, perhaps, is that adjustments can be parsed in increments that are familiar to American woodworkers—16ths, 32nds, even 64ths. Sixteen tpi breaks down to 1/16 inch per full revolution. Four turns thus is ¼ inch, while a quarter-turn is 1/64 inch.

But the ⅜-inch rod is also heavier than the Hitachi's stock 6-millimeter rod, which makes it less apt to flex. And if you replace the rod, you can use a longer piece, which helps align your router crank and keep it from wobbling.

Can you replace the rods on other routers? Some you can, yes, but not all. You have to evaluate the rod that's on your router and decide whether it *can* be replaced and whether it *should* be replaced.

On the Hitachi, replacement is a matter of drilling out and retapping the hole for the rod in the router base. The details of this process are laid out in the feature "Cutting Threads" in the appendix. Separate the motor from the base to do this. Then the yoke on the motor housing must be opened up to accommodate the larger-diameter rod. You can do this easily with a rattail file. The yoke is formed of a soft, easily filed material that's often called "pot metal."

Turn a couple of jam nuts onto the new rod, then turn it into the hole in the base. Turn the nuts down the rod. Jam the first against the base and the second against the first. Reinstall the motor on the base. Turn your new router crank on the rod, and you are ready to hang the machine in your router table.

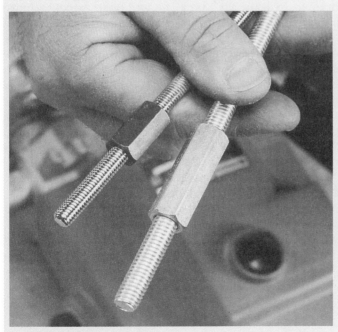

**The difference is obvious.** The Hitachi router's stock 6-millimeter rod is clearly smaller than a ⅜-inch rod. The latter rod makes it easier to adjust bit extension in predictable increments.

**Installing the new rod** is a matter of drilling out and retapping the mounting hole in the router's base. Some models have a mounting hole that extends all the way through the base, so you can work from the bottom, as shown. The "pot metal" used for most bases is very soft; be gentle. I broke out a piece of it getting the tap started.

**Epoxy the nut into the column.** Mix a very small amount of household epoxy according to the directions on the packaging. Dab it on selected flats of the nut, as shown, and thrust the nut into the column. Be discreet. If you apply too much epoxy, it will well into areas where you don't want it, botching the job.

**7. Chamfer or turn the column.** On most routers, the height-stop rod is nestled quite close to the router motor. Obviously, a 1½-inch-square column will not rotate in such close quarters, so it must be trimmed down.

Rip the column down to about 1 inch square, or smaller if it is possible. Reduce the section further by chamfering or rounding-over the edges.

Finally, crosscut the column to the final length. You may want to square the end of the column that the nut fits into, but be sure you don't inadvertently cut off the recess for the nut that you worked so diligently to create.

**8. Make the crank.** Use a piece of the column stock. Lay out the shape, as shown in *Router Crank Layouts*. Saw the crank to shape on the band saw, and sand the edges. If you want, you can chamfer or round-over the edges.

Drill the holes, a through hole for the crank handle, a stopped hole for the column. Determine the diameter of the hole for the column by measuring the column.

I used a red plastic knob for a handle. The particular knob I selected has a ⁷⁄₁₆-inch-deep insert. A 1¼-inch-long mounting bolt thus provides ¹⁄₁₆ of end-to-end play, contributing to the handle's freedom of movement.

**9. Attach the crank to the column.** Check the fit of the column in the hole. If necessary, sand down the column end so it will fit in the hole. Apply glue to the stopped hole in the plate, and insert the column.

**10. Epoxy the nut in place.** Leave the nut on the rod. Apply a small amount of epoxy to the nut, then slide the rod and nut home. (The rod helps keep the nut aligned while the epoxy sets.) I left the nut protruding just a skosh, so the nut and not the wooden column would rub on the yoke. (Actually, rather than have metal contacting metal, I used a nylon washer between the column's nut and the yoke.)

Be discreet in applying the epoxy. If you use too much or put it in the wrong places, the excess can ooze into the channel for the rod, which will transform the piece into scrap.

After the epoxy dries, remove the rod from the nut and reinstall it on the router. Then install the crank on the router.

## Super-Tuning the Router

To get the best out of the router crank, you need a router that plunges smoothly. But I haven't used too many plunge routers that worked right straight out of the box. You usually need to buff 'em a little. Literally.

Remove the motor from the base. This is a matter of removing the nuts from the height-stop rod and pulling the motor off the plunge posts. Set the springs aside.

Now polish those posts. If the router's plunge action has been very sticky, you may want to use fine-grit emery paper. Oftimes, you can improve the action simply by polishing the posts with something like a Scotchbrite pad. I work up the posts until they literally shine. ("Will this buffing affect the fit?" you ask. "Can I unknowingly remove a thousandth or two of metal from the posts and make them too loose in the bushings to function properly?" They are questions I asked, let me tell you. The several experts I consulted assured me it would take *hours* of buffing with emery paper to scour a thousandth off the rods. Polishing them will have only a positive effect on their performance.)

Work on the bushings that the plunge posts fit into. Roll the emery paper into a tube, and buff the bushings with it. Wipe the posts and bushings clean, then wax the posts really well.

When you reassemble the router, you may want to try this trick: Install only the spring that's on the side by the height-stop rod. Here's the rationale. The router is designed to plunge smoothly when force is applied to BOTH handles. When you use the crank (or any adjustment knob), you are in effect applying the force to only one handle, which throws the system out of balance. You can restore the balance by leaving out the one spring.

# Table Saw Extension Router Table

**Gain a router table without sacrificing precious shop space: Integrate a router mounting into your table saw.**

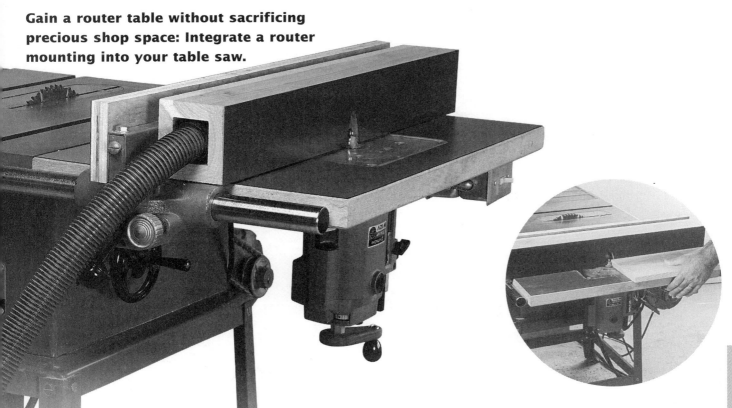

The router table is so useful that every shop, however small, should have one. I realize that in the typical home shop, space is at a premium, and I know that every stationary tool added to the inventory steals a little space from all the others.

Here's a solution: Integrate the router into the table saw. Now I'll be the first to admit that I resisted this approach. But having finally built an extension-wing router table, I can recommend it for small shops—as an easy-to-build first router table or as a workable secondary router table (which is its role in my home shop).

The advantages of this arrangement are several.

- A table saw is the first major investment of almost every woodworker, so you've got one in your shop (or you are about to get one!).
- The table saw is good and heavy, and its mass will help dampen vibration and add to the router table's stability.
- The broad expanse of the saw table means you've got a big router table.
- The table saw's rip fence can double as the basis for a router table fence.

This project is based on the router table top I made for my Rockwell (now Delta) contractor's saw, equipped with the standard rip fence moored to 1¼-inch-diameter rails. If you have a Delta contractor's saw, the specifics presented here should work for your saw. If you have a different brand, you may have to make some alterations. And certainly a different rip-fence mounting would also probably require some alterations to the router table top or its mounting approach.

My saw is positioned in my shop so that I don't have to address the router table from the front of the saw. I step around the saw to the right and work at the end of the extension table.

Included with this project is a boxlike facing for the rip fence. My misgivings about router tables of just this sort emanate from my fear of inadvertently routing the *steel* fence. Carbide-tipped cutters will cut aluminum but not steel. So when I made the fence facing, I made it 3½ inches wide, so I can just about bury a horizontal panel-raiser without encroaching on the fence's steel.

A plus of the fence design is that it serves as a conduit for dust and chips. I just plug the shop vacuum's hose into the hole at the end of the fence, and much of the router-generated debris is pulled through the fence opening away from the bit. Admittedly, there's a lot that ends up on my pants and shoes and on the floor. But every little bit of dust collection helps.

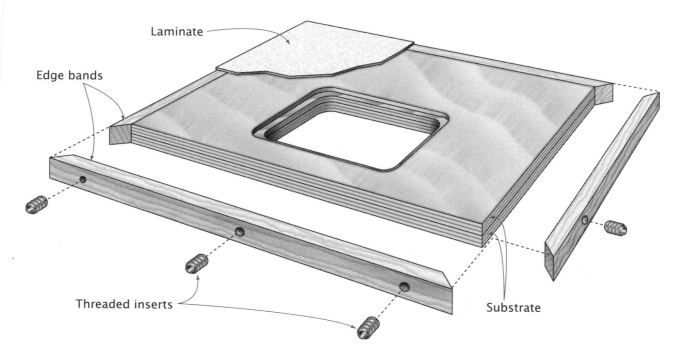

Laminate

Edge bands

Threaded inserts

Substrate

## Making and Installing the Tabletop

Before you being cutting work, evaluate your table saw carefully. You are about to make an extension wing for it. What should the dimensions of it be? (If you have a Rockwell/Delta contractor's saw, the dimensions specified here will work perfectly.) Can it be mounted to the saw as shown in the drawings? If not, how can you attach the new extension wing to the saw?

**1. Make the tabletop.** Cut two pieces of ¾-inch plywood to the dimensions specified by the Cutting List. Glue-laminate them face to face. Prepare hardwood edge-banding while the glue cures. When the clamps are off the plywood tabletop core, trim it to square the core and clean up the edges. Then apply the edge-banding. Flush-trim the edge-banding.

Apply the plastic laminate next. The top surface should get a piece of smooth, light-colored, unpatterned laminate, in my opinion. (I used a piece of battleship-gray laminate I found in the Rodale Press Design Shop, and it matches the color of the saw nicely and serves well mechanically. But it's too dark for me to easily see the setup lines I sometimes pencil on the tabletop.) Apply backer to the bottom surface. Trim the laminate with a 45-degree chamfering bit, forming the bevel around the tabletop at the same time.

If this is your first venture of this sort, turn to the chapter "Custom Router Table Top" on page 156 for more detailed information on making a tabletop.

### Cutting List

| Part | Qty. | Dimensions | Material |
| --- | --- | --- | --- |
| Substrate | 2 | ¾" × 16" × 25" | Plywood |
| Edge bands | 2 | 1" × 1⅝" × 18" | Oak |
| Edge bands | 2 | 1" × 1⅝" × 27" | Oak |

### Hardware

Plastic laminate, 19" × 28"

Backer, 19" × 28"

3 brass threaded inserts, ⁵⁄₁₆"-18

3 hex-head bolts with flat washers, ⁵⁄₁₆"-18 × 1"

2 brass threaded inserts, ⅜"-16

2 cap bolts, ⅜"-16 × 1½"

Acrylic plastic mounting plate, 7¾" × 10¼"

**2. Lay out the mounting holes.** I attached the router table top to the saw with bolts driven through the cast-iron saw table and the rip fence rails. To do this, I took advantage of existing holes in the saw table and the rails.

On the Rockwell/Delta saw, the standard stamped-steel extension wings are mounted using three ⅜-inch bolts run through the wing into threaded holes in the saw table. By using ⁵⁄₁₆-inch bolts, I could insert them through the saw table's holes, driving them into threaded inserts in the router table top. Using the smaller bolts even provided

Router Tables

## TABLETOP PLAN VIEWS

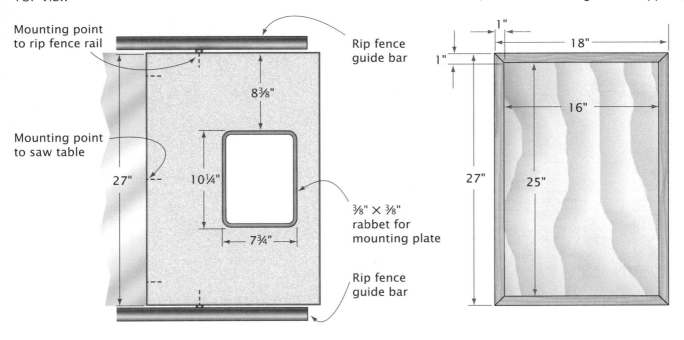

TOP VIEW

Mounting point to rip fence rail

Mounting point to saw table

27"

8⅜"

10¼"

7¾"

Rip fence guide bar

⅜" × ⅜" rabbet for mounting plate

Rip fence guide bar

TOP VIEW (Substrate with edge bands applied)

1"

18"

1"

16"

27"

25"

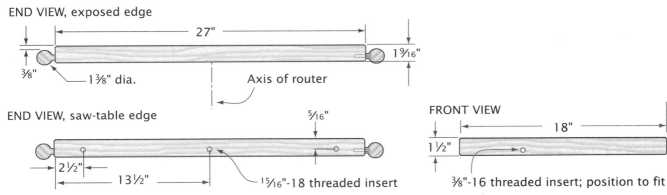

END VIEW, exposed edge

27"

1⁹⁄₁₆"

⅜"

1⅜" dia.

Axis of router

END VIEW, saw-table edge

⁵⁄₁₆"

2½"

13½"

¹⁵⁄₁₆"-18 threaded insert

FRONT VIEW

18"

1½"

⅜"-16 threaded insert; position to fit

a small measure of adjustability, so I could ensure that the router table top would be flush with the saw table.

In addition, the extension wing is attached to each fence rail with a single bolt. To mount the router table top, I used cap bolts inserted through the rail holes and turned into threaded inserts.

To lay out the holes for the five threaded inserts, I clamped some supports to the table saw (after removing the extension wing, of course). Then I set the tabletop in place and shimmed it as necessary to line it up and bring it flush with the saw table. Use a straightedge to check this. Fit a pencil through the appropriate holes, and mark on the edge-banding.

**3. Install the threaded inserts.** Not all threaded inserts are alike, so check to determine the required size for the pilot hole. Bore the pilot holes, using a drill or a plunge router.

To drive the inserts, use a bolt (of the appropriate size) with two nuts jammed together on it as a tool.

Thread the insert onto the bolt, right up to the nuts. Get the insert started into the wood, and turn the bolt with a wrench. The hard part is keeping the bolt perpendicular to the workpiece. When the insert is fully installed, use two wrenches to unjam the nuts, and turn the bolt out of the insert.

**4. Mount the tabletop on the saw.** Set the tabletop back on the temporary supports. Insert the bolts and tighten them. Make sure the tabletop is flush with the saw table.

**5. Cut out the mounting plate opening.** With the tabletop in place, it's an easy matter to cut the opening for the mounting plate, from which the router hangs. Rather than repeat something that's spelled out step by detailed step on page 168, I recommend you turn to that chapter, "Universal Router Mounting Plate." There you'll learn how to make the plate and attach the router to it. *And* you'll see how you can use it to guide the cutting of the router port in the tabletop.

**Putting a small bolt through a large hole** provides a measure of adjustability. It is pretty difficult to get the threaded inserts positioned in the tabletop edge with absolute precision. So the adjustability factor allows you to move the tabletop slightly to align it perfectly with the saw table.

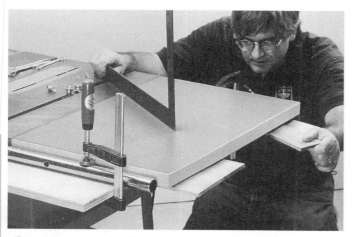

**Create some staging to support the tabletop** while you mark the insert locations. A piece of plywood clamped to the underside of the saw's fence rails supported my tabletop just about flush with the saw table. A couple pairs of builder's shims were all I needed to raise the tabletop into perfect position.

**6. Accessorize your router table.** Unlike the Floor-Standing Router Table on page 212, this one has no compartments or drawers for bits and other necessary stuff. After using the table a few times, I discovered the most time-consuming part of setup was finding the #@!!$ wrench. So I screwed a short strip magnet to the bottom side of the table, just for the wrench.

I also found myself running an extension cord every time I wanted to use the router table. So I sprang for the necessary electrical supplies to outfit the table with a switched outlet, as shown in the accompanying feature, "Power to the Router Table" on page 190. I mounted the box on the underside of the table saw, and I bundled the cable with the table saw's power cord so the number of cables snaking across the concrete shop floor is minimized.

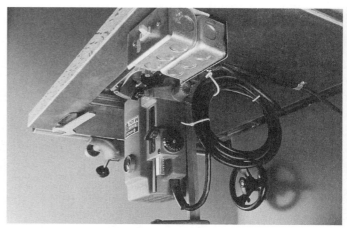

**It's not pretty, but it is orderly.** The router's handles were in the way. They'd jam against the bottom of the tabletop, limiting the depth of cut and preventing me from just lifting the router and plate out of the tabletop. So I removed them. The power cord dangled on the floor and made it hard to sweep up. So I rolled it into a coil and tied it. To lift the router out of the table, I unplug it. The strip magnet holds the collet wrench out of the way but close at hand.

## Making and Installing the Rip Fence Facing

Though this rip fence facing is billed as optional, I wouldn't do without it. As it has turned out, I use this router table a lot. And the table saw rip fence is a real plus. I can set its position quickly, even with one hand otherwise tied up. But the fence wouldn't be quite so useful without this box-section fence facing.

**1. Cut the parts.** The unit is simple enough that you can cut all the parts right off the bat. Joint and thickness the lumber, then rip and crosscut the parts to the dimensions specified by the Cutting List.

I used poplar for the fence parts. You could use any hardwood, but in retrospect, I think plywood would be a very good choice. While the tendency might be to use a utility material, you do need to use stable, straight-grained stock so that the fence stays straight and true.

**2. Cut the joinery.** You could cut the tongues and grooves that join the fence box on the router table, but of course you don't have one. You *can* do the job with a hand-held router, but frankly, it's easier to do it on the table saw.

Cut the grooves first. Set the blade height, and position the fence ¼ inch from the blade. Make a first pass on each of the four grooves. Reposition the rip fence, and make a second pass on each groove. If necessary, make a third pass to complete the grooves.

The tongues can be formed in much the same fashion. Don't change the blade height setting. Reposition the rip fence, as shown in the drawing, to make the shoulder cuts—four on each piece. Then move the fence closer to the blade, and trim off the remaining sliver of waste.

## RIP FENCE FACING EXPLODED VIEW

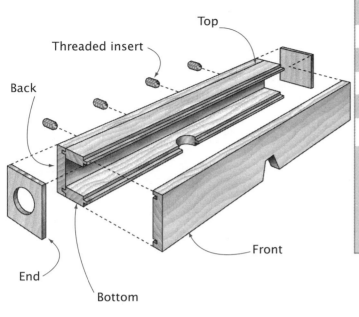

Threaded insert

Top

Back

End

Bottom

Front

| Part | Qty. | Dimensions | Material |
|---|---|---|---|
| **RIP FENCE FACING Cutting List** | | | |
| Front/Back | 2 | ¾" × 4" × 27" | Hardwood |
| Top/Bottom | 2 | ¾" × 2¾" × 27" | Hardwood |
| End caps | 2 | ¾" × 3½" × 4" | Hardwood |
| **Hardware** | | | |

Plastic laminate, 5" × 28"

8 oval-head wood screws, #6 × ¾" (for end caps)

4 threaded inserts, ¼"-20

4 hex-head bolts, ¼"-20 × 2½"

## SAWING FENCE JOINERY

### CUTTING THE GROOVES

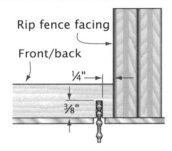

1. Set the blade height. Position the fence, as shown. Make a first pass on each groove.

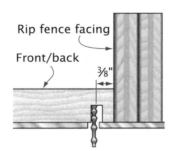

2. Move the fence the thickness of the blade to the right. Make a second pass on each groove. If the groove is not yet wide enough, move the fence a second time and make additional passes.

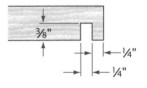

3. The completed, properly dimensioned groove.

### CUTTING THE TONGUES

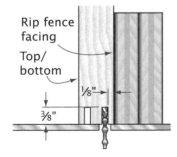

1. Keep the same blade height. But reposition the fence for the shoulder cut, as shown. Make two passes on each edge to define all four tongues.

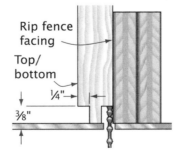

2. Move the fence closer to the blade to trim off the remaining waste.

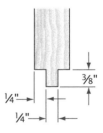

3. The completed, properly dimensioned tongue.

**Router Tables**

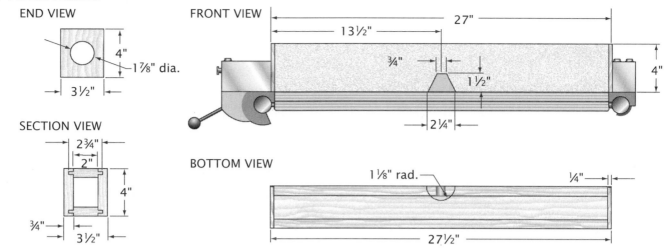

## RIP FENCE FACING

**END VIEW**

4"

1⅞" dia.

3½"

**SECTION VIEW**

2¾"

2"

4"

¾"

3½"

**FRONT VIEW**

27"

13½"

¾"

1½"

2¼"

4"

**BOTTOM VIEW**

1⅛" rad.

¼"

27½"

The end caps are rabbeted on all four edges. While this would again be a good router table operation, it can for this project be a table saw procedure. Set the blade height to ¾ inch, and position the fence ¼ inch from the blade. Stand the cap on end. Back it up with a good-sized scrap, and push it through the blade with the scrap. Repeat the process to cut the base of all the rabbets on both caps.

To make the shoulder cuts, lower the blade and reposition the fence. Make the cuts with the cap flat on the table saw, feeding the workpiece with a push stick. To avoid having the saw kick back the dartlike waste strips, position the fence so that the waste will fall to the left of the blade. This means you have the extra step of repositioning the fence after making two cuts on both caps.

**3. Cut the bit opening.** This is formed by cutting an arc in the bottom board, and a truncated triangle in the front. Fit the two parts together to lay out the cut. Use a saber saw to make the cuts.

**4. Assemble the fence box.** This is a pretty simple matter. Apply glue to the tongues and grooves, and fit the parts together. Wipe up any glue squeeze-out promptly. Check the assembly with a square as you apply the clamps, to ensure that the box is square. (Don't install the end caps until after the plastic is applied.)

**5. Apply the plastic laminate.** The purpose of the plastic laminate is to make the face slick, thus making it easier to feed work along the fence. It only needs to be applied to the face. It's a simple job.

Cut the laminate about 1 inch long and 1 inch wider than the fence face. Apply contact cement to both the laminate and the fence face. Allow the cement to dry. After it is dried, apply the laminate to the fence and burnish it down with a J-roller. With a flush-trimming bit in a router, trim the edges of the laminate. Be sure to run the trimmer into the bit opening.

**6. (optional) Install the end caps.** Install these if you plan to use the fence core as a channel for dust collection.

Bore a 1⅞-inch-diameter hole in the center of one cap. This is the opening for the shop vac hose. Fasten that cap over one end of the fence. Choose the end that suits you. Fasten the solid cap over the other end. It is best not to glue the caps in place. In use, the core of the fence can get impacted with chips, even when a shop vac is drawing through it, so leave yourself this clean-out option. Use screws to secure the caps.

**7. Prepare the router fence for mounting.** On my table saw, the rip fence has four ¼-inch-diameter holes in it, ostensibly for installing a facing. It is a simple matter to install threaded inserts in the back of the router fence, then insert bolts through the rip fence's holes and into the router fence.

But there's a hitch: The fastener heads will protrude on the side opposite the router fence. Thus, to have the router fence permanently attached to the rip fence's right side, you need also to have a facing attached to the left side. That way, you can countersink or counterbore the fastener heads into the facing.

So when I made the router fence, I also made a rip fence facing. For what it's worth, to make the facing, I glue-laminated two pieces of ½-inch birch plywood, then applied plastic laminate to one side. (Since the plywood is ¹⁄₆₄ inch scant of ½ inch thick, the plastic laminate brings the facing thickness to exactly 1 inch. As long as I remember to compensate by that 1 inch, I can use the rule etched into the rip fence rails to set the fence.)

To transfer the hole locations from the rip fence to the facing and the router fence, clamp the parts—one at a time, of course—to the rip fence. Then insert a bolt through the hole and tap it with a hammer, denting the wood. At the dents, drill the appropriately sized holes. Drive the threaded inserts. Counterbore the rip facing.

**8. Install the router fence.** This is largely a matter of driving the bolts that hold the parts together. But the face of the router fence should be square to the router table top. After bolting the fence in place, check with a square.

If the fence is out-of-square, loosen the fence and insert shims between the rip fence and the router fence. Depending upon how far out the fence is, a few layers of masking tape may cure the misalignment. Retighten the bolts and recheck the fence.

It is a trial-and-error process. Keep at it until you have the fence square to the tabletop.

## Using the Router Table

Using this router table isn't a whole lot different than using any other.

Because of the location of the router and the orientation of the saw's fence, you most frequently approach the router table from what is the saw's right rear corner. The drawing *Feed Direction* makes this clear. You've got to keep the area around the saw's right end clear so you can move around and maneuver a workpiece.

The fence is handy because it's right there on the saw. You can slide it into position quickly and set it. No clamps to fiddle with. And it won't shift out of position, either.

The disadvantage of using the saw's fence crops up when you are switching back and forth between the router table and the table saw.

Making moldings is a good example. To make narrow moldings, you want to rout the profile on a wide board, then rip the stick from the board, then rout the profile on the new edge, then rip it from the board. To do this, you have to keep shifting the fence back and forth. Let me tell you from experience, it'll drive you nuts.

In these circumstances, it's better to use a separate fence for the router table, so you can preserve the router table setup while using the rip fence for the saw operations.

In other particulars, such as changing bits, setting bit height, and controlling the workpiece, do with this router table as you would with any other router table.

**FEED DIRECTION**

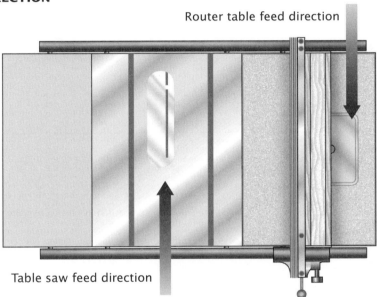

Router table feed direction

Table saw feed direction

When using the table saw's rip fence to guide a router cut, the feed direction is exactly opposite that for a saw cut. So the optimal post for a router woodworker is facing the right end of the saw.

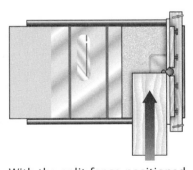

With the split fence positioned outboard of the bit, the feed direction mimics that of a saw cut. Stand in front of the saw and push the work, just as in making a saw cut.

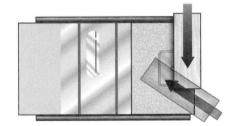

When using a bit's pilot to guide a cut, your working post is more flexible. The feed direction "rotates" clockwise around the bit.

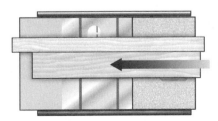

A long straightedge can be clamped across the saw table to guide a cut in an especially long or wide workpiece. This approach provides the best support for the workpiece. Position the fence "behind" the bit, and feed from the saw's right to its left.

# Power to the Router Table

If you are serious about router table work, you need a setup that incorporates a switched receptacle.

The advantages are several. Position the outlet next to the router, making it convenient to unplug when changing bits. (The main reason woodworkers fail to take this simple safety step is that it's inconvenient.) You can position an on-off switch where it's easy to find. (This is especially appealing when you need to kill the router *fast*.) You can add an outlet for something like a dust collector or a shop vacuum, making it switch-controlled: When the router goes on, so does the dust collector. (This works if your router has the "soft-start" feature, or if both router and dust collector are relatively low-amperage. But two high-amperage motors—say, a 14-amp router and a 12-amp dust collector—kicking on at the same instant can overload a 20-amp circuit, tripping the breaker.)

To start, get some electrical supplies. With the wiring diagram, there's a list of the stuff I used. Everything should be available at your local building supplies emporium—with the exception of the through box, which you can get at an electrical supply house.

Begin by attaching the receptacle box to the router table. Install the plug on one end of the appli-ance cable, and insert the other end into the switch box. Wire the switch following the wiring diagram, and install the switch plate. Likewise, wire the receptacle and install the receptacle plate.

Plug everything in, and you're ready to go.

## Hardware

1 through receptacle box

1 connector

1 single-pole switch

1 utility switch plate

1 duplex receptacle

1 utility receptacle plate

1' Romex cable, 12/2 with ground

1 grounding clip or screw

1 crimp ring (for ground conductors)

10' to 20' cord, 16/2 type SJ

1 plug

**WIRING DIAGRAM**

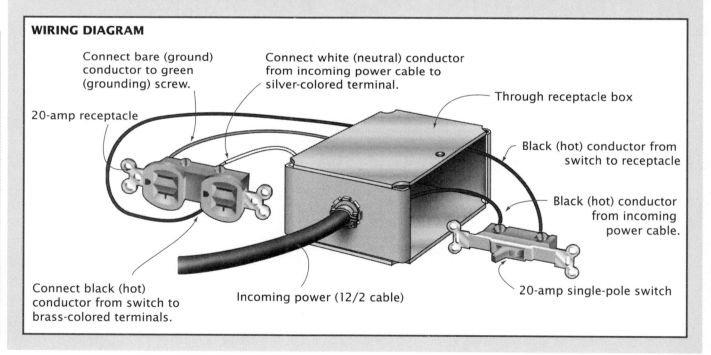

Connect bare (ground) conductor to green (grounding) screw.

Connect white (neutral) conductor from incoming power cable to silver-colored terminal.

Through receptacle box

20-amp receptacle

Black (hot) conductor from switch to receptacle

Black (hot) conductor from incoming power cable.

Connect black (hot) conductor from switch to brass-colored terminals.

Incoming power (12/2 cable)

20-amp single-pole switch

# Horizontal Router Table

**Turn the traditional router table on its ear. Use it to cut tenons, raise panels, and edge-groove boards.**

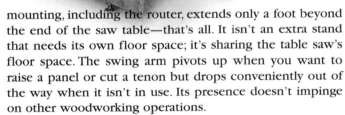

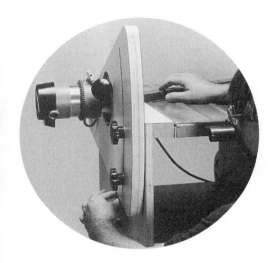

This project is an interesting—and space-saving—turn on the old horizontal router table idea. Mounting a router so the bit's axis is parallel to a work surface is the perfect setup for *any* operation that, performed on an ordinary router table, would require you to balance the workpiece on edge:

- Cutting tenons
- Cutting wide rabbets
- Grooving the edges of straight, flat boards
- Raising panels with a vertical bit
- Routing architectural molding with tall face-molding bits
- Cutting dovetail pins for sliding dovetails

The horizontal-mounting idea isn't particularly new, of course. Router magicians have been cobbling them up for years. But when Phil Gehret and Rob Yoder, two of my woodworking colleagues, first mounted a router on the end of a table saw, the general reaction was *Coool! What a smart idea.*

Piggybacking a horizontal router setup on the table saw saves space in the shop. The router is mounted at the left end of the table saw. Usually, you keep the area around that end clear so you can crosscut a board that's longer than 2 feet. Keeping that area clear means it's dead space. This mounting, including the router, extends only a foot beyond the end of the saw table—that's all. It isn't an extra stand that needs its own floor space; it's sharing the table saw's floor space. The swing arm pivots up when you want to raise a panel or cut a tenon but drops conveniently out of the way when it isn't in use. Its presence doesn't impinge on other woodworking operations.

The setup takes good advantage of the saw's mass, and it makes excellent use of the saw's broad, flat tabletop. You don't need a high-powered router for it; it's one setup in which any router will work (which is emphatically NOT true of regular router tables). As designed, this horizontal router mounting overcomes a fundamental shortcoming of most horizontal mountings: fine adjustment.

The design is clear-cut. A plywood support panel is attached to the rim of the saw's extension wing, and it's anchored to the saw housing so it is perfectly perpendicular to the saw table. Bolted to the support panel is a thick swing arm, which holds the router. As its name implies, this arm swings on a bolt, raising and lowering the router and bit. Fine adjustments to the cutting depth are made through a jackscrew, which can move the swing arm almost infinitesimal amounts. You adjust the bit height coarsely, by measuring the bit position as you move the arm with your hand. Then you move the jackscrew slide against the arm. Turning the jackscrew moves the arm in

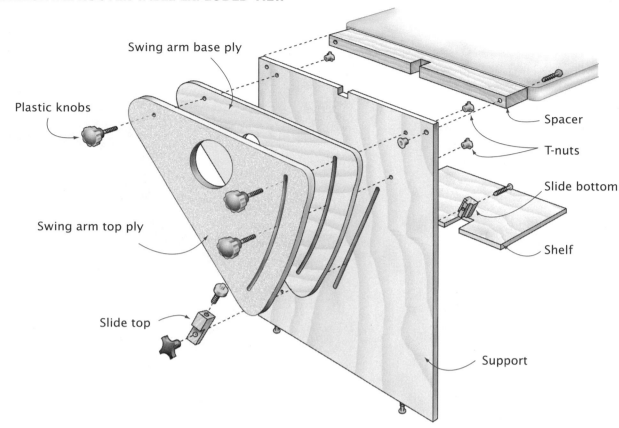

Plastic knobs

Swing arm base ply

Swing arm top ply

Slide top

Spacer

T-nuts

Slide bottom

Shelf

Support

## Router Tables

### Cutting List

| Part | Qty. | Dimensions | Material |
|---|---|---|---|
| Swing arm base ply | 1 | ½" × 18½" × 27" | Birch plywood |
| Swing arm top ply | 1 | ¾" × 18½" × 27" | Birch plywood |
| Support | 1 | ¾" × 27" × 33½" | Birch plywood |
| Spacer | 1 | 1½" × 2¼" × 27" | Hardwood |
| Slide top | 1 | 1½" × 1½" × 4¼" | Hardwood |
| Slide bottom | 1 | ¾" × 1½" × 1¾" | Hardwood |
| Shelf | 1 | ¾" × 11" × 21¾" | Plywood |

### Hardware

2 pieces plastic laminate, each 20" × 28"

1 jackscrew, ⅜"-16; #AJS-500 from Reid Tool Supply Co. (800-253-0421)

8 T-nuts, ⅜"-16

2 hex-head bolts with washers, ⅜"-16 × 2"

3 fluted plastic knobs with ⅜"-16 × 1½" steel studs; #DK-6 from Reid Tool Supply Co.

1 fluted plastic knob with ¼"-20 threaded insert; #DK-59 from Reid Tool Supply Co.

1 carriage bolt, ¼" × 2"

2 carriage bolts, ⅜" × 1½"

6 drywall screws, 2" long

2 hex nuts, ⅜"

such tiny gradations that you have to measure the cut to perceive the difference.

Equally important, the rig can be constructed and bolted to almost any floor-standing table saw in a matter of hours. The exotic hardware items are as close as your telephone and mailbox.

This setup is not a substitute for a router table. Rather it's a complement to the router table. In fact, I've got a router hung under the right-hand extension wing of my table saw (see the photo on page 183). I use the router table extensively. But "workpiece maneuverability" is a key fork in my decision tree. If I have to balance a workpiece on edge to machine it on the router table, I'll switch to the horizontal setup so I can lay it flat.

## Building the Horizontal Router Table

With a bit of careful layout work, this rig will come together easily. Before you start, make sure you have all of the materials specified by the Cutting List, especially the

# HORIZONTAL ROUTER TABLE PLAN VIEWS

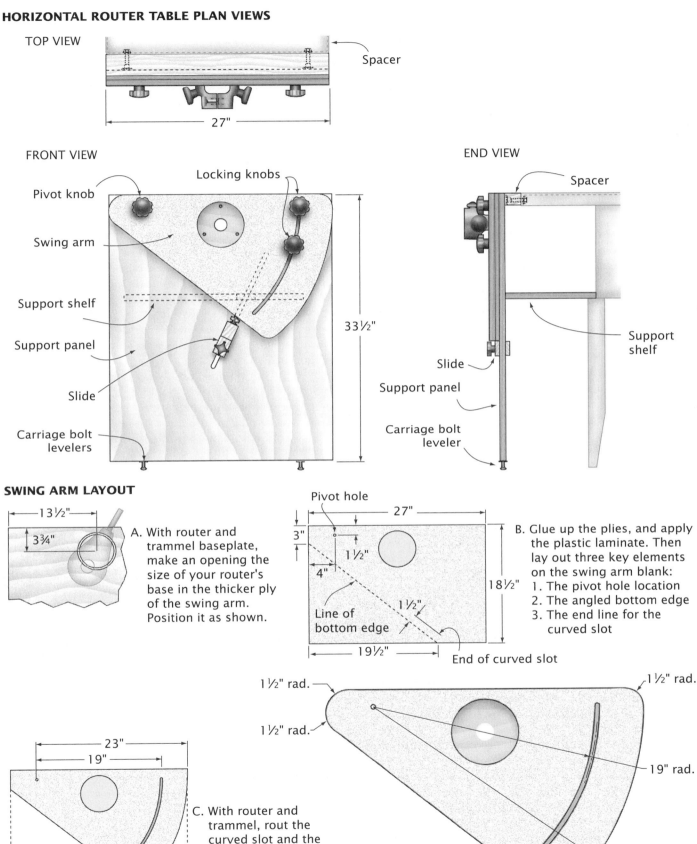

TOP VIEW

Spacer

27"

FRONT VIEW

END VIEW

Pivot knob

Locking knobs

Spacer

Swing arm

Support shelf

Support panel

Slide

33½"

Support shelf

Slide

Support panel

Carriage bolt levelers

Carriage bolt leveler

## SWING ARM LAYOUT

13½"

3¾"

A. With router and trammel baseplate, make an opening the size of your router's base in the thicker ply of the swing arm. Position it as shown.

Pivot hole

27"

3"

1½"

4"

Line of bottom edge

1½"

18½"

19½"

End of curved slot

B. Glue up the plies, and apply the plastic laminate. Then lay out three key elements on the swing arm blank:
1. The pivot hole location
2. The angled bottom edge
3. The end line for the curved slot

1½" rad.

1½" rad.

1½" rad.

1½" rad.

19" rad.

23"

19"

C. With router and trammel, rout the curved slot and the arm's curved front edge. Cut the arm's angled bottom edge.

23" rad.

1½" rad.

hardware. At least one of the hardware items, the jackscrew, you are unlikely to find in your local hardware store. Order the oddball parts from the recommended source, and when you have everything in hand, set to work.

## Building the Swing Arm

Start by building the swing arm. Doing it first makes it available for use in laying out and building the support assembly.

**1. Cut the two layers to size.** To make the arm as stiff as possible, you form it from two layers of birch plywood. One is ½ inch, the other ¾ inch. Cut the two pieces to the dimensions specified by the Cutting List.

**2. Rout the opening for the router.** In the completed arm, the router sets into a ¾-inch-deep recess and is bolted to the remaining material of the arm. The easiest way to create the recess is to cut completely through the thicker plywood layer before the two layers are glued together.

Since I used a Porter-Cable 690 router, which has a round base, cutting the opening was a simple matter of routing with a router and the Trammel Baseplate on page 39. Lay out the pivot point from the drawing *Swing Arm Layout,* and drill a pilot hole for the trammel's pivot. To keep the waste disk from shifting as the router bit breaks through the workpiece, use carpet tape to bond the area to be routed to waste backup.

If you use a router with a flat edge, trace the base on the workpiece. Then clamp a straightedge to the workpiece to guide the router as you rout the flat segment of the recess. Then switch to the trammel and rout the curved segment.

**3. Glue up the plies.** This is a glue-up that requires a lot of clamps. I used 12 medium-sized hand screws, spacing them fairly evenly around the periphery of the assembly. Adjust the clamps beforehand, so they are ready to apply without a lot of fumbling.

Examine the two pieces of plywood. They should be flat, but if either piece or both pieces are bowed, orient the convex face(s) in.

Use yellow glue, applying beads to the mating faces of both plies. Use a brush or scrapwood spreader to spread this glue out, so the entire surface has a thin coating of it. Lay one piece atop the other, and slide them around a bit to get a good, suction bond. Then align the edges and start applying the clamps. In my experience, if you get the edges clamped well, the interior of the glue-up, where it's difficult to apply any clamping pressure, will take care of itself.

**4. Apply the plastic laminate.** You need to cover both sides of the swing arm with plastic laminate. Cut two pieces of laminate so they slightly overhang the edges of the swing arm blank.

In a well-ventilated area, brush a thin layer of contact cement on one side of the swing arm blank and on one of the pieces of laminate. When the cement is dry (read the label for proper drying times), carefully lay the plastic laminate over the swing arm. You get only one chance at this—the two surfaces stick tight once they make contact. When the laminate is down, burnish the surface vigorously with a J-roller.

Repeat the process on the opposite side.

Trim the laminate flush with the edges of the blank using a router and flush-trimming bit. To open up the recess for the router, drill a hole through the laminate, somewhere in the middle of the recess. Set the router over the hole, with the bit extending through it. Switch on the router and feed toward the perimeter of the recess, until the bearing catches the edge. Then just rout around the inner edge of the recess.

**5. Rout the adjustment slot.** This is another router-and-trammel operation, but the trammel baseplate doesn't have the range for this job. You'll just have to work a little job-specific magic, which is what I did.

To begin, you need to lay out the pivot hole. While you are at it, lay out the beginning and end points of the curved adjustment slot, as shown in the drawing *Swing Arm Layout.* Drill the pivot using a bit matched to the pivot of your trammel. In my case, this was ⅜ inch (the final size of the hole).

Set up your trammel, and swing it from the arm's pivot, as noted. The arm blank should be clamped atop some scrap that will back up the cut *and* provide protection for the bench top. Begin routing the slot by plunge-boring a hole at each end of the slot. (If you have to work with a fixed-base router, drill these holes.) Now rout the slot.

**6. Cut the arm to shape.** The first step in this process follows naturally from the previous operation. Reset the trammel for a longer-radius arc. Using the same pivot point, rout the arc on the front edge of the arm.

(If need be, you can now drill the pivot hole to the required ⅜-inch-diameter size.)

Now lay out and cut the arm's angled bottom edge. To me, the best approach is to clamp a straight-edge to the arm, and rout off the waste. I'm going to use the router to round the arm's sharp corners next, so I may as well use it for this cut, too.

I used corner-rounding templates to shape the corners. (See the chapter "Boring Templates" on page 6.) Though two of the corners are way off square, you can get all four corners done neatly with the templates. Select the template with the appropriate radius, and align it on the workpiece. Then trim the arm flush using a router and either a pattern bit or a flush-trimming bit.

When the shaping is all done, chuck a bevel-trimming bit in your router and run it around the edges—both faces—of the arm. You'll find that square-cut plastic laminate edges are terribly sharp; bevel-trimming them takes that edge off and just may save you an annoying cut.

**7. Drill holes for the router-mounting screws.** This is easy enough. Drop the router's baseplate into the recess, and use it as a guide to drill the mounting-screw holes. Turn the arm over and countersink the holes.

**Basic tricks used in routing the arm's shape**
include trammel-guided, fence-guided, and template-guided cuts. Routing the arced edge involves the use of a trammel (*top*). To cut the angled bottom edge (*middle*), clamp a straight fence to the arm and feed a router along it. Complete the arm's shape by rounding the corners, using a template (*bottom*).

Now set the arm aside, and turn to the rest of the assembly.

## Building the Support Assembly

This stage involves laying out and building the support panel, gluing the spacer to it, then bolting the assembly to your table saw. This is the stage at which the unit really takes form.

**1. Cut the support panel.** The support is cut from ¾-inch birch plywood. To economize without sacrificing structurally, you can use BB-grade fir plywood. BB-grade has a smooth, finished veneer on both sides but doesn't necessarily look good.

In some situations, you may want to change the length of the support panel to match the height of your saw. My shop floor is concrete—a typical basement situation—so I can't fasten the panel to the shop floor. I designed the panel to end about 1 inch short of the floor. It is poised on two ⅜-inch carriage bolts, threaded into T-nuts in the panel's bottom edge, which serve as levelers.

Measure your saw, assess your shop situation, and cut the panel.

**2. Lay out and drill the locking-knob holes.** Study the drawing *Support Panel Layout,* and note the locations of holes for the pivot and locking-knob T-nuts. The most accurate way to lay out these holes is to transfer them from the swing arm. You ought to drill the counterbores first, and they are on the panel's back.

With a Forstner bit, drill the 1⅛-inch-diameter × ³⁄₃₂-inch-deep counterbores for the T-nut flanges at these spots, as shown in the drawing. Then drill the ⁷⁄₁₆-inch-diameter holes for the T-nut barrels, centering the holes using the marks left by the Forstner bit's center spur.

Tap the T-nuts into place.

**Mark the bolt-hole locations on the support panel.** Line up the arm on the *back* of the support panel. Insert a ⅜-inch bolt in the pivot hole and tap it with a hammer. The bolt will mark the panel. Insert the bolt in the adjustment slot at the top, and tap it again. Then work out the location of the second locking knob along the slot, insert the bolt there, and tap it.

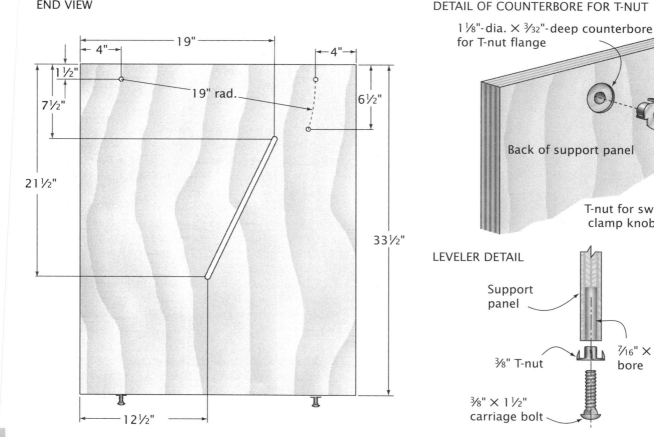

## SUPPORT PANEL LAYOUT
### END VIEW

19"

4"

4"

1½"

19" rad.

7½"

6½"

21½"

33½"

12½"

### DETAIL OF COUNTERBORE FOR T-NUT

1⅛"-dia. × 3⁄32"-deep counterbore for T-nut flange

Back of support panel

T-nut for swing-arm clamp knob

### LEVELER DETAIL

Support panel

3⁄8" T-nut

7⁄16" × 2" bore

3⁄8" × 1½" carriage bolt

**3. Lay out and rout the slot for the slide.** The location can be taken from the layout drawing.

Use a plunge router and a ½-inch straight bit to rout the slot. Set up the router. Determine the distance a guide fence must be offset from the slot's centerline (generally that would be the radius of the baseplate). Clamp a straightedge to the panel, parallel to the centerline of the slot, and offset the necessary distance.

Begin routing by plunge-boring through the panel at the beginning and end of the slot. Then rout out the waste between the two holes.

**4. Install the T-nuts for the levelers.** The levelers, as noted already, are carriage bolts that thread into T-nuts. The locations are shown in the drawing *Support Panel Layout.* Bore the clearance holes for ⅜-inch T-nuts, drilling deep enough for the bolt shanks.

Orient the T-nuts carefully before you drive them into place. It'll be obvious that the flanges are a good bit larger than the plywood is thick. I oriented the T-nuts so two of the spurs would bite into the wood, and that has proven satisfactory.

**5. Cut the spacer.** The spacer should be made from a hardwood like cherry, oak, or maple. Joint and plane the stock to the specified width and thickness, making sure the faces are parallel to each other and square to the edges. Crosscut it to the length specified by the Cutting List.

**6. Locate the mounting bolt holes.** As shown in the drawing *Assembly Detail,* the support assembly is attached to the table saw with bolts that pass through holes in the saw table and thread into T-nuts in the spacer. Since the particulars of saw tables vary from brand to brand, you will have to determine the best spots for the mounting bolts.

My Rockwell/Delta contractor's saw has stamped-steel extension wings, each of which has three oblong, ½-inch-wide mounting-bolt holes in its rims. I used two of these holes, but not the third, since it is dead-center, right where the router bit does its work. (Obviously, you must be cognizant of the ultimate location of the router bit; don't put a bolt where the bit will hit it the first time you use the equipment. *That* would dampen your enthusiasm, wouldn't it?)

In some cases, you may need to drill holes for the bolts through the rim of your saw table. Take a cue from the Delta design, and make the holes bigger than the bolts. That will help you adjust the support assembly flush with the saw table during installation.

In any event, transfer the hole locations from the saw table to the spacer. Clamp it to the saw table rim. Reach through the holes with a pencil, marking the bolt-hole locations on the spacer. Unclamp the spacer.

**7. Bore and counterbore the spacer.** As with the holes for the T-nuts in the support panel, the counterbore should be drilled first, then the shank holes. Again, use a

Router Tables

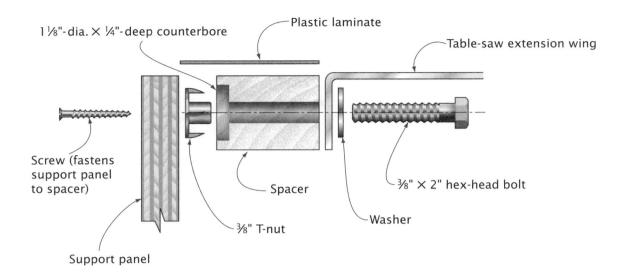

1⅛"-dia. × ¼"-deep counterbore

Plastic laminate

Table-saw extension wing

Screw (fastens support panel to spacer)

Spacer

⅜" × 2" hex-head bolt

⅜" T-nut

Washer

Support panel

Forstner bit to drill the counterbores. Make these counterbores ¼ inch deep. Then drill the ⅜-inch-diameter bolt holes through the spacers.

Insert the T-nuts in the counterbores, and seat them. To do this, you can thread a bolt into the T-nut, then tap the bolt with a hammer to drive the prongs of the flange into the wood.

**8. Assemble the spacer and the support panel.** The panel is glued and screwed to the spacer. Spread glue and clamp the parts together. While the clamps are still securing the parts, drill and countersink pilot holes for 2-inch-long drywall screws. Use about a half-dozen screws, evenly spaced across the panel. Just be sure to avoid the center section, where the bit will be cutting.

After the clamps are off, sand the top edge of the panel and the top of the spacers smooth and flush. Cement plastic laminate across this surface, and trim it flush all around.

**9. Mount the assembly on the saw table.** Thread two hex nuts on each of the two "leveler" carriage bolts, spinning them up to the head. Thread the bolts into the T-nuts in the panel's bottom edge.

Prop the assembly against the edge of the saw table. Fit a washer and a split washer on each mounting bolt. Insert the mounting bolts through the holes in the table's rim, and thread them into the T-nuts. As you tighten the bolts, try to bring the top surface of the support assembly flush with the saw table surface.

Adjust the levelers as necessary to push the assembly into proper alignment with the saw table. When the assembly is aligned, turn the first hex nut on each leveler against the T-nut, and jam the second against it, locking the leveler's position.

**10. Cut and fit the shelf.** The face of the support panel must be perpendicular to the surface of the saw table.

The shelf, while handy for table-saw accessories, is really an alignment device. It keeps the support panel from getting pushed in toward the saw housing or pulled away from it.

With a framing square, line up the panel. Measure from the panel's inner face to the side of the saw housing at the level you want to place the shelf. (As you can see from the photos, my saw's stand is a bit wider than the saw housing, so there's a ledge on which the shelf rests. That ledge dictated where the shelf would be.)

Cut the shelf from ¾-inch plywood. The shelf will interfere with the movement of the slide, so you'll have to notch it. Hold the shelf in position, and mark the width and depth of the notch. Cut it on the table saw, on the band saw, or with a saber saw.

**The support panel alignment is critical.** The panel's face must be perpendicular to the saw table, and the surface of the spacer must be flush with the saw table. Monitor these alignments with a framing square as you adjust the levelers and position the panel to measure for the shelf.

Router Tables

**11. Install the shelf and square the assembly.**
To hold the shelf in position while you drill pilots and drive the mounting screws, clamp two hand screws to the panel and rest the shelf on them. Fasten the panel to the shelf.

Although the shelf appears to be supported by the saw stand, it is fastened to the saw with screws. Three is plenty. Drill clearance holes through the saw housing for the screws, and drive them through the housing into the shelf's edge.

## Making the Slide

The slide is installed in the slot routed into the support panel. It provides fine adjustment of the swing arm position by way of a special piece of hardware called a jackscrew.

After roughly setting the arm position, you loosen the locking knob on the slide and move it up the slot until it contacts the edge of the arm. Tighten the knob. Then loosen the three knobs securing the arm. Raise the arm in measured fractions by turning the jackscrew. The jackscrew has 16 threads per inch, so turning its knurled nut a single revolution will move the arm $\frac{1}{16}$ inch. A quarter-turn moves the arm $\frac{1}{64}$ inch. That's fine adjustment. Anyway, when you've got just the setting you want, tighten the knobs on the swing arm.

Here's how to make the slide.

**1. Cut the slide body.** Because the two pieces forming the slide are small, it's a sound idea to do the heavy machining on a single (relatively) large piece, then separate the parts and trim them to final size. Regardless of what the Cutting List specifies for these parts, I'd recommend starting with a single piece of hardwood $1\frac{1}{2}$ inches square and 8 inches long.

**2. Cut the rabbets that form the tongues.** Since you are working with a single workpiece, you need to form only one tongue. It is easiest to do this on the table saw. Set the blade height to $\frac{1}{4}$ inch, and position the rip fence to cut the sides of the tongue. Then crank up the blade to $\frac{1}{2}$ inch, and reposition the rip fence. Cut so the waste falls to the outside of the blade, thus avoiding having these wafers kicked back at you.

**3. Drill the holes for the jackscrew and the locking bolt.** Do the $\frac{7}{16}$-inch-diameter hole for the jackscrew first. Bore into one end of the slide blank, penetrating just over 2 inches, as shown in the *Slide Detail*.

Now cut the blank into two pieces. One piece should be $4\frac{1}{4}$ inches long; this is the slide top. The slide bottom will be taken from the remainder. But drill a $\frac{1}{4}$-inch-diameter hole for the locking bolt next. Set up a fence and stop block on the drill press when you drill these holes, so the two parts will align when bolted together. Drill a hole in the slide top and one in the slide bottom, as shown in the *Slide Detail*.

**4. Complete and install the slide.** With a backsaw, cut a $\frac{3}{4} \times 2\frac{1}{4}$-inch knob clearance notch in the slide top, as shown in the *Slide Detail*. Then trim the slide bottom to final length.

## SLIDE DETAIL

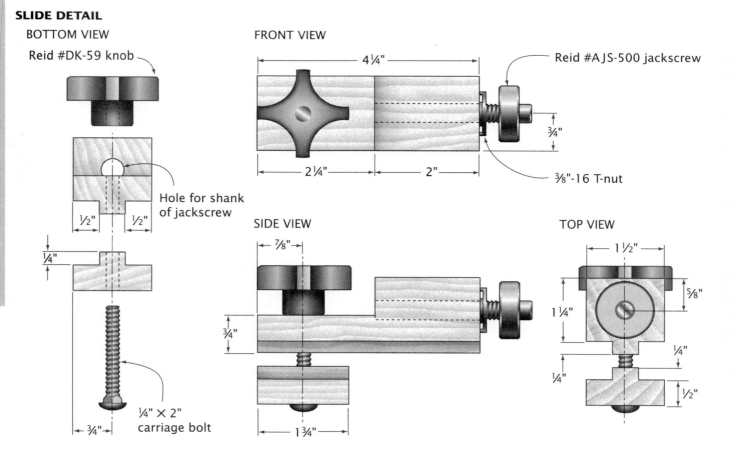

BOTTOM VIEW

Reid #DK-59 knob

Hole for shank of jackscrew

$\frac{1}{2}$"  $\frac{1}{2}$"

$\frac{1}{4}$"

$\frac{3}{4}$"

$\frac{1}{4}$" × 2" carriage bolt

FRONT VIEW

4$\frac{1}{4}$"

Reid #AJS-500 jackscrew

$\frac{3}{4}$"

2$\frac{1}{4}$"   2"

$\frac{3}{8}$"-16 T-nut

SIDE VIEW

$\frac{7}{8}$"

$\frac{3}{4}$"

1$\frac{3}{4}$"

TOP VIEW

1$\frac{1}{2}$"

$\frac{5}{8}$"

1$\frac{1}{4}$"

$\frac{1}{4}$"

$\frac{1}{4}$"

$\frac{1}{2}$"

Tap a T-nut into its hole, and turn the jackscrew into place. Push the carriage bolt through the slide bottom, and assemble the slide in its slot in the support.

### Installing the Router

You still aren't entirely ready to try out your new horizontal router mounting. You have to mount the router and also cut the slot for the bit in the support panel and the spacer. I performed the latter operation with the router.

Mount the router. Then fit it with the largest-diameter straight bit you have. Retract the bit into the router base. Settle the arm down as low as it'll go. Leave the locking knobs loose enough that you can move the arm, but don't leave the arm sloppy-loose.

Switch on the router, plunge the bit about ¼ inch into the support panel, and lock the depth. Then lift the arm and rout a slot up through the spacer. Lower the arm. Unlock the router and plunge a little deeper. Raise and lower the arm again.

Keep repeating the process until the slot is routed to the maximum depth that your router and the bit are capable of. If you ever get a large bit, it's a simple matter to enlarge the bit slot in the same fashion.

# Horizontal Routing

Okay, so you've built this nifty router mounting. Now what can you do with it? Darn near anything you can do with a regular router table and fence. I don't see this setup as a substitute for a router table. I see it as a complement to a router table.

But there are a few operations that are done better, easier, safer on the horizontal setup. These are the operations that on the regular router table perch the workpiece on edge. Among them are raising panels with a vertical panel-raising bit and profiling the face edges of broad pieces—baseboards, casings, crowns, and other moldings.

**When routing a broad architectural molding,** keep the workpiece flat on the table. By standing behind the swing arm at the corner of the table, you can more easily hold the stock against the swing arm as you feed it across the cutter. Of course, a couple of featherboards can help, too.

**An excellent way to raise panels** is to use a vertical panel-raising bit in this router table. Vertical panel-raising bits are smaller than wing-type panel-raising bits, they cost less than the bigger bits, and they can be powered by mid-sized routers. Set up the router and bit just as you would for cutting a tenon or routing a molding. Adjust the bit extension. Then adjust the swing arm so the bit's cutting edge is barely exposed above the table. Make fine adjustments to the height of the bit by rotating the jackscrew. For best results, especially in hardwoods, raise panels in two passes.

### Making a Slip Joint

The best single illustration of the horizontal router table's capabilities is to make a slip joint.

The slip joint is a simple variation on the mortise-and-tenon; it's really a slot-and-tenon joint, sometimes called an open mortise-and-tenon, a bridle joint, a saddle joint. It's a good joint for simple door frames, face frames, and the like. It offers more glue area than any other joint you could substitute. AND it is truly easy to set up and cut. To do it on the horizontal router table, all you need is a single bit and a sled. Layout work is as simple as layout work can ever be.

The process of routing the slot is a paradigm for slotting the edges of long, wide boards, for routing dovetail slots, and for other similar operations. Making the tenon for the slip joint is no different from making a tenon for a mortise-and-

**The slip joint is low-tech and easy to cut,** especially on the horizontal router table. In this simple variant of the mortise-and-tenon, the mortise is a slot into which the tenon slips.

tenon joint. This process is a paradigm for routing wide rabbets, and even for routing moldings and raising panels.

**1. Set up to cut the slot.** In the ideal—and probably unachievable—setup, the slot is exactly the width of the cutter. If you subscribe to the Rule of Thirds, use a ¼-inch straight bit for making the joint in ¾-inch stock.

Here's the extent of the layout work. On a sample of the stock make two marks, dividing the thickness into thirds. It doesn't have to be perfect; use a ruler if it comforts you to do so. Set that piece on the saw table, and set up the router.

Fit the bit in the collet. Raise the swing arm enough that the bit is up where you can see it. Adjust the bit extension first. Put the piece of stock against the swing arm, and adjust the router so the bit projection is a hair greater than the width of the stock. Now adjust the bit height by moving the swing arm. Set the stock beside the bit, and align the bit between the layout marks.

**2. Cut a test slot and fine-tune the setup.** Lay the stock flat on the saw table, its end butted against the swing arm. Bring the sled up behind it, then back the stock's end away from the swing arm. You shouldn't try to hog out the full-depth slot in a single pass.

Switch on the router and cut the slot. Keep the sled squarely against the swing arm. Feed the work into the bit, cutting a slot about ¼ inch deep. Pull the sled and work back and shift the work about ¼ inch closer to the arm. Make a second pass. Pull back, shift the work toward the arm, and make a third pass. Continue this routine until the slot has reached full depth.

Now roll the workpiece over and make a full-depth pass. This will probably widen the slot, but it definitely will center it on the workpiece.

Switch off the router and examine your cut. As long as the slot walls are ³⁄₁₆ inch thick or better, your setup is okay.

**3. Cut the slots.** Using the multipass procedure described in Step 2, cut the slots in all the workpieces.

**4. Revise the setup to cut the tenons.** Unlock the swing arm and lower the bit. Lay a slotted piece beside the bit and visually align the cutting edge of the bit with the slot wall. You want to make a cut that matches the wall's thickness.

Do NOT alter the bit extension.

**5. Cut a test tenon and fine-tune the setup.** Cut a tenon and a test piece of the working stock. Orient the stock and sled as you did for cutting the slot. Feed the work in the same way. Cut one side, then roll the stock over and cut the second.

Test the fit of the tenon in a slot.

- *If it is loose,* you must lower the bit.
- *If it is tight,* you must raise the bit.

It is that simple. Use the jackscrew for these adjustments. Remember that the change is doubled because you cut twice to form the tenon (and keep it centered).

Loosen the locking knobs and turn the jackscrew. Tighten the knobs. Cut a new test tenon (or recut the first one if it was too thick). Test the fit in the slot. If necessary, adjust the bit height again and cut a third test piece.

**6. Cut the tenons.** When the setting produces a tenon that fits the slots perfectly, cut tenons on the working stock.

**Routing the slip joint's slot** produces smooth, square surfaces. Back up the workpiece with the sled. Cut the slot in three or four passes. Hold the workpiece back from the swing arm, so the first cut is only ¼ to ½ inch deep. Move the workpiece closer to the arm on the second pass, as shown here, and butt it against the arm for the third pass. Then roll the workpiece over, and, with the workpiece butted to the swing arm, make a final pass to center the slot.

**The typical tenon can be routed quickly** on the horizontal router table. The amount of material being removed is modest, so a single pass can complete a cheek-and-shoulder cut. For a slip joint, two passes completes the tenon. For a mortise-and-tenon joint, a tenon can be completed in four passes, a speed that matches any other approach. The cheeks will be smooth, the shoulders square.

# Horizontal Savvy

With the router's orientation changed from vertical to horizontal, the methods for fine-tuning your cut must change. "Bit height" becomes a confusing term. Does it refer to an adjustment made on the router, as it does when working at a regular router table? Or does it refer to an adjustment made by moving the swing arm?

To me, the adjustment you make on the router itself is for *bit extension.* It governs how far out from the swing arm the bit extends. *Bit height,* when we're talking about the horizontal router table, refers to the height of the bit in relation to the plane of the tabletop.

When you begin to rout, you have to deal with feed direction. It's different: You feed from left to right. But let's not get ahead of ourselves. Do the adjustments first.

*Bit-extension adjustment:* Easy to do. You can stand beside the router and look straight down on the bit. Moreover, you don't have to worry about losing the router's bit-height setting when you loosen the clamp securing the motor in its base. You aren't fighting gravity in this adjustment.

Hold a rule next to the bit and move the router.

*Bit-height adjustment:* The swing arm's fine-adjustment system works great.

To get a coarse setting, loosen the locking knobs and lift the swing arm. When the setting *looks* right, tighten the knobs (particularly the two in the slot). Then bring the slide up so the nose of the jackscrew touches the swing arm. Be sure the jackscrew is about halfway out. This ensures that you can lower the arm as well as raise it to fine-tune the bit height.

Make a test cut and measure the cut itself. To deepen the cut, raise the arm. To make it less deep, lower the arm. In both situations, loosen the locking knobs—remember, the arm won't move when you do this—and turn the jackscrew clockwise to raise the arm, counterclockwise to lower it.

If you are a stickler, you'll want to remember that the jackscrew has 16 threads per inch. One complete revolution will alter its height $\frac{1}{16}$ inch. But you also need to know that the pivoting action of the swing arm and the location of the bit axis will halve that height change at the bit. Turn the jackscrew a complete revolution, and the bit height will change $\frac{1}{32}$ inch.

*continued*

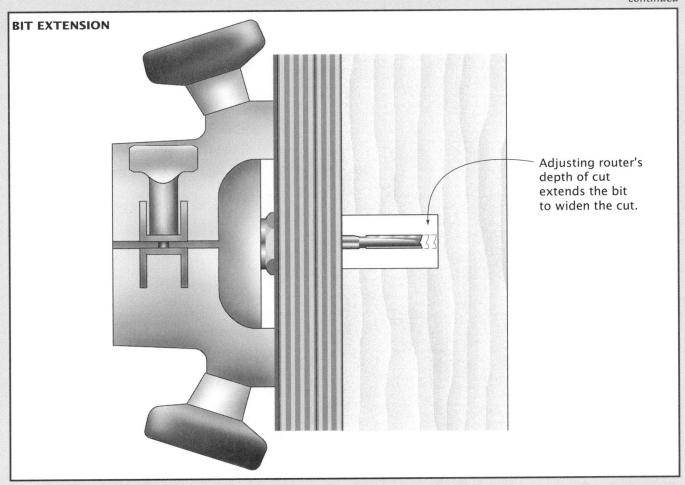

**BIT EXTENSION**

Adjusting router's depth of cut extends the bit to widen the cut.

# Horizontal Savvy—Continued

That *is* fine-tuning.

*Feed direction:* As I said, it is from left to right, unlike on a regular router table. This is because you're using what would be, on a regular router table, the back of the bit.

It's easy to figure out. Look at the bit as it extends into the tabletop bit opening. Look at the cutting edge. Does it remind you of the cutters on a jointer, the way they are pitched into the cut? It does me. I look at that router bit and I can just see it's going to spin toward the left—counterclockwise.

And because you always feed *against* the cutter rotation, I know I'm going to feed the stock from left to right. **In practical terms:** Feed from the front of the saw table to the back, just as you would when ripping or crosscutting.

## BIT ELEVATION

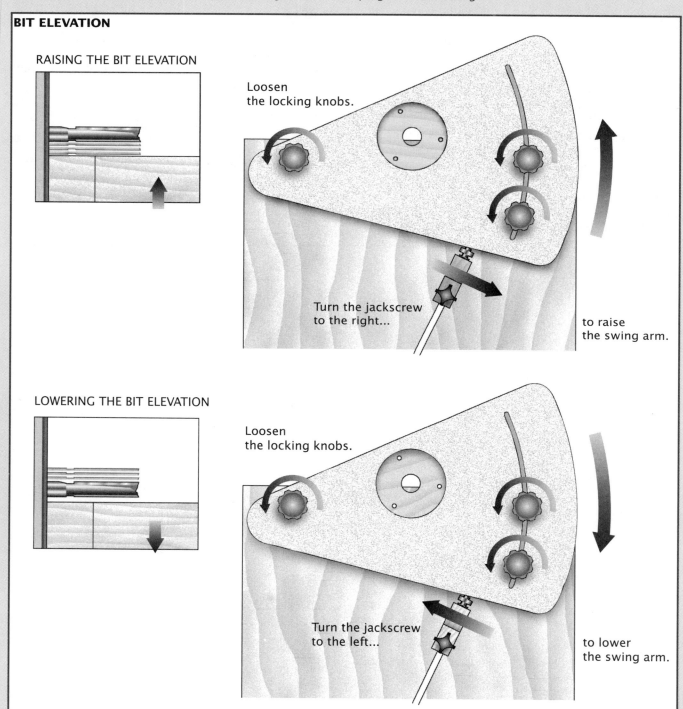

RAISING THE BIT ELEVATION

Loosen the locking knobs.

Turn the jackscrew to the right...

to raise the swing arm.

LOWERING THE BIT ELEVATION

Loosen the locking knobs.

Turn the jackscrew to the left...

to lower the swing arm.

Router Tables

# Bench-Top Router Table

**Your router won't be tied up in this router table. Removing it is as easy as popping a couple of toggle clamps.**

For the small shop, for the remote job site, or as an extra in a busy shop, this little bench-top router table is just the ticket. It has a bunch of practical features, but easily the best is the simple router-mounting system.

I know a lot of hobby woodworkers have only one router, and they don't want to mount it in a table because it *seems* to be tying it up. The approach presented here doesn't tie up your router, because flicking two toggle clamps frees the router from the table, totally ready to use for hand-held work.

Just insert the router (with the baseplate still installed) in the recess for it beneath the tabletop, and snap two toggle clamps closed. It's mounted, easy as that! Need the router for a hand-held procedure? Pop open the toggles and the router is free of the table and ready to go. No fiddling with mounting screws to remove a mounting plate and reinstall the baseplate, because the baseplate has been in place the whole time.

Making this little operation even easier to perform is a lift-top feature (which this router table shares with the larger Floor-Standing Router Table presented on page 212). The tabletop is hinged, and it tilts up in front, just about handing you the router. Because it is so easy to do, you'll just remove the router to change bits.

Equally impressive is how easy bit-extension adjustments become with this tilt-top feature. With the tabletop lifted, you can sight across the table surface to the bit without bending or stooping. The fence doesn't need to be moved to tilt the tabletop. Thus you can make a test cut, measure the cut itself, and lift the tabletop to adjust the bit without losing your fence setup. You can use both hands to adjust the router, because a commercial lid stay keeps the tabletop in the tilted-up position until you are ready to close it.

With a benchtop unit, the working surface is elevated closer to you than with a floor-standing unit. This is especially helpful, I think, when dealing with small workpieces. I tend to hunch over to keep a close eye on the operation, which in a protracted session is quite literally a pain in the neck. So for such sessions, it's often worthwhile to pull out this little table, set it on the workbench (or on a Shopmate), and clamp it down.

The unit's footprint is small, just 16 × 28 inches. The bottom extends well beyond the housing on the sides and at the back, so it is stable and well suited to clamping to a workbench. The base is a plywood box with buttresses. It is painted.

Almost as an afterthought, I routed a handgrip opening

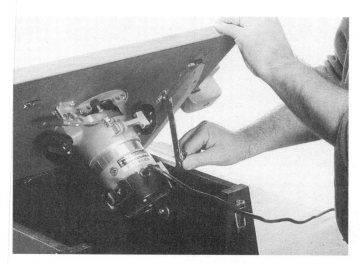

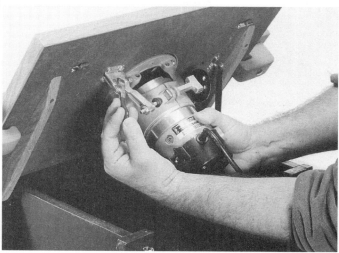

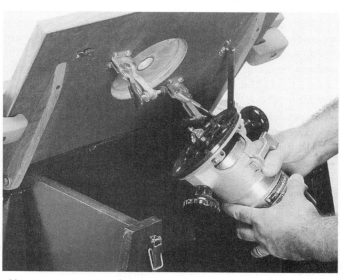

**No, your router is not possessed,** not by this router table. To reclaim the router for a hand-held procedure (or simply to change a bit), just lift the tabletop until the lid stay locks (*top*). Grasp the router with one hand, and pop open the two toggle clamps with the other (*center*). The router virtually falls out of its mounting recess. Note that its stock baseplate is still in place (*bottom*).

through the bottom on each side of the housing and behind it as well. The handgrips make it easy to carry the unit around, and one or another invariably doubles as a hanging hole. I hang it over a (big) nail to store it.

The tabletop is two layers of ½-inch plywood with oak edge-banding. It is covered on top with plastic laminate; on the bottom, with backer. The hinge leaves are oak, with hex-head lag screws used as hinge pins. Although the tabletop doesn't seem to jump or jiggle during use, I installed a couple of toggle latches to lock it down. That way the tabletop stays closed when it's being moved about.

A corollary of the toggle-clamp mounting approach is that there's no mounting plate. This is worthy of note because the bit opening is a hole in the tabletop, and that does have a drawback. It is that once you bore out the opening with a big bit, it will always be opened way up. As a consequence, you may want to limit yourself to using relatively small bits—say, under 1 inch in diameter—in this router table. It isn't suited to panel raising anyway.

I scaled the bench-top router table for a small, fixed-base router. I use a Porter-Cable 690 in it, but I think a Dewalt DW610, the Bosch 1606, and even Sears models would work. Plunge routers will be too tall, so if that's what you've got, be aware that you'll need to resize the base unit to accommodate your machine.

The plans that follow show a very basic fence. It is a simple straightedge with integral clamps. But from time to time, you may find it beneficial to have a more elaborate fence to use, one with vertical facings and even a dust pickup. For this, you should be able to adapt the Split Fence shown on page 237 to fit this router table.

This is a dandy little unit, even if I do say so myself. If you have all the hardware in hand, you can build it in a productive weekend, apply the finish over the next few evenings, and put it to work the following weekend.

## Building the Router Table

I've broken this project down into three components, each of which you build in turn: the base, the tabletop, and a fence. In actually doing the work, you'll probably bounce back and forth between the base and the tabletop, keeping the project moving forward on one front while the glue is drying on the other. The fence probably should be built to fit the tabletop.

### Building the Base

A base is little more than a plywood box. I angled the back and the front stiles to give the unit the appearance of being broadly based and very stable. And the buttress-like elements surely do contribute to the base unit's rigidity.

I planned from the start to paint the unit, so I glued solid-wood edge-banding to any exposed plywood edges. This process does add to the construction time, but probably no more than an hour.

You can make the base unit even simpler than it is. If

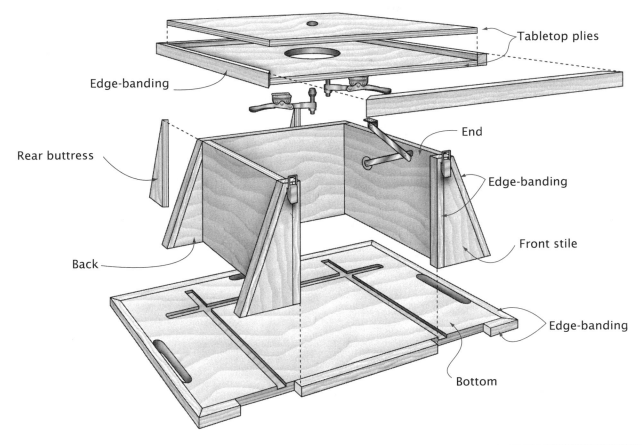

Tabletop plies

Edge-banding

Rear buttress

End

Edge-banding

Back

Front stile

Edge-banding

Bottom

## Cutting List

| Part | Qty. | Dimensions | Material |
|---|---|---|---|
| Bottom | 1 | ¾" × 14½" × 26½" | Plywood |
| Ends | 2 | ¾" × 10½" × 10½" | Plywood |
| Back | 1 | ¾" × 11" × 21" | Plywood |
| Rear buttresses | 2 | ¾" × 2¾" × 11" | Plywood |
| Front stiles | 2 | ¾" × 11" × 4" | Plywood |
| Edge-banding | 8 | ¾" × ½" × 12" | Poplar |
| Edge-banding | 2 | ¾" × ¾" × 16" | Poplar |
| Edge-banding | 2 | ¾" × ¾" × 28" | Poplar |
| Tabletop plies | 2 | ½" × 16" × 20" | Plywood |
| Edge-banding | 2 | 1" × ¾" × 17½" | Oak |
| Edge-banding | 2 | 1" × ¾" × 21½" | Oak |
| Top surface | 1 | 1⁄16" × 16" × 20" | Plastic laminate |
| Bottom surface | 1 | 1⁄32" × 16" × 20" | Laminate backer |
| Hinge straps | 2 | ¾" × 1" × 12¼" | Oak |
| Fence | 1 | 1" × 3" × 27¼" | Oak |
| Clamp blocks | 2 | 1½" × 1½" × 3½" | Oak |

## Hardware

6d finish nails

2 drywall screws, #6 × 1¼"

4 drywall screws, #6 × 1⅝"

2 hex-head lag screws, ¼" × 2"

4 flat washers, ¼" I.D.

2 Dzus toggle latches; #DTL-802A from Reid Tool Supply Co. (800-253-0421)

2 Dzus strikes; #DTL-800-9 from Reid Tool Supply Co.

8 panhead wood screws, #6 × ¾"

2 toggle clamps, De-Sta-Co #TC-215-U

8 panhead screws, #8 × 1"

1 folding lid stay with mounting screws, right-side mount

1 fender washer, ¼" I.D.

2 carriage bolts, ¼"-20 × 3"

2 plastic knobs, 1¾" dia. with ¼"-20 through insert; #DK-54 from Reid Tool Supply Co.

2 panhead screws, #6 × 1"

**Router Tables**

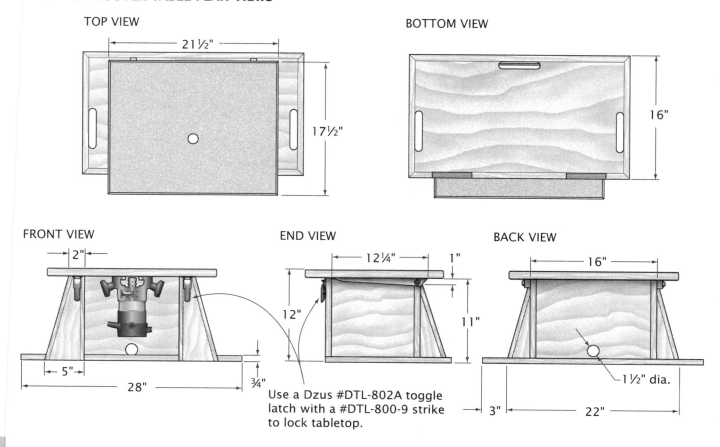

TOP VIEW

21½"

17½"

BOTTOM VIEW

16"

FRONT VIEW

2"

5"

28"

¾"

END VIEW

12¼"

1"

12"

Use a Dzus #DTL-802A toggle latch with a #DTL-800-9 strike to lock tabletop.

BACK VIEW

16"

11"

1½" dia.

3"

22"

quick-and-dirty is your style, then forgo the edge-banding and the buttress-like stiles and back. A plain plywood box will do just fine.

**1. Cut the parts.** All the plywood parts except the ends are edge-banded to conceal the plies. I used birch plywood, but you can use BB-grade fir plywood since the base is painted. For the edge-banding, I used poplar, simply ripping a few sticks to the thickness and width specified by the Cutting List.

To determine the buttress angle on the back, on the rear buttresses, and on the front stiles, I laid out the back. Then I set a sliding T-bevel from the layout and used it to adjust the table saw miter gauge.

To safely cut out the stiles and buttresses, lay them out with the back on a plywood piece 11 × 37 inches. Lay out one stile on each end of the piece. Cut the angles, then reset the miter gauge square to crosscut the stiles from the over-sized blank. Repeat the process to cut the buttresses from the blank. Then cut the angles on the back.

**2. Edge-band the stiles, buttresses, and back.** Cut and glue strips of wood to the exposed edges of the stiles and back. You can avoid all the frustration of clamping the angled parts if you nail the edge-banding as well as glue it. Use 6d finish nails, and countersink them and putty over the heads.

After the glue has set, trim the edge-banding flush with

the faces of the back and stiles. This goes easily if you use a router and the Flush-Trimming Baseplate on page 119.

**3. Dado the bottom for the ends and back.** The ends and back set into ¾-inch-wide × ¼-inch-deep dadoes routed into the base. The drawing *Bottom Layout* shows where to cut the dadoes.

**Guide a router along the Routing Straightedge** (see page 75) to cut the dadoes in the bottom. Especially with a D-handled router, it is a quick operation. Hold the work with one hand, and guide the router with the other.

Router Tables

**BOTTOM LAYOUT**

SECTION VIEW

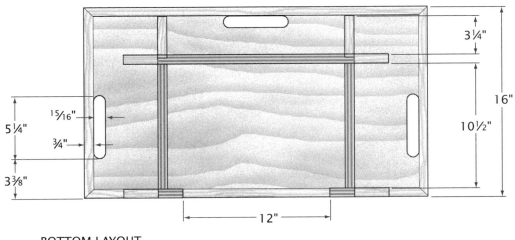

3¼"

16"

10½"

5¼"

¹⁵⁄₁₆"

¾"

3⅜"

12"

BOTTOM LAYOUT

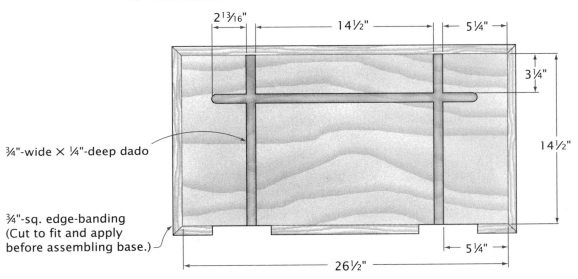

2¹³⁄₁₆"

14½"

5¼"

3¼"

14½"

¾"-wide × ¼"-deep dado

¾"-sq. edge-banding
(Cut to fit and apply
before assembling base.)

5¼"

26½"

**4. Edge-band the base.** While it might seem easier to apply this edge-banding after the base is assembled, you will then find that flush-trimming the edge-banding is somewhat problematic. The stiles will be in the way. So work sequentially around the bottom, measuring, cutting, and fitting the short strips of wood to the plywood edges.

Begin by standing the stiles in position and scribing a line along each edge on the base. X-out the area between the lines; no edge-banding will be applied here.

Apply strips across the ends of the bottom first. These strips are mitered on both ends. Measure, miter, and apply them. You can clamp them while the glue sets, or instead drive a few finish nails to secure them. Next measure, miter, and apply short pieces between the front corners and the scribe marks on the edge. It is better to have these a tad long than have them be too short. They can be pared back with a chisel for a perfect fit. Finally, cut and apply the strip that fits between the two stiles.

After the glue has set, trim the edge-banding flush. Check how the stiles fit. If necessary, pare back the ends of the edge-banding.

**5. Rout the handgrip openings in the bottom.** Make a template to guide this cut. Lay out the opening on the center of a 3-inch-wide × 16-inch-long piece of hardboard or plywood. Bore a 1-inch-diameter hole at each end, then saw out the remaining waste with a saber saw. Sand the edge of the opening smooth.

To rout the opening in the bottom, clamp the template to the workpiece. Fit a plunge router with a ⁵⁄₁₆-inch-O.D. template guide and a ¼-inch straight bit. Rout out the waste. After the opening is cut, round-over the edges on both sides of the workpiece with a ³⁄₁₆-inch roundover bit.

**6. Assemble the base unit.** Glue and nail the parts together. Start with the ends. Glue them into the dadoes. Then fit the back into place. Glue and nail it to the bottom and the ends. Glue and nail the buttresses and stiles in place last.

Go over the base, and countersink all the nails; then fill the holes. Sand the base. After the tabletop has been fitted—see Step 4 under "Building the Tabletop," below—apply primer, then a coat or two of paint inside and out.

**Router Tables**

## TABLETOP DETAIL

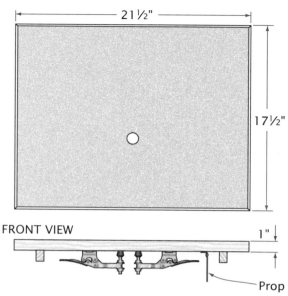

TOP VIEW

21½"

17½"

FRONT VIEW

1"

Prop

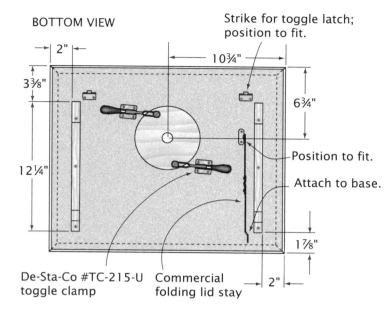

BOTTOM VIEW

Strike for toggle latch; position to fit.

2"

10¾"

3⅜"

6¾"

12¼"

Position to fit.

Attach to base.

1⅞"

De-Sta-Co #TC-215-U toggle clamp

Commercial folding lid stay

2"

## Building the Tabletop

The tabletop is pretty much a miniature of the Custom Router Table Top. The chapter of that name, which begins on page 156, details just how to construct such a tabletop.

**1. Cut a hole in one ply for the router.** Like the generic tabletop, this table has a two-ply core. The layers, however, are ½-inch plywood (not ¾-inch). The router mounts directly to the tabletop—there's no mounting plate; it fits into a ½-inch-deep recess in the underside. Now you *can* excavate the recess after assembling the tabletop, but it's a heck of a lot easier to simply rout a hole in one ply, then glue-laminate the core.

Lay out the center of the hole, drill a pivot hole, and use the Trammel Baseplate (see page 39) on a plunge router to cut the opening. Fit the opening tightly to the router you will be using in the router table.

**2. Make the tabletop.** Following the detailed instructions for making the Custom Router Table Top on page 156, make the tabletop shown in the drawings. The instructions there basically include these steps:

- Glue up the plies.
- Trim this core to square the edges.
- Apply oak edge-banding. Trim it flush, top and bottom.
- Apply plastic laminate to both top and bottom. Trim the laminate, and open up the router recess on the bottom.
- Bevel the edges of the tabletop.

**3. Cut and shape the hinges.** I made the hinges of oak, cutting them to the shape shown in the drawing *Hinge Layout*.

Cut the two oak workpieces to the dimensions specified by the Cutting List. Tape them together with masking

tape or packing tape (or with carpet tape between them). Lay out the hinge-pin hole and the shape of the hinges on the top workpiece.

Drill the hole for the hinge pin.

With the two hinges still taped together, miter the ends, as shown in the drawing, then cut the main taper. This last cut is done most easily on the band saw, but I did it on the table saw using a tapering jig. Peel off the remaining tape, separating the parts, and sand them, softening the edges.

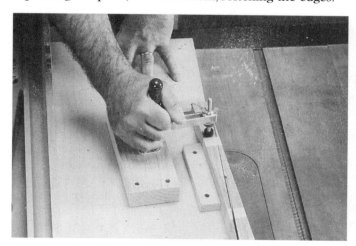

**Cutting the hinge taper** can be done safely on the table saw using a "carry board." With the two hinges taped together, clamp them to a scrap of plywood with a toggle clamp, as shown. The cut line should be aligned directly over the plywood's edge. Feed the jig along the rip fence, cutting off the waste.

**4. Fit the hinges to the base unit.** Bits of the back's "buttresses" must be pared away to allow the hinges to nestle squarely against the base's ends. Hold a hinge against one side and mark along its lower edge on the but-

## HINGE LAYOUT

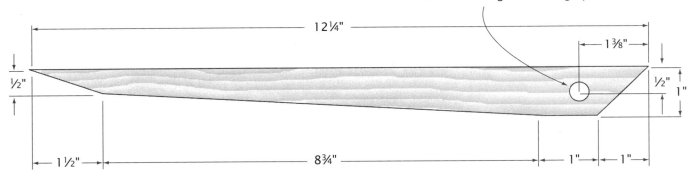

¼"-dia. hole for lag-screw hinge pin

12¼"

1⅜"

½"

½"

1"

1½"

8¾"

1"

1"

tress. With a back saw and chisel, trim the buttress. Repeat the process on the other side.

Chuck a ³⁄₁₆-inch bit in a portable drill. Hold a hinge in place against the base unit. Guided by the hole in the hinge, drill a pilot for the lag-screw hinge pin. Drill the second hinge-pin hole.

Temporarily mount the hinges on the base unit. Try to lift the hinge, and you'll see there's still interference between the buttress and hinge. Mark the material that must be removed, then pare it away.

**5. Attach the hinges to the tabletop.** Set the tabletop on the base, and carefully align so it overhangs the base exactly the way you want it to. Then scribe along the base ends on the tabletop. In turn, hold each hinge in place, and scribe along the ends on the underside of the tabletop.

Lift the top off the base and lay it on your workbench, bottom up. Set the hinges on the tabletop, about ¹⁄₁₆ inch outside of the lines. Drill and countersink pilot holes, and drive 1⅝-inch drywall screws through the hinges into the tabletop. Three screws in each hinge is enough.

**6. Install the toggle clamps.** The optimal position for the two toggle clamps will vary from router to router. The locations and orientation shown in the drawing *Tabletop Detail* works with a Porter-Cable 690 router, but they may not with a different model or brand. With the tabletop still on the workbench, set your router in place, and try the clamps in different locations. Don't be content to find a spot that works if the clamps are closed. You have to work the clamp to ensure that the spindle doesn't hang up on the body of the base or the depth-control knob or some other protuberance on the router.

When you've determined the best locations for the clamps, attach each to the tabletop with four #8 × 1-inch panhead screws.

Adjust the spindle of each clamp so the router is held firmly in place. Then remove the router and set it aside until the router table is completed.

**7. Mount the tabletop on the base unit.** Set the tabletop atop the base unit. Fit flat washers on the hex-head lag screws, and insert one through each hinge into

the pilot for it. Drive the screws with a wrench.

**8. Install the stay.** After experimenting with several different homemade props for the tabletop, I settled on a commercial folding lid stay. The folding stay cost me only $2, and it keeps the tabletop up until I am consciously ready to lower it.

To install the stay, you will have to experiment to find the best location. The drawing *Lid Stay Detail* provides a general idea of where to locate it.

**9. Install the toggle latches.** One toggle latch is mounted on each front stile. The strikes are installed on the underside of the tabletop.

## LID STAY DETAIL

SECTION VIEW

6⅛"

Position stay where strut tip will clear stile as tabletop is lowered.

3⅞"

Fender washer

6⁹⁄₁₆"

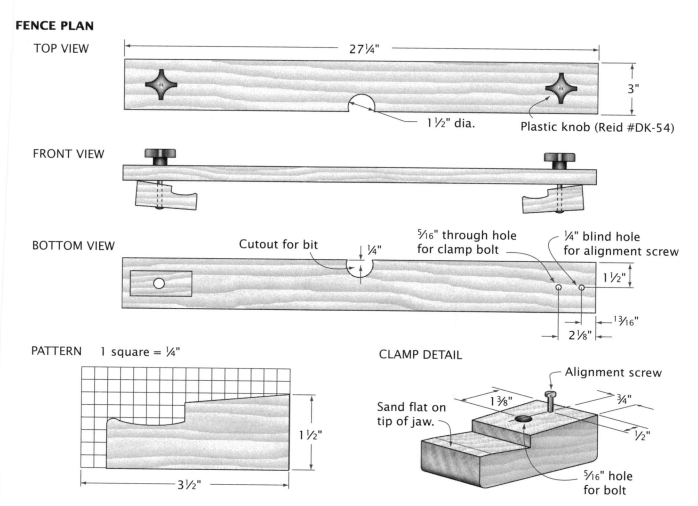

TOP VIEW

27¼"

3"

1½" dia.

Plastic knob (Reid #DK-54)

FRONT VIEW

BOTTOM VIEW

Cutout for bit

¼"

⁵⁄₁₆" through hole for clamp bolt

¼" blind hole for alignment screw

1½"

¹³⁄₁₆"

2⅛"

PATTERN     1 square = ¼"

1½"

3½"

CLAMP DETAIL

Alignment screw

Sand flat on tip of jaw.

1⅜"

¾"

½"

⁵⁄₁₆" hole for bolt

## Building the Fence

A router table isn't complete without a fence. The fence shown is real basic—a board with shop-made clamps. It has a cutout for a bit. This basic fence is my workhorse; it gets a lot of use.

**1. Cut and shape the clamp blocks.** The contour and dimensions of the clamp blocks are shown in the drawing *Fence Plan*.

The clamps are easiest to form with a band saw and a stationary sander. Enlarge the pattern, transfer it to a single board of the correct thickness, and then saw out the blocks. The sander will smooth and blend the edges.

As an alternative, you can saw out the clamp blocks with a table-mounted saber saw. Or you can rough them out on the table saw; the details of doing this are related in the directions for making the Split Fence, on page 237.

In any event, you should complete the clamp blocks by sanding or filing a narrow flat at the jaw's tip. Then round-over the exposed edges with sandpaper or a file.

**2. Drill the holes in the blocks.** The clamp blocks are mounted to the fence with ¼-inch carriage bolts. Each block has a panhead screw protruding from the top; the screw projects into a hole in the fence, keeping the block from twisting.

To provide a little play for the mounting bolts, bore ⁵⁄₁₆-inch holes through each block, as shown in the drawing. Also drill a pilot hole and drive the alignment screw into it. Leave the head protruding about ³⁄₁₆ inch.

**3. Prepare the fence.** Cut the fence to the dimensions specified by the Cutting List. The cutout for the bit can be created with a 1½-inch Forstner bit. The center of the hole should be ¼ inch from the fence's edge. After drilling this opening, lay out and drill the clamp-bolt holes. Finally, rout a chamfer on all the edges.

**4. Mount the clamps.** Insert the bolts in the holes in the clamp blocks, and seat the heads with a hammer blow. Slip the bolts through the fence, drop a flat washer over the shank, and turn the plastic knobs onto the bolts. Align the screws in the alignment holes, and the fence is ready to slide onto the tabletop.

## Using the Router Table

Hey, it's a router table! It's a small one to be sure. But on it, you can do just about anything you can on any floor-standing router table. Here's the drill.

**1. Clamp the unit to a workbench.** The need to

clamp the table stems from its lightness. Move the work too aggressively into the bit, and you may find an unfettered table sliding away from you. Not good. So clamp it.

What you clamp the unit to can range from a workbench to a saw table, from a pair of shop trestles to a Shopmate. Be careful about what you choose. With some aggressive routing, you may find a lightweight table wobbling, tipping, and skidding. A workbench with mass won't do this, and neither will a table saw. A Shopmate, with its wide stance and rubbery toes, provides a good base. Of

**A truly comfortable working height** is one of the pluses of a bench-top router table. Though its work surface is small, this router table is suitable for all sorts of operations. Clamp it to the workbench and you are ready for work.

**No router table should be without a starting pin.** But that doesn't mean it needs to be a pin stuck in a hole in the tabletop. With my bench-top router table, I use a triangular scrap clamped to the tabletop as a "starting pin," as shown here.

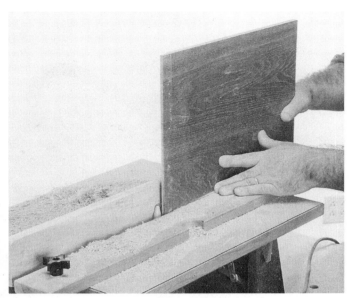

**A trap fence setup** is easy to arrange if you make two fences for the bench-top router table, one of them with a vertical facing. To create a trap fence, you simply position the low fence parallel to the vertical fence. The trap fence keeps the bottom of the workpiece from sliding away from the vertical fence and thus the bit. Try it. You'll find that it takes surprisingly little pressure to keep the workpiece against the vertical fence, and that even a 4-inch-high vertical fence is plenty high to support a tall workpiece.

course, in some shops, the bench-top router table will be set up permanently on an auxiliary table, while in smaller circumstances, it will be stored in an out-of-the-way spot and set up only when it is going to be used.

**2. Clamp the router under the tabletop.** Chuck the bit for whatever job you are doing in the router's collet. Lift the tabletop, fit the router into its recess, and snap the two toggle clamps closed. No need to remove the baseplate, remember. Hold a rule at the bit, and adjust the bit extension. *Now* lower the tabletop.

**3. Set the fence or starting pin.** Obviously you need some means of guiding and controlling the workpiece. If you are doing edge work with a piloted bit, use the starting pin. Otherwise, slide the appropriate fence onto the tabletop, set its position, and tighten the clamps.

**4. Rout.** Plug the router in. Switch it on. Rout. That's all there is to it.

The limitations of the unit will become clear to you as you use it more and more. I've already suggested, for example, that it isn't ideal for raising panels, primarily because you don't want to make that bit opening too big. You'll probably want to avoid milling very long molding strips, or broad panels. The tabletop isn't all that big, remember.

On the other hand, I've also suggested that its small size and its elevated stature (when clamped to a bench top) make it an excellent choice for small parts.

**Router Tables**

# Floor-Standing Router Table

**Build your own personalized router table from a menu of innovative and practical features: a lift top for easy router adjustments, two-stage dust collection, bit storage, and a lot more.**

When I set out to get a floor-standing router table for my shop, I mentally reviewed the memorable strengths and weaknesses of those I'd seen and used. And over the years, I've seen and used quite a number of different router tables, both shop-made and commercial.

Right off I knew that I'd build, rather than buy, the router table.

Look at what's available through woodworking catalogs: plastic laminate–covered tabletops mounted on trestle or post-and-apron leg assemblies. Here and there you'll see a tabletop mounted on a cabinet. The tabletops have the mounting-plate hole located dead-center, and a miter gauge slot plowed from one end to the other. Are these tables well made? For the most part, sure. The leg assemblies are tightly joined and reasonably rigid. The cabinets are marvels of economical construction, displaying a character typical of lumberyard kitchen cabinets. The tabletops are flat. The retail prices generally are reasonable.

But I knew that if I'd take the money and invest it in *materials* for a router table, I could build a much better table than I could buy. I could incorporate features that suited me, even if they suited no one else. So what did I want?

- An expansive tabletop with the router offset toward the front edge. Flat and heavy. No holes or slots in the tabletop. Laminate covering the entire top surface for long wear.

- A straight, true fence, one with a good dust pickup and maybe even adjustable facings. I didn't want to have to traipse to the clamp rack before setting the fence. I wanted to be able to clear the fence from the table quickly, without undoing bolts. Integral clamps thus would be essential.

- Ready access to the router, so I could change bits quickly and easily and make adjustments conveniently. I'm getting too old for the stooping and kneeling.

- Mass. I wanted a heavy piece that would dampen the vibrations of a powerful router making heavy cuts, a solid structure that wouldn't drift or dance away from me in mid-cut.

- Good dust collection. Why is sweeping the shop so burdensome? It isn't hard work, but I hate it. So I wanted to capture the router-generated mountain of dust and chips *before* it got to the floor.

- Orderly, logical bit storage. I've lost and misplaced scores of bits, largely because I don't know what I've got and where to put it when it isn't in the router's collet. A frequently used router table has two or three drawers for ½-inch-shank bits, a couple of others for ¼-inch-shank bits. Looking for a ⅜-inch roundover bit? You end up opening and closing all the drawers. I wanted to organize my bits, making a particular spot for each bit, so I don't have to look through them all to find just one. And organizing them by profile makes a lot more sense to me than segregating them by shank size. (Do you sense some irritability on this one?)

- Convenient storage for featherboards, sleds, and other jigs and accessories used with the router table.
- Switched outlets so both the router and the dust collection could be powered up at the same time.

I came up with a design that responds to each of these needs or desires. Few of the individual solutions are particularly original, I admit, but in aggregate, they yield a smashing piece of woodshop furniture. And the best of these features are unique to shop-made tables. Here's what it's got:

- a 1½-inch-thick, plastic laminate–covered tabletop made of birch plywood with semiconcealed hardwood edge-banding;
- a lift-top feature that allows you to adjust the router and change bits without bending, stooping, squinting, kneeling, and otherwise supplicating;
- a clamp-on fence—with its own built-in clamps—that doesn't interfere with the lift-top feature;
- a sturdy, hardwood, post-and-apron leg assembly to support the tabletop;
- a separate cabinet insert to house the router and to provide storage for bits, wrenches, and other accessories;
- two-level dust collection—it pulls chips off the tabletop through a fence-mounted pickup and from the router compartment beneath the tabletop—powered by a common shop vacuum;
- generous drawer for storage;
- electrical outlets inside the router compartment and on the cabinet back controlled by a switch.

This is an eclectic mix of features. I make no bones about it. I've borrowed brazenly from a bunch of smart designers. Specifically, the stand and upper cabinet design draws heavily on a router table designed by Ellis Walentine and Andy Rae. Woodworking writer Nick Engler claims credit for the lift-top concept, and his was the first working model I ever saw. Woodworker Fred Matlack suggested a slew of little tweaks and fixes throughout the development process.

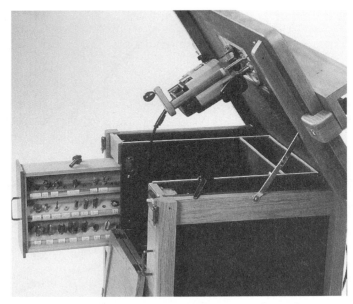

**The router table's upper cabinet** envelops the router (when the tabletop is lowered), capturing a lot of its dirt and muffling its noise. In addition, it furnishes orderly storage for bits and other essential paraphernalia, right at your fingertips.

**With the tabletop tilted up,** it is surprisingly easy to change bits and adjust the bit height. The router is suspended at a very convenient height, and you can use both hands to loosen and tighten the collet.

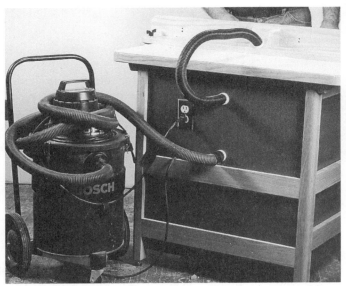

**A shop vacuum** collects all the dust the router table generates. Its hose is plugged into the lower port on the cabinet back. With the cabinet well sealed, the vac has enough suction to pull chips off the fence via the jumper hose to the cabinet's upper port.

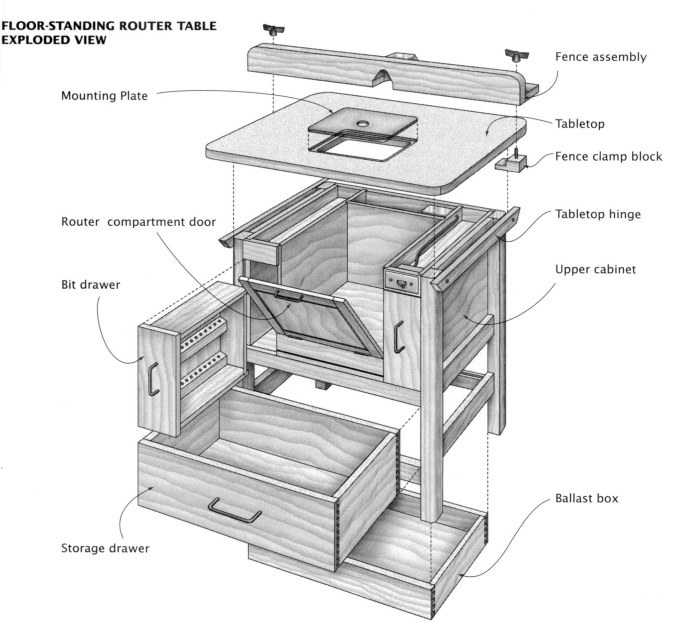

Mounting Plate

Fence assembly

Tabletop

Fence clamp block

Router compartment door

Tabletop hinge

Bit drawer

Upper cabinet

Storage drawer

Ballast box

It may not be the most beautiful router table you've ever seen, but it isn't bad-looking for a hard-working piece of shop furniture. My plan was to make the router table reasonably attractive, without getting into using really premium hardwoods. For the stand and the cabinet faces, I used oak and applied a clear finish (polyurethane). For the casework, I used plywood and poplar, and I painted them.

The completed table, fitted out as shown in the photos, is sturdy, rigid, and heavy. It doesn't wobble or sway, it doesn't vibrate, it doesn't shimmy or jitterbug. I expect it to serve me a long, long time.

A great benefit of the modular design is that you can build the router table in stages. Once you have the stand and the tabletop built, you can put the router table to use. When you get time, build the fence. That'll give you plenty of router table; you may never take the project any further.

But I'd recommend you add the case that houses the router and provides storage for bits and accessories. Still

later, you can finish out the unit by building the big storage drawer to fill the bottom of the stand. This is your custom router table, so make it serve your needs.

Is this the ultimate router table? Heck, no. Creative woodworkers are still noodling around out there in the workshops of America and the world beyond. New designs and configurations and accessories are bound to crop up. To my mind, there never will be an "ultimate" router table.

For now, though, this one is pretty darn good.

## Building the Router Table

This is modular shop furniture, made up of six separate components. At minimum, you need to build two of them—the stand and the tabletop—in order to have a working router table. Once these two are built, you can use the table, whether it be for your regular woodworking or to complete the other components.

Router Tables

## FLOOR-STANDING ROUTER TABLE PLAN VIEWS

TOP VIEW

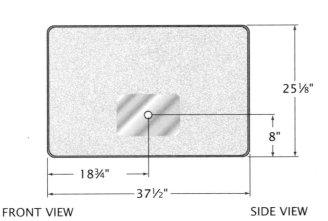

TOP VIEW OF STAND

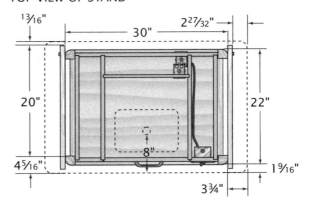

FRONT VIEW

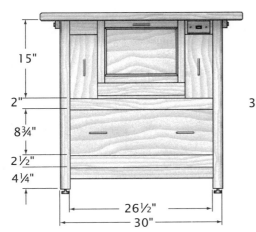

SIDE VIEW

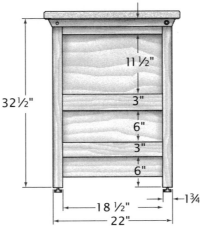

BACK VIEW

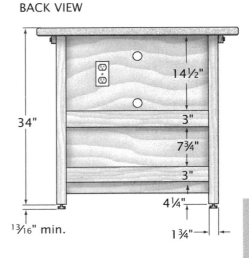

## FLOOR-STANDING ROUTER TABLE SECTION VIEWS

FRONT SECTION VIEW

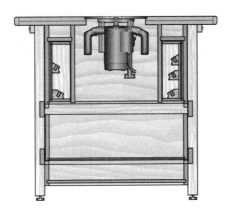

SIDE SECTION VIEW

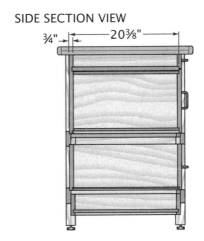

# Building the Stand

The foundation of the router table is the stand, so it makes sense to build it first. This stand is straightforward, just 4 legs and 10 rails, but it is strong and rigid. With screw adjusters installed, it can be set square and level, even on an undulating floor.

I used oak for the assembly. It is strong, attractive, and here in eastern Pennsylvania, readily available from local sawmills. The result is an open stand that's heavy enough to stay put, even under the stress of some pretty vigorous routing operations.

**1. Cut the parts.** Use straight-grained, defect-free stock for the stand. Mill stock to thicknesses of 1¾ inches and ⅞ inch. Rip and crosscut the legs and rails to the

| STAND Cutting List | | | |
|---|---|---|---|
| **Part** | **Qty.** | **Dimensions** | **Material** |
| Legs | 4 | 1¾" × 1¾" × 32½" | Oak |
| Side rails | 6 | ⅞" × 3" × 20½"* | Oak |
| Back rails | 2 | ⅞" × 3" × 28½"* | Oak |
| Front rail | 1 | ⅞" × 2" × 28½"* | Oak |
| Bottom front rail | 1 | ⅞" × 2½" × 28½" | Oak |
| Runners | 4 | ¾" × ¾" × 20¼" | Oak |
| Cleats | 2 | ¾" × ¾" × 25" | Oak |

### Hardware

drywall screws, #6 × 1¼"

4 T-nuts, 5⁄16"-18

4 adjustable glides; #AG-50 from Reid Tool Supply Co. (800-253-0421)

*Including tenons*

FRONT LEG

BACK LEG

¾"-rad. roundover

2½" (typ.)

¼" (typ.)

3" (typ.)

¼" (typ.)

⅜" (typ.)

2½"

⅜" (typ.)

¼" (typ.)

¼" (typ.)

12"

¼"-wide × ½"-deep rabbets

Front rail

3"

2½"

2½"

Side rails

6½"

8¼"

Back rails

1½"

2½"

2½"

9¼"

2"

6¼"

4½"

2"

⅞"

Mortises are all ⅜" wide and 1" deep.

4½"

2½"

Tenons are ⅜" thick and 1" long. Shoulder is ¼" wide all around.

Lower front rail

5⁄16" T-nut

Adjustable glide (Reid #AG-50)

dimensions specified by the Cutting List. Re-rip and crosscut remnants to form the runners and cleats.

**2. Rout the mortises in the legs.** Take the details of mortise sizes and locations from the drawing *Leg and Rail Joinery*, and lay out the four legs. Note that all the mortises are ⅜ inch wide. The mortises for the side rails are offset ¼ inch from the inside edge, while those for the front and back rails are offset ¼ inch from the outside edge.

I routed all these mortises using a plunge router and the Mortising Jig on page 124. Most of the mortises are 2½ inches long. Set up the jig and do these mortises. Then reset the jig for the shorter mortises and do them.

**3. Bore the holes for the adjusters.** The adjustable glides enable you to level the router table on an uneven floor. But they also allow you to raise the entire table an inch or so. The glides themselves have 5⁄16-inch-diameter shanks and are threaded into T-nuts. You need to drill ⅜-inch-diameter × 1½-inch pilots for the T-nuts and adjuster shanks in the center of each leg's foot end.

These holes can be drilled on the drill press, but the job can also be done using the plunge router and the mortising jig. You've got the jig set up and the correct bit in the router. Give it a try.

**4. Round-over the exposed arris of each leg.** Use a ¾-inch roundover bit. This would be easy on a router table (but since you are building a router table, it just may be that you don't have one).

To do the job with a hand-held router, dog a leg to the workbench, capturing the ends of the leg, so you can make

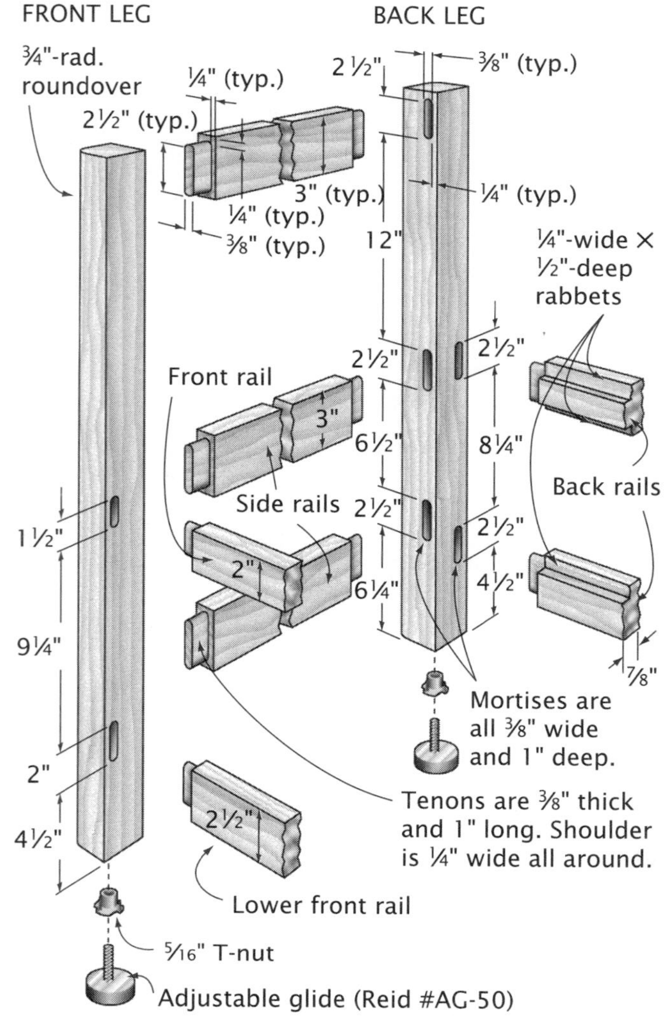

**To bore the adjuster holes on the mortising jig,** set up the jig's workrest for routing end mortises. Set up the router's edge guide to center the holes, and position the stops to prevent the router from moving laterally. One by one, clamp the legs in the jig and plunge-bore the holes.

Router Tables

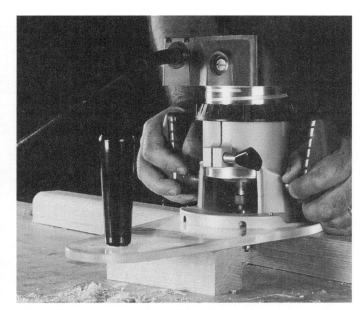

**Round-over one edge of each leg.** Attach a chunk of the leg stock to the router baseplate with carpet tape. The router will then be supported squarely by the leg and the scrap, making it easy to perform the operation accurately.

an end-to-end pass without interference. Round-over only one edge of each leg.

**5. Cut the tenons on the rails.** While the height of the tenons varies somewhat, they are consistently sized, with a length of 1 inch and a ¼-inch-wide shoulder all around. Assuming the rail stock was milled to a consistent and accurate ⅞-inch thickness, you only have to form the shoulder properly and the tenon size will be correct.

Here's another job that could be done quickly on a router table, if you had one. If you *do* have access to a router table, make a tenoning sled (see the chapter "Sleds" on page 246) and rout the tenons on the ends of the rails.

Otherwise, cut the tenons on the table saw, using a table-saw tenoning jig.

Round the edges of each tenon with a file, and test how each tenon fits its mortise.

**6. Rabbet the rails.** The upper back rail (which is really about mid-level) is rabbeted along its inner edges to accommodate and/or support the cabinets. (See the drawing *Leg and Rail Joinery*.) The rabbets are cut ¼ inch deep into the inner face of the rail and are ½ inch wide, measured from the edges.

Cut the rabbets on the table saw. Or rout them with a hand-held router. Tape a support block to the router baseplate to help steady the machine during the operation, as you did in rounding-over the legs.

**7. Assemble the side frames.** Apply glue to the mortises and tenons and join the parts. As you clamp these assemblies, check them with a square, and measure diagonally from head to foot to ensure that they are square. And make sure they are flat, too.

**8. Drive the inserts for the tabletop hinge bolts.** The tabletop mounting—in either the lift-top or fixed-top configuration—has bolts that penetrate the legs and turn into threaded inserts installed in the legs. In the lift-top configuration, the shank holes and inserts are in the back legs only. In the fixed-top form, all four legs must be drilled.

While it would be easy to drill these holes before assembly, the holes penetrate the top rail tenons, so you have to wait until after the side frames are glued up to make the holes. The assembled side frames are awkward to position on the drill press, but this is the best way to drill the holes. The holes should be perpendicular to the leg axis.

At each spot, drill the ⅜-inch-diameter, ⁷⁄₁₆-inch-deep pilot for the insert. Then switch bits and drill the ¼-inch-diameter shank hole on the same axis. Drive the inserts.

**9. Finish assembling the stand.** Apply glue to the mortises and tenons, and join the front and back rails to the side frame assemblies. If the joinery cuts were done accurately, the unit should come together square and true, but measure diagonals and check with a square to be sure.

When the glue has set and the clamps are off the stand, install the runners and cleats. Glue the runner to the rails, but not the legs. You can drive two or three drywall screws through each runner or cleat into the rails.

**10. Install the adjusters.** Upend the stand and drive a T-nut into each leg. Turn the adjustable glides into the T-nuts.

## Building the Tabletop

The work platform for this router table is a thick, broad, laminate-covered tabletop. Your preferences may lead you to have exposed edge-banding or to cover the edges, as well as the top, with laminate. The top I chose to make has semi-concealed oak edge-banding. To me, this is the most durable configuration, since the laminate protects the edge-banding as well as the substrate.

The 1½-inch-thick tabletop is certainly heavier than a 1-inch-thick one, which means it gives greater mass to the entire table. It seems more substantial.

**1. Make the tabletop.** Let me direct you to the chapter "Custom Router Table Top" on page 156. There you will find detailed, step-by-step directions for gluing up the substrate, applying the plastic laminate, and so on. The tabletop described in that chapter is the very tabletop used on this router table. (I believe you'll find that the tabletop section of the Cutting List here matches the Cutting List there. It's the same tabletop.)

**2. Make the hinges.** Rather than rush ahead and cut the mounting plate opening, get the tabletop installed on the stand. Then the top will be supported when you do cut the opening. The first step in mounting the tabletop is to make the hinges.

The mounting approach gives you the first of the

## TABLETOP CONSTRUCTION AND MOUNTING

### HINGE CLEAT LAYOUT

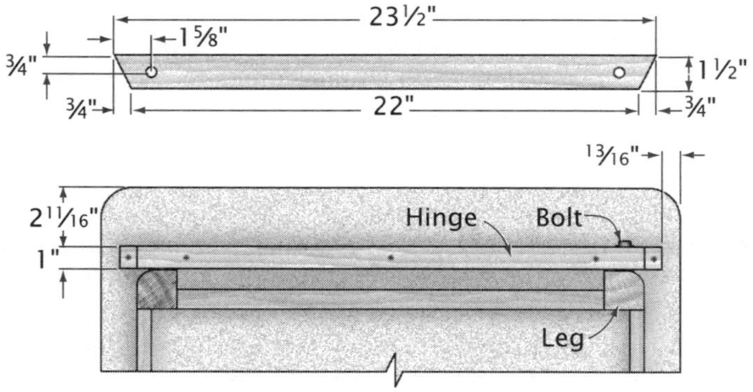

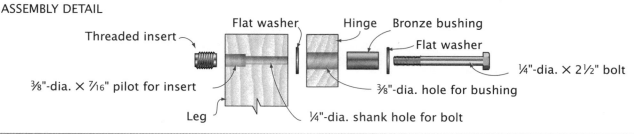

### TABLETOP LAYERS

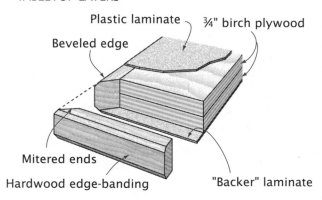

### ASSEMBLY DETAIL

| TABLETOP Cutting List | | | |
|---|---|---|---|
| **Part** | **Qty.** | **Dimensions** | **Material** |
| Core plies | 2 | ¾" × 23⅝" × 36" | Birch plywood |
| Edge bands | 2 | ¾" × 1⅝" × 37½" | Oak |
| Edge bands | 2 | ¾" × 1⅝" × 25⅛" | Oak |
| Surface covering | 1 | 1/16" × 26" × 38" | Plastic laminate |
| Bottom surface covering | 1 | 1/32" × 26" × 38" | Backer |
| Mounting plate | 1 | ⅜" × 8" × 11¾" | Phenolic plastic |
| Hinges | 2 | ⅞" × 1½" × 23½" | Oak |

### Hardware (for Attaching Tabletop to Stand)

4 brass threaded inserts, ¼"-20; #EZ-12 from Reid Tool Supply Co. (800-253-0421)

4 hex-head bolts, ¼"-20 × 2½"

2 bronze bushings, ¼" I.D. × ⅜" O.D. × 1" long; #OIB-80 from Reid Tool Supply Co.

8 flat washers, 5/16" I.D.

drywall screws, #6 × 2"

drywall screws, #6 × 2½"

2 Dzus toggle latches; #DTL-802A from Reid Tool Supply Co.

2 Dzus strikes; #DTL-800-9 from Reid Tool Supply Co.

8 panhead screws, #6 × 1" (for latches and strikes)

1 folding lid stay with mounting screws, left-hand mount*

*Buy a stay labeled for installation on the left. Even though it will be installed on the right side of the table, the left-hand stay is what you want.

router table's many choices. One option is the lift-top configuration. The other is the fixed-top option. One does not preclude the other. The construction difference between the options is two toggle latches or two bolts and threaded inserts. The cost isn't steep, and the work isn't irreversible. Make it a lift top. If you hate it, take off the toggle latches and install the extra two bolts.

Cut the hinge cleats to the dimensions specified by the Cutting List. Shape the ends of the cleats, as shown in the drawing *Tabletop Construction and Mounting*.

To locate the hinge-pin holes, clamp the hinge cleats to the stand. Insert a scratch awl through the holes in the legs, and mark the centers for the corresponding holes in the hinges. Drill the holes on the drill press.

**3. Install the hinges.** The best way to position the hinge cleats is to fit them to the stand and tabletop.

Begin by bolting the hinge cleats in place. If you opted to bore holes in all four legs, just bolt the cleats to the legs. Be sure to install the bushings, and the flat washers, so the cleats are exactly as they will be in the finished product. If you opted for the lift-top configuration, install the cleats with the hinge bolts, then clamp the free ends to the stand's front legs.

Now set the tabletop on the cleats and align it very carefully. Clamp the cleats to the table. You can crawl around beneath the stand, drilling pilot holes and driving screws, to join the cleats and tabletop. But it is easier to unthread the bolts (and unclamp the cleats from the legs), and move the tabletop to your workbench. Set it with the hinge cleats up, of course. Drill the pilots, drive the screws, and the hinges will be mounted.

**4. Mount the tabletop on the stand.** One task remains before bolting the tabletop in place. If you want to be able to lift the tabletop, you have to radius the tops of the back legs. A portable belt sander makes quick work of this detail.

Now set the tabletop in place and install the bolts.

Install the toggle latches next. Determine the position of each by holding the wire loop up and sliding the latch up the leg until the loop touches the underside of the top. Hold the latch in that spot while you lift the catch and mark through the screw holes on the leg. Drill pilots and screw the latches in place. Position the strikes and screw them to the underside of the top.

Attach the lid stay. This is attached to the top side rail and the tabletop. The drawing *Tabletop Construction and Mounting* provides a specific location. You may want to experiment a bit to determine the optimum location for the stay you buy. In any event, be sure you orient the stay so it folds to the front of the table; otherwise, it may collapse inadvertently.

**5. Make the mounting plate.** After completing and mounting the tabletop, turn to the chapter "Universal Router Mounting Plate" on page 163. In that chapter are detailed directions for making the mounting plate used in this router table.

**6. Install the mounting plate.** Stay with the mounting plate chapter for the directions on cutting the opening in the tabletop for the mounting plate. A couple of slightly different approaches are detailed there. Either one will work.

**Mount the tabletop squarely on the stand** by setting the tabletop (bottom-side up) on your workbench and up-ending the stand, with the hinges attached, on it. This way, you can easily align the stand on the tabletop. Then clamp the hinges to the tabletop, as shown, drill pilot holes, and drive screws through the hinges into the tabletop.

**To fit the stay** between the top rail of the stand and the hinge, I needed to rout a relief into the hinge. To do this, I made a template of ½-inch plywood. I bored two semicircles in the template edge with a Forstner bit, then cut away the waste from between them. I clamped the template to the right-hand hinge and used a template guide and ¼-inch straight bit to make the relief cut, as shown.

Where to place the mounting plate is for you to decide. Here are my thoughts for you to weigh as you decide.

The plans, taken from the router table shown in this chapter's photos, have the bit axis 8 inches from the front edge of the tabletop. This is better than the central location that is so prevalent. I'd bet that 75 percent of your router table work involves short, narrow workpieces. (This is a reason that small bench-top router tables are so serviceable.) Locating the router relatively close to the table's edge makes it easy to access for this 75 percent of your work.

When you have a large panel to rout, step to the rear of the table and address the bit from there. You have a nearly 30-inch-wide surface between the back edge and the bit axis with the router offset, which is a work surface that'll support a BIG panel. It's more support than you'll get from a table with the router in the central location.

In other words, the central router location is a compromise, a *bad* compromise. For most of your work, it is too far away from where you have to stand. And when you have a big workpiece, it's too close to all the edges, preventing the vast tabletop from being used to your advantage in supporting the work.

Put the mounting plate where you will. I recommend the offset location shown in the plans.

**7. Apply the finish.** Screw the mounting plate to your router, and drop it in place in the tabletop. You've now got a router table you can use. If this was your destination, you've reached it.

Before you celebrate, break out a can of finish and complete the job. Varnish the exposed wood—the edge-banding and the edge inside the cutout for the mounting plate.

Of course, if this Step 7 is but a stop on your journey, you may want to hold off on the finishing step until you've got the fence and cabinets built, then finish them all at the same time.

# Building and Installing the Ballast Box

If you intend to incorporate the lift-top feature into your router table, you need to confront the tip-over syndrome.

The fact is, this router table, like all other router tables, is top-heavy. Most of the weight is in the tabletop and the router, not the stand. Tilt the tabletop, and the weight is raised and thrown toward the back. In this attitude, it takes a very modest push to topple the router table. Bad news.

### BALLAST BOX Cutting List

| Part | Qty. | Dimensions | Material |
|------|------|------------|----------|
| Front/back | 2 | $\frac{3}{4}$" × 4" × 26$\frac{3}{8}$" | Poplar |
| Sides | 2 | $\frac{3}{4}$" × 4" × 19$\frac{3}{8}$" | Poplar |
| Bottom | 1 | $\frac{1}{2}$" × 19$\frac{3}{8}$" × 25$\frac{5}{8}$" | Plywood |

**BALLAST BOX CONSTRUCTION**

JOINERY DETAIL

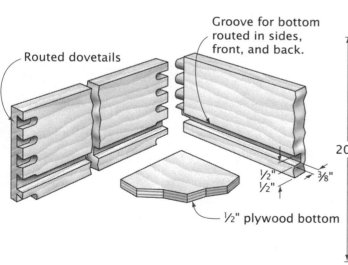

Routed dovetails

Groove for bottom routed in sides, front, and back.

$\frac{1}{2}$"
$\frac{1}{2}$"
$\frac{3}{8}$"

$\frac{1}{2}$" plywood bottom

TOP VIEW

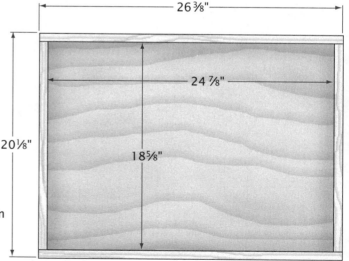

26$\frac{3}{8}$"

24$\frac{7}{8}$"

20$\frac{1}{8}$"

18$\frac{5}{8}$"

SIDE VIEW

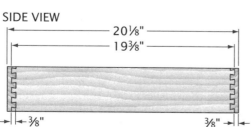

20$\frac{1}{8}$"
19$\frac{3}{8}$"
$\frac{3}{8}$"
$\frac{3}{8}$"

FRONT VIEW

4"

On the Bench-Top Router Table, the syndrome is countered by the base design. The pivot point is forward of the back edge of the base. But you want to be able to address the Floor-Standing Router Table from the back occasionally. That's the point of offsetting the mounting-plate location. If you cant the back posts, or scab on elongated feet, you'll be tripping over them at the most unpropitious moments.

My solution is a ballast box. It's nothing more than a fixed drawer suspended from the lower rails. You have access to this box only when the storage drawer is removed. What you do is fill it with ballast: scrap iron, a bag of concrete, sand bags, whatever you can come up with that's cheap and heavy. You need about 30 to 50 pounds.

**1. Cut the box parts.** The box is made of hardwood sides, front, and back, and a ½-inch plywood bottom. Because it is to be painted, you should use a wood that is relatively inexpensive and that takes paint well.

Cut the parts to the dimensions specified by the Cutting List.

**2. Rout the dovetails.** The front and back are joined to the sides with router-cut half-blind dovetails. Set up the dovetail jig and the router, and make all the test cuts necessary to get well-fitted dovetails. Then rout the dovetails on the workpieces.

**3. Rout the groove for the bottom.** As shown in the drawing *Ballast Box Construction,* the bottom is housed in a ½-inch-wide × ⅜-inch-deep groove. The groove is ½ inch from the bottom edges of the sides, front, and back. I made the groove in the front and back a stopped groove so it wouldn't show in the assembled box. The truth is, however, that the router table's legs conceal the joints in the ballast box, so you don't need to be too particular about the grooves from an appearance standpoint. I plowed the grooves on the router table. One setup does all four parts.

**4. Assemble the ballast box.** It's prudent to assemble the box without glue to check how the parts fit together, allowing you to make adjustments if necessary. When it goes together easily without glue, get out the glue, adjust the clamps, and set your cauls close at hand.

Apply glue to the tails, and assemble the box. Fit the bottom into its groove during assembly, but don't glue it there. Clamp the assembly until the glue sets, and use a wet rag to wipe up any glue squeeze-out before it sets.

**5. Screw the box to the stand.** The box, as previously pointed out, fits in the bottom of the stand, hanging from the lower rails. It butts against the bottom of the cleats attached to the lowest side rails.

Fit the box first. It may need to be sanded or planed to fit between the legs. When you get it to fit, clamp it in place and drive screws through it into both the front and back rails.

After getting it mounted, back out the screws, and remove the box for painting. You can reinstall it after both the box and the stand have been finished.

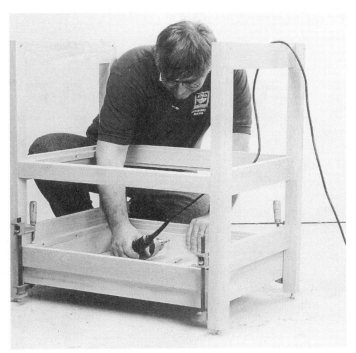

**Clamp the ballast box to the stand** while you drill pilot holes for the mounting screws, then drive the screws. It fits between the legs, up against the cleats attached to the lowest side rails. Assuming you have more sense than I do, you'll do the job at a comfortable working height by setting the stand on your workbench.

## Building the Fence

A router table isn't complete without a fence. This fence has three features worth talking about:

- a good dust pickup
- integral, adjustable clamps
- a broad, flat base

The dust pickup is made for a shop-vacuum hose, and it sets the hose as close to the tabletop surface as possible. What I've found is that dust and chips tend to pile up at any lip or ledge between the tabletop and the hose opening. So I eliminated that lip by setting the hose opening low and angling it toward the tabletop surface.

You can use this pickup with a hose direct from your shop vac, or you can incorporate it into the table-wide dust collector by running a short length of hose from the fence pickup to the router compartment.

The broad base and the integral clamps work together to provide solid clamping, regardless of the fence orientation. First of all, let me point out the clearance around the large plastic wing nuts that tighten the clamp blocks against the underside of the tabletop. All too often on commercial fences, these knobs are crowded against the fence facing: Tighten the knob, and you scrape your knuckles on the facing. Not with this fence.

The fence can be quickly removed from the table completely. Just loosen the clamp knobs and slide the fence

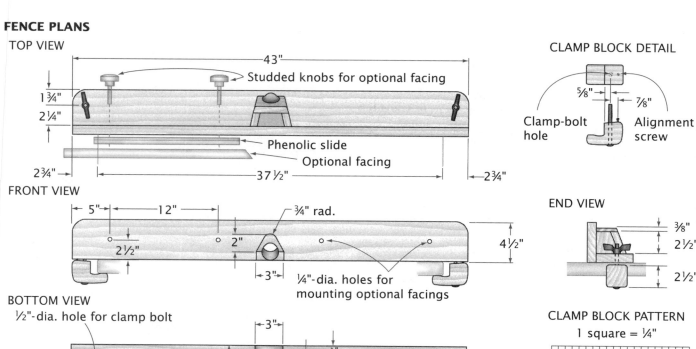

## FENCE PLANS

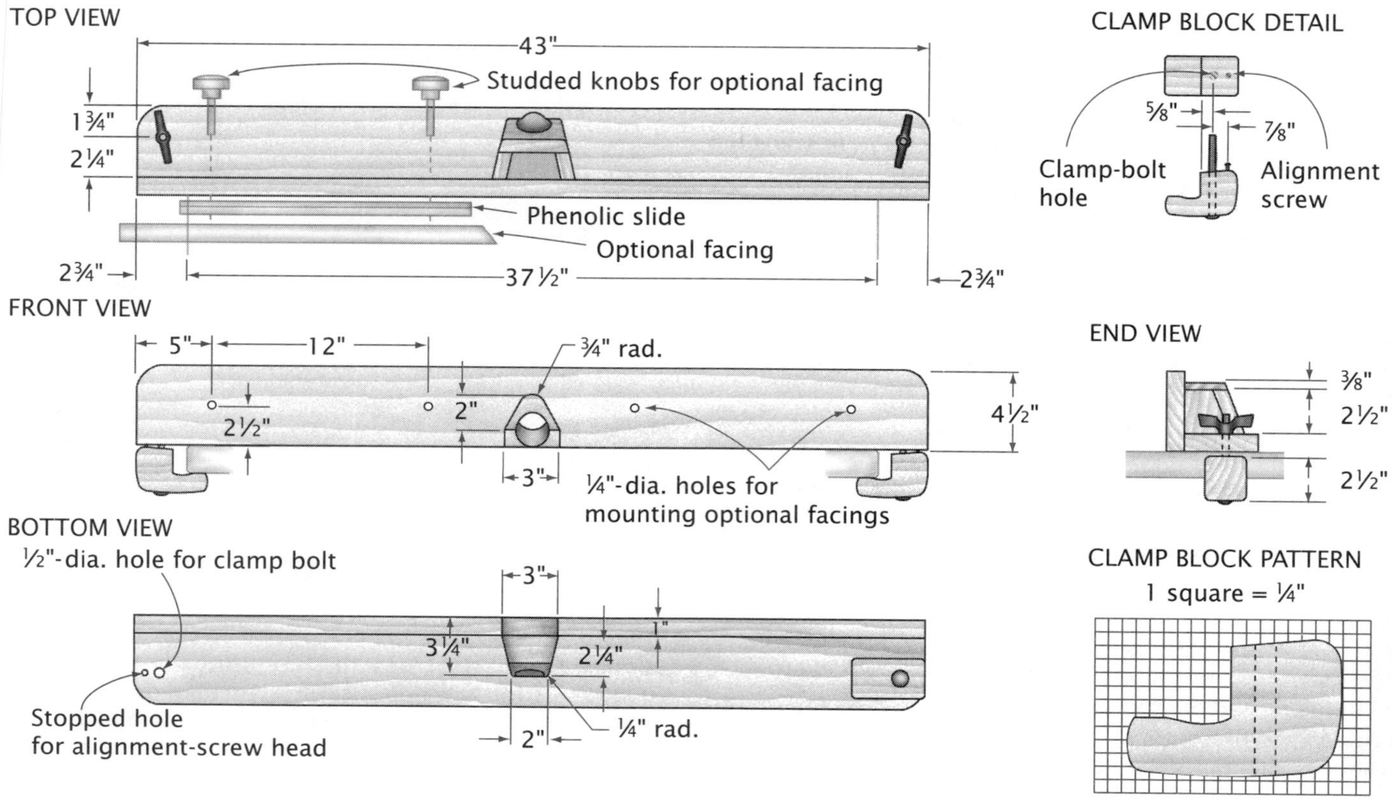

**TOP VIEW**

43"

Studded knobs for optional facing

1¾"
2¼"

Phenolic slide

Optional facing

2¾" — 37½" — 2¾"

**FRONT VIEW**

5" — 12"

¾" rad.

2½"  2"

4½"

3"

¼"-dia. holes for mounting optional facings

**BOTTOM VIEW**

½"-dia. hole for clamp bolt

3"

3¼"  2¼"

1"

Stopped hole for alignment-screw head

2"  ¼" rad.

**CLAMP BLOCK DETAIL**

⅝"  ⅞"

Clamp-bolt hole   Alignment screw

**END VIEW**

⅜"
2½"

2½"

**CLAMP BLOCK PATTERN**

1 square = ¼"

## FENCE
## Cutting List

| Part | Qty. | Dimensions | Material |
|---|---|---|---|
| Base | 1 | 1" × 4" × 43" | Oak |
| Facing | 1 | 1" × 4½" × 43" | Oak |
| Pickup sides | 2 | ¾" × 2½" × 2½" | Oak |
| Pickup back | 1 | ¾" × 3" × 3¼" | Oak |
| Pickup top | 1 | ⅜" × 2¼" × 4⁹⁄₁₆" | Clear acrylic |
| Clamp blocks | 2 | 2¼" × 2½" × 4" | Oak |
| Split facing plies (optional) | 4 | ½" × 5" × 21" | Baltic Birch plywood |
| Split facing laminate (optional) | 2 | ¹⁄₁₆" × 5½" × 22" | Plastic laminate |
| Split facing backing (optional) | 2 | ¹⁄₁₆" × 5½" × 22" | Backer |
| Split facing slides (optional) | 2 | ⅜" × ½" × 15" | Phenolic plastic |

## Hardware

4 brass roundhead screws, #6 × 1"

2 panhead screws, #8 × 1"

2 carriage bolts, ⅜" × 4½"

2 flat washers, ⅜" I.D.

2 plastic wing knobs; #85J94 from Woodcraft Supply (800-225-1153)

4 plastic knobs, 1¾" dia. with 1¼" studs; #DK-20 from Reid Tool Supply Co. (800-253-0421)

**Router Tables**

off the table. There won't be any loose parts to deal with, either. The clamps and knobs stay connected to the fence, whether the fence is on the table or off.

**1. Cut the parts.** Look over the parts and their dimensions, as specified by the Cutting List. My inner designer kept whispering to me, "Use oak so it matches the stand and cabinet facings." So I used oak for the wooden parts of the fence. You can use another wood, or you can face-glue two layers of ½-inch plywood to form the base and facing.

Select dry, straight-grained, defect-free stock for the base and facing. You want them to stay flat and true over the long haul. Joint, plane, rip, and crosscut the stock to the dimensions specified by the Cutting List. Each clamp block is formed by face-gluing three layers of ¾-inch hardwood stock.

Radius the back corners of the base and the top corners of the facing, as shown in the drawing *Fence Plans*. This can be done on the band saw. Or you can use a plunge router with either a trammel or corner-rounding templates to radius these corners.

**2. Cut the clamp blocks to shape.** The contour and dimensions of the clamp blocks are shown in the *Clamp Block Pattern* of the drawing *Fence Plans*.

The clamps are easiest to form with a band saw and stationary sander. You can enlarge the pattern, transfer it to the glued-up clamp blocks, then saw out the blocks. The sander will make quick work of smoothing and rounding the edges. (To make the blocks duplicates, all you have to do is

**Sticking a paper layout** to the clamp block is surely the easiest way to transfer the pattern to the workpiece. Enlarge the pattern on paper, and make a copy for each block you plan to cut. Use spray adhesive on the blank and the paper. When the adhesive has dried, lay the paper on the block and burnish it down.

stick them together with carpet tape and sand both at the same time.)

As an alternative, you can saw out the clamp blocks with a table-mounted saber saw. Or you can rough them out on the table saw; the details of doing this are related in the directions for making the Split Fence on page 237.

Finish shaping the clamp blocks by sanding or filing a narrow flat at the jaw's tip. Then round-over the exposed edges on your new router table. Be sure to use the starting pin.

**3. Drill the holes in the blocks.** The clamp blocks are hung on the base with ⅜-inch carriage bolts. To keep it from twisting out of position, each block has an alignment screw protruding from the top. This panhead screw projects into a hole drilled for it in the base.

Drill the ⅜-inch holes for the clamp blocks, as indicated in the *Clamp Block Pattern* of the *Fence Plans* drawing. Then drill a pilot hole for the alignment screw, and drive a #8 × 1-inch screw into it. Leave the screw protruding about ⅜ inch.

**4. Drill the holes in the fence base.** Following the drawing *Fence Plans*, lay out both the bolt holes and the alignment-screw holes on the fence base. I tend to worry about such stuff, so I set the fence base on the router table top to confirm that the hole locations were right. I wanted to allow a little side-to-side adjustment of the fence yet guarantee that the clamp block jaws would be in contact with the tabletop, regardless of the side-to-side positioning.

Drill the bolt holes using a ⁷⁄₁₆-inch bit. Then drill the alignment-pin holes with a bit somewhat larger than the screw head's diameter. You want the screws to keep the blocks from pivoting out of position, but you don't want them to jam in the holes.

**5. Cut the bit notches in the base and facing.** The notches, which are dimensioned for you in the drawing, house the bit. Lay out the notches. Notice that facing's notch has a ¾-inch-radius arc, which is formed by boring a 1½-inch-diameter hole. On the band saw or with a saber saw, saw in from the facing edge to the hole. In similar fashion, the notch in the base is formed by boring ½-inch-diameter holes at the corners, then sawing in from the edges to the holes and from hole to hole.

**6. Assemble the fence.** Use glue only. Be very precise, and be sure the face is square to the base. Particularly check the outside faces with a square. (Set the clamp blocks aside for now.)

After the glue has set and the clamps are off the fence, scrape off any glue squeeze-out and joint the bottom surface to ensure that it is perfectly square to the facing.

**7. Cut and attach the dust pickup sides.** The pickup sides are small, and their edges should be beveled to fit properly against the fence and the back. Exercise appropriate caution in cutting these parts on the table saw. If you have a chop saw or a sliding compound miter saw, use it to cut these parts.

Begin by ripping a foot-long piece of ¾-inch stock to the width specified by the Cutting List for the sides.

Use a sliding T-bevel to capture the angle of the notch in the base to the surface of the facing. Tilt the table-saw blade to this angle, and crosscut the board in two. Make one beveled crosscut on each piece. This beveled end butts against the facing.

To cut the back ends of the sides, you have to make a compound miter. Save the table saw's bevel angle, and swing the miter gauge to 22½ degrees. You need a scrap facing attached to the miter gauge to support the work-pieces as you make this cut, as I'm sure you'll see. Before you make the cuts, mark the sides so you don't mix them up and get the angles going the wrong way. (The bevels on the ends of each piece must be parallel).

Glue the sides in place.

**8. Cut and attach the dust pickup back.** The back is beveled top and bottom so it can lean against the ends of the sides yet still make full, flat contact with the base and present a flat surface for the pickup top. The bevel angle is the same as the miter angle on the ends of the sides.

Use the sliding T-bevel to capture the angle and set up the tilt of the table saw blade. Rip the back stock to width, beveling both edges as you do so. Miter the ends as shown in the drawing *Fence Plans*.

Glue the back in place. Apply a clamp to grip the back

to the base. The clamps applied to hold the back to the sides need the wedge-shaped cauls under their jaws.

**9. Make the hose port.** After the clamps are off, use a hole saw in a hand-held electric drill to make the port for the shop-vacuum hose. I bought a hole saw some time ago specifically to make ports for the shop-vac hose, and this is not the first time I've used it. It matches the connector's diameter, so I get a good fit. It didn't cost much, and I think it was a worthwhile investment.

The idea is to start the hole from inside the dust pickup, then complete it by sawing from the outside. The thickness to be penetrated is too great for a hole saw to cut through solely from one side or the other.

I started the hole from inside the pickup because this gave me better control over the angle and position of the hole. I just eyeballed the angle and endeavored to minimize the lip between the bottom surface of the fence and the hose port. If possible, extend the hole saw's pilot bit so it can do its job, which is to help you start and align the hole.

Cut until the hole saw bottoms. If the pilot has emerged through the pickup's back, you can move around and saw from the outside. If it hasn't, chisel out some of the waste and continue sawing from the inside until the pilot bit does emerge. Then you can shift your operation to the outside and complete the hole.

**10. Apply a finish.** I applied the same polyurethane used on the rest of the router table.

**To clamp the pickup sides to the fence,** you need a couple of clamps and a pair of wedge-shaped cauls. Apply a clamp to the side's top edge and the base bottom, as shown. Then set a caul against the back edge of the side and apply an additional clamp, squeezing the side against the fence facing.

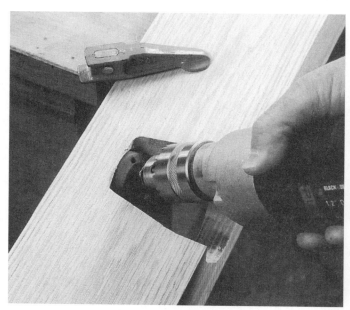

**Cut the vacuum hose port** with a hole saw in a portable drill. Turn the fence upside down and clamp it, as shown, at a corner of the workbench. The trick is getting the hole started in just the right spot without having the hole saw skip off the mark. I found that you can begin at an angle low enough for the pilot bit to bite into wood, then, before you get in too deep, change the angle of the hole by raising the drill as you saw.

**11. Cut and attach the dust pickup top.** The top is a piece of clear acrylic. I used ⅜-inch-thick stuff, since I had scraps of it left from making the mounting plate and other jig-and-fixture projects. You can use thinner material if that's what you have. Cut the top to shape. Scrape and chamfer the edges, and buff 'em for some sparkle. Then drill pilot holes and attach the top with four roundhead screws (I used brass screws to match the other hardware).

**12. Install the clamp blocks.** Slip a ⅜-inch carriage bolt through each clamp block. Fit the bolt through the base, drop on a flat washer, and turn the plastic wing knob onto the bolt. Tighten the knob firmly to seat the bolt's subhead into the block.

Loosen the knobs, and slide the new fence across the tabletop. Tighten the clamps to lock it in position.

**13. (Optional) Make and install movable facings.** The basic fence is great. But it's a benefit for certain operations to be able to move the fence facings, pulling them in close to the bit. This is a prime value of the Split Fence (see page 237), one you can have without building an entirely new fence. A lot of tips on constructing the facings can be gleaned from that chapter.

In brief, here's how to make these optional facings:

Cut and glue-laminate two pieces of Baltic Birch plywood (or the American-made variety, Apple Ply) to form each movable facing. (Yes, you need two facings.) Rip and crosscut the facings to trim and square their edges. To produce a tough, slick "working" surface, apply plastic laminate.

**The optional movable facings** for the fence are mounted on T-slides made from phenolic plastic. Turning two plastic knobs tightens the slide against the fence, securing the facing. Loosening the knobs frees the facing to be moved or removed. Note that the facings have plastic laminate on the fronts, and backer on the back.

Rout a T-slot in the back of each facing. Use a straight bit to groove each piece, then switch to a keyhole bit or T-slot bit to convert the groove into the T-slot.

To mount the facings, drill four ¼-inch holes through the fence's face. Locate the holes as shown in the drawing *Fence Plan.*

Now cut two 15-inch-long strips of ⅜-inch phenolic, cutting them the same width as the T-slots in the facings. Rabbet two edges of the phenolic to form T-slides. Test the fit of these slides in the slots in the facings, and sand them as necessary for a smooth-sliding fit. Now drill and tap holes in the slides for the studded plastic knobs. Insert the knobs in the holes in the fence, and screw them into the slides about three turns. Slip the facing onto the phenolic slide, adjust its position vis-à-vis the bit opening, and tighten the knobs to lock the facing.

## Building the Upper Cabinet

The next key component, the upper cabinet, houses the router, capturing a lot of the noise and chips it generates in use. It provides orderly storage for bits, collets, and wrenches. And it incorporates switched receptacles for the router and a shop vac or dust collector.

Although in general I've had a negative regard for doors on router compartments, I put one on this cabinet. With the lift-top feature, the door isn't an irritating barrier to router access. Now it's a barrier to chips and noise. And it is essential for dust collection.

Complementing the door is a panel I call a threshold. It prevents chips from spilling out of the router compartment, even when the door is open. The door is hinged to this panel, so it can drop open and thus out of the way.

The cabinet has two well-like storage bins for wrenches, collets, and other useful tools and supplies like a dust brush and a Scotch-Brite pad. The bins can be accessed only when the top is lifted. Because they are fixed bins, their contents can't be dumped inadvertently. The bin on the right also houses the metal electrical box for the switch and serves as the chase for the electrical cable that connects the switch to the table's two duplex receptacles.

In the space beneath each fixed bin is a bit storage drawer, which is a traditional drawer set on its side. To me, the drawer makes better use of the space available if it's oriented this way. Each drawer has wood strips, each with a line of ½-inch-diameter holes for holding the bits. The strips also have grooves for labels, so I can label each bit. Call me anal-retentive if you want, but it keeps the bits organized, and I can identify the size of each bit. I know exactly where to go for any bit, too, since each has a specific place.

The cabinet is a plywood case with oak face parts—drawer fronts, threshold, and door. The rabbet joints between the sides and back are concealed by the legs. I planned from the outset to paint the case, so I used birch plywood, which takes paint well. Other good choices for this construction would be medium-density fiberboard (MDF) and medium-density overlay (MDO), both of which take

## UPPER CABINET PLAN VIEWS

CASE FRONT VIEW

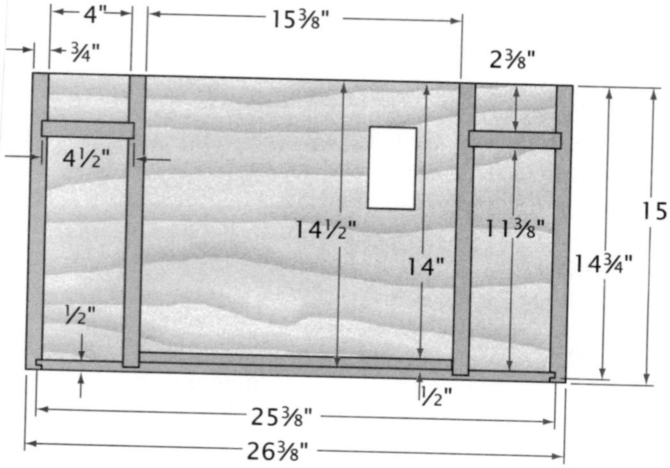
4"
¾"
15⅜"
2⅜"
4½"
14½"
14"
11⅜"
15"
14¾"
½"
½"
25⅜"
26⅜"

FACE FRONT VIEW

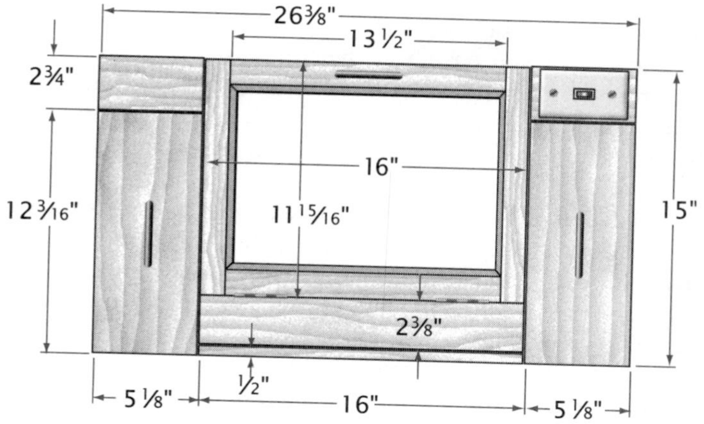
26⅜"
13½"
2¾"
12 3/16"
16"
11 15/16"
15"
2⅜"
5⅛"
½"
16"
5⅛"

TOP VIEW

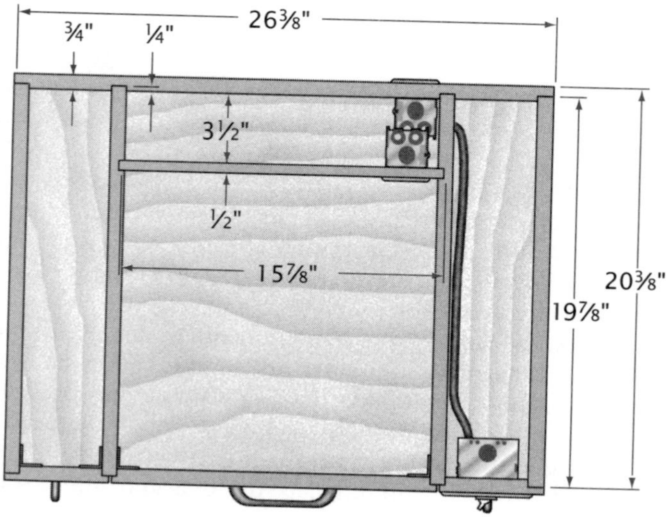
26⅜"
¾"
¼"
3½"
½"
15⅞"
20⅜"
19⅞"

BACK VIEW

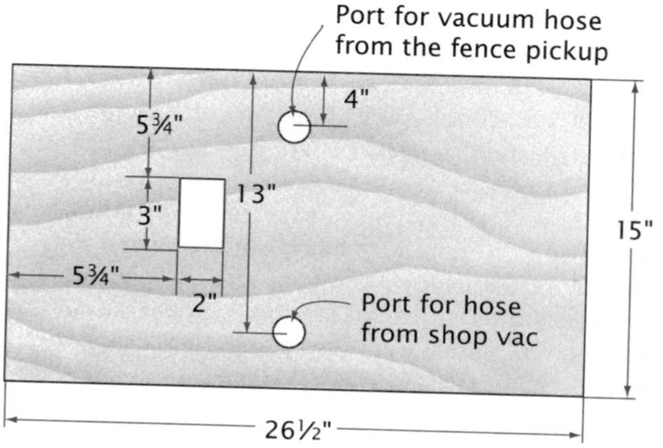
Port for vacuum hose
from the fence pickup
4"
5¾"
13"
3"
15"
5¾"
2"
Port for hose
from shop vac
26½"

ROUTER COMPARTMENT DOOR DETAIL

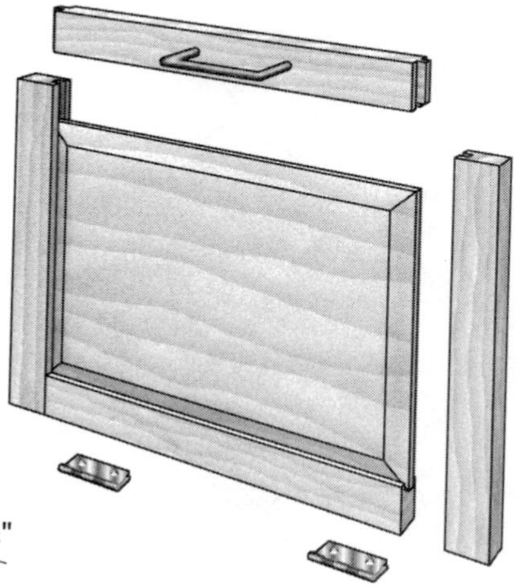

BIN FRONT DETAIL

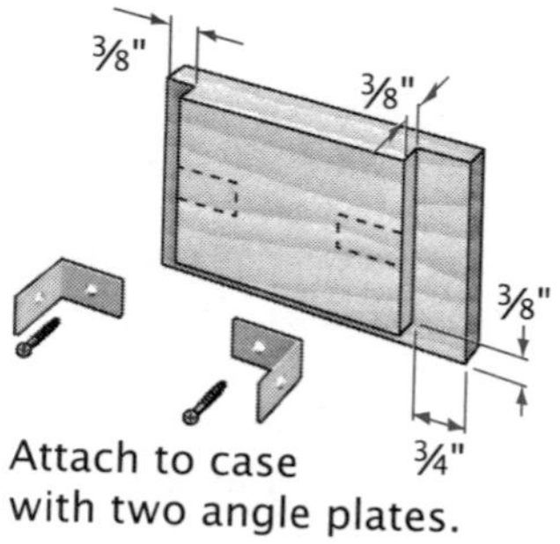
⅜"
⅜"
⅜"
¾"
Attach to case
with two angle plates.

THRESHOLD ASSEMBLY DETAIL

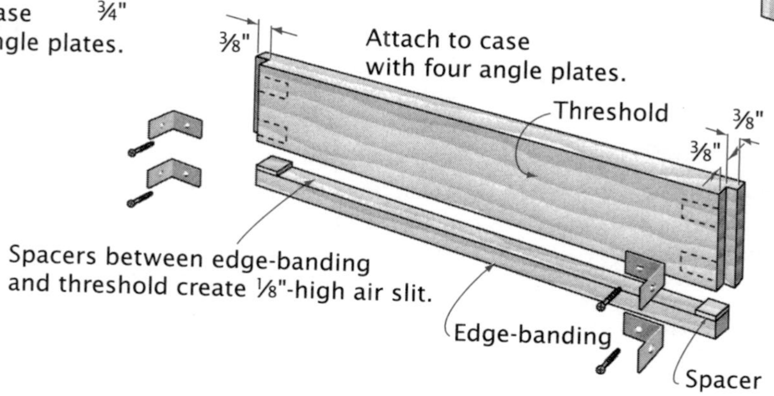
⅜"
Attach to case
with four angle plates.
Threshold
⅜"
⅜"
Spacers between edge-banding
and threshold create ⅛"-high air slit.
Edge-banding
Spacer

## UPPER CABINET
## Cutting List

| Part | Qty. | Dimensions | Material |
|---|---|---|---|
| Bottom | 1 | $\frac{1}{2}$" × 19$\frac{7}{8}$" × 25$\frac{3}{8}$" | Birch plywood |
| Back | 1 | $\frac{3}{4}$" × 15" × 26$\frac{3}{8}$" | Birch plywood |
| Sides | 2 | $\frac{3}{4}$" × 15" × 19$\frac{7}{8}$" | Birch plywood |
| Partitions | 2 | $\frac{3}{4}$" × 14$\frac{3}{4}$" × 19$\frac{7}{8}$" | Birch plywood |
| Recess bottoms | 2 | $\frac{3}{4}$" × 4$\frac{1}{2}$" × 19$\frac{7}{8}$" | Birch plywood |
| Dust baffle | 1 | $\frac{1}{2}$" × 14" × 15$\frac{7}{8}$" | Birch plywood |
| Bin fronts | 2 | $\frac{3}{4}$" × 2$\frac{3}{4}$" × 5$\frac{1}{8}$" | Oak |
| Router compartment threshold | 1 | $\frac{3}{4}$" × 2$\frac{3}{8}$" × 16" | Oak |
| Spacers | 2 | $\frac{1}{8}$" × $\frac{3}{8}$" × $\frac{3}{8}$" | Oak |
| Edge band | 1 | $\frac{1}{2}$" × $\frac{3}{8}$" × 16" | Oak |
| Router compartment door stiles | 2 | $\frac{3}{4}$" × 1$\frac{1}{2}$" × 11$\frac{15}{16}$" | Oak |
| Router compartment door rails | 2 | $\frac{3}{4}$" × 1$\frac{1}{2}$" × 13$\frac{3}{4}$" | Oak |
| Router compartment door panel | 1 | $\frac{5}{8}$" × 9$\frac{11}{16}$" × 13$\frac{3}{4}$" | Oak |
| Bit drawer fronts | 2 | $\frac{3}{4}$" × 12$\frac{3}{16}$" × 5$\frac{1}{8}$" | Oak |
| Bit drawer backs | 2 | $\frac{1}{2}$" × 3$\frac{7}{8}$" × 10$\frac{13}{16}$" | Poplar |
| Bit drawer sides | 4 | $\frac{1}{2}$" × 3$\frac{7}{8}$" × 19$\frac{5}{8}$" | Poplar |
| Bit drawer bottoms | 2 | $\frac{1}{4}$" × 10$\frac{13}{16}$" × 18$\frac{3}{4}$" | Birch plywood |
| Bit holders (bottom) | 2 | 1$\frac{3}{4}$" × 2$\frac{1}{8}$" × 18$\frac{1}{8}$" | Poplar |
| Bit holder (middle) | 1 | 1$\frac{3}{4}$" × 1$\frac{7}{8}$" × 18$\frac{1}{8}$" | Poplar |
| Bit holders (top) | 2 | 1$\frac{3}{4}$" × 1$\frac{3}{8}$" × 18$\frac{1}{8}$" | Poplar |

## Hardware

6d finish nails

3 wire pulls, 3", brass, with screws (for upper cabinet)

2 magnetic catches and strikes with mounting screws (for router compartment door)

1 pr. brass hinges, 2" × 1$\frac{3}{8}$" with mounting screws (for router compartment door)

2 brass threaded inserts, $\frac{1}{4}$"

2 roundhead stove bolts, $\frac{1}{4}$" × 1$\frac{1}{2}$" (for bit drawer stops)

6 brass angle plates, $\frac{1}{2}$" × 1" × 1", with screws

paint extremely well (better than the birch plywood I used).

If you want a natural wood appearance, you can invest in a choice hardwood plywood for the case. If you do this, be sure you cut the parts so the grain direction is oriented consistently (and logically) throughout the casework.

**1. Cut the case parts.** Before you cut anything, measure the space for the cabinet in the assembled stand. It's not unlikely that minor deviations from the plans have crept into your construction. (They did in mine.) The cab-

inet is designed to be about $\frac{1}{8}$ inch narrower than the span between the legs so that it can be set in place easily. The last thing you want is to build the cabinet to spec, then find it won't fit your stand.

So measure the stand and adjust the dimensions of the case parts as necessary.

As I said, all the case parts are cut from plywood. Note that the bottom and the dust baffle are $\frac{1}{2}$-inch material, while the other parts are $\frac{3}{4}$ inch. The dimensions are specified by the Cutting List.

**2. Cut the case joinery.** All the joint cuts can be made with a hand-held, fixed-base router. Because plywoods are undersized (in thickness), you'll get the tightest joints if you use a $^{23}\!/_{32}$-inch straight bit to rout the dadoes and grooves needed. Study the drawing *Upper Cabinet Plan Views*. Lay out the cuts, and use a T-square or straightedge to guide the router through the cuts.

Here's a list of the cuts needed:

- Rabbet the back for the sides and bottom.
- Dado the back for the partitions and bin bottoms.
- Dado the sides and partitions for the bin bottoms.
- Dado the partitions for the dust baffle.
- Groove the sides for the bottom.
- Rabbet the bottom for the sides.

**3. Assemble the case.** Use glue and finish nails to join the parts together. After the assembly work is complete, countersink all the nails and putty over the heads.

The assembly sequence is as follows: Lay the back on its back. Glue the partitions in place. Next, add the bin bottoms and the case bottom. Finally, attach the sides. Make sure the case is square, of course.

Don't install the dust baffle at this time. Test how it fits, but don't glue it in place, or it will be a hindrance when you install the electrical boxes and wire them.

Finally, bore the two dust collection ports in the case back. The locations are shown in the drawing *Upper Cabinet Plan Views*. The holes should be sized to accommodate your shop vac's hose.

**4. Cut (and glue up) the face parts.** These include the bin fronts, the bit drawer fronts, and the threshold parts. So that the upper cabinet would match the stand, I used oak for these parts.

Mill a batch of hardwood to the required thickness, ¾ inch. (While you are at it, prepare enough stock for the door parts—rails, stiles, and panel—as well. The stock for the rails and stiles should be ¾ inch thick; for the panel, ⅝ inch thick. Set the stock for these parts aside until you are ready to actually make the door.) Rip and crosscut the bin and drawer fronts and the threshold parts to the dimensions specified by the Cutting List.

Note that to make up the bit drawer fronts, you'll probably need to edge-glue two or three pieces. These drawer fronts are narrow and very tall, but the grain should run from side to side in order to match that of the other face parts. I edge-glued one panel, from which I ripped and crosscut both drawer fronts and both bin fronts.

In cutting these parts to size, I think it is a good idea to set them in place on the front of the case, so they'll fit the case you've built rather than the one depicted in the drawings.

**5. Rabbet the bin fronts, drawer fronts, and threshold.** The potential for error is significant here, I think. As you can see from the drawing *Bit Drawer*

*Construction,* each drawer front has rabbets of three different widths on it. In addition, the bin fronts have two different rabbet widths, as revealed in the drawing *Upper Cabinet Plan Views*.

If you aren't careful, you might find yourself mixing up the rabbets widths. What I did was label each part—left drawer, left bin front, right drawer, and so on. I marked the top and bottom edges of the parts as well. Then on the inside face, I labeled each edge with the width of rabbet needed. (Place these labels where they won't be removed as you rout the rabbets.) The lefts and rights are not duplicates, remember; they are mirror images.

I cut the rabbets on a router table using a 1-inch-diameter straight bit. Here's how to do it. Set the cut depth at the full ⅜-inch right at the start. So that the cut won't be too heavy, limit the *width* of cut. Make the initial cut no more than ⅛ inch wide, and make it on every edge that is to be rabbeted. Subsequently, the drill is to increase the width of cut in steps, and keep cutting the edges until each has been routed to the necessary width.

**Use a pusher** to back up the work as you rout the rabbets. This will prevent tear-out, especially as you rout across the end grain. Make a pusher from scrap stock by routing a rabbet in it so that it can nest into the rabbet being cut in the workpiece.

**6. Cut the remaining bit drawer parts.** The bit drawers are constructed like conventional drawers; they simply are oriented on their sides. Rather than confuse things, I've referred to "sides," "bottom," and "back" on the Cutting List, labeling the parts as in a conventional drawer orientation.

The sides and backs are cut from ½-inch-thick pieces of whatever you are using as your secondary stock. Check the Cutting List as you work, but fit the parts to the case. The drawer bottoms are ¼-inch plywood.

**BIT DRAWER CONSTRUCTION**

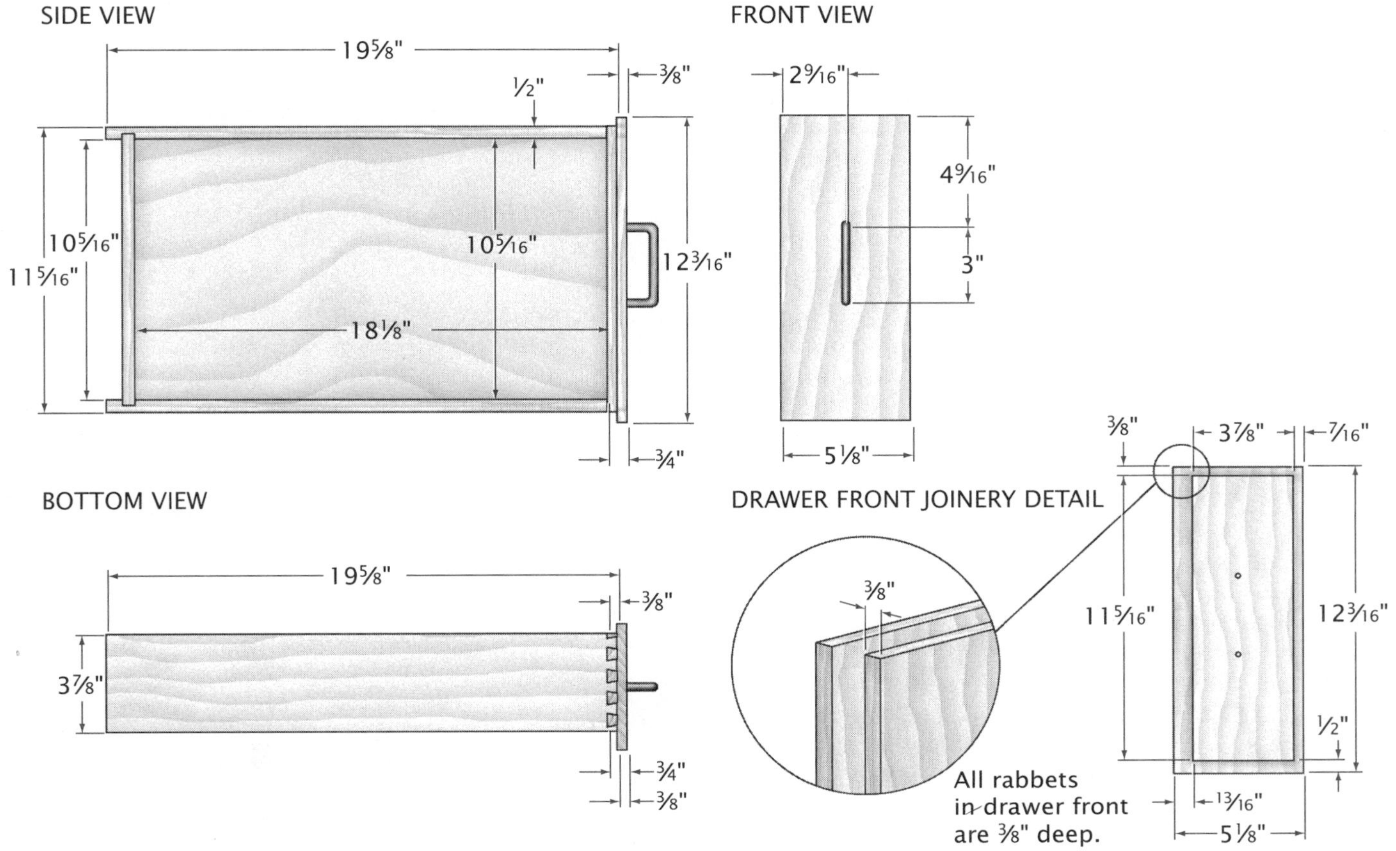
SIDE VIEW
19⅝"
½"
⅜"
10 5/16"
11 5/16"
10 5/16"
12 3/16"
18⅛"
¾"
FRONT VIEW
2 9/16"
4 9/16"
3"
5⅛"
BOTTOM VIEW
19⅝"
⅜"
3⅞"
¾"
⅜"
DRAWER FRONT JOINERY DETAIL
⅜"
⅜"
3⅞"
7/16"
11 5/16"
12 3/16"
½"
13/16"
5⅛"
All rabbets
in drawer front
are ⅜" deep.

**7. Rout the dovetails.** As you can see in the drawing, the front is joined to the sides with router-cut half-blind dovetails. Now you may be used to routing dovetails, but these are different because the drawer fronts are lipped. The lip (or rabbet) requires you to shift the drawer front's position in relation to the template. The piece has to be moved forward in the dovetail jig so the rabbet's shoulder is aligned where the drawer front's end usually is aligned. Obviously, you can't do this if the side is in the jig. So in this case, you have to do the sides and the fronts separately.

To align the drawer front accurately, use what I call a positioning gauge. It is simply a scrap of wood with a rabbet across one end. The depth of the rabbet must be the same as the width of the drawer-front rabbet. In this instance, you actually need two gauges, one with a ⅜-inch-deep rabbet and the other with a ½-inch-deep rabbet.

You also need a ½-inch-thick spacer to offset the drawer front from the alignment stop so that the first socket is a half-pin from the shoulder of the rabbet. (The spacer thickness is determined by subtracting the width of the drawer-front rabbet from ⅞ inch, the center-to-center spacing of ½-inch dovetails. The starting point for marking off these dovetails is the vertical edge with the ⅜-inch-wide rabbet.)

Here's how to set up: Fit the drawer front in the dovetail jig. The long edge with the ⅜-inch-wide rabbet must be at the jig's alignment pin. If that edge is on the right, move the front to the right-hand pin. If that edge is to the left,

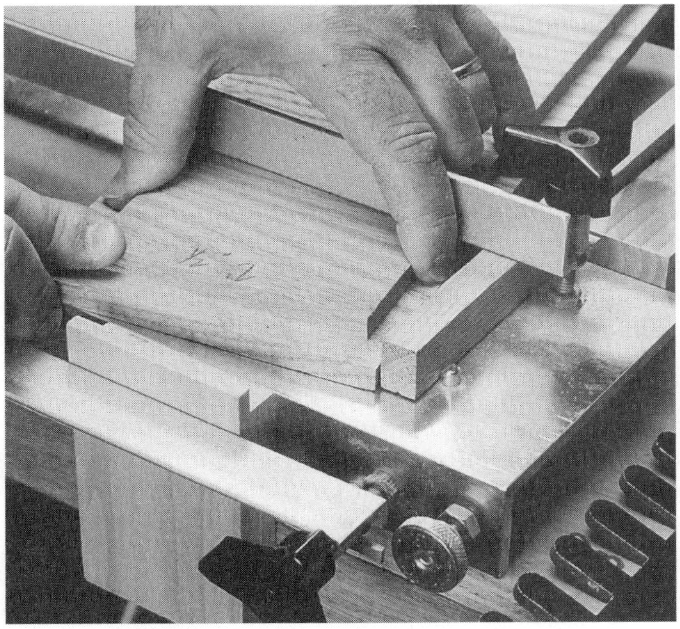

**Two simple, shop-made jigs** are needed when routing dovetails in lipped drawer fronts, like those used in the bit drawers. One is a spacer, which you set between the dovetail jig's alignment pin and the workpiece, as shown. The other is a positioning gauge, shown clamped at the front of the dovetail jig. When the workpiece's end is butted against the gauge, its shoulder will be properly positioned for the sockets to be routed.

slide the workpiece to the left-hand pin. Shift the workpiece enough to fit the spacer between it and the pin.

Now check the width of the rabbet across the workpiece's end. Clamp the appropriate positioning gauge in the front of the dovetail, where the drawer side usually is clamped. Pull the drawer front toward you, butting its end against the tab of the positioning gauge, the long edge with the ⅜-inch-wide rabbet against the spacer. Clamp the front, then rout the sockets.

Naturally, you have to switch to the other end of the jig to rout the sockets in the other end of the drawer front. And because the rabbet at that end of the drawer front is a different width, you have to switch to the other positioning gauge. (Don't forget to put the space between the workpiece and the alignment pin.)

After the sockets are routed in both drawer fronts, fit the drawer sides, one by one, in the dovetail jig and rout the pins. To help you position each side, and to prevent tearout, clamp a scrap of drawer-front stock in place of the drawer front.

**8. Cut the remaining drawer joinery.** The back is joined to the sides with dado joints. The bottom fits into grooves in the sides, front, and back.

Having cut the dovetails, do the dadoes and grooves. I cut the dadoes on the router table, guiding the workpiece along the fence with a scrap push-block. The block keeps the work square to the fence, and backs up the cut to boot. Groove the parts on the router table, too.

**9. Assemble the drawers.** This is routine. Apply glue judiciously to the dovetails and the dadoes. Join one side to the front, and set the bottom in place. Add the back, then the second side. Clamp the assembly and set it aside. Then repeat the process to assemble the second bit drawer.

Lay out the holes for the wire pull's mounting screws. The pulls are centered on the drawer fronts. Drill the holes, and mount the pulls.

**10. Make the bit holders.** I like to label my bits, so I designed bit holders that accommodate labels. Each holder begins as a square blank. You bevel the top at 30 degrees, then drill ½-inch-diameter holes into it, perpendicular to this surface. For the labels, you rout a very shallow dovetail groove on the front. As you can see in the drawing *Bit Holder Detail*, I installed two holders in one drawer and three in the other. The thickness and width of the individual holder varies according to its position in the drawer.

I used my secondary stock (poplar) for the holders. If you don't have stock of sufficient thickness, glue-laminate thinner pieces to build up the thickness required. Plane and rip the blanks, then bevel the top surface.

To bore the holes at the required angle, you need to hold the blank at an angle, so the top surface is perpendicular to the axis of the bit. Make a V-block from three scraps of ¾-inch plywood. Bevel an edge of one scrap at 30 degrees, and an edge of another at 60 degrees. Nail these strips to the third scrap, forming the V-block. Align the block under the bit, and clamp it to the drill press table. Cradle the

holder blank in the V-block, and drill the holes with a ½-inch Forstner bit. The holes should be ¾ to 1 inch deep.

The hole spacing is up to you. I spaced the holes in the lowest holder 1½ inches apart, figuring this is where the

**With a V-block aligned under the bit** and clamped to the drill press table, drilling the angled holes in the bit holders is easy. Lay out the hole positions on the holder, and set it in the V-block. Drill the first hole, then slide the holder, aligning the next mark under the bit. Drill it. Keep it up until all the holes are finished.

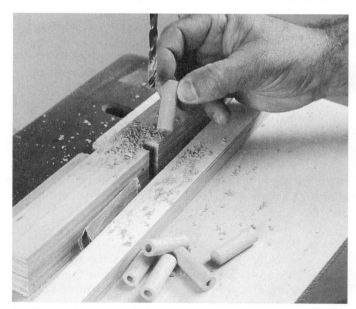

**Quarter-inch-shank bits fit ½-inch holes** if you use sleeves made from lengths of ½-inch dowel. To drill the dowels, hold them in a shop-made pinch clamp secured to the drill press table. Clamp the fence to the table, and drill a ½-inch hole that breaks the edge. Set the dowel in this hole and jam it with a pivoting jaw, as shown, while you drill a ¼-inch hole through it.

## BIT HOLDER DETAIL

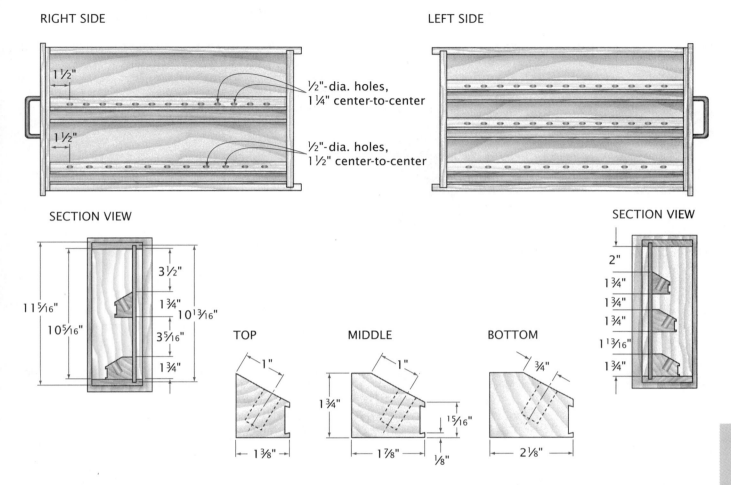

RIGHT SIDE

1½"

½"-dia. holes, 1¼" center-to-center

1½"

½"-dia. holes, 1½" center-to-center

LEFT SIDE

SECTION VIEW

11⁵⁄₁₆"

10⁵⁄₁₆"

3½"

1¾"

10¹³⁄₁₆"

3⁵⁄₁₆"

1¾"

TOP

1"

1⅜"

MIDDLE

1"

1¾"

1⅞"

⅛"

¹⁵⁄₁₆"

BOTTOM

¾"

2⅛"

SECTION VIEW

2"

1¾"

1¾"

1¾"

1¹³⁄₁₆"

1¾"

largest-diameter bits would go. In the other holders, the holes are 1 to 1¼ inches apart.

(If you are wondering why all the holes are ½ inch, the answer is that I made "sleeves" for ¼-inch-shank bits. Drill ¼-inch-diameter holes in the center of 1-inch-long pieces of ½-inch dowel. This allows you to put a ¼-inch-shank bit anywhere. You can even make sleeves with ⅛-inch stems for storing extra pilot bearings.)

Finally, set up the router table with a ¾-inch dovetail bit. Set the bit extension at about ⅛ inch. Set the fence, and rout a dovetail groove along the front surface of each bit holder. (If you don't have a ¾-inch dovetail bit, you can make the same groove in two passes using a ½-inch dovetail bit.)

**11. Install the bit holders.** Trim the holders to fit the drawers. The holders are secured in the drawers by screws driven through the bottom and back. Three screws suffice for each holder. The spacing I used is shown in the drawing. Note that if you put three holders on a drawer, it probably will be necessary to pare notches in the ends of two holders to accommodate the pulls' mounting screws.

**12. Rout the electrical box openings.** The upper cabinet is wired with switch-controlled receptacles inside the router compartment and on the back. The outlet inside

the cabinet is for the router, while the outlet in the cabinet back is for a shop vac or dust collector. Punch the switch on the cabinet front, and both the router and the dust collector power up. (This works only if the router has the "soft-start" feature; otherwise, two motors starting simultaneously will probably trip the circuit breaker.)

The full installation requires that three openings be cut, one in the back of the case, one in the dust baffle, and the last in the right-hand bin front. I routed them all using a template. You don't need a perfect opening, and if you prefer, you can cut the openings with a saber saw. But I like the router route.

Make a template in a piece of ½-inch MDF or plywood. Set a receptacle box on the template, and trace around it with a compass set to ¹⁄₁₆ inch. This is a ¹⁄₁₆-inch offset; use a ¼-inch bit with a ⅜-inch-O.D. template guide with the completed template to rout the openings. Cut out the template. Drill ⅜-inch holes in the corners, then saw from hole to hole with a saber saw. File the inside edges smooth.

Set up a plunge router. Clamp the template atop the work. Rout.

When routing the opening in the case, you can secure the template with carpet tape. Back up the cut with scrap, clamping or wedging it tight against the inside face of the case back. When routing the bin front, which is smaller than the template, you will have to bond the workpiece to scrap and surround it with blocking to help support the template.

Two final "rough-in" jobs: Drill a hole through the case back for the power cord; and drill a hole through the right partition for the cable that runs from the switch to the outlets. Locations are suggested in the drawings, though exact locations are up to you. Size the holes to accommodate the cable you use.

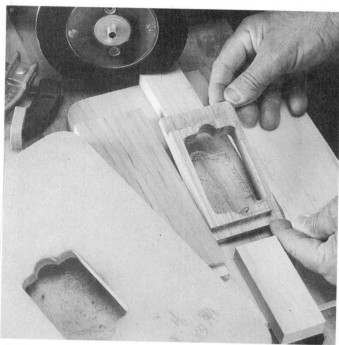

**Routing an opening** in the bin front for the electrical box is easier than trying to saw it, because of the part's small size. Using scraps, make a fixture to hold the bin front, then clamp the template on top and rout the opening. I used the template shown to rout openings in the case back and the dust baffle as well.

**13. Cut the door parts.** The router compartment door is assembled with cope-and-stick joints. I used a raised panel, though you could easily substitute a hardwood-plywood panel, or even a clear pane of acrylic or polycarbonate.

Rip and crosscut the rails and stiles for the door to the dimensions specified by the Cutting List. The stiles can run a little long, but the rails must be cut precisely to length. Cut the panel, or glue up stock to form the panel.

**14. Rout the sticking on the stiles and rails.** This is a router table operation. Tighten the sticking bit in the router collet, and adjust the bit's height to cut the desired profile. The objective in setting the bit height is to position the profile for its best appearance without getting the groove too close to the back. With the ¾-inch stock being worked, this shouldn't be too difficult. Make test cuts as necessary to establish the optimum bit height.

For a safe operation, set up the fence so the bit is mostly buried in the fence and the guiding edge of the fence is even with the edge of the bit's bearing. The more closely

matched the fence opening is to the bit contour, the better the fence will back up the cut and minimize—if not completely eliminate—chipping ahead of the cutter. Using the Split Fence (see page 237) makes this easy to accomplish. You simply shift the two fence elements toward the bit until they nearly touch it, then lock them down.

Set a couple of featherboards to keep the work tight to the fence.

When everything seems to be set up properly, cut the profile and groove in the inside edges of the stiles and rails. One pass should be sufficient to complete each cut.

**15. Cope the ends of the rails.** This operation is best done using a miter sled, plans for which are in the chapter "Sleds," which begins on page 246. With the sled plans are step-by-step directions for making the cope cuts. Turn to that chapter and follow its directions in coping the ends of the door rails.

**16. Raise the panel.** Do this on the router table, of course. After trimming the panel to the final dimensions, form all four edges with a panel-raising bit. Cut across the ends, then along the sides. Make shallow passes, working up the final cut depth.

**17. Assemble the door.** Before gluing the door's rails and stiles together, you should assemble it without glue to check that everything fits. Then apply glue to the joints. Begin to assemble the rails and stiles. Slide the panel into the frame before fitting the second stile in place, closing the frame.

Lay out the locations of the hinges that mount the door to the threshold. Carefully pare mortises for the hinges. Drill pilots for the mounting screws.

Lay out the holes for the wire pull's mounting screws. Drill these holes and install the pull.

**18. Assemble the cabinet face.** Most easily installed are the bit drawers; simply slide them into their compartments.

The two air-intake spacers are glued to the threshold edge-banding, which in turn is glued directly to the case between the bit drawers.

The threshold and the left-hand bin front are installed with brass angle plates. Fit these two parts in place. Use a plate as a guide to lay out the mounting-screw holes. Drill the pilots and install the plates, securing the parts to the case.

The right-hand bin front is secured by the receptacle box. Fit the box into the front, and attach it with tiny screws driven through the box's flanges. Set this unit in place in the case; I think you'll find you need to chisel recesses in the bin bottom for various screws and nubbins on the outside of the box. Do whatever is necessary to seat the box and the bin front properly. Then secure the works by driving 2½-inch-long screws through the appropriate holes in the box into the case.

On the threshold, lay out the mortises needed for the door's hinges. Pare these mortises and mount the door.

Determine the appropriate positions for the magnetic catches, and mount them.

With the parts all mounted, check the operation of the door and the drawers. Check the fit of the cabinet in the stand. If everything is copacetic, take it all apart (except the threshold edge-banding, of course).

**19. Finish the upper cabinet.** With the drawers and the door and all the fronts removed, prime and paint the plywood case. Mask off the threshold edge-banding so you don't get paint on it. Remove the pulls and other hardware from the front elements. Apply a clear finish to the door, the drawer and bin fronts, and the threshold.

When the finish is dry, remount the hardware and reassemble the cabinet.

**20. Wire the cabinet.** The box for the switch is already installed. Install the box for the "outside" receptacle in the case back. Pull the dust baffle from the case and install the box for the "inside" receptacle in it.

Run the cables next. Run a cable from the "outside" receptacle box to the switch box. This cable should be secured to the case with a couple of metal clips made for the job. Feed the power cord through its hole in the case and extend it into the "outside" receptacle box. Be sure to secure the power cord to the case so that when you catch your foot in the cord (someday), you won't rip out the con-

nections in the electrical boxes. A short piece of cable extends from the "outside" box to the "inside" box. Mount it in the "outside" box, then feed it into the "inside" box as you slide the dust baffle into place.

Follow the *Wiring Schematic* in connecting the circuits. Push the electric fixtures into the boxes, drive the mounting screws, and install the plates. Install the plug on the end of the power cord.

## Hardware for Wiring Case

3 steel receptacle boxes

12 roundhead screws, #4 × ½"

1 single-pole switch, 15 amp

1 switch plate

2 duplex receptacles, 15 amp

1 utility receptacle plate

1 receptacle plate

3' Romex cable, 12/2 with ground

2 grounding clips or screws

10' to 20' cord, 14/3 type SJ

1 plug

## WIRING SCHEMATIC

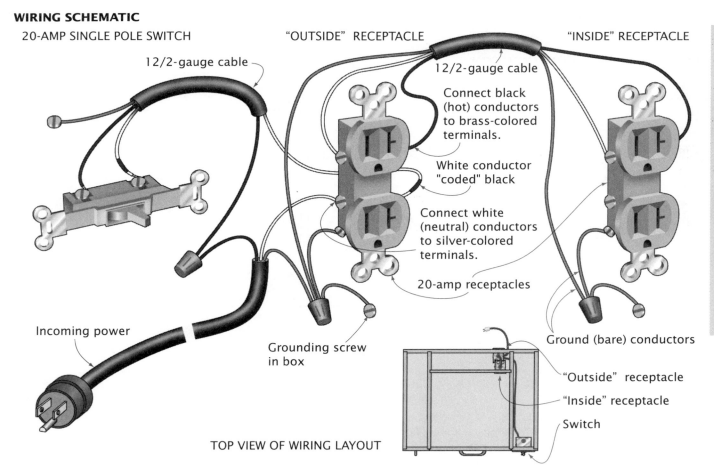

20-AMP SINGLE POLE SWITCH

"OUTSIDE" RECEPTACLE

"INSIDE" RECEPTACLE

12/2-gauge cable

12/2-gauge cable

Connect black (hot) conductors to brass-colored terminals.

White conductor "coded" black

Connect white (neutral) conductors to silver-colored terminals.

20-amp receptacles

Incoming power

Grounding screw in box

Ground (bare) conductors

"Outside" receptacle

"Inside" receptacle

Switch

TOP VIEW OF WIRING LAYOUT

Router Tables

# Building the Storage Drawer

The final element to make is a big drawer that rests on the runners attached to the bottom side rails. It provides a generous storage space for an extra router or two, extra mounting plates, sleds, featherboards, and other router table accessories. Although the plans here show an undivided drawer, it would be a simple matter to partition the space, providing tidy cubicles to organize the storage.

**1. Cut the drawer parts.** The storage drawer has its front and back joined to its sides with router-cut dovetails. The ¼-inch-plywood bottom is housed in grooves routed in the other parts.

The front is cut from oak so it matches the other front

**Installing the switch** is the last step in wiring the router table. Before you do this, you must secure the electrical box to the bin front and the case, then rough in the cable. Leave about a hand's length of cable extending from the box so you can wire up the switch. Note the black tape on the white conductor, a reminder that it is hot, not neutral.

| STORAGE DRAWER Cutting List | | | |
|---|---|---|---|
| Part | Qty. | Dimensions | Material |
| Front | 1 | ¾" × 8¹¹⁄₁₆" × 26⁷⁄₁₆" | Oak |
| Sides | 2 | ¾" × 8¹¹⁄₁₆" × 20" | Poplar |
| Back | 1 | ¾" × 8¹¹⁄₁₆" × 26⁷⁄₁₆" | Poplar |
| Bottom | 1 | ¼" × 19¾" × 25⁷⁄₁₆" | Plywood |
| **Hardware** | | | |
| 2 wire pulls, 3", brass, with screws | | | |

## STORAGE DRAWER CONSTRUCTION

EXPLODED VIEW

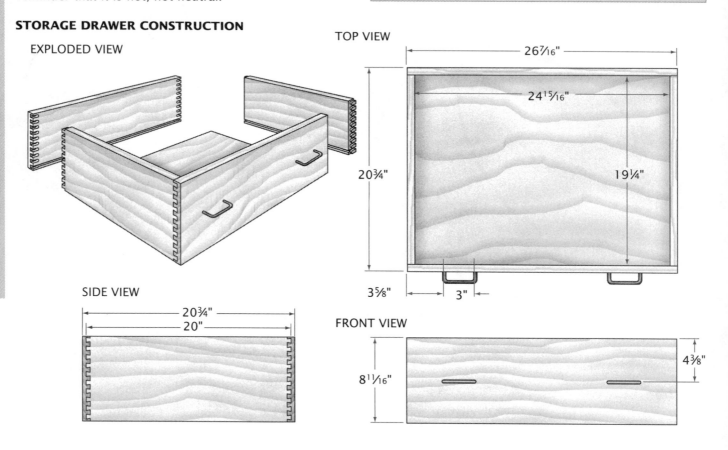

TOP VIEW

SIDE VIEW

FRONT VIEW

Router Tables

elements of the router table. The sides and back are made of poplar (or whatever you are using as your "secondary" wood). Joint and plane the stock to the required thickness. Measure the stand's lower area, and compare your measurements to the plans and the Cutting List. Presuming that no adjustments are needed, rip and crosscut the parts to the dimensions specified by the Cutting List. Cut the bottom from plywood.

**2. Rout the dovetail joinery.** Use any jig that will yield ½-inch half-blind dovetails. Set up the jig and router according to the manufacturer's instructions. Rout the dovetails.

**3. Rout the grooves for the bottom.** Do this on the router table, using a ¼-inch straight bit. Set the fence to guide the cut, and rout a ¼-inch-deep groove just shy of the bottom edge of both sides, as well as the front and back.

**4. Assemble the drawer.** Do a dry run to ensure that everything fits together properly and to set up the clamps and cauls. Then apply glue to the dovetails and assemble the drawer. Fit the bottom in place, but don't glue it into its groove.

Lay out the locations of the holes for the drawer pulls' mounting screws. Drill the holes and mount the pulls.

**5. Fit the drawer to the stand.** The drawer *should* fit; you checked the dimensions of the space for it before you cut the parts. But check the fit and see how smoothly the drawer operates. If necessary, sand or plane the sides and/or edges to achieve a good fit.

**6. Apply the finish.** Paint the back and sides, and apply a clear finish to the front. You don't need to paint the drawer edges, since they won't be seen when it is set in place in the router table.

## The Dust Collection System

Collecting all the dust and chips generated by a router table is a challenge. After all, making dirt just may be the *one thing* that routers do best of all. The conventional approach is to integrate a pickup into the fence, the theory being that suction to one side of the bit will capture all the chips and dust.

Well, if you've used a router table at all, you know that chips go everywhere. If you rout the edge of a board, a fence-mounted shop-vacuum pickup will capture a lot of the dirt. But if the bit has shear-cutting flutes, and if the bit is not fully elevated above the tabletop, it will throw much of the dirt below the

*(continued)*

### DUST COLLECTION SCHEMATIC

Chips drawn off the bit via the fence's dust pickup are carried into the plenum by the jumper hose. They drop to the bottom of the plenum and are sucked into the shop-vac hose.

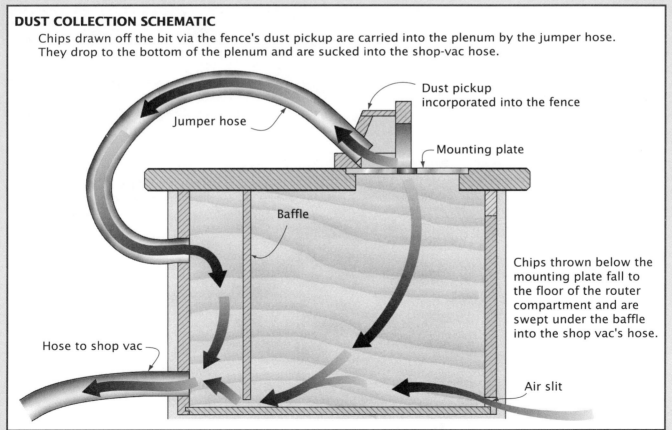

Jumper hose

Dust pickup incorporated into the fence

Mounting plate

Baffle

Chips thrown below the mounting plate fall to the floor of the router compartment and are swept under the baffle into the shop vac's hose.

Hose to shop vac

Air slit

tabletop surface. That fence-mounted pickup just can't get it all. You need some form of containment under the table, too.

What this router table's dust collection system provides is a two-level approach. It pulls dust and debris off the top of the table through the fence's pickup. And it sucks dust and chips from the router compartment as well. Both levels are cleared by one shop vacuum. The drawing *Dust Collection Schematic* shows how it is supposed to work.

The system depends upon the venturi effect in two places. One is the intake below the threshold. As air is pulled through the narrow slit, it speeds up, and this rush of air helps sweep the dust settling on the compartment floor toward the vacuum port. The dust baffle forms the second venturi, a ½-inch-high slot through which all the air in the compartment is pulled by the vacuum. Speeding up the air helps it keep the dust in suspension so it can be swept into the vacuum hose.

To make the system work as advertised, you have to be diligent about sealing the router compartment, so that air enters the router compartment only via the jumper hose from the fence's dust pickup, through the mounting plate's bit opening, and through the narrow slit beneath the threshold. The more free air in the system, the less effective the dust removal will be. If you run the system with the router compartment door open, the shop vac will be overwhelmed and won't be able to capture the router-generated debris. Even a dust collector with a 4-inch hose won't be able to clear the chips in this situation. But even seemingly insignificant infiltration will rob the system of effectiveness. If you find that chips and dust accumulate in both the fence's pickup and the router compartment, check for a gap between the case and the tabletop. You have to keep the system sealed.

To this end, I stuck foam weather stripping to the top edges of the case's back, dust baffle, and partitions, around the door, and even to the top of the threshold. Keep the door closed when you are routing.

When the shop vac is operating, it creates enough suction to pull the dust and chips from the fence into the router compartment.

It's a good system, and it captures a lot of the dirt.

Even so, it isn't perfect. If you rout a groove with a straight bit, the workpiece blocks that fence-mounted pickup. While some dirt is captured in the router compartment, chips blow out the groove, too. What I'm saying is that, as you build your two-level router-table dust collection system, you need to accept that you just can't contain and capture *all* the dust.

**Seal the router compartment well** to ensure that your shop vacuum isn't overwhelmed by too much air. Apply foam weatherstripping to the top edges of the case's back, partitions, and dust baffle to seal the gap between the case and the tabletop. This view shows the plenum formed by the dust baffle, as well as the two ports in the case back.

# Split Fence

**Here's a first-class fence for any router table. Its separate faces adjust independently for jointing operations and for near-zero clearance work.**

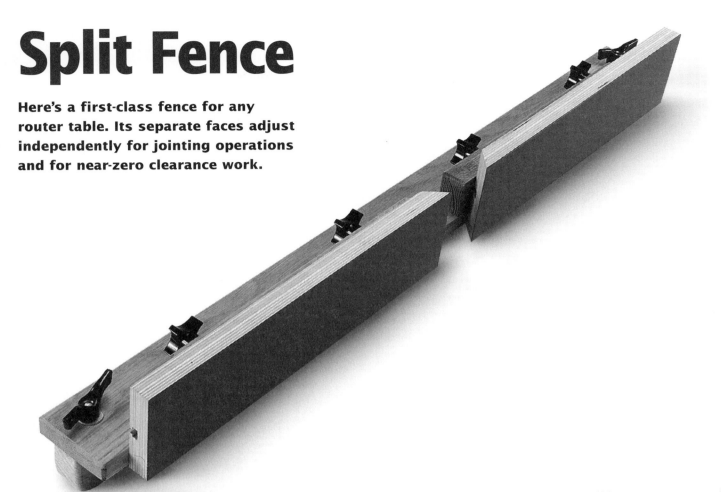

Every router table needs a first-class fence, one that's more than a straight board clamped to the tabletop. The straight board gets the routine work done, but this split fence does more than the routine. This fence has built-in clamps, which allow you to adjust the fence's position without fumbling with it, AND a separate clamp that takes two hands to work. With their big, plastic wing knobs, the built-in clamps are a cinch to use.

The fence has two faces that can be adjusted independently of one another. Surfaced with plastic laminate, the fence faces won't add any drag to the movement of your work across the router table. Moreover, the faces are high enough to support a tall workpiece.

The fact that the faces are adjustable in two planes means you can easily alter the gap between them to accommodate most any size bit. It means you can use your router table as a jointer. You'll be able to joint small parts, which are dangerous to machine on a jointer, and glue-laden sheet goods, which really abuse steel jointer knives. All you have to do is shim out the outfeed fence face.

These features alone are enough to make this a worthwhile workshop project. But there's more. You can remove the faces completely and use the fence without them. And the faces are sufficiently easy to make that they can be replaced quickly and inexpensively.

Why would they need replacement, you ask. Because the edges shrouding the bit will probably get chewed up enough to lose their effectiveness if you use a wide variety of bits. Close them in on a big profile bit enough times,

and they just won't close in on a small bit.

You can make a fence like this to fit any size router table. The plans and directions following show a version sized to the Floor-Standing Router Table (page 212) as well as one for my Table Saw Extension Router Table (page 183). The clamps on the latter are designed to grip the rip-fence rails rather than the tabletop.

## Making the Fence

The hardware is central to the easy function of this fence, and you won't get too far into this project before needing it. While the bolts are common, the plastic knobs will have to be ordered from a catalog. I'd recommend waiting until you have the hardware in hand before beginning.

**1. Cut the parts.** The fence requires only a few of them. The two fence faces are formed by glue-laminating two pieces of ½-inch plywood, so you need four pieces altogether. Since the faces must be flat, use a good-quality plywood (or MDF). I used standard birch plywood. The faces are relatively small, so you may be able to use left-over plywood from another project.

The other parts should be made of a straight-grained hardwood, like oak, maple, beech, or even cherry. Again, not a great deal of material is needed, but the parts are all different thicknesses and widths. Dress the hardwood to the required thicknesses, and cut the parts to the sizes specified by the Cutting List.

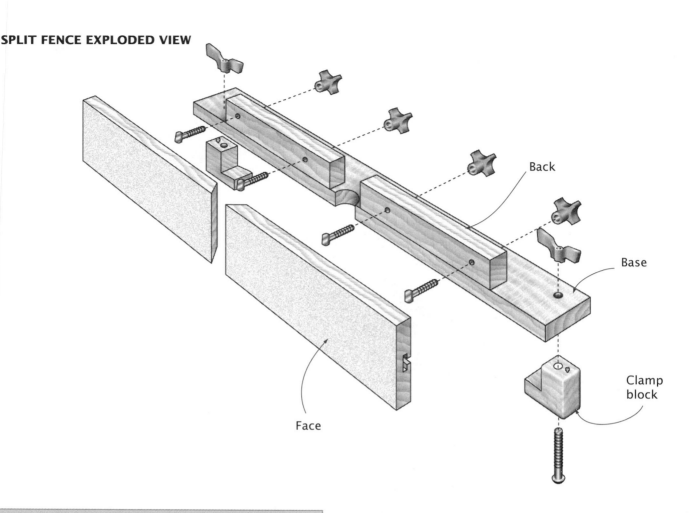

Back

Base

Clamp block

Face

## FLOOR-STANDING ROUTER TABLE SPLIT FENCE
### Cutting List

| Part | Qty. | Dimensions | Material |
|------|------|------------|----------|
| Base | 1 | 1" × 3½" × 39" | Hardwood |
| Backs | 2 | 1¼" × 2" × 14" | Hardwood |
| Face plies | 4 | ½" × 4½" × 17" | Plywood |
| Clamp blocks | 2 | 1¾" × 2½" × 3½" | Hardwood |

### Hardware

Plastic laminate, 2 pcs. 5" × 18" each

4 toilet bolts, ¼" × 2½"

4 plastic knobs, 4-prong, 1¾" dia. with ¼" through threaded inserts; #DK-59 from Reid Tool Supply Co. (800-253-0421)

2 carriage bolts, ⅜"-16 × 4½"

2 plastic wing knobs with ⅜"-16 threaded insert; #85J94 from Woodcraft Supply Co. (800-225-1153)

2 panhead screws, #6 × 1"

**2. Laminate the face plies.** Apply glue to the mating faces, and spread it thinly and evenly over the surfaces. Put the surfaces together and twist them a bit to get a good bond. Line up the edges and apply clamps.

**3. Glue the backs to the base.** Before actually gluing the backs in place, drill the holes for the toilet bolts that mount the faces to the fence. Lay out and drill the holes carefully, so they will be in the same plane, ensuring that after assembly, the faces will be level. This is easy enough to do if you have a drill press and can use a fence to position the workpieces. If you don't have a drill press, you can use a plunge router equipped with an edge guide for this operation. You do need a long bit to penetrate the 1¼-inch-thick backs.

Lay out the locations of the backs on the base. Apply glue and clamp the backs in place. With a wet rag, wipe off any glue squeeze-out before it sets.

**4. Make the clamp blocks.** Start with two blocks of straight-grained hardwood, cut to the dimensions specified by the Cutting List. The basic cuts can be made on the table saw. To do so, you must attach an auxiliary facing to the miter gauge. The facing should extend beyond the blade, regardless of which miter slot the gauge is placed in.

Make the cuts, as shown in the drawing *Making Clamp Blocks*. To avoid confusion as you work, it's a good idea to

## SPLIT FENCE PLAN VIEWS

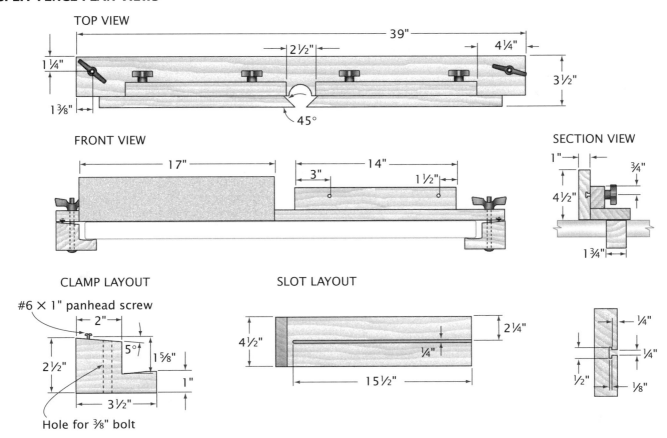

TOP VIEW

39"

2½"

4¼"

1¼"

3½"

1⅜"

45°

FRONT VIEW

17"

14"

3"

1½"

SECTION VIEW

1"

¾"

4½"

1¾"

CLAMP LAYOUT

#6 × 1" panhead screw

2"

5°

1⅝"

2½"

1"

3½"

Hole for ⅜" bolt

SLOT LAYOUT

4½"

2¼"

¼"

15½"

¼"

¼"

½"

⅛"

## MAKING CLAMP BLOCKS

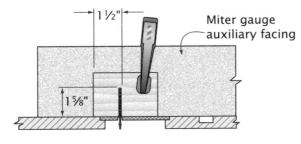

1½"

Miter gauge
auxiliary facing

1⅝"

1. Make the shoulder cut with the
miter gauge in the left-hand
slot. Clamp the workpiece to the
miter gauge facing.

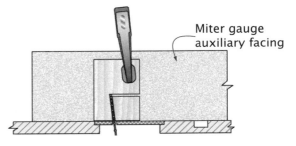

Miter gauge
auxiliary facing

2. Make the base cut with the blade tilted 5°
and the miter gauge in the left-hand slot.
Align the block so the cut intersects the end
of the shoulder cut. Clamp the workpiece to
the miter gauge facing.

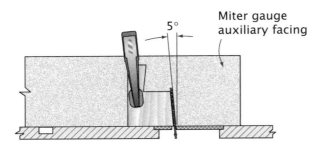

5°

Miter gauge
auxiliary facing

3. Make the top cut with the blade
tilted and the miter gauge in
the right-hand slot. Clamp the workpiece to the miter gauge facing.

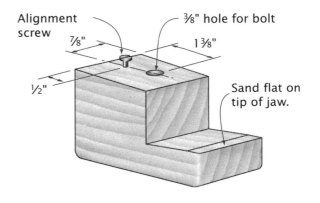

Alignment
screw

⅜" hole for bolt

⅞"

1⅜"

½"

Sand flat on
tip of jaw.

Router Tables

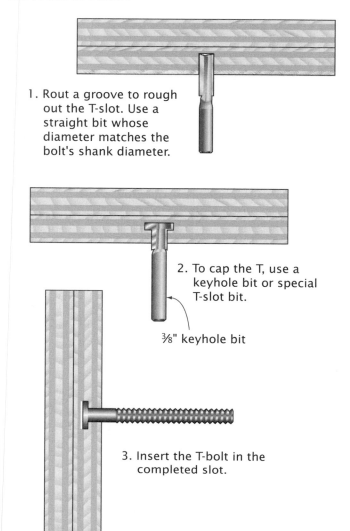

1. Rout a groove to rough out the T-slot. Use a straight bit whose diameter matches the bolt's shank diameter.

2. To cap the T, use a keyhole bit or special T-slot bit.

⅜" keyhole bit

3. Insert the T-bolt in the completed slot.

sketch the shape of the finished block on each workpiece. Pay attention to the grain direction. The blocks are small, so clamp the workpiece to the miter-gauge facing when making a cut.

Two of the cuts are made with the blade tilted 5 degrees. Some table saws tilt the arbor to the left, others to the right. I think it's a good idea to keep the workpiece close to the miter gauge itself, rather than hung out on the far side of the blade. So switch the gauge from one slot to the other, as appropriate, to accomplish this.

Set up the saw from the shoulder cut, and make it on both workpieces. Then make the base cuts, and finally the top cuts.

Finish shaping the clamp blocks by sanding or filing a narrow flat at the jaw's tip. Then round-over the exposed edges with sandpaper or a file.

**5. Drill the assembly holes.** The clamp blocks are mounted to the fence base with ⅜-inch carriage bolts. Left at that, the blocks would easily twist out of position, which would be pretty annoying when you are trying to adjust

the fence position on the tabletop. So each block has a small screw protruding from the top. The screw head extends into a mating hole on the base, keeping the block from twisting.

Bore the ⅜-inch holes through each block, as shown in the drawing *Making Clamp Blocks.* Bore matching holes through the fence base.

Drill pilot holes for the alignment screws, then drive a panhead screw into each block, as shown in the drawing. Leave the head protruding about ³⁄₁₆ inch.

To locate the hole positions in the base, mount the blocks on the base with the bolts and plastic wing knobs, line them up, and tighten the wing knobs enough to mark the base with the screw heads. Remove the blocks, and drill stopped holes for the screw heads.

**6. Rout the T-slots.** These slots, and the special bolts that fit in them, are what allow the fence faces to be adjusted in two planes (parallel to the base axis and perpendicular to the base axis). The bolts can be either T-slot bolts, purchased from a woodworking supply outlet, or common toilet bolts, purchased at the local hardware store. I used the toilet bolts.

The slots can be routed with either a keyhole bit or a T-slot bit. In either case, make sure the bit profile matches the bolt. I used a ½-inch keyhole bit.

Both keyhole and T-slot bits have a slender neck between the shank and the cutter. The neck is frail and breaks easily if you feed the work too aggressively. A good approach is to rough out the slot by routing a groove the size of the bolt shank with a straight bit. Then when you make the pass with the T-slot or keyhole bit, it is making a much lighter cut, alleviating the stress on the neck.

Make the cuts on a router table, and center the slots on the workpieces. The slots in the fences I've made are stopped on one end (the one closest to the bit), as shown in the drawings. They do have to be open at one end so you can fit the bolt heads in. A keyhole bit will allow you to make stopped slots because it is a plunge-cutting bit. With its tail end resting on the tabletop, hold the workpiece's leading end above the bit. Plunge it onto the bit, and feed in the correct direction, routing through to the end.

T-slot bits generally are not plunge-cutting bits. To avoid having to make a climb cut, which can be dicey, you can rout the slots from end to end.

**7. Apply plastic laminate to the faces.** Prepare the plywood faces by ripping and crosscutting them to clean and square up the edges. Trim the pieces of laminate to the dimensions specified by the Cutting List, which will make them about 1 inch longer and wider than the plywood faces.

Apply contact cement to the laminate and the faces, and let the cement dry. Carefully apply the laminate so there's some overhang on all edges. With a router fitted with a flush-trimming bit, trim the laminate.

Finally cut the 45-degree bevel across one end of each face.

Router Tables

**Flush-trim the fence faces if they overhang the base.** To do this, clamp the assembled fence in a vise, as shown. Set the router on the faces, with the bit's pilot bearing riding on the fence base. Rout from one end of the fence to the other.

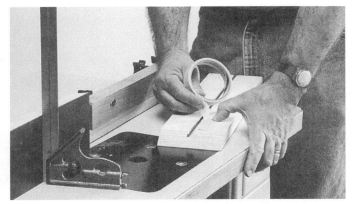

**Shim a face to get it properly aligned.** Tape is good for this purpose, since it won't fall off the fence if you make other adjustments during use. Apply a strip—or if necessary, several strips atop one another—right where it needs to be to force the face into alignment.

**8. Assemble the fence.** The front of the base/back unit must be square to the bottom. Check this with an accurate square before bolting the faces in place. If necessary, square these surfaces to each other on a jointer.

Now insert two toilet bolts into the slot in each face, and mount the faces on the fence. Tighten the plastic knobs to seat the faces firmly against the base/back unit. Bolt the clamps in place with 4¼-inch-long carriage bolts with plastic wing knobs.

**9. Fine-tune the fence.** This is a matter of setting the fence on the router table top, clamping it down, and doing whatever it takes to ensure that the faces are flush and parallel to each other and are square to the tabletop.

Deal with the seam between the fence and the tabletop first. The faces should touch the tabletop.

- *If there's a gap of ⅛ inch or less* between the faces and the tabletop, disassemble the fence and joint the base as necessary to eliminate the gap.
- *If there's a gap over ⅛ inch* between the faces and the tabletop, you just might be better off making new faces. You need to be wary of jointing the base too thin. But you must use your own judgment as to what constitutes "too thin."
- *If the faces overhang the base,* use a flush-trimming bit to rout them flush with the base's bottom surface. Don't do this on your jointer; the plastic laminate and the glues in the plywood will be too hard on the knives.

Now that you have a tight fit between fence faces and tabletop, address the other alignment concerns. Hold a long straightedge on the faces, checking their flatness from top to bottom, diagonally from corner to corner.

- *If one or both faces are humped or hollow,* toss the fence and make a new one that's really flat.
- *If both faces are flat but out of alignment with each other,* use shims to bring them into alignment. Strips of tape applied to the face backs are good.

Now use a square to check that the faces are square to the tabletop.

- *Minor discrepancies* can be corrected with shims.
- *Major discrepancies* should be corrected by disassembling the fence and jointing or rejointing the base/back unit.

## For a Table Saw Mounting

If you've got a router hanging from a table saw extension wing, you can adapt the split fence to use with it. The following directions and specifications are for a split fence made to go with the Table Saw Extension Router Table on page 183.

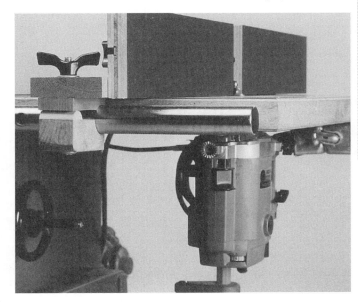

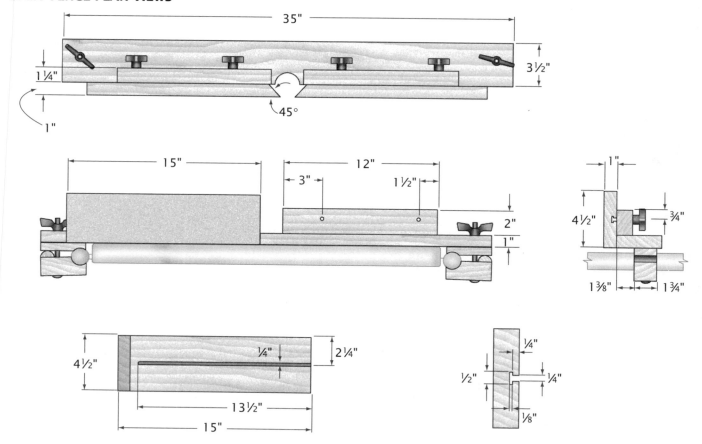

## TABLE SAW EXTENSION ROUTER TABLE SPLIT FENCE
### Cutting List

| Part | Qty. | Dimensions | Material |
|------|------|------------|----------|
| Base | 1 | 1" × 3½" × 35" | Hardwood |
| Backs | 2 | 1¼" × 2" × 12" | Hardwood |
| Face plies | 4 | ½" × 4½" × 15" | Plywood |
| Clamp blocks | 2 | 1¾" × 2⁹⁄₁₆" × 3½" | Hardwood |
| Fulcrums | 2 | 1" dia. × 1¾" | Hardwood dowel |

### Hardware

Plastic laminate, 2 pcs. 5" × 16" each

4 toilet bolts, ¼" × 2½"

4 plastic knobs, 4-prong, 1¾" dia. with ¼" through threaded inserts; #DK-59 from Reid Tool Supply Co. (800-253-0421)

2 carriage bolts, ⅜"-16 × 4½"

2 plastic wing knobs with ⅜"-16 threaded insert; #85J94 from Woodcraft Supply Co. (800-225-1153)

The big difference between this fence and the one designed for a regular router table is the clamp block design. Here, the clamps are designed to pinch the round rip-fence rails. But the overall length of this fence is different, too. Check the Cutting List and *Plan View* drawings for the details.

If you are going to build this split fence, follow the step-by-step directions under the heading "Making the Fence" (beginning on page 237) except for Steps 4 and 5. Instead, follow these steps:

**1. Cut the blanks.** The clamps consist of an upper jaw, which is glued to the underside of the fence base, and a lower jaw, which is bolted to the fence. Both the upper and lower jaws are formed from a single block of hardwood, as shown in the drawing *Making Clamp Blocks*.

Cut the two blanks required to the dimensions specified by the Cutting List. Rip a short piece of 1-inch-diameter dowel in half, then crosscut two 1-inch-lengths of the dowel halves.

**2. Bore the holes.** Two holes are bored in each clamp blank. One is for the rail, and the diameter of this hole must match that of the fence rails on your table saw. The second hole is for the clamp bolt.

The first hole must be bored with a Forstner bit so it can break the edge of the blank. The drawing specifies a 1⅜-inch diameter; but before you drill this hole, check the

Router Tables

## MAKING CLAMP BLOCKS

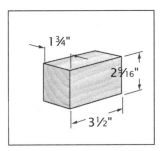

Start with a block of straight-grained hardwood.

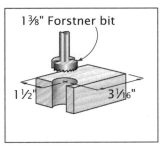

With a Forstner bit, drill a 1⅜"-dia. hole positioned to break through the edge, as shown.

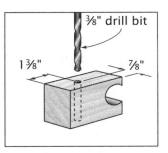

Drill a ⅜"-dia. hole for the clamping bolt.

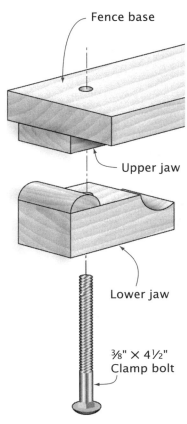

Fence base

Upper jaw

Lower jaw

⅜" × 4½" Clamp bolt

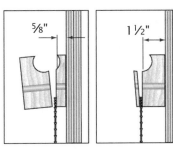

Rip the block in two, making the upper jaw ⅝" thick (*left*). Rip the lower jaw, making it 1½" thick (*right*).

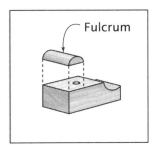

Rip a 1"-dia. dowel in half, and glue a piece to the lower jaw as a fulcrum.

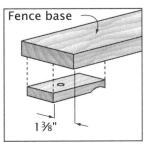

Glue the upper jaw to the fence base. Then extend the ⅜" hole through the fence base.

diameter of your table saw's fence rails. Adjust the diameter of this hole, if necessary. Lay out the centerpoint of the hole on each blank. Position each blank carefully on the drill press, and bore the hole.

Chuck a ⅜-inch bit in the drill press. Lay out the location of the clamp-bolt hole, and drill one through each blank.

**3. Cut the blocks.** On the table saw, rip the blanks in two, forming the upper and lower jaws. Re-rip the lower jaw, reducing it to the final thickness.

**4. Assemble the clamps.** Begin by gluing and clamping the split dowel pieces, which serve as fulcrums, to the lower jaws, as shown in the drawing. Then glue and clamp the upper jaw to the underside of the fence base.

When the glue has set and the clamps have been removed, bore the clamp-bolt hole through the fence base. Use the hole in the upper jaw as a guide, of course.

Insert a ⅜-inch × 4½-inch carriage bolt through the lower jaw, then through the fence. Secure the assembly with a large plastic wing knob. If you want to *ensure* that the jaws will open when you loosen the large plastic wing knob, fit a compression spring over the bolt before inserting it in the fence.

## Using the Split Fence

This fence is great because of the built-in clamps. Loosen the big wing knobs about a turn, and the fence can be slid across the tabletop. Turn those wing knobs back, and it is clamped securely. No separate clamps to fumble with. No loose parts to fall or drop on the floor when you're trying to hold a precise setting.

It is just a great all-purpose router table fence.

### Near-Zero Clearance

The split fence is also great because it can be adjusted to accommodate an infinitude of bit sizes and settings. It isn't absolute zero-clearance; but in router woodworking, chasing zero-clearance is tantamount to chasing unicorns.

Probably you've seen ads for commercial fences with plastic inserts for you to make zero-clearance inserts. But think about how you chase a particular setup, when seeking a particular molding profile, for example. You set up and make a test cut. Then you raise or lower the bit a hair. Another test. The fence gets yuxed in or out. Another test. Another bit height adjustment. Another test.

Well, with each adjustment, the zero is going out of the clearance between the bit and the insert.

**Adjust the facing spacing to suit the bit you are using.** The split fence allows you to set the fence around the bit without having to actually cut out a space for it. You can move the fence faces close in to a small bit (*left*), then pull them out for a large one (*right*). By having the fences close to the bit on either side, they can provide backing for the work.

But okay, you *do* want to close the gap between fence and bit as much as possible, and the fence's movable faces allow you to do that. To adjust the gap between the faces, just loosen the four knobs that secure them. Slide the faces in toward the bit or out away from it. Then retighten the knobs.

## Jointing

Your router can do a darn good job substituting for a jointer. Think seriously about using the router if

- you don't have a jointer;
- you want to joint glue-laden materials like plywood or medium-density fiberboard (MDF);
- you want to joint a board or panel that's too big to maneuver when it's standing on edge;
- you have an especially small, blocky, or thin workpiece.

With this split fence, you can do the job on the router table.

To joint on a router table, all you have to do is adjust the split fence's two faces separately, to serve as infeed and outfeed supports.

The faces are seated against the fence backs, and the entire unit has been trued. So all you have to do is shim out the outfeed face. If you want to remove about ⅟₁₆ inch of stock, try using some scraps of plastic laminate as shims. For

**The split fence is easy to set up for jointing.** Loosen the knobs securing the left-hand fence facing, and insert shims between the fence back and the facing (*left*). The thickness of the shims equals the amount of stock that will be removed in one pass. With this outfeed facing locked down, adjust the fence position so the outfeed facing is tangent to the bit's cutting edge. Check this with a straightedge, as shown above. You are then set to joint.

less of a cut, use scraps of backer or several thicknesses of card stock. For a heavier cut, rip some shims to the thickness you are aiming for. This is the easy part.

What's more challenging is aligning the fence properly with the bit. The outfeed half of the fence must be tangent to the bit's cutting edge. I do it this way:

1. Make a rough adjustment of the fence, and tighten one clamp.
2. Hold a straight edge against the outfeed face.
3. Fine-tune the fence position by moving its unclamped end. Adjust it so the bit's cutting edge just grazes the straightedge.
4. Tighten the second clamp.
5. Test the setting by making a partial cut. Feed a test piece by the bit until it nearly spans the entire fence. Switch off the router, and carefully check whether it is squarely against both faces of the fence. If it is, you are ready to joint the workpiece.

The ideal bit, in all these cases, is a fairly heavy but well-balanced straight bit. Always use a ½-inch-shank bit if possible.

The biggest constraint in using the router for jointing is the bit's cutting-edge length. The typical straight bit has a 1-inch cutting capacity, with longer ones extending that to 1½ inches. With the latter bit, you can barely handle a 6/4 (six-quarter) board.

Two manufacturers—Freud and Amana—make ½-inch straight bits with a 2½-inch cutting length. This is the longest straight bit I've seen. Cutting judiciously, you

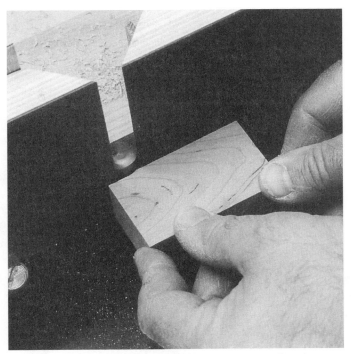

**From a safety standpoint,** the router may be the best tool for surfacing small workpieces. Maybe the piece is small and blocky. Maybe it's thin. These are the pieces that the jointer tends to jerk around or demolish, mauling your fingers in the process. Avoid this hazard—joint the piece on the router table.

should be able to joint up to 10/4 stock with this bit. And you can use it for many other straight-bit jobs, too. Freud's bit is catalog number 12-130; Amana's is 45427.

# Sleds

When you build (or buy) a router table, the tendency is to think you'll use your table saw's miter gauge on it. "Whenever I have to make a cut across the end grain," you think, "I can set the work in the miter gauge and guide the cut with that. Besides, I already have it."

The miter gauge is a table saw accessory. Leave it on the table saw. It isn't suited for router table work.

What you do need is a sled or two. What a sled does that a miter gauge doesn't is back up the work, preventing tear-out as the cutter exits the workpiece. A sled doesn't require a slot in the tabletop to guide it. Some sleds ride along the fence; others have a shoe that rides along the edge of the tabletop.

Following are plans for several different pushers or sleds that belong with your router table.

## Pusher

Looks like a handsaw handle, doesn't it? It should, since I traced around the most comfortable saw handle I could find to start the pattern for this pusher. In making it, I wanted something a little different from the usual scrapwood push stick.

The typical table-saw push stick takes about five minutes to make, three of which are spent rummaging through the scrap bin looking for juussst the right stick. The other two are spent at the band saw. But I wanted this pusher to do a little more than a push stick does.

And clearly, this is a more elaborate pusher.

- Using the notch in the toe, you can feed stock into the saw or router bit.
- Using the heel to hook the work puts the sole of the pusher flat on the workpiece. That way you can apply some downward force at the same time you are feeding it forward. This is a definite plus on the router table.
- Using the V-groove in the sole allows you to hold the work down, but also force it against the fence as you feed it. To do this, you tilt the pusher and catch the edge of the work in the groove. The heel hooks the end of the work. This is the most useful aspect of the pusher on the router table, especially when shaping the edges of relatively narrow sticks.

Given the versatility of the pusher, I wanted it to feel good in the hand, to feel natural to a woodworker. I wanted it to be used, after all. So the saw-handle grip is perfect. Make the thing from some pretty wood—you'll need more than a small scrap, I'm afraid—and it'll look just right in your shop.

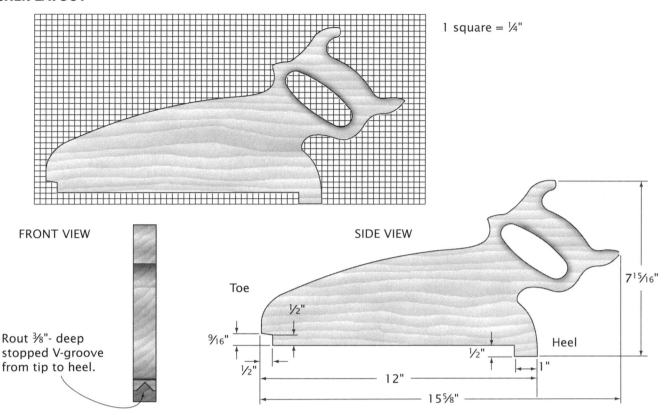

1 square = ¼"

FRONT VIEW

SIDE VIEW

Toe

½"

9/16"

½"

½"

12"

15⅝"

Heel

1"

7¹⁵/₁₆"

Rout ⅜"- deep stopped V-groove from tip to heel.

## Making the Pusher

I wanted to make this a router project (rather than a band saw project). I also wanted to make it easy to make duplicates. So I first made a template, then knocked out several pushers from the template.

**1. Make the template.** Enlarge the pattern shown in *Pusher Layout.* Or trace a saw handle and extend lines from the handle to connect it to the body layout taken from the plan.

Lay out the pattern on a piece of hardboard or ¼-inch plywood. Cut it on the band saw or with a saber saw. To cut the handle opening, drill holes to form the radii at each end, then cut out the waste between them with the saber saw. Sand and/or file the edges smooth and fair.

*Note:* What I found, after making a prototype pusher, is that pushing on the router table is a slightly different action than sawing. If you merely duplicate the handle position from the saw, it won't be right. Instead, rotate the handle up about 20 degrees.

**2. Rout out the pusher.** First off, select a nice piece of hardwood for this tool. Stick the template to the stock with carpet tape. Set this workpiece on an expendable piece of plywood or hardboard (to protect your workbench), and clamp it to the workbench. I located the clamps on the body and routed the handle, then shifted the clamps so I could rout out the rest of the pusher.

Use a plunge router; a ¼-inch spiral upcut bit if you

| PUSHER Cutting List | | | |
|---|---|---|---|
| **Part** | **Qty.** | **Dimensions** | **Material** |
| Pusher | 1 | 1" × 8" × 16" | Hardwood |

have a spiral upcut, a regular ¼-inch bit if you don't; and a 5/16-inch-O.D. guide bushing. Rout around and around the template, cutting incrementally deeper on each circuit. You can keep the bit cutting cooler if you stop and vacuum the chips from the cut after every circuit or two.

**3. Rout the V-groove.** Do this on the router table using a V-grooving bit, and guide the cut with the fence.

The groove is stopped. Measure 11 inches from the bit, and put a piece of masking tape on the tabletop. Rout until the toe of the pusher reaches the tape, then lift the workpiece up off the bit.

**4. Glue on the heel and notch the toe.** The heel is a ½ × 1-inch bit of the working stock. Glue it in place.

Then notch the toe, as shown in the drawing, using a back saw or on the band saw.

**5. Round-over the edges.** The final touches are to radius all the edges. I used a 5/16-inch roundover bit in a table-mounted router for this. Then sand the edges and faces.

**Router Tables**

## Using the Pusher

This is not complex. If you've used a push stick, you can use this pusher.

I was going to say that it doesn't take a lot of practice, but in a way it does. Using a pusher on a table saw is pretty much second nature for most woodworkers, but that's not so on the router table. One reason is that you don't channel

**With a V-groove in its sole,** this pusher is perfect for router table work. Tilt the pusher so the edge of the work nestles into the groove. The heel hooks the end and allows you to feed the work while simultaneously holding it down on the tabletop and in against the fence.

the work between the bit and the fence on a router table. If you just push the end of the stock, it tends to come away from the fence and thus away from the bit.

And that's where this pusher proves its worth. With that V-groove, you can apply the forces needed to keep the work on the tabletop, against the fence and bit, and moving forward, all while keeping your fingers well clear of danger.

What the pusher will not do is provide backup for the work. It doesn't prevent tear-out. For that you need either the push-block sled or the miter sled.

## Push-Block Sled

A big, thick block fitted with a handgrip is first-rate for feeding work across a cutter in conjunction with the fence. It has mass, so it is stable.

| PUSH-BLOCK SLED Cutting List | | | |
|---|---|---|---|
| Part | Qty. | Dimensions | Material |
| Base plies | 2 | ¾" × 6" × 12" | Plywood |
| Handgrip | 1 | 1" × 4⅝" × 5⅝" | Hardwood |
| **Hardware** | | | |
| 2 roundhead wood screws, #10 × 1½" | | | |

**PUSH-BLOCK SLED PLANS**

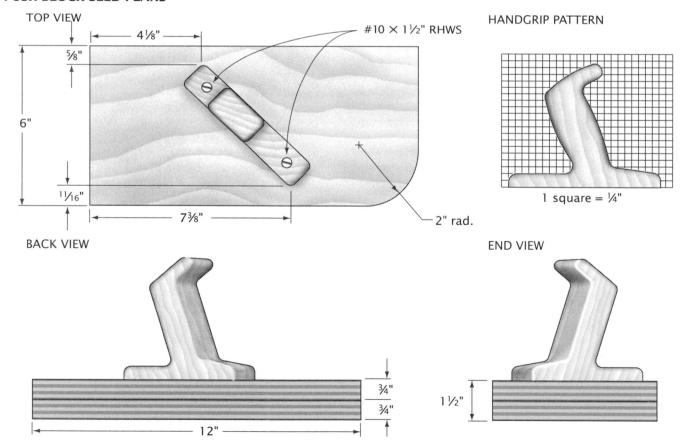

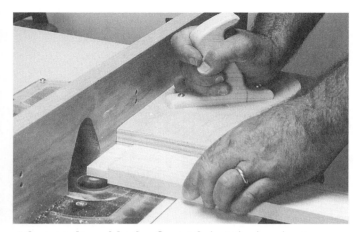

**It's a serious block of wood,** but the hand grip turns it into a router table sled. Backing up an end-grain cut, it both feeds the work, keeping it square to the fence, and backs it up, preventing tear-out.

This push-block sled provides good backup, so you won't get tear-out in the workpiece. Because of the orientation of the handgrip, you actually have two edges you can use. For cuts where the work is on end, flat against the fence, I tend to use the short edge. When the work is flat on the tabletop and I want the sled to help keep it square to the fence, I use the long edge.

Because it is routinely nibbled by whatever cutters you use, this sled gets chewed up. When tear-out starts occurring in the work, it's time to freshen up the sled. Simply saw off the damaged area on the table saw, exposing a fresh, square surface. Over time, of course, this prunes the sled so small it's useless. When it does, make another!

### Making the Push-Block Sled

Making the handgrip is the time-consuming part of this project. But that's the part that, over time, gets transferred from one base to another as the bases get chewed up in the course of your work. Spend some time on that grip so that it fits your hand comfortably.

**1. Make the base.** Cut two pieces of 3/4-inch plywood to the dimensions specified by the Push-Block Sled Cutting List. Glue them together face to face.

After the clamps are off the base, rip and crosscut it to true the edges and to make the corners perfectly square. If the corners aren't square, the workpieces you guide with it will be out-of-square.

I radiused the right rear corner of the base, cutting it on the band saw. This is a cue to orienting the sled. Even without thinking, I know which corner is the working one.

**2. Cut the handgrip.** I modeled my handgrip on a bench plane's handgrip. I removed the part from one of my planes to use as a pattern. But because the original wasn't quite big enough for my hand, I stretched it a bit. I also elongated the foot to provide places to put a couple of mounting screws. (Because it is useful on all sorts of pushers, I made a hardboard template so I can reproduce the outsized grip whenever I want.)

You can do what I did, or you can scale up the handgrip pattern. Lay out the grip on a block of 1-inch-thick hardwood. Note the grain direction.

Cut out the grip on the band saw or with a saber saw. Sand the cut edges. A sanding drum chucked in the drill press can smooth the inside radii. With a 1/4-inch or 3/8-inch roundover bit in a table-mounted router, machine the edges of the handgrip.

**3. Mount the handgrip.** Don't glue the handgrip to the base; you want to be able to move it to a new base someday. Use two #10 × 1½-inch roundhead wood screws, located as shown in the drawing *Push-Block Sled Plans.*

I cocked the handgrip so that pushing on it would advance the sled but would also keep it against the fence.

### Using the Push-Block Sled

This sled is always used with the fence, because the fence guides both it and the work. What the sled is doing is pushing the work, keeping it square to the fence, and backing it up so tear-out is prevented.

The angle of the handgrip makes it easy to keep the sled against the fence as it is advanced.

## Miter Sled

The miter sled combines the roles of miter gauge, push block, and chip breaker. Because it hooks over the table edge, it doesn't need to be used with the fence, nor does it require a slot.

When the sled is serving as a chip breaker, the bit cuts through the work and into the sled's fence, so the fence is, in a strong sense, a consumable. It's easy to replace the fence or even to make an entirely new sled, so you can make special sleds for different cuts. The sled shown has been used exclusively for the cope cuts made in conjunction with cope-and-stick work. It was made of scrap-bin materials.

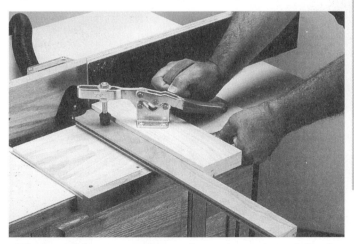

**When making a cope cut,** always have the rail firmly clamped to the sled. Feed the sled past the bit, making the cut. When the cut is done, you can simply ease the sled away from the edge of the tabletop and thus ease the work away from the bit. You don't have to pull the work back across the cutter.

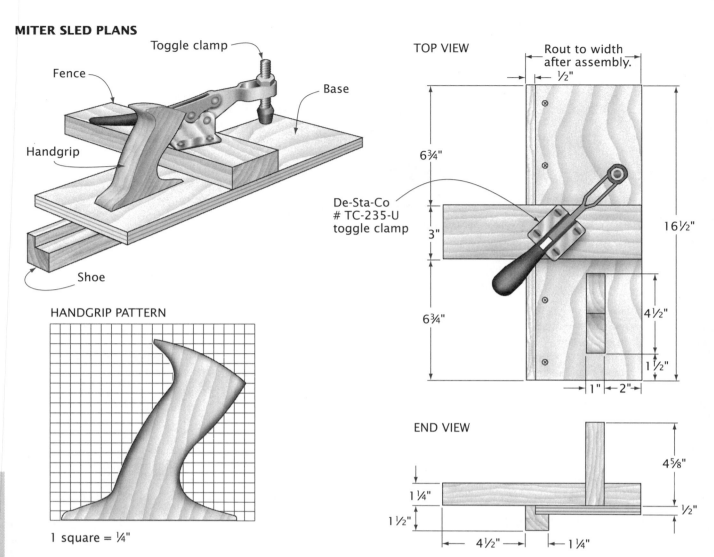

**Fence** · **Toggle clamp** · **Base** · **Handgrip** · **Shoe**

**HANDGRIP PATTERN**

1 square = ¼"

**TOP VIEW**

Rout to width after assembly.

½"

6¾"

De-Sta-Co # TC-235-U toggle clamp

3"

6¾"

16½"

4½"

1½"

1" · 2"

**END VIEW**

4⅝"

1¼"

1½"

½"

4½"

1¼"

## MITER SLED Cutting List

| Part | Qty. | Dimensions | Material |
|------|------|------------|----------|
| Base | 1 | ½" × 10"* × 16½" | Plywood |
| Shoe | 1 | 1¼" × 1½" × 16½" | Hardwood |
| Fence | 1 | 1¼" × 3" × 11"* | Hardwood |
| Handgrip | 1 | 1" × 4⅝" × 5⅝" | Hardwood |

## Hardware

6 drywall screws, #6 × 1"

1 toggle clamp, De-Sta-Co #TC-235-U; from Reid Tool Supply Co. (800-253-0421)

4 panhead screws, #14 × 1"

*The base width and fence length must be adjusted, as explained in the text, to the distance between the tabletop edge and the bit on your router table. See text.*

A practical feature of the sled is the toggle clamp. It keeps the work firmly in place, while freeing both of your hands to guide the sled. Its position is designed to keep the end of the work from bowing up away from the bit, which would give you an irregular cut.

For coping work, the clamp is almost essential. The reason? In action, the coping bit is self-feeding, and though you are moving the work counter to the bit's rotation, it will pull the work into it. The cut that starts square may end up slightly angled, and the matched joints you cut may not fit tightly. Although you may not believe this, that toggle clamp can clench the work a lot tighter than you can with your hand.

### Making the Miter Sled

This is a sled that should be custom-fitted to your router table. The base in particular must extend from the shoe to the edge of the bit. Naturally, that distance will vary from router table to router table. The sled shown is tailored to the Floor-Standing Router Table (page 212).

The sled is a consumable, as I noted earlier. The base and shoe will last a long time, but the fence will need periodic replacement. It makes sense to avoid gluing the parts together. I used screws exclusively.

**1. Cut the parts.** The base, fence, and shoe need to be flat and square. Cut the shoe and fence to the dimensions specified by the Cutting List. On the router table, measure from the tabletop edge to the bit axis, then subtract the radius of the pilot bearing of the bit you intend to use with the sled. Add ¾ inch to that measurement (the width of the rabbet in the shoe), and rip the base to that width. Crosscut it to the length specified by the Cutting List.

If you want the miter sled to slip especially easily, apply plastic laminate to the bottom surface of the base.

**2. Make and install the shoe.** Cut a rabbet for the base in the shoe, as shown in the drawing *Miter Sled Plans*. The rabbet is easily cut on the router table or the table saw.

Set the base into the rabbet, and drive three or four drywall screws through the base into the shoe. If you've covered one surface of the base with plastic laminate, be sure to orient it down, so it is the surface that rides on the router table.

**3. Screw the fence in place.** Note that the fence is positioned flush with the working edge of the base and that it overhangs the shoe by about 4½ inches. The extra length just provides fuller support for the workpiece. Be sure it is at right angles to the shoe. Drive screws through the base into the fence. Keep them back from the edge where the bit might hit them.

Screw the toggle clamp to the fence. The clamp specified is BIG, and because it is, it is strong. You can certainly use a smaller clamp, if you have one. The exact position of the clamp is not important, but the spindle should contact the work quite close to the working edge of the sled.

**4. Cut, shape, and install the handgrip.** You can enlarge the pattern included in the drawing, or you can contrive a layout of your own. The exact shape is less important than its fit in your hand; try to achieve the latter.

Cut the handgrip to shape on the band saw or with a saber saw. Round the edges with a roundover bit in a table-mounted router. Attach the grip to the base by driving two long drywall screws through the base into the grip.

**5. Trim the sled to fit the table and application.** For best results, you should limit your use of the sled to a particular application. The sled shown in the photos, for example, is used exclusively for the coping cuts made as a part of cope-and-stick work.

Fit the bit used for that application in the router table, and adjust its elevation for the application. Turn on the router, and make one pass with the sled and a scrap workpiece. The working edge of the base will be trimmed, as will the end of the fence. Both will perfectly match the cutter profile.

The sled is ready for some work.

**The cope-and-stick joint** is a contemporary joint, used primarily on cabinet doors. One pass along the edge of the rail or stile with the sticking bit cuts a decorative profile and a groove for the door panel. The coping bit machines the ends of the rails, forming a stub tenon and a negative of the decorative profile. The rail end thus can nestle snug against the edge of the stile with its tenon locked in the panel groove.

## Using the Miter Sled

Generally speaking, a miter sled is used without the router table fence. The shoe riding along the table's edge guides the sled, and thus the cut. The sled's fence keeps the workpiece in position and provides that all-important backup so the cutter doesn't "emerge" from the workpiece so much as pass from it into the sled fence. It is when the cutter "emerges" that it blows out splinters.

You can make a general-purpose miter sled, and it can function as your table-saw miter gauge does. That is, it will hold the workpiece so you can make a cut squarely across the end. But it won't provide cut-specific backup unless you add an auxiliary facing.

But for certain operations, like making cope cuts, you really want a tailored sled. The only difference between a general-purpose sled and a job-specific sled is that the latter is used exclusively with a particular bit. Its working edge has been trimmed with that bit, so it is a zero-clearance edge.

Because my miter sled is used for cope work, it seems appropriate to talk you through the coping operation. You'll then see the sled's role and the specifics of using it. And I believe you'll be able to move from this particular application to the more general uses a miter sled has.

The cope-and-stick joint is a relatively new one, used primarily in cabinet doors. It is routed with a special bit set. The sticking cut, made on the edges of the frame members, forms a decorative profile—a bead or an ogee, for example—and at the same time plows the panel groove. The coping cut, made across the ends of the rails, forms a negative of the profile and a stub tenon that fits into the panel groove. When the parts are joined, you get a nice tight joint.

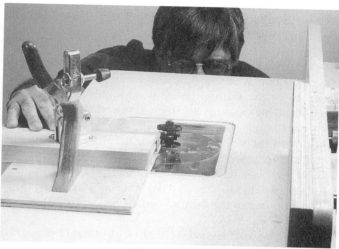

**Match the cope bit height** against a piece of the sticked stock to establish a rough setting. It is a quick and pretty reliable way to do it. Set the stock beside the bit, as shown, and adjust the bit to align with it. Check the setting with a test cut, but if you're careful, it should be right on.

You usually stick all the workpieces first. The sticking cut is made on the router table, with the work guided by the router table fence. Then you switch to the cope cutter, and get out your coping sled...

**1. Adjust the toggle clamp spindle.** The sled has a big toggle clamp. The clamp is important. Coping cutters have a tendency to pull the workpiece as the last corner clears the bearing. It's the same effect you experience when routing an edge with a hand-held router; as you get to the corner, you have to be very careful that you clear the corner without slipping around it. If you are using your fingers to hold the work on the sled, you may not be able to prevent this kind of self-feeding. The clamp *can*. So use it, and save yourself extra work.

Because stock thickness tends to vary slightly from job to job, you need to adjust the spindle to accommodate the thickness of the current run's stock. If you can move a piece of stock that's clamped in the sled, the spindle isn't set correctly; adjust it.

**2. Set the coping bit elevation.** The bit elevation is set in two stages. Right now, you need to establish a coarse setting so you can prepare the rest of the setup. Then you'll return to the elevation and fine-tune it using test cuts. For now, just adjust the bit by eye.

**3. Make a test cut.** Use the sled but not the fence. Lay the test workpiece in the sled without clamping it. Line up the end with the bearing on the bit, then snap the toggle clamp closed. Make the cut. Finally, with the router switched off, align the sled and the test piece with the bit and check to be sure the piece has been cut to the full depth.

Depending upon how good your eye is, you may get the position just right on the first try. But it is more likely that you'll need to sneak the test workpiece one way or the other to get the position set precisely.

**Positioning the workpiece in the sled** for the first cut helps you understand why you want to use the fence as a positioning stop. You must hunker down at tabletop level, and sight across the end of the test workpiece. Line up its end with the bearing on the bit.

**4. Set the router table fence as a stop.** To set it, set the sled with the test cut still clamped to it at one end of the tabletop. Bring the fence up to the scrap. The fence *must* be parallel with the front edge of the table or the setup won't be accurate. So slide the sled back and forth, lining up the fence with the end of the scrap. When it is aligned, lock it down.

The best arrangement is to use the Split Fence (see page 237 for plans) and to remove the outfeed section of the facing.

Hereafter, to position a workpiece in the sled, you merely have to slide it along the sled's fence until it butts against the fence. Flip the toggle to lock it down, and you're ready to cut.

**Cutting across end grain is perilous** because the cutter usually tears splinters out as it exits the stock. The sled's fence backs up the rail—preventing the tearout—when the rail's square edge is tucked against it, but that's only half the cuts. For the others, insert a coped piece of scrap into the stick cut before clamping the rail in the sled, as shown here. For the rail to be properly aligned in the sled, make sure the scrap is at least as long as the sled's fence.

**5. Refine your coarse bit-elevation setting.** Do this through test cuts. The cope cutter is designed to cut a profile that locks into the sticking cut. Fit your test cut to one of the stiles. Keep adjusting the bit height until the stile and rail surfaces are flush when assembled. (If the coped piece is proud of the sticked piece, lower the cutter. If the sticked piece is higher, raise the bit.)

**6. Prepare a coped backup strip.** The sled's fence serves to prevent the cutter from blowing out chips as it exits the good stock. But the sled fence has a square edge, so it can only do this when the flat edge of the rail is against it. For half your cope cuts, you'll have the sticked edge against the sled fence. For these latter cuts, make a coped-edge strip to serve as an auxiliary fence facing. The sticked edge of each rail will nest into the coped edge of the facing.

When the proper bit height is set, clamp a length of ½-inch plywood to the router table top along the fence. Then rout a cope *along the edge* of a strip of the working stock. This is the auxiliary sled fence facing.

**7. Trim the rails to finished length.** This has to be done before coping their ends. The width of the profile is what you must account for. For example, if you are making an 18-inch-wide door and using 1¾-inch-wide stiles, the distance between the stiles is 14½ inches. But the rails must be long enough to overlap the sticking profile. If it's ⅜ inch wide (which seems to be the standard), then you need to add ¾ inch to the length of the rails (⅜ inch for each stile, or twice the width of the profile). The easy way to measure the profile is to stick a rule into the groove and see how deep it is; the depth of the groove will match the width of the profile.

**8. Cope the workpieces.** With your setup tested and the rails trimmed to length, you should be ready to cut.

**A tenoning sled** makes fast work of router table tenon cutting. A large-diameter bottom-cleaning bit can cut a cheek and shoulder for the typical tenon in one pass. A stop on the sled's fence automatically positions the workpiece for the cut, so the shoulder will be square and perfectly aligned all the way around the rail.

As with the sticking cuts, the cope cuts should be completed in one pass. Repeating a pass *can* enlarge the cut and create a loose fit.

I cope one end of each workpiece. Then I bond the auxiliary facing to the sled with carpet tape and cope the other end.

# Tenoning Sled

A slightly different miter-style sled is one used for routing tenons. It's set apart from the cope-and-stick miter sled by two things—the fence that extends far beyond the base, and the separate workpiece stop. (Okay, it doesn't have any kind of handle either, but that's irrelevant.)

The purpose of the fence that extends over and beyond the bit is to back up the cut and to support a positioning stop. In this instance the cut's contour is as much horizontal as vertical, so you want that section of the fence over the bit.

I always use this sled with the same bit, a 1¼-inch mortising bit. The bit-side edge of the sled's base was cut by the bit, so the base edge indicates the edge of the cut. This is useful in lining up work for tenoning.

The stop clamps to the sled fence. You butt the workpiece against the stop and make a pass, which cuts the tenon cheek and shoulder. If the tenon is longer than 1¼ inches, then you make two passes, one with the work against the stop, one with it pulled back from the stop.

The toggle clamp is a style that closes when you push forward on the T-handle. Thus it can serve as a handgrip.

## Making the Tenoning Sled

This is another of those scrap-bin projects. There's more to the hardware than to the wood.

**1. Cut the sled and stop parts.** The dimensions of the parts are specified by the Cutting List. The width of the sled base must be determined by measuring from the table edge to the bit axis on your router table. To that measurement, add the thickness of the shoe.

In selecting and preparing the hardwood parts, be sure to joint and plane these pieces square and true, with parallel edges and faces. The particular wood you use isn't that significant. I used poplar.

**2. Assemble the base and shoe.** Glue and screw the base to the shoe first.

The second assembly step is to trim the base with the bit that will be used with the sled. Fit your tenon-cutting bit in the table's router. Adjust the elevation to the thickness of the base. With the shoe tight against the table's edge, make a pass with the sled, trimming the bit-side edge flush with the bit.

**3. Install the fence and clamp.** Position the fence perpendicular to the just-trimmed edge of the base, and screw it to the base and shoe. I drove two screws through the fence into the shoe, two through the base into the

## TENONING SLED PLANS

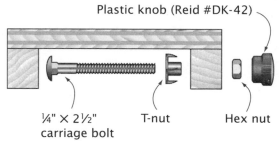

### STOP ASSEMBLY DETAIL

Plastic knob (Reid #DK-42)

¼" × 2½" carriage bolt

T-nut

Hex nut

Stop plate

Stop jaw

Toggle clamp

Bit cuts into fence.

Fence

Shoe

Base

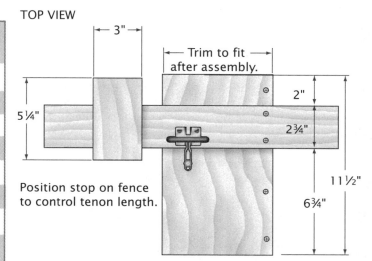

### TOP VIEW

3"

Trim to fit after assembly.

5¼"

2"

2¾"

11½"

6¾"

Position stop on fence to control tenon length.

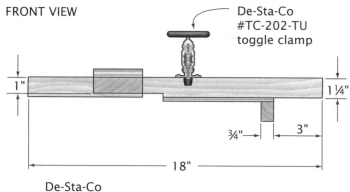

### FRONT VIEW

De-Sta-Co #TC-202-TU toggle clamp

1"

1¼"

¾"

3"

18"

De-Sta-Co #TC-215208 spindle (2⅛" overall length)

### TENONING SLED
### Cutting List

| Part | Qty. | Dimensions | Material |
|---|---|---|---|
| Base | 1 | ¼" × 9+"* × 11½" | Birch plywood |
| Shoe | 1 | ¾" × 1" × 11½" | Hardwood |
| Fence | 1 | 1¼" × 2¾" × 18" | Hardwood |
| Stop plate | 1 | ½" × 3" × 5¼" | Birch plywood |
| Stop jaws | 2 | ¾" × 1" × 3" | Hardwood |

### Hardware

12 drywall screws, #6 × 1"

1 toggle clamp, De-Sta-Co #TC-202-TU; from Reid Tool Supply Co. (800-253-0421)

1 spindle, De-Sta-Co #TC-215208; from Reid Tool Supply Co.

4 panhead screws, #8 × 1"

1 T-nut, ¼"

1 carriage bolt, ¼" × 2½"

1 hex nut, ¼"

1 plastic knob with ¼" threaded insert; #DK-42 from Reid Tool Supply Co.

*The base width must be adjusted, as explained in the text, to the distance between the tabletop edge and the bit on your router table. See text.*

fence. (Be sure these screws are placed where the bit can't contact them.) I didn't glue the fence, on the theory that I'd need to replace it from time to time. But the whole sled is so economical of materials and so quick to make that if it ever gets too chewed up, I can just replace the whole works.

Mount the toggle clamp on the fence. Position it so the spindle will contact the workpiece within ½ to ¾ inch of the tenon.

**4. Assemble the stop.** Drill a clearance hole through one stop jaw for the T-nut. Drive the T-nut into the hole. Turn the carriage bolt into the T-nut. Now glue and screw the stop plate to the two stop jaws. Finally, turn the hex nut and the plastic knob onto the bolt. Jam the two together to keep the knob from unthreading.

### Using the Tenoning Sled

With the sled and the right bit, tenoning is a snap on the router table. Here's how to do it, step by step.

**1. Set up the router table.** This is a matter of chucking the appropriate bit in the router and setting the coarse bit elevation. The bit can be a mortising bit, a large-diameter straight bit, or a bottom-cleaning bit. The mortising bit—which is designed for clearing hinge mortises, not mortises for tenons—and the bottom-cleaning bits are designed to clear a broad surface, leaving it clean and smooth. A straight bit is not as well suited design-wise but will be completely adequate.

The bit elevation should be measured from the top surface of the sled's base. Set the bit a skosh under, so you can measure test cuts and creep up on the just-right setting.

**2. Lay out a tenon on a test piece.** Use scraps of the working stock for the tests. The single layout line you need is one marking the tenon shoulder. Scribe it around the test piece.

If at all possible, use one of your mortises (rather than a ruler) to determine the correct tenon thickness.

**3. Set up the sled.** Lay the test piece in the sled, and align the shoulder line with the bit-side edge of the base.

Snap the toggle clamp closed, clamping the workpiece. (Adjust the spindle as necessary for the clamp to get a tight grip on the work.)

Now set the stop. Place it on the fence, butted against the end of the workpiece. Tighten its clamp.

**Work and roll is the routine** for cutting tenons on the router table. With the workpiece in the tenoning sled, its butt against the stop, make a pass, cutting the broad cheek. Pull the sled back, pop the toggle clamp, roll the workpiece onto its edge, hook the work with the clamp—you can't snap it closed when the work's on edge—and make another pass. Two more quarter-rolls and two more passes complete the tenon.

**4. Cut the test tenon.** Turn on the router and make a pass, cutting the first cheek and shoulder. Unbutton the clamp and roll the workpiece over. Make a pass, cutting the second cheek and shoulder.

Check the fit of this tenon in your mortise. Raise or lower the bit, as necessary, to refine the fit. Make another test cut and fit it to the mortise.

When you've got the settings right, cut the real work.

# Featherboards

**Held by mechanical clamps or vacuum, featherboards provide firm workpiece guidance on the router table—and prevent dangerous kickback.**

A featherboard, as you probably know, is a feed-control and safety device. It is simple to make, and very important to use.

In router table work, particularly when routing profiles on 3-foot and longer workpieces, I'll plant featherboards on the tabletop, one on each side of the bit, so they'll press the work against the fence. Then I'll clamp a couple more to the fence to press the work against the table. In addition to ensuring that the work doesn't drift or bow away from the bit, the featherboards prevent the work from kicking back. (In this regard, featherboards are terrifically useful on the table saw.)

What I want to do here is show you a couple variations on the featherboard and emphasize how easy they are to make and use. I also want to show you vacuum-clamped versions of the featherboard. If you have a vacuum system at your disposal, you'll discover that it is even easier to set the featherboards with vacuum than with mechanical clamps.

## Making a Basic Featherboard

Is there a typical featherboard? I doubt it. They have been made in all sizes and configurations. I've seen 2-inch-wide ones and 10-inch-wide ones. I've got a couple of 2-inch-thick ones. You can make yours 6 inches long or 18 inches long. Some are cut on the table saw, some on the band saw. There are even woodworkers who cut the "feathers" with a backsaw.

What usually happens is that you run into a situation where the featherboards you've got won't work. One's too big, another's too small. Or you don't have enough featherboards.

So you make more. It takes a trip to the scrap bin and 3 to 5 minutes at the saw. Bingo! You have another featherboard.

If you are just starting out, here's the scoop on cutting your very first one.

**1. Select a board to use.** As I've suggested, the width and length of a basic featherboard aren't all that important. The layout drawing shows a featherboard that's 4⅝ inches wide and 10 inches long, but that's arbitrary. (The feathers came out nice and even at that width when I "drew" the 'board on my computer. Would you agree that's arbitrary?) If you are making a featherboard for a particular immediate need, size it for the job.

As you sort through the scraps in your bin, look in par-

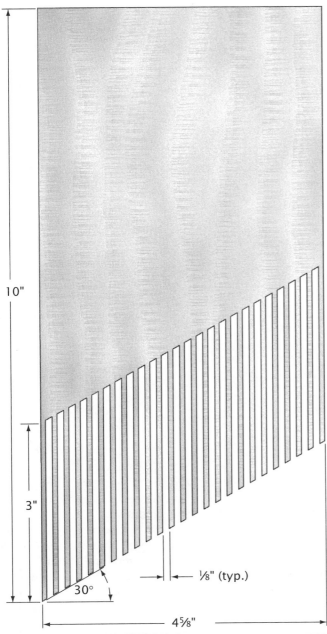

10"

3"

30°

⅛" (typ.)

4⅝"

## BASIC FEATHERBOARD CUTTING LIST

| Part | Qty. | Dimensions | Material |
|------|------|------------|----------|
| Featherboard | 1 | ¾" × 4⅝" × 10" | Hardwood |

ticular for a piece of oak or ash. These are naturally springy and work well for this use. But maple and cherry and poplar work, too. As a general rule, you ought to steer clear of the soft and the brittle woods.

**2. Miter the end.** The layout shows a 30-degree angle. That's fine. But you'll find, over time, that that angle is arbitrary, too. If you are making a job-specific featherboard, a very shallow (or very steep) angle may allow you

to position a featherboard in a very tight spot.

At any rate, make your first cut a miter. Scribe a line parallel to the mitered end but offset about 3 to 6 inches. This line marks the base of the feathers.

**3. Cut the feathers.** Some woodworkers swear by the band saw for this work, but I do it on the table saw. No layout—beyond the baseline—is necessary.

As you might expect, both the length and the thickness of the feathers affect the pliability of the 'board. Short feathers are stiffer than long feathers of the same thickness. Thick feathers, too, are stiffer than thin ones. If you have to make the 'board short so it will fit a confined spot, make the feathers thin.

Set the rip fence about ⅛ inch from the blade. Feed the blank into the blade, cutting as far as the baseline. Pull the work back. Move the fence ¼ inch away from the blade. Make a cut as far as the baseline, and pull the work back. I use a push stick to help me move the featherboard back off the blade.

Keep up this routine until you run out of featherboard width. If you move the fence ¼ inch after each cut, you should get a fully satisfactory set of feathers.

And that's all there is to it. Well, okay…you can modify the "body" of the 'board. Round it off, maybe radius the edges, drill a hole in it so you can hang it on a nail. You can even put some finish on it. But really, once the feathers are cut, it's ready to be put to work.

### Making a Featherboard with Thumbs

A featherboard that's very useful for the router woodworker is the "thumbed" style. It can be planted on a pretty narrow surface, like a router table fence, by applying clamps to the 1- to 2-inch-wide sections on one or both sides of the feathers. These clamping surfaces are what I call the thumbs.

As you can see from the layout drawing, the thumbs are ⅜ inch or so shorter than the feathers. While the particular version shown in the drawing, with its radiused corners, is a band-saw project, you can easily produce a workable model on the table saw. And if one thumb is all your application can accommodate, one thumb will be adequate.

## Using Featherboards

Setting a featherboard the first time can be a little frustrating.

The goal is to position the 'board so that its feathers move just a little as you feed the workpiece past it. Just a little flexing. There needs to be pressure, but not so much that you have to struggle to advance the workpiece. What you certainly don't want is a slip fit for the workpiece between the fence and the featherboard.

The slip fit, of course, is easy to achieve. It's the tight fit that you have to work for. I think it comes with practice.

Stand a workpiece against the fence. Slide the featherboard against it. Maneuver it to set the feathers squarely against the work—you don't want just the heel or the toe, you want the whole foot pressing against the work. Press it so the feathers flex just a little. Now clamp it. All you need

**Router Tables**

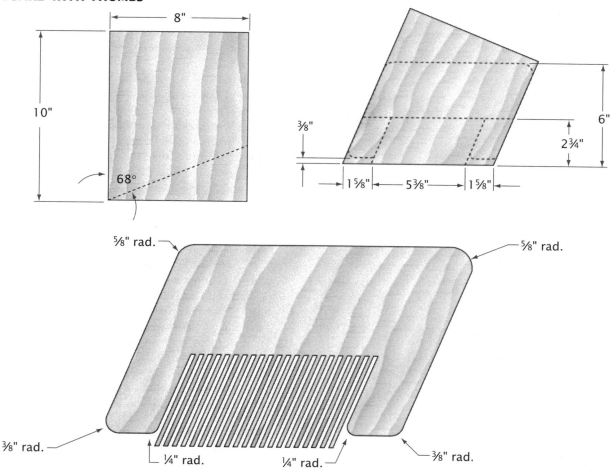

8"

10"

68°

3⁄8"

6"

2¾"

1⅝"  5⅜"  1⅝"

5⁄8" rad.

5⁄8" rad.

3⁄8" rad.

¼" rad.

¼" rad.

3⁄8" rad.

## FEATHERBOARD WITH THUMBS CUTTING LIST

| Part | Qty. | Dimensions | Material |
|------|------|------------|----------|
| Featherboard | 1 | ¾" × 8" × 10" | Hardwood |

**Sawing the feathers on the table saw** ensures that you get straight kerfs and feathers of a consistent thickness. Move the fence ¼ inch after each cut. A push stick can help you move the featherboard back from the blade.

is three hands, one to hold the 'board, two to apply the clamp. What usually happens, of course, is that you lose the tension 'til you get the clamps tightened.

Here are two tricks you can try. Set the featherboard against the work to establish its position. Lift the work from the table, and move the featherboard about 1⁄16 inch closer to the fence. Then clamp it. Now the channel is narrower than the workpiece, enough to put the work under pressure but not so much as to stall its passage.

The second trick is to set the featherboard just a bit cocked, and apply the first clamp. Then remove the workpiece and pivot the featherboard around that first clamp, properly aligning the tips of the feathers. Apply the second clamp.

Note that you need two clamps for each featherboard. With only a single clamping point, the featherboard will pivot and shift out of position. The clamping points can be virtually side by side, but as long as you have two, the 'board won't move. Be savvy in your choice of clamps, too. I've found that hand screws can vibrate loose unexpectedly. And the popular trigger-action quick-clamps, which you can apply with one hand, don't always hold securely either. The plastic pads on the jaws can slide on the work, and even work off their jaws. I use 'em, but not for clamping fences and featherboards to my router tables.

Where should featherboards be stationed?

Router Tables

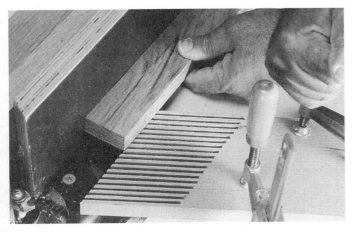

**Use a piece of the working stock** to help you position the featherboard. Hold it against the fence and align the featherboard so the workpiece just overlaps its tips, as shown. Secure the featherboard with two clamps.

**A three- or four-featherboard setup** is often required when routing moldings to ensure that the work doesn't bow or drift away from the cutter. This array features a "thumbed" featherboard clamped to the fence, and a couple of basic featherboards clamped to the tabletop.

**A tandem featherboard** cuts down on the number of clamps required. It speeds up setup, too, because if one featherboard is positioned properly, the second also will be.

In general they should be fore and aft of the bit, though the specifics of the operation have to be taken into account. I'm not comfortable with the idea of applying the featherboard's pressure directly at the bit. Pressing the work to the fence or the tabletop (or both) is what you want to do. Often, a featherboard or two clamped to the router table top and pressing the work against the fence suffices. Other times you want the featherboards clamped to the fence, pressing the work down onto the table. And when milling long moldings, you may have to festoon both tabletop and fence with featherboards.

All these featherboards require a cartload of clamps. You spend a lot time setting and removing the clamps, too. Following are some timesaving approaches.

## A Tandem Featherboard

A single clamp won't do on a featherboard; you need two to keep the device from pivoting out of position. Moreover, a single featherboard often won't do either; you need two to keep the work in line.

The tandem featherboard saves clamps and clamping time. It's so simple and obvious that you'll kick yourself for never having thought of it. (Well, at least I did when I saw one for the first time.) To make one, you simply screw a cleat to two featherboards, linking them together (see the drawing *Tandem Featherboards*).

One clamp applied to each 'board in the tandem will suffice. Set a tandem on the tabletop, with one featherboard on each side of the bit.

## Vacuum Featherboards

Vacuum simplifies setup dramatically. You don't need any mechanical clamps at all. Hold the featherboard in position firmly with one hand, and turn a valve with the other. The vacuum will instantly suck the featherboard to the tabletop or fence.

How easy is that?

You do need vacuum-clamping equipment. Review the chapter "Vacuum Clamping" on page 50 for the details on vacuum pumps, fittings and hoses, vacuum tape, and other supplies. You won't take the vacuum-clamping plunge in order to set featherboards; but if you've got the equipment, or you're planning on investing in a vacuum setup in the future, this is one of the applications.

You can probably convert the featherboards you already have, so long as the stock used is nonporous and the bodies are large enough to provide the minimum-sized vacuum chamber (10 square inches). All you have to do is drill a vacuum port, seal the featherboard, and install a fitting, then apply the vacuum tape.

If you want to start from scratch, here's that "basic" design, modified to work with vacuum.

**1. Lay out and cut the featherboard.** Use a stout, nonporous hardwood like maple or cherry. (Earlier I recommended oak and ash for featherboards, but they are

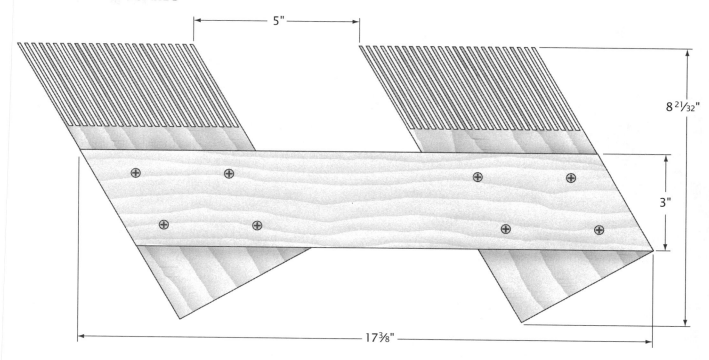

5"

8 21/32"

3"

17 3/8"

Router Tables

| TANDEM FEATHERBOARDS Cutting List | | | |
|---|---|---|---|
| Part | Qty. | Dimensions | Material |
| Featherboards | 2 | ¾" × 4⅝" × 10" | Hardwood |
| Cleat | 1 | ¾" × 3" × 18" | Hardwood |
| **Hardware** | | | |

8 drywall screws, #6 × 1¼"

problematic with vacuum because of their porosity.) Select a board that's free of defects. Miter one end of the board at about 30 degrees. Lay out the base of the cuts that form the feathers.

You can cut the feathers on the table saw or on the band saw.

**2. Drill the vacuum port and seal the board.** Once all the feathers have been cut, drill the vacuum port. The hole is a pilot for your vacuum fitting, so size the hole appropriately. The layout shows a through port, but you can, of course, use a T-port if you prefer.

Apply a couple of coats of a film finish to the board's body to seal it against porosity. Seal the bore of the vacuum port as well.

**3. Install the vacuum fitting(s).** Several options are available here. An easy approach is to seal a male quick-disconnect into the port with silicone caulk. If you think you'll be using multiboard setups, you may want to cut down on the number of female quick-disconnect fittings

needed. If so, opt to use a brass or nylon barbed hose connector. (You can just slip the vacuum hose over the barb; no other connector is needed.)

I was concerned by the idea of having the fitting jutting up out of the featherboard, so in the layout drawing, I show the use of an elbow fitting.

To install a threaded fitting into a solid wooden featherboard, just file a notch across the fitting's first few threads. It will act like a self-tapping screw, cutting its own threads in the wood. If you drilled the correct size pilot, you should get a sufficiently tight seal. If you do end up with a vacuum leak, back the fitting out and apply a bead of silicone caulk to the threads before redriving the fitting.

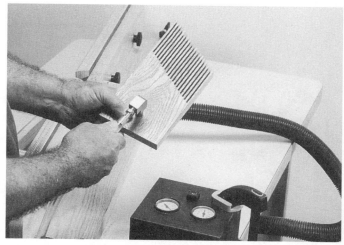

**A vacuum featherboard's advantage** is the ease with which it can be applied to the tabletop or fence. Hold it in place with one hand and pull the vacuum with the other.

## VACUUM FEATHERBOARD LAYOUT

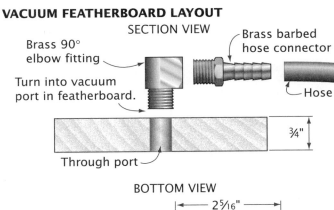

**SECTION VIEW**

Brass 90°
elbow fitting

Turn into vacuum
port in featherboard.

Brass barbed
hose connector

Hose

Through port

¾"

**BOTTOM VIEW**

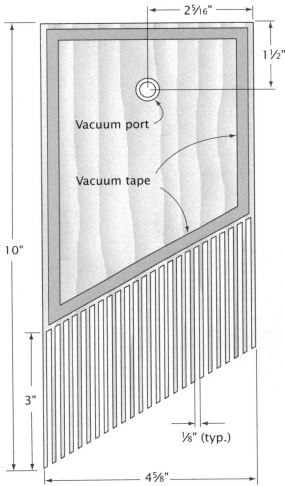

2⁵⁄₁₆"

1½"

Vacuum port

Vacuum tape

10"

3"

⅛" (typ.)

4⅝"

| VACUUM FEATHERBOARD Cutting List | | | |
|---|---|---|---|
| **Part** | **Qty.** | **Dimensions** | **Material** |
| Featherboard | 1 | ¾" × 4⅝" × 10" | Low-porosity hardwood |

### Hardware

Vacuum tape, ⅛" × ¼", approx. 24"

Brass 90° elbow, male/female

Brass barbed hose connector, male

**4. Apply the vacuum tape.** Make the vacuum chamber just as large as you can. Remember that the bigger the vacuum chamber area, the greater the clamping force you will have. I used a continuous band of tape around the featherboard.

## A *Vacuum* Tandem Featherboard

The tandem is a device for ganging two featherboards on a clamping plate. That way, you can set infeed and outfeed featherboards simultaneously. I wanted to use "standard" featherboards but fit them on a fence or along the front of the various router tables made for this book. This compromise works.

**1. Cut the featherboards and plates.** The featherboards are the vacuum featherboards described immediately above. Follow steps 1 and 2 on pages 259–260 to make two featherboards for each tandem.

The base ply of my prototypes is phenolic, which is a strong, nonporous material that's ideal for vacuum-clamping plates. The top plate is a strip of plywood. I used Baltic Birch for this, but you don't have to. Cut these parts to the dimensions specified by the Cutting List.

**2. Cut half-laps in the featherboards and top plate.** To joint the four components (two plates and two featherboards), I opted to cut half-laps in the featherboards and the top plate. The base fits into the laps in the featherboards, while the featherboards are locked into the laps in the top plate. The assembly is glued together with epoxy.

All the lap cuts are the same depth. To establish the correct widths and the correct positions, it is best to lay them out using the workpieces. Do the laps on the router table, using the Miter Sled (page 249) to guide the workpieces.

Do the featherboards first. Use the base to set the depth of cut. Then use it to lay out the laps. Cut them.

Do the top plate next. Check the depth of cut against the lapped featherboards, and adjust the bit extension if necessary. Lay out the laps on the plate under the featherboards, then cut them.

**3. Drill the vacuum port.** A nice thing about phenolic (and other plastics) is that you can actually cut threads in it with a tap. The plan here is to bore and thread a hole (the vacuum port) in the base for a nipple that extends up through the top plate. To accommodate the nipple, the top plate needs a clearance hole that's fractionally bigger than the outside diameter of the nipple.

Lay out and drill the vacuum port in the base. Then, using the appropriate tap—the one that's got the same thread as your fitting—cut threads. With phenolic, you don't need a tap lube, though you do with other plastics. (See the section "Cutting Threads" in the appendix.)

Bore the clearance hole. Make sure it aligns with the vacuum port.

**4. Assemble the tandem.** Epoxy holds it all together. Mix a batch of the glue, apply it, and assemble the parts.

# VACUUM TANDEM FEATHERBOARDS PLAN

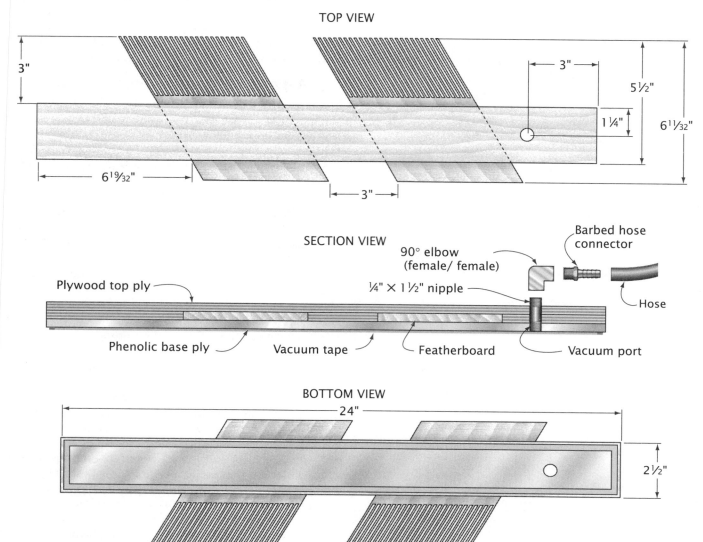

TOP VIEW

3"

3"

5½"

1¼"

6¹¹⁄₃₂"

6¹⁹⁄₃₂"

3"

SECTION VIEW

Barbed hose connector

90° elbow (female/ female)

Plywood top ply

¼" × 1½" nipple

Hose

Phenolic base ply

Vacuum tape

Featherboard

Vacuum port

BOTTOM VIEW

24"

2½"

## VACUUM TANDEM FEATHERBOARDS Cutting List

| Part | Qty. | Dimensions | Material |
|------|------|------------|----------|
| Featherboards | 2 | ¾" × 4⅝" × 10" | Nonporous hardwood |
| Base ply | 1 | ⅜" × 2½" × 24" | Plastic* |
| Top ply | 1 | ¾" × 2½" × 24" | Plywood |

### Hardware

Vacuum tape, ⅛" × ¼", approx. 54"

Brass nipple, male/male, 1½" long

Brass 90° elbow, female/female

Brass barbed hose connector, male

*Acrylic, polycarbonate, and phenolic are all suitable.

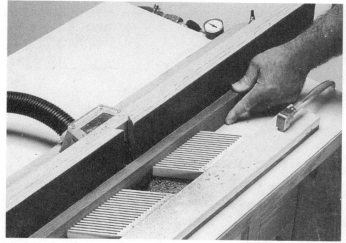

**The tandem vacuum featherboard** is designed to fit the narrow space between the table's edge and the router bit. Position it so the bit is between the featherboards, as shown.

Router Tables

**5. Install the vacuum fittings.** Turn the connector into the elbow and tighten it. Turn the elbow onto the nipple, and again tighten the parts together. Finally, turn the nipple into the vacuum port.

**6. Apply the vacuum tape.** Make the vacuum chamber just as large as you can, but confine it to the base ply (don't incorporate any of the featherboard bodies). I used a continuous band of tape around the ply, keeping it as close to the ply's edges as possible.

## Using a Vacuum Featherboard

Few setups in woodworking are easier than planting a vacuum featherboard, as I said. You position these 'boards in the same places, you just don't have to grapple with mechanical clamps. But in router woodworking, you usually use two to four featherboards at a time, so what you are really doing is trading the mechanical clamps for hoses and valves or pinch clamps.

Setting four vacuum featherboards requires three T-fittings and three pinch clamps, as well as the vacuum pump. Consult the drawing *Plumbing a Multiboard Setup.* The setting sequence is as follows:

1. Plumb the four featherboards, as shown in the drawing. Close all three pinch clamps tight.
2. Plant the tabletop infeed clamp first. It has no pinch clamp, you'll note. Set the position, then turn on the vacuum.
3. Set the tabletop outfeed featherboard next. Slide it into position, then open the pinch clamp. The featherboard will be sucked to the tabletop.
4. Set the two fence featherboards in the same manner. One by one, establish the position, then suck it to the fence by opening the pinch clamp.

Repositioning a featherboard is as simple as closing the pinch clamp to free the device. Then you can move it to a new spot and set it by opening the pinch clamp. (Repositioning that tabletop infeed featherboard, of course, would require releasing all four featherboards, *unless* you put a pinch clamp on its hose, too.)

Using the vacuum tandem featherboard simplifies the plumbing substantially, since you only need two lines. Set one tandem on the router table, positioning it so the bit is between the featherboards. Then set a tandem on the tall fence, again positioning it so the bit is between the featherboards.

## PLUMBING A MULTIBOARD SETUP

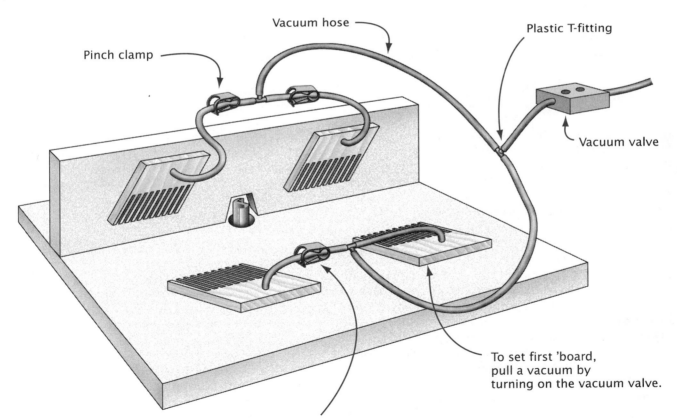

Pinch clamp

Vacuum hose

Plastic T-fitting

Vacuum valve

To set first 'board, pull a vacuum by turning on the vacuum valve.

To set the other 3 'boards, pull vacuum to them by opening the individual pinch clamps.

# Surfacing Baseplate

**Fit a router with a long, wide baseplate, and it becomes a planer, a hollowing machine, even a circle cutter.**

The name "surfacing baseplate" is something of a misnomer. This custom baseplate is really a multi-purpose, oversized fixture.

Yes, the primary use is for surfacing stock. But it has other uses as well. Any job in which the router must be suspended above the work—hollowing a broad recess, for example—is one for which this baseplate is suited. You can block it up and clamp it to a workbench, and it becomes a kind of overhead router fixture. Because the baseplate has so much surface area to either side of the router, it's also a kind of offset baseplate. Reposition the router off-center, and it really becomes an offset baseplate. If you are willing to drill a few extra holes in it, it can be a trammel.

Quite simply, here's what the surfacing baseplate is: a wide, flat platform fitted with two handle grips. Having once used a plywood fixture like this, I chose to make the one shown using clear acrylic. Especially with the stiffeners, it is suitably rigid, yet you can see through it and monitor your work.

Since I made it, I've used it for only a few projects, but in each case I was mighty glad I had the baseplate on hand. For a couple of those projects, nothing else would do. One example: I needed to flatten a warped plank that was too wide for my jointer. It was the kind of job the plate was

designed for. Worked like a charm, and the setup was simple and fast. Then there were the uses it got because, well, it was what I *had* that would work. Instead of cobbling up a trammel especially to rout a 17- to 18-inch-radius arc, for example, I just drilled a pivot hole in the far corner of this baseplate and used *it* as the trammel.

## Making the Baseplate

The baseplate doesn't take long to make. I spent about two hours on it. The stiffeners were made from cherry rippings selected from my too-big-to-toss scrap collection. The acrylic and the handles were purchased especially for this project.

**1. Cut the parts to size.** The surfacing baseplate has only three parts to make—the plate itself, plus two stiffeners.

I made my surfacing baseplate using ⅜-inch clear acrylic. The plate need not be acrylic. It need not be clear. Use phenolic. Use ¼-inch or ⅜-inch or ½-inch plywood, medium-density fiberboard (MDF), particleboard, or hardboard. The stiffeners will cancel the tendency of the thinner materials to sag.

# SURFACING BASEPLATE LAYOUTS

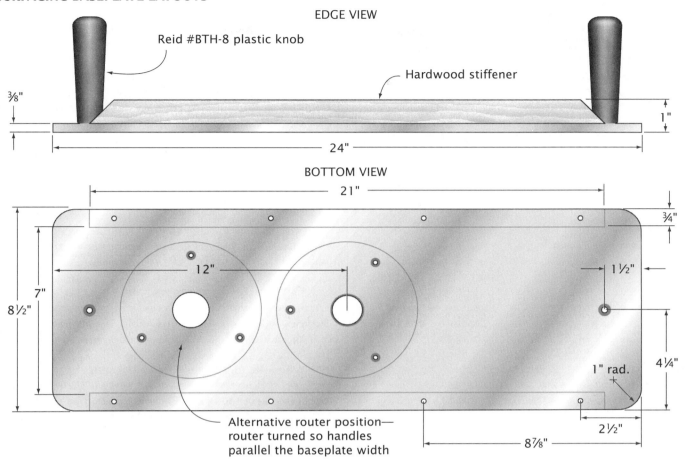

EDGE VIEW

Reid #BTH-8 plastic knob

Hardwood stiffener

3⁄8"

1"

24"

BOTTOM VIEW

21"

3⁄4"

12"

7"

8½"

1½"

1" rad.

4¼"

2½"

8⅞"

Alternative router position—
router turned so handles
parallel the baseplate width

| Cutting List | | | |
|---|---|---|---|
| **Part** | **Qty.** | **Dimensions** | **Material** |
| Plate | 1 | 3⁄8" × 8½" × 24" | Clear acrylic |
| Stiffeners | 2 | 3⁄4" × 1" × 21" | Hardwood |

## Hardware

2 tapered plastic knobs, 4¼" tall, with 3⁄8"-16 threaded insert; #BTH-8 from Reid Tool Supply Co. (800-253-0421)

2 flathead stove bolts, 3⁄8"-16 × 1"

8 flathead wood screws, #6 × 1"

The stiffeners can be any of these materials, but I used cherry.

Once you've selected your materials, cut the parts to the sizes specified by the Cutting List.

**2. Drill the baseplate holes.** At this point, lay out and drill the holes for the stiffener-mounting screws and the knob-mounting bolts. In the next step you'll deal with the router-mounting screws and the bit opening.

On the masking paper protecting the acrylic, lay out the locations and size of the screw holes. The eight holes for

the stiffener-mounting screws are 5⁄32 inch in diameter. The two holes for the knob's bolts are 3⁄8 inch in diameter. On the drill press, drill these holes.

You can use standard woodworking twist or brad-point drill bits for this. Use a slow, even feed rate, backing out of the hole frequently to reduce heat buildup. To prevent chipping as the bit breaks through the plastic, slow the feed rate even more as you reach bottom. And use a good backup board.

Next, chuck a countersink in the drill press (a metal-worker's single-flute countersink produces the best results in plastic, by the way). Countersink all the holes. For the most consistent results, use the drill press's depth stop. Use one setting for the bolt holes, a shallower setting for the screw holes.

**3. Locate and drill the router-mounting screw holes.** The usual approach is to attach the baseplate to the workpiece with carpet tape, then to drill the mounting-screw holes guided by the baseplate. Pertinent tips and alternatives can be found in "The Generic Baseplate" on page 63.

Select the drill bit you will use *before* you stick down the baseplate. Attach the baseplate to the top surface of the fixture, between the stiffeners. Be sure the plate is backed up well when you drill the holes. After the holes are drilled, switch to a countersink, turn the plate over, and counter-sink the holes. (I set up my baseplate right off the bat with

# Accommodating Template Guides

A wide spectrum of template work can be done with a stock router, just as it comes from the factory. And then one day, you need some magic. The template required for a particular project has an opening that's broader across than your router's baseplate. So when it's over the middle of the template, the router won't have any support.

You take down your surfacing baseplate, and you're ready to mount the router to it, when you realize...it's not configured to accept a template guide.

Oh, but it can be! The model shown in the photo has a bit opening for Porter-Cable-type template guides. This means it has a 1¼-inch-diameter hole, surrounded by a ⅟₁₆-inch-wide × ³⁄₃₂-inch-deep rabbet. It also means the opening must be carefully positioned so that it is concentric with the bit axis.

If you want to keep your options open, make your surfacing baseplate with a proper bit opening. Read the detailed directions for doing this, which are found in the chapter "Universal Router Mounting Plate" on page 163. Choose your approach, and apply it to the fabrication of this baseplate. Someday, you'll be glad you did.

two positions for the router. One is the central location, and here I lined up the router handles with the baseplate grips. The other location is offset, and at this location, I turned the router 90 degrees.)

Next, attach the router to the plate. You can either plunge-bore a bit opening with the router itself or use a V-grooving bit chucked in the collet to mark the bit opening centerpoint. If you take the latter approach, unmount the router before drilling the bit opening on the drill press.

**4. Polish the plate's edges.** This is a purely aesthetic step; you can leave the edges of the plate sharp-cornered and rough. But the fixture will look a lot better if you invest an extra ten minutes to buff its appearance.

Start at the corners. Round the four corners using a router and a flush-trimming or straight pattern bit, guided by a corner-rounding template. (See "Boring Templates" on page 6.) Round the corners at a 1-inch radius.

Next, work on the edges. Begin with a cabinet scraper, going over the edges of the acrylic to remove the saw marks. After the worst of the saw makrs have been removed, flame-polish the edges.

Flame-polishing is a technique that takes good advantage of the heat-sensitivity of acrylic plastic. Fire up a propane torch, and pass the flame slowly over the edges of the plate. The goal is to glaze the edges, and I think you'll find it takes quite a few very slow passes with the torch to melt the surface enough that the minute scratches blend together. When you get the technique down, though, you will find the edges take a right nice polish.

**5. Install the stiffeners.** Miter the ends of the stiffeners, as shown in the layouts. You can round-over the exposed edges on the router table, if you like. I used a ¼-inch radius bit. Sand the stiffeners and, if you are so inclined, apply a coat or two of finish.

When the finish is dry, attach the stiffeners to the plate with #6 × 1-inch flathead wood screws. Clamp the stiffeners in place, and drill pilot holes, guided by the holes in the plate. Then drive the screws. Make sure they are seated below the plate's surface.

**6. Assemble the baseplate.** All that remains to be done is to install the knobs (or handles). I used 4½-inch-tall post-type handles, though, of course, many other options are available. To mount the handles, I turned flathead stove bolts through the plate into the brass threaded inserts integrated into them.

With the handles installed and the router mounted on the plate, you are ready to install a bit and take the plate for a ride.

## Using the Surfacing Baseplate

To plane stock with a router, what you need, in addition to the surfacing baseplate, is a sturdy router, a large-diameter bottom-cleaning or dish-cutting bit, and tracks that will position the router and baseplate above the stock, allowing the machine to move side to side and back and forth in a level plane. In a nutshell, the procedure is to clamp the board to be planed between two tracks. Set the router on the tracks, with the bit set to remove about ⅟₁₆ inch of stock. Slide the router and baseplate up and down the tracks, methodically planing every square inch of the board.

The router can surface stock in ways that a planer or jointer cannot. It can excavate a recess. It can taper. You can use the surfacing baseplate for both of these operations.

First, let's look at a straightforward surfacing job, step by step.

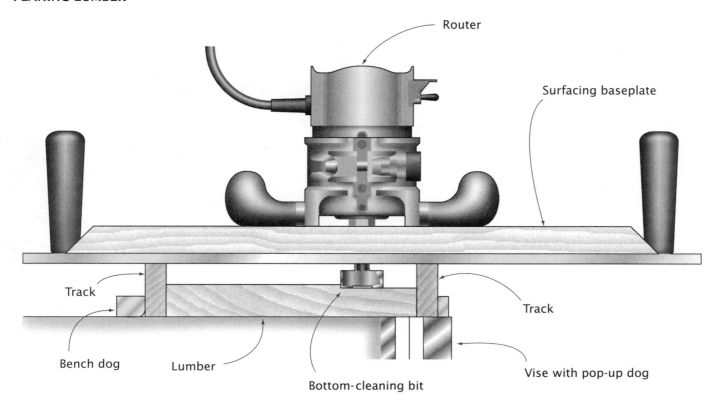

Router

Surfacing baseplate

Track

Track

Bench dog

Lumber

Vise with pop-up dog

Bottom-cleaning bit

**1. Take stock of the material to be surfaced.** Generally speaking, the router is not the proper tool for planing lumber. You can't beat the traditional jointer–planer–table saw ensemble to dress rough-sawn boards, making the faces smooth, flat, and parallel, the edges smooth, square, and parallel. But every once in a while you'll confront a special project where router-thicknessing is appropriate. Maybe it'll be centered around a curly maple board—beautiful but difficult to surface without tear-out. Perhaps it's a warped plank. If it's warped enough, it can be the devil to joint flat so you can feed it through the planer.

So the first chore is to study the material and confirm that it is, indeed, an appropriate router-surfacing project. Then figure out how to work it. How tall must the tracks be? How will you secure the stock and the tracks?

**2. Cut tracks to support the surfacing baseplate.** The real key to getting flat stock with parallel faces with the surfacing baseplate is accuracy in the tracks. Each track must be straight with parallel edges, and the two must be of identical height. The tracks must be about 4 to 6 inches longer than the workpiece so the bit can move off the edge of the work without the surfacing baseplate tumbling off the tracks.

**3. Secure the workpiece and the tracks.** The most troublesome stock to position for machining is warped stuff. What you need to do is set the warped stock on your workbench, and shim the corners as necessary so it doesn't rock (like shimming cabinets to level them during

installation). Try to set the board so you can get a flat surface with minimal stock removal. When the board is set, plant the tracks on each side of the board. This can be the problematic part of the job.

**Capture the workpiece between tracks,** as shown here. The spacers between the stock and the tracks allow you to surface all the way to the edges without chewing completely through the tracks.

**4. Set up the router.** You can use any of the following bits for surfacing: bottom-cleaning, straight, mortising, dish-cutting. The best bit to use is the one you already have, though clearly a 1¼-inch-diameter bottom-cleaning bit will do the job quicker than a ½-inch-diameter mortising bit.

The bit I like best for surfacing is designed chiefly for hollowing out compartments in a tray. It's called a dish cutter. What makes it ideal for surfacing? The cutting edges are radiused at the perimeter of the bit. This gives you a nice radius inside a recess, but it also means you don't have a hard edge between adjacent passes.

At any rate, you need to chuck whatever bit you are going to use in the router. Set the router on the tracks, and sight between the baseplate and the workpiece to set the bit extension. Don't make too deep a cut (i.e., more than ⅛ inch).

**Be methodical.** Sliding the surfacing baseplate–equipped router around willy-nilly *will* get the job done...eventually. But you'll get a smooth, flat surface more quickly if you start at one end of the board and move the router from side to side, methodically creeping forward a fraction of an inch after each pass.

After a first pass over the entire surface, make as many additional passes as necessary to flatten the board. Naturally, you need to adjust the depth of cut between passes. Then make a final skim cut to make the surface as smooth as you can get it with the router. Scraping and sanding will then remove any remaining swirl marks.

## Beyond Thicknessing

It's a small step from thicknessing a board to routing a recess in it.

If you are comfortable freehanding it, you can outline the area to be recessed. You don't need to set up tracks. The surfacing baseplate rests directly on the workpiece, with the bit projecting the most mimimal amount beneath it. To start, tip the router so the bit is poised above the middle of the area to be worked. Turn the router on, and lower the bit into the work. No plunge router needed, really. Because the baseplate is clear, you can see how close to the cutting lines you are.

This sort of work generates an incredible amount of chips. If you have a router that can be fitted with a dust pickup, by all means use it. It will keep the dust down and will make it easier to see your work.

If you are not comfortable working freehand, make a template. Attach it to the work. Then, with a guide bushing mounted in the surfacing baseplate, do the job as a template-guided one.

**Bits suitable for surfacing** include (*left to right*) a mortising bit (intended for routing hinge mortises), a dish-cutting bit, a bottom-cleaning bit, and a common straight bit.

**5. Surface the workpiece.** The conventional wisdom seems to be that you must make your sweeps in the direction that the grain runs. That isn't the case. Unlike a planer or jointer, the router bit's cutting action is the same, regardless of the direction from which it addresses the wood grain. It is just this cutting action that enables the router to plane curly maple and other twisted-grain woods. So sweeping back and forth across the board doesn't yield a lesser finish than coursing from end to end.

Be methodical, however. Whether you work back and forth or end-to-end, be an automaton. Sweep on one axis, then click over a notch in the other. Sweep, then click over. Sweep, then click over.

# Router Lathe

**Create elaborate patterned turnings—including spiral cuts—in table legs, bedposts, stair spindles, or columns!**

*Memo to marketing:*

Hey, Bob. Here's a suggestion for the Router Magic promotion piece.

Instead of showing the router lathe itself in the piece, *show what it produces!* Show some turnings (including spiral turnings). Then say, "ALL THESE THINGS WERE CUT WITH A ROUTER!!!! Hard to believe? *Router Magic* shows you how to do it."

Bob, I'm telling you. These turnings will really grab attention. An experienced woodworker knows you either cut spiral turnings on a device like this or you carve them by hand. Those eighteenth-century guys would invest hours and hours in carving a set of spiral turnings for something like a high-style tall clock. With this machine (what else can I call it but a machine?), a woodworker—even a hobby woodworker, for cat's sake—can knock out the same spiral turnings in a couple hours. It really is incredible when you think about it in those terms.

But even if you don't know how they are produced, the spirals just knock your socks off. So a woodworker who longs for the know-how to make attention-grabbing furniture will glom onto this machine.

Okay, okay. Yeah, yeah, yeah. You can go out and buy something like this. But if you want to buy one of these devices, Bob, you have two choices—an incredibly expensive industrial machine (expensive like two grand *plus* the router and bits) or a cheap-o-shoddy one (I mean cheap like three hundred bucks; you know, *that* cheap). And no one, I mean *NO ONE*, has published plans for such a device.

Should I point out that this is remarkably well conceived gizmo? Fred Matlack, who runs the design shop, cooked it up. He used one of those cheap-o-shoddy machines about four or five years ago when the shop guys were making a stunning tall clock for an *American Woodworker* article. That machine had only one ratio of linear travel per revolution, which was tight, too tight for attractive legs. The thing was short, too: too short for bedposts or any turning longer than a table leg. On top of that, it used cables to move the router, and they tended to stretch. (You get what you pay for, you know?)

So when I started this book project, I asked Fred if he could make a better one, one that a reasonably skilled woodworker could make. And here it is.

The bed is made of plywood. The mechanicals include some off-the-shelf bearings and gears. No real expensive stuff. Instead of cable, he used BICYCLE CHAIN. It's easy to find, cheap (you can use old chain—doesn't have to be new), real strong, and it won't stretch. This is brilliant! To

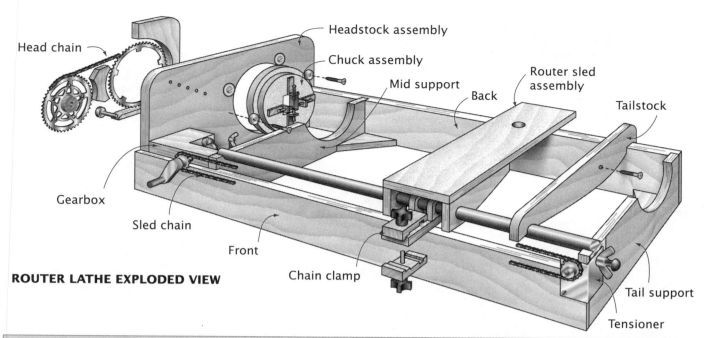

**ROUTER LATHE EXPLODED VIEW**

Head chain · Headstock assembly · Chuck assembly · Mid support · Back · Router sled assembly · Tailstock · Gearbox · Sled chain · Front · Chain clamp · Tail support · Tensioner

| Cutting List | | | |
|---|---|---|---|
| **Part** | **Qty.** | **Dimensions** | **Material** |
| Back | 1 | ¾" × 5½" × 43¾" | Birch plywood |
| Front | 1 | ¾" × 3¼" × 43" | Birch plywood |
| Mid/Tail supports | 2 | ¾" × 5" × 17⅜" | Birch plywood |
| Headstock end | 1 | ¾" × 12" × 17⅜" | Birch plywood |
| Retainer plate stock | 1 | ¾" × 12" × 12" | Birch plywood |
| Triangular gussets | 3 | ¾" × 3¾" × 3¾" | Birch plywood |
| Bearing sleeves | 7 | ⅝" dia. × ½" | Hardwood dowel |
| Gearbox case halves | 2 | ¾" × 3⅞" × 6" | Birch plywood |
| Gearbox support blocks | 2 | ¾" × 2½" × 4" | Birch plywood |
| Chip shield | 1 | ⅛" × 3½" × 3½" | Acrylic |
| Chip shield riser | 1 | ¼" × ¾" × 3½" | Hardwood |
| Chip shield riser | 1 | ¼" × ¾" × 2¾" | Hardwood |
| Large chuck disk | 1 | ¾" × 11" × 11" | MDF |
| Small chuck disk | 1 | ¾" × 9" × 9" | MDF |
| Transverse sprocket hub blank | 1 | 1" × 5" × 12" | Hardwood* |
| Drive sprocket hub blank | 1 | ¾" × 5" × 12" | Hardwood† |
| Crank plate | 1 | ¾" × 1⅝" × 4¼" | Birch plywood |
| Sled base | 1 | ¾" × 7" × 17¼" | Birch plywood |
| Sled bushing blocks | 2 | ¾" × 2½" × 8" | Birch plywood |
| Clamp bushing blocks | 2 | ¾" × 1¾" × 8" | Birch plywood‡ |
| Chain clamp base | 1 | ¾" × 3½" × 2½" | Birch plywood |
| Chain clamp jaws | 2 | ¾" × 2" × 1⅞" | Hardwood |
| Tailstock | 1 | ¾" × 3" × 18⅜" | Birch plywood |

use the chain, you've got to use bicycle sprockets. Bicycles have what . . . 10, 12, 18 speeds these days. So for all those speeds, bicycles need lots of different sizes of sprockets. And *that* means the router lathe you build to Fred's specs can have one heck of a lot of spiral ratios.

Okay, so basically, here's how it works. It's really pretty simple. You center your turning blank in the chuck. The router is screwed to a sled that can slide from one end of the lathe to the other. The bit sticks through the sled and touches the turning blank. You turn the crank on the front of the lathe, and two things happen simultaneously. The stock begins to rotate, Thing One. And, Thing Two, the router begins to travel down the length of the stock. The combination of the blank's rotation and the cutter's linear travel produces a spiraling cut.

This doesn't mean Thing One and Thing Two always have to happen simultaneously. The lathe has two separate bicycle-chain loops driven by the same crank. You can turn the crank to rotate the spindle without having the router move. And by hand, you can move the router without having the stock rotate. Through various combinations of these actions, you can round off a square blank, rout beads

## Hardware

#6 × 1¼" drywall screws (frame assembly, etc.)

1 steel plate, ¹⁄₁₆" × 2" × 2"

2 roundhead wood screws, #4 × ½"

7 ball bearings, ⅝" bore × 1⅜" O.D. × ½" long

7 hex-head bolts with nuts, ¼"-20 × 2"

21 flat washers, ¼" I.D.

2 wing nuts, ¼"-20

1 bevel gear, 24-tooth, Boston #L148Y-G

1 bevel gear, 12-tooth, Boston #L148Y-P

1 steel rod, ½" dia. × 6½"

1 steel rod, ⅜" dia. × 3¾"

1 bronze bushing, ½" I.D.(⅝" O.D.) × 3¼"

1 bronze bushing, ⅜" I.D.(½" O.D.) × 1½"

#6 × 1⅝" drywall screws (for mounting gearbox)

1 bicycle chainwheel
(or chainring), 52-tooth (chuck sprocket)

5 panhead screws, #8 × 1"
(for mounting chuck sprocket)

10 flat washers, ³⁄₁₆" I.D.

8 pcs. steel angle, 2½"× 2½" × ¼" × ¾" (chuck clamps)

8 roundhead stove bolts, ¼"-20 × 2" (clamp screws)

16 panhead screws, #8 × 1¼"
(chuck clamp mounting screws)

3 fender washers, ³⁄₁₆" I.D. (chuck retainers)

3 panhead screws, #6 × ¾" (for fender washers)

1 brass threaded insert, ¼"-20

1 roundhead stove bolt, ¼"-20 × 2"

1 bicycle chainwheel (or freewheel), 46-tooth
(transverse sprocket)

1 bicycle chainwheel (or freewheel), 32-tooth

4 roundhead screws, #4 × ½"

1 loop of bicycle chain, approx. 44 inches in circumference (head chain)

1 brass threaded insert, ¼"-20

1 roundhead stove bolt, ¼"-20 × 1½"

1 plastic knob with ¼"-20 blind insert;
#ROA-4 from Reid Tool Supply (800-253-0421)

1 roundhead stove bolt, ¼"-20 × 1¼"

2 bicycle freewheel sprockets, 13-tooth

1 pc. steel angle, 1½" × 1½" × ⅛" × 2¾"
(drive chain tensioner body)

2 roundhead stove bolts with nuts, ¼"-20 × 1¼"

1 roundhead stove bolt with nut, ¼"-20 × 1"

2 flat washers, ¼" I.D.

1 wing nut, ¼"-20

1 loop of bicycle chain, approx. 84 inches in circumference (drive chain)

1 cold-rolled steel shaft, 1" dia. × 36"

3 bronze bushings, 1" I.D. × 1¼" O.D. × 2"

1 brass threaded insert, ¼"-20

1 threaded rod, ¼"-20 × 2¾"

2 plastic knobs with ¼"-20 threaded inserts;
#DK-81 from Reid Tool Supply

2 flat washers, ¼" I.D.

1 piece aluminum conduit, ½" I.D. × 5"

*A hub, 2½" dia. × 1" thick, is cut from this blank.
†Two hubs, each 1⅝" dia., are cut from this blank.
‡Two bushing blocks, each 1¾" square, are cut from this piece **after** the necessary holes are drilled.

and coves into the blank, and, of course, rout those eye-popping spirals.

Anyone who builds one of these is going to have a lot of fun experimenting with it, Bob. I mean, they simply have to experiment with the gear ratios and different router bits to unleash its full potential. Or should I say, *"UNLEASH ITS FULL POTENTIAL!!!!"* But in the process, they'll be creating truly unique turnings.

Know what else? This lathe will allow you to do loonnngggg turnings, like bedposts. Six feet tall, whatever. It's the pass-through chuck that Fred designed. You start with this long square sticking out one end of the lathe. After you've turned a section, you loosen the chuck and shift the blank. Now you've got stock sticking out BOTH ends of the lathe. Turn the second section, then shift the blank a second time. Now the turning is sticking out the OTHER end of the lathe. You can't *buy* this capability, Bob. You gotta build it.

And one more thing you can do. Finials, Bob, even stylized flame finials.

Oh man! This is magical, Bob. (I know, I know. Not THAT word again.) But look again at the photo I've attached. *Look* at those turnings with their beads and coves, and especially those spirals. Check out that finial. No lathe was used, no *real* lathe, anyway. Just our home-built machine and a nothin'-special router.

Here's something else. A lot of woodworkers don't have a *clue* about turning. I'm one of them, I admit. (Hard to believe, isn't it?) I don't know what it is. Turning's an abstract skill, too abstract to tackle through book-learning (yes, that's the best kind, I know). It just seems like turning'll be too expensive to get into without some guarantee that you'll master it. So we either buy the turnings or build stuff without turnings.

Ahhh, but with this router lathe…Bob, I made a Windsor-style stool with nice double-bobbin legs. I'm making a table with turned legs. Not spiral-turned legs, just nice round tapers with a couple of beads top and bottom. So suddenly, I can do some basic spindle turning.

And hey, it's with my router.

So whaddayathink? This is the book's Grand Finale. The machine is darn easy to build, especially considering what it will do. Not every woodworker will build one, but the kinds of work it produces will grab *any* woodworker's attention. Let's make sure it's in the promotion piece, Bob. But show 'em what it'll do. That's what will grab 'em!

# Building the Router Lathe

This project may head some of you into unfamiliar territory. It involves some familiar materials—plywood and hardwood blocks and MDF—and familiar operations—ripping and crosscutting, cutting grooves and dadoes, routing disks and holes using a trammel.

But gears and sprockets? Bicycle chain? Cutting and drilling metal? Cutting threads? Oh, ye gods and little fishes!

Relax. Relax. It is all doable. The bicycle chain and sprockets can be purchased at a bicycle shop. You don't need new parts, because you won't be using them to propel a 170-pound load across the countryside. And while you are making your purchase, you can probably get some free pointers on making up the two chain loops you need.

The bearings and bevel gears and bushings all can be purchased at the same place; look in the Yellow Pages under the heading "bearings."

Metal parts? Try a welding shop or machine shop.

Keep this in mind: You are building a very inexpensive lathe that will do some things that even the most expensive shop lathes cannot do. It's worth a little trouble to find the oddball parts you need and to master the simple metal-working skills you need.

## Building the Frame

Starting with the frame is somewhat arbitrary, but it's an approach that gives you a sense of progress early on. It doesn't take long for the frame to take shape, giving you a concrete idea of what you are making.

After you have the frame assembled, you can work on the headstock, the gearing, and all the supporting paraphernalia.

**1. Cut the frame parts.** These include the front and back, the mid and tail supports, the headstock end, the retainer plates, and the triangular gussets. In building his original prototype, Fred used ½-inch medium-density fiberboard (MDF) for all but the back, which was made from ¾-inch plywood. In building my own unit, I used ¾-inch Baltic Birch for all the frame parts. Fred's lathe, of course, worked just fine; but I think the bulkier, stiffer frame is an improvement.

Almost all these parts will be further modified before assembly, but begin by cutting all but the mid and tail supports to the dimensions specified by the Cutting List. Shaping the two supports is eased by starting with a single panel 10 × 17½ inches; after making initial shaping cuts, this panel is cut in half to yield the two separate supports.

After cutting the three square pieces specified for the gussets, halve each square on a diagonal—this is easily done on the band saw—forming the triangles needed to brace the frame.

**2. Cut the joinery on the front and back.** The head panel, the mid support, and the tail panel fit into rabbets or dadoes cut across in the front and back, as shown in the *Top View* of the drawing *Router Lathe Plan Views*.

Lay out the locations of these cuts on the front and back. Clamp a T-square or other straightedge to the stock, and make the cuts with a straight bit.

**3. Shape the mid and tail supports.** Each support has two semicircular cutouts in its top edge, as shown in the drawing *Support Layout*. The larger of the two semicircles provides clearance for the stock being turned, while the smaller one cradles the sled shaft. I think the easiest way to make these cutouts is to cut two circles in one large panel, then cut it in half, splitting the holes.

## ROUTER LATHE PLAN VIEWS

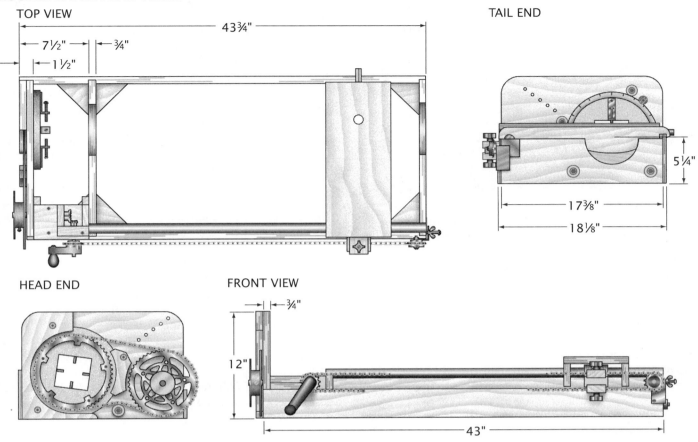

TOP VIEW

43¾"

7½"    ¾"

1½"

TAIL END

5¼"

17⅜"

18⅛"

HEAD END

FRONT VIEW

¾"

12"

43"

Lay out a centerline on the panel for the two supports. Mark the centerpoints of the two holes to be cut on this centerline. Bore the smaller hole with a Fortsner bit on the drill press. Rout the larger hole with a plunge router equipped with the Trammel Baseplate (page 39) or some other trammel.

Cut the workpiece in half, splitting the holes and forming the two supports.

In the finished lathe, the tail support is equipped with two bearings that carry the tail disk, which is used for especially long turnings. Lay out and bore the ¼-inch-diameter holes for the bearing-mounting bolts.

## SUPPORT LAYOUT

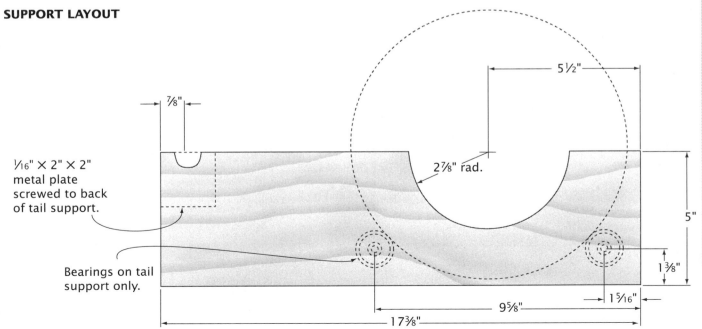

⅞"

5½"

1/16" × 2" × 2" metal plate screwed to back of tail support.

2⅞" rad.

5"

Bearings on tail support only.

1⅜"

1⁵⁄₁₆"

9⅝"

17⅜"

Turning

**Assemble the lathe frame** with glue and drywall screws. Join the mid and end supports to the back, then add the front. When you drive screws into the gussets, it will pull the frame into square.

**4. Begin assembling the frame.** Glue and screw the two supports to the front and back. Square the assembly, and glue and screw the gussets in place.

Cut the small steel plate for the tail support, and drill two mounting-screw holes in it. Screw the plate to the support in the upper front corner, where it can simultaneously serve as the retainer for the sled shaft and as a contact plate for the chain tensioner.

**5. Lay out the headstock end.** The frame's headstock—a subassembly—supports the chuck disk and the chain-drive assembly. The headstock consists of the headstock end, two retainer plates, and a handful of bolts, nuts, washers, screws, and bearings. The chuck disk fits into a hole in the headstock end. It rides on three bearings positioned around the hole's perimeter, which allow it to turn

freely. To keep it in place, the chuck disk is trapped between the retainer plates on the headstock end's outer face and several "trap washers" on the inner face.

The first step in making this assembly is to lay out the headstock end. Study the *Headstock End* section of the drawing *Headstock Layouts,* then duplicate the layout on the headstock end panel. Begin by laying out the centerpoint of the chuck disk hole, then scribing the 5-inch-radius hole with a compass. Reset the compass to swing a $5^{11}/_{16}$-inch radius, set the pivot on the hole's centerpoint, and scribe a second circle. The centers of the chuck support bearings will be on this circle. Mark the bearing centers.

Now lay out the rest of the holes. The $\frac{5}{8}$-inch-diameter hole is for a sprocket shaft, the arc of $\frac{1}{4}$-inch-diameter holes provide chain adjustment, and the $\frac{1}{4}$-inch-wide slot allows adjustment of the chain's tension.

**6. Lay out the retainer plates.** Following the *Retainer Plates* section of the drawing *Headstock Layouts,* lay out the centerpoint of the sprocket opening. Scribe the $9\frac{1}{4}$-inch-diameter hole, then add the cut lines that transform the blank into two retainers.

**7. Make the headstock holes.** The large-diameter holes in the headstock end and the retainer-plates blank can be routed using a plunge router equipped with the Trammel Baseplate. When making each of these cuts, stick the workpiece to scrap with carpet tape, making sure that the pivot-point area, especially, is securely bonded to the scrap.

After routing the large openings, bore the sprocket hole and the chain idler holes on the drill press. The chain-tension adjustment slot can be formed by drilling a hole at each end and sawing out the waste between them with a saber saw.

## HEADSTOCK LAYOUTS

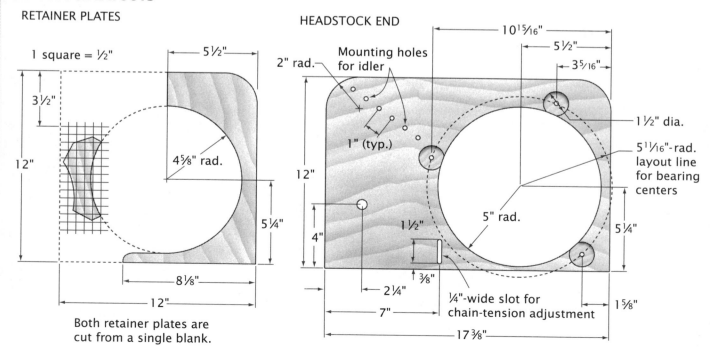

RETAINER PLATES

1 square = ½"

5½"
3½"
12"
4⅝" rad.
5¼"
8⅛"
12"

Both retainer plates are cut from a single blank.

HEADSTOCK END

10¹⁵⁄₁₆"
5½"
3⁵⁄₁₆"
2" rad.
Mounting holes for idler
1" (typ.)
12"
4"
1½"
2¼"
⅜"
7"
17⅜"
1½" dia.
5¹¹⁄₁₆"-rad. layout line for bearing centers
5" rad.
5¼"
1⅝"
¼"-wide slot for chain-tension adjustment

Turning

Wait to drill the openings for the bearings until after the end and the retainers have been joined.

**8. Assemble the headstock.** Before you can actually bond the headstock end and the retainers together, the retainer-plate blank has to be cut into the two pieces. Cut along the layout lines on the band saw (or with a saber saw).

Glue and clamp the retainers to the headstock end, as shown in the layout drawing. As you apply the glue, be careful to keep the glue back from the edges of the chuck disk opening. You don't want squeeze-out to deal with in this seam because it will interfere with the free rotation of the chuck disk.

When the glue is dry, round the top corners of the assembly, as shown in the drawing.

**9. Bore the bearing recesses.** Now is the time to bore the bearing recesses and the holes for the bearing-mounting bolts. The three centerpoints are laid out on the inner face of the assembly. The bearings are 1⅜ inches in diameter. To provide clearance, the recesses for them in the headstock should be 1½ inches in diameter.

Bore the recesses on the drill press with a Forstner bit, making them about ⅝ inch deep. Try to line up the holes precisely. Although it may seem to be extra busy-work, you may want to use a centering pin (or small-diameter bit) to align the workpiece on the drill press table. When the centerpoint is properly aligned and the workpiece clamped to the table, you can switch to the Forstner bit to bore the recess.

And if you take this tack, you can then switch to a ¼-inch bit and bore the mounting-bolt hole, thus ensuring that its axis will be concentric with that of the bearing recess.

In any case, once you've bored the recesses, bore the mounting-bolt holes.

**10. Mount the bearings.** The bearings have a bore of ⅝ inch, but the mounting bolts are ¼ inch. In the size disparity lies a bit of adjustability.

Fred's thinking was this: Even if you try, you can't really drill a hole centered on the axis of a dowel. Instead of being concentric, it'll be eccentric. So he drilled ¼-inch holes in short bits of ⅝-inch dowels to serve as sleeves between the bearings and the bolts. To adjust a bearing very slightly in relation to the chuck disk, he turns the sleeve. Because it is ever-so-slightly eccentric, it shifts the bearing position.

So begin the installation of the headstock bearings by drilling holes through seven pieces of ⅝-inch dowel. (Although there are only three headstock bearings, there are four other places the bearings are used on the lathe, so you might as well drill the sleeves for all of them at the same time.) Grip the dowel in a hand screw to hold it while you work on the drill press. The dowels tend to split, so don't feed too aggressively, and be prepared for a fairly high failure rate. Just remember, you only need seven good ones.

Assemble the dowel, bearing, and two washers on the bolt, as shown in the drawing *Headstock Assembly.* Feed

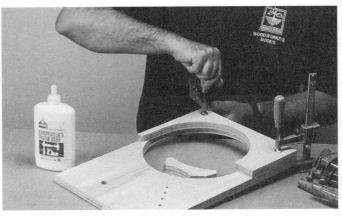

**Aligning the parts accurately** is essential. The outside edges of the large retainer plate can be aligned flush with those of the head end. It is helpful to pencil position lines around the small retainer plate during a dry run so that you can position it quickly after the glue is applied.

**HEADSTOCK ASSEMBLY**

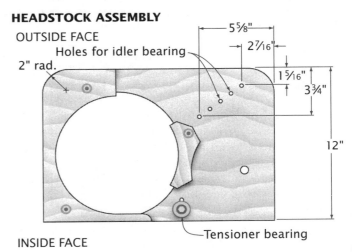

OUTSIDE FACE
Holes for idler bearing
2" rad.
5⅝"
2⁷⁄₁₆"
1⁵⁄₁₆"
3¾"
12"
Tensioner bearing

INSIDE FACE

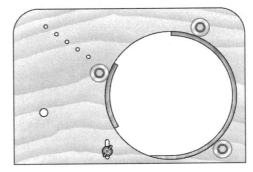

BEARING ASSEMBLY DETAIL
¼"- I.D. flat washer
Ball bearing
⅝" bore × 1⅜" O.D. × ½" long
¼"- I.D. flat washer
¼"-20 × 2" hex-head bolt

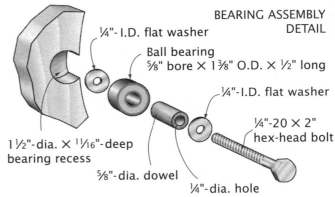

1½"-dia. × ¹¹⁄₁₆"-deep bearing recess
⅝"-dia. dowel
¼"-dia. hole

**Don't try too hard to center the holes** in the bearing mounting sleeves. Off-center holes provide a small measure of adjustability. To bore them, mark the "centerpoint" with an awl. Then pinch the sleeve in a hand screw, and drill the hole at the mark.

the bolt's shank through the mounting-bolt hole, and settle the bearing into its recess. Add a washer and nut on the bolt's shank, and tighten the nut with a wrench.

**11. Temporarily join the headstock to the frame.** *Temporarily* means no glue. You need to be able to remove the headstock to install the gearbox. But it's fun to see the frame take shape.

Fit the headstock assembly into the rabbets for it in the front and back. Drill pilot holes, and drive screws to secure the part.

## Constructing the Gearbox

The gearbox is the linchpin of this lathe's works. When you turn the crank, the router slides along the sled shaft and cuts the spindle chucked in the lathe. It's the gearbox that transfers the power from the crank to the spindle, so that when the router moves, so does the workpiece.

This vital unit is assembled from an assortment of parts, including some plywood, a couple of bronze bushings, stock bevel gears, and steel rods. The particulars of the gearbox emanate from the bevel gears. The brand and item number of the gears used in the prototypes are included in the Hardware List; they are off-the-shelf items at bearing dealers (look in the Yellow Pages under the heading "bearings"). The larger gear has a ½-inch bore, which dictates the use of a ½-inch shaft with it, while the smaller gear has a ⅜-inch bore, necessitating the use of a ⅜-inch shaft. Obviously, it would have been better if both gears had the same bore, but they don't. The sizes of the shafts dictate the sizes of the bushings needed. The bushings can be purchased from the same dealer that supplies the gears (and the bearings used elsewhere in the lathe). Cold-rolled steel rod can be purchased at a good hardware store or at the bearing store.

The key to smooth operation is precise construction, so follow the directions meticulously and work carefully.

**1. Cut the gearbox stock.** The gearbox's "case" is formed of two small pieces of plywood. Cut the two case halves to the dimensions specified by the Cutting List. Take extra care to ensure that the long edges are parallel and that the ends are perfectly square to the sides.

**2. Rout the bushing channels.** These channels

## GEARBOX CONSTRUCTION

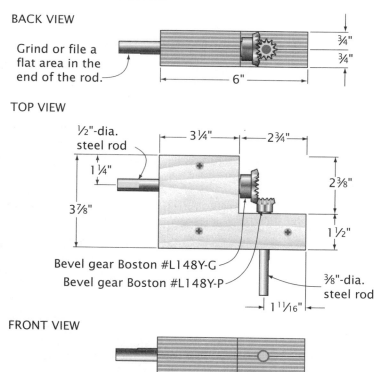

BACK VIEW

Grind or file a flat area in the end of the rod.

¾"
¾"
6"

TOP VIEW

½"-dia. steel rod
3¼"
2¾"
1¼"
2⅜"
3⅞"
1½"
Bevel gear Boston #L148Y-G
Bevel gear Boston #L148Y-P
⅜"-dia. steel rod
1¹¹⁄₁₆"

FRONT VIEW

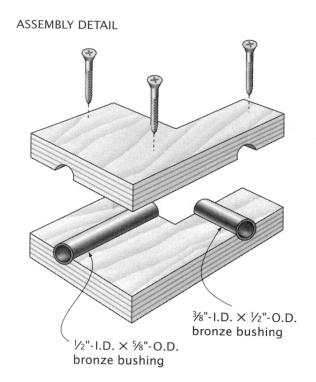

ASSEMBLY DETAIL

⅜"-I.D. × ½"-O.D. bronze bushing

½"-I.D. × ⅝"-O.D. bronze bushing

need to be cut precisely if they are to match up correctly when the case halves are mated. The easy way to do it is on the router table.

First, chuck a ⅝-inch core-box bit in a table-mounted router. Set the bit extension to ⁵⁄₁₆ inch, and adjust the fence to position the channel, as shown in the drawing *Gearbox Construction.* Check the accuracy of the setup by making a test cut in a piece of scrap. Then rout the channel in both halves of the gearbox case.

To cut the second channel, the router setup must be altered. Switch to a ½-inch core-box bit, and adjust the bit extension to ¼ inch. Adjust the fence to position the small channel, as shown in the drawing. Make test cuts in scrap to confirm the accuracy of this setup. That done, rout the small channel across both pieces of stock.

**3. Cut the clearance notch.** At this point your gearbox case is finished but for the notch that provides clearance for the bevel gears. Carefully lay out the notch, as shown in the drawing. Cut it on the band saw or with a backsaw.

**4. Prepare the bushings and steel rods.** Cut the bushings and steel rods with a hacksaw to the lengths specified by the Cutting List. Note that the larger-diameter bushing is cut ¾ inch longer than the channel in which it will be placed; the extra length is so it can extend through the headstock. Make the cuts squarely, and remove any burrs with a file or emery paper.

After the shafts have been cut to length, grind or file a short, narrow flat at each end. The gears and hubs that mount on these shafts are secured with setscrews. Without these flats, the setscrews will almost certainly slip.

**5. Assemble the gearbox.** First, push each bevel gear over one end of its shaft, and tighten the setscrews onto the flats. Then slip the shafts through their bushings.

One special note is in order at this point. The upper photo on this page shows the use of two or three short bushings on each shaft. You can buy long bushings, and you should. If forced to use short bushings, grease up the shafts so the epoxy won't stick to them. It worked for me.

Next, mix up some epoxy, and spread it in the grooves. (I used PC-7, which has a stiff, pastelike consistency, as you can see in the photo.) Don't be too generous with the epoxy; you don't want squeeze-out when you mate the case halves. That could foul the works.

Set the bushing and rod assemblies in place in one half of the case. While the case is open, you have to adjust the gears so they'll spin smoothly and mesh properly. This is a critical adjustment that you have to get right. Once you "close up" the case and the epoxy cures, the gearbox can't be readjusted; it can only be reconstructed. But the epoxy sets slowly, and thus you have time to fiddle with the works before closing up the case.

What you want is for the bevel gears to mesh so the individual teeth have some headroom. You'll find that if you force the gears tightly together, they bind when you try to spin the shafts. On the other hand, if there's too

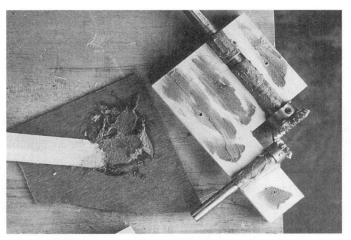

**With the epoxy applied** and the bevel gears, shafts, and bushings placed in a gearbox case half, you must adjust—for all time—the mesh of the bevel gears. When you have them adjusted just right, set the second case half in place and drive the screws.

much headroom, the teeth don't mesh consistently, and the action is erratic and jerky. Work with the gears and get them set just right.

Now use the bushing positions to hold the gear adjustment you've established. Work the bushing along the shaft so it nestles against the body of the gear. When the gears and bushings are aligned, set the second case half in place and screw the two halves together. Set the gearbox aside to cure.

**6. Mount the gearbox on the frame.** The gearbox is trapped between the headstock and the middle support; it's held level by the front and by blocks attached to the headstock and the middle support.

Begin the installation by unscrewing the headstock from the front and back. Move the headstock just enough to allow you to slip the gearbox's shaft through the hole for it

**A dry run eases the final assembly.** Here, it helped position the supports, which have been glued to the headstock and mid support. And it demonstrated that pulling the headstock only about ½ inch from the frame would provide the clearance necessary to insert the gear shaft through the opening for it.

in the headstock. Then slide the headstock back into place and clamp the assembly.

Next, seat the gearbox on the edge of the front, make sure it is level, and scribe along its bottom and inner edges on the headstock and the middle support. These marks indicate where the support blocks must be attached. Disassemble the headstock and gearbox. Cut the support blocks to the dimensions specified by the Cutting List, then notch them. Glue and screw the support blocks to the headstock and the middle support. Reassemble the gearbox and headstock. Complete the installation by driving a couple screws through the headstock into the gearbox and a single screw through the middle support into the gearbox. (I didn't use glue in this part of the assembly. I can always remove the headstock and the gearbox by withdrawing the assembly screws. And I just may want to change gear ratios someday, which would require me to make and install a new gearbox.)

Finally, cut and install the acrylic chip shield over the gears. To raise the shield clear of the larger bevel gear, you will have to apply a couple strips of ¼-inch-thick stock (rippings from the scrap bin, really) to the top of the gearbox. Set the shield on the strips, and screw it in place.

## Making the Chuck Assembly

This is the part of the lathe that holds the workpiece and causes it to rotate when you turn the crank.

The chuck hub consists of two disks of MDF, glue-laminated face to face. The hub fits into the opening in the headstock and rides on three bearings. On one side of the chuck hub are mounted four shop-made L-shaped brackets,

which are the means by which the workpiece is held. On the other side is attached a 52-tooth bicycle chainring.

Completing the chuck assembly is the transverse sprocket, which is mounted on the gearbox shaft that projects through the headstock. The transverse sprocket, which is also a chainring pirated from a bicycle, transfers the power from the gearbox to the chuck sprocket via standard bicycle chain. The sprocket shown in the drawings has 46 teeth, but a good bicycle shop will have a selection of usable chainrings. By changing this sprocket, you can adjust the distance the router travels per workpiece revolution.

Construction of the chuck involves some metalworking, which can be dealt with using a hacksaw, your drill press, and a tap. If you don't want to tackle it yourself, it—and other metal components of the router lathe—can be fabricated for you by a local machine shop.

If you expect to use your router lathe for turning extra-long workpieces, you will need a second chuck to serve as a tailstock. The tailstock chuck doesn't need the sprocket, but it is otherwise a duplicate of the headstock chuck. You can make both chucks at the same time, which is surely the most efficient way to do it. Or you can, at a later date, come back to this section, retrace the steps, and make that second chuck.

**1. Collect the sprockets for the chuck assembly.** You need at least two. The model shown has three. And if you want a lot of adjustability in your lathe, you can use even more. "Bike Parts" on page 282 provides some basic information about bicycle gears.

For the chuck sprocket, you need a 52-tooth gear,

## CHUCK CONSTRUCTION

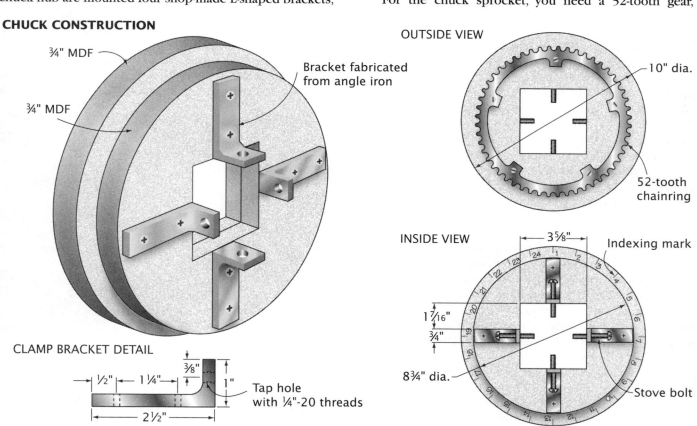

¾" MDF

¾" MDF

Bracket fabricated from angle iron

CLAMP BRACKET DETAIL

⅜"
½" | 1¼" | 1"
2½"

Tap hole with ¼"-20 threads

OUTSIDE VIEW

10" dia.

52-tooth chainring

INSIDE VIEW

3⅝"

Indexing mark

1⁷⁄₁₆"
¾"

8¾" dia.

Stove bolt

which means it has to be either a chainring or a chainwheel. For the transverse sprocket, you need a 46-tooth gear, and it can be either a chainwheel or a freewheel. For additional ratios of twist, select gears for the transverse sprocket that have fewer teeth than 46.

The gear you use for the chuck sprocket will have to be modified to create an unobstructed 5½-inch-diameter opening inside its toothed ring. The first task is to use a compass of some kind to mark the locations of the mounting-screw holes that have to be drilled. These must be on the same circumference line so that you can ensure the sprocket is concentric with the chuck, an essential for smooth operation. After scribing that line, reduce the radius of the compass and scribe the cut lines.

With a hacksaw, cut the webbing out of a chainwheel or amputate the mounting tabs of a chainring. Drill the mounting-screw holes on the drill press.

**2. Lay out the two disks for the chuck.** These two parts are made of medium-density fiberboard (MDF). This is the ideal material for this particular application. Cutting it leaves crisp edges, which, because of the material's density, won't be crushed or deformed by the bearings upon which the hub rides. This is one instance where substitutions are discouraged.

Begin by cutting two squares of MDF to the dimensions specified by the Cutting List. Mark the center of each square.

The large disk needs to have indexing marks added to its edge that divide it into 24 equal segments. Later these indexing marks are used when routing spiral turnings and in positioning flutes or beads on a turning. It's easiest to lay them out now, although you don't need to label them. Just mark the segments indelibly. If you've never done it, turn to page 110 in the chapter "Dowel-Turning Jig," and study the drawing *Index Wheel Layout Tricks*. This drawing shows

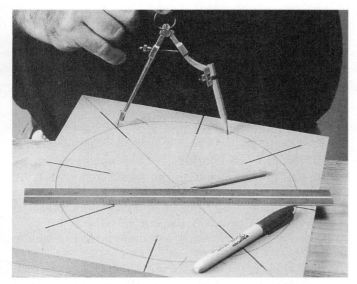

**Laying out the indexing marks** takes careful work with a compass. Making your marks on the chuck hub blank while it's still square will make the task a bit easier and the results more accurate.

how to divide a disk into 6 or 12 segments using a compass and rule. By carrying the process one step further, you can divide the clamping disk into 24 equal segments.

To complete the layout of the smaller square, work from the centerpoint and scribe a square 3⅝ inches on a side in the center of the piece. Eventually, this will be cut out to permit the workpiece to actually pass through the chuck. Radiating from the centerpoint and bisecting each of the scribed square's sides, mark lines on which the L-brackets will be placed.

**3. Rout the chuck disks.** Use a plunge router equipped with a trammel for this operation.

Using a tiny drill bit, bore a pivot hole through each square on the drill press. This is important since this hole will help you get the chuck components assembled as close to concentric as it will be possible to get them. You need the holes to be small, to be perpendicular to the faces, and to completely penetrate the square.

The size of the smaller disk isn't critical. If it turns out to be an eighth under or over the diameter specified, that's no big deal. But the larger disk has to be a close fit in the hole for it in the headstock. It may be worthwhile to make test cuts in hardboard or ¼-inch plywood to set up the trammel. Do this: Set the trammel, cut a sample disk, and fit it into the headstock opening. Adjust the trammel as necessary, and cut another test disk. When you've got the setup, rout the MDF.

When cutting the good stuff, stick the MDF to scrap with carpet tape. This will protect the workbench beneath the work, and it will keep the parts from shifting and jamming when the bit cuts through.

After the large disk is cut, check its fit in the headstock. Remember that the bearings have a small measure of adjustability. You want the disk to rotate freely, without play or chatter. If the disk is a skosh too big, you probably can tweak the trammel setting and recut the disk. And of course, if the disk is too small, toss it and start over.

**4. Lay out the mounting for the chuck sprocket.** This sprocket, which you prepared in Step 1, is screwed to the large disk, on the side opposite the index markings. The sprocket must be as close to concentric with the disk as possible. Since you laid out and drilled the gear's mounting-screw holes, you know the radius of the arc upon which they are located.

Using the drilled centerpoint as a pivot, scribe a circle of that radius on the appropriate side of the large chuck disk.

**5. Glue-laminate the chuck disks.** Glue the small disk to the large one. Drive a finish nail through the center hole of the small disk, so the tip protrudes on the other side. Apply glue to that side and set the small disk onto the large one, using the nail to align them. Be sure you don't cover the square laid out on the small disk, and that you apply the small disk to the side of the large disk that has the index markings on it. Clamp the disks together and allow the glue to dry.

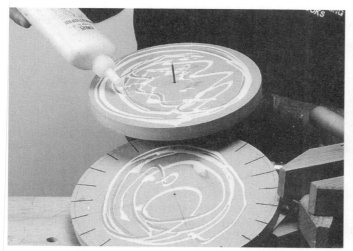

**A nail aligns the chuck disks** during glue-up. Drive it through the pivot hole in one disk, spread the glue, as shown, and join them, inserting the nail into the second disk's pivot as you do.

**Fender washers hold the chuck in place.** Position them around the edge of the headstock's opening, roughly as shown. Note that they don't have to project far beyond the edge to keep the chuck in place.

**6. Make the chuck clamps.** Cut four ¾-inch-wide sections of 2½ × 2½ × ¼-inch steel angle. With a hacksaw, this could take some time. If you have the option, have the angle iron cut at a metal shop. When you have the four pieces, cut down one extension of each to 1 inch, as shown in the drawing *Chuck Construction*.

Next, drill and tap the short arms for a ¼-inch-20 thread, as shown in the drawing. The twist-drill bits you use for woodworking will also bore holes in metal; it just takes longer. (Don't use brad-point bits, though; they aren't high-speed steel.) A detailed explanation of how to tap a hole is provided in the section "Cutting Threads" in the appendix.

Finally, drill two mounting-screw holes in the long extensions of the clamp brackets.

**7. Complete the chuck.** The first thing is to cut out the opening. Drill a large-diameter starting hole inside the layout lines. With a saber saw, cut out the waste. File the cut edges as necessary to clean and square them.

Next, mount the head sprocket. Very, very carefully align the chainring on the hub, centering all the mounting holes over the circle scribed on the outside of the large disk. When you've aligned it just right, tape it down with packing tape or masking tape so it can't shift, and drill pilot holes. Remove the tape, and as you screw the sprocket in place, slip a couple of flat washers under the sprocket at each screw. These washers will offset the sprocket from the chuck to provide clearance for the head chain.

Now mount the chuck clamps. Align each clamp on a layout line, drill pilot holes, and attach it with #8 × 1¼-inch panhead screws. After all four clamps are mounted, turn a roundhead stove bolt into the threaded hole in each clamp.

Finally, install the chuck in the headstock. Adjust the bearings as necessary to ensure a good fit. To keep the chuck in place, screw fender washers to the headstock, just at the edge of the hole. Position each washer so it just overlaps the chuck; three washers installed in this way, one more-or-less beside

each bearing, will be enough to keep the chuck in place.

**8. Cut the transverse sprocket hub.** With the chuck in place, the next element to make is the transverse sprocket assembly. As noted above, this sprocket is interchangeable, allowing you to change the distance the router moves per spindle revolution. The hub for this sprocket is designed to hold two different-sized sprockets. To change gears, so to speak, you just loosen the sprocket setscrew, pull the sprocket assembly off the gearbox shaft, flip it around, and remount it.

The assembly consists of two different bicycle crankset sprockets and a hub. The hub is a piece of 5/4 (five-quarter) hardwood, routed into a 2½-inch-diameter round and bored with a ½-inch centerhole. To center the sprockets, the hub is shouldered on both sides, so a very short stub tenon projects through the sprocket's bore. A sprocket is set over the stub, then screwed to the hub.

To make the hub, you obviously need the two sprockets in hand. Measure the bore diameters of these sprockets so you know what size to make the stubs. Select a decent-sized piece of 5/4 hardwood from which you will rout the hub (big enough to comfortably support your trammel-equipped plunge router). Drill a pivot hole in it, boring completely through the stock.

The stubs are formed by routing circular grooves around the pivot on both sides of the hub stock. Set the trammel to cut the radius of the sprocket bore. Set the router's plunge depth stop to limit the cut depth to the sprocket thickness (probably ³⁄₃₂ inch to ⅛ inch). Set the pivot and rout the groove in the stock.

Turn the stock over and repeat the process to form the second stub.

Rout the hub next. Reset the trammel to a 1¼-inch radius and the plunge depth stop to 1³⁄₁₆ inches (so you can cut completely through the stock). Reset the trammel pivot in the same pivot hole in the stock, and pass by pass, rout completely through the stock, creating the round hub.

## HUB DETAILS

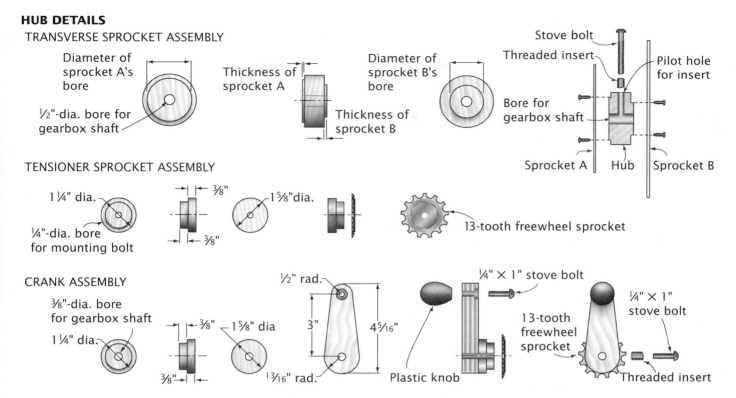

**TRANSVERSE SPROCKET ASSEMBLY**

Diameter of sprocket A's bore

½"-dia. bore for gearbox shaft

Thickness of sprocket A

Diameter of sprocket B's bore

Thickness of sprocket B

Stove bolt

Threaded insert

Pilot hole for insert

Bore for gearbox shaft

Sprocket A | Hub | Sprocket B

**TENSIONER SPROCKET ASSEMBLY**

1¼" dia.

¼"-dia. bore for mounting bolt

⅜"

⅜"

1⅝"dia.

13-tooth freewheel sprocket

**CRANK ASSEMBLY**

⅜"-dia. bore for gearbox shaft

1¼" dia.

⅜"

1⅝" dia

⅜"

½" rad.

3"

4⁵⁄₁₆"

¹³⁄₁₆" rad.

Plastic knob

¼" × 1" stove bolt

13-tooth freewheel sprocket

¼" × 1" stove bolt

Threaded insert

**9. Complete the sprocket assembly.** Three tasks remain here: drilling out the bore so the hub will fit on the gearbox shaft, installing the setscrew, and mounting the sprockets. Do the tasks in that order.

At the drill press, bore a ½-inch-diameter hole through the hub, centered on the pivot hole.

Stand the hub on edge—you can clamp it in a hand screw to keep it from rolling—and drill a pilot hole for the insert, penetrating the edge into the hub's bore. Drive the ¼-inch-20 insert into the hole. And here's a little tip: The hub is a small piece of wood. To avoid having the insert split it, make the pilot hole large enough that the insert's threads can't bite too deep. Apply some epoxy to the insert, then drive it into place.

When you install the sprocket assembly on the gearbox shaft, you can drive a roundhead stove bolt into the insert and tighten it against the flat filed on the shaft, thus locking the sprocket on the shaft.

Finally, mount the sprockets. Fit one over its stub, and drive a couple small screws into the seam between the metal and the wood. Turn the hub over, and mount the second in the same way.

**10. Install the head chain tensioner and idler.**
A tensioner is a device that adjusts the slack in the chain loop. In this case, the headstock tensioner is a 1⅜-inch bearing, whose mounting bolt passes through a slot. The chain passes over the bearing, and by adjusting the bearing position, you can alter the chain loop's slack.

The bearing used is the same as those that support the chuck. As with those bearings, you need a wooden sleeve. On a ¼-inch hex-head bolt, stack a flat washer, the bearing and sleeve, and another washer. Insert the bolt through the

slot in the headstock, add yet another washer, then add a metal wing nut.

The idler is a duplicate of the tensioner, but its role is different, and it is used only occasionally. If you need to use the smaller gear on the transverse sprocket, you'll discover you have an excess of chain. What you do is run the chain loop over the idler, which you position to take up *most* of the slack. You still use the tensioner to take up the last bit of slack.

The idler is mounted in one of the series of holes you drilled through the quadrant of the headstock above the gearbox shaft.

**Installing the head chain** takes only a minute. Catch a few links on cogs of both sprockets, then pull the chain slowly so both sprockets move, settling the chain into place. Then adjust the tensioner to take up the slack.

# Bike Parts

Bicycle gears and chain were selected for this project because they are available almost everywhere; they are relatively inexpensive, especially if purchased used; they provide a range of gear ratios; and they are durable. The only drawback to using these parts that I can think of is that they are unfamiliar to some woodworkers.

Here are the basics of what you need to know. Ask the mechanic at the bike shop where you buy the parts to clarify anything you don't understand, especially exactly how to break the chain. All you need to do this is an inexpensive device called a chain tool.

Let me start with the chain. You need about 11 feet of it altogether, so one old bike won't yield enough for the project. There are two basic widths. BMX and all one- and three-speed bikes use ⅛-inch chain. This is what we used. Derailleur bikes, those with ten speeds and up, use ³⁄₃₂-inch chain. *You can use either width,* but make sure that all the chain you get is either one width or the other.

Bicycles have a variety of sprockets or gears. You need both freewheel sprockets, which are mounted to the bike's rear wheel, and chainwheel (or chainring) sprockets, which are attached to the pedals.

The lathe's idler and crank sprockets are bicycle freewheel gears. On the lathe, both of these sprockets must be the same size, with the same number of teeth. We used 13-tooth sprockets, but freewheel gears range from 12 teeth up to 34 teeth. Large-diameter sprockets may get in your way, so stick with smaller ones. But don't feel locked into the 13-tooth size. Just get two the same.

The other sprockets are chainwheels or chainrings. On a bicycle, this is the big sprocket at the pedals. The difference between chainwheels and chainrings should be evident from the names: One is a toothed wheel, the other a toothed ring. Usually, a chain*wheel* is used on BMX and one- and three-speed bicycles, which have a single sprocket at the pedals. The chain*ring* is found on bicycles with ten or more speeds, as these have two or three sprockets at the pedals. These sprockets range in size from 24 teeth up to 56 teeth.

Our basic setup uses a 52-tooth gear on the chuck, and a 46-tooth gear and a 32-tooth gear on the transverse sprocket. All are chainwheels. The chainwheel used for the chuck sprocket has the webbing cut out and has mounting-screw holes drilled in it.

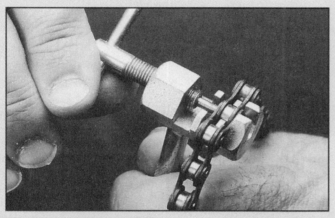

**Bicycle chain is easy to "break,"** if you use the correct tool. The chain is made up of links that are connected to each other with plates and pins. To "break" a chain loop, you use a chain tool (*top*) to push the pin out of a link, but not completely out of the plate. When done correctly, the pin will project from the outside of the plate, and you will be able to pull the link free (*bottom*). (Be careful: If you push the pin all the way out, you won't be able to get it back in.) You'll quickly see how easy it is to add and remove links to make up the specific length of chain you need.

**Bicycle sprockets** come in many sizes and configurations. Use a chainring, which has mounting tabs but not webbing (*lower left*), or a chainwheel, which has webbing (*center*), for the chuck sprocket and for the transverse sprocket. (At upper left is a chainwheel with the webbing cut out.) Freewheel gears (*right*) can be used for the idler and crank sprocket, as well as the transverse sprocket.

**11. Install the chain.** As noted, the lathe uses standard bicycle chain. What you must do now is make up a chain that can be looped around both sprockets on the headstock. Don't make it a tight fit; you need some slack, and the amount of slack can be adjusted using the chain tensioner. The chain on my lathe is about 44 inches long.

When you have the chain made up, install it on the sprockets. Make sure the chain runs over top of the tensioner.

Adjust the tensioner's position to give you the right amount of slack. You *do* need some slack; if the chain is too tight, the movement of the assembly will be jerky and halting. You want the sprockets to turn smoothly and quite freely. Tighten the wing nut to lock the tensioner.

## Building the Router Sled Assembly

The sled carries the router. It slides back and forth along a heavy steel shaft mounted at the front of the lathe, while following a template clamped to the lathe's back. The template contour dictates, in part, the shape of the spindle that the router cuts as it moves from one end of the spindle to the other. The sled is dragged on its journey by a chain loop that extends from the crank at the headstock to an idler at the tail support.

While the sled itself is simply a plywood rectangle to which the router is screwed, the apparatus that controls its movement is more complex. The sensible thing, to me, is to make and install the chain drive system, then make the sled, its guidance system, and the clamp setup that connects it to the chain.

**1. Make the sprocket hubs.** The drive chain system is a simple loop, with the chain running over two sprockets. Both the crank sprocket, which is mounted to the gearbox, and the idler, located at the tail end of the lathe, are identical. You need two 12- or 13-tooth freewheel sprockets and

**Routing the sprocket hubs is a two-step task.** With a trammel-equipped plunge router, cut the smaller-diameter circle, forming the stud over which the sprocket fits. Then reset the trammel and rout the larger diameter, cutting the hub free of the stock.

two wooden hubs. The 1⅝-inch-diameter hubs are shouldered so that the sprocket can drop over a 1¼-inch-diameter stub and seat against hub body. (Note that you may have to modify the hub specs somewhat to accommodate the particular sprockets you use.) The hubs are cut from ¾-inch-thick hardwood stock with your by-now familiar trammel-equipped plunge router.

Select a piece of hardwood that is big enough to support the router and trammel as you work. Sketch out where the hubs will be cut, then drill a pivot hole through the stock in the center of each spot. Stick the work to scrap, both to protect the workbench and to keep the hub from shifting as the cut is completed.

Rout the stub section first. Set the trammel to cut a ⅝-inch radius, and set the router's plunge depth stop to limit the cut depth to ⅜ inch. Set the pivot and rout a circular groove in the stock at each spot.

Reset the trammel to a ¹³⁄₁₆-inch radius and the plunge depth stop to ¹³⁄₁₆ inch, so you can cut completely through the stock. Rout out the two hubs.

Finally, bore out the pivot hole in each hub, the idler to ¼-inch diameter, the crank hub to ⅜-inch diameter.

**2. Make the crank.** Start by cutting and shaping the crank plate, as shown in the drawing *Hub Details*. Drill and countersink a ¼-inch hole at one end for mounting a knob, and drill a ⅜-inch hole at the other for the gearbox shaft.

Glue the appropriate wooden hub to the crank plate. Insert a ⅜-inch bolt through the hole in the crank plate and into the hub's bore to align the two parts during glue-up. Make sure you orient the hub correctly, as shown in the drawing. After the glue has dried, sand the edges.

Next, install a threaded insert for the setscrew. A ¼-inch roundhead stove bolt is used for a setscrew, so you need to use a ¼-inch-20 insert. Bore a pilot of the appropriate diameter for the insert, drilling into the seam between the crank plate and the hub and angling the hole into the center of the hub bore. Apply epoxy to the threaded insert, and drive it into the hole. Then turn the setscrew into the insert.

Finally, install the plastic knob on the crank.

**3. Epoxy the sprockets to the hubs.** The sprockets are bonded to the hubs with epoxy. Mix a small amount of this adhesive and apply it to the shoulders of the hubs. Fit a sprocket over the stub of each hub and seat it in the epoxy. Try to be neat, of course. Set the assemblies aside so they won't be disturbed while the epoxy cures.

**4. Make the tensioner body.** The tensioner is the means for taking up the slack in the sled chain. When the tension is backed off completely, the chain loop will be slack enough that you can remove it from the sprockets. This assembly consists of the idler sprocket (which has already been made), the tensioner body on which the idler is mounted, a pivot bolt, and an adjustment bolt. The body is a short length of steel angle.

Cut the steel angle to the length specified by the Hardware List.

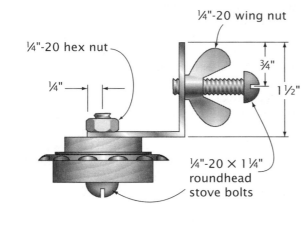

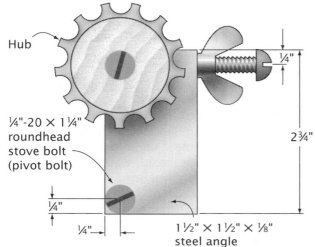

**Assemble and install the sled chain tensioner,** which pivots on the mounting screw at the bottom of its angle-iron body. After the sled chain is installed, turn the adjustment screw (*right*) to alter the angle of the tensioner and thus the degree of slack in the chain loop.

Lay out and drill a ¼-inch-diameter hole for the pivot bolt. Then lay out and drill holes for the idler mounting bolt and for the adjustment bolt. Both these holes must be tapped with ¼-inch-20 threads. The holes you drill, therefore, must be ¹³/₆₄ inch in diameter. Use a tap to cut the threads.

**5. Assemble and install the tensioner.** First, insert the pivot bolt into its hole in the tensioner body, then insert it through the mounting hole in the router lathe front. Secure with a washer and two ¼-20 hex nuts. Lock the nuts against each other when the slop has been taken out of the pivot's fit.

Next, attach the idler. Insert a roundhead stove bolt through the idler, and turn it into the appropriate hole in the tensioner body. Seat the bolt, then back it off a half-turn or so, allowing the idler to spin freely without sideplay. Thread a hex nut onto the bolt and jam it against the back of the tensioner body, thus preventing the bolt from loosening.

Finally, thread a metal wing nut onto another stove bolt, as shown in the drawing *Tensioner Construction,* and turn the bolt into the adjuster hole in the tensioner body. The bolt will contact the metal plate attached to the tail support. As you turn it further, it will force the tensioner to

pivot away from the plate. Tightening the wing nut against the tensioner bolt locks the adjustment-screw position.

**6. Install the crank.** This is easy. Back out the setscrew enough to allow the crank to be slipped onto the ⅜-inch shaft jutting out of the front of the gearbox. Line up the setscrew over the flat filed into the shaft, and tighten the screw.

**7. Install the chain.** The sled chain is common bicycle chain. Make up a chain that loops comfortably around both the crank sprocket and the idler, with a modest amount of slack. If you can fit it over the sprockets without moving one or the other to work it into place, you may have a link (or more) too many in the loop. I find that I need to fit the chain onto the idler, then get a link hooked on a cog of the crank sprocket and give the crank a turn to carry the chain fully onto that sprocket. When it is in place, there is some slack.

**8. Cut the sled parts.** The sled itself is a plywood rectangle. It is mounted on the sled shaft via bronze bushings that are trapped between wooden bushing blocks attached to the underside of the sled. Also trapped between these bushing blocks are two other bushing blocks that are attached to a clamp device. This clamp links the sled assembly to the drive chain. Check out the drawing *Sled Assembly;* all this is more simple than it sounds.

Begin making the sled assembly by cutting the parts. The sled base, the clamp base, and the bushing blocks for the sled can be cut to the dimensions specified by the Cutting List. To make it easier to bore and shape the smaller bushing blocks (those for the clamp), it is best to cut a single piece of ¾-inch plywood to 1¾ inches by, say, 8 to 12 inches for both blocks. Finally, to make it safer to fabricate the clamp jaws, you should cut a single piece of ¾-inch hardwood to a width of 4⅛ inches and a length of 6 to 8 inches for both jaws.

**9. Drill the bushing blocks.** Each bushing block, whether it be for the sled or for the clamp, has a shouldered bore. The through hole is 1⅛ inches in diameter, to provide plenty of clearance for the 1-inch-diameter sled shaft that extends through all these blocks. For two-thirds of its length, each bore is opened up to a 1¼-inch diameter. This is to accommodate the bronze bushings, which are the bearings that make the assembly slide smoothly and freely on the shaft.

The *Sled Assembly* drawing indicates how the three bushings are deployed. One is inserted in the left sled bushing block, and one in the right. Just fitting between the free ends of these bushings is the clamp subassembly, which has the third bushing trapped between its two bushing blocks.

In my opinion, the most accurate and troublefree approach to drilling these holes is to use Forstner bits in the drill press. When I made my blocks, I positioned a block on the drill press table, clamped it down, drilled the large-diameter, ½-inch-deep hole, then switched bits and completed the bore with the smaller bit. Although it involves extra bit changing, this approach ensures that the two holes are concentric. And that's important. Using a fence ensures that the holes in like blocks will be consistently positioned.

Pay particular attention here. You have to bore the sled bushing blocks in such a way that you end up with a left and a right, NOT two identical blocks. I aligned the holes in the blocks in relation to the top edges.

**10. Shape the bushing blocks.** While the sled's bushing blocks could be left square-cut, they look better if you taper or contour the bottom edges, as indicated in the drawing. The exact shape of the contour isn't that important. Simply lay out a line, and cut to it on the band saw or with a saber saw.

The clamp bushing blocks DO need to have the exposed corners rounded off, as indicated in the drawing, for the sled to have the necessary range of motion. Crosscut the blocks from the larger pieces, then shape the corners. The job can be done at the band saw or on a stationary sander.

**11. Assemble the chain clamp base.** The clamp parts still to be made are the base and two jaws.

Start with the base. Drill the hole for the threaded rod, as shown in the *Top View—Clamp* of the *Sled Assembly* drawing.

After you've drilled the hole, and before you unclamp the part from the drill press table, use the machine to help you drive a ¼-inch-20 threaded insert into the hole. Use a ¼-inch bolt with two nuts jammed together on it. Thread the insert onto the bolt, right up to the nuts. Chuck the bolt in the drill press. DON'T turn the machine on; this is a hand-powered operation. What the machine does is help you keep the insert perpendicular to the workpiece surface.

**Stand the chain clamp base on edge** to assemble it. Trap a bronze bushing between the bushing blocks, apply glue to their bottom edges, and clamp them to the base, as shown. Then drill pilot holes and drive drywall screws through the base into each bushing block.

Feed the insert into the hole, as if it were a drill bit, and turn the chuck by hand. Once the insert is well started into the wood, remove it from the chuck and finish driving the insert with a wrench. Then use two wrenches to unjam the nuts, and turn the bolt out of the insert.

Install the bushing blocks next. Jam one on either end of one of the bronze bushings. Glue and screw the clamp base to the bottoms of the bushing blocks.

**12. Cut the clamp jaws.** The clamp jaws are designed to pinch the chain that is looped across the lathe front. The chain passes through a groove cut into the underside of the jaw. When the jaw is loose, the chain moves freely through the groove and the sled doesn't move. But when the jaw is tightened, it jams the chain against the clamp base, and the sled assembly gets dragged along the sled shaft by the chain.

To make the jaws, make a series of cuts on the table saw, using the miter gauge to control the cuts. Make the cuts in a single, oversized workpiece, which you cut down as the final step in the process.

Cut the chain groove first. Set the blade height to ½ inch, and make the first pass ¼ inch from the butt end of the workpiece (you want to cut across the grain). Shift the workpiece to the right and make a second pass. If necessary to achieve the desired groove width, make a third pass.

For the next cut, lower the blade ¼ inch. Adjust the workpiece position, and cut the shoulder of the double rabbet.

Now lower the blade a second time, so the cut depth is only ⅛ inch. Make two or three passes to form the ¼-inch-wide, ⅛-inch-deep rabbet.

To complete the jaw's shape, crank the blade up to a height of 1⅛ inches. Move the rip fence to within ½ inch of the blade. Stand the workpiece on end, with the uncut face against the fence. Make one pass.

Turning

**Forming the chain clamp jaws is a table-saw operation.** After making a series of cross-grain kerfs, stand the workpiece on end and rip away the last bits of waste. Because the individual jaws are small, it is safer to make the cuts on an oversized workpiece and then trim the two jaws from it.

Now rip the workpiece in two, then crosscut the jaws from the waste. Finally, drill a mounting hole through each jaw.

**13. Assemble the sled.** Do the chain clamp assembly first. Turn a 2¾-inch-long piece of threaded rod through the threaded insert so that an equal length protrudes on each face of the clamp base. Apply a few drops of Loctite to the rod at the insert to "glue" it in position. Now slip a clamp jaw over the threaded rod on the assembly's top, add a flat washer, then turn a small plastic knob onto the rod. Turn the unit over and install the second clamp jaw.

First, drill the router bit clearance hole through the sled base, as shown in the *Top View—Sled* of the *Sled Assembly* drawing.

Cut a 5-inch length of aluminum electrical conduit that serves as the template follower, and drill holes for the mounting screws. Scribe a centerline bisecting the base, and mount the follower centered on that line. Accurate alignment is important.

## SLED ASSEMBLY

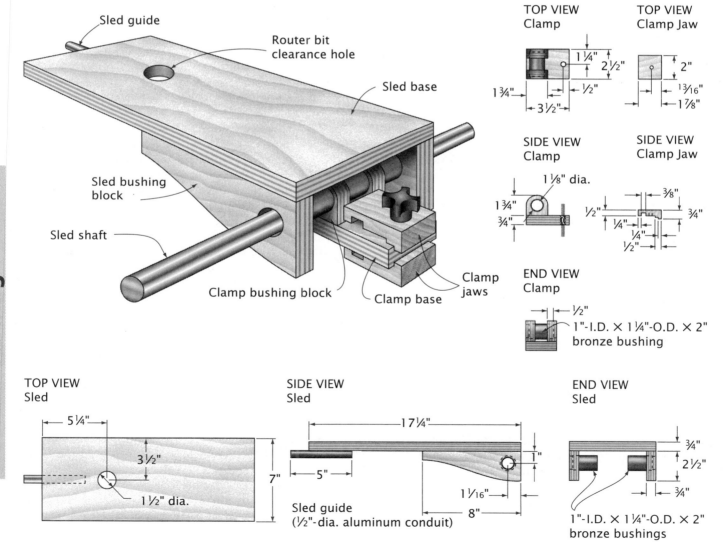

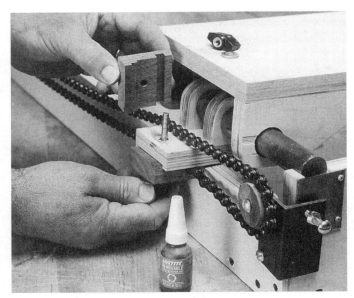

**Complete the assembly of the sled** by setting the chain clamp jaws over the threaded stud and the drive chain. Then turn the plastic knobs onto the stud.

Now glue and screw the bushing blocks to the underside of the sled base. To do this, I found it helpful to clamp the base at the very corner of the workbench. I installed a bushing in each bushing block and slid them onto the sled shaft. Then I applied glue to the blocks, set them on the base, and aligned them with its corners. After I clamped them to the base, I removed the shaft.

After the glue has cured, slide the sled shaft into one bushing of the sled. Fit the chain clamp unit into the gap—make sure it is oriented correctly—and feed the shaft through its bushings and on into the second sled bushing. Set the shaft into place on the lathe frame. See how the sled moves on the shaft. It's a good idea to wax the shaft, but *don't oil it*.

**14. Mount the router on the sled.** The router used on the lathe shown is a fixed-base model. It's got both ¼-inch and ½-inch collets and, at 1½ horsepower, has all the power needed for the work being done.

To make it easy to mount, I drilled a couple of holes right through the router base. Then we simply set the router in place (with its baseplate removed) and drove drywall screws through the base into the sled.

The first time you install the router on the sled base, you need to align it carefully. The bit axis must be dead-on the intersection of the workpiece centerline and the template follower's centerline.

## Making the Tailstock

The tailstock is designed to do just what its name implies: support the tail end of the turning stock. It has three elements that need to be positioned very accurately as you make it. The semicircular notch that fits over the slide bar is the first of them. The second is a square notch that fits over the back of the router lathe. Finally, there's a hole for a screw that acts as does a tail center on a regular lathe. Drive a screw through this hole into the center of the turning blank.

**1. Size the stock.** Cut the tailstock blank to the dimensions specified by the Cutting List.

**2. Shape the stock and drill the screw hole.** Lay out the three critical elements—the two notches and the screw hole—very carefully. They are important to the accuracy of the lathe. Follow the drawing *Tailstock Layout,* and lay out your tailstock.

Begin shaping the tailstock by boring the arc for the sled shaft. Use a 1-inch-diameter Forstner bit in a drill press. Then cut the profile of the tailstock on the band saw or with a saber saw. As you do so, carefully cut out the notch for the frame back.

Finally, lay out and drill the screw hole with a ⅛-inch-diameter drill bit. It is *essential* that this hole be properly located, meaning that it has to be aligned with the center of the chuck. If it is high or low, you won't be able to rout perfect cylinders.

The best way to fine-tune the tailstock is to mount a straight, true turning blank in the lathe, center it carefully, and measure the distance from the bench top to the blank's

**TAILSTOCK LAYOUT**

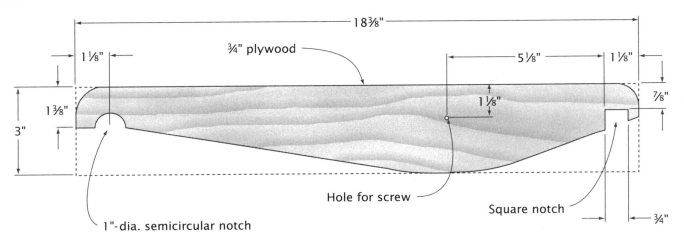

centerpoints at the headstock and the tailstock, and also from the lathe's back to the blank's centerpoints at both ends. Adjust the tailstock screw position as necessary.

**3. Install the tailstock chuck support bearings.** You should still have a handful of hardware to install. These are the bearings that support the tailstock chuck—the one used when routing extra-long workpieces. Bolt the bearings to the end support.

# Using the Router Lathe

You are going to need a bit of messin' around time to get a feel for how the router lathe works.

You won't be able to jump right into routing spirals, of course. First you've got to get the hang of the basics. Just mounting a blank will be a challenge the first time you do it. Rounding and tapering are the most elementary turning operations, and you've got to master them before you can embellish a spindle with rings, coves, and—yes—spirals. Along the way you'll learn how to make and use templates. Eventually, though, you'll learn to rout beautiful turnings with straight and twisted flutes and beads.

The first thing you are going to do—heck, you've probably done it again and again as you assembled the lathe—is

crank the crank and watch the chuck turn. You'll play with the chain clamp setup.

- Try it with both chain clamp jaws tightened. It locks up the whole works. Crank won't turn, nothing turns, nothing moves. You're never going to use it this way.
- Loosen both jaws. The crank turns and the chuck turns, but the sled just sits there. You'll use this setup a lot—for everything but routing spirals.
- Tighten just the top jaw. When you turn the crank clockwise, the sled moves left to right. When you turn it counterclockwise, the led moves right to left.
- Tighten just the bottom jaw. When you turn the crank clockwise, the sled moves right to left. When you turn it counterclockwise, the sled moves left to right.

One of the fundamental lessons you will learn when you tackle spirals is the importance of being very conscious of which way you are turning that crank, and which way the sled is going to move.

## Templates

The first time you set up to do a turning, and every time thereafter, you will need a template to guide the router. So you might as well read up on what—in router lathe terms—

## LAYING OUT A TEMPLATE

DOUBLE-BOBBIN LEG PROFILE

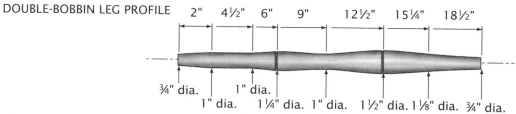

FIRST TEMPLATE

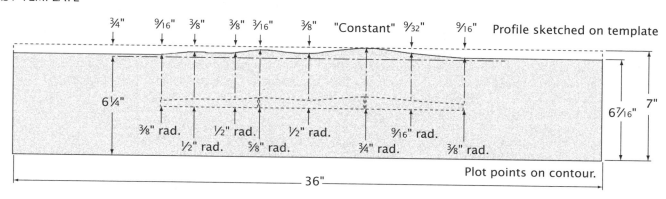

SECOND TEMPLATE

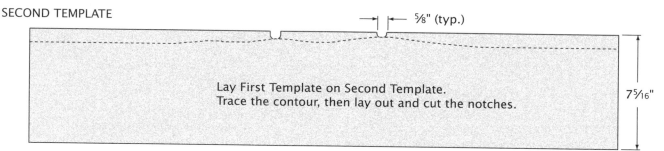

a template is, what it does, and how you make one.

In the sequences that follow, I'll come back to this topic, and show and tell you how to make the template needed for that particular process. And how to use it.

Any template does two things.

First, it lifts the sled's follower off the lathe back, providing clearance between the bottom of the sled and the turning blank. You can't have the sled resting on the blank: It won't spin, ya see.

Second, the template guides the router. Turning a cylindrical spindle? Use a template with a straight, level edge. Want a taper? Use one with a straight but sloping edge. Want undulations? Use a template with a undulating edge. Need a groove in a particular spot? Use a template with a notch to trap the follower, thus keeping the router in position.

Sometimes you need two templates for a single turning. One is used to shape the turning, the second to position and secure the router for adding grooves or beads. Other times, you may find it helpful to clamp stops to a template so you can work a turning one section at a time.

A template is easy to make, of course. Use hardboard or ¼-inch plywood. Lay out the profile and cut it on the band saw or with a saber saw. Use files and sandpaper to refine and smooth the edge.

The tricky part is the layout. Here's why: Because of the location of the router on the sled, the template cannot be a duplicate of the profile you want to produce. The rise and fall of the profile must be scaled up.

Here's a brief step-by-step on template making.

**1. Cut a piece of template stock.** Make it about 7 to 8 inches wide and 36 inches long. Right on the template stock, draw the profile you want, measuring and recording the radii of various features—high points and low points. You will plot each of these points in laying out the template's contour. See the drawing *Laying Out a Template,* which depicts how to make a two-part template for turning a double-bobbin chair leg. Note that you should scribe the turning's axis, then lay out the profile in relation to that.

**2. Locate the largest radius in the profile.** This will be the highest point on the template. You will calculate all the other points on the template contour in relation to this point. This radius is the "constant" in calculating other contour points.

**3. Lay out the template profile.** Using the largest radius as the distance, measure from the template edge and scribe the axis, making sure it is parallel to the template edge. You need both the edge and the axis line to plot the contour.

Now mark the extremities of the turning—the two ends, in other words. Between these points, mark the location of the other key radii.

Plot the contour points next. You need to do some math; I use the template as my scratch pad for this. To locate the plot point (X) for a particular radius (R), subtract that radius from the constant (C) (that's the largest radius on the

turning, remember). Divide the difference by 2, then multiply the quotient by 3. As an equation, that would be:

$$X = (C - R) \div 2 \times 3$$

Again, the drawing *Laying Out a Template* provides a specific example. Note that "X" is not the radius. You plot the point by measuring from the template edge, rather than the axis.

After all the points have been calculated and plotted, connect the dots, sketching a fair contour.

**4. Isolate fixed features for a separate template.** So far, the template has been contrived to guide the router as it is moved along the turning's axis. But some features of a turning are produced by planting the router in one spot. The V-grooves in the leg shown in the drawing are perfect examples.

You want some device to trap the router in a fixed position, so you can turn the crank and spin the turning without worrying that the router will slip or drift out of position, thus ruining the workpiece. A semicircle, one the same diameter as the follower, cut into the edge of the template is ideal.

But if you cut that into the template that's guiding the router as it is moved back and forth along the turning's axis, it is going to be an obstacle.

The solution is a complementary template that has just these fixed positions. After you shape the turning, you can replace the first template with the second. Then rout the grooves or rings.

**5. Cut the template contour.** With the template (and its mate) laid out, cut the edge on the band saw or with a saber saw. File and sand the edge as necessary to eliminate nibs, bumps, dips, and roughness.

## Rounding a Spindle

Here's the baseline operation. The first step in any turning you do is to knock the corners off your square blank and make it round. Here's how to set up and do it.

**1. Choose your stock and cut it to size.** Whenever you are working with long, thin sticks, you need to choose stock with straight and even grain. This serves two purposes, one practical and one aesthetic. Straight-grained wood is stronger and more resistant to splitting. That's important. You don't want your spindle to break up midway through the operation. But also, spindles look better when their profile isn't being challenged by the wood's figure. Save the highly figured wood for another use.

The router lathe will take stock 3½ inches square and smaller. Anything larger won't fit into the chuck. A blank smaller than 1 inch square can be problematic because of its flexibility. When the bit presses against it, it will bow. It will be difficult to get a smooth, round spindle.

In a single pass, the lathe will produce a 29-inch-long turning. To get that turning, you need a blank about 40

# Bits for Turning

You already have bits you can use with your new router lathe. But depending upon the router turnings you want to produce, you may need to expand your collection.

Right away, let's eliminate from consideration *any* bit with a pilot bearing.

But look at the other bits you have. Surely you have straight bits, a V-groover, and a core-box or two. With these bits you can produce round or tapered spindles. You can produce turnings with mildly curved tapers, sweeping vases, and, of course, coves and V-grooves. The double-bobbin leg included in the photo of turning, at the beginning of this chapter, was created with a straight bit and a V-groover. The workpiece shown in the photos depicting the spiral turning process was worked with a straight bit and two sizes of core-box bits. You can do useful and attractive turnings with a modest bit collection. So you don't need to buy more specialized bits immediately.

But when you do progress beyond the straight bits, V-groovers, and core-box bits, I'd recommend two specific profiles.

The first—a dish cutter—is a kind of "utility" bit. Because it is designed to cut on the bottom, it does a better job of rounding and tapering spindles. Almost every turning task you'd do with a straight bit will be done better by a dish cutter. Such bits are available in a variety of sizes, in both ¼-inch and ½-inch shank configurations.

The second profile is the point-cutting roundover bit. This is the bit used to cut rings and rounded shoulders. It cuts a groove in which both shoulders are rounded over. There is no flat between the roundovers, because the cutting edge comes to a point. Not every bit manufacturer makes point-cutting roundovers, so they aren't easy to find, especially in sizes other than miniscule.

Here are several good sources: Oldham (800-828-9000); Eagle America (800-872-2511); Woodhaven (800-344-6657); Highland Hardware (800-241-6748).

Here's the hitch: Point-cutting roundover bits are extremely fragile. The cutting edge arcs from the out-side edge to a very sharp point at the bit axis. There's no way to support the carbide at that point, so it is very prone to breakage. (I suspect this is why there are so few manufacturers of these bits.) The breakage is more likely to occur in handling than in use, I'd bet.

A variant of the point-cutting roundover is the plunge-cutting roundover. This bit produces a groove with a narrow flat between the quarter-round shoulders. This is a sturdier bit, but because of the flat, the cuts it makes may not be as versatile.

A number of sources also have groove-cutting profiles identified as ogees and "classical." Check them out in catalogs, and decide for yourself whether they can be incorporated in turnings.

So the message on bits is this: You can do some interesting turnings with bits you have already. But to really unleash the magic, you need to do some shopping.

**A good bit collection** for router-lathe work would include core-box bits large and small, two sizes of dish cutters, a 60-degree V-groover, some point-cutting roundover bits, and even a groove-forming profile cutter or two.

inches long. Bear in mind, however, that with the second chuck serving as a tailstock, the lathe can accommodate a blank much longer than 40 inches. You just can't turn any more of it than about 29 inches at one time.

The shortest blank you can do anything with is about 14 inches. And at that length, just about all you can do is cut a groove about 3½ inches from one end.

Here's the deal with all this "waste" stock: The design of the sled dictates that the axis of the bit can't come closer than 3½ inches to the mid support or the tailstock. This means you will have a 3- to 3½-inch-long segment at the tail end of the blank that can't be turned. Likewise, when the sled hits the mid support, the bit axis will be 3½ inches from it. And from that point to the chuck, the distance is about 9½ inches. So you will have 13 inches of stock that you can't turn on any spindle blank.

By ganging turnings on a long blank, you can reduce the overall waste.

A blank does not absolutely have to be dressed and squared. It should be roughly square to begin, but a blank ripped from rough stock—one with two or three rough surfaces, in other words—can be centered reasonably well.

So to begin your very first turning, prepare a blank about 2½ inches square and 40 inches long.

**2. Center the stock in the router lathe.** Just as in standard lathe turning, centering the stock in the router lathe is a crucial step. Finding the center of the bottom of the leg stock is easy. Just draw diagonal lines across the end grain. The point where the lines intersect is the center of the stock. When the time comes, you just drive a 2-inch drywall screw through the tailstock into that point on the blank.

Centering the top of the leg stock between the bolts of the clamping disk is a little trickier. I start by drawing a centerline along each face of the blank. Start at the butt of the blank, and make the lines about 2 inches long.

When you go to fit the blank in the lathe, you'll discover that the sled is in the way. With the sled's follower resting on the lathe back, there isn't enough room beneath the sled for a 2½-inch-square blank. What I do is tip the sled up and prop it up with a scrap of wood.

With the sled now propped out of the way, I position the leg stock in the chuck and turn the clamp screws in enough to support the stock. Then I jump to the tail end long enough to drive that tailstock screw into the blank's centerpoint. With the tail end mounted, I can focus on centering the head end of the blank.

Return to the headstock and adjust the clamp screws so each screw is on one of the centerlines. This is all it takes to roughly center the blank. (And with experience and practice, you may be able to get to this point without marking those centerlines. You'll be able to eyeball it.)

**Centering stock in the chuck** involves trapping it between four screws. Centerlines drawn on the stock help get the initial setting. To fine-tune it, clamp a scrap at one corner of the blank, as shown. Adjust the screws until each corner just brushes the scrap as the stock rotates.

To fine-tune the setup, use a scrap of wood as a gauge. Rest it on the mid support and butt its end against the blank. Turn the crank very slowly, spinning the blank. What you want to do is hold the "gauge" against a corner of the blank. If the blank is centered, you can turn the blank and all four corners will brush the gauge. When it is off-center, two consecutive corners will brush the gauge, but the third and fourth corners will miss. You have to adjust the clamp screws to push those corners closer to the gauge.

It's a trial-and-error process that gets easier the more times you do it.

**3. Set up a template.** With a blank centered in the lathe, it should be evident that a "template" is necessary. When you are merely rounding a blank, the template is just a strip taller than the lathe back that can support the sled's follower. For the task at hand—rounding that 2½-inch square—a 6½- to 7-inch-wide, 3-foot-long piece of hardboard or ¼-inch plywood is all that's needed.

Cut this template. Then stand it against the lathe back, its bottom edge on the bench top, and clamp it to the lathe. Remove the prop from under the sled, and lower the sled onto the template.

**4. Adjust the bit depth.** Chuck a bit appropriate for the job in your sled-mounted router. To me, the ideal bit is a large-diameter dish cutter. But you can use a bottom-cleaning bit, a mortising bit (designed for cutting hinge mortises), or a large-diameter straight bit.

Adjust the depth of the bit to cut ⅛ to ¼ inch deep into the stock. As an aid to adjusting the bit depth, simply lower the sled until the bit rests on the corner of the turning blank, and then measure the distance between the follower and the top edge of the template. Adjust the bit until the distance equals *half* the amount of stock you want to remove in the first pass.

**5. Round the turning area.** The action will seem more like surfacing than rounding. What you do is slide the router back and forth over the stationary blank, cutting from end to end. This approach involves little cranking, and it completes the work in a remarkably short time.

Slide the sled as far to the head end of the lathe as it will go. Switch on the router, and lower the sled until the follower rests on the template. The bit should engage the blank. Grasping the router's knob or the sled itself, slide it smoothly and steadily to the tail end of the lathe, then back to the starting position.

Now give the crank a nudge, turning the blank about 10 degrees. Make another pass from the head end to the tail and back again.

Use the crank to turn the blank another 10 degrees, then pass the router from end to end and back.

And that's how it is done. You just repeat and repeat this process until you've routed the entire blank. This first pass will actually only round the corners of the blank. It will still have prominent flats. To make it really round, you'll have to extend the bit another ⅛ to ¼ inch and make another series

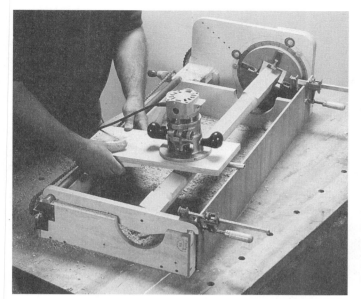

**To round a spindle,** slide the router back and forth along the blank by hand, turning the blank only a few degrees between passes. You can grasp the sled itself or a knob on the router as you move it. Note the straight level template clamped to the lathe back.

**To taper a spindle,** you need to use a template that tapers from one end to the other. It is obvious here that the template is more steeply angled than the actual taper it produces. Note that the corners have been knocked off the waste at the foot of the turning so the sled can pass over it.

of passes, routing the entire blank. Then, after extending the bit yet again, you have to do it a third time (maybe even a fourth and fifth). On the final series of passes, turn the blank only about 5 degrees per pass and advance the bit only $\frac{1}{16}$ inch. This will yield the smoothest surface.

When you are finished, you will have a smooth, even round.

## Tapering a Spindle

Routing a taper follows exactly the same procedure as rounding. The only difference is the template. Instead of using a straight, level guide edge, you use a straight, sloped guide edge. The steeper the slope, the sharper the taper.

Make the template following the guidelines set out in the section "Templates" on page 288.

Once you've made it, set to work. You don't need to round the blank first. You can use the taper template and a square blank. Just set the cutting depth with the follower poised at the deepest point of the taper so you won't overload the router. You'll probably start with half-length passes, and the smallest section of the turning may be round before you even begin knocking the corners of the fattest section.

One problem you may confront is that the degree of taper is so pronounced that you can't even get the spindle started. The sled settles onto the blank before the follower reaches the lowest point on the template. What you have to do is put spacers under the template temporarily. Start routing with the template elevated the same amount at both ends. After the corners are off the blank, you can remove the spacers and lower the template.

But now the corners on the unrouted waste at the tailstock end of the blank will hit the sled. Just knock off these corners with a chisel or drawknife. It is waste. Take off enough to allow the sled clearance.

## Routing a Leg

The best way to show you how this router lathe works is to walk you through a project. A table leg is a good turning to use as a practice project.

The leg, shown in the drawing *Table Leg Template Layouts,* was designed by my colleague Rob Yoder. It consists of three inset beads at the top, a taper, two protruding beads, and a straight foot. Routing this turning isn't difficult once you have the two templates made. But determining the contour of the first template is a little tricky. In addition, this turning introduces you to the intricacies of accounting for the bit diameter in laying out the template.

**1. Lay out and analyze the turning.** The first step, of course, is to cut a piece of template stock and to lay out the turning profile on this stock.

Having done that, analyze the profile in terms of how it can be reproduced on the router lathe. Note that the leg has a square section, which is where the apron will join it. Just below that is a 2½-inch-long segment that is 2¼ inches in diameter. It is embellished with the inset beads. Next is a $16\frac{7}{16}$-inch-long taper, gradually reducing the turning's diameter to 1¼ inches. At the end of this taper are the two protruding beads, which have a maximum diameter of 1¾ inches. Finally, there's a 2-inch-long foot that is 1¼ inches in diameter. Any stock beyond that is waste.

All the beads have a ¼-inch-radius section, and they converge, rather than having a flat between them. You can plan to rout them with a ¼-inch point-cutting roundover bit. Because they are fixed elements, the template notches should be on the second template.

The first template needs to produce the contour, which is pretty straightforward except for the protruding beads.

Turning

## TABLE LEG PROFILE

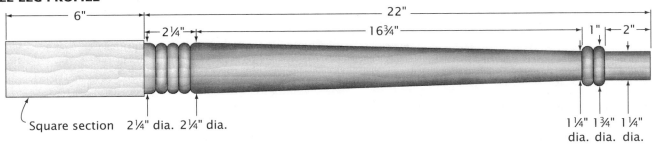

Square section   2¼" dia.   2¼" dia.

6"   2¼"   16¾"   22"   1"   2"

1¼"   1¾"   1¼"
dia.   dia.   dia.

The template must also have a positive stop to locate the shoulder between the square and turned sections. This template's basic contour, shown in the drawing *Table Leg Template Layouts,* is not too hard to figure out. The tricky part is calculating the dimensions. You must account for the diameter of the bit as you work this out.

To account for the bit size, subtract its diameter from the diameter of the follower, then divide by 2. In the drawing, we are using a 1¼-inch-diameter dish cutter. The follower is ⅝ inch in diameter. When the follower is against a stop, the bit is extending ⁵⁄₁₆ inch beyond the stop. So, as shown in the drawing, to limit the length of the cut to 19 inches (the distance from the square shoulder to the protruding beads), the stops must be 18⅜ inches apart.

Note that if you use a bit smaller in diameter than the follower, the stops would have to be farther apart than the length of the turned area.

**2. Lay out the templates.** I think you can study the layout drawing and figure out the rationale for how the two templates are laid out. If you have the same bits I used, then you can duplicate the templates shown.

But if you must use something other than the dish cutter I used, you'll have to redo the first template. There's, of course, no substitute for the point-cutting roundover bit for producing the beads.

**3. Clamp the first template to the router lathe.** To position the template so waste is minimized, you should slide the router sled as close to the headstock as possible, and prop it up. Set the template against the back and adjust its lateral position so its stop is against the follower. Clamp the template.

Because you've got to switch templates to complete a turning (and you have to complete a turning before removing it from the lathe), you need to trace along its ends on the lathe. That way, you can position the second template between the marks and be confident that the beads will end up in just the right places. (You might even clamp or screw a stop to the lathe back to aid in positioning the templates.)

**4. Cut the leg blanks.** By waiting until now to cut the blanks, you can save a bit on material. With the template in place, you can determine how long each blank must be.

## TABLE LEG TEMPLATE LAYOUTS

ACCOUNTING FOR BIT DIAMETER

⁵⁄₁₆"   ⅝"   Sled base
Dish-cutting bit   Follower
1¼"

FIRST TEMPLATE

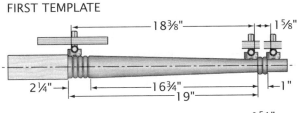

18⅜"   1⅝"
2¼"   16¾"   1"
19"

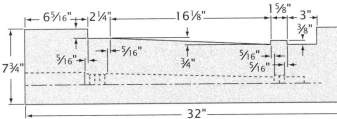

6⁵⁄₁₆"   2¼"   16⅛"   1⅝"   3"
3⁄8"
7¾"   ⁵⁄₁₆"   ⁵⁄₁₆"   ¾"   ⁵⁄₁₆"   ⁵⁄₁₆"
32"

SECOND TEMPLATE

Trim the "ears" from the template.

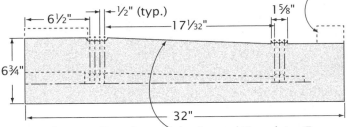

6½"   ½" (typ.)   17¹⁄₃₂"   1⅝"
6¾"
32"

Lay the First Template on the Second Template. Trace along the top edge. Transfer the "bead stop" locations from the profile sketch on the First Template.

Slide the sled to the tail end of the template. Set the tail-stock in place on the lathe, and measure from it to the chuck. That's how long the blank must be.

**5. Rout the turning's basic profile.** The process here is exactly like that in rounding or tapering a spindle. Set the bit extension, turn on the router, and move the router sled back and forth, guided by the template. As you near the turning's foot, you'll have to lift the sled slightly to get it over the bump for the protruding beads. After each pass, turn the blank a few degrees. When you've routed back and forth through a full rotation of the blank, reset the bit extension and repeat the process.

You do have to monitor your progress by measuring the girth of the turning. It is possible to turn the blank smaller than you want if you aren't careful.

When the basic profile is done and the turning is to the correct diameter, it is time to switch templates and router bits.

**6. Rout the beads.** Prop the sled up (relatively) out of the way. Switch the templates, being careful to align the second template exactly the way the first was.

Switch bits. Use a ¼-inch-radius point-cutting roundover bit. Remove the prop and lower the sled's follower onto the template. Adjust the bit extension so it cuts about ⅛ inch deep.

Now make a first pass on each bead. Tip the router up very slightly, and poise the follower over one of the "bead stops" on the template. Turn on the router, and lower the sled so the follower drops straight into the stop. Crank the turning through two or three full rotations. (It should go without saying that the chain clamp jaws are loose throughout this entire turning project.) Lift the router just enough to poise the follower on the center of the next bead stop. Lower the router and crank. Lift, shift, lower, and crank.

**Using a template** is essential with the router lathe. Each arc of this template retains the follower, in effect parking the router in one spot, so its bit makes a cut around the circumference of the spindle. With a point-cutting roundover bit, the template produces three full beads.

To avoid burning the wood when cutting elements like these beads, Fred likes to start cranking before the follower has bottomed on the template. If you try it, you'll note that the sled tends to pull to one side, which can cause a deformed cut. You have to be cautious. Experience, says Fred, will teach you which way and how much to compensate.

After you've completed a first pass on all the beads, readjust the bit extension. You should be able to complete the beads with this pass, so you want to adjust the bit carefully. Do not cut too deep.

Make the second round of cuts the same way you did the first round.

## Routing Spirals

Now for the fun part. The ability to rout spirals on turnings is a feature unique to the router lathe, and it really is a simple operation.

Spiral turnings can be used as table legs or bedposts, on clocks and mirror frames, and in many other applications. The lathe allows you to spiral the cuts clockwise or counterclockwise, so you could make a table with the legs on the left spiraling one way and the legs on the right spiraling the other way. You can do a turning with the cuts spiraling from the bottom *up* in one direction and from the top *down* in the other, meeting in the middle. You can even cut crossing spirals.

Routing spirals calls into play all the gears and chains that are integral to the lathe's design. You turn the crank and the spindle turns while the router migrates from one end of the lathe to the other.

With the lathe set up—like the prototype—with the 2:1 gearbox ratio and the 52-tooth chuck gear and the 46-tooth transverse gear, the router will move 15 inches along the spindle each time the spindle makes one complete revolution. Referred to as "1 in 15 inches," this ratio is decent for table leg–length turnings, though it may be a bit loose for shorter turnings. You can lengthen the spiral by using a smaller transverse gear; the alternate gear on the prototype lathe has 32 teeth and moves the router 21 inches per spindle revolution. Want an even looser spiral? Stop by a bicycle shop and buy a still-smaller gear.

If you want a tighter spiral than 1 in 15 inches, you have to build a gearbox with a less-than 2:1 ratio. Buy a set of 1:1 bevel gears, and build a new gearbox. Install it, and see what spiral ratios are produced using the sprockets you have. And go from there.

To illustrate the operation, let me show you how to rout spiraling coves into a mildly tapered spindle.

**1. Make the template.** Start by making the template shown in the drawing *Spiraled-Spindle Template*. The template has a straight taper, bounded by notches. You trap the sled's follower in a notch to rout a cove around the spindle. The coves, cut with a ¾-inch core-box bit, set off the spiraled section from the rest of the spindle.

In addition to the template shown, you need a plain rectangular template to guide the rounding of the spindle.

## SPIRALED-SPINDLE TEMPLATE

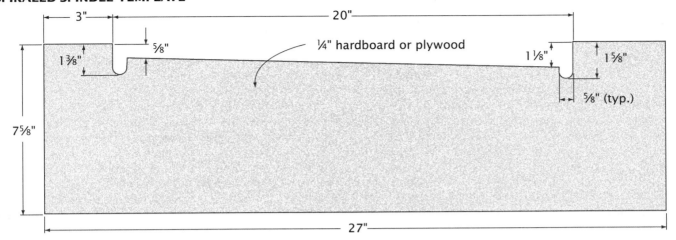

¼" hardboard or plywood

3" — 20" — 27"

5/8" · 1 3/8" · 7 5/8" · 1 1/8" · 1 5/8" · 5/8" (typ.)

**2. Rough out the spindle.** Cut a spindle about 2¼ inches square by about 36 inches long. Center it in the chuck, then round the turnable segment of it. Use a straight, level template and whatever bit you favor for this operation.

When the spindle is turned to a 2-inch round, switch templates and cut the taper. To prevent the sled's follower from dipping into the notch at either end of the taper, clamp a scrap block at the very edge of each one. Then with the same bit you have been using, cut the taper.

**3. Rout the coves.** Switch to a ¾-inch core-box bit, and remove the stops blocking the notches.

Set the bit extension so the cut will be about ⅛ to ¼ inch deep. Lift the router sled slightly, and poise the follower above one of the template notches. Switch on the router, lower the router, and turn the crank to rotate the spindle two or three complete revolutions. Now lift the router and slide it along the shaft, lining it up over the other notch. Lower the router and crank the spindle to cut the second cove.

If necessary, adjust the cutting depth and make a second pass at each cove, cutting both to the final depth.

**4. Set up the lathe to rout the spirals.** Several adjustments have to be made.

First, you need to switch to a ½-inch core-box bit. The plan is to cut eight shallow coves into the tapered portion of the spindle with this bit. Chuck the bit in the router, and adjust it so it will penetrate about 3/32 inch into the spindle. To check the depth, tilt the router sled down so that the bit is resting on the stock, and then measure the distance between the follower and the template edge. The depth of cut will be two-thirds of that distance.

Next, you must reclamp the stops over the notches. You don't want the follower to dip into the notches.

**5. Rout the first spiral cove.** To rout a spiral, you must align an indexing mark on the chuck with the registration mark on the headstock. You must set the sled at either the headstock or tailstock end, then tighten the appropriate chain clamp. When you are ready to rout, lift

the router so the bit is just clear of the work, switch it on, lower the bit to the work, and turn the crank, dragging the router to the other end of the turning. There you lift the router again and switch it off. You've got a spiral cut.

It's easy. But you must be mindful of the details.

*Detail 1:* Figure out how many spirals you want before cutting a single one. Determine which index numbers you'll use to space the spirals evenly around the spindle. There are 24 index marks on the chuck. In this exercise, you'll do eight cuts, so you use every third index mark; that is: 3, 6, 9, 12, 15, 18, 21, and 24.

*Detail 2:* The drive train has a little play in it. You want to keep this play under control by always turning the crank in the same direction. If, when setting up, you overshoot the index mark, do NOT back up the chuck by reversing the direction you are cranking. Instead, crank the chuck all the way around to the mark. This keeps the slack taken up.

In addition, always cranking in the same direction is a habit that can save you some work. Imagine routing the eighth spiral clockwise after routing the first seven *counter*clockwise.

*Detail 3:* Don't forget the chain clamp. You will be tightening and loosening the clamp again and again as you rout a series of spirals. Coordinate the clamp you use—top or bottom—with the direction you turn the crank and the sled's starting position.

For example, I tend to crank counterclockwise. To me, the top clamp seems easier to use. So I post the sled at the tailstock to begin each spiral cut. Thus, when I tighten the top clamp and turn the crank counterclockwise, the router will be dragged to the headstock.

Here's the drill:

1. Loosen the clamp, and slide the sled to its starting position.
2. Turn the crank in the chosen direction to align the appropriate chuck index mark with the headstock registration mark.
3. Tighten the clamp.
4. Make the cut, then switch off the router.
5. Go to Step 1.

So go through the motions in your head and maybe with the lathe, with the router switched off. When you are confident you are ready to make the chips fly, position the router, line up index mark #3, tighten the clamp, and rout the first spiral.

**6. Rout the rest of the spirals.** With one spiral cut under your belt, the rest will be a piece of cake.

Loosen the chain clamp, and slide the router sled back to the starting position. Crank the spindle through its revolution, aligning the index mark #6 with the registration mark. Tighten the chain clamp. Rout a another spiral.

The next spiral will start from index mark #9, and then #12, and then #15—but you get the picture. The last spiral you rout will be at index mark #24.

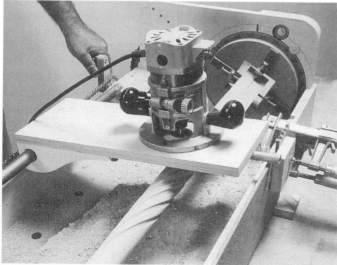

**Routing spirals** requires you to be methodical above all else. Always turn the crank in the same direction. Align the index mark on the chuck with the registration mark on the headstock (*top*) to set the spindle in the proper starting position. With the router in its starting location and its clamp tightened, turn the crank (*bottom*) to simultaneously rotate the spindle and drag the router, making the spiral cut.

## Extended Turnings

It would be a shame if the router lathe's unique turnings had to be confined to turning blanks that could fit between the headstock and tailstock. But the lathe's unique design allows you turn a blank of any practical length.

Want to rout a 5- or 6-foot-long bedpost? You can do it! Want to turn a couple of posts for the porch? It'll be a lot of work, but you can do it. All you need is a tailstock chuck to match the headstock chuck. With it in use, the turning blank can pass through the tailstock just as it does through the headstock. You can have a couple feet of stock jutting out of both ends of the lathe while you work the middle.

The tailstock chuck is a duplicate of the headstock one, though you don't need the indexing marks on it. In use, this auxiliary chuck simply rests on the two support bearings bolted to the tail support. It won't topple off the bearings because it is clamped to the blank, and the blank in turn is clamped to the headstock chuck, which is securely mounted in the headstock. Got that?

To set up an extended blank for turning, roughly center it in the tailstock chuck first. Feed the head end through the headstock chuck, and set the tailstock chuck on the support bearings. Now center the blank in the headstock chuck. That done, refine the centering of the work in the tailstock chuck. The blank can now be turned just as if it were a 3-footer.

To do an extended turning, you have to customize the design to conceal transitions between turned segments. You probably won't have much success producing a continuous round or taper that's longer than the 29 inches the lathe can work at one time. When you shift the workpiece position, you have to recenter it in two chucks, and the likelihood of the second setup matching the first alignment is slim to none. Thus, you won't be able to seamlessly blend two sections together. So use a feature like a bead or cove to isolate the sections.

**Routing a long workpiece** calls the auxiliary chuck into play. The open-centered chuck design allows you to "step" the blank through the lathe, working it section by section. Here the midsection of a long post is being rounded. Extending the turning simply requires you to loosen the chuck clamps and shift the post toward the tailstock. Then you recenter the blank and continue routing.


Turning

# Creating a Finial

A finial is a decorative turning used at the tip of a post. It's usually created as a faceplace turning, rather than a spindle turning. The top is turned to a point; it isn't sawed off.

The most elaborate finials that come to my mind are the flame finials hand-carved for Queen Anne highboys. While the router lathe won't produce anything as exquisite as a flame finial, it will enable you to shape a finial and decorate it with spiral beads, grooves, or coves.

Once you've mastered the art of turning spindles and decorating them with all manner of spirals, you may want to experiment with finials. The photos show the setup for a finial turned on the router lathe by Fred Matlack. The turning stock is supported by the chuck and an auxiliary support clamped to the workbench to the left of the headstock. You work the end of the stock, and bear in mind that the stock has to project beyond the lathe frame's middle support if it is to be within the router's reach.

To give the router bit better access to the stock's end, Fred shifted it to the edge of the sled nearest the headstock. He cut a template, which he used both to shape the finial and to guide the routing of spiral coves into it.

**Routing a spiraled finial** is a router lathe exclusive. You can shape a finial like this on a lathe, but you'd have to hand-carve the coves. The graceful template clamped to the lathe back was used to both shape and spiral this finial. The block clamped to the template is the starting block for the spirals.

**A special tail support** is needed to support the finial blank's free end. A simple but effective one can be cobbled from scraps and clamped to the workbench, as shown.

# Jig-Making Materials and Hardware

A lot of jigs. That's what I've seen in the course of developing this book. A LOT of jigs. I've built a lot of them, too. Some two or three times. The best of them, of course, have already been described in detail. What I want to talk about here is some of the materials used to make the jigs in this book.

Router jigs don't have to be fancy. Some are made as one-use throwaway items, such as when you want to attach a special fence or stop to the router without damaging the factory baseplate. These are the jigs you probably will cobble up using materials from the scrap bin.

This doesn't mean, of course, that these particular jigs won't be high-quality. If you ordinarily work with decent materials, then your scraps will be decent, too. It's just that you probably will feel less regret at tossing a jig you made with materials you had already decided to toss out.

The majority of the jigs I've included in *Router Magic* are built to be used again and again—a flush-trimming baseplate, for example, or a trammel, a mortising jig, or a T-square. For these, you just might want to invest in new, specialized materials and hardware. So as this book winds down, I want to pass along some of the things I learned about these special jig-making materials and hardware.

## Sheet Goods

Depending upon your experience level and the nature of the woodworking you do, you may be thoroughly familiar with sheet goods. Surely, every router woodworker has worked with plywood and hardboard, which are stocked by home centers as well as lumberyards. For making jigs especially, you ought to venture beyond the common construction sheet goods.

### Plywood

Take plywood for example. It's a material found in a great many of the *Router Magic* jigs. We all know that it is stable, that it is relatively unaffected by changes in humidity. Its stability makes it a good material to use when you want a jig to retain its accuracy for a long time.

But you shouldn't use just any kind of plywood. You should use a hardwood plywood or, even better, a *premium* hardwood plywood like Apple Ply or Baltic Birch plywood. Unlike construction plywood, hardwood plywood has smooth, hard face veneers on both sides of the sheet.

Plywood is made by gluing thin face veneers ($\frac{1}{40}$ to $\frac{1}{28}$ inch) to a core of wood plies or composite material like particleboard or medium-density fiberboard. Veneer-core (VC) plywood is the variety most commonly found in

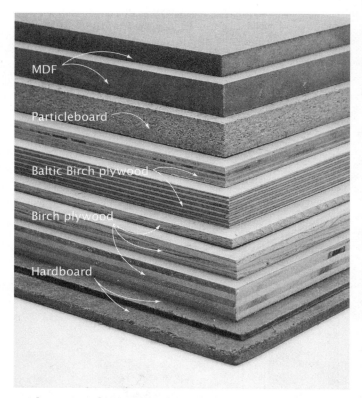

**A bonanza for router jig making** resides in this stack of fairly common sheet goods. All those shown make good jigs, but some make *great* jigs.

small shops. The core is made from plies glued together in alternating grain directions. This crossing of the grains gives VC plywood its uniform strength and dimensional stability. It is relatively lightweight and does a good job of holding fasteners.

Typically, a $\frac{3}{4}$-inch-thick sheet of VC plywood has seven plies—five core plies and two face veneers. Higher-grade plywood has a greater number of plies (usually 13 in a $\frac{3}{4}$-inch-thick panel), which mades the panel stiffer and more stable. This is important in the typical jig. With a high-quality plywood such as Baltic Birch or Apple Ply, a raw edge can be sanded and polished for a decorative effect. For most VC plywoods, you can expect small voids in the core (under 1-inch diameter) due to knotholes. While voids won't greatly affect the strength of the panel, edges will need to be filled, or better yet, banded with solid wood.

Common thicknesses for hardwood plywood are $\frac{1}{4}$ inch, $\frac{1}{2}$ inch, and $\frac{3}{4}$ inch. Keep in mind that these sizes are nominal. Generally, the panel you buy will be thinner than the stated size: For example, $\frac{3}{4}$-inch plywood is typically $\frac{23}{32}$ inch thick ($\frac{1}{32}$ inch under the nominal size). Although panels are usually 4 × 8 feet, European sheets like Baltic Birch are metric system and come in odd sizes (odd to us Americans). Typical is 150 × 150 centimeters (roughly 5 feet square).

### Medium-Density Fiberboard

A very useful sheet good that's becoming more available is medium-density fiberboard. It's been a popular material among commercial cabinetmakers for years but only recently has it found its way into retail building supply outlets.

Commonly called "MDF," medium-density fiberboard is used when a surface or substrate that's extremely flat and smooth is needed. MDF is made from what used to be considered waste—wood chips. The chips, from both hardwoods and softwoods, are ground into fibers, blended with a small amount of urea glue and paraffin waxes (for moisture resistance), then blown into a forming machine. A continuous mat emerges from the forming machine and passes into a hot press, which squeezes it FLAT under tremendous pressure (up to 50,000 pounds). Then the panel is sanded to a specific thickness and sawed to size.

Unlike plywood, MDF thicknesses are very precise: A ¾-inch-thick panel is right on the money. Wholesale suppliers stock sheets in ¼-inch, ½-inch, and ¾-inch thicknesses, though you may not find all thicknesses in a given retail outlet. The standard panel size is ½ inch over 4 feet by 8 feet. MDF is heavy, about half again as heavy as a comparable piece of plywood.

The dense, homogeneous character of MDF gives it great stability, making it an ideal material for jigs and fixtures. I think it is particularly fine for templates. A router bit's pilot bearing won't compress its dense edges (or dive into a void between plies). MDF's uniform surface makes it an excellent substrate for laminates. Routing its edges produces sharp, crisp profiles. The faces are smooth enough to obviate the need for sanding, but the edges should be sanded lightly before finishing in order to remove nap left after machining.

Common woodworking glues bond well to the surface of MDF, but the porous edges should be sized before gluing. (A thin coat of white or yellow glue works fine.)

But MDF isn't a problem-free material. One hitch is that, left unsealed, MDF will wick up moisture and swell, causing permanent changes in dimension. A film finish or surface veneer will protect boards from absorbing moisture. Another hitch is that large MDF panels have a tendency to sag under load, even under their own weight, because the material has no grain to provide stiffness. With the typical jig or fixture, this isn't a problem, but it can be if you use MDF for a router table top. To prevent sagging, you need to design a support structure. Covering both faces with plastic laminate will stiffen the panel, negating its tendency to sag. A third problem also stems from MDF's grainlessness: Regular wood screws strip out. Use deep-threaded screws for good grab. For even better holding power, use knock-down fasteners.

Finally, MDF turns to powder when you machine it. I mean POWDER. This is fine dust that gets everywhere; good dust collection and a dust mask are musts.

### Hardboard

Hardboard is similar to fiberboard in that it is made from ground-up fibers. Because it's commonly available in precise and uniform thicknesses of ⅛ inch and ¼ inch, and because it has a burnished surface that's smooth and slippery, this type of board is well suited to jig and fixture work.

Several grades of hardboard are available, and for jig making, the rule of thumb is the harder the better. Tempered hardboard, sometimes referred to as Masonite (the brand name of International Paper Company's board), is a high-density hardboard that's been resin-impregnated and heat-cured. This tempering process enhances the board's hardness, strength, and water resistance. The type of hardboard I'd recommend has two smooth faces, but a screenbacked hardboard, which has a smooth face and a textured face, is also available.

Tempered hardboard is a good choice for quickie baseplates (those job-specific ones you make in haste, then toss just as quickly). It is quite uniform with no voids or splinters, but you may have to apply several coats of sealer to prevent the edges from getting fuzzy. If you need to glue it to another part, its surface needs to be roughed up first (120-grit works well).

### Particleboard

Particleboard is widely available and cheap, so it is attractive to many woodworkers. It is considered an excellent substrate for plastic laminates and thus is widely used for countertops and cabinetry.

It is generally available in a wider selection of thicknesses than plywood or MDF. All the standard thicknesses—from ¼ inch to ¾ inch—are stocked, as well as thicker panels like 1 inch, 1¼ inches, and 1½ inches. Panels are typically 48½ inches wide by 96½ inches long.

Often called flakeboard or chipboard, particleboard is made from chips that are compressed under heat and pressure. The resulting panel is, like MDF, heavier than plywood but less strong than plywood. Unlike MDF, its internal density is low, and also unlike MDF, it has rough edges that result from the large chips used to make it. Like MDF, working with particleboard requires good dust collection.

The upshot is that particleboard is a pretty poor choice for making jigs. You especially should avoid using particleboard where strength and edge quality are important. It makes unsatisfactory templates because router bit pilots are likely to dig into the edge.

## Plastic Laminate

Because it wears well, slides smoothly on wood, and is easily machinable, plastic laminate is a great material to use in making a router table and accessories and in making router jigs and custom baseplates. It is readily available and is easy to bond to wood. (Some of it is even supposed to *look* like wood, though we all know it doesn't even come close.)

The material is made by impregnating several layers of kraft paper with phenolic plastic resin. The color and pattern is in a separate sheet of paper, impregnated with melamine

**Plastic laminate** is attached with contact cement and cut with a flush-trimming bit. As easy as it is to apply, it provides slick, durable surfaces for hardworking router jigs and fixtures. The fanned-out samples are only representative of all the available colors and textures.

plastic resin, which covers the core. The surface can be embossed with a design or texture. The paper layers and the plastics are bonded together under high heat and pressure. The resulting material is hard and durable—easily cleaned, and scratch- and wear-resistant. For all this, it isn't expensive.

In the router workshop, plastic laminate can be used to cover anything that needs a wear-resistant, slick, easily cleaned surface. Router table tops. Fence facings. You can use it to advantage on the base of a sled or the edges of a straight-edge. If a stable, flat surface is needed, the laminate should be applied to both sides of the core to prevent warping. In some instances, it's appropriate to apply laminate to both surfaces; but where one surface will be hidden from view, you can save money by applying what's called backer to the hidden side. Backer is laminate without the color layer.

Sold in several grades, the most commonly used is the horizontal grade, which is about ¹⁄₁₆ inch thick. Many sheet sizes are available, ranging in width from 30 inches up to 60 inches, and in length from 8 to 12 feet. Most lumber-yards sell several different brands and will have an incredible assortment of 1 × 2-inch samples to choose from. Order the color and finish you want, select the sheet size, and in a few days—most likely—your plastic laminate will be ready for you to pick up, tied up in a 2- to 3-foot-diameter roll.

In a nutshell, the procedure for working with laminates is: Cut a piece of plastic laminate to a size just a few fractions of an inch larger than the plywood, MDF, or other substrate it is to cover. Bond it to the substrate; contact cement is the most popular glue for this. The laminate is positioned so its edges overhang those of the substrate just a little. With your router or laminate trimmer and a flush-trimming bit, zip around the edges, trimming away the excess laminate and making it flush with the substrate's edges. Perfect!

There's a little more to working with plastic laminates than that, but the router is the key tool used throughout the process. In addition to trimming the edges to finish a lami-nate project, you can also use the router to cut the pieces you need from the laminate sheets to start the project.

## Plastics

For jigs and fixtures, I *love* this stuff. Clear baseplates make it so much easier to see what the router is doing as you work. Clear mounting plates can make it easier to change bits in a table-mounted router. And that's just the beginning of the benefits.

You won't find plastics at the local building center, but there's probably a plastics dealer near you. Your wood-working power tools will cut and bore and shape plastic as well as they do wood.

### Acrylic and Polycarbonate

Acrylic and polycarbonate, two common plastics, are very popular for custom baseplates, bit guards, and other jig-and-fixture applications.

Acrylic may be more familiar to you as Plexiglas, the brand manufactured by Rohm and Haas, or as Lucite, the brand made by DuPont. There are other brands, as well as generics. This name game is true also of polycarbonate: You may have heard of General Electric's Lexan, or Rohm and Haas's Tuffak, without knowing both were brands of polycarbonate, and without knowing that you could buy a "generic" polycarb and save a little money.

Both acrylic and polycarbonate plastics are pretty com-monly available. They're stocked by plastics dealers—check your Yellow Pages—in sheets in a range of thicknesses, lengths, and widths; but you can usually buy odds and ends that are perfectly suited for baseplates, mounting plates, and other jig work.

The practical difference between the two types of plastic? The acrylic is crystal-clear, rigid, and quite strong, and as such is well regarded as a less-fragile glass substitute. Nevertheless, it is possible to break. Polycarbonate, con-versely, is very hard to break (it's the stuff safety glasses are made of), but it is less rigid than acrylic. Under stress, poly-carb will tend to give, and the stress of supporting an 18-pound router can produce measurable sag. So make durable, unbreakable baseplates for hand-held routing from polycarb, and router-table mounting plates from acrylic.

Both materials are quite easily worked with carbide-tipped woodworking tools. These plastics are popular primarily because they are available in clear sheets. Ostensibly, a baseplate made of either affords a nearly unob-structed view of the work at hand. But both plastics scratch easily, so after being used a while, baseplates made from them become webbed with scratches and thus fairly opaque.

## Phenolic

Phenolic plastic is gaining popularity for custom baseplates, mounting plates, and other jig-making uses. It's the material that the factory baseplates have been made of for years. Phenolic sheet is a hard, dense material made by applying heat and pressure to layers of paper or cloth impregnated with synthetic resin. The layers can be made of cellulose paper or cotton, synthetic fabric, or glass fabric. Under the heat and pressure, a chemical reaction—polymerization—transforms the layers into an industrial laminated plastic.

Phenolic wears and slides extremely well, it's heat-resistant, and depending on a particular phenolic's composition, it can be very rigid and strong. It machines well and doesn't tend to melt and stick like the other plastics. Typically, phenolic plastic is brown or black.

The range of grades is bewildering, and it's difficult to know whether a particular piece will be suitable for your purpose. Try NEMA XX, the lowest grade. The cost of ¼-inch phenolic in this grade is comparable to the cost of ⅜-inch acrylic, and so is the strength.

The problem with phenolics is availability. The plastics dealer who sells you scraps of acrylic and polycarb is unlikely to have scraps of phenolic around. Few of the wholesale-retail dealers even stock phenolics.

There are, however, a few mail-order tool companies offering small pieces of phenolic material.

## How to Work Plastic

Plastic has some worthy uses in woodworking, especially in making strong, practical baseplates and mounting plates, naturally slick router-table sleds, and virtually bulletproof router-table bit guards.

The plastics we are talking about here are easily worked with typical woodworking tools—saws, drills, sanders. And, yes, routers. Now there *are* saw blades and drill bits that lend themselves better to plastic work than others. But as a practical matter, you don't need to get too lathered about special tooling. Every plastic jig in this book was made using whatever woodworking blade was in the table saw or band saw at the time the cut was made, and with absolutely standard twist-drill and Forstner bits. Both tooling and workpieces emerged from these experiences in good shape.

Acrylics and polycarbonates are easily scratched. For this reason, most of these plastics are covered on both sides with protective masking paper. Leave the paper on while you work. Do your layouts with a pencil on the masking paper. After you've cut it, bored the holes, and scraped the edges, peel the paper off.

### Cutting

Almost any rigid plastic, from a laminate to an acrylic to a phenolic, can be cut on your table saw with a carbide-tipped combination blade. The band saw, fitted with a metal-cutting blade, cuts plastics well, especially curves. Of the portable power saws, the saber saw is the most versatile, since it will handle a range of cuts, from bevels to curves. It's especially good for cutting tight-radius curves. And don't forget the

**The band saw cuts plastic with ease.** Acrylic and polycarbonate usually come with a protective masking applied, so you can draw layout lines on the paper. The black phenolic being cut here has masking tape applied so layout lines will be visible.

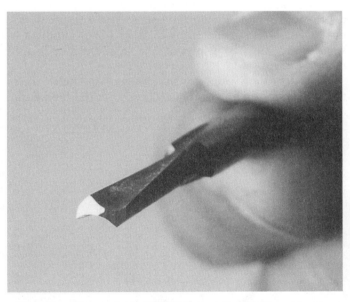

**Bosch makes a straight bit** just for cutting plastics (catalog number 85611M). It's a ¼-inch bit with two 1-inch-long flutes. The cutter geometry gives a surprisingly smooth finish. According to Bosch, this geometry also reduces heat buildup, thus helping to prevent the bit from being "welded in the cut."

router. With a carbide-tipped bit, you can cut your plastic and plunge-bore holes. Equipped with either a pattern bit or a flush-trimming bit, your router will produce as many plastic duplicates as you want from a pattern.

Acrylics and polycarbonates are thermoplastics, which means they are sensitive to heat. Generate too much heat in working them, and they'll gum up that work. So when cutting, back the blade out of the cut as soon as it starts to bind. The length of the band saw blade keeps it cool, so this is less of a problem with the band saw. (In addition, the band saw blade clears chips well, producing a very smooth cut.)

## Drilling and Counterboring

Drilling holes in plastic is more problematic than cutting it because of its incompressibility, brittleness, and/or low softening temperature. The usual advice is to use a high-speed twist bit that's been reground slightly to keep it from splitting or cracking the plastic. The idea is to change the cutting edges from an acute angle to a right, or even an obtuse, angle. What usually happens with an unaltered bit is that it augers into the plastic like a screw, rather than boring a hole.

Back up the plastic with a clean board and clamp it to a bench top or in a vise, or to the drill press table. Feed the bit into the work slowly and steadily; the drill's speed should be 500 to 1,000 rpm. If the hole is deep and the material a thermoplastic, back the bit out often to clear the chips. Don't stop the bit in the hole; it may get stuck there. As the tip nears the breakthrough point, slow the bit even more.

All this advice notwithstanding, I've found that standard brad-point bits and even Forstner bits work just fine. Drill the hole with an in-and-out action so that things have a chance to keep cool—cool enough, anyway, to prevent the plastic from melting. A standard countersink similarly works just fine for countersinking mounting holes, although a single-flute countersink produces a smoother cut than a multi-flute one.

Be particularly careful when drilling large holes, since this operation can create enough heat to soften the plastic

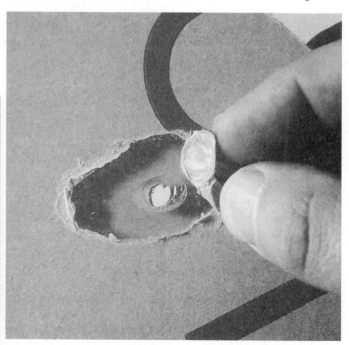

**An overaggressive feed rate caused the chipping** at the hole drilled in this plastic baseplate. To avoid this problem, be sure you have good backing beneath the workpiece. As you near breakthrough, ease up on the feed rate so that the bit bores through, rather than punches through.

and make it stick to the bit. A good approach is to use the templates described in the chapter "Boring Templates" on page 6.

## Joining Plastics

Plastic can be joined to plastic or to wood or to metal. Use common mechanical fasteners like bolts and screws. Or use glue. Though both approaches are familiar to every wood-worker, there are some novel twists in how these apply to plastics.

Take the fastener approach first. Here are a few twists:

- Cut threads in acrylic or polycarbonate with a tap. You then can turn a machine screw directly into the plastic, eliminating the need for a nut. (See "Cutting Threads" on page 304.)
- Use self-tapping screws designed for use in metal. When turned into a pilot hole, a self-tapping screw will cut its own threads. (Repeatedly screwing and unscrewing this fastener destroys the threads, however, so use it only where assembly is a once-and-done proposition.)
- Use wood screws in acrylics and polycarbonates. Clamp the assembly together and drill a pilot hole, making it slightly smaller than the screw's outside diameter, and as deep as the screw is long. With a propoane torch, heat the screw 'til it's deep blue. *Push* it into the pilot hole. The plastic will melt and conform to the screw's shape. When the screw is cool, remove it with a screwdriver, and replace it with a new screw.

You can, of course, just use machine screws with nuts, or bolts with nuts. Easy and familiar and practical and effective. Connect, for example, two pieces of plastic, a piece of plastic and a block of wood, or a plastic bit and a metal part. Use washers for best results.

When it comes to *bonding* plastic to plastic, wood, or metal, forget the familiar glues. They probably won't be satisfactory. Instead, you need epoxies and special cements and solvents.

Although you may never have used contact cement or epoxy, you certainly have heard of them. Less familiar, perhaps, is synthetic rubber adhesive, which refers to the range of caulklike adhesives stocked by every hardware store and building center. (Silicone-based adhesives work here, too.) Solvent and acrylic cement are probably new to you; both are sold by the same retailer who sells the plastic.

Of the latter two bonding agents, solvent *sounds* easier to use, but for router jigs-and-fixtures work, the acrylic cement may work better.

The solvents effectively weld the plastics together. The parts to be joined are assembled, then the solvent—usually methylene dichloride—is applied along the seams with a brush or syringe. So long as the joint is perfectly matched, capillary action pulls the solvent into the joint. There it softens the plastics, allowing them to intermingle and, as the solvent evaporates, to fuse. If the joint is not perfectly fitted, the solvent will be pulled in only here and there, and the bond will be spotty.

You can circumvent this somewhat by soaking one part in a shallow puddle of the solvent, then pressing it to the other part. Still, when using the solvent, it's best to have tight-fitting joints.

The acrylic cement, on the other hand, works best in gappy joints. Two constituents, a resin and a hardener, are mixed, and the resulting syruplike cement is applied with a syringe. Usually, it will form a reinforcing fillet along the seam.

### Polishing the Edges

If you are as meticulous about finishing your jigs and fixtures as you are about finishing your woodworking projects, you may want to smooth and polish the cut edges of your plastic baseplate. It's a several-step process, and if you're like me, you'll probably compromise by scraping the rough spots and beveling the edges just enough to eliminate their sharpness.

Uncompromising? Then scrape those edges next to remove the saw scars, then buff and polish the edges to bring them to a high gloss.

For the first step, use a regular cabinet scraper. Clamp the plastic between wooden cauls in a vise. Position the scraper across the plastic's edge, tilting it back toward you at an angle of about 60 degrees. Pull the scraper toward you; never push it away. Use moderate pressure and long strokes to avoid creating depressions in the piece. Use a file to smooth interior cutouts where a scraper won't fit. Smooth-cut rasps and bastard-cut mill files are best. Rub chalk over the file to keep it from sticking.

Buffing can be done either by hand or mechanically. Use a buffing compound, selecting one used for metal. Apply the compound to the buffer, then buff the plastic with it. Next, wash the plastic with soap and water to remove the abrasive buffing compound; and finally, polish your baseplate with paste wax.

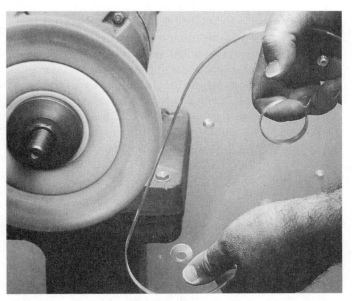

**Give the edges a final polish.** In working with a buffing wheel, you must be careful that the work doesn't catch in the wheel and get yanked from your grasp. Begin in the middle on an edge, as shown, and pull the work up, so you buff toward the bottom of that edge.

**Use a cabinet scraper** to remove saw marks from the edges of plastic. For me it works best to drag the scraper toward me, rather than pushing it away, the usual technique. It doesn't take many strokes to remove all the scratches. This works on phenolic and polycarbonate as well as the acrylic shown.

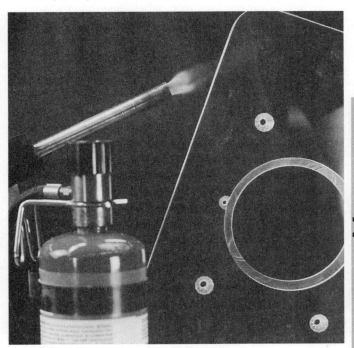

**Edges can be "flame-polished"** with your propane torch. Sweep the flame slowly over the edge, and the heat will melt the plastic enough to smooth out the roughness and add a sheen. While you don't want to dwell on one spot too long, it does take more than a few seconds to heat the plastic enough to "polish" it.

# Cutting Threads

Taps and dies cut threads in metal and plastic. Taps cut internal threads (in holes, in other words), while dies cut external threads (on rods and pipes, for example). As an enterprising router woodworker, you just may find it handy to have two or three sizes of taps and dies in your tool cabinet.

Do you, for example, want to upgrade your router's baseplate-mounting screws? Might you want to tap a hole in a plastic mounting plate or another jig part? Might you need to cut threads on a trammel or edge-guide rod? If you do, then you need to learn a little about taps and dies.

Neither are difficult to use, but you ought to understand some rudiments of thread jargon. The basic dimension of a threaded fastener is its diameter. But the number of threads per inch and the thread classification may also be pertinent under some circumstances. Ever find a nut that wouldn't thread onto a bolt, though they were the same diameters? Well, you had one piece threaded in the National Coarse standard and one in the National Fine standard. Typically, the ¼-inch bolt you buy at the local hardware store will have 20 threads per inch, which is the National Coarse (NC) standard for that size fastener. National Fine (NF) has 28 threads per inch.

As a practical matter, to cut threads, you need to know the diameter of the thread, as well as the number of threads per inch (tpi). Whether it is in the NC or NF classification is irrelevant, though it will be one or the other. (See the chart "Tap Drill Sizes" on page 306.)

Each tap or die is marked with the size of the hole or shaft and the number of threads per inch. If the diameter is less than ¼ inch, the size is given in terms of machine-screw gauges. Thus a tap marked 10-24 NF will cut threads to accept a 10-gauge machine screw with 24 threads per inch, which is the National Fine standard. A ⅜-16 NC tap will cut threads for a ⅜-inch bolt with 16 threads per inch, which is the National Coarse standard.

As you create a threaded hole, make sure you start with a hole of the correct size. Check the tap you will use *first*. Embossed on its side will be the size of drill bit to use to bore the hole. Check out the drill sizes in the tap drill chart, and be welcomed to the wacky world of machinists. Few of the bits are spec'd by diameter; rather they have number or letter designations. The store that has the taps and dies will also have bits in the number and letter designations.

You can buy taps and dies individually or in sets from good hardware stores, including Sears. By mail order, you can buy individual taps, dies, drill bits, and related accessories from Reid Tool Supply Co. (800-253-0421). A typical set will include a dozen or more of the most common taps, matching dies, a tap wrench used to turn the tap, and a diestock used to turn the die, and perhaps a reamer and a thread gauge. As a collection of precision tools, a tap-and-die set won't be inexpensive. And such a set is undoubtedly more than you need. You can save by buying just the tap or two you need, along with a simple tap wrench, the necessary drill bits, and a can of cutting oil.

The thread gauge, by the way, comes into play when you want to cut threads to match a stock nut or bolt. Use the blades in the gauge in a trial-and-error process to determine the number of threads per inch you must cut. A measurement with a dial caliper will tell you the diameter. This in turn will tell you the corresponding tap or die to use.

To tap threads, clamp the work to a workbench or in a vise at a comfortable working height. Unless you are cutting threads in cast iron or brass, you need to use a lubricant. Turpentine is a suitable lubricant for aluminum or copper, and soapy water works with plastics. Steel requires an oil-base lube. You can buy suitable cutting oil where you get the tap. Apply a few drops to the tap's threads before you start, then add more with each turn, dripping it on the tap shank just above the hole.

The first few threads you cut will determine the course the tap will follow, so align the tap carefully. You don't want the threads to be cocked. If it will help, set a try square beside the tap and line up the tap with the vertical leg of the square.

When starting out, turn the wrench clockwise while exerting moderate downward pressure. Once the initial threads are cut, the pressure isn't necessary; the threads will pull the tap into the hole as you turn it. After each turn or two of the tap wrench, back off a quarter-turn or so to cut off burrs and allow filings to clear.

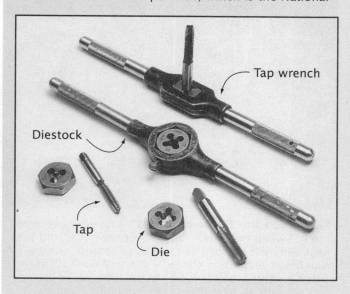

Tap wrench

Diestock

Tap

Die

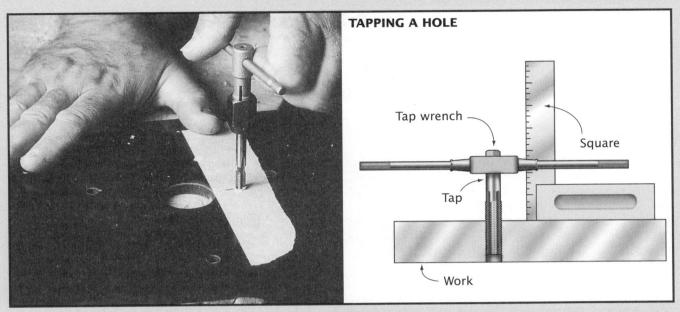

## TAPPING A HOLE

Tap wrench

Square

Tap

Work

**If you can drive a screw,** you can tap a hole. Drill a hole of the correct size, then turn the tap into that hole. The masking tape was applied to this phenolic mounting plate so the hole location could be laid out.

To thread a rod with a die, you must clamp the rod in a vise. With a file, bevel the end of the rod, then mark where to want the threads to end. Fit the diestock over the rod, and adjust the guide fingers to the diameter of the rod. Remove the diestock and fit the die into it. Put the diestock back over the rod, line up the guide fingers with the top of the rod, and, grasping the center of the diestock in your fingers, carefully turn it onto the rod until the die gains a firm purchase. Then grip the handles, and, exerting downward pressure, turn the unit clockwise. Every one or two turns, back off the unit about a quarter-turn. Continue in this manner until you complete the threads.

*(continued)*

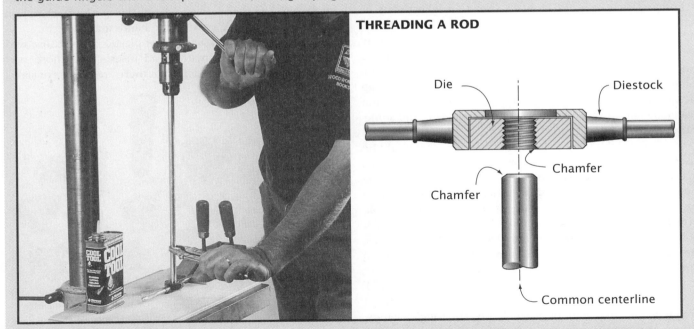

## THREADING A ROD

Die

Diestock

Chamfer

Chamfer

Common centerline

**The challenge** in cutting threads on a rod is ensuring that they are square to the rod's axis. Use the drill press. Tighten the rod to be threaded in the chuck. Clamp the diestock to the drill press table. DON'T turn the machine on. Instead, turn the rod with locking-grip pliers while advancing the quill. Once you have the threads started, you can move the work to a vise and continue in a more conventional manner.

### Tap Drill Sizes

| Size | National Coarse | | | National Fine | |
|---|---|---|---|---|---|
| | TPI | Bit Size | | TPI | Bit Size |
| 6 | 32 | 63 | | 40 | 33 |
| 8 | 32 | 29 | | 36 | 29 |
| 10 | 24 | 25 | | 32 | 21 ($\frac{5}{32}$")* |
| 12 | 24 | 16 | | 28 | 14 ($\frac{3}{16}$")* |
| ¼" | 20 | 7 ($\frac{13}{64}$")* | | 28 | 3 ($\frac{7}{32}$")* |
| $\frac{5}{16}$" | 18 | F (¼")* | | 24 | I ($\frac{17}{64}$")* |
| $\frac{3}{8}$" | 16 | $\frac{5}{16}$" | | 24 | Q ($\frac{21}{64}$")* |
| $\frac{7}{16}$" | 14 | U ($\frac{23}{64}$")* | | 20 | $\frac{25}{64}$" |
| ½" | 13 | $\frac{27}{64}$" | | 20 | $\frac{29}{64}$" |

*Approximate size—in most cases slightly oversized.*

## Hardware

Almost every woodworking jig or fixture has some hardware in it. Well, okay, templates probably don't have hardware, and various positioning gauges don't have hardware. But even custom baseplates need mounting screws.

Just the right piece of hardware can simplify a jig, make it work better, more efficiently, even more safely. How to secure a fence or stop? How to speed an adjustment or setup? How to hold the work? How to ensure accuracy?

The answers to all these jig-design questions just may be readily available bits of hardware. So aside from the bookstore and the supermarket, my favorite place for shopping is the hardware store. When trying to work out a jig design, it's a great resource. I roam the aisles, looking at the fasteners and fittings and gewgaws and widgets. And sometimes the answer is there.

I don't think I need to list all the fasteners that might be useful in making jigs. You know about and use drywall screws, machine screws, stove bolts, carriage bolts, hex-head bolts, washers and fender washers, stop nuts, and wing nuts. As you tackle the various jig projects in this book, you'll run across the less commonplace hardware bits that solved problems for me—nylon washers, plastic sleeves, bronze bushings, coupling nuts, threaded rod, compression springs, T-nuts, threaded inserts, and the like.

But two special categories of essential jig-making hardware aren't found in the local hardware stores that I frequent. I'm talking about plastic knobs and toggle clamps. These are items I buy through the mail. Although most woodworking catalogs show assortments of both, I buy primarily through the Reid Tool Supply catalog, which has an intoxicating range of knobs and clamps, as well as many other intriguing items intended for machinists.

## Plastic Knobs

The very best jigs and fixtures do not count "makeshift" amongst their characteristics. It is clear, when you study one, that the various parts were made to perform specific functions. To me, the use of metal wing nuts or wooden cranks is the mark of a makeshift jig. Sure, makeshift jigs usually do what they were contrived to do. But if the jig is a keeper, why not style it a bit and make it easier to use? Why not use knobs and levers and crank wheels that perform exceptionally well and that are easy on the hands and eyes?

There are three basic types of plastic knobs: those with threaded studs, those with blind inserts, and those with through inserts. Within each type, there are dozens of styles,

**The right plastic knob** can be the difference between sweetness and misery when using a jig. So many sizes and styles are available, as you can see, that you should be able to find one that's perfect for any jig-making application.

ranging from tiny knobs you grasp between fingers and thumb up to bulky handgrips. There are ball shapes, football shapes, mushrooms, even teardrops. Round knobs can be knurled, fluted, or both. There are three- and four-pronged styles, starlike patterns, even oversized wing knobs.

The studded knobs are like bolts or machine screws that are to be tightened by hand, rather than with a wrench or screwdriver. There are dozens of applications for such hardware in jig making. A catalog search will turn up everything from bantam knobs with ½-inch-long 8-32 studs to husky grips with 2-inch-long ⅜-inch studs.

The other two types of knobs are like nuts designed to be tightened by hand. With the through insert, whatever threaded shank the knob is turned onto can pass completely through the knob. With a blind insert, the threaded shank will "bottom" in the insert.

Going beyond knobs, you can find hand wheels, cranks, and levers. If you haven't found what you need to simplify your jig and make it easier to use, you probably haven't looked hard enough.

## Toggle Clamps

Many of the jigs in this book—the sled for coping cuts shown in the chapter "Sleds" on page 246, for example, or the mortising jig shown in the chapter "Mortising Jig" on page 124—are equipped with toggle clamps.

These clamps are not just for looks. Depending upon the application, the toggle clamp can be a labor-saving trick, a practical clamping solution, or a safety device. In some applications, it is all three.

Consider its role on a coping sled, for example. If you are doing cope cuts, you need to clamp the workpiece. The reason is that the rotation of the cutter will pull in on the workpiece. If you allow that to happen, your router will act like a tree trimmer's chipper for a split second. Then something will probably break and go flying across the room. I don't want to be there when it happens, and neither do you.

Now, you may have strong fingers, and they may be strong enough to clench the workpiece sufficiently tight to prevent this disaster. But a toggle clamp is a strong, untiring device that's superior to fingers for the job.

And unlike screw-action clamps of various kinds, toggle clamps are NOT inconvenient or time-consuming to use. At the flick of your wrist, a toggle clamp will snap closed on a workpiece, cinching it tightly in place. Another flick of the wrist pops the clamp open, instantly freeing the workpiece.

Toggle clamps are available in four basic types—hold-down, straight-line, pull-action, and squeeze-action, as shown in the drawing *Toggle Clamp Types*. There are a variety of sizes and styles, with horizontal, vertical, and T-handles, straight and flange mountings, solid and U-bar clamping arms, and high and low profiles. The first two types—hold-down and straight-line—are the best adapted to woodworking. Flip back through the book; you'll see that the jigs that have toggle clamps have some form of hold-down type.

Several spindles and spindle accessories may be useful. I'd recommend that you replace the standard spindle with a slightly longer one. The extra spindle length allows you to accommodate a greater range of workpiece thicknesses. In situations where you need to adjust the spindle often to accommodate workpieces of different thicknesses, it will benefit you to ditch the hex nuts used to adjust and lock the spindle. Use a couple of check nuts, or a check nut and a wing nut instead. The check nut–wing nut combination allows you to make spindle adjustments without using wrenches.

Finally, don't be put off by the cost of toggle clamps. Remember that you can use the same clamp on any number of jigs and fixtures. It takes only two to four screws to mount a clamp. It's easy to buy one clamp and use it on whatever jig is in use. An alternative is to make the sort of mounting pad shown in the chapter "Shop-Built Slot Mortiser," which begins on page 131.

## TOGGLE CLAMP TYPES

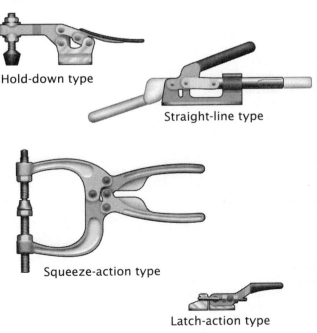

Hold-down type

Straight-line type

Squeeze-action type

Latch-action type

**Toggle clamps** are made in an almost bewildering assortment of sizes and styles. This small selection conveys the range of sizes, and it includes clamps I've found useful in making jigs and fixtures for router woodworking.

Appendix

# Index

Note: Page references in **boldface** indicate tables.

Index

**Index**

**Index**

Index